Economic Foundations of Private Law

Elgar Critical Writings Readers

The Economics of the Environment
Edited by Wallace E. Oates

Industrial Organization
Edited by Oliver E. Williamson

The Economics of Transaction Costs
Edited by Oliver E. Williamson and Scott E. Masten

Economic Foundations of Private Law
Edited by Richard A. Posner and Francesco Parisi

Wherever possible, the articles in these volumes have been reproduced as originally published using facsimile reproduction, inclusive of footnotes and pagination to facilitate ease of reference.

For a list of all Edward Elgar published titles visit our site on the World Wide Web at http://www.e-elgar.co.uk

Economic Foundations of Private Law

Edited by

Richard A. Posner

Judge
United States Court of Appeals for the Seventh Circuit
and Senior Lecturer
University of Chicago Law School, USA

and

Francesco Parisi

Professor of Law, George Mason School of Law
and Co-Director, Program in Economics and the Law, J.M. Buchanan Center
for Political Economy, George Mason University, USA

An Elgar Critical Writings Reader
Cheltenham, UK • Northampton, MA, USA

Published by
Edward Elgar Publishing Limited
Glensanda House
Montpellier Parade
Cheltenham
Glos GL50 1UA
UK

Edward Elgar Publishing, Inc.
136 West Street
Suite 202
Northampton
Massachusetts 01060
USA

This book has been printed on demand to keep the title in print.

A catalogue record for this book is available from the British Library

Library of Congress Cataloguing in Publication Data

Economic foundations of private law / edited by Richard A. Posner and Francesco Parisi.
p. cm. – (Elgar critical writings reader)
Includes bibliographical references and index.
1. Civil law–Economic aspects. 2. Law and economics. I. Posner, Richard A. II. Parisi, Francesco. III. Elgar critical writings reader

K487 E3 E264 2003
330.1–dc21

2002027147

MIX
Paper from responsible sources
FSC
www.fsc.org
FSC® C013604

ISBN 1 84376 071 1 (paperback)

Contents

Acknowledgements

The editors and publishers wish to thank the authors and the following publishers who have kindly given permission for the use of copyright material.

American Economic Association for articles: Harold Demsetz (1967), 'Toward a Theory of Property Rights', *American Economic Review*, **57** (2), May, 347–59; Richard A. Posner (1987), 'The Law and Economics Movement', *American Economic Review*, **77** (2), May, 1–13; Robert D. Cooter and Daniel L. Rubinfeld (1989), 'Economic Analysis of Legal Disputes and Their Resolution', *Journal of Economic Literature*, **XXVII**, September, 1067–97.

Georgia Law Review for article: William M. Landes and Richard A. Posner (1981), 'The Positive Economic Theory of Tort Law', *Georgia Law Review*, **15** (4), Summer, 851–924.

Harvard Law Review Association for article: Guido Calabresi and A. Douglas Melamed (1972), 'Property Rules, Liability Rules, and Inalienability: One View of the Cathedral', *Harvard Law Review*, **85** (6), April, 1089–128.

Hofstra Law Review Association for article: Guido Calabresi (1980), 'About Law and Economics: A Letter to Ronald Dworkin', *Hofstra Law Review*, **8** (3), Spring, 553–62.

Journal of Law and Economics and the University of Chicago for articles: R.H. Coase (1960), 'The Problem of Social Cost', *Journal of Law and Economics*, **III**, October, 1–44; William M. Landes (1971), 'An Economic Analysis of the Courts', *Journal of Law and Economics*, **XIV** (1), April, 61–107.

Journal of Legal Studies and the University of Chicago for articles: Harold Demsetz (1972), 'When Does the Rule of Liability Matter?', *Journal of Legal Studies*, **I** (1), January, 13–28; John H. Barton (1972), 'The Economic Basis of Damages for Breach of Contract', *Journal of Legal Studies*, **I** (2), June, 277–304; Isaac Ehrlich and Richard A. Posner (1974), 'An Economic Analysis of Legal Rulemaking', *Journal of Legal Studies*, **III** (1), January, 257–86; Paul H. Rubin (1977), 'Why is the Common Law Efficient?', *Journal of Legal Studies*, **VI** (1), January, 51–63; George L. Priest (1977), 'The Common Law Process and the Selection of Efficient Rules', *Journal of Legal Studies*, **VI** (1), January, 65–82; Anthony T. Kronman (1978), 'Mistake, Disclosure, Information, and the Law of Contracts', *Journal of Legal Studies*, **VII** (1), January, 1–34; Steven Shavell (1980), 'Strict Liability Versus Negligence', *Journal of Legal Studies*, **IX** (1), January, 1–25; Steven Shavell (1984), 'Liability for Harm Versus Regulation of Safety', *Journal of Legal Studies*, **XIII** (2), June, 357–74; Louis Kaplow and Steven Shavell (1994), 'Why the Legal System is Less Efficient than the Income Tax in Redistributing Income', *Journal of Legal Studies*, **XXIII** (2), June, 667–81.

Notre Dame Journal of Law, Ethics and Public Policy for article: Richard A. Posner (1985), 'Wealth Maximization Revisited', *Notre Dame Journal of Law, Ethics and Public Policy*, **2** (1), Fall, 85–105.

RAND for article: Steven Shavell (1980), 'Damage Measures for Breach of Contract', *Bell Journal of Economics*, **11** (2), Autumn, 466–90.

Southern California Law Review for article: Robert D. Cooter (1982), 'Economic Analysis of Punitive Damages', *Southern California Law Review*, **56**, 79–101.

Yale Law Journal Company and William S. Hein Company for articles: Alan Schwartz (1979), 'The Case for Specific Performance', *Yale Law Journal*, **89**, December, 271–306; Charles J. Goetz and Robert E. Scott (1980), 'Enforcing Promises: An Examination of the Basis of Contract', *Yale Law Journal*, **89** (7), June, 1261–88 and 1321–2; Ian Ayres and Robert Gertner (1989), 'Filling Gaps in Incomplete Contracts: An Economic Theory of Default Rules', *Yale Law Journal*, **99** (1), October, 87–130.

Every effort has been made to trace all the copyright holders but if any have been inadvertently overlooked the publishers will be pleased to make the necessary arrangement at the first opportunity.

In addition the publishers wish to thank the Library of the London School of Economics and Political Science, the Marshall Library of Economics, Cambridge University, the Library of the University of Warwick and B & N Microfilm, London for their assistance in obtaining these articles.

The Economic Foundations of Private Law: An Introduction

Richard A. Posner and Francesco Parisi

This volume collects some of the seminal papers in law and economics, with special emphasis on some foundational contributions to the economics of property, contracts and torts. Despite some of the early resistance of legal academia to the application of economics to nonmarket behavior, these contributions have unveiled essential bonds between legal and economic analysis, providing an important illustration of the fruitfulness of economic analysis in the study of law.

1. The Methodological Foundations of Law and Economics

In many respects, the impact of law and economics has exceeded its early ambitions. One effect of the incorporation of economics into the study of law was to irreversibly transform traditional legal methodology. Legal rules began to be studied as a working system – a clear change from the Langdellian tradition, which had relied almost exclusively on the self-contained framework of case analysis and classification, viewing the law as little more than a filing system. Economics provided the analytical rigor necessary for the study of the vast body of legal rules present in a modern legal system. This intellectual revolution came at a fortuitous moment, when legal academia was actively searching for a tool that would permit a critical appraisal of the law, rather than merely strengthening the dogmatic consistencies in the system.

This marriage of law and economics has also affected the economic profession, contributing to the expansion of the original domain of microeconomic analysis – the study of individual and organizational choices in the market – to the study and understanding of other institutions and non-market phenomena.

The Law and Economics Movement

In spite of notable antecedents traceable to Adam Smith's discussion of the economic effects of legislation regulating economic activities (1776), and Jeremy Bentham's theory of legislation and utilitarianism (1782 and 1789), it was not until the mid-20th century – through the work of Henry Simon, Aaron Director, Henry Manne, George Stigler, Armen Alchian, Gordon Tullock, and others – that the links between law and economics became an object of serious academic pursuit. The regulation of business and economic law fell within the natural interest of economists, so that the first applications of economics to law tended to focus on areas related to corporate law, tax law and competition law.

In the 1960s, however, the pioneering work of Ronald Coase and Guido Calabresi brought to light the pervasive influence of economics in all areas of the law. The methodological breakthroughs occasioned by Coase and Calabresi allowed immediate extensions to the areas of tort, property and contract. The analytical power of their work was not confined to these fields, however, and subsequent law and economics contributions demonstrate the explanatory and analytical reach of its methodology in a number of other areas of the law.

A difference in approach is discernable between the law and economics contributions of the early 1960s and those that followed a decade later. While earlier studies appraise the effects of legal rules on the normal functioning of the economic system (i.e. they consider the impact of legal rules on the market equilibrium), the subsequent generation of studies utilizes economic analysis in order to achieve a better understanding of the legal system. Indeed in the 1970s a number of important applications of economics to law gradually exposed the economic structure of virtually every aspect of a legal system: from its origin and evolution, to its substantive, procedural and constitutional rules.

An important ingredient in the success of law and economics research has come from the establishment of specialized journals. The first such journal, the *Journal of Law and Economics*, appeared in 1958 at the University of Chicago. Its first editor, Aaron Director, should be credited for this important initiative, successfully continued by Ronald Coase. Other journals emerged in the following years: in 1972 the *Journal of Legal Studies*, also housed at the University of Chicago, was founded under the editorship of Richard Posner; in 1979, *Research in Law and Economics*, under the editorship of Richard Zerbe, Jr.; in 1981, the *International Review of Law and Economics* was established in the United Kingdom under the editorship of Charles Rowley and Anthony Ogus (later joined by Robert Cooter and Daniel Rubinfeld); in 1982, the *Supreme Court Economic Review*, under the editorship of Peter Aranson (later joined by Harold Demsetz and Ernest Gellhorn); in 1985, the *Journal of Law, Economics and Organization*, under the editorship of Jerry Mashaw and Oliver Williamson (later joined by Roberta Romano); in 1994, the *European Journal of Law and Economics* was launched under the editorial direction of Jürgen Backhaus and Frank Stephen; and, most recently, in 1999, the *American Law and Economics Review*, under the editorship of Orley Ashenfelter and Richard Posner. These specialized journals provided – and continue to provide – an extremely valuable forum for the study of the economic structure of law.

Methodological Debates in Law and Economics

Despite the powerful analytical reach of economics, it was clear from the outset that the economist's competence in the evaluation of legal issues was limited. While the economist's perspective could prove crucial for the positive analysis of the efficiency of alternative legal rules and the study of the effects of alternative rules on the distribution of wealth and income, economists generally recognized the limits of their role in providing normative prescriptions for social change or legal reform.

Recognition of the positive nature of the economic analysis of law was not sufficient to dispel the many misunderstandings and controversies in legal academia engendered by the law and economics movement's methodological revolution. As Coase (1978) indicated, the cohesiveness of economic techniques makes it possible for economics to move successfully into another field, such as law, and dominate it intellectually. But methodological differences played an important part in the uneasy marriage between law and economics. The Popperian methodology of positive science was in many respects at odds with the existing paradigms of legal analysis. Rowley (1981) characterizes such differences, observing that positive economics follow the Popperian approach, whereby testable hypotheses (or models) are derived by means of logical deduction, then tested empirically. Anglo-American legal analysis, on the other hand, is generally inductive: lawyers use individual judgments to construct a general premise of law. Much work has been done in law and economics despite these methodological differences, with a reciprocal enrichment of the analytical tools of both disciplines.

Law and economics rely on the standard economic assumption that individuals are rational maximizers, and study the role of law as a means for changing the relative prices attached to alternative individual actions. Under this approach, a change in the rule of law will affect human behavior by altering the relative price structure – and thus the constraint – of the optimization problem. Wealth maximization, serving as a paradigm for the analysis of law, can thus be promoted or constrained by legal rules.

The early years of law and economics were characterized by the uneasiness of some traditional legal scholars in the acceptance of the notion of wealth maximization as an ancillary paradigm of justice. Although most of the differences gradually proved to be largely verbal – and many others were dispelled by the gradual acceptance of a distinction between paradigms of utility maximization and wealth maximization – two objections continue to affect the lines of the debate. The first relates to the need for specifying an initial set of individual entitlements or rights, as a necessary prerequisite for operationalizing wealth maximization. The second springs from the theoretical difficulty of defining the proper role of efficiency as an ingredient of justice, vis-à-vis other social goals. Calabresi (1980) claims that an increase in wealth cannot constitute social improvement unless it furthers some other goal, such as utility or equality. Denying that one can trade off efficiency against justice, he argues instead that efficiency and distribution are ingredients of justice, which is a goal of a different order than either of these ingredients. Calabresi thus defends law and economics as a worthy examination of certain ingredients of justice, rather than a direct examination of justice itself.

Wealth Maximization and the Law

In his well-known defense of wealth maximization as a guide for judicial action, Posner (1985) distinguishes wealth or expected utility from market prices. While market prices may not always fully reflect idiosyncratic valuations, they avoid an undertaking of interpersonal utility comparisons, with the opportunity for *ex post* rationalization of positions taken on emotional grounds. Posner's view is sympathetic to the premises of a property right approach to legal relationships, and he stresses the importance of an initial distribution of property rights prior to any calculation of wealth maximization. His paradigm of wealth maximization serves as a common denominator for both utilitarian and individualist perspectives. By combining elements of both, Posner provides a theory of wealth maximization that comes closer to a consensus political philosophy than does any other overarching political principle.

The intellectual resistance that has attended the birth of law and economics can only be temporary. Both legal practitioners and policymakers are becoming increasingly aware of the important role of economic analysis in understanding the law, and we have already mentioned notable contributions to mainstream economic theory from lawyers in the law and economics movement. Likewise, as Coase (1978) noted, economists have come to realize that the other social sciences are so intertwined with the economic system as to be part of the system itself. For this reason, law and economics can no longer be appraised as a branch of applied microeconomics; rather it must be seen as contributing to a better understanding of the economic system itself. The study of the effects of other social sciences on the economic system will, Coase predicts, become a permanent part of the field of economics.

Coase also examines the reasons for the movement of economists into the other social sciences, and attempts to predict the future of this phenomenon. Groups of scholars are bound together by common techniques of analysis, a common theory or approach to the subject, and/or a common subject matter. In the short run, Coase maintains, one group's techniques of analysis may give it such advantages that it is able to move successfully into another field and maybe even dominate it. In the long run, however, the subject matter tends to be the dominant cohesive force. While the analytical techniques employed by economists – such as linear programming, quantitative methods, and cost–benefit analysis – may recently have aided the entry of economists into the other social sciences, Coase predicts that such a movement can only be temporary. After all, the wisdom possessed by economists, once its value is recognized, will be acquired by some of the practitioners in these other fields (as is happening in the field of law).

As the domain of law and economics continues to expand, its perspective on methodological issues has not been stagnant. While this survey emphasizes the wide range of substantive applications, some degree of controversy still surrounds several of the methodological, normative, and philosophical underpinnings of the economic approach to law. Most of the ideological differences tend to lose significance because their operational paradigms often lead to analogous results when applied to real cases. Some scholars, however, perceive that the current state of law and economics as comparable to the state of economics prior to the advent of public choice theory, insofar as an understanding of 'political failures' was missing from the study of market failures. (Buchanan, 1974; Rowley, 1989) Public choice may indeed inject a skeptical – and at times disruptive – perspective into the more elegant and simple framework of neoclassical economics, but this added element may well be essential to enable a better understanding of a complex reality. In a way, the systematic incorporation of public choice theory into the economic approach to law may serve to bridge the conflicting normative perspectives in law and economics, at least by bringing the debate onto the more solid ground of collective choice theory.

Redistribution Through Legal Rules

The wealth maximization paradigm also finds adherents outside the Chicago school of law and economics. Most scholars in our discipline have reached the conclusion that redistributive goals should not be utilized in the design of legal rules. In many legal relationships with a working price system (e.g. contract law, etc.), redistribution through legal rules would be impossible. Any attempt by legal planners to effectuate a transfer of wealth via the legal system (e.g. with the selection of income-biased contract rules) would immediately be frustrated by price adjustments in equilibrium. In other areas of the law where there are no *ex ante* price mechanisms to offset the wealth effects of redistributive legal rules (e.g. in most tort situations), the legal system has the potential of effective redistribution between the parties. However, even in such cases, the common wisdom in law and economics suggests that redistribution through the legal system is generally both inappropriate and undesirable. Among the most notable discussions of the important trade-offs between efficiency and redistribution, Kaplow and Shavell's (1994) article stands for the basic proposition that, if redistribution of income in society is desired, it can be 'accomplished more efficiently through the income tax system than through the use of legal rules' (Kaplow and Shavell, 1994: 677). Regardless of whether society elects to implement a progressive tax system (e.g. raising income tax rates for higher income individuals) or whether it employs progressive legal rules (e.g. requiring wealthy individuals to pay greater tort damages than poor individuals for the same accident), or a combination of the two, both options are inefficient because they distort individual (labor and behavioral) incentives. Kaplow and Shavell thus suggest that a modified yet progressive tax system coupled with the most efficient legal rule (i.e. a rule that does not take into account an individual's income) is the preferable way to achieve redistribution. All individuals are better off under this regime because society collects additional resources in the tax system, saves resources by not implementing an inefficient legal rule, and creates for itself the option value of being able to use the surplus resources for any or all purposes, including improvement of the conditions of the poor.

Kaplow and Shavell consider nonempirical arguments for and against their proposition that a modified income tax scheme with an efficient (and non-redistributive) legal rule is the superior way to achieve wealth redistribution. If redistribution takes place through the legal system, parties will have skewed incentives, leading to inconsistent and, therefore, inefficient outcomes. This, in turn, will reduce the surplus available for redistribution via taxation. Alternatively, inefficient legal rules will induce individuals to attempt to renegotiate contractual arrangements, opting out of the inefficient legal rules. This would impose unnecessary transaction costs with a dissipation of valuable resources. Finally in terms of distributive equity the potential of redistributive legal rules is limited since the redistribution would only affect those actors involved in accidents, whereas redistribution through tax law takes place on a comprehensive basis with a more uniform impact of the costs and benefits of redistribution, and possibly a substantial reduction of administrative costs.

2. The Hypothesis That the Common Law is Efficient

An important premise of law and economics is that the common law (i.e. judge-made law) is the result of an effort – conscious or not – to induce efficient outcomes. This premise is known as the efficiency of the common law hypothesis. According to this hypothesis, first intimated in Coase (1960) and later systematized and greatly extended by Posner in numerous books and articles, common law rules attempt to allocate resources in either a Pareto or Kaldor–Hicks efficient manner. Further, common law rules are said to enjoy a comparative advantage over legislation in fulfilling this task because of the evolutionary selection of common law rules through adjudication. Several important contributions provide the foundations for this claim; however, the scholars who have advanced theories in support of the hypothesis often disagree as to its conceptual basis.

An Economic Theory of Adjudication

Among the first to articulate an economic theory of adjudication, Landes (1971) considers the effect of the public provision of court services on the level of litigation. He suggests that because users of the judicial system pay only nominal fees, queues develop to ration the limited supply of court services. As a method of reducing these queues and the resulting court delays, Landes contemplates the payment of a money price and its potential impact on the use of courts and the demand for trials. He predicts that a money price for courts would increase the ratio of pre-trial settlements to total disputes. As to criminal adjudication, Landes observes that, contrary to popular belief, most criminal cases are disposed of ('settled') before trial, either by a guilty plea or by a dismissal of the charges. He then develops a theoretical model that examines the dynamics of a decision to settle or go to trial. Underlying his model is the behavioral assumption that both prosecutors and defendants rationally seek to maximize their utility, subject to given constraints. Landes' model shows that the decision to settle or to pursue litigation is influenced by factors such as the probability of conviction, severity of the offense, resources available to and used by the prosecutor and the defendant, the relative costs of trial and settlement and degree of risk aversion. Through Landes' contribution, the theory of the legal process began to develop the first empirically falsifiable hypotheses, which Landes himself tested using data from both state and federal courts.

A general theory of adjudication was subsequently advanced by the work of Ehrlich and Posner (1974). They outline a theory of the legal process which holds that the choice of the degree of precision in the formulation of legal commands is largely based on the desire to minimize social costs. Specific legal rules and general legal standards lie at opposite ends of the specificity–generality spectrum. Ehrlich and Posner articulate the criteria for determining the optimal degree of specificity, given cost minimization as a dominant consideration. They discuss the benefits that precision brings to the legal system, including increased predictability and the consequential reduction in litigation expenditures, increased speed of dispute resolution, and reduced information costs associated with adjudication. Yet, precision also involves costs: the costs of rule formulation (often substantial, given the high transaction costs of statutory decisions); allocative inefficiency arising from both the over- and underinclusive effects of rules; and information barriers for the layman, who is more likely to understand general standards than specific rules which employ technical language.

The Evolutionary Selection of Efficient Common Law Rules

Among the leading themes in the economics of the legal process is one exploring the claim that a common law process generates efficient rules. Rubin (1977) provides an important contribution to the emerging efficiency of the common law hypothesis. He maintains that the efficiency of the common law is best explained by an evolutionary model that finds parties more likely to litigate over inefficient rules rather than efficient ones. The pressure for the common law to evolve to efficiency, he argues, rests on the desire of parties to create precedent because they have an interest in future similar cases. Rubin thus considers three basic situations: where both parties are interested in creating precedent, where only one party is interested in creating precedent, and where neither party has such an interest.

Where both parties have an interest in future similar cases, and the current legal rule is inefficient, the party held liable will have an incentive to force litigation. Parties will continue to use the courts until the rule is changed. If the current rule is efficient, however, there is no incentive to change it, so it will remain in force. Where only one party has an interest in future similar cases, the incentive to litigate will depend on the allocation of liability. If liability falls on a repeat player, litigation will likely occur, whereas the other party would have no incentive to litigate. As a result, precedents will evolve in the interested party's favor, whether or not the rule is efficient. In the event that neither party is interested in precedents, the legal rule – whether efficient or not – will remain in force, and parties will settle out of court because they lack the incentive to change the current rule. Rubin thus concludes that the common law becomes efficient through an evolutionary process based on the utility maximizing decisions of litigants, rather than on judges' desires to maximize efficiency.

Rubin's analysis was extended by Priest (1977), who articulated the idea that the common law tends to develop efficient rules independently of judicial bias in decision making. Indeed, he asserts, efficient rules will develop even despite judicial hostility toward efficient outcomes. Priest parts with Rubin, however, on the source of the tendency toward efficiency, rejecting Rubin's conclusion that this tendency occurs only where both parties to a dispute have an interest in future similar cases and therefore have an incentive to litigate. Instead, he asserts that litigation is driven by the costs of inefficient rules, rather than the desire for precedent.

According to Priest's analysis, inefficient rules impose greater costs on the parties subject to them than do efficient rules, thereby making the stakes in a dispute greater. Where the stakes are greater, litigation is more likely than settlement. Consequently, out of the complete set of legal rules, disputes arising under inefficient rules will tend to be repeatedly litigated more often than disputes arising under efficient rules. This means that the rules not contested will tend to be efficient ones. Because they are less likely to be reviewed, including by judges hostile to efficient outcomes, these rules tend to remain in force. Further, as inefficient rules are reviewed, the process of review provides the chance that they will be discarded in favor of efficient rules that are, in turn, less likely to be reviewed. Thus, the selection of efficient legal rules continues through the adjudication process.

The Decision Whether to Settle or Go to Trial

An important component of the theories advanced by Rubin (1977) and Priest (1977) is the criteria for the selection of disputes for litigation. In fact, only a small fraction of disputes go to trial, and even fewer are appealed. Priest and Klein (1984) develop a model of the litigation process that explores the relationship between the set of disputes litigated and the set of disputes settled. According to their one-period model of dispute resolution, the proportion of plaintiff victories in any set of cases will be influenced by the shape of the distribution of disputes, the absolute magnitude of the judgment, litigation and settlement costs, and the relative stakes of the parties. Priest and Klein show that the set of disputes selected for litigation, rather than settlement, will therefore constitute neither a random nor a representative sample of the set of all disputes. They then derive a selection hypothesis: where both parties have equal stakes in the litigation, the individual maximizing decisions of the parties will create a strong bias toward a success rate for plaintiffs at trial (or appellants on appeal) of 50 percent, regardless of the substantive standard of law.

When the assumption that both parties have equal stakes in the dispute is relaxed (e.g. where one of the parties is a repeat player and has a stake in future similar cases), the rate of success in litigation begins to deviate from the hypothesized baseline, and the model predicts that the repeat player will prevail more frequently. Priest and Klein present a great deal of data, both derived from their own empirical investigations and from the major empirical studies of the legal system since the 1930s. While they caution, because of measurement problems, against the conclusion that these data confirm the selection hypothesis, the data are nonetheless encouraging.

Legal disputes are resolved at various stages of a sequential decision-making process in which parties have limited information and act in their own self-interest. An efficient resolution occurs when legal entitlements are assigned to the parties who value them the most, legal liabilities are allocated to the parties who can bear them at the lowest cost and transaction costs are minimized. Following these premises, Cooter and Rubinfeld (1989) review economic models of legal dispute resolution, attempting to synthesize a model that provides a point of reference necessary to both an understanding of the courts, and deliberation over proposed changes in legal rules. In the first stage of a legal dispute, the underlying event, efficiency requires balancing the cost of harm against the cost of harm avoidance. Because Coasian bargaining is typically not possible, the social costs of harm are externalized. Therefore, an initial allocation of entitlements is essential to creating incentives for efficient levels of activity and precaution. During the second stage, the harmed party decides whether or not to assert a legal claim. This requires the balancing of immediate costs, such as hiring an attorney, and the expected benefits from asserting a claim. In the third stage, after a legal claim is asserted, but before trial, courts encourage parties to bargain together to reach a settlement. If the parties cannot privately settle their dispute, the court performs this function in the final stage, trial. Using their hybrid economic model of suit, settlement, and trial, Cooter and Rubinfeld come to examine the incentives parties face as they proceed through the litigation process, and make predictions based on the decisions available to the parties, with a discussion of some of the concerns that arise from the pursuit of efficiency that pervades normative economic analysis.

3. The Coase Theorem and the Economics of Property Rights

Coase's (1960) article on the 'Problems of Social Cost' has occasioned one of the most intense and fascinating debates in the history of legal and economic thought. Coase challenges the Pigouvian approach to externalities by demonstrating that, in the absence of transaction costs, generators of externalities and their victims will negotiate to an efficient allocation of resources, independent of the initial assignment of rights among them. Coase's descriptive statement was first articulated in the form of a theorem by Demsetz (1967), who redefined Coase's proposition in the following terms:

> There are two striking implications of this process that are true in a world of zero transaction costs. The output mix that results when the exchange of property rights is allowed is efficient and the mix is independent of who is assigned ownership (except that different wealth distributions may result in different demands).

The implicit premise of the Coasian analysis draws upon a fundamental postulate of microeconomic theory: the free exchange of goods in the market moves goods toward their optimal allocation, such that, when every possibility of beneficial exchange is satisfied, resources will reach their optimal allocation according to the criterion of Pareto efficiency. The law creates many subjective juridical positions that are also susceptible of exchange and transfer.

Applying by analogy the postulate concerning the free exchange of goods in the market, Coase maintains that the transferability of rights in a free economy leads toward their best use and to a Pareto efficient final allocation. A non-optimal allocation of legal entitlements will thus be cured by the voluntary transfer of individual rights in the marketplace. Coase's assertion that in the absence of transaction costs the initial assignment of property rights is irrelevant to overall welfare (positive Coase theorem) established a far-reaching framework for analyzing the effect of alternative assignments of property rights and liability rules in the presence of transaction costs (normative Coase theorem). In confuting the conclusions of the Pigouvian tradition, Coase gives life to a model with much broader potential: a revolutionary new perspective for the evaluation of an unlimited number of legal and social issues. The relevance of the seminal contributions that came to complement Coase's analysis reach well beyond the specific area of property rights and externalities, offering a methodological framework that has proved capable of turning several legal constructs on their head.

An Economic Theory of Property Rights

Historically the study of property rights and institutions has engaged the attention of economists, philosophers and lawyers alike. Private property is often explained as the unavoidable by-product of scarcity in a world where common pool losses outweigh the sum of contracting costs and the enforcement of exclusive property rights. At the turn of the 20th century, the underlying assumption in the economic literature was that private property emerged out of a spontaneous evolutionary process because of the desirable features of private property regimes in the creation of incentives for constrained optimization. This understanding of the relationship between scarcity and the emergence of legal entitlements, which had characterized mainstream property right theory, was found incapable of serving as the sole conceptual framework for the understanding of this institution. Through Alchian (1965) and Demsetz (1967 and 1972), it became clear that issues of incentives, as well as scarcity, were at the core of the property right problem.

Alchian (1965) discusses various aspects of property rights, focusing mainly on the distinction between private and public ownership. While there are a number of differences between these two types of ownership, they stem essentially from the inability of a public owner to sell his share of public ownership. Alchian examines the implications of permitting the free transfer of public ownership, noting that a conversion to private property will change the incentive structure, as well as the method of achieving governmental objectives. He derives a theorem, positing that the costs of any decision or choice are less fully thrust upon the decision maker under public ownership than under private ownership. This means that under public ownership, the cost–benefit calculation is affected by a misalignment of incentives. Public agencies would thus be expected to impose special constraints on public employees or agents, in order to induce a closer convergence of incentives. As a result of this structural agency problem, public ownership is often more costly – less efficient – than private ownership.

Alchian's analysis is extended by Demsetz (1967), who outlines additional elements of an economic theory of property rights. In discussing the concept and role of property rights, their emergence, and evolution, Demsetz centers his analysis on the primary allocative function of property rights, the internalization of externalities. Property rights confer the right to benefit or harm oneself or others, and internalization is precluded when the adjustment of property rights cannot take place because of impediments to exchange. A necessary condition for the emergence of property rights is that the benefits obtained through internalization exceed the costs of establishing and monitoring the property rights.

Demsetz uses this framework to appraise several property right structures, including communal ownership, private ownership and state ownership. Because of the potential for group and intergenerational externalities, communal ownership results in great welfare losses: under such a property regime, the effects of one owner's activities on his fellow owners (and subsequent generations of owners) will not be fully captured by the private cost borne directly by the decision maker. These externalities are not likely to be internalized, given the high transaction costs involved. Conversely, under a private property regime, both costs and benefits are borne directly by the individual owner. This creates incentives for the efficient use of resources, except for the externalities that the private owner may impose on the property rights of others. Transaction costs here are significantly lower than in the case of communal ownership, because it will often be sufficient for a few owners to reach an agreement that takes the externalities into account.

Resource Allocation and Transaction Costs

Demsetz (1972) examines and refutes two criticisms of Coase's (1960) analysis. One criticism suggests that where there is a suboptimal allocation of resources between two industries, in the long run different liability rules will alter the profitability of remaining in, or out of, each industry. That industry which must bear the cost of liability will suffer a decrease in its rate of return, with the result that resources will exit the industry. Therefore, the argument goes, even if there are no transaction costs, the market will allocate resources differently in the long run, depending on the liability rule. Approaching the problem as one of constrained optimization of conflicting activities, Demsetz demonstrates that the long-term effects of a change in the liability rule do not erode Coase's conclusions. The problem, rather than being one of liability rules, is one of pervasive scarcity of resources. Another criticism of Coase's analysis suggests that a change in the liability rule can lead to extortion; those who own the legal entitlement will threaten to exercise their entitlement beyond the optimal level, so as to receive a larger payment in exchange for the release of the entitlement. According to Demsetz, however, the possibility of this type of strategic behavior does not alter the final allocation of resources between the competing activities; the problem is symmetrical and, under competitive conditions, disappears. Along similar lines, Stigler (1989) demonstrates that a stable property or tort law will not affect the distribution of income. Demsetz also discusses problems resulting from lifting the assumption of zero transaction costs. Articulating the normative core of the Coase theorem, he observes that the introduction of significant transaction costs into the choice of liability rule analysis does affect resource allocation. One liability rule may be superior to another because the difficulty of avoiding costly interactions is usually different for the interacting parties. Accordingly, the normative predicament indicates that the rule of liability should be based on which party can avoid the costly interaction at the lowest cost.

When two or more parties have conflicting interests in the same resource, the law must decide which party shall prevail, i.e. which party shall receive the entitlement. Once the entitlement decision is made, the law must decide how the entitlement is to be protected and whether it may be transferred. Articulating a concept of entitlements protected by property, liability, or inalienability rules, Calabresi and Melamed (1972) develop a framework that integrates the approaches of property and tort. Calabresi and Melamed allow for a wide range of concerns to be balanced through the assignment of a particular entitlement. Their considerations include economic efficiency and distributional goals, while allowing for the weighing of 'other justice reasons'. In a world of zero transaction costs a Pareto optimal allocation of resources occurs, regardless of the initial entitlement. Calabresi and Melamed outline how, given the reality of transaction costs, an economic efficiency approach selects one allocation of entitlements over another.

Entitlements are protected by property rules (transfer of the entitlement involves a voluntary sale by its holder), liability rules (the entitlement may be destroyed by another party if he is willing to pay an objectively determined value for it), or rules of inalienability (transfer of the entitlement is not permitted, even between a willing seller and a willing buyer). Entitlements cannot be enforced solely through property rules because, even if the transfer would benefit all parties, high transaction costs (especially the holdout problem) may prevent an efficient reallocation. Calabresi and Melamed demonstrate how liability rules often achieve a combination of efficiency and distributive results that would be difficult to achieve under a property rule.

The utility of models predicting behavior in a zero transaction cost world is that they guide the law – whose object is to develop rules which approximate the zero transaction cost world as closely as possible – in responding to legal problems arising in a positive transaction cost environment. Two major impediments to bargaining (i.e. sources of transaction costs) take the form of externalities and holdouts, which Epstein (1993) shows stand in inverse relationship to each other. He defines the optimal legal rule as that which minimizes the sum of these externality and holdout costs in any particular institutional setting. Epstein demonstrates, through examples in property, restitution and tort, how Coase's transaction costs model plays the central organizing role in developing legal responses to many private law problems. Along similar lines, Parisi (1995) observes that the implicit normative component of the Coasian analysis expects the legal system to mimic what the single owner of interfering resources would do. Notwithstanding the obvious measurement and information problems, Epstein (1993) stresses the importance of the 'single owner test': where resources are under the command of two or more persons, the legal arrangement should attempt to induce all the parties to behave in the same way that a single owner would. Epstein concludes that where the single owner test yields a unique result, that result should be adopted as the legal rule. Where the single owner test does not yield clear results, however, no corollary principle will provide a decisive answer to the particular problem.

In sum, the vast and important literature that developed around Coase's theorem suggests an alternative approach: one based on the evaluation of the relative costs of alternative assignments of rights. In 1960, Coase entrusted legal and economic scholars with the challenging task of deriving the implications of his theorem in their areas of research, and his invitation was successfully taken up by many who experimented with the unparalleled analytical potential of Coase's approach in the evaluation of difficult normative choices.

4. The Economics of Contract Law

A natural area for the application of law and economics, contract law provides a set of legal rules and remedies that facilitate transactions in the marketplace and provide the institutional and legal framework for the understanding of a core element of the economics of exchange. The law and economics literature addresses numerous important issues, ranging from the definition of the essential elements of an enforceable contract to the study of alternative remedies and excuses to performance.

The Optimal Enforcement of Contracts

Concerning the requirements for enforceability of a contract, the law and economics scholar is faced with an immediate trade-off: strict enforcement of all promises may deter future promising, while nonenforcement would reduce reliability. The Anglo-American legal tradition generally draws a primary distinction on the basis of the gratuitous versus onerous nature of the promise. At common law, gratuitous promises were generally not legally enforceable. There are, however, a number of exceptions. From an economic standpoint, Posner (1977) attempts to answer why gratuitous promises are made by rational economic actors, and when such promises should be legally enforceable. Rational economic actors do not make promises unless they confer utility on the promisor. Posner argues that a gratuitous promise confers utility on the promisor over and above the utility to him of the promised performance, by increasing the present value of an uncertain future stream of transfer payments. In developing optimal rules for enforcing gratuitous promises, Posner notes that promises should not be enforced where the enforcement cost exceeds the gain from enforcement. Thus, in deciding whether to enforce gratuitous promises, one must compare the utility of the promise to the promisor and the social cost of enforcing the promise.

To illustrate the theory that contract law develops in light of efficiency considerations, Posner examines some areas in which case law has created exceptions to the general rule that gratuitous promises will not be enforced. For example, promises based on past consideration are generally enforced. Posner states that this type of promise confers a high utility of the promise to the promisor, while the costs of enforcement are low. Similar conclusions are reached with respect to promises under seal, charitable pledges and contract modification. All these examples show judicial enforcement of some gratuitous promises tracks with the economic rules for enforcing gratuitous promises developed by economic analysis.

Goetz and Scott (1980) attempt to develop a general model for determining the most efficient rules for contract enforcement. Tautologically, optimal rules are those that maximize the aggregate welfare of the parties, by balancing the beneficial and the harmful effects of promising. Goetz and Scott elaborate on this conceptual framework, describing an enforcement mechanism that promotes the socially optimal number and types of promises. A promise conveys information about the future, based on which a promisee can adapt his plans. If the promisor performs, the promisee may gain from 'beneficial reliance'. If the promisor breaches, the promisee may suffer from 'detrimental reliance'. Legal rules that encourage self-protection by promisees result in concurrent reductions in both detrimental and beneficial reliance.

The act of promising creates both costs and benefits. Self-interested behavior considers only internal benefits and costs. However, the law can cause individuals to consider the external effects of their decision making, and thus internalize them, by creating incentives and imposing costs (i.e. damages). To induce optimal promise making, the promisor's costs of promising must be adjusted to reflect external effects on the promisee. Goetz and Scott discuss the role of damages in optimizing this interaction through an analysis of nonreciprocal and reciprocal promises.

The enforcement of nonreciprocal promises shapes the behavior of both the promisor and the promisee. A determination of optimal damages must take into account both the beneficial and detrimental reliance induced by the promise, resulting in a prospective net reliance damage rule that encourages promisors to internalize the externalities and make precautionary adjustments. Where self-sanctions are effective and the prospect of improved information is poor, however, nonenforcement of nonreciprocal promises is the optimal choice. In the case of reciprocal promises, the bargaining process accomplishes most of the behavior regulation that the legal system must perform for nonreciprocal promises. Bargainers are able to adjust the volume and form of promising by varying the price of the promise.

Contract Incompleteness and Default Rules

An important part of the economic analysis of contract law comes from the realization that the economic model of a perfect contract is never realized under real-world conditions. The legal system has to provide rules for filling gaps in incomplete contracts. These gap-filling provisions are generally called default or suppletive rules. All legal systems provide rules for filling gaps in incomplete contracts that govern unless the parties contract around them, as distinct from the imperative and nonderogable rules that cannot be changed by contractual agreement. Ayres and Gertner (1989) set out to develop a theory of how courts and legislatures should set default rules.

Typically, high transaction costs are cited as the primary source of contractual incompleteness. The costs of contracting can be minimized when lawmakers choose default rules that most parties would have wanted. However, the costs of *ex ante* bargaining can encourage parties to shift the process of gap filling to the courts, *ex post*, which is inefficient. By penalizing parties for inefficient gaps, courts could give parties an incentive to negotiate *ex ante*. Consistent with this observation, Ayres and Gertner refute the general view that default rules should always mimic what the parties would have wanted, and introduce the concept of 'penalty defaults', which are designed to give at least one of the contracting parties the incentive to contract around the default rule. By purposefully establishing a default rule that the parties would not want, parties are encouraged to reveal information to each other and to the courts. Ayres and Gertner thus distinguish between 'tailored' and 'untailored' default rules. The former attempt to provide precisely what the parties would have contracted for, while the latter constitute a single standard that represents what the majority of contracting parties would want.

Ayres and Gertner also consider a second source for contract incompleteness: strategic behavior. Relatively better informed parties may strategically withhold information that would increase the total gains from contracting, in order to increase their own share of the gains. By setting penalty defaults that induce knowledgeable parties to reveal information by contracting around the default, lawmakers can reduce the opportunities for this rent-seeking behavior. Still, penalty defaults must not be imposed indiscriminately. Considerations include the likelihood that the penalty will induce the desired information transfer, the benefit of the information revealed and the costs of contracting around the default.

Dealing With Asymmetric Information and Opportunistic Behavior

The issue of strategic withholding of information that would be relevant to the other contracting party is crucial for the determination of the validity of any contractual arrangement. Defects in the formation of a contracting party's consent could result from the use of duress or fraud, or from a party's mistaken belief as to an essential element of the contract. In the latter case, an important question emerges as to whether a party to a contract, who knows or should know that the other party is mistaken about a particular fact, has a duty of disclosure to the other party. In some common law cases dealing with unilateral mistake, courts have held that a promisor who is mistaken about some important fact is excused from his obligation to perform or pay damages when the error is or should be known to the other party. Other contract cases, however, hold that a party with knowledge does not have a duty of disclosure to the other party. Kronman (1978) attempts to explain this apparent inconsistency in the law of contracts, suggesting that the key lies in a distinction between two types of information: that which is the result of a deliberate search, and that which is casually acquired.

Rational contracting parties minimize the risk of mistake by assigning it to the party who is the better risk avoider. When one party is mistaken and the other knows or should know of the mistake, courts apply an efficient compound liability rule: while the initial responsibility for the mistake is imposed on the mistaken party, liability later shifts to the other party because it may be the better risk avoider and therefore is in a better position to correct the mistake. In these cases the information is typically acquired casually, at little or no cost, so disclosure is required. The imposition of a disclosure requirement on casually-acquired information does not create a disincentive to invest in the production of socially-useful information.

Where nondisclosure is permitted, however, the information involved is usually the product of a deliberate and costly search. Only by permitting nondisclosure can parties be induced to invest in the acquisition of such information. To ensure that a party benefits from the information it acquires deliberately, a property right in the information must be assigned to that party. When determining which party is the better risk avoider, the cost of deliberately acquiring the information must be considered. Kronman concludes that both the disclosure and nondisclosure requirements, as applied, are not inconsistent and indeed, promote efficiency, placing the risk of a unilateral mistake on the better risk/cost avoider.

Remedies for Breach of Contract

One important function of contract law is to provide remedies in the event of breach of contractual obligations, so as to compensate a disappointed promisee by putting him in as good a position as he would have enjoyed had the promisor not breached. There are normally two methods for achieving this purpose: requiring the breaching party to pay damages, and requiring the breaching party to render specific performance. Historically, different remedies have emerged as preferred solutions across various legal systems (e.g. the English common law inclination to use damages as a default remedy, and the German civil law preference for specific performance). In the Anglo-American legal tradition, damages remain routinely available to a disappointed promisee, while the remedy of specific performance is rarely applied.

A) RELIANCE, EXPECTATIONS, AND CONTRACTUAL DAMAGES

Barton (1972) and Shavell (1980a) examine the area of damages for breach of contract in search of an underlying economic theory. Traditionally, the frameworks that have been used in the determination of damages for breach of contract have been related to the protection of the expectation (an attempt to put the plaintiff in as good a position as if no breach had occurred) and the maintenance of incentives (the setting of a penalty which makes it more desirable to honor a contract than not). The classic Anglo-American common law measure of contract recovery is expectation damages. Asserting that the model for damages in market transactions does not exhibit the problems encountered in contemporary contract law, Barton's (1972) analysis focuses on contractual obligations for which there is no market in which the object of the contract can readily be bought or sold. With nonmarket transactions, expectations (and related damages) become difficult to estimate. The protection of the plaintiff's interests cannot be pursued through incentive maintenance, in that the total costs of completing the transaction may exceed the total benefits, making it economically inefficient to induce performance through penalties.

Under the appropriate bargaining conditions, a negotiated allocation of risk will be optimal. Therefore, when parties with equal bargaining power and equivalent knowledge of the risks fairly bargain for an allocation of the risks or measure of damages, courts should enforce the contract as written. However, parties often do not allocate each risk, normally because of the transaction costs involved. If the risk later materializes and a party breaches, it then falls upon the courts to allocate the risk, thereby adding an unstated term to the contract. Barton suggests that the goal of the law of damages should be to encourage the party that is best able to appreciate the risk to negotiate toward its optimal allocation.

Under conditions of perfect cognitive competence and low transaction costs, the parties would be able to anticipate and provide for all possible contingencies in their contract. Complete contingent contracts are those that specify the obligations of the parties and the payments to be made in the event of breach under every conceivable contingency. If mutually agreed upon, such a contract would be Pareto efficient. Most real life contracts, however, are not Pareto efficient complete contingent contracts, and on these grounds parties may seek to escape their obligations under the terms of the contract. Most contracts must therefore be enforced by means of an assessment of damages that determine the amount of money, if any, that the breaching party must pay the other party. Shavell (1980a) shows how a damages measure for breach of contract may create incentives for parties whose contracts fail to provide for various contingencies, such that they will act in a way that approximates what would have been agreed upon under a Pareto efficient complete contingent contract.

Damages measures influence the decisions regarding breach and reliance. A party will breach only if his position after breaching and paying damages will be better than if he performs. The amount of damages a nonbreaching party receives may be a function of his level of reliance, so that varying reliance can affect the probability of breach. The expected value of a contract to each party can therefore be determined, as can the desirability of the various damages measures. One damages measure is Pareto superior to another if, using the first measure, both parties can assure themselves of a higher expected return. Shavell analyzes four common damages measures (expectancy, reliance, restitution and no damages) in two different cases, and derives several conclusions. The payment of damages for breach tends to promote only Pareto efficient breaches by forcing a potential breacher to internalize the loss that would be imposed on the other party, although the payment of damages may lead to an excessive level of reliance on the part of the potential victim. With a similar logic, Shavell shows that expectation damages are generally Pareto superior to reliance damages.

B) SPECIFIC PERFORMANCE OF THE CONTRACTUAL OBLIGATION

Considering the alternative class of remedies for providing relief to the victim of contractual breach, Schwartz (1979) argues that specific performance should be as routinely available as damages. In his view, specific performance is the most accurate method of achieving the goal of compensating a disappointed promisee, yet is available only at the discretion of the courts. Schwartz examines the arguments in favor of the restrictive use of specific performance, and refutes each in turn.

One argument touts damages as fully compensatory, so that specific performance is unnecessary. Schwartz argues that damages are actually often undercompensatory: a request for specific performance itself serves as evidence that damages would be inadequate. Another argument holds that restricting specific performance is efficient because it reduces both pre-breach and post-breach negotiation costs. Schwartz replies that expanding the remedy of specific performance would not result in greater transaction costs than the damages remedy. Instead, it would produce efficiency gains by minimizing the inefficiencies of undercompensation, reducing the need for liquidated damages clauses, minimizing strategic behavior, and saving the costs of litigating complex damage issues. Schwartz also rejects the argument that specific performance increases the administrative costs of the parties and the courts because of the difficulty of supervision. He suggests that courts can eliminate much of the cost by appointing special masters. As to whether requiring specific performance interferes with a promisor's liberty more than requiring the payment of damages, Schwartz notes that while the argument may have validity in the context of personal services contracts, it has none where roughly fungible goods and corporate services are concerned. In this way, Schwartz argues that defenses to requests for specific performance that rest on the unfairness of contract terms or prices should be eliminated, and that the defense based on difficulty of supervision should be greatly restricted.

5. The Economics of Tort Law

The positive economic theory of tort law maintains that the common law of torts is best explained as if judges are trying to promote efficient resource allocation, i.e. maximize efficiency. The relevant variables for the tort problem are the cost of accidents, the cost of accident avoidance (prevention), and the administrative costs of the justice system. Every legal system chooses among several liability rules (e.g. negligence, strict liability, etc.) and safety standards to minimize the overall cost of accidents.

The Learned Hand Formula of Negligence

The relatively simple structure of a tort problem provides one of the most fertile areas for the application of economic analysis. The legal and economic theory of negligence liability identifies the boundaries of liability through a balance of the social value of the interest in jeopardy and of that of the risk-creating activity. This definition – that is currently accepted by North American doctrine – is clearly summarized by the *Restatement (Second) of Torts* § 291:

> Where an act is one which a reasonable man would recognize as involving a risk of harm to another, the risk is unreasonable and the act negligent if the risk is of such magnitude as to outweigh what the law regards as the utility of the act or of the particular manner in which it was done. (*The Restatement (Second) of Torts* §§ 292 and 293, indicate the criteria to use in verifying utility of conduct and magnitude of risk.)

American case law in a sense anticipated the results of economic analysis, adopting the simple and formal logic of economics to adjudicate tort cases. Already in 1947, Judge Learned Hand, in the celebrated decision of *United States* v. *Carroll Towing Co.* (159 F.2d 169 (2d Cir. 1947)), clarified the trade-offs between the above-stated variables, using a mathematical formula. This rule became a milestone in the law of torts, and it is now known as the Hand formula of negligence. The formula defines negligence as a function of three variables: a) the probability of a harmful event occurring (magnitude of risk); b) the seriousness of the damage that may result from this event (gravity of harm); and, c) the cost of preventing the occurrence of the harmful event (burden of prevention). In the original formula, (P) indicates the magnitude of risk; (L) indicates the gravity of the loss; and (B) indicates the burden of prevention (i.e., the cost of adequate precautions). According to the Hand formula, conduct is negligent if the cost of adequate precautions is less than the cost of the injury multiplied by the probability of its occurrence, i.e. if $(B) < (PL)$.

Although the Hand formula does not directly consider the social value of the risk-creating behavior, it produces the proper incentives for the evaluation of such behavior. By imposing a balance between risk and prevention, the result in *Carroll Towing* encourages individuals to weigh the cost of prevention against the utility of the behavior. When deciding whether to engage in an activity, the reasonable person will consider whether the utility derived from the activity justifies the risk of liability and/or the cost of prevention (this is, indeed, the question of the *Restatement (Second) of Torts* § 291, comment 'a', which asks whether 'the game is worth the candle'). According to this logic, individuals will respond to liability rules by undertaking the socially optimal level of precaution. A vast region of law and economics literature has explored the wisdom of this tort doctrine, often with the use of formal economic models, bringing to light the importance of using marginal (rather than total) values in the assessment of liability. Along similar lines, after establishing a positive economic model of tort law, Landes and Posner (1982) conclude that the Hand formula of negligence, as applied, coincides with the economic model of due care.

Negligence Versus Strict Liability

Landes and Posner (1982) thoroughly develop an overarching economic model that in their view underlies the positive economic theory of tort law, and compare the model's predictions to the actual rules of tort liability. The model assumes that individuals maximize their expected utility, that both injurers and victims are risk neutral (risk neutrality is assumed with no prejudice to a subsequent introduction of risk aversion), and that victims and injurers are complete strangers, with no cost-effective opportunity to enter into a voluntary contract prior to the accident. Situations of joint care (where it is optimal for both the victim and the injurer to take some care) and alternative care (where it is optimal for one party to take care, but not the other) are distinguished, as are level of care (the amount of precaution a party takes when engaging in an activity) versus level of activity (the amount of activity a party engages in). Comprehensively analyzing and comparing liability rules in the context of the economic model, Landes and Posner illustrate that if a change in the victim's activity level is likely to reduce the cost of accidents, strict liability may be a superior rule compared to a negligence standard. They evaluate the legal application of strict liability, using as examples the common law's treatment of damage by animals (domestic and wild) and ultrahazardous activities. They conclude that the common law imposes strict liability in the same instances as would the economic model: where optimal accident avoidance requires altering the defendant's activity level rather than his care or the plaintiff's activity or care.

Landes and Posner's analysis points out that the legal system tends to favor negligence with a defense of contributory negligence over strict liability without such a defense. Contributory negligence, though, can lead to incorrect results in certain alternative care cases and therefore deviate from the economic model. Such deviations explain the emergence of defenses to contributory negligence, such as last clear chance and attractive nuisance, where the costs of accident avoidance are lower to the injurer than to the victim.

Shavell (1980b) compares the efficiency of negligence and strict liability rules in both the 'unilateral case', where the actions of injurers but not of victims are assumed to affect the probability or severity of losses, and the 'bilateral case', which also takes account of the possibility that potential victims may affect losses. He considers both the market and the nonmarket case, and his model assumes that parties are risk neutral and take liability rules as given, and that the legal system is free of administrative costs. Liability rules that maximize social welfare are considered efficient. For unilateral care cases, where injurers and victims are strangers, strict liability rules force the injurer (or seller, for the market case) to consider accident losses when choosing the appropriate level of activity and care, and are therefore efficient. Because injurers must only exercise due care, negligence rules may produce inefficient activity levels. For the bilateral care case, there is no single liability rule that induces efficient behavior. Under a negligence rule, injurers (or sellers, for the market case) will tend to choose levels of activity that are too high, while victims, who bear the residual loss, will generally reduce their level of activity. A strict liability rule will have the converse effect.

Tort, Contract and Regulation

Starting from the premise that both contract and tort are essentially about the exchange of property rights, Bishop (1983) notes that contract and tort law are remarkably similar, both being designed to provide crucial terms otherwise lacking because of the high cost of bargaining. He explores the areas where contract and tort converge and diverge through an analysis of four fundamental problems of insurance and information, and the doctrinal devices that seek to mitigate their effects. These problems include remote contingencies; adverse selection; actions by the insured, after the contract of insurance but before any loss, which make the loss more likely (moral hazard 1); and actions by the insured, after the loss, which aggravate the loss (moral hazard 2). For example, both contract and tort law provide default rules for remote contingencies. Decision makers assign probabilities, based on the information available, to various events. Many events have a very low probability, so that parties will have little incentive to bargain over them. Tort deals with remote contingencies through a remoteness doctrine (foreseeability). In contract, the problem is dealt with through the doctrines of frustration, impossibility and common mistake.

Rejecting the convergence thesis, Bishop observes that while liability has expanded in both contract and tort, and the two areas definitely overlap, contract and tort have not converged into one grand law of obligations. Unlike many civil law systems, the common law still relies on different conceptual frameworks to address substantially similar issues in tort and contract. For example, tort law copes with moral hazard problems by inducing efficient behavior, where the victim could have avoided the injury more cheaply than the tortfeasor, through contributory and comparative negligence rules. There is no readily equivalent rule in contract, even though in the case of a contractual duty of care, the failure of a victim to take inexpensive precautions is equally wasteful and undesirable. *Ex post* contribution to the harm is, however, disciplined with similar principles in torts and contracts: both systems deal with actions taken by the victim after the accident or breach which aggravate the loss, with a rule requiring the plaintiff to take reasonable steps to mitigate his loss.

Society can control activities that create a risk to others by using two very different approaches: liability in tort and safety regulations. After assessing both approaches in terms of four general determinants (differential knowledge, incapacity to pay for harm, escaping suit, and administrative cost), Shavell (1984) concludes that both approaches are desirable as typically employed: liability in the case of typical torts and regulation in the case of activities normally subject to safety standards. Two of the four determinants generally favor liability: administrative costs and differential knowledge. Under the liability approach, administrative costs are incurred only if harm occurs; under regulation, they are incurred whether or not harm occurs. As to knowledge, private parties have an advantage because they are in a superior position to estimate benefits to be derived from their activities, and are in at least as good a position to estimate risk. Notwithstanding public-choice concerns, in certain contexts regulatory authorities may possess an advantage because private parties have an insufficient incentive to gather information. The other two determinants tend to favor regulation. Under regulation, insolvency of the tortfeasor becomes irrelevant if safety standards can be enforced as a precondition for engaging in the activity. Conversely, when the parties' assets are less than the potential harm, there may be insufficient incentives to adopt adequate precautions. A similar logic applies to the chance that private parties might escape liability following a lawsuit, which would dilute the incentives to undertake efficient precautions but would not stand in the way of an effective enforcement of *ex ante* safety standards.

The Function of Punitive Damages in Tort

An important issue in tort law is related to the applicability of punitive damages (i.e. damages in excess of the actual harm) to the tortfeasor. Legal systems across the world are divided on this controversial issue. By means of an economic model, Cooter (1982) develops standards for deciding when punitive damages (in addition to merely compensatory damages) are appropriate in tort disputes governed by a fault-based rule. Describing the legal standard of care as a threshold, Cooter notes that when a potential injurer crosses the threshold (the point where diligent conduct becomes negligence with consequential liability) the expected cost of liability jumps abruptly to a positive value. Because it is often cheaper to comply with the legal standard of care than bear liability, noncompliance is usually unintentional. Cooter argues that because the purpose of punitive damages is to deter future injuries and punish offenders, they should not be imposed where fault is unintentional.

Cooter's model shows that unintentional fault is better corrected through compensatory damages, and that the purposes of punitive damages are best met where fault is intentional. His model assumes that intentional fault usually involves gross noncompliance. This is so because although there is an abrupt jump in liability costs when the fault threshold is crossed with a moderate degree of noncompliance, there is no similar discontinuity when moving from moderate noncompliance to gross noncompliance. To deter such behavior, Cooter suggests that punitive damages should be a function of the illicit benefit or extraordinary cost that prompted the intentional fault (which will normally result in a large award to the plaintiff).

Conclusion

The extent and the steady expansion of the law and economics scholarship in the areas of law considered in this volume has made the task of selecting representative articles all the more difficult. In the spirit of the present collection, we have presented some of the seminal contributions to this field of research. While considering only a very small sample of the existing scholarship, this volume will, the editors hope, illustrate the breadth and analytical power of economic analysis in the study of legal problems. In this introduction to the economic foundations of private law we have attempted to portray the important interface between economics and law.

The growth rate of this field of research unquestionably underscores the relevance and importance of the economic approach to the theory and practice of law. The growing influence of these seminal writings in the judicial profession, and in the legal and economic academic world, underscores the relevance and importance of these early contributions and the growing maturity of the new law and economics movement. These papers have indeed provided the important foundations for the development of an overarching economic theory of law and, most importantly, have opened new areas of research for present and future generations of jurists and economists alike.

Bibliography

Alchian, Armen (1965), 'Some Economics of Property Rights', *Politico*, **30** (11), 816–29.

Ayres, Ian and Robert Gertner (1989), 'Filling Gaps in Incomplete Contracts: An Economic Theory of Default Rules', *Yale Law Journal*, **99**, 87–130.

Barton, John H. (1972), 'The Economic Basis of Damages for Breach of Contract', *Journal of Legal Studies*, **1**, 277–304.

Bentham, Jeremy (1782), *Of Laws in General*.

Bentham, Jeremy (1789), *Introduction to the Principles of Morals and Legislation*.

Bishop, William (1983), 'The Contract–Tort Boundary and the Economics of Insurance', *Journal of Legal Studies*, **12**, 241–66.

Buchanan, James (1974), 'Good Economics – Bad Law', *Virginia Law Review*, **60**, 483–92.

Calabresi, Guido (1980), 'About Law and Economics: A Letter to Ronald Dworkin', *Hofstra Law Review*, **8**, 553–62.

Calabresi, Guido and A. Douglas Melamed (1972), 'Property Rules, Liability Rules, and Inalienability: One View of the Cathedral', *Harvard Law Review*, **85**, 1089–128.

Coase, Ronald H. (1960), 'The Problem of Social Cost', *Journal of Law and Economics*, **3**, 1–44.

Coase, Ronald H. (1978), 'Economics and Contiguous Disciplines', *Journal of Legal Studies*, **7**, 201–11.

Cooter, Robert D. (1982), 'Economic Analysis of Punitive Damages', *Southern California Law Review*, **56**, 79–101.

Cooter, Robert D. and Daniel L. Rubinfeld (1989), 'Economic Analysis of Legal Disputes and Their Resolution', *Journal of Economic Literature*, **27**, 1067–97.

Demsetz, Harold (1967), 'Toward a Theory of Property Rights', *American Economic Review (Papers and Proceedings)*, **57**, 347–59.

Demsetz, Harold (1972), 'When Does the Rule of Liability Matter?', *Journal of Legal Studies*, **1**, 13–28.
Ehrlich, Isaac and Richard A. Posner (1974), 'An Economic Analysis of Legal Rulemaking', *Journal of Legal Studies*, **3**, 257–86.
Epstein, Richard A. (1993), 'Holdouts, Externalities, and the Single Owner: One More Salute to Ronald Coase', *Journal of Law and Economics*, **36**, 553–82.
Goetz, Charles J. and Robert E. Scott (1980), 'Enforcing Promises: An Examination of the Basis of Contract', *Yale Law Journal*, **89**, 1261–322.
Kaplow, Louis and Steven Shavell (1994), 'Why the Legal System is Less Efficient than the Income Tax in Redistributing Income', *Journal of Legal Studies*, **23**, 667–81.
Kronman, Anthony T. (1978), 'Mistake, Disclosure, Information, and the Law of Contracts', *Journal of Legal Studies*, **7**, 1–34.
Landes, William M. (1971), 'An Economic Analysis of the Courts', *Journal of Law and Economics*, **14**, 61–107.
Landes, William M. and Richard A. Posner (1982), 'The Positive Economic Theory of Tort Law', *Georgia Law Review*, **15**, 851–924.
Parisi, Francesco (1995), 'Private Property and Social Costs', *European Journal of Law and Economics*, **2**, 149–73.
Posner, Richard A. (1977), 'Gratuitous Promises in Economics and Law', *Journal of Legal Studies*, **6**, 411–26.
Posner, Richard A. (1985), 'Wealth Maximization Revisited', *Notre Dame Journal of Law, Ethics, and Public Policy*, **2**, 85–105.
Priest, George L. (1977), 'The Common Law Process and the Selection of Efficient Rules', *Journal of Legal Studies*, **6**, 65–82.
Priest, George L. and Benjamin Klein (1984), 'The Selection of Disputes for Litigation', *Journal of Legal Studies*, **13**, 1–55.
Rowley, Charles K. (1981), 'Social Sciences and the Law: The Relevance of Economic Theories', *Oxford Journal of Legal Studies*, **39**, 391–405.
Rowley, Charles K. (1989), 'The Common Law in Public Choice Perspective: A Theoretical and Institutional Critique', *Hamline Law Review*, **12**, 355–83.
Rubin, Paul H. (1977), 'Why is the Common Law Efficient?', *Journal of Legal Studies*, **6**, 51–63.
Schwartz, Alan (1979), 'The Case for Specific Performance', *Yale Law Journal*, **89**, 271–306.
Shavell, Steven (1980a), 'Damage Measures for Breach of Contract', *Bell Journal of Economics*, **11**, 466–90.
Shavell, Steven (1980b), 'Strict Liability Versus Negligence', *Journal of Legal Studies*, **9**, 1–25.
Shavell, Steven (1984), 'Liability for Harm Versus Regulation of Safety', *Journal of Legal Studies*, **13**, 357–74.
Smith, Adam (1776), *An Inquiry into the Nature and Causes of the Wealth of Nations*.
Stigler, George J. (1989), 'Two Notes on the Coase Theorem', *Yale Law Journal*, **99**, 631–36.

Part I
The Methodology of Law and Economics

[1]

RICHARD T. ELY LECTURE

The Law and Economics Movement

By RICHARD A. POSNER*

In the last thirty years, the scope of economics has expanded dramatically beyond its traditional domain of explicit market transactions.[1] Today there is an economic theory of property rights, of corporate and other organizations, of government and politics, of education, of the family, of crime and punishment, of anthropology, of history, of information, of racial and sexual discrimination, of privacy, even of the behavior of animals—and, overlapping all these but the last, of law.[2]

Some economists oppose this expansion, in whole or (more commonly) in part.[3] There are a number of bad reasons, all I think closely related, for such opposition, and one slightly better one.

1) One bad reason is the idea that economics *means* the study of markets, so that nonmarket behavior is simply outside its scope. This type of argument owes nothing really to economics, but instead reflects a common misconception about language—more specifically a failure to distinguish among three different types of word or concept. The first type, illustrated by the term "marginal cost," is purely conceptual. The term is rigorously and unambiguously defined by reference to other concepts, just as numbers are; but (again like numbers) there is no observable object in the real world that it names. (Try finding a firm's marginal costs on its books of account!) The second type of word, illustrated by "rabbit," refers to a set of real-world objects. Few such words are purely referential; one can speak of a pink rabbit or a rabbit the size of a man without misusing the word, even though one is no longer using it to describe anything that exists. Nevertheless, the referential function dominates. Finally, there are words like "law," "religion," "literature"—and "economics"—which are neither conceptual nor referential. Such words resist all efforts at definition. They have, in fact, no fixed meaning, and their dictionary definitions are circular. They can be used but not defined.[4]

One cannot say that economics is what economists do, because many noneconomists do economics. One cannot call economics the science of rational choice, either. The word "rational" lacks a clear definition; and, passing that difficulty, there can be noneconomic theories of rational choice, in which few predictions of ordinary economics may hold; for example, because the theory assumes that people's preferences are unstable. There can also be nonrational economic theories; an example is the type of survival theory in industrial organization in which firms that randomly hit on methods of lowering their costs expand vis-à-vis their rivals; another example is Marxism. One cannot call economics the study of markets either, not only because that characterization resolves the question of the domain of eco-

*Judge, U.S. Court of Appeals for the Seventh Circuit; Senior Lecturer, University of Chicago Law School, 1111 E. 60th St., Chicago, IL 60637. I thank Gary Becker, Frank Easterbrook, William Landes, Geoffrey Miller, Richard Porter, George Stigler, Geoffrey Stone, and Alan Sykes for comments on a previous draft and Nir Yarden for research assistance.

[1]See, for example, Gary Becker (1976); Jack Hirshleifer (1985, p. 53); George Stigler (1984); Gerard Radnitzky and Peter Bernholz (1986).

[2]For a recent conspectus of economic analysis of law, see my book (1986).

[3]See, for example, Ronald Coase (1978). Coase is of course a leading figure in the economics of property rights, so his opposition is far from total.

[4]For an excellent discussion, see John Ellis (1974, ch. 2).

nomics by an arbitrary definitional stop but also because other disciplines, notably sociology, anthropology, and psychology, also study markets. About the best one can say is that there is an open-ended set of concepts (such concepts as perfect competition, utility maximization, equilibrium, marginal cost, consumers' surplus, elasticity of demand, and opportunity cost), most of which are derived from a common set of assumptions about individual behavior and can be used to make predictions about social behavior; and that when used in sufficient density these concepts make a work of scholarship "economic" regardless of its subject matter or its author's degree. When economics is "defined" in this way, there is nothing that makes the study of marriage and divorce less suitable a priori for economics than the study of the automobile industry or the inflation rate.

2) The "extension" of economics from market to nonmarket behavior is sometimes thought to be premature until the main problems in the study of explicit markets have been solved. How can economists hope to explain the divorce rate when they can't explain behavior under oligopoly? But this rhetorical question is just a variation on the first point, that economics has a fixed subject matter, a predefined domain. The tools of economics may be no good for solving a number of important problems in understanding explicit markets; that is no reason to keep hitting one's head against the wall. Economics does not have a predestined mission to dispel all the mysteries of the market. Maybe it will do better with some types of nonmarket behavior than with some types of market behavior.

3) Next is the idea that to do economics in fields that have their own scholarly traditions, such as history or law, an economist must master so much noneconomic learning that his total educational investment will be disproportionate to the likely fruits of "interdisciplinary" research; hence economists should steer clear of these fields. Besides disregarding the possibility of collaboration between economists and practitioners of other disciplines, this argument assumes that economics means something done by people with a Ph.D. in economics. It may be easier for an anthropologist to learn economics than for an economist to learn anthropology. Maybe the fraction of one's training in economics that is irrelevant to the economic analysis of anthropological phenomena is larger than the fraction of anthropological training that is irrelevant; or maybe economic theory is more compact than the body of knowledge we call anthropology. (It probably is easier to learn economics well than to learn Chinese well.) Or it might simply be (this has happened in law and economics) that a given anthropologist had more of a knack for economics than a given economist had a knack for anthropology. It is only by defining economics, in rather a medieval way, as the work done by members of a particular guild (the guild of economics Ph.D.s) that one will be led to conclude that if the economics of law is done by lawyers, or the economics of history by historians, it cannot be "real" economics. The emergence of nonmarket economics may have resulted in a vast but unrecognized increase in the number of economists!

The idea that nonmarket economics is somehow peripheral to economics is connected with the fact that there has been little fruitful analysis of explicit markets besides economics, though admirers of Max Weber's analysis of the role of Protestantism in the rise of capitalism may want to challenge this assertion. Almost by default, explicit markets became thought of as the natural subject matter of economics. But the fact that other areas of social behavior, such as law, have been extensively studied from other angles than the economic is no reason for concluding that these areas cannot be studied profitably with the tools of modern economic theory.

4) Still another bad reason for hostility to nonmarket economics is fear that it will bring economics into disrepute by associating the economist with politically and morally distasteful, bizarre, or controversial practices (such as capital punishment, polygamy, or slavery before the Civil War) and proposals—whether specific policy proposals such as education vouchers, or the idea, which is basic to nonmarket economics,

that human beings are rational maximizers throughout the whole, or at least a very broad, range of their social interactions. If economics becomes associated with highly sensitive topics, it may lose some of the appearance of scientific objectivity that economists have worked so hard to cultivate in the face of obvious difficulties including the fact that much of traditional microeconomics and macroeconomics is already politically and ethically controversial, as is evident from current debates over free trade, deregulation, and deficit spending. But this complaint, too, is part of the fallacious idea that there is a fixed domain for economics. If there were, it would be natural to recoil from economic ventures at once peripheral and controversial. But if I am right that there is no fixed, preordained, or natural domain for economics—that politics, punishment, and exploitation are, at least a priori, as appropriate subjects for economics as the operation of the wheat market—then it is pusillanimous to counsel avoidance of particular topics because they happen to be politically or ethically (are these different?) controversial at the present time.

5) A slightly better reason for questioning the expansion of economics beyond its traditional boundaries is skepticism that economic tools will work well in the new fields or that adequate data will be available in them to test economic hypotheses. Maybe these are domains where emotion dominates reason, and maybe economists can't say much about emotion. And explicit markets generate substantial quantitative data (prices, costs, output, employment, etc.), which greatly facilitate empirical research—though only a small fraction of economists actually do empirical research. These points suggest a functional as distinct from a definitional answer to the question of the appropriate bounds of economics: economics is the set of fruitful applications of economic theory. But a detailed survey of nonmarket economics is not necessary in order to make the point that the economic approach has been shown to be fruitful in dealing with such diverse nonmarket subjects as education, economic history, the causes of regulatory legislation, the behavior of nonprofit institutions, divorce, racial and sexual wage differentials, the incidence and control of crime, and (I shall argue) the common law rules governing property, torts, and contracts[5]—successful enough at any rate to establish nonmarket economics as a legitimate branch of economics and to counsel at least a temporary suspension of disbelief by the skeptics and doubters. Indeed, so familiar have some of these areas of nonmarket economics become in recent years (for example, education viewed through the lens of human capital theory) that many young economists no longer think of them as being outside the traditional boundaries of economics. The distinction between "market" and "nonmarket" economics is fraying.

I

A

The particular area of nonmarket economics that I want to focus on is the economics of law, or "law and economics" as it is often called. Because of the enormous range of behavior regulated by the legal system, law and economics could be defined so broadly as to be virtually coextensive with economics. This would not be a useful definition. Yet to exclude bodies of law that regulate explicit markets—such as contract and property law, labor, antitrust and corporate law, public utility and common carrier regulation, and taxation—would be cripplingly narrow. But if these bodies *are* included, in what sense is law and economics a branch of *non*market economics? (I do not suggest that this is an important question; it may, indeed, be an argument for discarding an increasingly uninteresting distinction.)

As with any nonreferential, nonconceptual term, the only possible criterion for a definition of law and economics is utility—not accuracy. The purpose of carving out a separate field and calling it law and economics

[5]For a few examples see Becker (1981; 1975); Orley Ashenfelter and Albert Rees (1973); Robert Fogel and Stanley Engerman (1971); Isaac Ehrlich (1974); David Pyle (1983); Stigler (1971).

(or better, because clearer, "economics of law") is to identify the area of economic inquiry to which a substantial knowledge of law in both its doctrinal and institutional aspects is relevant. Many economic problems in such areas of law as taxation and labor do not require much legal knowledge to solve. Although taxes can be imposed only by laws, often the details of the tax law either are not relevant to the analyst, as where he is asking what the effect on charitable giving of reducing the marginal income tax rate is likely to be, or are transparent and unproblematic.

Similarly, in the field of labor, you can study the effects of unemployment insurance on unemployment without knowing a great deal about the state and federal laws governing unemployment insurance, though you must know something. But suppose you wanted to study the consequences of allowing the defendant in an employment discrimination case to deduct from the lost wages awarded the plaintiff (if the plaintiff succeeds in proving that he was fired because of race or sex or some other forbidden criterion), any unemployment benefits that the plaintiff might have received after being fired. You could not get far in such a study without knowing a fair amount of nonobvious employment discrimination law: Is there a uniform judicial rule on deduction or nondeduction of such benefits? Could the benefits be deducted but then be ordered paid to the state or the federal government rather than kept by the employer? Does the law insist that the employee who wants damages for employment discrimination search for work? How are those damages computed? The economics of law is the set of economic studies that build on a detailed knowledge of some area of law; whether the study is done by a "lawyer," an "economist," someone with both degrees, or a lawyer-economist team has little significance.

The law and economics movement has made progress in a number of areas of legal regulation of explicit markets. These include antitrust law, and the regulation of public utilities and common carriers; fraud and unfair competition; corporate bankruptcy, secured transactions, and other areas of commercial law; corporate law and securities regulation; and taxation, including state taxation of interstate commerce, an area that the courts regulate under the commerce clause of the Constitution.[6] In none of these areas is participation by economists, or (if we insist on guild distinctions) by economics-minded lawyers, particularly controversial any more, though some die-hard lawyers continue to resist the encroachments of economics and of course there is disagreement among economists over many particular issues; this is notable in antitrust. An area of legal regulation of explicit markets that is just beginning to ripen for economics is intellectual property, with special reference to copyrights and trademarks. Patents have long been an object of economic study.

The areas of law and economics about which economists and lawyers display considerable unease are the (sometimes arbitrarily classified as) nonmarket areas—crime, torts, and contracts; the environment; the family; the legislative and administrative processes; constitutional law; jurisprudence and legal process; legal history; primitive law; and so on. All the reasons that I gave at the outset for why some economists resist the extension of economics beyond its traditional domain of explicit market behavior coalesce in regard to these areas. And because they are also close to the heart of what lawyers think distinctive about law—of what they think makes it something more than a method of economic regulation—this branch of economic analysis of law dismays many lawyers. Furthermore, lawyers tend to have more rigid, stereotyped ideas of the boundaries of economics than economists do, in part because most lawyers are not aware of the extension (which is recent, though its roots go back to Adam Smith and Jeremy Bentham) of economics to nonmarket behavior. Indeed, a demarcation

[6]The work in these areas is summarized in my book (pts. 3–5 and ch. 26). It is of some interest to note that the economic analysis of secured financing is now dominated by economically inclined lawyers. See Robert Scott (1986) and references cited there.

which places secured financing on one side of the divide and contract law on the other seems entirely artificial. The distinction between market and nonmarket economics may be as arbitrary as it is uninteresting.

B

I want to try to convey some sense of the economic analysis of "nonmarket" law. Its basic premises are two:

1) People act as rational maximizers of their satisfactions in making such nonmarket decisions as whether to marry or divorce, commit or refrain from committing crimes, make an arrest, litigate or settle a lawsuit, drive a car carefully or carelessly, pollute (a nonmarket activity because pollution is not traded in the market), refuse to associate with people of a different race, fix a mandatory retirement age for employees.

2) Rules of law operate to impose prices on (sometimes subsidize) these nonmarket activities, thereby altering the amount or character of the activity.

A third premise, discussed at greater length later, guides some research in the economics of nonmarket law:

3) Common law (i.e., judge-made) rules are often best explained as efforts, whether or not conscious, to bring about either Pareto or Kaldor-Hicks efficient outcomes.

The first two premises lead to such predictions as that an increase in a court's trial queue will lead to a reduction (other things being equal—a qualification applicable to all my examples) in the number of cases tried, that awarding prejudgment interest to a prevailing plaintiff will reduce settlement rates, that "no-fault" divorce will redistribute wealth from women to men, that no-fault automobile accident compensation laws will increase the number of fatal accidents even if the laws are not applicable to such accidents, that substituting comparative for contributory negligence will raise liability and accident insurance premium rates but will not change the accident rate (except insofar as the increase in the price of liability insurance results in fewer drivers or less driving), that increasing the severity as well as certainty of criminal punishment will reduce the crime rate, that making the losing party in a lawsuit pay the winner's attorney's fees will *not* reduce the amount of litigation, that abolition of the reserve clause in baseball did not affect the mobility of baseball players (the Coase theorem, restated as a hypothesis), that the 1978 revision of the bankruptcy laws led to more personal-bankruptcy filings and higher interest rates, and that abolishing the laws that forbid the sale of babies for adoption would reduce rather than increase the full price of babies.

I have given a mixture of obvious and nonobvious hypotheses derived from my basic premises. Notice that I do not say intuitive and counterintuitive hypotheses, because all are counterintuitive to people who believe, as many economists and most lawyers do, that people are not rational maximizers except when transacting in explicit markets, or that legal rules do not have substantial incentive effects, perhaps because the rules are poorly communicated or the sanctions for violating them are infrequently or irregularly imposed.

C

Thus far in my discussion of the economic analysis of legal regulation of nonmarket behavior I have focused on the effects of legal change on behavior. One can reverse the sequence and ask how changes in behavior affect law. To make this reversal, though, one needs a theory of law, parallel to the rational-maximization theory of behavior. The economic theory of the common law, defined broadly as law made by judges rather than by legislatures or constitutional conventions or other nonjudicial bodies, is that the common law is best understood not merely as a pricing mechanism but as a pricing mechanism designed to bring about an efficient allocation of resources, in the Kaldor-Hicks sense of efficiency.[7] This theory implies that when behavior changes, law will

[7]See my book (pt. 2); and William Landes and myself (1987).

change. Suppose that at first people live in very close proximity to each other. Natural light will be a scarce commodity in these circumstances, so its value in exchange may well exceed the cost of enforcing a property right in it. Later, people spread out, so that the value of natural light (in the economic sense of value—exchange value rather than use value) falls; then the net social value of the property right (i.e., the value of the right minus the cost of enforcing it) may be negative. These two states of the world correspond roughly to the situations in England and America in the eighteenth century. The English recognized a limited right to natural light; they called this right "ancient lights." When American courts after independence decided which parts of the English common law to adopt, they rejected the doctrine of ancient lights—as the economic theory of the common law predicts they would.

Another example is the adoption of the appropriation system of water rights in the arid American West. In wet England and the wet eastern United States, the riparian system prevailed. This was a system of communal rights, which is a kind of halfway house between individual rights and no rights, and is inefficient for scarce goods. The appropriation system is one of individual rights, and was and is more efficient for areas that are dry (i.e., where water is scarce rather than plentiful)—which is where we find the appropriation system, as the economic theory of common law predicts. Or consider the different responses of the eastern and the western states to the problem of fencing out vs. fencing in. Fencing out refers to a property rights system in which damage caused by straying cattle is actionable at law only if the owner of the crops or other goods damaged by the cattle has made reasonable efforts to fence. Fencing in refers to a system where this duty is not imposed, so that the owner of the cattle must fence them in if he wants to avoid liability. The former system is more efficient if the ratio of crops to cattle is low, for then it is cheaper for the farmer than the rancher to fence. If the ratio is reversed, fencing in is a more efficient system. In fact, the cattle states tended to adopt fencing out, and England and the eastern states fencing in. Many similar examples could be given.[8]

Two objections to this branch of economic analysis of law must be considered:

1) One is that a theory of law is not testable, because when one is examining the effects of behavior on law rather than of law on behavior, the dependent variable tends not to be quantitative: it is not a price or output figure but a pattern of rules. However, the scientific study of social rules is not impossible; what else is linguistics? Fencing in vs. fencing out (or ancient lights vs. no ancient lights, or riparian vs. appropriative water rights) is a dichotomous dependent variable, which modern methods of statistical analysis can handle. And if a continuous variable is desired, it can be created by using the year in which the particular law was adopted (earlier adoption implying a more strongly supported law), the severity of the sanctions, or the expenditures on enforcement, to distribute states or nations along a continuum.

2) James Buchanan (1974), along with a number of neo-Austrian economists, holds that law should not be an instrumental variable designed to maximize wealth. Judges should not be entrusted with economic decisions—they lack the training and information to make them wisely. They should use custom and precedent to construct a stable but distinctly background framework for market and nonmarket behavior. But this is an objection to normative economic analysis of law—to urging, for example, that the common law (and perhaps other law) be changed to make it approximate the economic model of efficient law better—and the more interesting and promising aspect of economic analysis of law is the positive. I say this not because of a general preference for positive to normative inquiry, but because so little of a systematic nature is known about law. Law is not so well understood that one can hold a confident opinion about whether the right way to improve it is to

[8]See sources cited in fn. 7, from which the above examples are taken.

make the judges more sophisticated economically or more obedient to precedent and tradition.

II

Much of what I have said so far is old hat, at least to those familiar with the law and economics movement, so let me turn to some novel applications of economic analysis to law: applications to free speech and religious freedom, respectively.

A

It has long been recognized that the process by which truth emerges from a welter of competing ideas resembles competition in a market for ordinary goods and services: hence the influential metaphor of the "marketplace of ideas." It is also well known that because of the incompleteness of patent and copyright law as a system of property rights in ideas, the production of ideas frequently generates external benefits. Aaron Director (1964) and Ronald Coase (1974) have emphasized the peculiarity of the modern "liberal" preference for freedom in the market for ideas to freedom in markets for ordinary goods and services (both freedoms having been part of the nineteenth-century concept of liberty), and have attributed this preference to the self-interest of intellectuals.

Economists have paid scant attention, however, to the details of legal regulation in this area. Over the past seventy years or so, the courts have developed an elaborate body of doctrine through interpretation of the First Amendment's guarantee of free speech. Both the effects of this body of doctrine on the marketplace of ideas and the economic logic (if any) of the doctrines present interesting issues for economic analysis.

So far as effects are concerned, I suspect they have been few. Despite the high-flown rhetoric in which our courts discuss the right of free speech, they have countenanced a large number of restrictions—on picketing, on obscenity, on employer speech in collective bargaining representation elections, on commercial advertising, on threats, on defamatory matter, and on materials broadcast on radio and television. Although Americans appear to enjoy greater freedom of speech than citizens of the Western European nations, Japan, and other democratic nations at an equivalent level of development to the United States, the gap appears to have narrowed, not broadened, since the Supreme Court began to take an aggressive stance toward protection of free speech in the 1940's. It may be that as nations become wealthier and their people better educated and more leisured, the gains from restricting free speech—gains that have to do mainly with preserving social and political stability—decline relative to the costs in hampering further progress and in reducing the welfare of producers and consumers of ideas. These trends, I conjecture, are sufficiently pronounced to bring about (save possibly in totalitarian counties) dramatic increases in free speech regardless of the specifics of free-speech law.

The American law[9] has several interesting economic characteristics.

1) In the evolution of free-speech law, the first mode of regulation to go is censorship of books and other reading matter; the law's greater antagonism to censorship than to criminal punishment or other *ex post* regulation (for example, suits for defamation) being expressed in the rule that "prior restraints" on speech are specially disfavored. Censorship is a form of *ex ante* regulation, like a speed limit. The less common the substantive evil (the costs resulting from an accident due to carelessness, in the case of the speed limit, or the costs resulting from a treasonable or defamatory newspaper article, in the case of censorship), and also the more solvent the potential injurer,[10] the weaker the case for *ex ante* regulation is. With the growth of education and political stability, the social dangers of free speech have de-

[9]Well summarized, and in a form accessible to nonlawyers, in Geoffrey Stone et al. (1986, pt. 7).

[10]If the probability of apprehension and punishment is substantially less than one, the expected punishment may not deter wrongdoing even if the punishment, when imposed, takes away the offender's entire wealth and utility.

clined; and suppose the fraction of books and magazine articles that contain seriously harmful matter is today very small. Then the costs of a scheme in which a publisher must obtain a license from the public censor to publish each book are likely to swamp the benefits in weeding out the occasional prohibitable idea, especially since publishers have sufficient resources to pay fines or damage judgments for any injuries they inflict. It makes more economic sense in these circumstances to rely on *ex post* regulation (through criminal punishment or tort suits) of those ideas that turn out to be punishable. Censorship is retained, however, in areas, such as that of classified government documents, where the probability of harm is high and where in addition the magnitude of the harm if it occurs may be so great (for example, from disclosing sensitive military secrets) that the threat of punishment will not deter adequately because the wrongdoer will lack sufficient resources.

Many of these arguments could of course be made against *ex ante* regulation of safety, as by the Food and Drug Administration and OSHA. One difference is that while the First Amendment forbids overregulating the marketplace of ideas (and also, as we are about to see, the religious marketplace), no constitutional provision seems directed at forbidding overregulation of markets in conventional goods and services.

2) Consider now the onerous limitations that the Supreme Court has placed on efforts to sue the media for defamation. If we assume that news confers external benefits, then, since a newspaper or television station cannot obtain a significant property right in news, there is an argument for subsidizing the production of news. A direct subsidy, however, would involve political risks—though we have run them occasionally, as in the establishment of the Corporation for Public Broadcasting. A form of indirect subsidy is to make the victims of defamation bear some of the costs of defamation that the tort system would otherwise shift to the defamer. Notice, however, the curious effect of this method of subsidization, which may make it on balance inefficient. Because it is impossible to insure one's reputation, the victims of defamation cannot spread the costs of being defamed to other members of the community. The costs are concentrated on a narrow group, resulting in a deadweight loss if risk aversion is assumed. Moreover, public service is made less desirable, resulting in a decline in the quality of government. It would be difficult to prevent the decline by raising government salaries. The salary increase would have to be large enough to cover not only the expected cost of uncompensated defamation, but also the risk premium that risk-averse people would demand because they cannot buy insurance. Even if salaries are raised, the composition of public service will shift in favor of risk preferrers and people with little reputation capital. Finally, the difficulty of monitoring government outputs leads to heavy emphasis on economizing on visible inputs, for example by paying low salaries to government officials; and the problem of false economies is aggravated if the costs of government service are raised by curtailing the right of government officials to protect their reputations through suits for defamation.

3) The Supreme Court has distinguished between public and private figures, giving private figures a broader right to sue for defamation than public ones. This distinction may make economic sense. The external benefits of information about public figures are greater than those of information about private figures, and therefore the argument for allowing some of the costs to be externalized is stronger. Moreover, a public figure, being by definition newsworthy, has some substitute for legal action: he can tell his side of the story, which the news media will pick up.

4) A related point is that if the main reason for limiting efforts by government to regulate the marketplace of ideas is to foster the provision of external benefits, we would expect, and to a certain extent find, that the limitations on regulation are more severe the greater the likelihood of such benefits. Consider: Maximum protection for freedom of speech is provided to scientific and political thought, in which property rights cannot be obtained. Slightly less protection is given art, which enjoys a limited property right under

the copyright laws.[11] Even less constitutional protection is given to pornography and commercial advertising. And none is given to threats and other utterances that manifestly create net external costs.

Pornography appears to create no external benefits (no one but the viewer or reader himself benefits—and he pays), and may create external costs. Commercial advertising, a particularly interesting case, also creates few external benefits—since most such advertising is brand-specific and its benefits are captured in higher sales of the advertised brand—and it creates some external costs: competitor *A*'s advertising may go largely to offset *B*'s, and vice versa. This analysis implies that if the logic of free-speech law is basically an economic logic, commercial advertising that is not brand-specific, such as advertising extolling the value of prunes as a laxative, would receive greater legal protection than brand-specific advertising.

B

The First Amendment also forbids the government to make any law (1) respecting an establishment of religion or (2) prohibiting the free exercise of religion. The Supreme Court has enforced both clauses aggressively in recent years.[12] The economic effects of the Court's doctrines as well as their possible economic logic are interesting topics that economists (with the partial exception of Adam Smith) have not addressed.

There is, it is true, a nascent economic analysis of religion. Corry Azzi and Ronald Ehrenberg (1975) have formulated a simple (maybe too simple, given the variety of religious beliefs) economic model of religion, which assumes that people want to increase their expected utility from a happy afterlife.[13] The model leads to such predictions as that women will spend more time in church than men because the cost to women in foregone earnings is less, and that men will spend more time in church as they get older because as they approach the end of their working life it is optimal for them to switch from investing further in their earning capacity to investing in the production of afterlife utility. The authors find support in the data for their predictions.[14] My focus is different. I ask, what have been the effects on religious belief and observance of the Supreme Court's enforcement of the First Amendment? To avoid potential misunderstanding, I emphasize that I am offering no opinion on either the validity of any religious belief or the legal soundness of any of the Court's decisions.

Three major strands in the Court's modern decisions should be distinguished:

1) In its school-prayer decisions, and other decisions under the establishment clause, the Court has interpreted the concept of an "establishment" of religion very broadly, in effect forbidding the states and the federal government to provide direct support, financial or even symbolic, for religion. These decisions make a kind of economic sense, though perhaps only superficially. Public education (the principal arena of modern disputes over establishment of religion) involves the subsidizing of schoolchildren and their parents. Parents willing to pay the full costs of their children's education can and often do send their children to private schools. If they choose a public school instead, this may be because some of the costs will be paid by others, including persons who do not have school-age children as well as taxpayers in other parts of the state or nation. The principal economic argument for externalizing some of the costs of education is that education (with possible exceptions, as for vocational education and "phys. ed.") confers external benefits; that we all (or most of us, anyway) benefit from living in a nation whose popu-

[11] Only the specific work of art is protected; an artistic innovation (perspective, chiaroscuro, the sonnet, blank verse, etc.) is not.

[12] See Stone et al. (pt. 8).

[13] See also Ehrenberg (1977); Paul Pautler (1977); Barbara Redman (1980).

[14] For criticism of some of their results, see Holley Ulbrich and Myles Wallace (1984).

lation is educated. Therefore, to justify on economic grounds a public school's spending money on prayer and other religious activities, either these activities would have to be shown to produce positive externalities also (as by making schoolchildren more moral, or at least better behaved in school), or there would have to be economies from combining secular and religious instruction in the same facility, or private persons would have to volunteer to pay the incremental cost of the public school's religious activities, so that there would not be a subsidy.

If the Supreme Court were willing to accept any of these justifications—provided, of course, that they were adequately supported by evidence—then one might conclude that the Court was taking an economic approach to the issue in religion in the public schools. But, in fact, the modern Court forbids virtually every public school religious activity, whether or not any of these justifications is present. If none is present, it can indeed be argued that religious persons would be enjoying a public subsidy of religion if the activity were permitted. Parents willing to pay the full costs of education in a school that conducts prayer or engages in other religious activities can always send their children to a private school that offers such activities, thereby bearing the full cost of those activities rather than shifting a part of it to others in the community. Concern with public subsidies of religion may explain the Court's insistence that Christmas nativity scenes supported by public funds have a secular purpose, that is, confer benefits on nonreligious as well as religious persons. But the Court has not worried about the fact that the benefits may be greater for the latter persons, so that an element of subsidy remains. Nor has it explained its unwillingness to search for similar secular justifications for public school religious activity—such justifications as reducing the rowdiness of schoolchildren.

Further complicating the picture, the Supreme Court has declined to hold that the exemption of church property from state and local taxes is an unconstitutional establishment of religion. However, the consequence of the exemption is that the churches receive public services for which they do not pay. This is fine if they generate benefits for which they cannot charge, but the Court has not required that they show that. So here may be a large judicially sanctioned public subsidy of religion.

2) In its "free exercise" decisions, the Court has sometimes required public bodies to make costly accommodations to religious observance. An example is forbidding the denial of unemployment benefits to a person whose religion forbids him to accept a job offer that would require working on Saturdays. So the Court with one hand (establishment clause cases) forbids the subsidizing of religion and with the other (free-exercise cases) requires such subsidies.

3) In cases involving contraception, abortion, illegitimacy, obscenity, and other moral questions about which religious people tend to hold strong views, the Court in recent years has almost always sided with the secular against the religious point of view.

The decisions in both groups 1 and 2 favor religious rivalry or diversity (not competition in the economic sense: as we shall see in a moment, to subsidize rivalry as in 2 retards rather than promotes competition in the economic sense). Any public establishment of religion will tend to favor major religious groups over minor ones and can thus be compared to government's placing its thumb on the scales in a conventional marketplace, by granting subsidies or other benefits to politically influential firms. Refusing to accommodate fringe religious groups will have effects similar to those of establishing a religion because employment policies, and other public policies and customs, are chosen to minimize conflict with the dominant religious groupings.[15] It is no accident that the official day of rest in this country is the sabbath recognized by the mainline Christian groups. Fringe groups will therefore benefit from a rule requiring accommodation of their needs.

[15]As stressed in Michael McConnell (1985).

But since the costs of accommodation are borne by employers, consumers, taxpayers, other employees, etc., the group 2 cases actually subsidize fringe religious groups. And since it is no more efficient for government to subsidize weak competitors than strong ones, it may not be possible to defend the accommodation cases by reference to notions of efficiency. In addition, the group 1 cases may go further than necessary to prevent public subsidies of established religious groups, by neglecting the various justifications that might be offered for public support of religion—although allowing the property-tax exemption may correct (or for that matter, overcorrect) that tendency. The most important point to note, however, is that the Supreme Court has required government to subsidize fringe religious groups both directly and by discouraging religious establishments that inevitably would favor the beliefs and practices of the dominant sects in the community. By doing these things, the Court probably has increased religious diversity and may therefore have promoted religion, on balance, notwithstanding the "antireligion" flavor of some of its establishment cases.

The group 3 decisions favor religion, too —more precisely, private religious organizations—but in a subtler sense, which may be entirely unintended, even unrecognized, by the courts. By marking a powerful agency of government (the federal judiciary) as secularist, and, more important, by undermining traditional values through invalidation of regulations that express or enforce those values, these decisions increase the demand for organized religion, viewed as a preserver of traditional values. If the government enforced the value system of Christianity, as it used to do, people would have less to gain from being Christian. The group 1 cases have a similar effect. By forbidding teachers paid by the state to inculcate religious values, the courts have increased the demand for the services provided by religious organizations. And allowing the property-tax exemption lowers the costs of these organizations.

Of course, there may be no net increase in the provision of religious services if a public school in which teachers lead prayers or read to students from the Bible is treated as a religious organization, but my concern is with the effect on private organizations. Similarly, a government that rigorously repressed abortion might be thought of as the enforcement arm of the Christian sects that regard abortion as immoral; but by thereby assuming one of the functions of private religious organizations, it would be competing with those organizations and thus reducing the demand for the services provided by them.

There is a further point. As Adam Smith pointed out (1937, pp. 740–50), the effectiveness of a private group's monitoring and regulating the behavior of its members is apt to be greater, the smaller the group (this is the essence of cartel theory), from which Smith inferred that the more religious sects there were, and hence the smaller each one was on average, the more effective would religion be in regulating behavior. This implies that legal regulations which have the effect of atomizing rather than concentrating religious organization may improve the society's moral tone even if they diminish the role of government in inculcating moral values directly.

It may be hard to believe that the moral tone of our society has actually improved since the Supreme Court adopted its aggressively secularist stance, but economic analysis suggests that the situation might be worse rather than better if the Court had weakened private religious organizations by allowing government to compete more effectively with them in inculcating or requiring moral behavior. Since government and organized religion are substitutes in promoting moral behavior, an expansion in the government's role as moral teacher might reduce the demand for the services of organized religion. I say "might" rather than "would" because, to the extent that the government's role as moral teacher is taken seriously, a government that seeks to promote religiously based moral values may help "sell" religious values, and the organizations that promote them, over their secular substitutes. But this assumes what history suggests is unlikely: that the government will find a way of supporting religion on a genuinely nonsectarian basis rather than establishing a particular sect and thereby weakening competing sects and maybe religion as a whole.

To prove, in the face of the conventional wisdom to the contrary, that the Supreme Court's apparently antireligious decisions have promoted religion would be a formidable undertaking, and here I offer only two fragments of evidence. The first is the rapid growth in recent years of evangelical Christianity, formerly a fringe religious grouping and one marked by emphatic adherence to traditional values.[16] The second is the startling difference in religiosity between the United States and Western Europe. Not only does a far higher percentage of Americans believe in an afterlife than the population of any western European country other than Ireland,[17] but this percentage has been relatively constant in the United States since the 1930's, while it has declined substantially in Europe over the same interval.[18] Almost all Western European nations have an established (i.e., a taxpayer-supported and legally privileged) church (or churches, as with the state churches of Germany), and some require prayer in public schools.[19] To the extent that establishment discourages the rise of rival sects, it reduces the religious "product variety" offered to the population, and I would expect the demand for religion to be less. The American system fosters a wide variety of religious sects. Almost every person can find a package of beliefs and observances that fits his economic and psychological circumstances. And by preventing the government from playing a shaping role in the moral sphere the Supreme Court in recent years has, I have conjectured, increased the demand for religion as a substitute institution for the regulation of morals.

No doubt the Supreme Court's causal role in all this is smaller than I have suggested. The tradition of religious diversity in the United States is very old, and the Court's contribution to maintaining it may be slight. Nevertheless, economic analysis suggests that the religious leaders who denounce the course of the Court's decisions and the secular leaders who defend it may be arguing contrary to their institutional self-interest.

C

My discussions of free speech and religion can be connected as follows. One possible reading of the First Amendment (I do not suggest the only, or a complete one) is that it forbids government to interfere with the free market in two particular "goods"—ideas, and religion. Government may not regulate these markets beyond what is necessary to correct externalities and other impediments to the efficient allocation of resources. This seems an appropriate description of how modern courts interpret the amendment; the principal though not only exceptions are the cases that forbid what might be called "efficient" establishments (establishments that do not involve a subsidy to religious persons beyond what can be justified on secular grounds) and the cases requiring accommodation of religion in the sense of subsidizing fringe religious groups. There is no compelling economic argument for such a subsidy unless something can be made of Adam Smith's point that the more separate religious sects there are, the more effective religion is in bringing about moral behavior—and morals supplement law in correcting negative externalities such as crime and fostering positive ones such as charity.

But a lecture is not the place to prove a new economic theory. All that is feasible is to suggest that a particular theory holds promise and is thus worth pursuing. I hope I have persuaded you that what may loosely be called the economic theory of law has a significant potential to alter received notions, generate testable hypotheses about a variety of important social phenomena, and in short enlarge our knowledge of the world.

[16]See *The Gallup Report* (1985, pp. 3, 11).

[17]See *The Gallup Report*, p. 53.

[18]See *The Gallup Report*, pp. 9–10, 40, 42, 53.

[19]On the religious establishments of Western Europe, see, for example, E. Jürgen Moltman (1986); E. Garth Moore (1967); Franklin Scott (1977, pp. 571–75); Frederic Spotts (1973).

REFERENCES

Ashenfelter, Orley and Rees, Albert, *Discrimination in Labor Markets*, Princeton: Princeton University Press, 1973.

Azzi, Corry and Ehrenberg, Ronald, "Household Allocation of Time and Church Attendance," *Journal of Political Economy*, February 1975, *83*, 27–56.

Becker, Gary S., *The Economic Approach to Human Behavior*, Chicago: University of Chicago Press, 1976.

______, *Human Capital: A Theoretical and Empirical Analysis, With Specific Reference to Education*, NBER, New York: Columbia University Press, 2d ed., 1975.

______, *A Treatise on the Family*, Cambridge: Harvard University Press, 1981.

Buchanan, James M., "Good Economics—Bad Law," *Virginia Law Review*, March 1974, *60*, 483–92.

Coase, Ronald H., "Economics and Contiguous Disciplines," *Journal of Legal Studies*, June 1978, *7*, 201–11.

______, "The Market for Goods and the Market for Ideas," *American Economic Review Proceedings*, May 1974, *64*, 384–91.

Director, Aaron, "The Parity of the Economic Market Place," *Journal of Law and Economics*, October 1964, *7*, 1–10.

Ehrenberg, Ronald G., "Household Allocation of Time and Religiosity: Replication and Extension," *Journal of Political Economy*, April 1977, *85*, 415–23.

Ehrlich, Isaac, "Participation in Illegitimate Activities: An Economic Analysis," in Gary S. Becker and William M. Landes, eds., *Essays in the Economics of Crime and Punishment*, NBER, New York: Columbia University Press, 1974, 68–134.

Ellis, John M., *The Theory of Literary Criticism: A Logical Analysis*, Berkeley: University of California Press, 1974.

Fogel, Robert W. and Engerman, Stanley L., *The Reinterpretation of American History*, New York: Harper & Row, 1971.

Hirshleifer, Jack, "The Expanding Domain of Economics," *American Economic Review*, December 1985, Suppl., *75*, 53–68.

Landes, William M. and Posner, Richard A., *The Economic Structure of Tort Law*, Cambridge: Harvard University Press, forthcoming 1987.

McConnell, Michael, "Accommodation of Religion," *Supreme Court Review*, Chicago: University of Chicago Press, 1985, 1–59.

Moltmann, E. Jürgen, "Religion and State in Germany; West and East," *Annals of the American Academy of Political and Social Science*, January 1986, *483*, 110–17.

Moore, E. Garth, *An Introduction to English Canon Law*, Oxford: Clarendon Press, 1967.

Pautler, Paul A., "Religion and Relative Prices," *Atlantic Economic Journal*, March 1977, *5*, 69–73.

Posner, Richard A., *Economic Analysis of Law*, Boston: Little, Brown, 3d ed., 1986.

Pyle, David J., *The Economics of Crime and Law Enforcement*, New York: St. Martin's Press, 1983.

Radnitzky, Gerard and Bernholz, Peter, *Economic Imperialism: The Economic Approach Applied Outside the Field of Economics*, New York: Paragon House, 1986.

Redman, Barbara J., "An Economic Analysis of Religious Choice," *Review of Religious Research*, Summer 1980, *21*, 330–42.

Scott, Franklin D., *Sweden: The Nation's History*, Minneapolis: University of Minnesota Press, 1977.

Scott, Robert E., "A Relational Theory of Secured Financing," *Columbia Law Review*, June 1986, *86*, 901–77.

Smith, Adam, in Edwin Cannan, ed., *The Wealth of Nations*, London: Methuen, 1937.

Spotts, Frederic, *The Churches and Politics in Germany*, Middletown: Wesleyan University Press, 1973.

Stigler, George J., "Economics—The Imperial Science?," *Scandinavian Journal of Economics*, No. 3, 1984, *86*, 301–13.

______, "The Theory of Economic Regulation," *Bell Journal of Economics*, Spring 1971, *2*, 3–21.

Stone, Geoffrey R. et al., *Constitutional Law*, Boston: Little, Brown, 1986, pts. 7 and 8.

Ulbrich, Holley and Wallace, Myles, "Women's Work Force Status and Church Attendance," *Journal for the Scientific Study of Religion*, December 1984, *23*, 341–50.

The Gallup Report, Report No. 236, Princeton: The Gallup Poll, May 1985.

[2]

AN EXCHANGE

ABOUT LAW AND ECONOMICS: A LETTER TO RONALD DWORKIN

*Guido Calabresi**

August 29, 1979

Professor Ronald M. Dworkin
Oxford University
Oxford, England

Dear Ronny,

In the course of preparing the Cooley lectures for the University of Michigan I had occasion to read your exchange with Dick Posner which clustered around the Cornell-Chicago conference of this April and May[1] and which, I take it, will be the basis of both

---

* Sterling Professor of Law, Yale University; Arthur Goodhart Professor in Legal Science, University of Cambridge (1980-81).

1. The papers from this conference are published in a symposium entitled *Change in the Common Law: Legal and Economic Perspectives*, 9 J. LEGAL STUD. 189 (1980). I was originally scheduled to attend the conference which was organized by Mario J. Rizzo. Unfortunately a series of unexpected events made it impossible for me to be there. I received the conference papers from the editors of the *Hofstra Law Review* and read them at the end of the summer of 1979 while I was working on the Thomas M. Cooley Lectures, which I delivered at the University of Michigan Law School in October 1979, under the title: Nonsense on Stilts? The New Law and Economics Twenty Years Later. This paper was not written to be more than a letter to Professors Dworkin and Posner (who received a copy) commenting on their interesting exchange. As is my habit, the Cooley Lecures were delivered from notes, and I am now in the course of writing them up. They include, among other things, a fuller statement of my views on the subjects touched on, rather casually, in this letter. It did not seem to me inappropriate, nevertheless, to let the editors of the *Hofstra Law Review* publish this letter as a "Comment," especially since they hoped, correctly as it turned out, that publication would stimulate some more excellent thoughts from Professor Dworkin.

A footnote is not the place to answer Professor Dworkin fully, but a few comments can be usefully made. It seems to me that the differences between him and me are largely verbal, which is not to say unimportant. It is true that I speak of trade-offs between wealth and its distribution, but I try not to speak of trading off equality (largely because it means too many different things). And, even when I speak of wealth and its distribution, I as often use "recipe" language (*see, e.g.*,

your and his contributions to the *Hofstra Law Review* symposium. Despite the perhaps unnecessarily provocative language in your first article,[2] language which I fear will lead some to misunderstand the piece to mean that efficiency in the production of wealth is irrelevant to a "just" society, I found myself substantially in agreement with it. If I may oversimplify your fuller and more complex discussion, it seems to me that you make two points that are hard to challenge. (Indeed, I think I may have made them myself from time to time,[3] though certainly not as systematically.):

(1) That without starting points—whether termed rights, enti-

---

"blend" and "ingredients" at p. 558 *infra*, and "mix" at p. 559 *infra*) as what Dworkin assumes to be "compromise" language (like "trade-offs"). In fact, the whole tone of my letter is to ask that we concentrate on what blend of wealth, its distribution, and "other justice" notions leads to what can go by the name of justice. Dworkin asks, instead, what blend or recipe leads to "deep equality." Dworkin, *Why Efficiency?* 8 HOFSTRA L. REV. 563, 568-70 (1980). He is entitled to use that phrase, of course. But while I have no great confidence in the term "justice," I must say that I find the term "deep equality" somewhat misleading and even loaded. In my view of justice, what can be called "deep equality," is close enough to permit its use without stretching language. (I certainly have never suggested that I was a teleological utilitarian, *see, e.g., id.* at 572.) But other views of justice—other blends—do exist, and to assert that the goal of the blend of wealth and its distribution is deep equality psychologically stacks the deck against some of these. (Psychologically, not logically, since Dworkin does not define deep equality and so one could introduce what to some would seem like mighty inegalitarian notions into the term, though perhaps only at some cost to the ordinary meaning of words.) In the end, however, what one calls the "value term" may be less important than the functional issues, reached at the end of both my letter and Dworkin's paper, on when specific institutions like courts are likely to be good in defining or achieving the blend and when, instead, they are not.

Two other notes: Dworkin is precisely correct in his discussion on p. 568-69 of the type of regret one feels at an inability to make a Pareto improvement on a fair distribution and the type of regret-sacrifice that one does not feel. He is equally correct in his statement on pp. 582-83 that the Pareto criterion can only be treated as an all-or-nothing criterion and that *any* move that involves a deviation from the result ordained by what he calls the "fanatical" Pareto criterion requires justification in some non-Paretian moral theory. Since I have been saying this, and its close cousin (that "what *is*, is Pareto optimal—unless what *is* can be unanimously changed," and then, of course, it will be) for some time, *see, e.g.*, G. CALABRESI & P. BOBBITT, TRAGIC CHOICES 83-87 (1978); Calabresi, *On the General State of Law and Economics Research Today and its Current Problems and Prospects*, in LAW AND ECONOMICS 9, 11-12 (G. Skogh ed. 1978); *cf.* Dahlman, *The Problem of Externality*, 22 J. L. & ECON. 141 (1979) (advocating a similar position), I was particularly pleased to find Dworkin making so elegant and rigorous (more than I could) a statement of the point.

2. Dworkin, *Is Wealth A Value?*, 9 J. LEGAL STUD. 191 (1980).

3. *See, e.g.*, G. CALABRESI, & P. BOBBITT, *supra* note 1, at 32-34; Calabresi, *supra* note 1, at 12-15; Calabresi & Melamed, *Property Rules, Liability Rules, and Inalienability: One View of the Cathedral*, 85 HARV. L. REV. 1089 (1972).

tlements, bodily security, or what have you—it is hard to give any meaning to the term "an increase in wealth."[4] What is viewed as wealth, at the very least, must depend on the desires of individuals. Since these desires in turn depend on the characteristics of individuals, one must, at a minimum, justify in terms other than wealth maximization why a person "owns," rather than just possesses, the characteristics that give rise to his or her desires. In a way, this is merely a more general way of stating that my superior intelligence, my ability to hit a baseball as well as Rod Carew, or my possession of two good kidneys will affect my wants differently depending upon whether kidneys, intelligence, or batting skill belong to society, to those who wish or need to use them, or to me.

To put it still another way, each individual's desires are dependent on, indeed are a function of, his or her initial "wealth." Since wealth necessarily, in this sense, includes whether one starts off advantaged or disadvantaged by having a specific characteristic (like brains, kidneys, or batting skill) in that society, it is hard to know what to make of a statement that maximizing wealth is a good thing, unless one has accepted something, other than wealth maximization, as a ground for initial starting points.

One can get a starting point, of course, if one takes existing starting points to be "inevitable." But this is simply contrary to fact. Possession of a characteristic may be inevitable, but ownership is not. And possession without ownership can put one at a distinct disadvantage. That is, it can alter completely the starting point; viz., the plight of the beautiful slave and of the slave who is strong enough to do horrible, killing work. One can also get a starting point if one is willing to accept historical starting points as "just," or if one is willing to make some fairly strong assumptions (which I am inclined to believe most of us do) about "similarity among individuals regardless of characteristics" in their desire for "happiness" or "utility."[5] But this merely emphasizes that simple "desire for wealth" is not a meaningful starting point, because while one may be able to give meaning to a desire for happiness, say, apart from other characteristics, one cannot give meaning to "wealth" and hence to a desire for wealth in such an abstract state.

4. The term is Posner's. *See* Posner, *Utilitarianism, Economics, and Legal Theory*, 8 J. LEGAL STUD. 103 (1979).

5. Tony Kronman is currently arguing, persuasively, that an analogous assumption is implicit in Rawls. Kronman, *Talent Pooling*, NOMOS (forthcoming). *See generally* J. RAWLS, A THEORY OF JUSTICE (1971).

(2) That even with a starting point it is hard to see how an increase in wealth constitutes an improvement in a society unless it furthers some other goal, like utility or equality. Even an efficiency move that makes some *A* wealthier without making any *B* poorer —an extraordinary situation—is not a move toward a better society unless one is prepared to make the frequently plausible, but not necessary, assumption that the change also made that *A* happier and did not make any *B* less happy, or that *A* is made happier and that any *B* made less happy by *A*'s greater wealth deserves to be less happy because envy is "bad." In either event, the efficiency move is, as you say,[6] merely instrumental and needs to be attached to some account of what it is instrumental toward before it can be evaluated. The same is true, a fortiori, in the ordinary situation in which *A*'s greater wealth makes some *B* poorer.

It seems to me that at the end of your and Dick's polemic he does not really disagree with this last point; rather he does not find it necessary to specify the complex mixture of desirable goals (utility is too simple for him) which he claims wealth maximization serves better than any other *testable* instrument. Not being a philosopher, I would not myself require a precise complex of goals to be spelled out. I am even skeptical of such an exercise in an open society.[7] Posner's concept of wealth maximization would be enough for me if I thought it were, in practice, a better instrument than any other available one for furthering a plausible, if not completely coherent, complex of goals that were apparently adhered to by most people in a society, even if with no great consistency. Were that the case, the furthering of wealth maximization simpliciter might indeed be a worthwhile aim of some institutions (even judges, perhaps) in that society.

The trouble is that wealth maximization, apart from its distribution, does not seem to me (and I would warrant to most) to further even that muddle of aims which I, more tolerantly than you, would accept. It only necessarily serves "utility" on the most peculiar, not to say absurd, assumption about the relationship between wealth and utility, namely, that $1 is as likely to be worth as much to the rich person as to the poor person. One can be quite an agnostic about interpersonal comparisons and still say that *that* particular assumption is a lousier one than most. It clearly does not serve equality. It might, ironically, serve a bastardized maximin,

6. Dworkin, *supra* note 2, at 195.

7. *See generally* G. CALABRESI & P. BOBBITT, *supra* note 1.

but only under a series of uncertain empirical assumptions, perhaps more commonly made in the nineteenth century than today, about the trickling down of wealth. (I say bastardized, because the poor who would benefit, even under these assumptions, would usually be the next generation of poor. Thus, the beneficiaries are those who would benefit in the future from economic growth and not the currently least advantaged.) In any case, one would be hard put to explain why even this would not occur sooner if one self-consciously traded off some wealth maximization for some speedier redistribution, assuming a trade-off were needed.

I do not doubt that there exists an unspecified complex of goals—that can be spoken of in justice-value terms—that are better served by wealth maximization, without redistribution, than by other "measurable" instruments. I also do not doubt that Dick Posner, in a not totally systematic way (of which as I said I do not disapprove), "holds" these goals. I only suggest that in holding to these, he is in a very small minority. And, I would suspect that most people would say, and indeed do say, "Your goals, Richard, are fine for you, but without a lot more in the way of equality (pass, for now, of what) they are totally unacceptable to me."

All this leads to the part of your polemic with Dick that I find less successful. And that, as you might have suspected, is Part IV, where you speak of me and of the more "modest" efficiency-as-value theorists.[8] My argument with you here is less with your analysis than with its applicability to me. I do not, and never have, held that one can trade off efficiency and justice. I will admit that I am clearer on this point in some of my writings than in others. But even *The Costs of Accidents*,[9] which is the one to which you advert[10] and which is perhaps the least clear, should be clear enough. I do say of any system of accident law that it has two principal goals. "First, it must be just or fair; second, it must reduce the costs of accidents."[11] I do not find *any* passage in which I say that "these goals may sometimes conflict so that a 'political' choice is needed about which goal should be pursued."[12] What I do say is quite different:

> Though I list justice or fairness as a goal, it will soon be apparent that . . . I do not treat it as a goal of the same type as cost

8. Dworkin, *supra* note 2, at 201-05.
9. G. Calabresi, The Costs of Accidents (1970).
10. Dworkin, *supra* note 2, at 201.
11. G. Calabresi, *supra* note 9, at 24.
12. Dworkin, *supra* note 2, at 201 (footnote omitted).

> reduction but as a veto or constraint on what can be done to achieve cost reduction. Viewed this way fairness becomes a final test which any system of accident law must pass.[13]

I then criticize "claims . . . that justice is in some sense a goal concurrent with accident cost reduction" on the ground that "[t]hey seem to suggest that a 'rather unjust' system may be worthwhile because it diminishes accident costs effectively," and conclude that "justice is a totally different order of goal from accident cost reduction. Indeed . . . it is not a goal but rather a constraint that can impose a veto."[14] None of this supports trade-offs, I think.

Justice language *is* different from efficiency and, I think, wealth distributional language. As a result it only confuses things to talk about trading justice for efficiency. This is consistent with the assertion that both wealth-efficiency and its distribution are, in your terms, at least ingredients of justice. They certainly are in utilitarian theories. It may even be that, in some theories, equality of distribution of wealth is, in your terms, a "component of value."[15] I do not think it is in utilitarian theories, and I wonder whether there is value in a society in which all equally starve to death. But that is neither here nor there.

What is more to the point is that "modest" theorists, like myself, do contend that it is possible to speak of trade-offs between efficiency-wealth maximization and wealth distribution. Indeed, we would say that it is nearly impossible not to do so and still make some sense out of what goes on in just about every society one can look at. In your "last" reply to Posner you do the same when you say, "The question is not whether redistribution inhibits efficiency or whether a great decline in efficiency hurts the poor. It is whether justice is better served by some redistribution at the cost of some efficiency."[16] I would go further and say that an appropriate blend of efficiency and distribution is highly instrumental toward, and closely correlated with, achieving what many would view as a just society.

Some would go further (and on some utilitarian assumptions it is easy to see how) and say that the appropriate blend *is* the just

13. G. CALABRESI, *supra* note 9, at 24 n.1.

14. *Id.* at 25.

15. Dworkin, *supra* note 2, at 195.

16. R. Dworkin, Unpublished Comments at 14 (1979) (commenting on Posner, *The Value of Wealth: A Comment on Dworkin and Kronman*, 9 J. LEGAL STUD. 243 (1980)) (on file at *Hofstra Law Review*).

society, or would be if it could be defined and achieved. I have been more reluctant than many to go that far. I have always believed that efficiency and distributional language does not translate directly into justice language; that there are components of the just society that could only be encompassed in the terms efficiency and distribution if these terms were given a meaning far different from their ordinary ones. Hence the discussion of "Other Justice" in *The Costs of Accidents*[17]—which has been misinterpreted by some to imply that I believe that "justice" is a value separate from efficiency and distribution and to be traded off against them. "Other Justice," as I have made clear in later writings, was meant to suggest that an appropriate mixture of wealth-efficiency and its distribution does not guarantee a just society.[18] To put it another way, equating an appropriate efficiency-distribution mix with justice requires assumptions that are neither intuitively obvious nor so widely accepted as to permit me to say, "Solve the problem of that mix and you have justice."

Whether one wants to call these constraints (within which efficiency and distribution must work if they are to be instrumental toward justice), "rights" or, as I did, "veto points," is not terribly interesting. More interesting would be the question of what one ought to do if, in fact, an agreed upon efficiency-distribution mix ran into one of these veto points. Ought one to assume that such rights are definable with sufficient precision and absoluteness that either (a) an error has been made in the efficiency-distribution mix or assumptions, or (b) in the particular case at hand the instrument fails to further the goal?[19] Or may one, instead, use the clash to question whether what one thought was a right is, in fact, a right? Mistakes are made by all, and what may seem to be rights may just be perpetuations of historical injustices. If one believes the "instrument" generally leads very near the "good," one is more apt to take this last position and use the clash to force a reexamination not only of the efficiency-distribution assumptions, but also of the asserted veto.

Where does all this leave law and economics? Not in bad shape, I think. Clearly, the relationship between the instruments (efficiency, distribution) and the goal (justice) needs to be studied.

17. G. CALABRESI, *supra* note 9, at 24-26.

18. *See* Calabresi & Melamed, *supra* note 3, at 1102-05.

19. A utilitarian might say, "That mix which in other cases furthers utility does not do so here."

Intuitively most people would, I would guess, think the fit reasonably close. Sufficiently so, in fact, to assign to some institutions the task of furthering a given mixture in a given context. Enough also to justify criticizing institutions or laws when they blatantly fail in furthering either of the instruments, or what plausibly seems an appropriate mixture of the two.

But why not say, instead, that all should study the "goal" directly? That assumes that all should be philosophers, and, more important, that the best way to get to a point is always to focus directly on it, rather than on some road signs that point toward it. This is an assumption that is, I think, patently false. If, moreover, it be the case that some institutions are pretty good at finding road signs while others are better at defining the end point and suggesting when the road signs are apt to head away rather than towards the goal, it would be silly to ask both sets of institutions to be concerned either with the end point or with the road signs.

I believe that law-and-economics is concerned with the road signs. I also believe that this is both an intellectually worthy and difficult task. It is especially difficult because finding road signs that are not too misleading to be worth spending time on (like "wealth maximization" simpliciter) requires the lawyer-economist to make assumptions about distribution.[20]

Such assumptions about distribution have not been made and studied in any systematic fashion by economists in the past. Philosophers, like Jules Coleman, are trying to make a start at examining economics from this point of view.[21] And certainly the kind of work Sen is doing[22] and the kind of work Little did[23] (which characteristically Sen is among the few wise enough to appreciate) suggests that a great deal can be done. I would also not shrug off old Abba Lerner—after all, in the absence of knowledge to the contrary, the guess that any member of a species of animal is more like other members of that species[24] than different from them is not a silly guess.

20. Assumptions which I would argue, but cannot do here, are no more precarious than those which traditionally have been made by economists in talking about efficiency.

21. *See* Coleman, *Efficiency, Exchange, and Auction: Philosophic Aspects of the Economic Approach to Law*, 68 CALIF. L. REV. 221 (1980).

22. *See, e.g.*, Sen, *Social Choice Theory: A Re-examination*, 45 ECONOMETRICA 53 (1977); Sen, *The Welfare Basis of Real Income Comparisons: A Survey*, 17 J. ECON. LITERATURE 1 (1979); Sen, *Utilitarianism and Welfarism*, 76 J. PHILOSOPHY 463 (1979).

23. I. M. D. LITTLE, A CRITIQUE OF WELFARE ECONOMICS (2d ed. 1957).

24. *See, e.g.*, A. LERNER, THE ECONOMICS OF CONTROL 23–40 (1944).

But once again that is all beside the point, which in the end is simply: if lawyer-economists do not make the mistake of claiming too much for what they are doing, and if they are willing to work at defining and analyzing pretty good instruments leading toward the just society, philosophers ought not be troubled. Indeed, they might even find it profitable to reexamine critically their conclusions as to particular rights and particular manifestations of justice when the lawyer-economists' instruments seem to conflict with, rather than further, the results which the philosophers' particular conception of justice would seem to call for. Conversely, the lawyer-economist should be highly skeptical of the empirical assumptions on which he or she has based his or her analysis when such a conflict exists. This factual failure is as likely to be the source of the conflict, as is the more obvious possibility: namely that the best instruments or ingredients are not the "goal" or even components of the "goal" and so may at times mislead.

I have not, and this may seem odd to you, said anything in this letter about the role of courts in all this. That is too large a topic, and is in any case separate from the topics treated above. I know you believe that courts are eminently suited to further the "goal" directly and are not suited to define and work out the "instruments." Dick Posner, conversely, thinks courts good only at furthering what, for him, is at least a crucial instrument—wealth maximization. (I assume that by now you have disabused him of the notion that it is the "goal.") He also thinks we can show empirically that they have been doing just that.

I find it hard to explain judicial behavior in America simply in terms of wealth maximization. But I find it equally hard to explain it only in terms of ultimates or principles. In other words, my guess would be that courts do decide policies as well as principles, and perhaps more often the first than the second. The policies are based, and again I am guessing, on that mixture of efficiency and distribution that in the particular context is thought by the court to be instrumental toward justice and, in particular, does not violate any fairly precisely defined rights or veto points.

Whether that is an appropriate task for that institution is another matter and one that I wish to pass for now. My only thought on that at this point is that such a discussion works better in context than in the abstract. I find it difficult, in other words, to consider that issue apart from the capabilities of other institutions. For that reason, discussions of the role of courts that do not distinguish England from America (let alone both of these countries from Italy and France) seem to me prima facie suspect. One can say: "If they are assigned task *X* (policies, for example) because they are the most suited to that task in that society, they are no longer courts." But that, I think, would just trivialize a very important issue in the allocation of functions in a society.

Enough, enough. As you can see, your excellent paper set me off on many a tangent, and for that as well as for your acute analysis I am grateful to you and to Dick Posner who, in a way, set you off.

Best always,
Guido

[3]

WHY THE LEGAL SYSTEM IS LESS EFFICIENT THAN THE INCOME TAX IN REDISTRIBUTING INCOME

*LOUIS KAPLOW and STEVEN SHAVELL**

In economic analysis of law, normative judgments about legal rules are usually based on the rules' efficiency, regardless of their effects on the distribution of income. As a consequence, the economic approach is often criticized. Such criticism would be moot if the income tax system—understood here to include possible transfer payments to the poor—could be used freely to achieve any desired distribution of income. But income taxes and transfer payments distort incentives to work, limiting the degree to which it is socially desirable to employ the income tax system to redistribute income. The question therefore arises whether legal rules[1] should be used to take up some of the slack and promote distributional objectives,[2] even if at a sacrifice to efficiency.

In this article, we develop the argument that redistribution through legal rules offers no advantage over redistribution through the income tax system and typically is less efficient.[3] The reason is that using legal

* Professors, Harvard Law School, and Research Associates, the National Bureau of Economic Research. We are grateful for comments from Jennifer Arlen, Reuven Avi-Yonah, David Charny, A. Mitchell Polinsky, Alvin Warren, and participants in a workshop at Georgetown University Law Center.

[1] For purposes of this article, the term "legal rules" refers to rules other than those that define the income tax and welfare system.

[2] Our discussion concerns the overall distribution of income or wealth, not entitlement to payment based on desert.

[3] The first model establishing this point is in Steven Shavell, A Note on Efficiency vs. Distributional Equity in Legal Rulemaking: Should Distributional Equity Matter Given Optimal Income Taxation? 71 Am. Econ. Rev. 414 (1981). A related argument is made in Aanund Hylland & Richard Zeckhauser, Distributional Objectives Should Affect Taxes but Not Program Choice or Design, 81 Scand. J. Econ. 264 (1979). (For extensions and further applications, see Louis Kaplow, Should the Government's Allocation Branch Be Concerned about the Distortionary Cost of Taxation and Distributive Effects? (Discussion Paper No. 137, Harvard Law School Program in Law and Economics 1993).)

It does not appear, however, that the point is understood in legal academia. See, for

[*Journal of Legal Studies*, vol. XXIII (June 1994)]
 0047-2530/94/2302-0001$01.50

rules to redistribute income distorts work incentives fully as much as the income tax system—because the distortion is caused by the redistribution itself—and also creates inefficiencies in the activities regulated by the legal rules.

To illustrate, suppose that high-income individuals are subject to an income tax of 30 percent and that, in principle, further redistribution to the poor would be desirable. Would we want to adopt an inefficient legal rule because it redistributes an additional 1 percent of high earners' income to the poor? Under such a regime, high-earning individuals would surrender 31 percent of each additional dollar of income: 30 percent would go to the tax authority, and 1 percent would be taken by the legal system. Now assume, instead, that an efficient legal rule is retained and the income tax rate for high earners is raised to 31 percent. Then they would be in the same position and would be induced to work the same amount as under the inefficient regime. (The increase in the tax rate from 30 to 31 percent does not reduce their incentive to work because it is offset by the 1 percent decrease in the implicit tax that was associated with the inefficient legal rule.) The added tax revenue could be given to the poor, just as under the regime with the inefficient legal rule. Hence, redistribution using the 31 percent income tax and the efficient legal rule differs in only one respect from redistribution using the inefficient legal rule with the 30 percent income tax: because redistribution is accomplished in the presence of an efficient legal rule, resources would, by definition, be saved. With this savings, all individuals could be made better off (for example, by reducing taxes and increasing payments to the poor).

---

example, Guido Calabresi, The Pointlessness of Pareto: Carrying Coase Further, 100 Yale L. J. 1211, 1224 n.36 (1991) ("far from obvious that, as a general matter, tax and welfare programs *are* more efficient than a mixture of these and of other rules of law"); Duncan Kennedy, Distributive and Paternalist Motives in Contract and Tort Law, with Special Reference to Compulsory Terms and Unequal Bargaining Power, 41 Md. L. Rev. 563, 613 (1982) (inefficiencies from compulsory terms and from redistribution through taxation "involve exactly the same kinds of waste," leaving a difficult empirical question as to which is preferable); Anthony T. Kronman, Contract Law and Distributive Justice, 89 Yale L. J. 472, 508 (1980) (because taxation and contractual regulation both have efficiency costs, determining the preferable means of redistribution raises an empirical question that "must be resolved on a case-by-case basis, in the light of detailed information about the circumstances likely to influence the effectiveness of each method of redistribution"). In addition, Jennifer Arlen does not take into account the existence of the income tax system in arguing that legal rules should reflect parties' wealth. See Jennifer H. Arlen, Should Defendants' Wealth Matter? 21 J. Legal Stud. 413 (1992) (discussed in note 14 *infra*); see also *id*. at 428 (noting that basing liability on defendants' wealth would affect incentives to accumulate wealth, but claiming that "no matter what the outcome of [further analysis of the issue], it is clear that the conventional analysis . . . is not theoretically sound").

More generally, we show that, *even though the income tax distorts work incentives, any regime with an inefficient legal rule can be replaced by a regime with an efficient legal rule and a modified income tax system designed so that every person is made better off.* In Section I, we present the analysis leading to this conclusion. In Section II, we discuss briefly the general role of legal rules in redistribution and when, if ever, it is efficient for legal rules to take into account parties' wealth.

I. Analysis

We provide here an informal demonstration of our result: given any regime with an inefficient legal rule (notably, one intended to help achieve a redistributive goal), there exists an alternative regime with an efficient legal rule and a modified income tax system in which all individuals are better off. For concreteness, we will use a specific example in our analysis, but it will be clear that our argument does not depend on the particulars of the example. (For a formal proof, and discussion of certain qualifications, see the Appendix.)

Suppose that individuals engage in an activity that may cause accidents, the likelihood of which may be reduced by potential injurers' exercise of care. It is a familiar result that the strict liability rule—under which individuals pay for the harm they cause—leads to efficient behavior. Suppose that each individual's expected net accident costs under this rule, denoted $\hat{a}$, are \$1,000. These equal the cost of care, harm suffered, and damages paid, less damages received.

Compare this efficient legal rule to an inefficient one that redistributes income from higher- to lower-income individuals. (Redistribution might be accomplished, for example, by setting damages higher when the injurer is wealthy and lower when the injurer is poor. Such a redistributive legal rule would be inefficient: it would induce the wealthy to take more care and the poor to take less care than is efficient.) Let us denote the net expected accident costs—the cost of care, harm suffered, and damages paid, less damages received—individuals bear under this rule by $a(y)$; that is, an individual's accident costs are a function of his income, y. (Expected accident costs must be a function of income if the rule is to redistribute income relative to a rule under which everyone's accident costs are the same.)

In particular, suppose that relative to the efficient rule the poorest (those with income of \$0) benefit by \$500 and the richest (those with income of \$100,000) lose \$1,000, with a linear relationship in between. Figure 1 depicts accident costs under this inefficient rule and also under the efficient strict liability rule. Relative to the efficient rule, the ineffi-

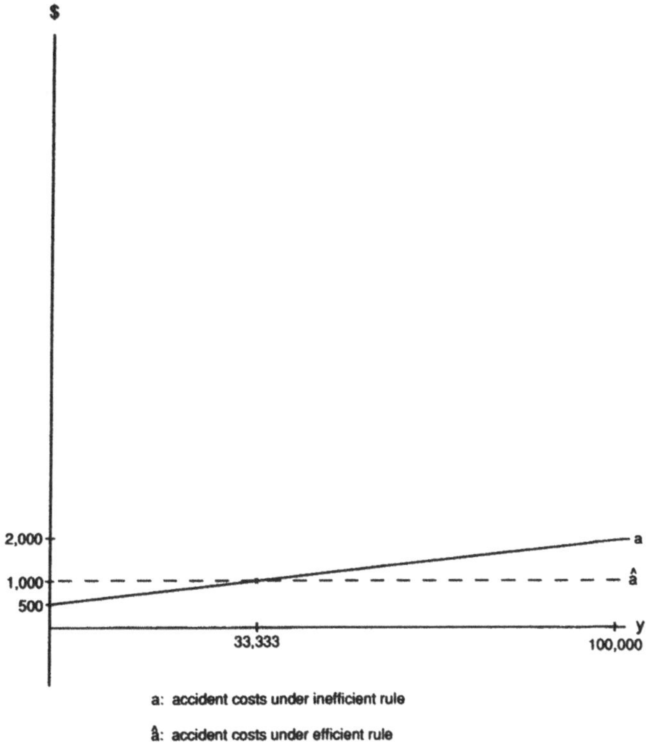

FIGURE 1

cient legal rule redistributes from those with incomes over $33,333 to those with lower incomes.

To complete the description of the regime with the inefficient rule, assume that there is an income tax with a rate of 20 percent. In particular, individuals pay tax on 20 percent of their income to the extent it exceeds $10,000; individuals with income under $10,000 receive transfer payments equaling 20 percent of the difference (so those earning no income receive $2,000).[4] This tax system, denoted t, is illustrated by the solid line in Figure 2.

In Figure 2, we also show a dashed line for $t + a$, which represents individuals' total payments under the tax system and on account of accidents in the regime with the inefficient legal rule. It is this combination that determines an individual's welfare level and work incentives. With

[4] This may be familiar to some readers as a negative income tax. It also is analogous to a conventional income tax combined with a welfare system.

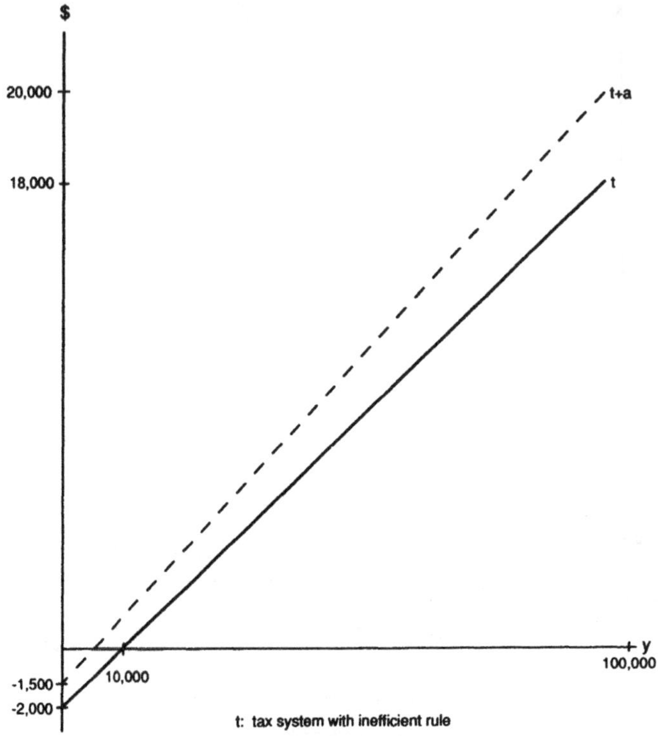

t: tax system with inefficient rule

t+a: tax system plus accident costs with inefficient rule

FIGURE 2

regard to the latter, we emphasize that when an individual with income *y* contemplates earning additional income by working harder, his total marginal expected payments equal the sum of his marginal tax payment and the expected marginal cost on account of accidents.[5]

Having described the regime under the inefficient legal rule, we will demonstrate that all individuals can be made better off in a regime with the efficient legal rule and an altered income tax system. Consider the

[5] Of course, the extent to which individuals accurately perceive both their marginal tax rate and the amount implicitly taxed by the legal system is an empirical question. We think it plausible that if the legal system redistributed a significant amount of income, individuals would take this into account. (After all, individuals often would not need to understand the effects of legal rules; rather, they might simply observe, for example, the resulting high prices of products bought disproportionately by the rich.) If they misestimated the extent of redistribution, there is no compelling reason to assume that their guesses would be too low rather than too high.

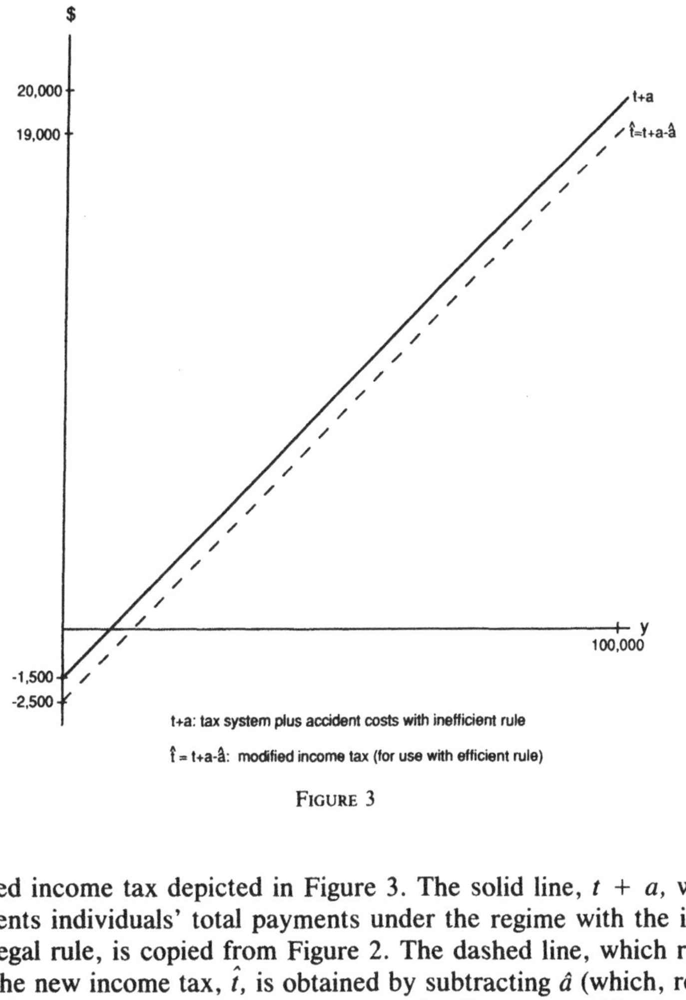

FIGURE 3

modified income tax depicted in Figure 3. The solid line, $t + a$, which represents individuals' total payments under the regime with the inefficient legal rule, is copied from Figure 2. The dashed line, which represents the new income tax, $\hat{t}$, is obtained by subtracting $\hat{a}$ (which, recall, equals \$1,000 for all income levels) from the line $t + a$. The two tax regimes are compared in Figure 4.[6]

We can now describe individuals' behavior and welfare under the efficient legal rule combined with the new income tax. The total effect of the tax and accident costs is given by the sum $\hat{t} + \hat{a}$. But, by construction, this expression is identical to $t + a$ for any income level. (After all, $\hat{t}$ is constructed by subtracting $\hat{a}$ from $t + a$. When $\hat{a}$ is added back, the result must equal $t + a$.) Thus, individuals who earn income y have

[6] The schedule $\hat{t}(y)$ is steeper than $t(y)$—that is, more redistributive—by precisely the amount by which $a(y)$ is steeper than $\hat{a}$, as depicted in Figure 1.

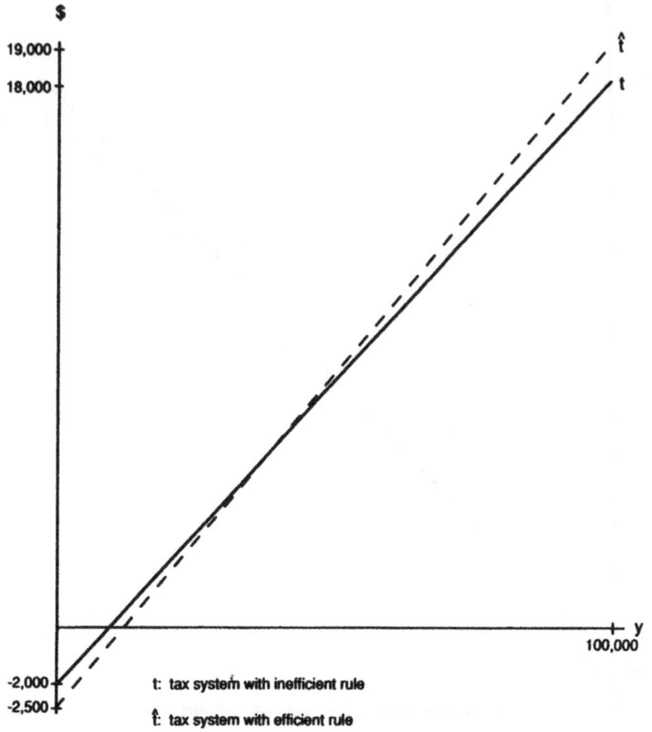

FIGURE 4

the same level of welfare under each regime. Moreover, each individual (whatever his ability) will choose to earn the same income under each regime because his incentives will be unchanged: a marginal dollar earned will result in the same incremental costs (taxes plus accident costs) under both regimes.

Although work effort and an individual's after-tax welfare are identical under the two regimes, the state collects more tax revenue in the new regime because it involves a more efficient legal rule. To see why this must be true, we first compare total available resources in each regime. Because individuals' work effort is unaffected by the new regime, total earnings will be the same. But the inefficient rule by definition wastes resources relative to the efficient rule, so total resources must be greater under the new regime. Yet the new income tax leaves individuals with the same income as in the initial regime. Thus, it must be that the new tax collects all the resources saved by the efficient legal rule. Indeed, the new tax was constructed precisely to produce this result.

To illustrate, consider the case in which individuals' income is uniformly distributed over the range from $0 to $100,000. It is straightforward to calculate that the per capita cost of the inefficient legal rule is $250. The per capita revenue under the original income tax, t, is $8,000, and per capita revenue under the modified income tax, $\hat{t}$, is $8,250. Indeed, the modified tax collects greater revenue by an amount that just equals the resources wasted by the inefficient legal rule.

The conclusion is that adopting the efficient legal rule, with an appropriate change in the income tax, leaves all individuals equally well off but leaves the government with a surplus. With this additional revenue, the government can make each individual better off—for example, by lowering taxes (for the poor, increasing transfers) by a fixed amount for each individual or spending the funds on a public good that benefits everyone.[7]

II. Discussion

(*a*) *Factors bearing on redistribution through legal rules.* In this article, we have emphasized that redistribution through legal rules is less efficient than redistribution through the income tax. Other more familiar considerations of feasibility and accuracy also favor redistribution through the income tax system.[8] Specifically, the income tax system (including transfer programs) can redistribute from all the rich to all the poor,[9] whereas legal rules have substantially less redistributive potential. First, when parties are in a contractual relationship, it is well understood that redistribution usually is not accomplished because prices generally adjust to reflect the expected cost of legal rules.[10] Second, when redistri-

[7] In practice, redistribution through the income tax rather than through legal rules would not literally make everyone better off. Inevitably, some would gain more than others and a few might lose. Systematic distributive effects across income levels can be avoided by adjusting the income tax, which leaves the possibility of sporadic unequal treatment within income classes. There is, however, no reason that such inequality would be greater when using the income tax rather than legal rules to redistribute income. For reasons noted in Section II(*a*) one might expect legal rules to fare worse on this account.

[8] See, for example, A. Mitchell Polinsky, An Introduction to Law and Economics 124–27 (2d ed. 1989).

[9] Many exceptions, such as adjustments for numbers of dependents, presumably reflect aspects of distributional policy. Others, such as those that result from tax evasion and welfare fraud, may be addressed in many ways (increasing enforcement, augmenting income taxes with luxury taxes). It would be surprising, however, if courts could more accurately determine true income in, say, private tort disputes than in tax evasion or welfare fraud enforcement proceedings.

[10] Contract rules may affect distribution if prices are also regulated, but then the price regulation itself may be used to accomplish redistribution among such parties. Also, there may be some incidental distributive effects of contract rules, such as when some individuals must expend resources to opt out of default rules that are suitable for others.

bution is possible, it tends to be limited to those few who become parties to lawsuits. And even then, redistribution may be haphazard. (A pro-plaintiff rule may be redistributive if plaintiffs, on average, are poorer than defendants, but unless this is uniformly true, the redistribution will flow in the wrong direction in some cases.)[11] The latter problem can be avoided only if the legal rule depends directly on parties' incomes, a policy that few have proposed. Furthermore, if one is prepared to go that far, it becomes difficult to understand why one would administer redistribution in such an ad hoc and inefficient manner rather than through the income tax system.[12]

An argument sometimes offered in favor of redistribution through legal rules is that the tax system falls short of optimal redistributive taxation—perhaps because of the balance of political power in the legislature. This argument raises questions that we do not seek to address about the function of courts in a democracy. In any case, it seems unlikely that courts can accomplish significant redistribution through the legal system without attracting the attention of legislators. Also, much legal reform presently under consideration, such as tort reform, is in the jurisdiction of legislatures.

These points, combined with this article's efficiency argument, suggest that normative economic analysis of legal rules should be primarily concerned with efficiency rather than the distribution of income. Nonetheless, analyzing distribution may be important, because those formulating income tax policy need to be aware of any significant distributive effects of legal rules that would not otherwise be apparent, such as from studying information on the actual distribution of income. Distributive effects, of course, are identified by economic analysis that examines the costs and benefits of legal rules—the same sort of analysis used to determine which rules are efficient.

(*b*) *Is it ever efficient for legal rules to take account of parties' wealth?* We have argued that it is inefficient for legal rules to take into account parties' wealth in order to redistribute income. We now consider whether there may be other reasons for legal rules to depend on parties' wealth.

Because the poor are more risk-averse than the rich, the efficient allo-

[11] Even when a party appears to be rich, the redistributive effect may be more limited. For example, when corporations pay more for injuries to third parties, consumer prices and wages will be affected.

[12] Thus, although we did not consider the possible additional administrative costs of increasing the amount of redistribution through the income tax, it seems plausible that these costs would be less than those of achieving significant, well-targeted redistribution through legal rules.

cation of risk might appear to justify taking wealth into account in the design of legal rules. For example, poor injurers might be assessed lower damages, the law's generosity providing them implicit partial liability insurance. Yet, if liability insurance is available in the marketplace, it is inefficient to adjust damages to reflect risk aversion.[13] Insurance purchases will provide the optimal degree of risk mitigation; furthermore, imposition of damages fully equal to harm is necessary to induce potential injurers and their insurers to take complete account of harm that might be caused. Thus, any adjustment in legal rules due to parties' risk aversion, as evidenced by their wealth, must be premised on a failure in insurance markets.[14]

Nevertheless, it often is efficient for damages to reflect the victim's income. When an injury involves lost future earnings, the level of earnings indicates the extent of economic loss.[15] In addition, under a negligence rule, sometimes it is efficient for the standard of care to depend on parties' income. To illustrate, suppose that a precaution that reduces expected accident costs by $15 takes an hour of effort. This precaution would be efficient for individuals who can otherwise earn only $10 an hour but not for those whose opportunity cost is $20 an hour.[16]

[13] This is demonstrated in Steven Shavell, On Liability and Insurance, 13 Bell J. Econ. 120 (1982).

[14] Jennifer Arlen, *supra* note 3, argues that, when parties are risk-averse, their wealth should affect the level of liability—even in the presence of perfect insurance markets and complete insurance. Her result derives from the assumption that the rich value wealth less at the margin than the poor (which is formally equivalent to the assumption that individuals are risk-averse). Therefore, social welfare is advanced by using the legal system to transfer wealth from the rich to the poor; in her model, this is accomplished by imposing higher liability on the rich. Yet she describes the social desirability of higher liability on the rich as an aspect of optimal deterrence, not as the masked transfer of wealth that it is. In fact, a complete analysis of her model would lead to the conclusion that the socially ideal outcome involves damages that fully equalize the wealth of the victim and the injurer. Indeed, if the victim were rich, he would pay "damages" to the injurer! Obviously, it would not be socially desirable to take parties' wealth into account in the manner Arlen suggests unless the income tax were unavailable for redistributive purposes. For further discussion of Arlen's article, see Thomas J. Miceli & Kathleen Segerson, Defining Efficient Care: The Role of Income Redistribution, 24 J. Legal Stud. (1995, in press).

[15] The argument assumes that injurers have some advance knowledge of the economic loss they might cause. If they knew only average losses for all victims, a rule providing that damages equal average harm would be equally efficient. See Louis Kaplow & Steven Shavell, Accuracy in the Assessment of Damages (Working Paper No. 4287, National Bureau of Economic Research 1993).

[16] An implicit assumption in this argument is that it is not possible simply to hire someone else to undertake the precaution. Also, note that under a rule of strict liability, damages should equal $15 rather than assessing higher damages on the rich in order to induce them to take the same care that others take.

III. Conclusion

Redistribution is accomplished more efficiently through the income tax system than through the use of legal rules, even when redistributive taxes distort behavior. Redistribution through legal rules causes the same inefficiency as taxes with regard to the labor-leisure choice: the distortion is caused by the redistribution itself and is not particular to the mechanism by which it is accomplished. And when redistribution involves choosing less efficient legal rules, additional costs are incurred. This argument, along with others that are more familiar, suggests that it is appropriate for economic analysis of legal rules to focus on efficiency and to ignore the distribution of income in offering normative judgments.[17]

APPENDIX

Formal Proof and Remarks

The model parallels the illustration in Section I. Individuals exercise care x and cause accidents with probability $p(x)$, with $p' < 0, p'' > 0$. An accident causes harm of h, which is borne equally by all individuals.[18] Individuals differ in their ability α to earn income y through labor effort ℓ, where $y(\alpha) = \alpha\ell$ and (for notational simplicity) α is distributed uniformly on the interval [0,1]. Individuals who cause accidents pay damages of d. The income tax schedule is $t(y)$.

We begin with an inefficient legal rule in which damages are $d(y_I, y_V)$, where y_I is the injurer's income and y_V is the victim's income. (Allowing damages to depend on parties' incomes makes redistribution possible.) Each individual chooses labor effort, ℓ, and care, x, to maximize expected utility, which is

$$EU = y - \ell - t(y) - x - \bar{p}h - p(x)\int_0^1 d(y, y_V(\alpha))\,d\alpha + \int_0^1 p(x(y_I(\alpha)))\,d(y_I(\alpha), y)\,d\alpha, \tag{A1}$$

where $\bar{p}$ is the average probability that others will cause a person harm and where, recall, $y = \alpha\ell$. The first four terms on the right side are income, work effort, income tax payments, and care. Next, utility is reduced by the expected harm a person suffers, $\bar{p}h$. The final two terms represent payments made and received under the legal rule. Payments are made when a person causes an accident, which has probability $p(x)$; damages, in turn, depend on a person's own income, y (when one is the injurer), and each possible victim's income ($y_V(\alpha)$ is the income earned by the type of individual who has ability α)—the integral measures the total over

[17] Conventional efficiency analysis of legal rules that abstracts from the distribution of income typically will yield the same result as an analysis that fully incorporates both the distributive effects of legal rules and adjustments to the income tax system. The conventional approach, however, is preferable on grounds of simplicity.

[18] Alternatively, it could be assumed that each individual bears harm with equal probability, so that the expected harm is the same for each individual.

all possible victims. Payments are received when one is injured; each type of individual causes an accident with probability $p(x(y_I(\alpha)))$ and pays damages reflecting his income—the integral measures the sum over all types who might injure a person.[19]

We now compare this regime to one with an efficient legal rule and a modified income tax system. The efficient rule is $\hat{d} = h$; as is well known, under strict liability when injurers pay damages equal to harm caused, all costs are internalized, so actors are induced to take the level of care that minimizes the sum of the cost of care and expected harm. We denote this efficient level of care as $\hat{x}$ and observe that it is independent of one's income level. It will be useful to denote the inefficiency caused by the damages rule $d(y_I, y_V)$ by

$$\pi = \int_0^1 \Big[[x(y(\alpha)) + p(x(y(\alpha)))h] - [\hat{x} + p(\hat{x})h] \Big] d\alpha. \qquad \text{(A2)}$$

Because the damage rule d is inefficient, π is positive. (The integrand is positive whenever $x(y(\alpha))$ is unequal to efficient care $\hat{x}$.)[20]

In the regime with the efficient damages rule $\hat{d} = h$, let the modified income tax be

$$\hat{t}(y) = t(y) + \Big[x(y) + \bar{p}h + p(x(y)) \int_0^1 d(y, y_V(\alpha))d\alpha - \int_0^1 p(x(y_I(\alpha)))d(y_I(\alpha), y)d\alpha \Big] - \Big[\hat{x} + p(\hat{x})h \Big]. \qquad \text{(A3)}$$

Note that, as in Section I, the new income tax, $\hat{t}(y)$, is constructed by beginning with the initial income tax, $t(y)$, adding total accident costs under the initial, inefficient regime and subtracting total accident costs under the efficient regime. The former total (under the inefficient rule) is the first term in large brackets: the cost of care, harm suffered, and expected damage payments, minus expected damage awards received. The latter (under the efficient rule) is the second term in large brackets: the cost of care and expected damage payments (harm suffered is precisely offset by expected damage awards received). As a result of the first adjustment, the new income tax changes with income in exactly the way that accident-related costs did under the inefficient liability rule. Thus, if higher-income individuals paid more in damages, now they pay more in taxes instead.

We next demonstrate that the expected utility of individuals will be the same under the new tax $\hat{t}(y)$ and the efficient legal rule as it is under the initial income tax and the inefficient rule. Recall that, under the efficient legal rule, all individuals (regardless of income) choose the same level of care, $\hat{x}$. Also, as just noted, expected harm suffered is just offset by expected damage awards received because damages equal harm. Hence, in the new regime, individuals choose labor effort ℓ to maximize expected utility, which is

[19] The last four terms together correspond to the expression $a(y)$ in the notation of Section I.

[20] In particular, whenever the damage rule d results in an expected payment exceeding h (as it would when injurers are relatively wealthy, if the rule is redistributive in a manner that favors the poor), injurers will take excessive care. Similarly, when the damage rule d results in an expected payment less than h (as when injurers are relatively poor), injurers will take too little care.

$$E\hat{U} = y - \ell - \hat{t}(y) - \hat{x} - p(\hat{x})h. \tag{A4}$$

If one uses (A3) to substitute for $\hat{t}(y)$ in (A4) and compares the result to (A1), the expression for expected utility in the initial regime, it is apparent that, for any income level y,

$$E\hat{U} = EU. \tag{A5}$$

Because expected utility is the same for any level of labor effort, ℓ, individuals of any given ability will choose the same labor effort under both regimes. This, in turn, implies that their welfare will be identical under both regimes.

Finally, we show that tax revenues are greater under the modified income tax. In particular,

$$\int_0^1 \hat{t}(y(\alpha))d\alpha = \int_0^1 t(y(\alpha))d\alpha + \pi. \tag{A6}$$

This follows directly from the definitions of $\hat{t}(y)$ in (A3) and π in (A2). After all, $\hat{t}(y)$ is constructed to equal $t(y)$, plus the total accident costs under the inefficient rule minus the total accident costs under the efficient rule. And π is defined to equal just this difference in accident costs. (The only difference between the bracketed expressions in [A3] and the right side of [A2] is that the former includes terms for damages individuals pay and receive. But when one integrates over all individuals, the total of damages paid and received are equal, so these components are precisely offsetting.)

One can define a new tax by $\hat{t}(y) - \pi$. (That is, the savings in accident costs are uniformly rebated, in a lump-sum manner, to the entire population.) Under this tax, labor effort will be unchanged (since the tax differs from $\hat{t}(y)$ by a constant),[21] so revenues will now be the same as under the initial tax, $t(y)$. Each individual is better off by π.

Remarks. (a) Generality of the result. It should be apparent that our result does not depend on the nature of the activity (for example, one could incorporate victim care), the form of the legal rule, the income tax system,[22] or the distribution of ability. The result might appear to depend on some features of the utility function—notably, risk neutrality, the lack of income effects, and care being independent of ability. Relaxing these assumptions would make determination of the efficient legal rule more complicated. It would remain true, however, that if the redistribution accomplished through an inefficient legal rule were instead achieved through a modification of the tax system, resources would be saved and all individuals could be made better off.

(b) Excise taxes versus legal rules as redistributive devices. Reasoning similar to that in our article suggests the superiority of excise taxes over legal rules as

[21] The utility function (A1) involves no income effects; if there were income effects, the argument would hold except that the amount of rebate that would restore budget balance would be less than π.

[22] For convenience, we examine the distribution of income with an income tax as the redistributive tool. In a dynamic analysis, one might wish to distinguish the distribution of consumption or wealth from the distribution of income (and consider consumption or wealth taxes in addition to an income tax), which would raise the issue of distorting savings. One can think of the labor-leisure distortion as exemplifying any distortion that results from a general redistributive tax.

redistributive tools. Suppose, for example, that there is an inefficient legal rule that requires excessive care by owners of yachts. Moreover, assume that this rule has desirable distributive features because yacht owners are usually wealthier than those injured by yachts. The inefficiency caused by this rule will have three components: excessive care is by definition more costly than the harm prevented; yachting is made more expensive, which distorts choices between yachting and other activities (for example, playing golf); and income buys less for the rich, which distorts their labor-leisure choices.

Consider the alternative of using an efficient legal rule combined with an appropriate excise tax on yachting, the proceeds to be distributed to low-income individuals (perhaps the victims of yachting accidents). Distortions of the amount of yachting and labor-leisure decisions would remain the same: the rich would pay more on account of the excise tax rather than on account of bearing higher accident costs (the sum of prevention costs and expected liability payments).[23] But the first inefficiency, excessive care, would be avoided. Thus, the excise tax would allow more efficient redistribution than the legal rule.

Observe, however, that an excise tax is a less efficient means of redistribution than the income tax, because the excise tax distorts the amount of yachting whereas the income tax does not.[24] Thus, if one wishes to redistribute income, the most efficient choice typically will be the income tax, the second choice would be an excise tax (as with luxury taxes), and the worst alternative would be an inefficient legal rule with desirable distributive consequences.

(c) Qualifications and the relationship between our result and those in the literature on optimal taxation. Our result is analogous to results on optimal taxation. In simple cases, specific commodity excises are inefficient in the presence of an optimal income tax.[25] This conclusion does not hold generally, however, because taxes or subsidies on particular commodities might have

[23] Analogous to the effects of excise taxes are subsidies for particular purchases. The familiar argument is that in-kind welfare assistance (for example, free housing rather than cash of equal market value) is inefficient because it distorts choices such as that between housing and food purchases, in addition to creating potential work disincentives for the poor that would result from cash assistance as well. Although one might justify in-kind welfare programs on other grounds—for example, because we paternalistically wish to force the poor to spend on food and housing—it is difficult to apply such arguments in the context of redistribution through legal rules. (We would not channel redistribution through a tort rule because we wished the poor to be in more accidents caused by the rich.)

[24] Under the Ramsey tax rule, the efficiency of such an excise tax would depend on the elasticity of demand for yachting. But, as explained in the following remark and note 25, this analysis is inapplicable in the presence of an income tax. An excise tax, however, may be superior if the amount of yachting were excessive, as it might be under a negligence rule. See Steven Shavell, Strict Liability versus Negligence, 9 J. Legal Stud. 1 (1980).

[25] For a useful survey of the literature and discussion of the ideas presented in this remark, see Joseph E. Stiglitz, Pareto Efficient and Optimal Taxation and the New New Welfare Economics, in 2 Handbook of Public Economics 991, 1023-27 (Alan J. Auerbach & Martin Feldstein eds. 1987). The survey explains why the familiar Ramsey tax rule—that tax rates on commodities should vary inversely with demand elasticities—is inapplicable in the presence of an income tax. (When an income tax is present, one can raise revenue without causing any distortion in choices among commodities. Hence, differential taxation of commodities is only useful when it reduces the labor-leisure distortion, as explained in the text.)

indirect effects that reduce the distortion of an income tax. In particular, by taxing complements of leisure and by subsidizing substitutes, one can reduce the labor-leisure distortion and thereby improve welfare by more than the inefficiency that results from distorted purchases of the taxed or subsidized commodities.

Analogously, if there were legal disputes involving activities that were strong complements of or substitutes for leisure, one might select rules that provided additional penalties or subsidies relative to what an efficient rule would involve. (As the excise tax discussion suggests, however, this would be the most efficient choice only if taxes or subsidies on the activities themselves were infeasible.) Such penalties and subsidies, however, are not conventionally redistributive: whether an activity should be penalized or subsidized depends on how the activity affects the labor-leisure choice, not on whether it is undertaken disproportionately by the rich. Thus, although a complete and sophisticated analysis does not demonstrate that it could never be efficient to change legal rules from what narrowly seem to be the most efficient ones, there is no general argument for adjustments of a conventionally redistributive type.[26]

[26] For discussion of other qualifications, see Kaplow, *supra* note 3.

[4]

ARTICLES

WEALTH MAXIMIZATION REVISITED

RICHARD A. POSNER*

Some years ago, I published an article in which I argued that "wealth maximization" provides an ethically attractive norm for social and political choices, such as those made by courts asked to determine whether negligence or strict liability should be the rule for deciding whether an injurer must compensate his victim.[1] This article gave rise to a flurry of criticisms,[2] to which I replied[3]—without convincing many of the critics.[4] I am pleased to have this opportunity to reconsider my position. Perhaps as a result of my new perspective as a judge, I find myself slightly more sympathetic to some of the criticisms than I once was—but only slightly more.

I. WHAT IS WEALTH MAXIMIZATION AND WHERE DOES IT COME FROM?

To most people who are not economists, the word

---

* Judge, U.S. Court of Appeals for the Seventh Circuit; Senior Lecturer, University of Chicago Law School. This is the revised text of a lecture given at the Thomas J. White Center on Law & Government at Notre Dame Law School on September 5, 1985. I am grateful to Gary Becker, Jules Coleman, Frank Easterbrook, Steven Shavell, George Stigler, David Strauss, and Cass Sunstein for helpful comments on a previous draft. The reader is asked to grant the usual indulgences in reading a paper originally intended for oral delivery.

1. Posner, *Utilitarianism, Economics, and Legal Theory*, 8 J. LEGAL STUD. 103 (1979), which appears in slightly different form in R. POSNER, THE ECONOMICS OF JUSTICE ch. 3 (1981).

2. *See, e.g.*, Coleman, *Efficiency, Utility and Wealth Maximization*, 8 HOFSTRA L. REV. 509 (1980); Dworkin, *Is Wealth a Value?*, 9 J. LEGAL STUD. 191 (1980); Kronman, *Wealth Maximization as a Normative Principle*, 9 J. LEGAL STUD. 227 (1980); Weinrib, *Utilitarianism, Economics, and Legal Theory*, 30 U. TORONTO L.J. 307 (1980).

3. *See* R. POSNER, *supra* note 1, ch. 4; Posner, *A Reply to Some Recent Criticisms of the Economic Theory of the Common Law*, 9 HOFSTRA L. REV. 775, 786-94 (1981).

4. *See, e.g.*, N. MERCURO & T. RYAN, LAW, ECONOMICS AND PUBLIC POLICY 130-37 (1984); Coleman, *The Normative Basis of Economic Analysis: A Critical Review of Richard Posner's* The Economics of Justice (Book Review), 34 STAN. L. REV. 1105 (1982).

"wealth" suggests money. But to an economist, it refers to weighting preferences for the things that people want, either by willingness to pay for a thing, if you do not own it, or by unwillingness to part with it voluntarily, if you do own it. So, if I am unwilling to part with my house for less than $100,000, and no one is willing to pay more than $90,000 for it, society's wealth is $10,000 greater than it would be if the house were taken from me and given to the highest bidder (I am not a bidder, because I am the owner). This would be so even if I were paid $100,000 for the house (which would require taxation, since no one will voluntarily pay $100,000 for it). I would be no wealthier than before, and the rest of the community would have $100,000 less, incompletely offset by a house worth only $90,000 to its new owner.

Now suppose that I want a car and would pay $10,000 for it, and the present owner would sell it for $5,000. Society's wealth will be increased if I am allowed to buy the car from him for any amount between $5,000 and $10,000 (ignore selling costs). Suppose the price is $7,500. After the transaction I will have $2,500 plus a car worth $10,000 to me. I will thus have total wealth (ignoring the house and any other wealth I have) of $12,500, and he $7,500, for a total of $20,000, whereas before the transaction our combined wealth was only $15,000.

Granted, both examples ignore a fundamental problem—how it is that I initially came to have the house, and he the car. I shall come back to that problem, but for now, I just want to explain what wealth means.

Wealth is not limited to market commodities such as houses and cars. As a matter of fact, the value of houses and cars is not always reducible to market values. The house I value at $100,000 might not be valued at more than $90,000 by anyone else because it has sentimental associations for me, and likewise with the car. In this case, the real value would exceed market value. Or, I might work for a lower salary than I could make, simply because I liked the work I did for that lower salary so much; that would mean that I derived part of my wealth from working and part from the pecuniary income that I earned by working.

These examples help to show that money, to an economist, is not wealth, but just a measure of one's entitlement to houses, cars, rewarding work, leisure, privacy, and countless other "things" that constitute a person's wealth; everyone's wealth added together constitutes the nation's wealth. The wealth of a nation is the present value of the flow of benefits, measured as suggested above, from the consumption of goods and services, tangible and intangible, by its people. Monetary measures of social income or wealth[5] such as Gross National Product or National Income are inadequate and inaccurate measures of a nation's wealth. When I used money as a component of wealth earlier, it was just a shorthand term for the things that money can buy.

The economist uses the concept of income or wealth in this broad sense all the time, but calls it "utility," meaning, however, something quite different from what utilitarian philosophers mean. To compound the confusion, the economist uses the word "wealth" to mean something different from the economic concept of "utility." To the economist, "utility" differs from "wealth" because utility is adjusted for people's preference for risk or (more commonly) aversion to risk, in the sense of the variance of possible outcomes of an uncertain event. If you were given gratis a fifty percent chance of winning ten dollars (and an equal chance of winning nothing), your "wealth" (in the narrow economic sense) would rise by five dollars, which is the expected utility of the chance to someone who is risk neutral. But if you were risk averse, the increment in your expected utility would be less than five dollars, so you would sell the ticket to someone less risk averse, or risk neutral, or risk preferring, if you could, and you would thereby increase your utility. If you were risk preferring, the chance would be worth more than five dollars to you. Thus "wealth," in my sense, is a synonym for expected utility. Bear in mind that wealth is a function of willingness to pay (or unwillingness to part with, but for present purposes, the difference is unimportant). If you will pay more for the fifty percent chance than its certain equivalent (because you are a risk preferrer), then it is worth more to you; its expected utility determines your willingness to pay, and hence describes the effect of the chance on your wealth. For example, if you would pay six dollars for the chance, the gift of it would increase your wealth by six dollars.

Wealth, in my sense, equates to utility in the economic sense but is distinct from the utilitarian concept of utility as happiness, however broadly (or narrowly) happiness is de-

5. "Income" is a flow concept, "wealth" the corresponding stock concept. The important thing to bear in mind is that income (and therefore wealth, which is the discounted present value of anticipated future income) refers to real rather than monetary phenomena—to housing or transportation services or leisure, not to wages or dividends.

fined, though wealth and happiness are positively correlated. (Ask anyone whether he or she would turn down an unconditional gift of money!) I might be made deliriously happy by being given a ticket to a Notre Dame football game, but if I am outbid by another football fan, it means that wealth maximization requires that I not get the ticket, even though the person who outbids me might derive less pleasure from the game than I would have derived. The refusal of modern economists to make "interpersonal comparisons of utility" means in effect that they use wealth rather than happiness as the criterion for an efficient allocation of resources.

People find it easier to picture wealth maximization in actual transactions than in potential transactions, but one of the most important uses of the concept is in connection with potential transactions. I refer to the analysis of the welfare loss (in my terminology, the wealth loss) caused by monopoly. In Figure 1, the monopolist, in order to increase his profits over the competitive (= zero) level, reduces his output to q_m, at which level the market-clearing price is p_m. Those customers who continue to buy the product at its new, monopoly price incur a wealth loss measured by the rectangle ABCF; but their loss is the monopolist's gain, so there is a wash. The

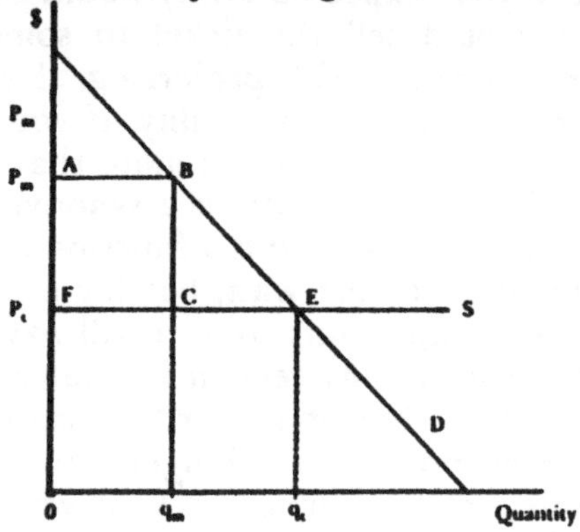

Figure 1

net social loss from monopoly is the triangle BEC. This is the consumer surplus that is lost by those who are deflected to substitute products by the higher price, but that is not transformed into producer surplus (profit). In what sense is it a loss? At the competitive price and output, these consumers (all but the last, represented by the intersection of D and S, at point E) would have been willing to pay more for the product than they were charged. In other words, the product increased their wealth by more than the purchase price—as is still true of those consumers who continue to buy the product at its current price. The idea of consumer (and producer) surplus, a legacy of the great English economist Alfred Marshall, shows that wealth is not money. This is the crucial insight in making wealth maximization a standard of social welfare.

The welfare loss of monopoly is the least controversial, though no longer the only, ground on which economists denounce monopoly.[6] This denunciation illustrates the normative use of the concept of wealth maximization,[7] and my position in this paper amounts to nothing more than expanding the normative domain of the concept. If you think back to the house and car examples with which I began, you will realize that they were both cases where the objective was to maximize surplus value—the value that measures what people are willing to pay (or what they demand) over and above market price, the price paid by the marginal buyer (p_m'. in Figure 1).

Anyone who is inclined to say that wealth is not a value in an ethical sense should ask himself whether he agrees that monopolies and cartels are bad because they lead to a reduction in the value of output. If he agrees with this traditional economic criticism, then he believes that wealth is a social, ethical value—whether he knows it or not. He also believes that interpersonal comparisons of wealth are possible—that is, that it is possible to compare the loss of surplus to the consumer with the gain to the monopolist. It is by such comparisons that one can determine whether a given transaction, policy or institution is wealth maximizing. Of course, the information costs may be formidable, but there is no objection in principle to measuring aggregate wealth.

II. Criticisms

The most basic criticism of an ethic of wealth maximization is one that I share: that you cannot deduce "ought" from "is"; you cannot prove, deductively or inductively, that

6. *See, e.g.*, J. Hirshleifer, Price Theory and Applications 249-52 (1984).

7. And makes quite extraordinary the assertion that wealth maximization requires monopoly because monopoly leads to higher prices. *See* N. Mercuro & T. Ryan, *supra* note 4, at 132; Kornhauser, *A Guide to the Perplexed Claims of Efficiency in the Law*, 8 Hofstra L. Rev. 591, 596-97 (1980); Coleman, *supra* note 2, at 523-24. This is known in the economic literature as the Earl of Lauderdale's fallacy. *See* G. Stigler, The Theory of Price 196-97 (3d ed. 1966).

social decisions ought to conform to some ethical theory. The lack of provability imparts a pervasive uncertainty to ethical debates; it is not clear what it means to prevail in an ethical argument. Ethical arguments do not convince doubters but rather provide rationalizations for ethical positions taken on emotional grounds. Indeed, more ethical arguments have been won on the battlefield than in the lecture hall; and if the fascist powers had won World War II, the dominant ethical views in this society would probably be different today. Perhaps—speaking descriptively and in the long run—might is responsible for most opinions of what is right.

My goal is therefore quite modest. I do not seek to "convert" anyone to wealth maximization. I merely want to persuade you that it is a reasonable, though not a demonstrably or a universally correct, ethic (I shall explain later why my goal is so limited). But to do this I shall have to consider the principal arguments against its being even that.

A. *Asking versus Offer Prices, and the Derivation of Property Rights*

The first argument is that the idea of wealth maximization does not tell us whether to maximize in terms of asking or offering prices; in my example of a house, the asking price was $100,000 but the offer price was only $90,000. I reject this argument. The concept of wealth maximization tells us when to use asking and when to use offer prices, provided—an important qualification to which I shall return in a moment—that property rights have been assigned.

If the costs of voluntary transactions are low, the equilibrium prices, which provide the logical and natural means of measuring wealth, will be asking prices; for whenever an offer price is higher than an asking price, the offer will be accepted.[8] If the costs of voluntary transactions are prohibitive, however, then offer prices[9] may exceed asking prices indefinitely; and if, but only if, an involuntary transaction is possible at a cost less than the difference between offer and asking price, the offer price (that is, the hypothetical offer price)

8. At the margin, of course, the offer and asking price will be the same; but there may be many intramarginal holders of the good or service transacted in the market, and for them the asking prices will exceed the offer prices and provide the correct measure of value. The house example illustrates this point.

9. Hypothetical offer prices, that is, if transactions are prohibitively costly, no one will bother to make offers.

rather than the asking price will provide the correct guide for social choices designed to maximize wealth. Suppose millions of people would be willing to pay in the aggregate $1 billion for clean air, and the polluters would be willing to stop polluting the air for $100 million. But because there are so many polluters and pollutants, voluntary transactions are prohibitively costly. One way to look at this case would be to say that clean air is not really worth $900 million (benefits minus costs), because we have left out the transaction costs. These transaction costs, which exceed $900 million, are just like any other costs—like transportation costs, for example—and, when added in, show that the clean air really has no net value.

Transaction costs differ from transportation costs, however, because they sometimes can be circumvented by substituting a legal institution for the market as the method of allocating resources. In deciding whether this is possible in a particular case, we must have an idea of the value of an allocative change without regard to transaction costs, before we can decide whether that value exceeds the cost of the legal institution necessary to bring about the allocation.[10] If, in my example, the institution would cost less than $900 million, then society would be made wealthier by the legally coerced allocation of the rights in the air to the victims of the pollution. But $900 million may be an underestimate. Recall that asking prices can exceed offer prices. It might be that although the victims of air pollution would be willing to spend only $1 billion for cleaner air, once they had cleaner air they might demand $2 billion to give it up. This would be the relevant figure if the victims were deemed to own clear air, rather than if the polluters owned the right to dirty the air; and, precisely since asking and offer prices may differ,[11] and differ greatly, this assumption may affect the outcome of the hypothetical transaction—an important point to which I shall return in a moment. If the cost of abating pollution was $1.5 billion, the difference between deeming the victims the owners of the right and deeming the polluters the owners of the right would be crucial.

10. Thus the social engineer is interested in the value of a transaction ex transaction costs in the same way that a transportation engineer is interested in the value of a transaction ex transportation costs.

11. For empirical evidence, including evidence on air pollution, see Knetsch, *Legal Rules and the Basis for Evaluating Economic Losses*, 4 INT'L REV. L. & ECON. 5 (1984).

But the present point is simply that, given well-defined property rights, the question of whether wealth maximization concerns offer prices or asking prices is a pseudo-question. Wealth is maximized by creating a system which allows offer and asking prices to be compared, and offers to be accepted if, but only if, the offer price exceeds the asking price, and which imposes acceptance if, but only if, transaction costs make it impossible for the market to compare a (higher) offer price with a (lower) asking price, as in the pollution example.

Because asking and offer prices may differ, it is necessary to have a way of deciding who may charge an asking price and who must make offers; this is a question about property rights. For present purposes, a property right means the right not to be divested of the use, control, and enjoyment of a thing (tangible or intangible) at a price below one's asking price. Once property rights are assigned, it becomes clear who may charge asking prices and who must make offers. Wealth maximization can then proceed through the operation of the free market, and through market surrogates where the costs of market transactions are prohibitive and the costs of legal transactions tolerable.

It would, of course, be possible to take the assignment of property rights as given, and use wealth maximization to guide the shifting of the rights through trade and substitutes for trade. But I think one can go further and without circularity, can suggest how property rights should be assigned in the first place in order to maximize a society's wealth. And this is not so academic an endeavor as it may seem.

In my pollution example, there is no "natural" assignment of property rights over the use of the air; one could say that people have a right to breathe clean air, and polluters must buy that right, or equally that polluters have a right to emit pollutants as a byproduct of their activities, and people must buy that right (the "purchase" in either case would be an involuntary transaction, because market transactions are assumed to be unworkable). I do not know how to solve this particular problem; that is, I do not know whether in determining how much pollution is optimal we should use the asking or offer prices of clean air, which may of course differ, though presumably by little if we are talking about small changes in the cleanliness of air. If we are talking about whether the air shall be breathable or lethal, the difference between asking and offer prices could be enormous, since offer prices are limited by one's wealth, and asking prices may be infinite when the asker's life is at stake. However, cases of this kind—where wealth maximization provides no guidance to the initial assignment of property rights *and* asking and offer prices are likely to differ greatly—are rare; they reveal a limitation to an ethics of wealth maximization, but not a fatal limitation.

One can say a good deal about how property rights should be assigned in order to maximize wealth. For example, wealth maximization does not imply assigning property rights to whomever, regardless of his budget, gets the most pleasure out of the property in question, though he might have the highest asking price.[12] This approach appears to collapse wealth maximization into utility maximization in the sense used by utilitarian philosophers; worse, it actually disserves wealth maximization. If property rights were assigned on the basis of who would charge the highest asking prices, society would soon be impoverished. The method of assignment would destroy incentives to work and invest—unless rights could be sold free of any governmental power to take them away from their new owner; but that would depart from a system of assigning property rights so as to maximize utility in the utilitarian sense.

Bear in mind that wealth is a stock concept, not a flow concept; one's wealth is the present value of the stream of future income or other benefits generated by one's human and physical capital. The stream would be pitifully small if property rights were assigned and reassigned on the basis of who derived the most pleasure from having what property. People would cultivate the faculty of enjoyment rather than of hard work; little producer and consumer surplus would be created.

If you asked a random group of economists how to assign property rights in a new society with a literate population so as to maximize the prices (times quantities), explicit and implicit ("shadow"), asking and offer, in the society, they would almost certainly begin by giving each mentally competent adult the property rights to his own labor.[13] They would, in short, reject slavery, an inefficient institution under modern conditions. With unimportant exceptions, the costs of moni-

12. Might, not would, because if he also got great pleasure out of other things, the money he could get for a given item of property might be very valuable to him because it would enable him to buy other pleasurable things.

13. The qualification implies, of course, the persistence of institutions of quasi-slavery, as one might characterize (but for the pejorative overtones) the condition of children and mental incompetents.

toring the output of a slave today would be much higher than the costs of monitoring a free man's output through contract. Although some slave owners would be quite wealthy, the society as a whole (which includes the persons who have been made slaves) would be poor. Society's wealth would be eaten up to a great extent by "agency costs." Arguably, this, rather than moral progress unrelated to material conditions, may be the main reason that slavery is no longer a common institution.

I recognize that some will count it a very great defect of my ethical system that it does not condemn slavery as always and everywhere bad. But partly, this is just a reaction to a word that has intensely pejorative connotations. Is it "slavery" to make a prison inmate work? Was indentured servitude, whereby immigrants to this country in the colonial period got their passage paid in exchange for becoming indentured servants for a period of years, "slavery," and therefore, bad? Was it an advance or retreat of civilization when victorious tribes began enslaving rather than killing the male population of the vanquished group? The answers are not so clear as to justify a blanket condemnation of all forms of involuntary servitude.

With natural resources, the initial assignment of property rights is not critical because presumably whoever gets the rights will sell or rent them to those who can get the most value out of them. The problem of the discrepancy between offer and asking prices will not be important here, because resources whose only use is "utilitarian" in the lay sense will tend to be valued at very near the market price. But this happy picture ignores important sources of friction. In particular, those who in the initial distribution receive no rights in natural resources will, in order to buy from those who do, have to borrow against inherently uncertain prospects. The same uncertainty makes it hard for the society to assign the property rights at the outset to those who can get the most value from them. Perhaps the best that can be done is, as in the nineteenth-century Homestead Acts, to parcel out the rights in an egalitarian fashion. This will give everyone some physical capital and therefore make it easier for the able and ambitious to rise.

An important application of this point suggests that the implications of wealth maximization are not entirely "illiberal," as those who deride it as capitalist ethics—which it is—may think. The maximization of wealth requires that people with productive potential have opportunities to develop that potential. This in turn requires means to identify such people and enable them to rent the tools they need to realize their potential. Because the potential of young children is not apparent unless they are given educational opportunities, and because it is difficult to borrow against one's future earnings (because the loan can be enforced only by making the borrower the lender's slave if he defaults—creating all the agency-cost problems of slavery), there is a solid argument based on wealth maximization for subsidizing education, especially (though not only) for the poor. The argument, however, need not imply government operation as distinct from financial support of the schools.

After rights are assigned, the free market can be relied on to reallocate them from time to time to those who value them the most as shown by willingness to pay an offer price equal to the current owner's asking price. Problems of monopoly, the needs of public finance, the problem just discussed of financing investments in human capital, external benefits and costs associated with such phenomena as charity (a source of external benefits) and crime (external costs), and concerns with political stability will require, however, some redistribution through the tax and government expenditure system. In short, a lightly regulated capitalism starting from conditions of broad equality will maximize a society's wealth. The history of this country, and, more generally, a comparison of capitalist and noncapitalist societies, illustrate the benefits of light regulation though it is no longer possible to describe our capitalism as lightly regulated.

B. *The Instrumental Character of Wealth Maximization*

I am reasonably satisfied that the objection based on the fact that wealth cannot even be measured unless property rights are first assigned can be met to the degree required in ethical discourse. I now move on to a second and more serious objection, which is that the ethic of wealth maximization rests on air. One does not value wealth for itself but for something else, and once we identify the something else, we can orient our social institutions toward accomplishing that end and cease pursuing the merely instrumental goal of maximizing wealth.

The values which provide the underlying ethical appeal of wealth maximization pull us in two seemingly opposite directions: toward utilitarianism and toward individualism. Wealth maximization promotes prosperity, and prosperity (not always but usually) engenders happiness. Wealth maximization also protects individual rights, and therefore promotes individualism. But, presumably, wealth maximization promotes each of these desiderata (particularly the second) to a lesser extent than a philosophy aimed directly at either one of them would do—a point that will now be illustrated and evaluated.

1. Wealth and Happiness

It is easy to think of examples where wealth maximization is at least superficially opposed to utilitarian goals—though, as the examples are rather extreme, maybe they should not trouble us much. But set aside that point and suppose as an example that a quantity of pituitary extract is being auctioned off. There are two bidders: one is a poor family whose child will be a dwarf unless he gets the extract; the other is a wealthy dilettante who wants to use the extract to grow a giant gerbil. The dilettante is the high bidder (let us assume away any imperfection in capital markets by supposing that even if the family could borrow against the child's future earnings, its offer price would still be lower than the dilettante's).

The result of wealth maximization in this case seems clearly contrary to the dictates of utilitarianism, besides being quite offensive. Yet these reactions may be superficial. We must consider, for example, who will get the pituitary extract if the dilettante is forbidden to buy it. More important, we must consider that, in the long run, there may be more and cheaper pituitary extract, and fewer dwarves, if the society does not try to allocate the product to those who will derive the greatest happiness from it. Or people may be sufficiently altruistic, even toward strangers, to support, as a component of the government's tax and expenditure system, a program for buying pituitary extract at market prices and giving it to children whose families are unable to afford it. Reliance on private charity may seem an obvious alternative to a public program but might not be efficient because of a free-rider problem. If I want fewer dwarves, I will benefit from your charitable contribution as much as you do, without having to make a contribution myself. The result will be a lower level of contributions than most people desire and, in the absence of free-rider problems, would make. This is an inefficient result which, in principle anyway, justifies government intervention even in a society dedicated to wealth maximization.

The real divergence between wealth maximization and utilitarianism occurs where utilitarianism is contrary to virtually everyone's moral intuitions. Suppose someone has such a well-developed sense of pleasure that he receives twice as much pleasure from a dollar than one who happens to be frugal and self-denying. Is that a reason for transferring a dollar from the second to the first person? A utilitarian would have to say it was a reason, although it might well be outweighed by the adverse effect on happiness in general if people's wealth were up for grabs in this way. Even worse, suppose a sadist got more pleasure from hurting people than his (involuntary) victims suffered pain; the sadist's conduct would be happiness-maximizing, and therefore good.

Utilitarianism makes the individual an input into the achievement of an aggregate quantity, the total happiness in society. This fact is the dark side of the most attractive feature of utilitarianism—its tolerance for different conceptions of the good. Somehow utilitarianism manages to be both radically individualistic and shockingly communitarian. It is so individualistic in its premises that it gives the same status to the sadist and the pleasure-loving scamp, on the one hand, as to the heroic physician or brilliant engineer on the other. At the same time, it is so aggregative that it invites us to consider the possibility of redistributing wealth and power from the productive and hard-working and self-restrained to people of unbridled appetites and vicious disposition.

What is missing from utilitarianism is any very direct concern with the productive side of human activity; all the focus is on the consuming, the appetitive. Perhaps this matters little in practice, because consumption is dependent on production, and the pleasure-loving will have few pleasures in a society that does not give its members incentives to produce. Indeed, the pleasure-loving might work particularly hard in order to get control of the resources that they need in order to maximize their pleasure and might support institutions that reward productive people. Nonetheless, it seems odd to give consumption moral precedence over production, to sacrifice the frugal for the pleasure-loving.

Wealth maximization reverses the order, and this is a mark in its favor. In a society dedicated to wealth maximization, the power to consume is limited by the ability to obtain claims on resources, and this ability depends on the production of goods or services that others value in trade. This is true even when the consumer is spending inherited money, as might have been the case with our wealthy dilettante buying pituitary extract for his gerbil. A person who accumulates more money than he spends during his lifetime is, in effect, deferring some of his spending until after his death, when it will be done by surrogates, his heirs. In deciding how much to accumulate and how much of that accumulation will go to his heirs rather than to charity, the testator will take into account the likelihood that his heirs will spend the money he leaves them in foolish or offensive ways. If, after taking this possibility (a form of "agency cost") into account, he nevertheless leaves them money, they become, in effect, his agents to spend it after his death. Any interference with their expenditures is an interference with his disposition of assets accumulated through his productive efforts.

Granted, he may not have accumulated his wealth by productive efforts; he may have stolen the money, or obtained it by monopolization, or inherited it from someone who had stolen it. These would be grounds for interfering with its expenditure in the next generation according to the testator's wishes. But if all illegitimate (i.e., unproductive) sources of wealth are assumed away as incompatible with wealth maximization, then in a society dedicated to wealth maximization, the right to consume will depend on productive activity.

To defend wealth maximization rigorously, it would of course be necessary to assign some ethical value to productivity. That would not be difficult but will not be attempted here. Although there is some well-merited skepticism about various aspects of modern life, very few people who live in wealthy societies would like to live in poor ones; and very many people who live in poor ones would, if allowed, move to wealthy ones. So there seems to be something good in a practical sense about wealthy societies, unless you think (as few economists do) that wealthy societies have become wealthy by exploiting poor ones. And if there is something good about wealthy societies, there must be something good about the people who make societies wealthy—and they are not the hedonists and the sybarites but the frugal and the hard-working. It is curious, but true, that to aim directly at maximizing happiness, by distributing and redistributing wealth to those who would get the most pleasure from it, is self-defeating because it results in a poor and unhappy society. Wealth maximization is a more effective instrument for attaining the goals of utilitarianism than utilitarianism itself. Stated otherwise, wealth maximization is the correct rule of decision in a system of rule utilitarianism.

Wealth maximization does not completely exclude governmental redistributions of wealth, as we saw in discussing the free-rider problem that depresses private charity. But it authorizes only those redistributions that conform to the altruistic feelings that most people harbor or that otherwise serve the interests of the productive people in the society. The free-wheeling redistributions of a utilitarian society are ruled out. This is also a mark in favor of wealth maximization.

A further criticism of wealth maximization that I will merely note and not try to answer is that, like utilitarianism, it assigns too much weight to individual preferences. Compare the sadist who assaults an involuntary victim and a sadist who obtains equivalent satisfaction from a mutually voluntary transaction with a masochist. The two sadists have similar standing in a system unflinchingly dedicated to maximizing happiness, provided that in the first case the sadist's pleasure exceeds his victim's suffering; but in a system of wealth maximization, the second sadist is a distinctly better man. The successful producer of an infantile television show who earns $500,000 a year would, in a system of wealth maximization, be counted as a better, more productive person than a laborer who earns $10,000. But the producer may not be more productive than a scientist who earns only $50,000, as the scientist may confer large external benefits on society, that is, benefits that he does not capture in a higher income for himself.

2. Wealth and Individual Rights

If wealth maximization has affinities with utilitarianism, it also has affinities with the individualist political philosophy that has been made respectable among professional philosophers in recent years through the work of Robert Nozick—though it has antecedents in the writings of Hobbes, Locke, Kant, Jefferson, and other classic expositors of Western liberalism. The premise of individualist political philosophy is that a person is defined by the possession of faculties such as reason and of rights thought appurtenant to the possession of such faculties. The conclusion is that the role of the state is to protect those rights, including the right to engage in voluntary exchange. In wanting to protect voluntary exchange, the individualist philosopher comes close to being a wealth maximizer. But he may also deduce rights that may be inconsistent with wealth maximization, as in Professor Epstein's suggestion that individualism implies that tort liability to strangers should be strict liability, even if negligence liability (or no liability) would be more efficient. In Epstein's view, if you run someone down, you must pay his damages because you have invaded his rights, even if you were faultless in the sense of being unable to avoid the accident at reasonable, perhaps at any, cost.[14]

A counterargument is possible, however.[15] If negligence is really cheaper than strict liability, then the sum of accident (first-party) and liability (third-party) insurance costs will be less under negligence than strict liability, and all drivers will prefer the former. Hence, negligence liability can be derived by a hypothetical voluntary transaction, which is a standard method of justifying institutions in an individualist philosophy. Stated differently, if a change (say from strict liability, assuming that is the regime initially deduced from individualist premises, to negligence liability) makes everyone better off by his own rights, it is hard to see it as trammeling anyone's individual rights. And if we are reasonably confident that the change would be adopted unanimously if we could somehow put it to a vote, this ought to come close enough to real (expressed) unanimity to satisfy the claims of individualism—as should also, I would contend, near unanimity, provided that the sacrifice by the opponents is a very small one in both an aggregate and an individual sense. That is, if ninety-five percent of drivers would have much lower insurance rates from a switch to a negligence standard, and none of the other five percent would pay more than a few dollars a year in additional premiums, it would be hard to condemn the change on individualist grounds without being accused of fanaticism.

C. *The Problem of Inalienable Rights*

Some implications of individualism, however, are quite hard to reconcile with wealth maximization, and these deserve separate consideration. Almost everyone writing in the individualist tradition thinks slavery improper even if the slave became such through a voluntary transaction, as in contracts of indentured servitude, which, as I mentioned, were common in eighteenth-century America—though most individualists will make a narrow and partial exception for mili-

14. *See* Epstein, *A Theory of Strict Liability*, 2 J. LEGAL STUD. 151 (1973).

15. For a slightly fuller treatment of this point, see R. POSNER, *supra* note 1, at 94-99.

tary service. Torture and lynching are other examples where the individualist will be inclined to say that the practice violates essential personhood even if it could be shown to maximize wealth, as it could be in the (far-fetched) example where a person is lynched in circumstances of absolute certainty that he is guilty and that the legal punishment would have been death if he had stood trial. In this case, the only effect of lynching is to reduce the costs of administering the legal system. A somewhat more plausible case is eliminating the privilege against self-incrimination, to make everyone (or nearly everyone) better off *ex ante*, by increasing the probability of convicting guilty people. The feeling against these practices runs very deep in our culture. It is bound up with a general aversion to cruelty that dates only from the humanitarian movement of the nineteenth century; yet Hobbes, who emphatically supported the privilege against self-incrimination,[16] was a man of the seventeenth century—and no softy.

Long after lynching, slavery, and torture were all thoroughly reprobated, it still would not have been thought unjust for the state to allow a man to starve who could not earn a subsistence income by his best efforts. Today it would be thought unjust, though not by all individualist philosophers in the sense in which I am using the term. There is for good or ill nothing in the ethic of wealth maximization which says that society has a duty to help the needy. It has a duty not to hurt them, to leave them alone; but it has no duty, and in a strict ethic of wealth maximization no right, to force the productive people to support the unproductive. Being needy does not establish a claim. A right implies a duty; and there is no basis in a system of wealth maximization for implying a duty to help someone you have not hurt. Charity is an important part of personal ethics, but except where the charitable impulse is impeded by free-rider problems, a political duty of charity cannot be deduced from the premises of wealth maximization. In this regard, wealth maximization is at one with individualist political philosophy, but both are out of phase with powerful currents of contemporary moral feeling; both, perhaps, neglect the role of luck in wealth and poverty and by doing so give excessive moral status to the condition of being a productive person.

All of the examples I have discussed are sufficiently troublesome to make me regard wealth maximization as an incomplete guide to social decision-making. But within the

16. *See*, T. Hobbes, Leviathan, pt. 2, ch. 21 (London 1651).

broad limits indicated by these examples, wealth maximization does provide a reasonable guide to social decision-making and, in particular, builds a bridge between utilitarian and individualist philosophies—and not an adventitious bridge, either. Wealth maximization shares with utilitarianism an emphasis on the moral value of individual preferences and desires, and with individualism a hostility to coercion.[17] It does not banish coercion entirely, because where market transaction costs are prohibitive, wealth maximization allows, and indeed requires, the state to use its powers to mimic the market—if this can be done at a cost lower than the gain in value brought about by the market-mimicking transaction. But the limited forms of coercion that are legitimate in a system of wealth maximization promote social welfare so broadly that they can be deemed to command almost universal consent. The institutions of criminal, property, tort, and contract law—indeed of common law in general—are of this character.

The strong hold that both utilitarianism and individualism have over American social thought suggests that a political philosophy which draws on both may command a broader support than either. The pluralistic and—let us face it—materialistic character of our civilization makes it inevitable that government will and should try to promote the greatest happiness of the greatest number, rather than decide what preferences are legitimate and whose preferences should count the most. But pushed to an extreme, utilitarianism creates a potential for wealth redistribution that is inconsistent with a commitment to individual autonomy (as illustrated by the claims of the "utility monster" to have wealth redistributed to him because he is especially efficient at processing it into happiness, though only his own). Yet too rigid a commitment to individual autonomy would diminish the happiness of the society to an intolerable extent—a point with many potential illustrations from the writings of Kant and his followers, including Rawls, who to maximize the position of the least fortunate would be willing to impose enormous sacrifices on the rest of the society.[18]

---

17. The civilizing influence of capitalism—and what is wealth maximization but the ethics of capitalism?—is emphasized in Haskell, *Capitalism and the Origins of the Humanitarian Sensibility* (pts. 1 & 2), 90 AM. HIST. REV. 339, 547 (1985).

18. *See, e.g,* J. RAWLS, A THEORY OF JUSTICE 152-54 (1971); Arrow, *Some Ordinalist-Utilitarian Notes on Rawls's Theory of Justice,* 70 J. PHIL. 245, 251 (1973); Hodges, *Punishment,* 18 PHIL. & PHENOMENOLOGICAL RESEARCH

Wealth maximization perhaps comes up short by not recognizing either inalienable (i.e., nonsalable) rights—a deficiency (if it is a deficiency) that it shares with utilitarianism—or claims to public assistance—a deficiency, in terms of contemporary intuitive morality, that it shares with individualism. In a system of wealth maximization, the needy (dramatically including the child in my pituitary-extract example) have no right to coerce even minimum assistance. Yet this characterization of wealth maximization is only approximately true. It would be more accurate to say that wealth maximization reflects the distributive preferences of the people who produce the wealth of the society. To the extent that such people are altruistic, but the full expression of their altruism is frustrated by free-rider problems, government is authorized (indeed, required) to undertake redistributive efforts. If altruistic feelings were not widespread, philosophers would not consider a political philosophy that made no room for the hard-hearted rather than hard-headed. To the wealth maximizer, altruism is neither good nor bad; but given that it exists, there is a legitimate if limited role for public wealth redistribution. If altruism did not exist, the absence of such redistribution would not be felt to be unjust.

It must also be emphasized that it is a *political* philosophy that I am expounding. You may be a bad person if you are selfish; but it may not be the proper role of the state to change your values and preferences.

III. Application to Law

Despite all I have said, or perhaps because of some of what I have said, I am sure that many of my readers will continue to regard wealth maximization as a dubious guide to social decision-making in general. But the case for using it to guide courts, in areas where the Constitution or legislation does not deprive them of initiative or discretion in the matter, is a powerful one—though with some limitations along the lines suggested above.

The legal profession long pretended that with unimportant exceptions, discretion—power—was something that bad judges seized, while good judges deduced the outcomes of their cases from rules laid down by higher or prior courts, legislatures, and the framers of the Constitution. Today, however, it is generally recognized that even the best judges

---

209 (1957-1959).

cannot decide difficult cases simply by deduction from premises found in authoritative sources of legal guidance (which is why the cases are called difficult)—that they have and must exercise substantial discretion. The question arises, in what frame of reference should that discretion be exercised? Pragmatic? Utilitarian? Christian? Darwinian? Rawlsian? Nozickian? I suggest that wealth maximization provides the most acceptable frame of reference. I shall not attempt to argue this position fully here but will content myself with the following rather summary points:

1. Wealth maximization combines, as I have said, elements of utilitarianism and individualism, and in so doing comes closer to being a consensus political philosophy (I do not suggest it is one) in our contentiously pluralistic society than any other overarching political principle. This point is concealed by the fact that the term "wealth maximization" is not a term in common usage. It would be easy to show, however, that many invocations of fairness and justice, "balancing" and due process and other familiar principles or methods of judicial decision-making are proxies for wealth maximization.[19]

2. The principal complaint likely to be leveled against wealth maximization as a guide to judicial action is its lack of a strong redistributive component; as we have seen, it validates some redistribution of wealth from rich to poor but much less than is desired by many reflective and influential students of social justice. Any possible collisions between wealth maximization and the strong modern feelings against slavery, lynching, and torture, however, are made moot by the constitutional prohibitions against these practices.[20]

Given the absence of anything approaching a consensus on the optimum distribution of wealth, however, it is very hard to see how courts could adopt a redistributive ethic to guide their decisions. For this and another reason—that courts do not have flexible instruments for redistribution compared to the (overtly) taxing, spending, and regulatory branches of government—a sensible division of labor has the

---

19. This is a major theme of my book, R. POSNER, ECONOMIC ANALYSIS OF LAW (2d ed. 1977); the forthcoming third edition will be published in March, 1986.

20. The Thirteenth Amendment forbids slavery; the due process clauses of the Fifth and Fourteenth Amendments lynching; the Fifth Amendment torture to obtain incriminating evidence; and the Eighth Amendment torture as a method of inflicting punishment on convicted criminals.

courts focus on wealth maximization (making the pie as big as possible) while legislatures focus on redistributing some of that wealth (reslicing the pie).

My interest in wealth maximization grew from and remains centered upon its role, both actual and desirable, in guiding judicial decision-making in "common law" areas, broadly defined to include any field where judge-made law is important; where judicial discretion—lawful and legitimate judicial discretion—is important. By a happy coincidence, as I have said, many of the questions on which the unflinching embrace of the implications of wealth maximization might yield results contrary to widespread moral intuitions, such as lynching and torture, have been taken out of the area of judicial discretion by constitutional provisions. The domain in which wealth maximization is allowed to operate in the law is, not surprisingly, the domain in which the principle of wealth maximization—once it is correctly understood, and not confused with the ethics of Mammon or Midas—expresses fundamental values of our political culture.

Part II
The Efficiency of the Common Law Hypothesis

[5]

AN ECONOMIC ANALYSIS OF THE COURTS*

WILLIAM M. LANDES

Columbia University and the National Bureau of Economic Research

"The object of our study, then, is prediction, ... The prophecies of what the courts will do in fact, and nothing more pretentious, are what I mean by the law." Oliver Wendell Holmes, Jr., The Path of Law (1897).

In the folklore of criminal justice a popular belief is that the accused will have his case decided in a trial. Empirical evidence does not support this belief. Table 1 indicates that most cases are disposed of before trial by either a guilty plea or a dismissal of the charges. What factors determine the choice between a pre-trial settlement and a trial? What accounts for the large proportion of settlements compared to trials? How are certain aspects of the criminal justice process such as the bail system and court delay related to the decision to settle or to go to trial? The main purpose of this essay is to answer these questions by means of a theoretical and empirical analysis of the criminal justice system using standard tools of economic theory and statistics.

A theoretical model is first developed that identifies the variables relevant to the choice between a settlement and a trial. The basic assumption of the model is that both the prosecutor and the defendant maximize their utility, appropriately defined, subject to a constraint on their resources. It is shown that the decision to settle or go to trial depends on the probability of conviction by trial, the severity of the crime, the availability and productivity of the prosecutor's and defendant's resources, trial versus settlement costs, and attitudes toward risk. We then analyse the effects of the bail system and court delay on settlements, and consider several proposals for improving the bail system and reducing court delay. These include "preventive detention," monetary compensation to defendants not released on bail, and the imposition of a money price for the use of the courts. The model is further useful in

* This paper has been approved for publication as a report of the National Bureau of Economic Research by the officers and Directors of the National Bureau, in accordance with the resolution of the Board governing National Bureau reports (see the Annual Report of the National Bureau of Economic Research). I would like to thank Professors Gary Becker, Solomon Fabricant, Laurence Miller, Sherwin Rosen, Finis Welch and Neil Wallace, and Elisabeth Landes for helpful criticisms. I also received useful comments at seminars at the NBER, Columbia, Rochester, U.C.L.A. and the University of Chicago.

TABLE 1
DISPOSITION OF CRIMINAL CASES

Area (Year)	Number of Defendants	Trials Number	Trials Per cent	Guilty Pleas Number	Guilty Pleas Per cent	Dismissed Number	Dismissed Per cent
132 State County Courts (1962)	7,510[a]	1,394	19	5,293	70	823	11
U.S. District Courts (1967)	31,535	4,208	13	23,131	73	4,196	13

Sources: Lee Silverstein, Defense of the Poor in Criminal Cases in American State Courts, A Field Study and Report (2 v. 1965); Ann. Rep., Admin. Off. of the United States Courts, 1967.
[a] Number of felony defendants in sample.

evaluating the frequently made argument that the criminal justice system discriminates against low income defendants. This proposition is analysed by relating a defendant's income or wealth to his decision to settle or go to trial, the probability of his conviction, and his sentence if convicted. The interactions of these factors with the bail system and court delay are also examined.

The second part of this study is an empirical analysis from published data on the disposition of cases in state and federal criminal courts. Multiple regression techniques are used to test the effects on the demand for trials (or conversely, settlements) and on the probability of conviction of the following: (1) pre-trial detention; (2) court queues; (3) the size of the potential sentence; (4) judicial expenditures; (5) subsidizing defendants' legal fees; and (6) demographic variables such as population size, region, county income, per cent nonwhite and urbanization. Finally, in the appendix a theoretical and empirical analysis on the demand for civil cases is presented.

I. THE MODEL

We make the following assumptions.

(1) There are n defendants.

(2) The probability of conviction in a trial for the ith defendant ($i = 1, \ldots, n$) depends on the prosecutor's and defendant's inputs of resources, R_i^* and R_i respectively, into the case. That is,

$$P_i^* = P_i^*(R_i^*, R_i; Z_i)$$

and

$$P_i = P_i(R_i^*, R_i; Z_i) \quad (1)$$

where P_i^* is the prosecutor's and P_i is the defendant's estimates of the probability of conviction by trial. P_i^* can be greater, less than, or equal to P_i. Z_i

denotes other factors affecting the level of P^*_1 and P_1; for example, the availability of witnesses, the defendant's past record, his alibi, etc. Inputs of R^*_1 would tend to raise P^*_1 and P_1, while inputs of R_1 would tend to lower them so that

$$\frac{\partial P^*_1}{\partial R^*_1} \geqslant 0 \qquad \frac{\partial P^*_1}{\partial R_1} \leqslant 0$$

$$\frac{\partial P_1}{\partial R^*_1} \geqslant 0 \qquad \frac{\partial P_1}{\partial R_1} \leqslant 0 \qquad (2)$$

(3) The sentence, S_1, the defendant would receive if convicted in a trial is known to the prosecutor and defendant and independent of R^*_1 and R_1.[1]

(4) Initially, there is no money charge for the use of the courts nor a non-money cost in terms of court delay or queues.

Prosecutor

Let the prosecutor's decision rule be to maximize the expected number of convictions weighted by their respective S_1's—he prefers longer to shorter sentences—subject to a constraint on the resources or budget available to his office (B).[2] This decision rule coincides with the social optimum in the following sense. If expected sentences are regarded as prices the community charges for various offenses, then the prosecutor's behavior is equivalent to maximizing the community's welfare for a given resource level.

[1] There is some justification for this assumption other than mathematical simplicity since most crimes carry statutory penalties which are presumably known to both parties and independent of R^*_1 and R_1. However, statutory penalties usually set a minimum and maximum sentence for the defendant convicted in a trial, and within this range the sentence received would partly depend on R^*_1 and R_1. To allow the sentence to be a function of R^*_1 and R_1 would substantially complicate the model at this point (for example, two sentences would have to be included—the defendant's estimate and the prosecutor's estimate) without substantially changing the analysis of the trial versus settlement decision. In a later section on wealth effects, I allow the sentence to be a function of resource inputs.

[2] Other decision rules are possible; for example maximizing the expected number of convictions without weighting by the S_1's. The difficulty here is that the prosecutor, in order to increase his convictions and conserve his resources, would often be willing to drop a murder charge against a suspected murderer if the latter agreed to plead guilty to a minor offense (for example, a traffic violation). A simple way of eliminating this in the model is to weight by the S_1's. (See the analysis of a settlement presented below.) Note that fines could be included in S_1 by specifying a rate at which the prosecutor transforms fines into sentences keeping his utility constant.

The prosecutor maximizes E(C) where

$$E(C) = \sum_{i=1}^{n} P_i^* S_i + \lambda(B - \sum_{i=1}^{n} R_i^*), \tag{3}$$

which yields the equilibrium conditions

$$\frac{\partial P_1^*}{\partial R_1^*} \cdot S_1 = \frac{\partial P_2^*}{\partial R_2^*} \cdot S_2 = \ldots\ldots\ldots, = \frac{\partial P_n^*}{\partial R_n^*} \cdot S_n \cdot \tag{4}$$

Thus, the prosecutor allocates greater resources to cases, *ceteris paribus,* where the sentence is greater and where P_i^* is more responsive to changes in R_i^*.[3] If all n defendants need not be prosecuted, one would also predict charges would be dismissed when the prosecutor sees little chance of conviction regardless of his resource input into the trial, or given a conviction he expects a negligible sentence. The formulation of (3) is sufficiently general to give the prosecutor discretion over the type of charge brought against each defendant. The charge selected would be one that maximized E(C). Further, the maximization of E(C) together with the assumption that $\partial P_i^*/\partial R_i^* \geqslant 0$ imply that the prosecutor would suppress any evidence that reduces the probability of conviction.

Scarce resources provide an incentive for the prosecutor to avoid a trial and negotiate a pre-trial settlement with the defendant. From (3) and (4) it follows that if the prosecutor's transaction costs of a settlement equal his optimal resource expenditure on a trial, he would be willing to offer the suspect a reduction in the sentence below S_i in exchange for a plea of guilty (which makes $P_i^* = P_i = 1$).[4] However, since trial costs probably exceed these transaction costs, he would be willing to offer a further sentence reduction as the savings in resources can be used to increase the conviction probabilities in other cases. If ΔS_i denotes the sentence reduction that is a positive function of the difference between the prosecutor's trial costs and transaction costs of a settlement, then

$$So_i = P_i^* S_i - \Delta S_i \tag{5}$$

[3] We assume the price of a unit of R_i^* is \$1.00 and $\partial^2 P_i^*/\partial R_i^* < 0$. It should also be noted that (4) does not necessarily have a unique solution unless one assumes that the prosecutor takes as given the defendant's inputs, R_i's. If he readjusts his inputs of R_i^* to changes or anticipated changes in any of the R_i's, then the defendants may in turn readjust their R_i's, and so forth. This process need not converge to a unique solution.

[4] The prosecutor's transaction costs of a settlement would equal his time spent explaining the terms of the offer to the suspect and judge, paperwork in his office, etc. These costs will generally be less than his total costs of reaching a settlement since the latter may involve substantial negotiating or bargaining costs in order to arrive at a sentence more preferred than the minimum sentence he is willing to offer in a settlement.

where So_i is the minimum sentence the prosecutor is willing to offer the defendant for a guilty plea.[5] From (5) we note that the terms offered the defendant will be more favorable the lower P_i^* and S_i, and the greater the prosecutor's resource saving from a settlement. Finally, suppose that certain cases bring the prosecutor considerable notoriety only if a trial occurs. If notoriety were desired, the sentence variable, S_i, could be increased by a notoriety factor (for example $S_i(1 + j_i)$ where j_i is a positive function of the amount of notoriety and is $\geqslant 0$). Hence in some cases So_i could be greater than $P_i^* S_i$ and even S_i. Unless otherwise stated, we assume $So_i < P_i^* S_i$.

Defendant

If the defendant goes to trial, the outcome is either of two mutually exclusive states of the world: a conviction state with an endowment Wc defined as

$$Wc = W - s \cdot S - r \cdot R \tag{6a}$$

or a non-conviction state with an endowment Wn defined as

$$Wn = W - r \cdot R. \tag{6b}$$

W is his wealth endowment prior to arrest, s equals the present value of the average pecuniary and non-pecuniary losses per unit of jail sentence, r is the average price of a unit of R, and S and R are defined as before.[6] I assume Wc is non-negative.

Let U be a continuous utility function over the defendant's endowment. His expected utility from going to trial is then

$$E(U) = PU(Wc) + (1 - P)U(Wn). \tag{7}$$

Since inputs of R lower P, Wc and Wn, the defendant would select a level of R to maximize E(U) such that

$$-P'(U(Wn) - U(Wc)) = r(PU'(Wc) + (1 - P)U'(Wn)) \tag{8}$$

where $P' = \frac{dP}{dR}$ and U′ denotes the marginal utility (>0) of the endowment in each state.[7] The left-hand side of (8) represents marginal returns

[5] A settlement that releases resources from any one case will increase the R_i^*'s in other cases. Thus, the R_i^*'s that initially satisfy (4) are not the final equilibrium values because adjustments take place as cases are settled. Moreover, these adjustments raise the So's in cases not yet settled. I largely ignore these secondary effects in the analysis.

[6] The subscript i is deleted since it is explicit that we are now dealing with one defendant.

[7] The qualification stated in footnote 3 regarding the prosecutor's equilibrium inputs of R^* also applies to the defendant's equilibrium inputs of R.

of R and the right-hand side, marginal costs of R.[8] An analysis of the determinants of the optimal R is presented later.

Trial versus Settlement

Let $r \cdot \hat{R}$ equal the defendant's transaction costs of a settlement.[9] Note that the defendant's trial costs, $r \cdot R$, are greater than $r \cdot \hat{R}$ because a defendant going to trial will in the process of rejecting a settlement incur most of the costs in $r \cdot \hat{R}$, and in addition he has expenditures on the trial. The defendant would choose between a trial or settlement on the basis of whether his expected utility from the former, E(U), were greater or less than his utility from the latter. Similarly, the prosecutor would choose the alternative that maximizes his conviction function, E(C). Therefore, a necessary condition for a settlement is that both the defendant and prosecutor simultaneously gain from a settlement compared to their expected trial outcomes. This requires that

$$\pi = U(W - s \cdot So - r \cdot \hat{R}) - E(U) > 0 \tag{9}$$

because one can then find a negotiated sentence somewhat greater than So, the minimum offer of the prosecutor, that leaves the defendant with a utility from a settlement greater than E(U) and at the same time increases E(C) for the prosecutor above its value in a trial. Although (9) explicitly allows for the prosecutor's and defendant's transaction costs of a settlement, the attempt to reach mutually acceptable terms may in certain cases involve substantial bargaining costs that are large enough to prevent a settlement even though $\pi > 0$. In spite of this qualification, I will assume that $\pi > 0$ is not only a necessary but also a sufficient condition for a settlement. Alternatively, $\pi < 0$ is a necessary and sufficient condition for a trial. These conditions are Pareto optimal in that if $\pi > 0$, both parties expect to gain from a settlement, and if $\pi < 0$, both parties expect to gain from a trial.

[8] The second-order condition for the optimum R requires that the rate of change of marginal returns be less than the rate of change of marginal cost. That is,

$$-P''[U(Wn) - U(Wc)] + rP'[U'(Wn) - U'(Wc)] < -rP'[U'(Wn) - U'(Wc)] - r^2[PU''(Wc) + (1-P)U''(Wn)]$$

where $P'' = d^2P/dR^2$, and $U'' =$ the rate of change of U'. P" is assumed > 0 to indicate diminishing marginal product of R in reducing P. If $U'' = 0$, the last three terms above are zero and hence marginal returns are falling while marginal costs are constant. If $U'' \neq 0$, marginal costs may be rising, falling or constant with increases in R since the two terms on the righthand side are of opposite sign. Similarly, when $U'' < 0$, marginal returns may actually rise since $rP'[U'(Wn) - U'(Wc)]$ is positive but when $U'' > o$, marginal returns must fall.

[9] Similar to the definition of the prosecutor's transaction costs (see *supra* note 4), $r\hat{R}$ would be generally less than the defendant's total costs of negotiating a settlement since $r\hat{R}$ excludes bargaining costs.

We can derive the following implications from (9) regarding the likelihood of settling and the resulting sentence.

1. Although the precise sentence in a pre-trial settlement is indeterminate, it must lie between the extremes defined by (9). Within this range it would depend on the relative bargaining strengths of the parties involved. In general, one would expect a smaller negotiated sentence the smaller the probability of conviction in a trial. A smaller P raises E(U) and thus lowers the maximum sentence accepted by the defendant, while a smaller P^* reduces the minimum acceptable to the prosecutor. For identical reasons, a lower sentence if convicted by trial, S, should lead to a lower negotiated sentence.

2. π will be positive and a settlement chosen whenever

$$s \cdot So < r(R - \hat{R}) \tag{10}$$

since this implies $U(W - s \cdot So - r\hat{R}) > U(Wn)$, and by definition $U(Wn) \geqslant E(U)$. This result is independent of the defendant's attitude toward risk and his estimate of the conviction probability because regardless of the trial outcome he is always better off with a settlement. (10) implies that a trial is less likely for offenses with small expected sentences (since So depends on S and P^*) relative to the defendant's differential cost of going to trial, $r(R - \hat{R})$.[10] Except when explicitly stated to the contrary, I now assume $s \cdot So > r(R - \hat{R})$ so that Wn is greater than $(W - s \cdot So - r\hat{R})$.

3. If both parties agree on the probability of conviction by trial ($P^* = P$), a settlement will take place for defendants who are risk averse ($U'' < 0$) or risk neutral ($U'' = 0$).[11] When $P^* = P$, one can show that a trial is equivalent to an unfair gamble (that is, the expected trial endowment is less than the settlement endowment).[12] Risk neutral suspects maximize their expected endowment and, therefore, refuse the trial "gamble," and *a fortiori* risk averse suspects also refuse the "gamble." On the other hand, a trial can still occur for a risk preferrer ($U'' > 0$) even though $P^* = P$.[13]

[10] This provides an explanation for why many persons plead guilty to traffic violations instead of spending considerable time in traffic court disputing them.

[11] U'' denotes the rate of change of U' with respect to one's endowment.

[12] A trial is an unfair gamble if

$$(W - s \cdot So - r\hat{R}) - (P \cdot Wc + (1 - P)Wn) > 0, \tag{i}$$

which can be rewritten as

$$s \cdot \Delta S + r(R - \hat{R}) > 0 \tag{ii}$$

using (5), (6a, 6b) and the assumption $P^* = P$. Since we have assumed $s.\Delta S$ and $r(R - \hat{R})$ are both positive, (ii) holds and the gamble is unfair.

[13] Given risk preference, a negative π, which leads to a trial, would be more likely the greater the preference for risk, the larger $r\hat{R}$, and the smaller $s \cdot \Delta S$ and rR. To prove this differentiate (9) partially with respect to these variables. The partial derivatives are negative for $r\hat{R}$, and positive for $s \cdot \Delta S$ and rR, indicating that π falls with respect to increases in $r\hat{R}$, and decreases in $s \cdot \Delta S$ and rR.

4. Suppose the prosecutor and defendant differ in their estimates of the trial conviction probability. If $P^* < P$, a trial becomes an even less favorable gamble in comparison to $P^* = P$, and hence risk averse and risk neutral suspects would continue to settle.[14] Risk preferrers are also more likely to settle since π in (9) rises. $P^* > P$ is the more interesting case because this provides an explanation in addition to risk preference of why trials occur. When $P^* > P$ a trial becomes a more favorable gamble compared to $P^* = P$, and hence π falls, increasing the chances of a trial. Moreover, if $P^* > P$, one can show that the likelihood of a trial is generally greater for defendants accused of crimes that carry stronger penalties.[15, 16]

Several additional points are worth noting in regard to the settlement versus trial decision:

5. The greater the savings in costs from a settlement, other things the same, the smaller So and $r\hat{R}$, and the more likely a settlement. This suggests that policy measures designed to eliminate or subsidize the defendant's legal fees, which in turn reduce the cost differential between a trial and a settlement, will increase the proportion of trials.

6. Suppose a not-guilty verdict in a trial produces pecuniary and nonpecuniary returns to the defendant. This would raise $E(U)$ and make a trial more likely. Similarly, publicity gains to the prosecutor from a trial would raise So, as previously noted, and also make a trial more likely.

7. The question of whether the defendant did in fact commit the crime he is charged with does not explicitly enter the analysis. The prosecutor and defendant have been assumed to react to the probability of conviction and other variables in choosing between settling and going to trial, while their behavior has not been directly influenced by the actual guilt or innocence of

[14] As P^* falls, So falls, which in turn increases $(W - s \cdot So - r\hat{R})$. Similarly, the increase in P lowers $(PWc + (1 - P)Wn)$. Thus, the value of (i) in footnote 12 rises relative to the case where $P^* = P$. Since (i) is already > 0 when $P^* = P$, it is obviously > 0 when $P^* < P$.

[15] Differentiating π with respect to S and noting that $So = P^* \cdot S - \Delta S$ (see (5)) yields $\partial\pi/\partial S \lesseqgtr 0$ according as

$$\frac{P}{P^*} \lesseqgtr \frac{U'(W - s \cdot So - r\hat{R})}{U'(Wc)}. \tag{i}$$

$\partial\pi/\partial S < 0$ when $U'' \geqslant 0$ since $U'(W - s \cdot So - r\hat{R}) \geqslant U'(Wc)$ and $P < P^*$. Thus, risk preferring and risk neutral defendants are more likely to go to trial as S rises given $P^* > P$. When $U'' < 0$ (risk aversion), both sides of (i) are < 1, and the sign of $\partial\pi/\partial S$ is indeterminate. However, if the degree of risk aversion is weak (the righthand side of (i) is close to one), risk averters are also more likely to go to trial as S rises.

[16] In another sense, the likelihood of a trial is *always* greater for large than for small sentences. We have already shown in (10) that a trial will not occur when $s \cdot So$ is less than the difference in costs between a trial and a settlement, $r(R - \hat{R})$. Thus, for very small sentences $r(R - \hat{R})$ is likely to dominate and a settlement will take place.

the defendant. However, this factor may enter in two ways. First, the amount and quality of the evidence against the defendant seems likely to diminish in the case of an innocent person. This would reduce the probability of conviction in a trial or even lead the prosecutor to dismiss charges more readily since P^* may be close to zero. Second, an innocent person may have an aversion to lying so that he would have a greater reluctance to plead guilty to an offense than a guilty person. This can be interpreted as imposing psychic losses on a guilty plea for an innocent suspect which would reduce $U(W - s \cdot So - r\hat{R})$ in (9) and hence increase the likelihood of a trial.

8. We observed in the introduction that a large fraction of cases are settled before trial. Our analysis predicts this if in most cases the prosecutor and suspect agree on the expected outcome of a trial, the costs of a trial to both parties exceed their settlement costs, and suspects are generally risk averse in their trial versus settlement choice.

Wealth and Sentence Effects

In this section two further questions are considered. (1) Do the resources invested by the defendant in a trial rise as the sentence increases? (2) Do the resources invested increase with the level of the defendant's initial endowment or wealth? The latter question is directly related to the widespread claim that the criminal justice system works less favorably for low income suspects than for affluent ones[17] because if the defendant's investment of resources rises with wealth, then both the probability of conviction in a trial and a negotiated sentence would tend to be lower for wealthier defendants.

To determine the effect of an increase in the sentence, we take the total differential of the first-order condition in (8) with respect to S and R.[18] This yields $dR/dS \gtreqless 0$ according as

$$\frac{-P'}{r \cdot P} \gtrless -\frac{U''(Wc)}{U'(Wc)} \qquad (11)$$

where $-U''(Wc)/U'(Wc)$ is a measure of absolute risk aversion. From (11) it follows that $dR/dS > 0$ for defendants who are risk preferrers or risk

[17] See Patricia M. Wald, Poverty and Criminal Justice, in U.S. Pres. Comm'n on Law Enforcement and Admin. of Justice, Task Force on the Admin. of Justice, Task Force Report: The Courts, at 139, app. C (1967).

[18] The differential is $\frac{dR}{dS} =$

$$\frac{s(P'U'(Wc) - rPU''(Wc))}{-P''(U(Wn) - U(Wc)) + 2rP'(U'(Wn) - U'(Wc)) + r^2(PU''(Wc) + (1-P)U''(Wn))}.$$

The second-order condition for E(U) to be a maximum requires that the denominator be < 0. Hence, $dR/dS \gtreqless 0$ as $P'U'(Wc) - rPU''(Wc) \lesseqgtr 0$.

neutral. If defendants are risk averse, the sign of dR/dS is uncertain. It is more likely to be positive the more responsive P to increases in R, the lower r, and the smaller the level of absolute risk aversion.[19] In sum, for a group of defendants differing in their attitudes toward risk, we might expect to find a greater investment of resources on average for defendants charged with crimes carrying longer sentences. Note that this need not lead to an observed negative relation between the probability of conviction and the severity of the crime since we have previously shown that an increase in the potential sentence also induces the prosecutor to allocate more resources to the case.

The value of one's time is generally related positively to one's income and wealth. In consequence, an increase in the defendant's wealth will lead to an increase both in r and s, the prices per unit of R and S respectively. To show this for r, let R be produced by both inputs of market goods such as the services of lawyers, expert witnesses, etc. and inputs of one's time. The optimal input combination is where the marginal products of the inputs over their respective marginal factor costs are equal. Since defendants with greater wealth attach higher prices to their time input, they would not only substitute more market intensive methods of producing R, but would also have a higher r.[20] Moreover, it follows from the equilibrium condition in (8) that a rise in r will lead to fewer inputs of R. In contrast, the increase in s as wealth rises will usually result in an increase in R.[21] Thus, to predict the net effect of an increase in wealth, which increases both r and s, one would have to determine the relative magnitudes of these two offsetting forces. In addition, a change in wealth even if s and r were to remain constant may change the equilibrium input of R if tastes for risk depend on wealth. We analyse below the case of risk neutrality and in the mathematical appendix we consider non-neutral tastes for risk.

The total differential of (8) with respect to W and R, assuming risk neutrality, gives $dR/dW \gtreqless 0$ according as

$$-P'E_s \gtreqless E_r\ (r/s \cdot S) \tag{12}$$

[19] (11) may also be rewritten as

$$\frac{e}{rR/Wc} \gtrless -Wc\frac{U''(Wc)}{U'(Wc)}$$

where e is the elasticity of P with respect to R, rR/Wc is the share of R in the suspect's conviction wealth, and $-Wc\,U''(Wc)/U'(Wc)$ is a measure of relative risk aversion. The value of the latter is often argued to hover around 1. (See Kenneth Arrow, Aspects of the Theory of Risk-Bearing, 33-37 (1965)). Thus, if rR/Wc were small, one would expect $dR/dS > 0$ for risk averse suspects.

[20] If higher income or wealth defendants are more productive in their use of time to produce R, then the marginal product of time would be positively related to income. This would work to offset the substitution of market inputs for time as income wealth rose. Further, r need not increase with wealth.

[21] The condition under which $dR/ds > 0$ is identical to that for $dR/dS > 0$ in (11).

where $E_s = \partial s/\partial W\ (W/s)$ and $E_r = \partial r/\partial W\ (W/r)$. E_r will be <1 since the price of market inputs is unaffected and some substitution of market inputs for time takes place as wealth rises. E_s can be assumed equal to 1 because as a first approximation the per unit value of time in jail is proportional to wealth. The optimality condition for R (see (8)) becomes with risk neutrality $-P' = r/s \cdot S$, and, therefore, dR/dW will be positive when $E_s > E_r$.[22] Thus, the amount of resources invested in a trial would tend to rise and the probability of conviction would tend to fall with increases in wealth. Note that this result also implies a lower negotiated sentence for wealthier defendants.[23]

Suppose that the penalty for conviction is not a jail sentence but instead a money fine. E_s would equal zero with a fine since changes in the value of time do not alter the dollar value of a fine, and dR/dW would be negative. Therefore, the effect of wealth on R reverses when penalties are in terms of money and not time for risk neutral defendants.[24] Once risk aversion or preference are introduced, the effect of changes in wealth on R cannot in general be specified unless one has explicit knowledge of additional parameters of the defendant's utility function. Nevertheless, one can presume that if the deviation from risk neutrality is small, the effects of wealth on R will follow the effects for risk neutrality.

II. Some Applications

The Bail System

In the United States the typical procedure for bail is that shortly after the defendant's arrest a bond is set as security for his appearance at trial. If the

[22] An identical result holds when R affects not only P but also S. With risk neutrality, the first-order condition for the optimal R becomes

$$-P'(s \cdot S) - P(s \cdot S') = r \tag{i}$$

where $S' = \partial S/\partial R \leqslant 0$. The total differential of (i) with respect to W and R yields $dR/dW \gtreqless 0$ as

$$E_s[-P'(s \cdot S) - P(s \cdot S')] \gtreqless E_r r, \tag{ii}$$

which gives $dR/dW \gtreqless 0$ as

$$E_s \gtreqless E_r \tag{iii}$$

[23] An increase in R that is anticipated by the prosecutor would lower P^* and hence his minimum offer, So, while the reduction in P would raise the defendant's expected utility from a trial and lower the maximum sentence he would accept to settle. Other things the same, these forces should work to lower the negotiated sentence.

[24] G. S. Becker, Crime and Punishment: An Economic Approach, 76 J. Pol. Econ. 354 (1968), presents a similar argument without presenting a proof. However, he argues that the incentive to use time to reduce the probability of a sentence is unrelated to earnings, and the incentive to use money to reduce the probability of a fine is also unrelated to earnings. These results would follow when in the former case R is produced solely by time and in the latter case R is produced solely by market inputs. However, once R is produced by both time and market inputs there is always an incentive to substitute market inputs for time as earnings rise.

defendant can post the amount of the bond through a deposit of cash or other assets, or have a professional bondsman do it for him, he is released until trial. The bondsman's fee runs about 10 per cent of the value of the bail bond. If the defendant does not meet the bail requirement, he remains in jail. The bond is generally forfeited should the released defendant fail to appear at trial.

Several implications of the bail system can be derived from our model.

(1) Bail costs would be deducted from the defendant's endowment, W, so that both $U(W - s \cdot So - r\hat{R})$ and E(U) in (9) would fall. For defendants released on bail there would be no obvious change in π (since equal dollar amounts are subtracted from $(W - s \cdot So - r\hat{R})$, Wc and Wn) and hence no reason to expect a change in their use of trials compared to settlements. Bail costs for defendants not released would equal the opportunity cost of their time in prison plus losses from restrictions on their consumption and freedom. These costs would be greater for a trial than a settlement because the delay in reaching trial generally exceeds the time taken to negotiate a settlement.[25] This in turn would lower E(U) relative to $U(W - s \cdot So - r\hat{R})$ in (9), raise π and make a settlement more likely for defendants not released on bail. Thus, given a positive time differential between a trial and settlement one would predict proportionately more settlements among defendants not released than those released on bail.[26]

(2) The defendant in jail is restricted in his use of resources to reduce the probability of conviction. This can be interpreted as either raising the costs or lowering the marginal products of his market and time inputs. For example, in the case of market inputs, detention would hamper consultation with lawyers, and in the case of time inputs, the defendant would have greater (even prohibitive) difficulty in seeking out witnesses and in engaging in other investigatory activities. These factors increase the marginal cost of

[25] Empirically, the time difference appears to be positive. For example, in the 89 United States district courts the median queues in 1967 were as follows: jury trial = 5.7 months; court trial = 3.9 months, and settlement (guilty plea) = 1.9 months. See, 1967 Ann. Rep. Admin. Off. of the United States Courts, 269-71, table D6.

[26] Two additional points should be noted. (a) If the defendant not released on bail were given credit toward his sentence for time in prison prior to disposition of his case, the only bail deduction in (9) would be from Wn, the defendant's endowment if he is not convicted. π would still rise. However, the rise in π would be negatively related to the probability of conviction. In the limit, if the probability of conviction equaled 1, court delay would leave π unchanged. (b) Bail costs of defendants released on bail will generally *not* be greater for a trial than a settlement. The bondsman's fee is independent of whether the defendant goes to trial or accepts a settlement, and a majority of felony defendants who make bail use bondsmen. (See, Lee Silverstein, Bail in the State Courts —A Field Study and Report, 50 Minn. L. Rev. 621, 647-52 (1966). And the returns from assets (except cash) used as security for bail bonds will continue to be received by the owner.

producing a given R and lower the defendant's input of R.[27] Thus, other things the same, the probability of conviction by trial should be greater for defendants not making bail than for those making bail.[28] As noted earlier, a higher probability of conviction by trial also leads to worse terms in a settlement. One should add that for these reasons the prosecutor always has an incentive to request the judge to set high bail charges.

(3) Finally, if making bail is positively correlated with income, then the effects of pre-trial jailing, cited above, would fall most heavily on low income defendants.

Proposals for bail reform generally focus on eliminating income as an indirect criterion of pre-trial release. The Federal Bail Reform Act of 1966 requires that criminal defendants in federal courts (which cover a small minority of criminal defendants) be released prior to trial unless there is reason to believe they would flee. The "President's Commission" suggests placing greater reliance on release of defendants without bail, accompanied by certain restrictions on their behavior (for example, restrictions on travel, associations), while simultaneously confining suspects whose release would pose a significant threat to the community, regardless of their financial ability to make bail,[29] the latter provision being a form of "preventive detention." If these reforms were to result in the pre-trial release of more defendants and more low income ones we would predict the following: a decline in the negative correlations between income and the effects of pre-trial jailing outlined above; a reduction in the fraction of defendants convicted since fewer defendants would be restricted in their use of R; and an increase in the demand for trials as differential bail costs between a trial and settlement go to zero for more defendants.[30] The latter would probably increase court delay.

[27] Defendants not making bail may have available added resources for legal services that would have been used to finance bail. These can offset the higher costs of R so that the probability of conviction need not increase. However, it is also possible that their resources will decline should the loss in income (excluding a consumption allowance) exceed the cost of financing bail. In the latter case, capital market difficulties would presumably have prevented their release.

[28] Critics of the bail system have recognized this point. For example, see Report of the Att'y Gen. Comm. on Poverty & the Admin. of Fed. Crim. Just. 74-76 (1963). Also note that the increase in cost of R for jailed defendants may be partly offset by the greater availability of "legal" advice from other inmates. However, if this factor were sufficiently important, one would observe defendants who were able to meet bail requirements accepting pre-trial detention instead.

[29] U.S. Pres. Comm'n on Law Enforcement and Admin. of Justice, Task Force on the Admin. of Justice, Task Force Report: The Courts, at 38-40 (1967). [Hereinafter, The Courts.]

[30] Other effects could be added. For instance, a predicted increase in crime from reducing the average probability of conviction, and a savings in resources used for pre-trial detention.

These reforms leave persons detained in the same position as before and, moreover, their position relative to defendants released may worsen if the latter group does not pay for their release. Suppose those detained were paid a monetary compensation that increased with the length of their detention. We could then eliminate much of the discriminatory aspects of the bail system while still detaining persons believed to be dangerous. A higher marginal cost of R for detained suspects would still be present but they would have additional resources to mitigate the adverse effects of this on the probability of conviction. Compensation would reduce the defendant's incentive for a settlement as the differential bail costs between a trial and settlement decline and approach zero for full compensation. If compensation were paid out of the prosecutor's budget, the latter's incentive for a settlement would increase given that the payment were greater for a trial than a settlement. This in turn would lower his minimum offer, So, and raise $U(W - So - r\hat{R})$ in (9). Hence, the incentive for a settlement need not fall with compensation. Note as So falls this tends to reduce the positive difference between negotiated sentence for defendants not released compared to defendants released on bail.[31]

Court Delay

It is widely recognized that the courts are burdened with a larger volume of cases than they can efficiently handle. The results are often long delays prior to trial, and hasty considerations when cases reach trial.[32] This is not surprising since users pay a nominal money fee, if any, and a queue develops to ration the supply.

To understand the implications of non-money and money pricing on the demand for courts, assume initially there is a money price, M, paid by the loser that clears the market.[33] We also assume that the prosecutor's budget is not increased to cover these court costs. M affects both the prosecutor's and defendant's demand for trial. First, it reduces the minimum sentence offered by the prosecutor, So in (5), by a positive function of $(1 - P^*) \cdot M$. This, in turn, raises π in (9) and increases the likelihood of a settlement. Second, it lowers the defendant's wealth if convicted by trial, Wc, by an amount equal to M, reducing E(U) and raising π in (9). This also increases the chance of a settlement. The larger is M, the greater the increase in π, and the more settlements that take place. Thus, a downward sloping demand curve for the courts

31 For a detailed analysis of alternative bail systems see my paper, Rules for an Optimal Bail System (unpublished).

32 The Courts, *supra* note 29, at 80-90.

33 This does not mean that defendants are immediately brought to trial. Some time is required by both defendant and prosecutor to prepare a case for trial. Current delays are alleged to run considerably in excess of this.

is generated. Further, one can venture from the analysis of (9) that as M rises, the reduction in quantity demanded of trials (hereafter, trial demand) will be primarily from cases where there is not a significant disagreement between the prosecutor and defendant over the probability of conviction, and where the sentence if convicted by trial tends to be small.[34] Put differently, cases that still go to trial as M rises are where there are significant disagreements over the probability of conviction and where penalties are severe. Moreover, changing the allocation of the payment of M has little effect on the above results since whether the loser or winner pays M, or both share M, a money price always increases π in (9) and reduces trial demand.

Compare this pricing scheme with one in which the courts are heavily subsidized, taking the extreme example of a zero money price. As M goes to zero, So and Wc rise, π falls and without an increase in supply, trial demand would exceed supply. Let us assume trial dates are allocated on the basis of waiting time since arraignment and a trial queue develops. The queue will reach an equilibrium size because, as we will show, trial demand is a decreasing function of waiting or queueing time. An increase in the queue imposes losses on the prosecutor as it (a) reduces the number of convictions in the current year from cases commenced in that year by delaying trial convictions,[35] and (b) ties up resources in a case for a longer period of time. These losses increase as the queue lengthens, inducing the prosecutor to offer a lower sentence in exchange for a guilty plea. Although $U(W - s \cdot So - r\hat{R})$ in (9) then rises (as So falls) the incentive for the defendant to settle as the queue grows will depend on whether or not he is released on bail. For defendants not released, the longer the queue the higher the bail costs of a trial and hence the lower their expected utility from a trial.[36] This factor, together with the response of the prosecutor, leads to the prediction that the demand for trials will fall as the queue lengthens for defendants not released on bail. On the other hand, for defendants released on bail the net effect on their expected utility of an increase in the queue is unclear. The discounted loss from a sentence received in a trial would diminish or increase as the penalty is pushed into the future, depending on whether earnings are rising at a slower or faster rate than the defendant's discount rate. In addition, the defendant's

[34] Optimal values of P*, P, R* and R may change as M rises since the prosecutor and defendant must now allocate some resources to losses from expected court fees.

[35] Even if the prosecutor had no time preference with respect to convictions, an increase in the queue would still impose losses on him. For example, suppose the prosecutor is in office for 5 years. An increase in the queue during his tenure would lead to fewer convictions and a lower weighted conviction function than a constant queue because he will have left to his successor a greater stock of cases than his predecessor had left to him.

[36] This would be partially offset by giving credit towards the eventual sentence for time spent in jail awaiting trial. We would be unchanged as the queue lengthened, providing the time spent in jail awaiting trial was less than S, but Wn would still fall. Hence, E(U) would continue to fall as the queue increased.

earnings may be adversely affected during the period he is free on bail due to his being under indictment. If on balance their expected utility falls or remains constant and the prosecutor's losses rise, one would expect an increase in π and a reduction in trial demand as the queue lengthens for defendants free on bail. However, one would predict that the demand for trials among defendants released would be less responsive to an increase in the queue than the demand among defendants not released since the cost of an increase in the queue is greater for the latter than the former group.

FIGURE I

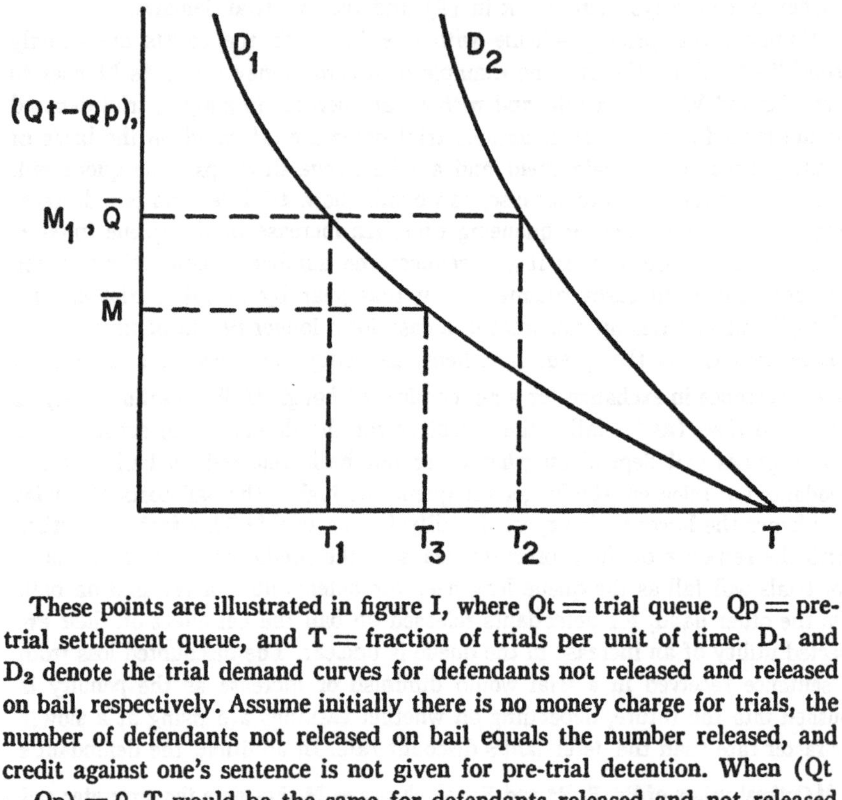

These points are illustrated in figure I, where Qt = trial queue, Qp = pre-trial settlement queue, and T = fraction of trials per unit of time. D_1 and D_2 denote the trial demand curves for defendants not released and released on bail, respectively. Assume initially there is no money charge for trials, the number of defendants not released on bail equals the number released, and credit against one's sentence is not given for pre-trial detention. When (Qt — Qp) = 0, T would be the same for defendants released and not released since the differential bail costs between a trial and settlement are zero for both groups. As (Qt — Qp) rises, due to a reduction in supply of trial services, the differential bail costs rise by a greater amount for the not released than for the released defendants and hence the reduction in trials will tend to be greater for the former than the latter group. Thus, D_1 diverges from D_2 as (Qt — Qp) increases. If the equilibrium queue initially equaled $\overline{Q}$, T would equal T_1 for defendants not released and T_2 for defendants released. Suppose a money charge for trials is established that is sufficient to reduce (Qt — Qp) to zero, keeping the number of trials constant. As a first approximation, the demand curves for trials of the released and not released defendants would be identical because the differential bail costs between a trial and settlement are now zero for both groups.[37] If the defendant's trial fee were set at M_1, a price that equals the maximum amount that defendants who are not released would pay at the margin for the same number of trials in order to reduce (Qt — Qp) to zero, the aggregate number of trials demanded would be less than the available supply as $2T_1 < T_1 + T_2$.[38] In order for demand to be equated with supply, the defendant's court fee must be less than M. Let $\overline{M}$ in figure I equal the market clearing court fee. At $\overline{M}$ the fraction of trials for each group would equal T_3 and by assumption, $2T_3 = T_1 + T_2$. Thus, a money charge for the courts that kept constant the number of trials can lead to an increase in the use of the courts on the part of defendants not released on bail, and a reduction in use among defendants released on bail. Moreover, if the supply curve of trials were positively sloped with respect to a money price, one would also expect an increase in the total number of trials.

In sum, we should note that although a zero money price is often advocated as a means of not discouraging low income defendants from using the courts, its effect can be the opposite. A zero price operating with a bail system that tends to detain in jail low income defendants will discourage the latter group from going to trial. In contrast, an appropriate money price may reduce the demand for the courts of defendants released on bail, and by reducing the trial queue can increase the use of the courts by defendants who do not make bail.[39] Surprisingly, the literature that criticizes court delay makes no mention of the possibility of charging a money price, which not only reduces delay, but can distribute the use of the courts more equally among defendants independent of their ability to make bail.

[37] Note that the demand curves may differ. For example, if the average wealth of released defendants exceeds that of jailed defendants and the wealth elasticity of trial demand is not zero, then the demand curve of the former group will be the right of D_1. However, as long as it is still to the left of D_2, the results that follow will still hold.

[38] The prosecutor's court fee as (Qt — Qp) falls to zero must be large enough to keep So constant. If other methods of allocating court fees (for example, winner or loser pays) were used, we could no longer assume that D_1 is the demand curve when trials are priced. Although the geometry would become more complicated when different pricing schemes are used, the results of the analysis would not be substantially altered.

[39] An alternative scheme that would produce similar results is to continue a zero money price for the courts but allow defendants to buy and sell their places on the queue. This would presumably reduce the differential costs between a trial and settlement for defendants not released on bail relative to those released, and hence lead to a shift in court use from the latter to the former group. For example, if \$X = the equilibrium price for a place in the queue that makes (Qt — Qp) = 0, the differential trial cost would be \$X for both defendants released and not released, and their trial demands would be approximately equal.

III. Empirical Analysis

In the legal area readily accessible and systematically collected data are quite limited. However, two sources of data were found that make it possible to test a number of the important hypotheses in the theoretical model. The first source is an American Bar Foundation (ABF) study, in which over 11,000 felony defendants in 1962 were sampled from state court dockets in nearly 200 counties.[40] From this sample we can estimate for several counties within most states the number of defendants released on bail and their average bail charge, the number going to trial, and the number dismissed, acquitted and sentenced. The second major source of data is for the 89 U.S. district courts where annually published statistics on civil and criminal cases are available.[41] These data contain information of civil and criminal court queues, the number of cases going to trial, the disposition of cases, and the number of criminal defendants receiving subsidized legal services. It should be added that most criminal defendants have their cases decided in state not in U.S. courts. In 1962 about 300,000 persons were charged with felonies in the state courts, while about 30,000 criminal defendants annually have their cases disposed in the U.S. district courts.[42]

The Demand for Trials

The theoretical analysis suggests the following demand function for criminal trials:

$$T = f(B, Q_t, Q_p, S, D, U) \qquad (13)$$

where T is the fraction of defendants going to trial, B is the fraction of defendants released on bail, Q_t and Q_p are the average trial and pre-trial settlement queues respectively, S is the average sentence if convicted by trial, D is the average cost differential between a trial and settlement, and U is the combined effect of all other factors.[43] We would predict on the basis of our

40 Lee Silverstein, Defense of the Poor in Criminal Cases in American State Courts, A Field Study and Report (2 v. 1965). Note that a felony is generally defined as any crime punishable by imprisonment of more than one year.

41 See various years of the Ann. Rep. Admin. Off. of the United States Courts and Fed. Offenders in the United States District Courts 1967.

42 Lee Silverstein, *supra* note 40, at 7-8 and Ann. Rep., Admin. Off. of the United States Courts, *supra* note 41. The types of offenses also differ in the state and U.S. courts. Offenses in the U.S. courts include forgery, counterfeiting, interstate transportation of stolen goods and vehicles, postal theft, and violation of immigration laws, liquor laws and other federal statutes, while it includes few cases of murder, assault, robbery, and other "violent" crimes. The latter types of offenses are concentrated in state courts. The one exception is the U.S. district court in the District of Columbia which handles all criminal offenses in the area. In the empirical analysis of the U.S. Courts I have excluded the District of Columbia in order to have comparable offenses across districts.

43 U would include factors derived from the π function (equation (9)) such as the distribution of estimates of the probability of conviction by trial, and attitudes toward

model that B, Q_p, and S will have positive effects on T, while Q_t and D will have negative effects on T. Unfortunately, data limitations prevent us from estimating the partial effects of these variables in a single equation. The ABF sample of state county courts has no data on queues or cost differentials between trials and settlements, while the data for the U.S. courts contain no information on bail. Therefore, the analysis will use the ABF data to test bail effects, and the U.S. data to test queue effects. At the same time we will point out possible biases and alternative interpretations of the results that arise from leaving out either the bail or queue variables.

State County Courts

Least-squares multiple regression equations were estimated across state county courts in 1962. These equations were of the following general form:

$$T = \alpha + \beta_1 B + \beta_2 S + \beta_3 Pop + \beta_4 Re + \beta_5 NW + \beta_6 Ur + \beta_7 Y + u. \quad (14)$$

The variables in (14) are defined as follows:

T: the fraction of defendants in a county court whose cases were disposed of by trial in 1962. Cases where a plea of guilty was made at time of trial are not counted as trials.

B: the fraction of defendants in each county released on bail in 1962.

S: the average time served of first-released prisoners in 1964 who had sentences of one year or longer. S is an estimate of the average sentence, if convicted by trial, of felony defendants in 1962. Releases in 1964 are used because the average time served in state prisons of first-released prisoners was about two years, and hence 1964 should be the average release year for defendants sentenced in 1962.

Pop: County population in 1960.

Re: Region dummy variable that equals 1 for counties in South and 0 for non-South counties.

NW: per cent nonwhite population in county in 1960.

Ur: per cent urban population in county in 1960.

Y: median family income in county in 1959.

Weighted regressions on T are presented in table 2 for counties in the U.S., the non-South and South.[44] In the U.S. and non-South equations

risk. I have not been able to directly measure these variables and hence they are largely ignored in the empirical analysis. U also includes several demographic variables that will be specified in the statistical estimation of (13).

[44] Observations were weighted by the $\sqrt{n}$ where n is the number of defendants sampled in each county. The range of n is from 3 to 349 with a mean of 58, and n generally rises with the size of the county population. Weighted regressions were computed because of the likelihood of larger variances in the residuals as n declined. However, unweighted regressions were also computed, and as it turned out the weighting made little difference in the results.

TABLE 2

WEIGHTED REGRESSIONS AND T-VALUES FOR CRIMINAL TRIALS IN 1962, STATE COUNTY COURTS[a]

Equation Number	Area	Counties	Dependent Variable	Regression Coefficients and T-Values[b]								R^2[c]
				α	B	S	Pop	Re	NW	Ur	Y	
2.1	U.S.	132	T	—.065 (.624)	.348 (4.071)	—.0002 (.087)	.037 (3.312)	.098 (2.723)	.014 (.106)	.062 (.709)	—.002 (.101)	.26
2.2	N.S.	100	T	.002 (.027)	.498 (6.521)	.003 (1.515)	.038 (4.263)		—.217 (1.548)	.129 (1.513)	—.043 (2.552)	.45
2.3	South	32	T	.229 (.833)	—.012 (.059)	—.009 (1.746)	.463 (3.215)		.109 (.488)	—.570 (2.716)	.095 (2.042)	.48

Sources: T and B from Lee Silverstein, Defense of the Poor in Criminal Cases in American State Courts, A Field Study and Report (2 v. 1965); Pop, NW, Ur and Y from U.S. Bureau of the Census, County and City Data Book 1962; S from U.S. Bureau of Prisons, National Prisoner Statistics Detailed Reports: State Admissions and Releases, 1964, table R-5.

[a] Although the ABF sample covered nearly 200 counties, many had to be excluded because there was no reporting on the number of defendants who made bail. I have no reason to believe that the group of excluded counties would have differed systematically from the counties included in the regression equation. Two counties in New Jersey were excluded because no data on S were available for New Jersey.

[b] T-values in parentheses.

[c] All R^2's are unadjusted in table 2 and all other tables unless explicitly stated to the contrary.

(*2.1 — 2.2*) the regression coefficients (β_1) of the bail variable have the predicted positive sign and are always highly significant, while in the South the β_1 coefficient is not significantly different from zero. Before discussing these results in greater detail, an interesting interpretation can be given to the bail regression coefficient. T can be written as

$$T = \frac{\lambda_1 N_1 + \lambda_2 N_2}{N} \qquad (15)$$

where N is the number of defendants, N_1 is the number not released on bail, and N_2 is the number released. λ_1 and λ_2 are the average propensities to go to trial of the not released and released group respectively. The theory predicts that $\lambda_2 > \lambda_1$, providing that the trial queue is longer than the settlement queue. Since $N_1/N + N_2/N = 1$ and $N_2/N = B$, (15) can be rewritten as

$$T = \lambda_1 + (\lambda_2 - \lambda_1)B. \qquad (16)$$

Therefore, from a set of observations on T and B, the intercept in a simple regression of T on B would be an estimate of λ_1 and the beta coefficient on B would be an estimate of $(\lambda_2 - \lambda_1)$. A positive beta coefficient would be consistent with the prediction that $\lambda_2 > \lambda_1$. The interpretations of these regression coefficients are modified with the addition of other independent variables, X_i, which enter the regression indirectly through their influence on λ_1 and λ_2. For example, let

$$\lambda_1 = c_1 + \sum_{i=2}^{j} \beta_i X_i \qquad (17)$$

and

$$\lambda_2 = c_2 + \sum_{i=2}^{j} \alpha_i X_i. \qquad (18)$$

By substitution into (16) we have,

$$T = c_1 + (c_2 - c_1)B + \sum_{i=2}^{j} \beta_i X_i + \sum_{i=2}^{j} (\alpha_i - \beta_i)B \cdot X_i. \qquad (19)$$

Estimates of equation (19) were not successful because of the large amount of multicollinearity resulting from the inclusion of interaction variables. This tended to eliminate statistical significance from any of the independent variables. However, if we set $\alpha_i = \beta_i$ for all $i = 2$, ——, j, the interaction variables drop out and (19) reduces to the form of equations estimated in table 2. It also follows from (17) and (18) that when $\alpha_i = \beta_i$ the regression coefficient on B is a measure of $(\lambda_2 - \lambda_1)$, the difference in trial propensities between defendants released and not released on bail.

Estimates of $(\lambda_2 - \lambda_1)$ from table 2 for the U.S. and non-South imply, for example, that the release of an additional 20 defendants on bail, other things the same, would lead to a desired increase of about 7 to 10 trials as a result of the reduction in trial costs associated with making bail. One can also get a rough idea of the increased demand for trial if the existing bail system were replaced with a system of preventive detention that released all defendants except a few "hard-core" criminal suspects (for example, 10 per cent). The weighted means of T and B are about .18 and .45 respectively. Therefore, the release of additional defendants to bring the number released to 90 per cent would lead to an increase in the fraction desiring trials from 18 per cent to between 34 and 40 per cent, or roughly a 100 per cent increase in desired trials.[45]

Although no direct measures of trial queues are available in the ABF data, longer trial queues are generally thought to exist in large urban areas. If the county population variable is interpreted as an imperfect proxy for the difference between trial queues and settlement queues, the sign of the regression coefficient on the population variable would depend on the relative strength of two opposing forces. On the one hand, longer queues discourage trials, but on the other hand, longer queues may be the result of an increased demand for trials. In table 2, β_3 is positive and significant in all regressions which suggests that the positive association of trials with queues dominates.

Further evidence on the effects of population size appears in table 3 where separate regressions are given for counties in the non-South with populations greater than 450,000, between 100,000 and 450,000, and less than 100,-000, and in the South with populations greater than 200,000 and less than 108,000. In table 3 not only does B continue to have a positive effect on trials in all non-South equations, but β_1 or $(\lambda_2 - \lambda_1)$ has a systematically greater value as county size rises (.09 in eq. 3.3, .31 in 3.2, and .75 in eq. 3.1), which is precisely what one would expect if $(Qt - Qp)$ was positively correlated with county population.[46] $(\lambda_2 - \lambda_1)$ is statistically significant in the non-South except in counties of less than 100,000. This result could be observed if the difference between $(Qt - Qp)$ was negligible in small counties. Moreover, the empirical finding that β_1 increases as county population size rises is indirect evidence that $(Qt - Qp)$ is in fact larger in counties with bigger populations.

[45] This is the increase in trials desired with no change in the trial queue. With an increased demand and unchanged court capacity the queue would presumably grow so that the actual increase in T would be less than the desired increase. In fact, if the courts were fully employed, the queue would grow until the costs of waiting were just sufficient to make desired trials equal to the previous level of trials.

[46] If we refer to Figure I, *supra*, we note that at a given value of $(Qt - Qp)$ the difference between D_2 and D_1 equals $\lambda_2 - \lambda_1$ and as $(Qt - Qp)$ increases, $\lambda_2 - \lambda_1$ increases due to the increase in bail costs of defendants not released compared to defendants released.

TABLE 3

WEIGHTED REGRESSIONS AND T-VALUES FOR CRIMINAL TRIALS IN 1962 BY COUNTY POPULATIONS, STATE COUNTY COURTS

Equation Number	Area	Counties	Dependent Variable	Regression Coefficients and T-Values							R^2
				α	B	S	Pop	NW	Ur	Y	
3.1	Non-South >450,000	30	T	.312 (1.011)	.750 (4.589)	.004 (.923)	.045 (2.864)	—.479 (1.778)	—.063 (.238)	—.081 (2.468)	.37
3.2	Non-South 100-450,000	27	T	—.041 (.200)	.309 (2.619)	.001 (.223)	.101 (.493)	.114 (.157)	—.120 (.616)	.014 (.430)	.31
3.3	Non-South <100,000	43	T	.151 (1.777)	.085 (1.126)	—.001 (.895)	.044 (.084)	.010 (.058)	.099 (1.556)	—.026 (1.562)	.17
3.4	South >200,000	17	T	—.194 (.417)	—.010 (.036)	—.016 (2.667)	.524 (2.674)	.590 (2.249)	—.642 (1.394)	.188 (3.633)	.81
3.5	South <108,000	15	T	.255 (.783)	—.186 (.775)	.0001 (.013)	—4.269 (2.402)	—.252 (.974)	—.067 (.342)	.088 (1.200)	.59

Source: Table 2, *supra.*

Let us briefly consider the empirical results for the South. The three regression coefficients on the bail variable in the South in tables 2 and 3, were negative and not significantly different than zero. One possible explanation is that (Qt — Qp) is negligible for counties sampled in the South so that (λ_2 — λ_1) would approach zero, and hence the regression coefficients on bail would not be significant.[47] A second explanation is that greater measurement errors in the bail variable may exist in the South compared to the non-South, which would lower the value of regression coefficients on bail in the South relative to the non-South. Along these lines it might be argued that justice is more informally administered in the South, particularly in rural areas, and this would produce poorer records on bail. (A similar argument may be used to rationalize the non-significant but positive bail coefficient in non-Southern counties of less than 100,000). However, it is questionable whether this argument should be given much weight since a non-significant bail variable was also observed for the South in counties with populations greater than 200,000.

Although a sufficient explanation is not available for the South, the overall results of tables 2 and 3 give strong support to the hypothesis that the frequency of trials is greater among defendants released on bail than those not released. A positive and statistically significant relationship between bail and trials was observed for the U.S. and the non-South, and the latter region included more than 3/4 of our observations. This finding is consistent with the prediction of the theoretical model that the costs of going to trial compared to settling are increased by not making bail, which in turn reduces the likelihood of a trial.

Several additional comments on the results in tables 2 and 3 are in order. (1) It might be argued that the bail variable is a proxy for wealth so that a finding that T increases with B is due to differences in wealth and not to greater trial costs for those not released. First, there is nothing in the theoretical analysis that indicates that wealth directly affects the choice between a trial and a settlement. If wealth were positively correlated with the ability to make bail, one would observe wealthier defendants going to trial, but the theoretical explanation lies with differences in costs not differences in wealth. Second, the empirical analysis of the U.S. courts in the next section contain indirect estimates of a defendant's wealth which show that increases in wealth have no observable positive effect on trials. (2) A second criticism, which if valid would weaken my conclusion that increases in B lead to increases in T, is that spurious correlation exists between B and T. The argument can be made that defendants planning to plead guilty will not be willing to incur

[47] Data for the federal courts indicate that queues are somewhat lower in the South. In 1966, the mean civil Qt's were 22.0 and 15.7 months for the non-South and South, and the mean criminal Qt's were 6.3 and 5.3 months in the two areas. However, (Qt — Qp) for criminal cases was 3.8 and 3.5 months in the non-South and South.

the costs of making bail, while those planning to go to trial will incur these costs. If this were true, an increase in T would lead to an observed increase in B and not the reverse. Although this argument has some plausibility, it has a defect. A defendant planning a guilty plea presumably desires the most favorable terms in a settlement. We showed in the model that one effect of not making bail is to raise the probability of conviction in a trial, which in turn results in worse settlement terms. Therefore, it is not obvious that the defendant planning to settle will find it any less desirable to post bail than the defendant planning a trial since both suffer losses from not being released on bail. (3) The regression coefficients on sentence variable, S, do not support the hypothesis that the likelihood of a trial is greater for defendants accused of crimes carrying longer sentences. In 4 of 8 equations in tables 2 and 3 the sign of S was positive, and in only one equation (3.4), where S had a negative effect, was the variable significant. The inconclusive behavior of S may partly be attributed to the data. The theoretical analysis calls for a variable that measures the average severity of offenses for defendants sampled in each county in 1962, while data limitations have forced us to use the average time served by all felons in a state who were first released in 1964. Fortunately, the regressions for the U.S. courts provide us with a stronger test of the sentence hypothesis because data on sentences in the U.S. courts correspond more closely to the theoretical requirements. (4) The NW, Ur and Y variables, which are included in the regressions of tables 2 and 3, should be viewed as demographic characteristics of counties rather than as indicators of socio-economic classes of defendants since the relation of these variables to defendants may be remote. There are no prior expectations on the effects of these variables on trials, and their regression coefficients do not show a consistent pattern. In table 2 Y and NW have negative effects on T in the non-South and positive effects in the South, while Ur has a positive effect in the non-South and a negative effect in the South. About two-thirds of the NW, Ur and Y regression coefficients are not statistically significant.[48]

U.S. Courts

Least-squares regression equations were estimated across U.S. district courts in 1967 of the following form:

$$T_1 = \alpha + \beta_1 Q_t + \beta_2 Q_p + \beta_3 S + \beta_4 D + \beta_5 Re + \mu. \qquad (20)$$

All variables are in natural logs except Re and hence the beta coefficients are elasticity measures. The variables in (20) are defined as follows:

T_1: ratio of defendants whose cases were disposed of by trials during 1967 to

[48] Regressions were also estimated without the NW, Ur and Y variables. The regression results for the bail, population and sentence variables were largely unaffected.

the total number of defendants disposed of in 1967. Regressions were also fitted on T_2 which equals the ratio of trials to defendants for 1968.

Q_t: weighted average of median time intervals from filing to disposition by court trial and by jury trial in 1967, where weights are the proportion of court and jury trials respectively.

Q_p: median time interval from filing to disposition by a plea of guilty in 1967.

S: weighted average of sentences received by convicted defendants whose cases were disposed of in 1967, where weights are the proportion of convicted defendants receiving each type of sentence.[49]

D: proportion of criminal defendants disposed of in 1967 who are assigned counsel by the court under provisions of the Federal Criminal Justice Act of 1964. The Act provides for counsel when defendants are unable to pay all or part of their legal fees.[50] Thus, D is a direct measure of the fraction of defendants with subsidized legal counsel. Since the ability to pay for counsel is related to the defendant's wealth, D would also serve as a rough measure of the fraction of defendants with low incomes or wealth.

R: region dummy variable where 1 is assigned to district courts in South and 0 to district courts in non-South.

Data on Q_t are available for only 44 of 89 district courts in 1967 (see note b to table 4), while data on Q_t and Q_p are not available for other years. Regressions were first estimated for the 44 districts in 1967. However, in order to incorporate observations for the remaining districts, and to work with years other than 1967, a proxy variable for Q_t was used that can be computed for all years and districts. The proxy for Q_t in year m is the ratio of pending cases (Pc) at the end of year m-1 to the average annual number of cases that go to trial ($\overline{T}$) in years m and m-1. One would expect Pc to estimate the backlog and $\overline{T}$ to roughly measure the availability of trial services, and hence $Pc/\overline{T}$ should serve as a measure of Q_t even though not all pending cases eventually go to trial.[51] The accuracy of $Pc/\overline{T}$ as an estimate

49 Obvious problems arise in evaluating a diversity of sentences that include imprisonment, fines, probation with and without supervision, suspended sentence, etc. The Administrative Office of the U.S. Courts has devised a common set of values for these sentences (see Fed. Offenders, *supra* note 41, at 4) that assign 0 to suspended sentences and probation without supervision, 1-4 for fines and various terms of probation with supervision, and 3-50 for imprisonment with sentences that range from 1 to more than 120 months. Although higher values are generally given to more severe sentences, the method is still arbitrary. For example, why all fines and probation with supervision from 1 to 12 months are both assigned the value 1 is never explained. Nevertheless, the use of this variable as an estimate of the average potential sentences of accused defendants in each district seems preferable to using just the mean prison sentence since the latter group includes only 38% of all defendants disposed of in 1967 while the former group includes 77%. Both measures suffer because they exclude defendants not convicted when the relevant theoretical variable is the average potential sentence faced by all defendants before disposition of their case.

50 See The Courts, *supra* note 29, at 59-61.

51 There were 10,771 pending criminal cases in the beginning of fiscal year 1967, and 3,924 trials in the 1967 fiscal year. Since the average trial queue is about six months, this

of trial queues was checked by running simple regressions of Q_t, Q_p, and $(Q_t - Q_p)$ on $Pc/\overline{T}$.[52] These equations indicate that $Pc/\overline{T}$ is positively and significantly related to Q_t and $(Q_t - Q_p)$, accounting for nearly half the variation in these variables. Although $Pc/\overline{T}$ is also positively related to Q_p, it is substantially more important in explaining variations in Q_t and $(Q_t - Q_p)$. Therefore, $Pc/\overline{T}$ is not merely a measure of general delay in the disposition of criminal cases, but, on the contrary, is a measure of differential delay between trials and guilty pleas. This result allows us to estimate regressions for all 89 district courts in 1967, and to check the stability of the model over time by fitting equations to an earlier year, 1960, in which direct data on queues were absent.

If equation (20) estimates a demand curve for trials, the theoretical analysis predicts that β_1 on Q_t (and $Pc/\overline{T}$) will be negative, and β_2 on Q_p will be positive. However, single-equation estimates may identify a supply curve instead, if the demand for trials varied more than the supply across districts. In the latter case, higher observed values for Q_t would have resulted from shifts to the right in demand curves, giving rise to a positive β_1. Similar behavior would produce a negative β_2 if a reduction in guilty pleas lowered Q_p. I have attempted to deal with this identification problem in two ways: (1) Equation (20) includes S and D variables that are expected to lead to shifts in the demand for trials. By holding S and D constant, the likelihood of identifying a demand curve is increased. A region variable, R, also enters equation (20), but it is not obvious that R operates more on the demand than supply side of trials. (2) Regressions have been estimated with a 1968 trial variable, T_2, against 1967 values of Q_t and Q_p. If defendants and prosecutors form their expectations about current queues on the basis of last year's queue, then Q_t in 1967 could still be inversely related to T_2 even though demand shifts in 1967 had caused a positive correlation between T_1 and Q_t.

Regression estimates of equation (20) are presented in table 4 for the

---

would suggest as a first approximation that roughly one-half of the trials in 1967 were from pending cases in the beginning of the year. Thus, about 20% of pending cases would go to trial.

[52] The regression equations for the 44 districts in 1967 were

$$Q_t = \underset{(14.961)}{1.272} + \underset{(5.689)}{.420}(Pc/\overline{T}) \qquad R^2 = .44$$

$$Q_p = \underset{(4.087)}{.489} + \underset{(1.603)}{.167}(Pc/\overline{T}) \qquad R^2 = .06$$

$$(Q_t - Q_p) = \underset{(4.155)}{.516} + \underset{(5.844)}{.629}(Pc/\overline{T}) \qquad R^2 = .45$$

$Pc/\overline{T}$, Q_t, Q_p, and $(Q_t - Q_p)$ are in natural logs, and all observations are weighted by $\sqrt{n}$ where n is the number of defendants disposed of in each district in 1967.

TABLE 4
WEIGHTED REGRESSIONS[a] AND T-VALUES FOR CRIMINAL TRIALS IN U.S. DISTRICT COURTS, 1960, 1967 AND 1968

Equation Number	Year	Dis-tricts	Depen-dent Variable	Regression Coefficients and T-Values								R^2
				α	Q_t[b]	Q_p	$Pc/\bar{T}$	S	D	Re	E(T)[c]	
4.1	1967	44	T_1	−2.814 (4.853)	−.246 (1.666)	.629 (4.201)		.610 (2.255)	.392 (2.529)	.159 (1.249)		.61
4.2	1967	44	T_1	−2.646 (6.321)		.608 (6.027)	−.407 (5.698)	.413 (1.976)	.151 (1.199)	−.039 (.379)		.78
4.3	1968	44	T_2	−1.999 (3.533)	−.250 (1.803)	.591 (3.788)		.296 (1.116)	.461 (3.166)	.095 (.822)		.57
4.4	1968	44	T_2	−1.880 (3.920)		.532 (4.494)	−.311 (3.849)	.143 (.598)	.349 (2.627)	−.047 (.430)		.67
4.5	1967	89	T_1	−2.750 (6.894)		.578 (5.882)	−.463 (6.573)	.495 (2.518)	.194 (1.620)	−.087 (.856)		.66
4.6[d]	1960	86	T	− .365 (.323)			−.410 (5.142)	.315 (1.246)		.037 (.293)	1.287 (3.954)	.42
4.7[e]	1960	43	T	1.294 (.996)			−.208 (2.338)	.242 (.805)		.054 (.372)	1.958 (5.751)	.58

NOTES TO TABLE 4

Sources: T_t, Q_t, Q_p, $Pc/\overline{T}$ for equations 4.1 through 4.5 are from 1967 Ann. Rep., Admin. Office of the United States Courts, tables D6, D1, C7; T_s for equations 4.1 through 4.5 is from 1968 Ann. Rep., Admin. Office of the United States Courts, table D6; S and W for equations 4.1 through 4.5 are from Fed. Offenders in the United States District Courts 1967, tables D10, D11; T, $Pc/\overline{T}$, E(T) in equations 4.6 and 4.7 from 1960 Ann. Rep. Admin. Office of the United States Courts tables C7, D1, D3, D4; S for equations 4.6 and 4.7 from U.S. Bureau of Prisons, Federal Prisons 1960, table 20.

[a] Weighted by $\sqrt{n}$ where n is the number of defendants disposed (equations 4.1 through 4.5) and the number of cases commenced (equations 4.6 and 4.7). All variables except Re are in natural logarithms.

[b] Q_t is the district average of the medium court trial queue and median jury trial queue. Data on either median were available only if there were at least 25 observations for that type of trial. 44 out of 89 districts had figures on at least one of two trial queues. Since most trials are jury trials (about 67 per cent), 29 out of the above 44 districts did not publish any information on court trial queues. The latter were estimated by assuming the ratio of the court trial to jury trial queue in the circuit (the 89 district courts are divided into ten circuits) was equal to the ratio in the district. Information was available on the aggregated circuit level, and hence the median court trial queue in a district could be directly estimated. Estimates were generally required in districts that had a small proportion of court relative to jury trials. Therefore, any errors in estimating the court trial queue would have a small effect on the weighted average Q_t. Finally, note that in 5 districts the queue for court trials but not jury trials was available. The procedure described above was then used to estimate the jury trial queue.

[c] E(T) in the ith district equals $\sum_{j=1}^{16} T_j^* \, 0_{ji}$ where T_j^* is the proportion of defendants in the jth offense category whose cases were disposed of by trial for all districts taken together in 1960, and 0_{ji} is the proportion of defendants accused of the jth offense in district i. There were 16 offense categories. Thus, variations in E(T) across districts are due solely to differences in the composition of offenses. E(T) was devised to take account of the possibility that differences in the fraction of trials across districts were the result of E(T) rather than the queue. Data did not permit a similar calculation for 1967-1968.

[d] In 1960 there were 86 district courts. By 1967 there were 89 district courts as several were eliminated and new ones were added. There are several small differences between the 1960 and 1967 data. They are: (1) T is the ratio of the number of cases that went to trial over the number of cases commenced in 1960. This differs from 1967 where the trial data are for defendants not cases, and the denominator is disposed defendants not commenced cases. In a given year the number of new defendants is about 25 per cent greater than the number of cases commenced indicating that the number of cases with more than one defendant exceed the number of defendants involved in more than one case. Since this is reflected in the numerator of the trial variable as well, the correlation in a given year between T for cases and defendants would be very high; (2) S in 1960 is the average prison sentence of convicted defendants, and excludes defendants who were fined or put on probation with supervision. The latter groups are included in the 1967 S variable.

[e] Regressions computed from districts in 1960 that match those districts in 1967 that had data on Qt.

years 1960, 1967, and 1968. In districts where Q_t and Q_p are available, the regression results strongly support the hypothesis that increases in Q_t, holding Q_p constant, have significant negative effects on T_1 and T_2, and increases in Q_p, with Q_t constant, have significant positive effects on T_1 and T_2. When $Pc/\overline{T}$ is substituted for Q_t, in equations 4.2 and 4.4, $Pc/\overline{T}$ has the predicted negative sign and is statistically significant, while Q_p has the same effects on T_1 and T_2 as before.[53] Further, when the sample is expanded to include all 89 districts in equation 4.5, the signs and significance of Q_p and $Pc/\overline{T}$ are similar to the results for the 44 districts. This suggests that any biases in estimating the effects of queues on trial demand due to excluding 45 districts in equations 4.1-4.4 are probably of small magnitude. Estimation of regressions for 1960 indicate that for all districts (equation 4.6) the queue, as measured by $Pc/\overline{T}$, had about the same effects as in 1967 and 1968. However, for districts in 1960 that match the districts in which Q_t were available in 1967 (equation 4.7), the regression coefficient of $Pc/\overline{T}$ was still negative but with a smaller absolute value. The latter partially results from the absence in 1960 of a measure of Q_p. Since Q_p and $Pc/\overline{T}$ are positively correlated, part of the positive effect of Q_p on trials would be picked up by $Pc/\overline{T}$ which, in turn, would diminish the negative effect of $Pc/\overline{T}$ on trials. I have tested this for 1967 by re-estimating equation 4.2 without Q_p, which reduces the regression coefficient of $Pc/\overline{T}$ from —.407 to —.331.

Although the regressions in table 4 are consistent with the hypothesis on Q_t and Q_p, these results contain an interesting puzzle. In both equations 4.1 and 4.3, trials are substantially more responsive to changes in Q_p than Q_t. One possible explanation is that errors in measurement are more important in Q_t than Q_p. Q_t is based on a sample of defendants that in each district averages less than 25 per cent of the sample size of Q_p, and in addition, Q_t often had to be estimated because either data on the jury trial queue or the court trial queue were absent (see note b in table 4).[54]

The effects on trial demand of the remaining variables in table 4 may be summarized as follows: (1) S has a positive sign in all regressions as pre-

[53] The significance of Q_p improves with this substitution, and the R^2's rise. The former is due to the substantially higher correlation between Q_p and Q_t than between Q_p and $Pc/\overline{T}$ (.54 compared to .24), while the latter is related to some spurious negative correlation since trials are present in the denominator of $Pc/\overline{T}$ and the numerator of T_1 and T_2. This spurious correlation probably explains why the absolute value of the regression coefficient of $Pc/\overline{T}$ is larger than Q_t.

[54] Errors in measurement of Q_t would also bias downward the regression coefficient of Q_p since the regression coefficient of Q_t on trials and the partial correlation between Q_t and Q_p are of opposite signs. See G. C. Chow, Demand for Automobiles in the United States, A Study in Consumer Durables app. I (13 Contributions to Economic Analysis 1957).

dicted by the theoretical analysis, and is statistically significant in the 1967 equations. The lack of significance in equations 4.3 and 4.4 is probably due to the fact that T_2 denotes defendants going to trial in 1968, whereas S refers to defendants sentenced in 1967. The non-significance of S in 1960 reflects the less comprehensive measure of S in that year. S is the average prison sentence in 1960, while in 1967, S includes defendants who were fined, placed on probation, and sentenced to prison. (2) D measures the fraction of defendants with subsidized legal counsel. These subsidies reduce the cost of a trial relative to a settlement, providing unsubsidized legal fees are greater for the former than the latter, and this in turn increases the demand for trials. The results of table 4 support this hypothesis. β_4 is positive in all regressions and significant in 4 out of 5 equations. This finding is relevant to the previous analysis of state courts where it was shown that defendants making bail had higher trial propensities. The latter was explained in terms of cost differentials between a trial and settlement that were greater for defendants not making bail. However, an alternative explanation was that wealthy persons were more likely to go to trial, and hence the observed relation between bail and trials resulted from the positive correlation between wealth and the ability to make bail. The analysis of the U.S. courts does not support this view. If differences in wealth *per se* were an important determinant of trial demand and wealthier defendants were more likely to go to trial, then β_4 would have had a negative sign since D should be inversely related to the fraction of wealthy defendants in a district. Thus, the results in table 4 together with the findings for state courts, indicate that the cost differential between trials and settlements is an important factor in trial demand and not differences in wealth among defendants.[55] (3) The South dummy variable, Re, had no systematic effect on trials in table 3, which contrasts with the strong positive effect of Re in the state data. This is not surprising since the region effect in the state courts may have picked up the effect of lower trial queues in the South, whereas queues were held constant in the U.S. courts.

The Probability of Conviction

State County Courts

The theoretical analysis predicted that if the defendant were not released on bail, the costs of his resource inputs would rise, leading to a reduction in

[55] If one still believed that wealth was an important variable in trial demand, then the observed positive coefficients of β_4 would show that wealthier defendants were *less* likely to go to trial. This contradicts the results of the state data which showed that wealthier defendants were *more* likely to go to trial. One final note is that if wealth were a determinant of the ability to make bail in the U.S. courts, then β_4 could have a negative sign. However, the Bail Reform Act (to the extent it is effective) would have reduced or eliminated the correlation between wealth and the ability to make bail.

these inputs and an increase in the probability of conviction. Therefore, a decline in the fraction of defendants making bail should result in an increase in the fraction of defendants convicted. A major difficulty in testing this hypothesis relates to the direction of causation between the bail and conviction variables. At the time bail is set a prima facie case is often made against the accused. If the preliminary evidence points to his guilt, a higher bail bond is likely to be set, which would lower his chance of being released. Hence, a selection process would take place before the final disposition of cases whereby defendants with a higher probability of conviction would be less likely to make bail. I have attempted to deal with this problem by including as independent variables both the fraction of defendants released on bail (B) and the average money bail charge (C) in regressions on the fraction of defendants convicted. Since setting a high money bail is a method of detaining a defendant with a high initial probability of conviction, then including C as an independent variable has the effect of holding constant differences across counties in these probabilities.[56] This in turn would remove from the regression coefficient on B any negative correlation due to higher conviction probabilities reducing the fraction of defendants released on bail.

Weighted regression equations of the form

$$P = \alpha + \beta_1 B + \beta_2 Pop + \beta_3 R_e + \beta_4 NW + \beta_5 Ur + \beta_6 Y + \beta_7 C + \beta_8 T + u \qquad (21)$$

are presented in table 5. B, Pop, Re, NW, Ur, Y and T are defined as before (see p. 79) and P and C are defined as follows:

P: the fraction of felony defendants sentenced to prison in each county. Some convicted felony defendants received only fines so that P understates the total number of defendants receiving penalties. However, data available in a few counties indicate that the fraction of defendants receiving only fines was negligible.

C: average dollar amount of bail set for defendants in each county.

The negative and statistically significant effect of B in equation 5.1 reflects in part the negative correlation described above that runs from P to B. C has a positive effect on P in equation 5.2, suggesting that defendants with greater conviction probabilities had C set at higher amounts.[57] As expected both the absolute value of the regression coefficient on B and its significance are

[56] The inclusion of C is only an approximation to holding constant variations in the probabilities because C may reflect other factors as well. For example, the severity of the offense, variations in the fraction of defendants not appearing for trial, attitudes of judges, etc.

[57] Data on C are available in only 70 of the 132 counties used in analysis of trials in county courts. The exclusion of 62 counties does not create any obvious biases since a regression computed for all 132 counties without C (equation 5.7) yields similar coefficients to equation 5.1.

TABLE 5

WEIGHTED REGRESSIONS AND T-VALUES FOR CRIMINAL CONVICTIONS IN 1962, 70 COUNTY COURTS IN U.S.

Equation Number	Dependent Variable	Regression Coefficients and T-Values									R^2
		α	B	Pop	Re	NW	Ur	Y	C	T	
5.1	P	.683	—.438	.010	.063	—.127	.076	—.006			.23
		(4.771)	(3.821)	(.748)	(1.141)	(.809)	(.581)	(.235)			
5.2	P	.655	—.369	.007	.062	—.142	.105	—.019	.015		.25
		(4.545)	(2.917)	(.544)	(1.129)	(.909)	(.800)	(.663)	(1.280)		
5.3	P	.676	—.247	.020	.051	—.090	.056	—.017	.011	—.289	.30
		(4.808)	(1.822)	(1.447)	(.947)	(.585)	(.431)	(.632)	(.989)	(2.130)	
5.4	Ds + A	.076	.227	—.019	.033	.010	.103	—.031	.015	—.299	.30
		(.641)	(1.978)	(1.566)	(.719)	(.074)	(.940)	(1.330)	(1.520)	(2.600)	
5.5	Ds	.115	.150	—.012	.063	—.042	.101	—.031	.013	.011	.19
		(1.044)	(1.408)	(1.114)	(1.482)	(.348)	(.994)	(1.440)	(1.442)	(.101)	
5.6	A	—.039	.077	—.006	—.030	.052	.002	.0002	.002	.288	.67
		(1.019)	(2.089)	(1.653)	(2.039)	(1.236)	(.056)	(.020)	(.565)	(7.789)	
5.7	P[a]	.824	—.430	.016	—.073	.091	.014	—.028			.17
		(7.409)	(4.307)	(1.283)	(1.729)	(.631)	(.147)	(1.292)			

Sources: See table 2 *supra*, for all variables except C. C is from Lee Silverstein, Bail in the State Courts—A Field Study and Report, 50 Minn. L. Rev. 621, tables 2, 3 & 4 (1966).

[a] Equation 5.7 is for all 132 counties where data on B are available whereas equations 5.1 through 5.6 are for 70 counties where data on C are available.

reduced when C is entered. We have previously shown that defendants released on bail have greater propensities to go to trial. One would like to determine to what extent the observed effect of B on P in 5.2 is due to differences in the method of disposition of cases (that is, trials versus settlements) between defendants released and not released on bail. In equation 5.3 a trial variable (T) has been added. T further reduces the regression coefficient of B and its significance because defendants going to trial are less likely to be sentenced to prison (that is, the regression coefficient on T is negative and significant) and more likely to make bail. In sum, the results of equations 5.1—5.3 support the hypothesis that the probability of conviction is increased for a defendant when he is not released on bail. At the mean values of P and B (both are about .5) the regression coefficient on B in 5.3 implies that the frequency of prison convictions is .38 for defendants released on bail and .62 for defendants not released, holding C and T constant. Observe that the coefficient of B is reduced by about 40 per cent when C and T are held constant—15 per cent due to C and 25 per cent due to T.

Regressions are also presented in table 5 on the fraction of defendants dismissed (Ds) and the fraction acquitted (A). These results confirm the previous findings that defendants released on bail are less likely to be convicted. The regression coefficients on B are positive in all three equations where C and T are held constant, and statistically significant in two. Note that 15 per cent of defendants in the sample were acquitted or dismissed, 50 per cent were sentenced to prison, while the remaining 35 per cent were generally given suspended sentences or placed on probation. The latter type of sentences, where the defendant's costs are small in comparison to prison sentences, should probably be viewed as non-convictions. For this reason P would be a better measure of convictions than $1 - (Ds + A)$. The positive though non-significant coefficients on C in the Ds and A regressions suggest that increases in defendants sentenced to prison as C rises, which are found in equations 5.2 and 5.3, come from a reduction in probations and suspended sentences rather than from fewer dismissals and acquittals.

Other findings in table 5 may be summarized as follows. (1) The population variable generally has a positive effect on convictions, indicating that longer trial queues across counties tend to increase the fraction of convictions. One should be cautious with this interpretation because of the uncertain relation between queues and population size and the lack of strong statistical significance of the population variable. (2) The demographic variables, NW, Ur and Y are not statistically significant in any regression. (3) An additional problem relates to the interpretation of the regression coefficient of B. Although a negative effect of B on convictions is found, this could be due to a greater average wealth rather than to a lower cost of resources for defendants released on bail. The relationship between wealth and convictions will be examined in the analysis of the U.S. court data.

Data on judicial expenditures in 1966-1967 are available for twenty counties with populations greater than 450,000. A reasonable assumption is that these expenditures are positively correlated with the size of the prosecutor's budget in a county. We would then predict from the theoretical analysis that the proportion of defendants convicted would be greater in counties with larger judicial expenditures per defendant. This hypothesis is consistent with findings in table 6 where judicial expenditures, denoted by J, have a positive effect on convictions in all regressions.[58] The primary effect of an increase in J is to reduce the proportion of cases dismissed while there is no significant effect on acquittals. Moreover, the increase in the fraction of defendants going to prison as J rises can be accounted for solely by a reduction in dismissals. At the mean values of J, Ds and P, a 15 per cent rise in J reduces Ds from .13 to .11 and increases P from about .50 to .52. Thus, the major economizing move as judicial expenditures fall is to reduce the number of cases prosecuted —hence an increase in dismissals.

U.S. Courts

Two conviction variables are used in regressions computed across U.S. district courts in 1967.

P: the fraction of defendants sentenced to prison.
F: the fraction of defendants receiving a fine only.

Prison sentences were more numerous than fines as the weighted means of P and F were .38 and .07 respectively in the 89 districts.

Of considerable interest in table 7 is the behavior of the variable D, the proportion of defendants assigned counsel by the court. D has a positive and significant effect on P, and a negative though non-significant effect on F in all equations. This suggests that increases in wealth of defendants reduce (increase) the frequency of convictions for offenses carrying prison sentences (fines) since D serves as a proxy variable for the fraction of lower income defendants in a district (see p. 86). These findings are consistent with a "wealth" hypothesis developed in the theoretical section which predicted for risk neutral defendants that (a) when penalties were in the form of jail sentences a rise in wealth would lead to an increase in the defendant's resource inputs and a subsequent fall in the probability of conviction and (b) when penalties are in the form of fines an increase in wealth would lower his inputs and raise the probability of conviction. A related interpretation of

[58] J is not divided by the number of defendants in a county because this information is not available. However, population size, which is probably positively correlated with the number of defendants in a county, is held constant in the regression equations.

TABLE 6

WEIGHTED REGRESSIONS AND T-VALUES FOR CRIMINAL CONVICTIONS IN 1962, 20 COUNTY COURTS IN U.S.

Equation Number	Dependent Variable	Regression Coefficients and T-Values										R^2
		α	B	Pop	Re	NW	Ur	Y	C	T	J	
6.1	P	.813	−.539	.028	−.033	.399	−.120	.013	−.015	−.378		.55
		(1.841)	(1.495)	(1.208)	(.262)	(.869)	(.222)	(.172)	(.603)	(1.487)		
6.2	P	.396	−.369	−.011	.147	.249	−.554	.123	−.008	−.255	.007	.67
		(.851)	(1.079)	(.350)	(.975)	(.584)	(1.011)	(1.347)	(.365)	(1.066)	(1.796)	
6.3	Ds + A	.903	.042	.042	−.157	−.124	.904	−.257	.017	.186	−.011	.82
		(2.887)	(.182)	(2.035)	(1.539)	(.433)	(2.453)	(4.191)	(1.155)	(1.145)	(4.052)	
6.4	Ds	1.013	−.141	.045	−.125	−.097	.775	−.241	.010	−.088	−.010	.76
		(3.308)	(.626)	(2.237)	(1.255)	(.344)	(2.149)	(4.010)	(.643)	(.555)	(3.862)	
6.5	A	−.110	.183	−.003	−.032	−.028	.129	−.016	.008	.275	−.001	.82
		(.755)	(1.704)	(.333)	(.663)	(.206)	(.747)	(.565)	(1.126)	(3.617)	(.579)	

Sources: See tables 2 and 5, *supra*, for variables except J. J is from U. S. Bureau of the Census, Criminal Justice Expenditure and Employment for Selected Large Governmental Units 1966-1967, tables 16 & 20 (State and Local Gov't Special Studies No. 51, 1969).

TABLE 7

WEIGHTED REGRESSIONS AND T-VALUES FOR CRIMINAL CONVICTIONS IN U.S. DISTRICT COURTS,[a] 1967

Equation Number	Dis-tricts	Depen-dent Variable	Regression Coefficients and T-Values							
			α	Qt	Qp	Pc/$\bar{T}$	D	Re	T_1	R^2
7.1	89	P	.593 (11.730)		—.096 (3.587)	.022 (1.069)	.086 (3.226)	.032 (1.319)	.046 (1.858)	.34
7.2	89	F	—.057 (1.711)		.061 (3.469)	—.012 (.875)	—.026 (1.471)	—.027 (1.707)	—.040 (2.441)	.27
7.3	44	P	.612 (6.217)		—.119 (2.656)	.030 (.955)	.081 (2.049)	.028 (.852)	.049 (.984)	.37
7.4	44	P	.502 (6.825)	.094 (2.717)	—.154 (3.815)		.086 (2.378)	.021 (.701)	.042 (1.232)	.46
7.5	44	F	.015 (.292)		.050 (2.227)	—.002 (.149)	—.012 (.591)	—.019 (1.151)	—.005 (.204)	.32
7.6	44	F	.018 (.449)	.002 (.108)	.047 (2.149)		—.011 (.558)	—.019 (1.158)	—.002 (.104)	.32

Sources: See table 4, *supra*, for all variables except P and F. P and F are from Federal Offenders in the United States District Courts 1967, table D10.

[a] All variables are in natural log form, except P, F, and Re.

the increase in P as D rises is that court assigned lawyers are less effective and of a lower quality than privately hired lawyers. This is not at variance with the "wealth" hypothesis because higher quality lawyers can be counted as more units of the defendant's resource inputs than lower quality ones. However, the quality explanation would also predict that privately hired lawyers would reduce the conviction rate on fines, and the reverse is found in table 7.[59]

An increase in delay between a trial and settlement is associated with an increase in the fraction of defendants sentenced to prison. The coefficients are positive for Qt and $Pc/\bar{T}$ and negative for Qp in the P regressions in table 7. We also observed in the state data that the population variable (interpreted as a proxy for trial delay) had a positive effect on convictions. One reason for the positive association between trial delay and prison convictions may be that the prosecutor becomes more selective with respect to the cases he prosecutes as trial delay increases. That is, he selects from an inventory of cases the ones he believes to have the greatest probability of conviction and the highest sentences if convicted in order to maximize his weighted conviction function. Moreover, if the prosecutor views fines as light penalties in comparison to jail sentences,[60] we would expect a negative relation between trial delay and the frequency of defendants fined. The equations on F give some support to this hypothesis although the regression coefficients on the Qt and $Pc/\bar{T}$ variables are not significant.

IV. Summary and Conclusions

The model developed in this essay utilizes two behavioral assumptions: the prosecutor maximizes the expected number of convictions weighted by their sentences, subject to a budget constraint, and the defendant maximizes the expected utility of his endowments in various states of the world. Both participants can influence the probability of conviction by their input of resources into the case, and cases are disposed of either by a trial or a voluntary pre-trial settlement between the prosecutor and defendant. A settlement

[59] A possible reconciliation is that higher quality lawyers are able to lower the defendant's conviction costs by shifting penalties from prison sentences to fines. This explanation would be consistent with both a positive effect of D on P and a negative effect of D on F. Another possible interpretation of the observed effects of D on P and F is that in districts where wealth is higher (and hence D lower) the types of crimes committed are more likely to be those carrying fines rather than jail sentences.

[60] The Administrative Office of the U.S. Courts assigns the value 1 to fines and 3 to imprisonment of 1 to 6 months in calculating a weighted average of the severity of all sentences (See Fed. Offenders, *supra* note 41, at 35, table 10 and note 49, *supra*). This indirectly suggests that fines are of small magnitude compared to jail sentences of a few months.

results in either a dismissal or a guilty plea. The major implications of the model are the following:

1. A settlement is more likely to take place (a) the smaller the sentence if convicted by trial, (b) the greater the resource costs of a trial compared to a settlement, (c) the greater the defendant's aversion to risk, and (d) the greater the defendant's estimate of the probability of conviction by trial relative to the prosecutor's estimate. We further showed that if the defendant and prosecutor agree on the expected outcome of a trial, a decision to go to trial is analogous to accepting an unfair gamble. In this instance, a settlement would result for risk neutral and risk averse defendants.

2. The defendant's investment of resources into his case is related both to the sentence if convicted by trial and to wealth. Generally, the resource investment is greater for crimes carrying larger sentences. Under the special assumption of risk neutrality (or presumably where the deviation from risk neutrality is small), increases in the defendant's wealth lead to greater resource investments when penalties are jail sentences and to smaller investments when penalties are money fines.

3. Court delays increase the opportunity costs of a trial compared to a settlement for defendants not released on bail. This leads to a smaller likelihood of going to trial for these defendants than for defendants released on bail. The greater the court delay the greater the difference in trial demand between the two groups. Pre-trial detention also raises the marginal costs of the defendant's resources and hence lowers his input. Therefore, defendants not released on bail are likely to have higher conviction probabilities in a trial and receive longer sentences if they settle than defendants released on bail. If making bail is a positive function of wealth, then the effects of pre-trial jailing fall primarily on low income defendants. We argued that paying a defendant not released on bail for time spent in jail prior to disposition of his case, or alternatively, crediting him for this time towards his eventual sentence and paying him only if he is not convicted would eliminate much of the "discriminatory" aspects of the current bail system.

4. In the absence of money pricing for the courts a trial queue arises to ration the limited supply. An equilibrium queue is reached because trial costs increase with the length of the queue. Queues could be reduced by charging a money price for trials, which reduces demand, leading to more settlements. Various methods of allocating the court fee—loser pays, winner pays, defendant and prosecutor share the cost—are consistent with a downward sloping demand curve for trials. Pricing trials will not only reduce delay but can also distribute trials more equally among defendants independent of their ability to make bail.

Available data on criminal defendants in state county courts and in U.S.

district courts enabled us to test a number of the hypotheses developed in the theoretical analysis. Multiple regressions were estimated for various cross-sections in selected years from 1957 to 1968. The principle findings of the empirical analysis may be summarized as follows.

1. The propensity to go to trial was smaller for defendants not released on bail than defendants released, holding constant the average sentence and several demographic variables. This was observed for state county courts in the United States as a whole, and the non-South. Moreover, results from the U.S. district courts indirectly indicate that increases in wealth do not increase trial demand. Thus, the observed relation between bail and trials in state courts is probably due to cost differences as predicted by the model rather than to differences in wealth that are positively correlated with the ability to make bail.

2. The absolute difference in trial propensities between defendants released and not released on bail increased as county population rose. One explanation for this finding is that court delay is greater in counties with larger populations. Note that direct measures of court delay were not available for the state courts.

3. Trial demand was negatively related to trial delay and positively related to settlement delay across U.S. district courts for 1960, 1967, and 1968. Thus, as the queue differential between a trial and settlement increased, the demand for trials fell.

4. Subsidizing defendant's legal fees in the U.S. district courts increased the demand for trials. This is consistent with the hypothesis that as the cost differential between a trial and settlement falls, the demand for trials increases.

5. District courts in which the average sentence was greater had proportionately more trials as predicted by the model. However, the results for the sentence variable in the county courts were inconclusive. The latter may be due to the crudity of the sentence variable used in counties.

6. The probability of conviction as measured by the proportion of defendants sentenced to prison was greater for defendants not released on bail than for defendants released on bail in county courts. This was observed in regressions which held constant, among other factors, both the size of money bail and the method of disposition (that is, trial or settlement). Money bail was included as an independent variable to reduce spurious correlation between the conviction and bail variables since defendants who were more likely to be convicted were also likely to have bail set at higher amounts, reducing their chance of release on bail. Regressions using the proportion of defendants acquitted and dismissed as the dependent variable supported the finding that defendants not released on bail were more likely to be convicted.

7. Convictions leading to prison sentences were lower in districts where estimates of the average wealth were higher, while convictions resulting in monetary fines were greater where average wealth was higher. One interpretation of this result is that the effect of wealth on the defendant's investment of resources into his case depended on whether penalties were jail sentences or fines.

8. Conviction rates were higher in district courts where trial delay was greater, and in county courts where judicial expenditures were larger. The former may result from a greater selectivity on the part of the prosecutor with respect to cases he prosecutes as the backlog increases. The latter was consistent with the hypothesis that the size of the prosecutor's budget determined the proportion of defendants convicted.

APPENDIX A

Civil Cases

We can extend our model to make it applicable to civil cases. The plaintiff replaces the prosecutor. Damages replace sentences. Both the plaintiff and defendant maximize their expected utility. It is assumed that civil trials decide both the question of the defendant's liability and the amount of damages. Only the defendant's guilt was at issue in criminal cases; the sentence if convicted was fixed and known prior to trial. A similar assumption for damages is not justified because statutory penalties generally do not exist for various types of civil suits. This modification requires that the plaintiff and defendant form expectations not only on the probability of the defendant being found liable, but also on the size of damages. With these changes, the analysis of civil cases remains quite similar to the model for criminal cases. To avoid excessive duplication I present only a brief outline of the civil model and its more important results.

In civil suits the plaintiff and defendant each select a level of resource inputs that maximizes his expected utility in the event of a trial. The plaintiff's inputs raise both the estimates of the probability that the defendant will be found liable and the amount of damages awarded in a trial, while the defendant's inputs lower these estimates. The plaintiff will determine a settlement payment ($=X$) that yields him the same utility as his expected utility from a trial. X would be the minimum sum accepted by the plaintiff to settle. If the payment of X by the defendant yields him a higher utility than his expected utility from a trial, a settlement will take place. This follows because one can find a payment somewhat greater than X that gives both parties a higher utility from a settlement than their expected utilities from a trial. It can further be shown that a settlement is likely when the following factors are present: (1) both parties have similar expectations on the probability that the defendant will be found liable in a trial; (2) both parties have similar estimates of the settlement, given that the defendant is found liable in a trial; (3) neither party has strong preferences for risk; (4) the costs of a trial including lawyer's fees, time costs of the plaintiff and defendant, court fees, etc. exceed the costs of a settlement. Alternatively, the more dissimilar the plaintiff's and defendant's estimates of liability and damages (providing the plaintiff's estimates are higher), the greater their preference for risk, and the lower court costs relative to settlement costs, the more likely a trial.[61]

The analysis of charging a money price for the courts, as opposed to queuing costs, is similar for civil and criminal cases. For example, a money price (M) will raise the maximum settlement offered by the defendant in a civil suit and lower the minimum settlement accepted by the plaintiff. M narrows the gap between what the defendant offers and what the plaintiff is willing to accept (providing the former was initially less than the latter sum), and increases the likelihood of a settlement. Moreover, the greater M the fewer civil cases that go to trial. As M falls to zero, the demand for trials will increase and a queue is likely to develop. The queue rations demand in the following way. As the queue lengthens, the discounted value of damages awarded in a trial fall. This would lower both the amount the plaintiff will accept and the amount the defendant will offer in a settlement. However, there are probably some costs to the defendant from trial delay. For example, his ability to dispose of assets (particularly if they are directly involved in the suit) and his ability to obtain funds in the capital market may be adversely affected by his being involved in litigation. If, on the average, the gains and costs of delay to the defendant offset each other, or the costs dominate, then the defendant's settlement offer would remain constant or increase as delay increases. The net effect would be a reduction in desired trials as the queue lengthened, since the defendant's settlement offer remains constant or increases while the plaintiff reduces the amount he is willing to accept.

There are several additional points on court delay that should be noted. (1) The analysis of queuing in civil cases is almost identical to criminal cases where the defendant is released on bail. In the latter, the prosecutor reduces his minimum sentence offer as delay increases, while the defendant's response is affected by two offsetting forces. Delay pushes his potential sentence from a trial further into the future, reducing its present value, while simultaneously his current earnings may be adversely affected by being under indictment. (2) A system analogous to the bail system could be instituted for civil cases. This would require, for example, defendants in civil suits to either pay a sum to the court per unit of time, or forgo the returns from all or part of their assets by depositing them with the court during the period between filing and disposition of the case. One effect of this procedure would be to make trial demand more responsive to a change in the queue as the costs of delay rise to the defendant. This is similar to the greater

[61] This result is similar to one derived by R.H. Coase, The Problem of Social Cost, 3 J. Law & Econ. 1 (1960). Coase shows that with well-defined property rights, and in the absence of transaction costs, a private agreement will be reached between individuals that internalizes externalities. If we interpret the absence of transaction costs in civil cases as the availability of information on damages at zero cost and zero bargaining costs of a settlement, and we generalize Coase's notion of well-defined property rights to include identical expectations over property rights or liability decisions in a trial, then Coase's theorem on private agreements would also include pre-trial settlements in the absence of risk preference.

responsiveness of criminal trial demand for defendants not released on bail relative to those released. (3) A requirement that the defendant pay interest on any sum awarded the plaintiff in a trial would have little effect on trial demand or court queues. Interest payments would raise both the defendant's settlement offer and the minimum sum acceptable to the plaintiff in a settlement. Hence, as a first approximation it would not close the gap between the defendant's offer and the plaintiff's acceptance sum and, therefore, would have no effect on the trial versus settlement decision. (4) Differences in the rate at which the plaintiff and defendant discount future damages awarded at a trial can give rise to differences in the response of trial demand to a change in the queue. The higher the plaintiff's discount rate relative to the defendant's, the larger the plaintiff's losses and the smaller the defendant's gains from an increase in the queue. This, in turn, would reduce the sum acceptable to the plaintiff by a greater amount than it reduces the defendant's offer, making a settlement more likely.

We can test the hypothesis that the demand for civil trials is negatively related to the length of the trial queue. The statistical specification of the demand function is

$$T = \alpha + \beta_1 Q_t^* + \beta_2 E(T) + \beta_3 Re + \mu . \qquad (22)$$

Data were from the 86 U.S. district courts in 1957-1961. The variables are in natural log form except Re and are defined as follows:

T: the ratio of the number of trials from cases that commenced in 1957 over the number of cases commenced in 1957.[62]

Q_t^*: Estimate of the expected trial queue in 1957 where Q_t^* is an exponentially declining weighted average of 1957, 1956 and 1955 median trial queues.[63] Q_t, the

[62] A frequency distribution of civil cases by length of time from filing to disposition by trial is published for each year from 1957-1961. (After 1961 only median trial queues are available.) This allows us to trace over time the eventual disposition (that is, trial or settlement) of cases commenced in 1957 assuming all of the latter cases are disposed of within four years from the date of filing. Since civil trial queues average about one-and-one-half years in the U.S. courts, a frequency distribution of trials is an important advantage in estimating T. For example, if the number of trials in a given year were used as the numerator of T, it would be difficult to choose an appropriate denominator for T because the trials were from cases commenced over several different time periods with an average queuing time to trial of one-and-one-half years. Moreover, it would be equally difficult to choose a value for the expected trial queue. Frequency distributions of trials are not available for criminal cases, but the above problems are not as great since criminal queues average about six months.

[63] Derived from the assumption that persons form expectations of future queues on the basis of past expectation and adjustment based on ratio of current value to previous expected value. That is,

$$Q_{t_y}^* = Q_{t_{(y-1)}}^* \left[Q_{t_y} / Q_{t_{(y-1)}}^* \right]^{\gamma} \qquad (i)$$

where Q_t^*'s are expected and Q_t's are actual median queues in a district, y is the year, and γ is the adjustment coefficient. (i) can be rewritten as the following infinite series:

$$Q_{t_y}^* = Q_{t_y}^{\gamma} \cdot Q_{t_{(y-1)}}^{\gamma(1-\gamma)}, \ldots \cdot Q_{t_{(y-\infty)}}^{\gamma(1-\gamma)\infty} \qquad (ii)$$

TABLE 8
WEIGHTED REGRESSION EQUATIONS[a] AND T-VALUES FOR CIVIL TRIALS IN U.S. DISTRICT COURTS, 1957-1961

Equation Number	Area	Districts	Regression Coefficients and T-Values					R^2
			α	Q_t*	Q_t	E(T)	Re	
8.1	U.S.	86	−.307 (.413)	−.410 (5.444)		.354 (1.051)	−.337 (4.014)	.28
8.2	U.S.		−.422 (.563)		−.369 (5.188)	.352 (1.032)	−.314 (3.757)	.27
8.3	Non-South	52	.164 (.238)	−.429 (6.033)		.546 (1.770)		.45
8.4	Non-South		.196 (.285)		−.400 (6.079)	.596 (1.940)		.46
8.5	South	34	−2.005 (1.087)	−.376 (2.080)		−.255 (.288)		.12
8.6	South		−2.399 (1.283)		−.323 (1.818)	−.386 (.420)		.10

Sources: 1956-1962 Ann. Rep., Admin. Off. of the United States Courts, tables C1, C3 and C5.
[a] Each observation weighted by $\sqrt{n}$ where n equals the number of cases commenced in 1957.

median trial queue in 1956, was also used as an estimate of the expected trial queue.

E(T): Expected fraction of trials in a district are estimated by dividing civil cases commenced in each district in 1957 into five broad groups, and then multiplying each group by the fraction of trials in that group for all U.S. district courts in 1957.[64] Therefore, the inclusion of E(T) allows us to hold constant differences in the distribution of types of cases across districts.

Q_t* in 1957 was approximated in the empirical analysis by using three previous values for Q_t. In logs this becomes

$$\log Q^*_{t_{57}} = \gamma \log Q_{t_{57}} + \gamma(1-\gamma)\log Q_{t_{56}} + \gamma(1-\gamma)^2 \log Q_{t_{55}}. \qquad \text{(iii)}$$

γ was initially set equal to .4, but to have the weights sum to 1 all weights were proportionally raised by a factor of 1.2755.

[64] Fraction of trials for various categories are as follows:

1. U.S. Plaintiff (excludes land condemnation and forfeiture cases)	.031
2. U.S. Defendant (ex. habeas corpus)	.188
3. Federal Question (ex. habeas corpus)	.123
4. Diversity	.151
5. Admiralty	.081

Note that 53,343 civil cases were commenced in 1957 in 86 U.S. District Courts and the number of cases excluded above were 4,613. These were excluded because data on queues and trials for each district do not include these types of cases. Note that when the U.S. government is involved in a suit as a defendant there is much greater likelihood of a trial than when the U.S. is the plaintiff. One explanation is that the costs to the defendant from delay (that offset the gains from the reduction in the present value of a trial settlement), such as his inability to dispose of assets or to obtain funds in the capital markets, may not be present when the defendant is the U.S. government. Hence,

Re: Region dummy variable that equals 1 for district courts in South and 0 for non-South district courts.

Table 8 presents regression estimates of equation (22). Separate regressions were also computed for districts in the non-South and South. All regression coefficients on Q_t^* and Q_t have the predicted negative signs, are highly significant, and are of similar magnitude. In sum, these results support the hypothesis that the demand for trials is negatively related to the size of the trial queue.

A difficulty in interpreting the findings of table 8 arises from the way in which the trial variable is measured. An unknown number of civil cases that would come under the jurisdiction of the U.S. courts are settled before they are filed. Since these cases are excluded from the denominator of T, the true proportion of civil cases going to trial in a district each year is less than the observed fraction. This measurement error in T will not bias the regression coefficients if the error is uncorrelated with the independent variables. However, we can show that the error in T is likely to be positively correlated with the trial queue, and this in turn will bias downward the absolute value of the queue elasticities.[65]

In table 8 E(T) has a positive and significant effect on T in the U.S. and non-South, but a negative and non-significant effect in the South. Overall, E(T) was less important than trial queues in explaining variations in T across districts. Re which is significant at the .01 level, indicates that the fraction of civil trials was about 30 per cent lower in the South holding the queue and E(T) constant. This result is puzzling in view of the finding that Re had no significant effect on the demand for criminal trials in the U.S. courts. A possible explanation is that the average size of damages in civil suits in the South is considerably lower than in

---

for a given queue one would expect more trials when the U.S. government is the defendant than when it is the plaintiff.

[65] Let t = the number of trials in a district, F = the number of cases filed, and C = the number of cases filed plus those settled before filing. Further, assume that $K \cdot F = C$, where $K > 1$. Suppose the relationship between t/C and Q_t^* is

$$t/C = Q_t^{*\beta} e^{\mu} \qquad \text{(i)}$$

while the estimating equation is

$$t/F = Q_t^{*\hat{\beta}} e^{\hat{\mu}} \qquad \text{(ii)}$$

where μ and $\hat{\mu}$ are error terms. (ii) can be rewritten as

$$\log K + \log(t/C) = \hat{\beta} \log Q_t^* + \hat{\mu}. \qquad \text{(iii)}$$

Let $E = \log K$, $Y = \log(t/C)$ and $X = \log Q_t^*$, and let e, y, and x denote deviations from their respective means. The least-squares estimator of $\hat{\beta}$ is

$$\hat{\beta} = \beta + \frac{\Sigma x e}{\Sigma x^2}, \qquad \text{(iv)}$$

which will be an unbiased estimator of β only if Cov $(x, e) = 0$. However, it is more likely that as Q_t^* rises, K will also rise, since the incentives to settle (both before and after filing) increase with the size of Q_t^*. This implies that Cov $(x, e) > 0$. Given that β and $\hat{\beta}$ are negative, this would result in $|\hat{\beta}|$ underestimating $|\beta|$.

the non-South. Thus, the negative effect on T of lower damages would be picked up by the Re variable.

APPENDIX B

Mathematical Notes: Wealth Effects

In this section we analyze the effect of changes in W on R when the defendant has non-neutral tastes for risk. Risk aversion is assumed. The case of risk preference can easily be worked out from the example of risk preference. Inputs of R are assumed to reduce both P and S (that is, $S' = \partial S/\partial R < 0$) in contrast to the assumption in section 1 that S was a constant and independent of R.

The first and second-order conditions for E(U) to be a maximum may be written, respectively, as

$$-P'(U(Wn) - U(Wc)) - sS'PU'(Wc) - r(PU'(Wc) + (1 - P)U'(Wn)) = 0 \quad (23)$$

and

$$-P''(U(Wn) - U(Wc)) + 2rP'(U'(Wn) - U'(Wc)) + r^2(PU''(Wc) + (1 - P)U''(Wn)) - 2sS'P'U'(Wc) - sS''PU'(Wc) + 2rsS'PU''(Wc) + (sS')^2PU''(Wc) < 0. \quad (24)$$

Relative risk aversion at Wn is defined as follows:

$$A(Wn) = -WnU''(Wn)/U'(Wn). \quad (25)$$

A(Wc) is similarly defined at Wc. Taking the total differential of (23) with respect to W and R, noting that (24) is negative, and substituting A(Wn) and A(Wc) gives $dR/dW \gtreqless 0$ as

$$U'(Wn)\left[-P'k - r'(1 - P) + \frac{r(1 - P)A(Wn)k}{Wn}\right] + U'(Wc)\left[P'm - s'S'P + \frac{sS'PA(Wc)m}{Wc} - r'P + \frac{rPA(Wc)m}{Wc}\right] \gtreqless 0 \quad (26)$$

where $r' = \partial r/\partial W > 0$, $s' = \partial s/\partial W$, $k = (1 - r'R)$ and $m = (1 - s'S - r'R)$. Note that $0 < k < 1$, $0 < m < 1$ and $k > m$. m and k are both positive because an increase in W must increase both Wn and Wc. Even with further simplifying assumptions the sign of (26) is indeterminate. For example, suppose $A(Wn) = A(Wc) = 1$ and let $Er = r'(W/r)$ and $Es = s'(W/s)$ where $0 \leqq Er, Es \leqq 1$. This gives $dR/dW \gtreqless 0$.

$$\frac{U'(Wn)}{U'(Wc)} \gtreqless Wn\,\frac{[-P'(W - E_ssS - E_rrR)Wc - sS'P(W - (E_sWc + E_ssS + E_rrR)) - rP(W - (E_rWc + E_ssS + E_rrR)]}{Wc[-P'(W - E_rrR)Wn + r(1 - P)(1 - E_r)W]}. \quad (27)$$

The sign of dR/dW cannot be determined from (27) without additional information about the defendant's utility function, the elasticities of s and r with respect to W, and the productivity of R in reducing S. If $E_s = E_r = 1$, (27) becomes

$$\frac{U'(Wn)}{U'(Wc)} \gtrless \frac{Wc}{Wn}. \qquad (28)$$

In the special case of a Bernoulli utility function, where the utility of wealth equals its logarithm, then $dR/dW = 0$, since $U'(Wn)/U'(Wc) = Wc/Wn$.

In general, the effects of changes in wealth on the defendant's input of resources are indeterminate once non-neutral tastes for risk are introduced. This conclusion is valid even when the strong assumption is made that relative risk aversion equals one for all levels of the defendant's wealth. Nevertheless, one still presumes that if the deviation from risk neutrality is small, the effects of wealth on R will be similar to those for risk neutrality.

[6]

AN ECONOMIC ANALYSIS OF LEGAL RULEMAKING

ISAAC EHRLICH and RICHARD A. POSNER***

THIS article continues and amplifies the examination of the legal process from the standpoint of economics begun by one of us in the last issue of the *Journal*.[1] In a study of the process, as distinct from the substantive content, of law, the social decision to regulate particular conduct—killing, or prices, or whatever—in a particular way is a given and the analysis focuses on the machinery of the legal system used to bring about compliance with the decision. The focus of the previous article was legal procedure. The present article discusses the degree of precision or specificity with which a legal command is expressed as a determinant of the efficiency of the legal process, a point on which the previous article touched only briefly.[2] We are *not* concerned here with the question why some activities are regulated and others not.

If we want to prevent driving at excessive speeds, one approach is to post specific speed limits and to declare it unlawful per se to exceed those limits; another is to eschew specific speed limits and simply declare that driving at unreasonable speeds is unlawful. Any choice along the specificity-generality continuum will generate a unique set of costs and benefits. This article discusses the conditions under which greater specificity or greater generality is the efficient choice and makes a preliminary effort to appraise the efficiency of the choices actually made by the legal process. Many of the concepts discussed in the following pages will be familiar to lawyers and other students

* Assistant Professor of Business Economics, Graduate School of Business, University of Chicago; Research Associate, National Bureau of Economic Research.

** Professor of Law, University of Chicago; Research Associate, National Bureau of Economic Research.

Our study has been supported by a grant from the National Science Foundation to the National Bureau óf Economic Research for research in law and economics. It is not an official Bureau publication since it has not yet undergone the full critical review accorded Bureau publications, including approval by the Bureau's board of directors.

Kenneth Culp Davis, Michael Graetz, Duncan Kennedy, George J. Stigler, and James B. White commented helpfully on a previous draft.

1 See Richard A. Posner, An Economic Approach to Legal Procedure and Judicial Administration, 2 J. Leg. Studies 399 (1973).

2 See *id.* at 448-51. For an earlier treatment see Gordon Tullock, The Logic of the Law 47-50 (1971). For an interesting perspective on the subject of this article that is quite different from our own see James B. White, The Legal Imagination: Studies in the Nature of Legal Thought and Expression 537-66 (1973).

of the legal process but we hope by placing them in an economic framework to facilitate both rigorous analysis and (eventually) systematic empirical investigation.

I. Preliminary Issues

1. To facilitate exposition, we will sometimes treat the specificity-generality continuum as if it were a dichotomy between "rules" and "standards." The term "standard" denotes in our usage a general criterion of social choice; efficiency (and its counterparts in legal terminology, such as reasonableness[3]) is an example. A standard indicates the kinds of circumstances that are relevant to a decision on legality and is thus open-ended. That is, it is not a list of all the circumstances that might be relevant but is rather the criterion by which particular circumstances presented in a case are judged to be relevant or not. In an automobile collision case governed by the negligence standard these circumstances would be the speed and weight of the vehicles, their design, the time of day, the layout of the highway, the weather, and any other factors that might affect the question how the sum of the expected accident costs and the accident-avoidance costs could have been minimized.

A rule withdraws from the decision maker's consideration one or more of the circumstances that would be relevant to decision according to a standard. Suppose that if it is proved that the following car in a rear-end collision was driving within 100 feet of the preceding car, the driver of the following car will be liable for the costs of the accident. This is a rule rather than a standard because, were the case to be decided under the general negligence standard, other circumstances besides the distance between the two cars would have to be considered, such as the ability of the driver of the preceding car to avoid stopping short. The simplest kind of rule, then, takes the form: if X, then Y, where X is a single, simple, determinate fact (*e.g.*, the car's speed) and Y is a definite, unequivocal legal consequence—a judgment of liability or nonliability—that follows directly from proof of X (*e.g.*, driver has violated traffic code). It should be clear, therefore, that we are using the term "rule" in a somewhat special sense; "general rule" would be a contradiction in our usage.

The difference between a rule and a standard is a matter of degree—the degree of precision. The efficiency standard itself could be regarded as a rule of social choice designed to implement a broader standard (the greatest happiness of the greatest number of people), while a rule that required the weighing of many circumstances (unlike our hypothetical rear-end rule, which required the weighing of only one, distance) would be like a standard.

[3] Cf. Richard A. Posner, A Theory of Negligence, 1 J. Leg. Studies 29 (1972).

Our fundamental concern is with precision of law rather than with choosing between rule and standard as such.

2. The issue of legal precision should not be confused with Professor Davis' contrast between "rule" and "discretion."[4] The problem with which Professor Davis has been primarily concerned is the lack of effective social control over subordinate officials, such as policemen and immigration officers. He believes that this problem can best be solved by defining the duties of these officials in greater detail. This approach, even if correct (we express some doubt below), identifies only one benefit of greater specificity. We are interested in the full range of benefits and of costs associated with movement along the specificity-generality axis. At the same time we are not concerned here with a basic issue in the rule vs. discretion literature: whether greater use of rules produces substantively better regulation.

3. Another familiar dichotomy is "rule-principle." The term "principle" has been used in discussions of judicial decision-making to denote a maxim, sentiment, or policy informing the decisional process and it has been argued —misleadingly in our opinion—that an account of judicial decision-making that emphasizes decision according to rule ignores the fact that principles may lead a judge to depart from an existing rule or formulate a new one.[5] The classic instance in which it is argued that rules must bend to principles is the inheritance by an individual who murdered the person from whom he inherits. Here, the rule that testamentary dispositions are to be enforced when certain formalities (a written will, witnessed in a certain way, etc.) are complied with is said to collide with the principle that no man should be permitted to profit from his wrongdoing.

But there is no real conflict between rule and principle here.[6] The question is simply the correct rule to govern a special class of testamentary dispositions, that in which the donor is murdered by the heir. A rule enforcing testamentary dispositions in favor of murdering heirs would be unsound. Whatever the testator's intentions at the time that he drafted his will, it is likely that had he been able at the moment of his death to revoke the bequest he would have done so. And the law permits people to revoke their wills at any time before death. We give effect to the testator's real desires and to the policy underlying the revocability of wills during the testator's lifetime by refusing to enforce the bequest to the murdering heir. In so doing we also reduce the incentive to commit murder.

4 See Kenneth Culp Davis, Discretionary Justice—A Preliminary Inquiry (1969), and, in the context of monetary policy, Henry C. Simons, Economic Policy for a Free Society 160-83 (1948).

5 See Ronald G. Dworkin, The Model of Rules, 35 U. Chi. L. Rev. 22 (1967).

6 This we take to be the view also of Hart and Sacks, who have a long section on the murdering-heir problem in their legal process materials. See Henry H. Hart, Jr. & Albert M. Sacks, 1 The Legal Process 75-110 (temp. ed. 1958).

Properly understood, "principles" are simply the considerations that are relevant in determining the content of a rule. The murdering-heir case is one where the law is incompletely detailed. A new rule must be created to decide the case soundly.

4. Rule and standard are not merely alternative forms in which to express the commands of the law. Standards are also criteria of rules. If the standard governing automobile accident cases were income equality rather than efficiency, the specific rules of accident law would be different from what they are. But while rules may implement standards, they need not do so, as can be seen by a comparison of rules, such as those of common law fields like torts, that derive (we believe) from coherent and intelligible social policies, with rules, characteristic of much of the economic legislation of modern welfare states, that are the outcome of a power struggle between opposing political factions, such as the rules of taxation.[7] (We do not suggest that all legislative rules are of this character.)

If the social goal is efficiency, a set of particular rules of accident law can be formulated to maximize attainment of the goal; arguably, most of the rules and doctrines of tort law are of this type.[8] One doubts that the rules of tax law (governing rates, deductions, and the like) could be derived in similar fashion. Taxation has goals—to raise revenue, to foster certain notions of distributive justice, and to avoid creating incentives to engage in inefficient activities—but they are often, perhaps typically, in conflict; they do not constitute a single, coherent standard. It does not follow that there are no rules of taxation; there are more rules of taxation than of negligence. But they do not comprise a logical system in the sense that, told "the purpose" of the system and something about the activities taxed, one could deduce the rules—at least it would be much harder to do so than in the case of the tort system.

If this analysis is correct, arbitrariness, political favoritism, covert influence, and the like—the very abuses associated with "discretionary justice" —may sometimes be more prevalent in an area, such as taxation, where decision is guided primarily by rules than in one where a less exact standard is operating. This point has been obscured by the lawyer's characteristic agnosticism concerning the content of a legislative or administrative rule: Professor Davis is not concerned with the question whether the rules of tax law are the product of a political process fraught with abuse but only with whether abuses occur in the process of enforcing the rules. This is perhaps

[7] A contrast suggested in Duncan Kennedy, Legal Formality, 2 J. Leg. Studies 351 (1973), and in the notion of "reasoned elaboration" emphasized throughout the Hart and Sacks materials (see note 6 *supra*). The notion is that courts, but not legislatures, are obligated to justify rationally their rules and decisions.

[8] See reference in note 3 *supra*.

why he is so confident that greater precision will make the law substantively sounder and fairer.

II. The Optimum Precision of Legal Obligation: A Static Analysis

We shall consider in this part the benefits and costs associated with different choices along the continuum between the highly specific rule and the highly general standard and discuss the optimum choice—the choice that maximizes the excess of benefits over costs. Our analysis will be rather abstract owing to the problem of measuring the relevant costs and benefits and to the absence of a readily identifiable empirical counterpart to the concept of precision of legal obligation (it is obvious that simply counting the number of rules in an area of law will not yield a reliable measure of it). We emphasize, however, that the *concept* of legal precision is unambiguous—the fewer and simpler the facts to which definite legal consequences attach, the more precise is a legal obligation. And we do not despair of measuring legal precision, especially within (rather than across) fields of law. We do not doubt, for example, that the so-called "per se" rules of antitrust law can be shown to be more precise than the "Rule of Reason" under which some antitrust questions are decided.

Several points should be kept in mind throughout the analysis:

1. Rules are addressed to two audiences: people who might violate (or be accused of violating) the law, and participants in the process of determining whether a violation has occurred (judges, lawyers, etc.). The effects of the choice between rule and standard on the first group we shall call effects on "primary behavior," as contrasted with the effects of the choice on law enforcement and other activities of the legal system.

2. The legislature's choice whether to enact a standard or a set of precise rules is implicitly also a choice between legislative and judicial rulemaking. A general legislative standard creates a demand for specification. This demand is brought to bear on the courts through the litigation process and they respond by creating rules particularizing the legislative standard. Thus an appraisal of the efficiency of a legislative decision to enact a standard requires consideration of the differences in costs and benefits between legislative rules and judge-made rules (precedents).

Sometimes the demand for specificity is satisfied by private rulemakers rather than by courts. This is especially likely to occur in areas where courts use standards rather than rules. Potential defendants may be unwilling to let their employees make the difficult decisions involved in applying a standard to particular circumstances, so they formulate rules of conduct to guide the employees. We do not discuss these private rules in this article but they are undoubtedly an important feature of legal regulation.

3. The analysis in this part is primarily static. We postpone to Part III a discussion of how the costs and benefits of a rule or standard are affected by changes through time in the relevant social or economic conditions.

A. *Elements of the Model*

1. *Benefits of Rules.* a. *Primary behavior.* A perfectly detailed and comprehensive set of rules brings society nearer to its desired allocation of resources by discouraging socially undesirable activities and encouraging socially desirable ones. This is because detailing the law efficiently (the importance of this qualification will become clear later) results in an increase in the expected gain from engaging in socially desirable activity relative to that from engaging in undesirable activity.

It does this by increasing the (subjective) probabilities that the undesirable activity is punishable and that the desirable is not. The cost of an activity includes any expected punishment costs. The expected punishment cost of engaging in an activity is the product of (1) the subjective probability of the participant's being apprehended and convicted and (2) the cost to him of the penalty that will be imposed if he is convicted. The probability of apprehension and conviction, in turn, is the product of (1) the probability that the activity in which the person is engaged will be deemed illegal and (2) the probability that, if so, he will be charged and convicted for his participation in it. The more (efficiently) precise and detailed the applicable substantive standard or rule is, the higher is the probability that the activity will be deemed illegal if it is in fact undesirable (the kind of activity the legislature wanted to prevent) and the lower is the probability that the activity will be deemed illegal if it is in fact desirable. Thus the expected punishment cost of undesirable activity is increased and that of desirable activity reduced.

Although this conclusion is independent of individuals' attitudes toward risk, its implications are particularly striking under certain plausible assumptions about those attitudes. Suppose that most people who engage in socially undesirable activities (criminals, tortfeasors, and other violators) are risk preferring while most people who engage in socially desirable activities are risk averse. Then an increase in specificity, by reducing the variance in outcomes associated with engaging in a particular activity, would tend to have a disproportionately deterrent effect on undesirable activity and a disproportionately encouraging effect on desirable activity. This is because people who like risk may invest in risky activities resources greater than the expected gain, while people who dislike risk may invest in the avoidance of risky activities resources greater than the expected cost of these activities, and the elimination of risk discourages both kinds of investment.

As one example of the foregoing analysis, consider the Supreme Court's concern with the "chilling" effect on participation in socially desirable activity of vague criminal statutes punishing conduct closely related to the expression of ideas.[9] If such a statute, because of its uncertain scope, *might* be applied to the expression of ideas itself, that expression becomes burdened by an expected punishment cost. The additional cost may be slight[10] yet may still cause a significant reduction in an activity that is relatively unremunerative to begin with, as is much of the activity within the scope of the constitutional guarantees of freedom of speech, press, and assembly. The fact that the activity is relatively unremunerative to the individual does not mean that its abandonment or curtailment could not impose substantial social costs. Activity not particularly valuable in the market place may be highly valuable socially. The private value of ideas tends to be lower than their social value due to the absence of an effective system of property rights.

To anticipate a bit, a finding that an uncertain statute is a source of heavy social costs in the context of expressive activity should not conclude the analysis. Those costs must be compared with the costs in reduced prevention of socially undesirable activity as a result of the loopholes that must arise (for reasons explained later) when the legislature reformulates the statutory prohibition in more specific terms. The Court has not considered these costs, perhaps assuming that they can be avoided by moderate expenditures on carefully formulating the desired prohibition.

The "chilling" of socially valuable behavior by an uncertain law is a potentially serious problem whenever criminal penalties are involved. This may explain why the Constitution has been interpreted to require greater specificity in criminal than in civil statutes. Not only do criminal sanctions tend to be severe (costly) but it is normally impossible to purchase insurance against criminal liability. The average individual can avoid the risk of being subjected to a criminal penalty only by avoiding criminal activity. But if what constitutes criminal activity is uncertain this is not enough: he can eliminate the risk only by avoiding, in addition to clearly criminal behavior, all other behavior that is within the penumbra of the vague standard. And he may very well do this, even though the penumbral activity is quite valuable privately as well as socially: a rational individual, especially if he is risk averse, may incur heavy costs to avoid even a slight risk of criminal punishment. Thus the social costs of vague criminal standards might be high.[11]

[9] See, *e.g.*, Thornhill v. State of Alabama, 310 U.S. 88, 97-98 (1940); Smith v. California, 361 U.S. 147 (1959).

[10] The probability that the courts would uphold what is by assumption an invalid application of the statute would be small.

[11] The analysis of the effect of a vague standard is closely parallel to that of legal

We offer two additional observations about the impact of precision of legal obligation on primary behavior. First, it has an indirect effect on that behavior through its effect on law enforcement activity (public or private), a point developed in the next subsection. Second, efficient *statutory* rules can be expected to have a greater effect on primary behavior than efficient judge-made rules. The statute precedes the precedent. The legislature's choice is between promulgating its own rule and leaving it to the courts to fashion a rule after a case (or series of cases) comes to them—the latter a protracted process. In addition, the statutory rule is likely to have a broader scope than the judge-made rule. Since the parties to a lawsuit, who define the issues in the suit, are generally individuals or individual firms that are not interested in obtaining a broad rule, a court tends to create a rule limited to situations very similar to that of the case at hand. The nature of the legislative process is such that ordinarily only substantial interest groups, rather than single individuals, can invoke it. The result is that most legislative rules control a relatively broad span of activity.

b. *Legal-system behavior.* Here we consider the benefits of greater precision of legal obligation in terms of its effects on behavior within the legal system.

(1) An increase in precision increases the probability of convicting the guilty and of acquitting the innocent ("guilty" here meaning engaged in socially undesirable activities and "innocent" engaged in socially desirable activities). Stated differently, it increases the marginal productivity of expenditures by the law enforcer (public or private) on prosecuting the guilty, reduces the marginal productivity of his expenditures on prosecuting the innocent, reduces the marginal productivity of the guilty defendant's litigation expenditures, and increases the marginal productivity of the innocent defendant's litigation expenditures. The combination of these effects should induce an increase in prosecutorial resources in cases involving guilty defendants, a decrease in defendants' expenditures in those cases, an increase in defense expenditures in cases where the defendant is in fact innocent, and a decrease in prosecutorial expenditures in those cases.[12] The net result should be a further increase in the probability of convicting the guilty and of acquitting the innocent, resulting in a further increase in the efficiency of primary behavior.

(2) The reduction in the amount of socially undesirable activity brought about both directly and (through the greater efficiency of law enforcement

error. See Richard A. Posner, *supra* note 1, at 410-15; Isaac Ehrlich, The Deterrent Effect of Capital Punishment: A Question of Life and Death, nn.12-13 (unpublished manuscript, Univ. of Chi. Grad. Sch. of Bus., July 1973).

12 Changes in the level of a litigant's expected expenditures will induce changes in the level of the other party's expenditures. These complex interactions are discussed in Richard A. Posner, *supra* note 1, at 429-33. It is unlikely that they would alter our conclusions, and we ignore them here.

expenditures) indirectly by rule precision should reduce the total number of cases brought and hence the total amount of resources devoted to legal dispute resolution. In addition, fewer cases will be brought that arise out of socially desirable activities. Also, the sum of the parties' expenditures in those cases that are litigated may be lower. This is because a rule withdraws from a lawsuit many of the issues that would have been litigable were the case decided under a standard and it seems likely that there are diminishing—often very rapidly diminishing—returns to proof of a point.

(3) If a legal dispute occurs, the fact that the outcome of the dispute, if it is litigated, will be determined by application of a rule rather than a standard should make it easier for the parties to predict the outcome. According to the economic analysis of the settlement of legal disputes out of court, an increase in the predictability of the outcome of litigation should result in an increase in the settlement rate.[13] Since the costs of litigating are generally higher than the costs of settling a dispute out of court, an increase in the settlement rate (at least within a broad range) should reduce the total costs of legal dispute resolution.

Greater certainty as to outcome might have an indirect effect on the settlement rate as well as the direct effect just discussed. The costs of settling a dispute will be lower if outcome is more certain, for there will be less disagreement over the outcome and this will facilitate the negotiation of a mutually satisfactory settlement price. A reduction in the costs of settlement may increase the settlement rate by increasing the attractiveness of settlement relative to that of litigation as a method of legal dispute resolution. This assumes that the costs of litigation do not fall by the same amount. The cost of obtaining a more favorable outcome by litigating rather than by settling might actually rise since the greater definiteness of a rule reduces the effect of litigation expenditures, strategy, and advocacy on the outcome of the litigation. This is another reason for expecting a shift from litigation to settlement as a method of resolving legal disputes.

When the rules in question are judicial rather than statutory, our conclusion that decision by rule reduces the costs of the legal process must be qualified. Precedents are produced by activity of lawyers and judges in court. This is a costly activity, and although the rules produced yield, as we have seen, reductions in outlays on the courts, the net cost of judicial rulemaking must be positive—otherwise the optimum number of such rules would be infinite.

(4) The choice of rule versus standard affects the speed, and hence indirectly the costs and benefits, of legal dispute resolution. Because of the sequential character of a trial, an increase in the number of issues to be

[13] See, *e.g.*, Richard A. Posner, *supra* note 1, at 423-26.

litigated will lengthen the trial. Decision by standard therefore increases the interval between an incident giving rise to a legal dispute and final judicial resolution of the dispute. The principal effects, so far as relevant here, are to increase the costs of legal error through the effect of delay in causing evidence to decay and to foster settlements in some classes of cases.[14]

(5) Rules reduce the costs of organizing and communicating information for use in resolving legal disputes. A rule that the driver of the following car is liable in a rear-end collision amounts to saying that since experience has shown that the driver of that car can usually avert the collision at moderate cost, the benefits of determining the question still another time are likely to be less than the costs of doing so. The rule summarizes what has been learned in the prior adjudications.

Oliver Wendell Holmes many years ago remarked the process by which the general standard of negligence had been transformed, over time, into specific rules of accident law.[15] In his view, after a particular type of accident case had been decided the same way by many juries applying the negligence standard, so that it was now clear how such a case should be decided under that standard, it was appropriate to withdraw the issue from the jury and make it an issue of law—to substitute, in other words, a rule for a standard.

A consumer looking for a refrigerator does not visit every store where refrigerators are sold, to compare brands, prices, etc. He samples from among the stores, continuing the sampling process until the expected value of the information yielded by an additional observation is just equal to the cost (in his time, etc.) of the additional search involved in making that observation.[16] The process described by Holmes is similar. Initially a particular type of case is decided under a general standard which permits a broad-ranging factual inquiry. Successive decisions convey information about how such cases should be decided. A point is eventually reached at which the additional information imparted by another decision under the standard is not worth the additional costs (discussed earlier) of decision by standard as compared to decision by rule. So a rule is adopted, based on the information previously obtained, to control subsequent decisions.

This analysis assumes that the relevant primary behavior is homogeneous, so that (as we shall see) governance by rule is clearly appropriate, and the problem is to discover the basic homogeneity. Such a process of discovery has long been at work in the antitrust area, for example, where over the years more and more practices have been ruled illegal per se after a period in which they were judged under a reasonableness standard. The courts

[14] See *id.* at 420-21, 445-46.

[15] Oliver Wendell Holmes, Jr., The Common Law 111-29 (1881).

[16] See, *e.g.*, George J. Stigler, The Economics of Information, in The Organization of Industry 171 (1968).

eventually discovered that evidence as to the circumstances that the standard permitted them to consider never changed the ultimate outcome of a case, so they substituted rules for the standard.

(6) Decision according to rule facilitates the social control of decision makers. Where the correct outcome of a litigation is highly uncertain due to the number of circumstances that must be weighed and the uncertain weight of each, detection of an incompetent or corrupt outcome is more difficult.

The last two points stress the utility of rules in reducing mistakes and usurpations by adjudicators. This function is obviously quite similar to that performed by the rules promulgated by bureaucratic organizations to direct and control the behavior of their employees.

We note in closing that the *net* benefits of legal rules may be smaller in cases where private rules are an alternative. The creation of a legal rule may simply shift the rulemaking function from the private to the public sector.

2. *The Costs of Legal Rules*. Several different sorts of cost are associated with greater precision of legal obligation. Some of these costs arise from the fact that making law more precise often involves making it more detailed in order to minimize the costs of overinclusion and underinclusion, which, as we are about to see, are generated by precise rules.

a. Obtaining and correctly evaluating information concerning the various combinations of events or circumstances under which the general standard that the set of rules is designed to implement should be activated are costly. The cost is presumably greater the more heterogeneous the conduct sought to be regulated (more on heterogeneity below).

b. Formulating a rule, once the appropriate scope of the desired prohibition has been determined, involves a cost. This cost, we conjecture, is greatest when the rule is a statutory rule and the conduct to be regulated is politically controversial. The formulation of a statutory rule requires negotiation among the legislators. This makes legislative production an extremely expensive form of production: the analysis of transaction costs in other contexts suggests that the costs of legislative negotiation are likely to be substantial due to the number of legislators whose agreement must be secured.[17] The costs of negotiation will be even higher when a proposed rule is controversial, that is, costly to a politically effective segment of the community.

Transaction costs tend to increase rapidly with the number of parties whose agreement is necessary for the transaction to occur. This suggests that there are practical limits to increasing the size of a legislature. Hence (to anticipate Part III) as the amount and complexity of social activity increase over time, we can expect to find that legislatures, rather than expanding, will delegate more and more of the legislative function to bodies that

[17] Cf. James M. Buchanan & Gordon Tullock, The Calculus of Consent: Logical Foundations of Constitutional Democracy ch. 8 (1962).

do not produce rules through negotiation among a large number of people —*i.e.*, to executive and administrative agencies and to courts—as has in fact happened. We are similarly led to predict that delegation will be less common in systems (such as the British) where party discipline in the legislature is tight and the legislature is (effectively) unicameral; both circumstances reduce the costs of arriving at agreement on legislation. A related prediction, one also supported by at least casual observation, is that over time judicial interpretation of statutes will become more flexible. As the costs of legislative enactment increase, courts will be more reluctant to apply principles of strict statutory construction, which have the effect of confining to the legislature the task of keeping statutes up to date.

c. Greater specificity of legal obligation generates allocative inefficiency as a result of the necessarily imperfect fit between the coverage of a rule and the conduct sought to be regulated. Our earlier assumption of a perfect fit was unrealistic. The inherent ambiguity of language and the limitations of human foresight and knowledge limit the practical ability of the rulemaker to catalog accurately and exhaustively the circumstances that should activate the general standard. Hence the reduction of a standard to a set of rules must in practice create both overinclusion and underinclusion. Some conduct is prohibited that would be permitted if the standard that the rules are designed to implement were applied directly to it; other conduct is permitted that would be prohibited under a direct application of the standard. Both effects impose social costs similar to those that an indefinite standard imposes since, as we saw earlier, such a standard, *in application*, will both over- and underinclude.

The problem of underinclusion can be solved by backing up the rule with a standard. It can be made unlawful to drive more than 60 miles per hour *or* to drive at any lower speed that is unreasonably fast in the particular circumstances. The result of adding a standard is, however, to sacrifice some benefits from governance by rules.

The problem of overinclusion is frequently dealt with by delegation to enforcement officials of authority to waive application of the rule: the policeman need not give a traffic ticket to the speeding driver who is en route to a hospital in an emergency. In principle one could rewrite the rule to specify all the possible exceptions; but in practice it may be cheaper to allow *ad hoc* exceptions to be made at the enforcement level—as recognized by even the severest critics of official discretion. Again, however, some benefits of governance by rules are sacrificed by recognizing exceptions based on implicit use of an overriding standard.

Our discussion of overinclusion requires two qualifications. First, where the sanction for violation of a legal rule or standard imposes on the violator a cost just equal to the social costs of the violation—simple damages in tort or contract actions approximate such a sanction—socially valuable violations will not be deterred. A rule that makes injurers liable for all of their accidents whether or not they are negligent (strict liability) should not deter them from engaging in behavior that results in nonnegligent (efficient) accidents, since, by definition, their liability will be less than the benefits they obtain from such activity.[18] The rule may have inefficient consequences because the right to be compensated for all accidental injuries may reduce the safety incentives of potential victims below the efficient level. However, this consequence results not from the substitution of a rule for a standard but from the form of the sanction—payment of damages to people injured by the violation. Were the sanction payment of the damages to the state rather than to victims, the inefficient consequences of substituting a rule for a standard would disappear.

Even if the substitution of a rule for a standard does not result in deterrence of socially beneficial behavior, as in the last example, it may still increase the costs of the legal process by increasing the scope of liability and hence the number of legal disputes.[19] This effect of overinclusion might be offset by underinclusion. But where an overly inclusive rule is backed up by a general prohibition in order to avoid underinclusion (loopholes), there is no such offsetting effect.

Strict criminal liability is occasionally imposed (*e.g.*, for adulteration). Its effects differ from those of strict civil liability. Since a fine or other criminal penalty, unlike simple damages, may impose on the convicted defendant a cost independent of the social cost of his conduct, criminal punishment may deter conduct that yields social benefits in excess of its social costs. Hence we are not surprised to find that strict criminal liability is imposed much less commonly than strict civil liability.

Another respect in which our analysis of overinclusion needs to be qualified involves situations where the costs of transactions among the people subject to the rule are low. An example of a rule operating in such a context is the Statute of Frauds, which provides that certain types of contract (*e.g.*, for the sale of land) are unenforceable unless reduced to writing. If the criterion for enforcing contracts for the sale of land were a reasonableness or efficiency standard, many oral land contracts would have to be enforced as expressing the true intentions of the parties. But it does not follow that the Statute of Frauds frustrates many valuable transactions. Since prospective contracting parties can assure enforcement by making a written contract, the major cost associated with the Statute of Frauds, viewed as an overinclusive rule, is not the prevention of valuable transactions[20] but the legal

[18] See Richard A. Posner, Strict Liability: A Comment, 2 J. Leg. Studies 205 (1973).

[19] See Richard A. Posner, *supra* note 1, at 443.

[20] Some valuable transactions will be frustrated, however, as a result of some people's ignorance of the requirement of a writing.

and negotiating expenses necessary to comply with the rule. These expenses are probably modest. The major benefit is a reduction in the cost of resolving contract disputes. The cost of proving the existence and terms of a contract is reduced; the probability of an erroneous decision is reduced; and the predictability of the outcome of contract litigation is increased.[21]

The problems of overinclusion and underinclusion are more serious the greater the heterogeneity (or ambiguity, or uncertainty) of the conduct intended to be affected. If speeding were a homogeneous phenomenon—as it would be, for example, if driving at a speed of more than 70 miles per hour were always unreasonably fast and driving at a lesser speed never unreasonably fast—it could be effectively proscribed by a uniform speed limit of 70 with no residual prohibition of unreasonably fast driving. But speeding is in fact heterogeneous. It includes some driving at very low speeds and excludes some very fast driving, depending on a multitude of particular circumstances. A single speed limit or even a large number of separate speed limits must exclude a great deal of conduct that is really speeding and include a great deal that is not really speeding.

d. We have thus far emphasized costs incurred in the production of rules and in people's adaptive behavior toward rules. Another (albeit overlapping) type of cost is the cost of hiring experts—lawyers—to advise and counsel on compliance with the law and to operate tribunals and represent the parties before them when a legal dispute arises.

It might appear that rules, by reducing the law's uncertainty, would reduce the demand for experts in its interpretation. It is true that the substitution of rules for standards may reduce the number of legal disputes and hence the demand for trial lawyers. But the conduct of litigation is a relatively minor source of the legal profession's income. So far as the much more important activity of lawyers in counseling and advising is concerned, the substitution of rules for standards may increase the demand for lawyers' services. Some scraps of evidence support this view. The application of broad standards such as negligence is often entrusted to laymen (jurors); and revolutionary regimes frequently establish popular tribunals in which lawyers do not participate at all, either as judges or as advocates, to decide cases under very general standards. There seems to be some affinity between the felt appropriateness of a lay decision and the choice of standard over rule as the criterion of decision. Why?

A standard is generally a policy, a goal of social action, a societal value—terms that do not denote legal artifacts. Many standards, such as efficiency (reasonableness), have a large intuitive element which makes them compre-

[21] Cf. Richard A. Posner, *supra* note 1, at 402, 426, 435-36.

hensible without special training, while most legal rules are not understood unless studied. Indeed, part of the process of reducing a standard to a set of rules is the elimination of value-laden terms. In some areas of the law, such as automobile driving and (to a limited extent) the income tax, the frequency of the layman's exposure to legal problems makes it worth his while to learn the rules and having done so he can operate in those areas most of the time without any legal assistance. But in other areas either the rules are too complex or their application too infrequent to warrant a layman's mastering the rules. This may be why a distinct profession of lawyers has emerged.

The demand for lawyers is affected not only by the choice between rule and standard but also by whether the rule is statutory or judge-made. Precedents, unlike statutory rules, are typically implicit rather than explicit rules. Higher levels of ability and training are required to master implicit rules. Hence we predict that lawyers will be more numerous and better paid in countries where many legal rules take the form of precedents—such as the United States—and also that competition with lawyers from members of other professions will be more intense in areas of the law characterized by explicit rules, as we observe with accountants in the tax area.

e. We have assumed up to now that an increase in the specificity of a legal prohibition always increases the certainty of the prohibition. This is incorrect; it may reduce it, thereby imposing the sorts of cost usually associated with standards. Compare the following alternative methods of defining the crime of statutory rape: sexual intercourse with a female under 16; sexual intercourse with a female who the defendant knows or should know is under 16. The first rule is more precise on its face than the second, but more uncertain in its application to primary behavior because it may be hard for potential defendants to determine age accurately. The first rule may induce the defendant (especially if risk averse) to confine his attentions to females obviously much older than 16. Observe, however, that it imparts greater certainty than the second rule to the litigation process since, in a legal proceeding, the female's actual age can be ascertained more readily than the defendant's knowledge. As we saw earlier, greater certainty at the litigation stage indirectly increases the efficiency of primary behavior.[22] So the costs of the first rule may be lower than the costs of the second rule after all.

This example makes clear that precision can be measured only by reference to whom the rule is addressed to. It may be precise to one audience (adjudicators), imprecise to another (potential violators). The example also suggests an additional point about the costs of overinclusion: they may be low if the lawful conduct deterred (here, intercourse with females who look younger than 16 but are not) is not considered socially very valuable.

[22] See text following note 12 *supra*.

B. *Implications of the Model*

The elements discussed in the preceding subpart can be brought together in a formal model which can be solved for the optimum number (precision) of statutory and of judge-made rules. The model is based on a social loss function having, as its principal components, the social loss from activities that society wants to prevent, the social loss from the (undesired) deterrence of socially desirable activities, and the costs of producing and enforcing statutory and judge-made rules, including litigation costs. Efficiency is maximized by minimizing the social loss function with respect to two choice variables, the number of statutory rules and the number of judge-made rules. (The mathematical appendix to this article presents a formal version of the model and derives its equilibrium conditions.)

What, the reader may ask, is the practical value of our model-building? The model enables us to test a theory about the nature of the legal process. The theory is that considerations of cost have played an important role in shaping the legal process, specifically with respect to the choice of the degree of precision with which to formulate the commands of the law and the allocation of rulemaking responsibilities among legislatures, courts, and other bodies. The model yields a number of specific, testable implications. If these implications are refuted by empirical study of the legal system, the theory will be disproved. If they are confirmed by empirical study, the theory can be regarded as provisionally supported.

A fundamental implication of the model is that anything that increases the benefits, or reduces the costs, of legal precision, other things remaining the same, will increase the optimum number (precision) of rules. It follows that if economic optimality is important to the actual choices made by society in designing a legal system, we can expect to find (1) more efficient (optimally precise) rules in the criminal area, (2) more overinclusive rules in areas where the sanction is simple damages or where transaction costs are low, and (3) more rules in areas where the relevant primary behavior is homogeneous.

The severity of most criminal penalties is an indication that society considers criminal activity to be socially very costly. That severity also increases the amount of deterrence of those socially desirable activities that might be penalized by mistake. Both considerations suggest that the optimal expenditure on identifying and formulating efficiently detailed rules of criminal liability will be high and that such rules will therefore be produced in great number, especially where, as in the free-speech example, the socially desirable activities that the vague criminal standard might reach are more valuable socially than privately. The economic analysis of rulemaking also predicts that the insistence on precision in criminal rules will be greater the more severe the penalty prescribed for a particular offense. Casual observation supports these predictions of the economic model.

We should expect the proportion of *overinclusive* rules to be higher in areas where either the sanction is simple damages or transaction costs are low than in areas where either the sanction is a punitive one or transaction costs are high, other things being equal. The reason is that the costs of overinclusion, *i.e.*, the social loss from forgoing socially desirable activities because they are prohibited by a rule, are lower in the former circumstances. Again casual observation bears out the predictions of economic analysis. Thus we observe greater use of strict liability in tort and contract than in criminal contexts and we observe heavy use of quite arbitrary rules in areas of the law such as commercial and real-property law where the parties subject to the rules can transact around them at moderate cost. Another area where we can expect, and find, a good deal of overinclusion is illustrated by our statutory-rape example: where the innocent activity that is deterred is not deemed socially very valuable.

The costs of detailedness are lower, the more homogeneous the conduct affected; problems of overinclusion and of underinclusion are less serious. Hence we predict that rules will be more common (other things being equal) in areas of homogeneous conduct—kiting checks compared to murder. We also predict that rules will be more common the older the problem with which they deal. At first a problem area may seem immensely complex and various, but over time elements of commonality will emerge. A tendency toward greater precision of legal obligation as an area of law matures is revealed by casual observation, but there are serious problems in objectively measuring homogeneity and in holding other factors constant (the maturation of a problem area may be accompanied by changes in underlying social or economic conditions that give rise to new problems).

The model also yields a number of implications with respect to the allocation of rulemaking between the legislative and judicial branches of government. For example, as suggested earlier, we expect (and observe) more delegation of legislative power by the United States Congress than by the British Parliament because the costs of producing legislation are lower under the parliamentary system with its well disciplined parties and its effectively unicameral legislature.

A necessary condition of equilibrium in the formal model is that the marginal cost of statutory rules exceed that of judge-made rules. This is because the marginal benefits of statutory rules tend to be greater. Since part of the social cost of any rule is the cost resulting from imperfect specificity, this condition implies that perfect specificity is less likely to be attained in statutory than in judge-made rules, which corresponds to observation. The greater costs of statutory rules may also explain why such rules are generally more difficult to revise or modify than judge-made rules—assuming, reasonably, that the costs of revising a rule are similar to those of creating a new rule.

The model also implies that an increase in the marginal cost of producing statutory rules will lead to a reduction in the optimal number of statutory rules and an increase in the optimal number of judge-made rules. This has interesting consequences for a class of rules that we have ignored thus far —those promulgated by executive or administrative bodies. Assuming that the cost of such rules is lower than that of statutory rules, we would expect administrative rules to be more detailed, and leave less room for supplementary judge-made rules, than statutory rules, and again this appears to be a true description of the real legal system. In a complete analysis, the substitution effects on private rules would also have to be considered; but we exclude private rules from our analysis.

Statutory rules and judge-made rules, although substitutes in reference to exogenous changes in the marginal cost of each, may be complements in reference to other changes. For example, the effect on the optimal number of judge-made rules of an increase in the loss from socially undesirable activities is ambiguous, since, although the marginal social benefits of such rules will be higher, statutory rules are substitutes for judge-made rules.

The model implies that, other things being equal, rules will be more precise the higher the level of economic (or other) activity in the society. The benefits of detailing a rule will be greater the larger the amount of activity governed by it, while the costs of detailing the rule are likely to be independent of the scale (as opposed to the complexity or variety) of the regulated activity.

The model has some interesting implications concerning the legal profession and the financing of the judiciary. Since, as just mentioned, statutory and judge-made rules are substitutes, an exogenous decrease in the former will lead to an increase in the demand for the latter. This helps explain the traditional hostility of the legal profession to the displacement of judge-made ("common law") rules by statutory codes: as noted earlier, the demand for legal services is apt to be greater, the greater the reliance of the legal system on precedent rather than statute. We may also have explained the traditional hostility of the profession to legislative delegation of rulemaking to agencies: the alternative would be delegation to the courts.

We suggested in the last subpart that the importance of precedents in the American legal system may help explain why we have so many more lawyers than other countries do. The model may also help explain why we rely so heavily on litigation to generate legal rules: the costs of producing legislative rules is high in our system, as we have seen, and this serves to increase the optimal number of judicial rules.

Since many judge-made rules are produced in private litigation, there may be a divergence between private and social costs and benefits. In the absence of corrective measures we would expect underproduction of judge-made rules in private litigation because the parties will not take into account the value of any rules they help produce in guiding other people's primary and litigation behavior. This may explain why the government picks up part of the tab for private litigation. The subsidization of judicial salaries, courthouse maintenance, and certain other costs involved in the production of rules results in an increase in that production. A corollary is that subsidization of the courts is unjustifiable on economic grounds in cases where the use of the courts cannot be expected to contribute to the formation or modification of legal rules.

Lastly, the model demonstrates why the process of deciding a case is, in practice, generally *not* one of searching for the optimal resolution of the conflict giving rise to the dispute. Such an approach would imply that decision was always by general standard (*e.g.*, efficiency) rather than by rule, and would be extremely costly. The use of rules to approximate the results that would be reached by case-by-case cost-benefit analyses is fully consistent with the view that the legal system has as a primary goal the maximization of efficiency.

The discussion in this subpart is hardly a proof that the economic model explains the actual choices made by the legal system. But it demonstrates the ability of the model to generate empirically testable hypotheses and the existence of at least suggestive evidence that notions of economic efficiency play a larger role in the legal process than commonly believed. The remainder of the article develops additional implications and evidence.

C. *Implications for the Economic Theory of Deterrence*

Previous economic studies of deterrence explored the effect of changes in the probability and severity of punishment and showed that this probability is determined by the resources devoted to apprehension and conviction, the burden of proof imposed on the prosecutor, and other factors.[23] The specificity of the prohibition has not been mentioned as a variable influencing the probability of punishment and hence the amount of deterrence. Yet it should now be clear that one method of increasing deterrence is to specify the prohibited conduct more exactly.[24]

[23] See, *e.g.*, Gary S. Becker, Crime and Punishment: An Economic Approach, 76 J. Pol. Econ. 169 (1968); Isaac Ehrlich, The Deterrent Effect of Criminal Law Enforcement, 1 J. Leg. Studies 259 (1972); Richard A. Posner, Economic Analysis of Law ch. 25 (1973).

[24] Assuming that the loophole effect (underinclusion) is avoided by backing up the specific prohibition with a general prohibition.

Increasing deterrence through greater specificity of prohibition resembles increasing deterrence through lightening the prosecutor's burden of proof.[25] Both techniques increase the probability of conviction, but the first may do so more effectively. Even if the prosecutor is not required to present much evidence of guilt, the defendant can always invest resources in proof of innocence. When the criterion of guilt is made extremely specific, however, the productivity of additional expenditures by the defendant on the litigation may decline sharply. For example, if the only issue in a speeding case is the speed at which the defendant was driving, an expenditure of resources (say on obtaining witnesses) that might be productive were the issue the reasonableness of his speed in the particular circumstances may be completely futile.

The two techniques are also similar in the nature of the costs that they involve, although the first—greater specificity—may be preferable in this regard too. A relaxation in the prosecutor's burden of proof, other things remaining the same, will result in an increase in the punishment costs borne by innocent people. Assuming some imprecision, the enactment of a specific prohibition is bound to involve the prohibition of—and hence the imposition of expected punishment costs on—innocent activity, too, as in the example of the flat speed limit. However, warned by the specific prohibition that they may be subjecting themselves to criminal liability, those engaged in the innocent activity covered by the prohibition can discontinue the activity as a means of avoiding legal jeopardy. Discontinuance will impose costs. The activities that are substituted must be less valuable—otherwise they would have been substituted before the threat of punishment increased their relative attractiveness. The costs of discontinuance, however, are necessarily smaller than the punishment costs of continuing the activity[26]—otherwise the activity would be continued. People whose exposure to criminal punishment was increased as a result of a reduction in the prosecutor's burden of proof might also want to take steps, including discontinuance of certain lawful activities, to avoid potential liability. But they might find this a good deal more difficult (costly) to do. It is cheaper to avoid a traffic ticket by driving within the speed limit than to take measures that assure one's never being prosecuted for any crime. The specific prohibition indicates precisely what change in one's activities is necessary, and sufficient, to avoid the risk of criminal punishment.

We conclude that increasing the specificity of prohibition is apt to be a more efficient technique for raising the level of deterrence than relaxing the prosecutor's burden of proof would be, or, stated otherwise, that a com-

[25] Analyzed in Richard A. Posner, *supra* note 1, at 410-15.

[26] The expected punishment costs will of course be higher than the product of the probability and severity of punishment if the potential defendant is risk averse.

bination of a heavy burden of proof with highly specific substantive rules of criminal law may be optimal—a pattern we observe in fact. (A complete analysis, however, would consider the interaction of other factors such as severity of penalties.)

The present discussion suggests an explanation of why, in the criminal area, society evinces so marked a preference for rulemaking by legislatures rather than by courts, a preference expressed in the rule that courts may not create new crimes. With the definition of crimes confined to legislatures, and given that legislatures act prospectively,[27] uncertainty with respect to criminal liability is minimized. A person is never forced to speculate about the probable reaction of a court or jury to conduct that, while not the subject of a specific prohibition, might be deemed contrary to some standard of good behavior. He can avoid possible entanglement in the criminal process by refusing to engage in well specified courses of conduct.

III. The Dynamics of Legal Rules

Thus far we have largely ignored the costs and benefits associated with the time dimension of legal regulation. Clearly, however, the efficient (or just) solution to a problem may change over time with changes in the economic and technological factors shaping the problem. For example, the development of the air brake, the spark arrester, the electric crossing signal, the steel car, and other railroad safety devices successively altered the relative costs of accident avoidance by railroads and by potential victims of railroad accidents, obsoleting rules of railroad accident law based on the relative costs of avoidance by injurer and by victim as they had existed prior to the development of the safety devices in question. An important cost of legal regulation by means of rules is thus the cost of altering rules to keep pace with economic and technological change.

Obsolescence is not so serious a problem with regulation by standard. Standards are relatively unaffected by changes over time in the circumstances in which they are applied, since a standard does not specify the circumstances relevant to decision or the weight of each circumstance but merely indicates the kinds of circumstance that are relevant. The standard of efficiency, and its legal counterpart in the accident area, due care, directs the decision maker to determine what behavior by the parties would have minimized the sum of the expected accident costs and the accident-avoidance costs. This precept can be obeyed even though the relevant costs, and hence the optimizing course of conduct, change radically over time. One is therefore not sur-

[27] Unlike courts, legislatures do not impose sanctions for acts committed before the announcement of the rule forbidding those acts. We discuss retrospective and prospective rulemaking further in Part III *infra*.

prised that the negligence standard has changed little since it was introduced some 150 years ago, while specific rules of accident law have changed frequently and substantially.

In general, the more detailed a rule is, the more often it will have to be changed. The greater detailedness of a very precise rule is thus also a source of additional costs, the costs of changing rules. These include the costs, discussed earlier, of producing the new rule plus additional costs arising from the fact that change in the law is a source of uncertainty. A transaction may be subject to a precise and definite rule but if there is a possibility that the rights of the parties to the transaction will in fact be determined by application of a different rule those rights are uncertain. Another name for uncertainty in this context is imperfect precision: if a rule can be changed, one can no longer say definitely that if circumstance X is present, legal consequence Y will follow. Thus the greater the amount of detail in a rule, the lower will be the costs of imperfect precision in one respect and the higher they will be in another.

The rule of stare decisis, which requires that a court adhere to precedent, is founded, in part anyway, on an awareness of the costs in uncertainty of changing rules.[28] Courts in this country do not follow the rule rigidly. It would be highly inefficient for them to do so. As a precedent "ages," a point is eventually reached at which the social costs generated by its imperfect fit with current reality exceed the benefits of having minimized uncertainty as to which rule would be followed. The principal effect of rigid adherence to stare decisis would therefore be to increase the demand for statutory rulemaking regardless of relative cost. Until very recently, the English courts did follow the rule of stare decisis rigidly, but the costs of such adherence were lower for the English than they would have been for Americans if, as suggested earlier,[29] the costs of statutory rulemaking are lower in England than in America.

An important (and testable) implication of this analysis is that stare decisis will be followed more faithfully in substantive areas where transaction costs are low than in areas where they are high. This is because the effect of imprecision in deterring socially valuable activity is less in the former areas.[30]

A legislature is completely free to change a judge-made rule, or its own prior rule. Formally, to be sure, legislative rulemaking is prospective: a statute governs only disputes arising after the rule was enacted. A court if it

[28] Cf. Robert E. Keeton, Creative Continuity in the Law of Torts, 75 Harv. L. Rev. 463 (1962).

[29] See p. 268, *supra*.

[30] See pp. 269-70, 273, *supra*.

announces a new rule will ordinarily (not invariably) apply the rule to the case before it even though the parties at the time of entering into the transaction giving rise to the case believed the transaction to be governed by the old rule. But this difference between legislative and judicial rulemaking is one of degree only: a change in zoning law, though in form prospective, will alter existing property values.

Although legislatures are not subject to any form of stare decisis, they frequently achieve a similar result by "grandfathering" existing activities —that is, by exempting them from the operation of a new rule. In addition, we hypothesize that the marginal costs of legislative production rise very rapidly with legislative output. This imposes some constraint on the practical ability of legislators to revise legislation (or, for that matter, judicial precedents) frequently. If legislators are unlikely to revise legislation frequently in any event, a rule of legislative stare decisis may be largely unnecessary to protect reliance on existing statutes.

The analysis of the dynamics of legal rules may help explain why the number of legal rules has evidently grown over time, at least in the period since the Industrial Revolution. The great increase in the volume of economic activity has increased the costs both of failing to deter socially undesirable activity and of deterring socially desirable activity. This should, by our earlier analysis,[31] have increased the demand for, and hence the quantity supplied of, rules unless the costs of rulemaking have risen equally rapidly.

The dynamic analysis may also explain why the relative importance of legislatures and especially of agencies in the production of rules has grown over time. The trend is noticeable in the torts area among many others. Detailed judge-made rules of liability, so characteristic of the nineteenth century,[32] have given way in this century to detailed traffic and other safety codes that, through the doctrine of "negligence per se," operate as rules of tort liability as well. We hypothesize that the trend is due in part to a decline in the costs of production of legal rules by legislatures and by executive and administrative agencies relative to those of production by the judicial process due to a rise in the rate of economic and technological change over time. Judicial processes are ill suited to the rapid alteration of rules. The delays of the judicial process, coupled with its dependence on a sequential sampling process (described earlier) for the formulation of rules, produce significant lags in judicial response to changing conditions. These lags, more serious in a rapidly changing than in a slowly changing society, may not infect legislative (or nonjudicialized executive or administrative) processes to the same degree. A factor working in the same direction is that

[31] See p. 274, *supra*.

[32] See Richard A. Posner, *supra* note 3.

judicial rulemaking activity lays a foundation for inexpensive legislative rulemaking: legislatures often adopt (codify) the rules made by the courts. The costs of statutory production in this form are presumably low; the benefits, which consist of replacing implicit by explicit rules and hence increasing the certainty of legal obligation and reducing the demand for lawyers' services, may be substantial.

We must also consider, however, the increase over time in the cost of statutory rulemaking brought about by the fact, emphasized earlier in this paper, that legislatures cannot be expanded to handle a rising workload without very sharp increases in the costs of enactment. This problem has been met by increased delegation to administrative agencies (as well as by more flexible principles of statutory construction on the part of both courts and agencies[33]). The importance of agencies, relative to courts, as sources of rules has increased dramatically, and this is consistent with the view that society is seeking to adapt to changes over time in the relative costs of different methods of producing rules.

Finally, we can explain why constitutional provisions are typically vaguer than statutory provisions and why courts generally interpret constitutional provisions more flexibly than they do statutes (sometimes converting a precise constitutional provision into a vague one by refusing to adopt a literal interpretation). The costs of changing constitutional rules are very high. The need for such changes (or, stated differently, the costs of not changing) can be minimized by forgoing precision at the constitution-drafting stage or by courts' treating constitutional rules as though they were standards.[34]

Conclusion

We have sketched in this paper a theory of the legal process according to which the desire to minimize costs is a dominant consideration in the choice between precision and generality in the formulation of legal rules and standards. (We do *not* suggest that the determination of the substantive content of legal rules and standards is dominated by considerations of efficiency to the same extent.) This theory yields a number of testable hypotheses concerning the structure of legal rulemaking and the allocation of rulemaking responsibilities. An admittedly casual survey of existing evidence has uncovered some support for a number of these hypotheses, though systematic empirical work, and considerable refinement of the theory, remain to be done.

[33] See p. 268, *supra*.

[34] Some states have very detailed constitutions. But these are generally states in which amendment is relatively simple (cheap). This is consistent with our analysis.

Mathematical Appendix

The Optimal Precision of Public Rules Under Static Conditions

Our main thesis has been that the extent of efficient precision of public rules as well as the optimal balance between rules promulgated by the legislative, executive, and judicial branches of government is, assuming no externalities in the production of those rules, determined so as to minimize social costs. We have identified the principal components of the social loss function pertinent to this problem as (1) the social loss from activities or outcomes that society wants to prevent, including the loss from the undesired deterrence of activities society wants to promote, henceforth to be denoted by the general function D; (2) the enforcement costs of public rules, including the costs incurred by courts in the production of judge-made rules, to be denoted by the general function C; and (3) the costs of producing statutory and administrative rules, to be denoted by the general function L. Both costs and benefits associated with public rules are defined net of the costs and benefits of the private provision of these rules. For methodological convenience, our formal analysis focuses on the two-way choice between statutory and judge-made rules (precedents) and avoids an explicit analysis of the related choice of administrative rules. The main implications of our analysis also apply, however, to the creation of legal precision through administrative rules.

It is difficult to define rigorously empirical counterparts of the degree of precision of different rules. Theoretically, the precision of a given law can be measured by the number of elementary situations or circumstances that are identified by that law to be either included in or excluded from the universe of circumstances to which a sanction applies. Thus, precision refers to the information content of a law rather than to the number of provisions included in a given law. We shall denote these theoretical measures of the precision of legislation and judge-made rules by the continuous variables r and j, respectively.

According to the analysis developed in Part IIA, each of the general functions D and C include both r and j as arguments. Specifically, we have argued that an increase in efficient precision[85] of the law reduces the incentive to engage in, and thus the social loss from, a socially undesirable activity, including the opportunity costs of forgoing socially desirable activities. Consequently, we assume that the partial derivatives of D with respect to r and j are both negative: $\partial D/\partial r < 0$ and $\partial D/\partial j < 0$. We have also argued that an increase in r reduces the total cost of law enforcement activity directly through reduction in litigation costs, and indirectly through the expected decrease in the number of violations of public rules, or $\partial C/\partial r$

[85] By "efficient precision," we mean precision that does not increase the social costs of the regulated activity. The theoretical constructs r and j are thus defined to exclude any rules that either list the "wrong" set of conditions and circumstances to which a legal sanction is attached or so reduces the opportunities for private production of rules or agreements in particular conflict situations as to offset completely the benefits of public rules.

< 0. In contrast, we have argued that an increase in r always raises the cost of producing statutory rules, including the social costs arising from overinclusive and, sometimes, from underinclusive aspects of rules and from their general rigidity. Formally, then, $\partial L/\partial r > 0$. Finally, as demonstrated below, under a static equilibrium involving a finite level of precision of judge-made rules, we also expect an increase in j to cause a net increase in the total cost of law enforcement activity (notwithstanding its potential negative effect on future litigation and enforcement costs), or $\partial C/\partial j > 0$.

Abstracting from any externalities inherent in the production of, especially, judge-made rules, many of which arise out of private lawsuits, and ignoring the role of potentially conflicting private interests of legislators and lawyers in determining the balance between statutory and judge-made rules, we can find the optimal values of r and j by minimizing the social loss function

$$N = D(r,j) + C(r,j) + L(r) \tag{1}$$

with respect to the choice variables r and j.[36] The first-order necessary conditions for equilibrium are given by:

$$N_1 = \frac{\partial N}{\partial r} = \frac{\partial D}{\partial r} + \frac{\partial C}{\partial r} + \frac{\partial L}{\partial r} = 0 \tag{2}$$

and

$$N_j = \frac{\partial N}{\partial j} = \frac{\partial D}{\partial j} + \frac{\partial C}{\partial j} = 0. \tag{3}$$

An immediate conclusion that can be derived from equations (2) and (3) is that in an equilibrium position involving a finite value of j, the marginal cost of judge-made rules must be positive in order that the positive marginal social benefits they confer are exactly offset.[37] This conclusion only applies at the margin, however, and need not apply to the majority of judge-made rules that are produced under static conditions. *A fortiori,* the net marginal costs of producing statutory rules—the sum of $\frac{\partial C}{\partial r}$ and $\frac{\partial L}{\partial r}$—also must be positive in equilibrium.

[36] In equation (1), the total cost of statutory rules, L, is specified as a function of r alone. In principle, however, these costs may also be influenced by the degree of precision of judge-made rules, j, because rules promulgated in court could in some cases reduce the costs of negotiating agreements among legislators concerning the efficacy or desirability of further specification of a related legal principle. This would generally be the case if a statutory rule simply formalized a set of judicial precedents. In our formal analysis we distinguish between statutory and judge-made rules according to their original production source—we are not concerned here with their final labeling. We therefore ignore the possible effects of the level of j on the marginal cost of r.

[37] If the marginal social benefits associated with the judicial ruling in private litigation are zero, as would be the case when the ruling applied to unique circumstances unlikely to recur in conflict situations involving persons other than the litigants themselves, then the marginal social benefits are zero, and the optimal marginal costs of judge-made rules should also be zero. Put differently, the costs of such rules should be borne entirely by private litigants with no implicit public subsidization of their production. The optimal number of such judicial rulings would be determined by the same set of factors that determines the incentives to go to court.

The production of detailed statutory and judge-made rules as a means of increasing the precision of a particular legislation is analogous to the production of closely-related goods in different firms. If both "goods" and both "firms" were identical, one might generally expect the same contribution to the precision of legislation to be made by either statutory or judge-made rules, provided that the marginal costs of their production were ultimately rising. But statutory and judge-made rules are not perfect substitutes, and the costs associated with their production are intrinsically different, as we have argued in the text. Specifically, judge-made rules are initiated largely as a result of private litigations, and these are likely to apply to a relatively narrow range of circumstances surrounding a regulated activity. In contrast, statutory rules generally apply to a broader and more general set of circumstances. The marginal deterrent effect of statutory rules on participation in socially undesirable or less than optimal activities (0) may then be expected to exceed that of judge-made rules, or, since $\frac{\partial 0}{\partial r} < \frac{\partial 0}{\partial j}$,

$$\frac{\partial D}{\partial r} \equiv D_0 \frac{\partial 0}{\partial r} < \frac{\partial D}{\partial j} \equiv D_0 \frac{\partial 0}{\partial j}. \tag{4}$$

Assuming the validity of equation (4), our analysis implies that in equilibrium, the marginal cost of statutory rules must exceed that of judge-made rules, since, by subtracting equation (3) from equation (2), one finds that

$$\frac{\partial C}{\partial r} + \frac{\partial L}{\partial r} - \frac{\partial C}{\partial j} = -\left[\frac{\partial D}{\partial r} - \frac{\partial D}{\partial j}\right] > 0. \tag{5}$$

Put differently, and perhaps more intriguingly, since part of the social cost of a detailed law stems from over- and underinclusion of relevant facts and circumstances and from rigidities and other imperfections, one may expect such imperfections to be more prevalent in statutory than in judge-made rules. This conclusion is consistent with the suggestion that statutory rules tend to be more out of date or anachronistic than judge-made rules, for the remaking of a statutory rule, which essentially amounts to the production of a new rule, is more costly than the remaking of a judge-made rule.

Values of r and j that satisfy equations (2) and (3) would minimize equation (1) locally if the following set of second-order conditions is also satisfied:

$$N_{rr} \equiv \frac{\partial^2 N}{\partial r^2} = D_{rr} + C_{rr} + L_{rr} > 0 \tag{6}$$

$$N_{jj} \equiv \frac{\partial^2 N}{\partial j^2} = D_{jj} + C_{jj} > 0 \tag{7}$$

$$\Sigma \equiv N_{rr} N_{jj} - [N_{rj}]^2 > 0, \tag{8}$$

where $N_{rj} \equiv \frac{\partial^2 N}{\partial r \partial j} = D_{rj} + C_{rj}$. It is plausible to expect an increase in the level of efficiently detailed statutory or judge-made rules alone to be associated with diminishing marginal social benefits and with increasing marginal social costs, due to diminished opportunities for the production of private rules, on the one hand, and to diminishing returns to scale in the production of precise public rules on the other. Therefore the signs of D_{rr}, D_{jj}, C_{rr} and C_{jj} are expected to be positive. The inequality signs in equations (6) and (7) are thus satisfied. *A fortiori*, since r and j provide a similar service in reducing socially undesirable activities and litigation costs, the signs of D_{rj} and C_{rj} are also expected to be positive. Presumably, however, $D_{rj} \leqslant D_{rr}, D_{jj}$ and $C_{rj} \leqslant C_{rr}, C_{jj}$, because judicial rules, which may in many cases further detail related statutory rules, partly complement the negative effects of the latter on the incentives to participate in undesirable activities and to go to court. These assumptions concerning the relative magnitudes of D_{rj} and C_{rj} provide the sufficient conditions to satisfy equation (8).

The optimality conditions summarized in equations (2), (3), (6), (7) and (8) have so far been explicitly defined as functions of the endogenous variables of the legal system, r and j. However, the social loss functions D, C, and L also depend on exogenous variables. These include the extent of external economies and diseconomies that are associated with activities under public regulation, factors affecting the magnitudes of the cost of producing r and j and the costs of producing private agreements in the absence of explicitly defined public rules, and related variables that change over time and across different areas of the law.

We now develop some comparative-statics implications that are associated with such changes. One may first notice that an exogenous increase in r, due, say, to various institutional changes (or historical reasons), leads to a reduction in the optimal value of j. Formally, let r be an increasing function of the exogenous parameter α; then, denoting the optimal value of j by j*, one obtains:

$$\frac{dj^*}{d\alpha} = \frac{-D_{rj} - C_{rj}}{N_{jj}} = \frac{(-)}{(+)} < 0. \tag{9}$$

Put differently, statutory and judge-made rules are found to be substitutes in the sense that an exogenous increase in statutory precision reduces the optimal amount of judicial precision. More generally, an increase in the marginal cost of producing statutory rules can be shown to decrease the optimal precision of these rules and increase the optimal precision of judge-made rules. For, if $\frac{\partial L}{\partial r}$ is an increasing function of the exogenous parameter, β, then

$$\frac{dr^*}{d\beta} = \frac{-(\partial L/\partial r \partial \beta) N_{jj}}{\Sigma} = \frac{(-)}{(+)} < 0, \tag{10}$$

and

$$\frac{dj^*}{d\beta} = \frac{-(\partial L/\partial r \partial \beta)(-N_{rj})}{\Sigma} = \frac{(+)}{(+)} > 0. \tag{11}$$

The converse must also hold, of course, and can be proved by a similar analysis.

This analysis implies that legal systems in which statutory rules are less costly to produce due, say, to an effectively unicameral legislature will exhibit relatively little tendency to delegate legislative power to the judicial or executive branch of government. Other systems, such as that in the United States, will exhibit a greater tendency to delegate such power.

Although r and j appear to be substitutes in terms of the effect of an increase in the shadow price of each, they may be complements with respect to a change in other parameters. For example, the partial effects of an increase in the marginal social damage from violations of a certain law, D_0, and thus in the marginal social benefits from efficiently detailed rules pertaining to this law, are given by

$$\frac{dr^*}{d\gamma} = \frac{-\frac{\partial O}{\partial r}(D_{jj} + C_{jj}) + \frac{\partial O}{\partial j}(D_{rj} + C_{rj})}{\Sigma} \frac{\partial D_0}{\partial \gamma}$$

$$= \frac{(+) + (-)}{(+)} = \frac{(+)}{(+)} > 0 \tag{12}$$

and by

$$\frac{dj^*}{d\gamma} = \frac{-\frac{\partial O}{\partial j}(D_{rr} + C_{rr} + L_{rr}) + \frac{\partial O}{\partial r}(D_{rj} + C_{rj})}{\Sigma} \frac{\partial D_0}{\partial \gamma}$$

$$= \frac{(+) + (-)}{(+)} = \frac{?}{(+)} = ? \tag{13}$$

where γ is an exogenous shift parameter associated with D_0, and $\frac{\partial D_0}{\partial \gamma} > 0$.

Equation (12) is positive in sign by equation (4), and by the assumptions that $D_{rj} \leqslant D_{rr}$, D_{jj} and $C_{rj} \leqslant C_{rr}$, C_{jj}. In contrast, the sign of equation (13) is ambiguous: the increase in D_0 increases the marginal social benefits from judge-made rules but at the same time increases the marginal social benefits from statutory rules by an even greater amount. Since r and j are substitutes, the optimal value of j may or may not rise, depending upon the magnitude of the offsetting effect from a rise in the level of r* relative to the direct effect of the rise in the social benefits from precision. A direct implication of this analysis is that in areas of legislation in which the costs of producing precise rules are not substantially different, the degree of precision with which legal rules are promulgated will be positively correlated with the degree of severity attributed to violations of the respective rules. Rules governing felonies in criminal law may thus be expected to be more precise than those governing misdemeanors, especially as far as statutory rules are concerned.

The marginal social benefits from statutory and judge-made rules are a function not only of the social damage from pursuing illegal and other suboptimal activities, D_0, but also of the overall deterrent effect of precise rules, given by the terms

$\frac{\partial O}{\partial r}$ and $\frac{\partial O}{\partial j}$. The latter effects may be expected to be monotonically increasing functions of the size of the "market" in which public rules apply. In contrast, the costs of producing precise public rules are primarily related to the composition and structure of the legislative and the judicial branches of government and are largely independent of the market size—the overall number of potential violations and illegal disputes within the relevant legal jurisdiction. Formally, then, the effect of market size on the optimal values of r and j can be addressed through the partial effect of a change in the absolute magnitudes of $\frac{\partial O}{\partial r}$ and $\frac{\partial O}{\partial j}$ due to a shift in the exogenous parameter δ alone. The results are given by

$$\frac{dr^*}{d\delta} = \frac{-D_0(D_{jj} + C_{jj}) + D_0(D_{rj} + C_{rj})}{\Sigma}\frac{\partial O}{\partial r\partial\delta} = \frac{(+) + (-)}{(+)} = \frac{(+)}{(+)} > 0, \tag{14}$$

and by

$$\frac{dj^*}{d\delta} = \frac{-D_0(D_{rr} + C_{rr} + L_{rr}) + D_0(D_{rj} + C_{rj})}{\Sigma}\frac{\partial O}{\partial j\partial\delta} = \frac{(+) + (-)}{(+)} = \frac{(+)}{(+)} > 0, \tag{15}$$

where $\frac{\partial O}{\partial r\partial\delta} < 0$.

A uniform increase in the overall deterrent effect of efficiently detailed public rules due to an increase in market size is thus found to have an unambiguous positive effect on the optimal level of precision of both statutory and judge-made rules, a conclusion that may be testable against the historical trends in the degree of legal detailedness within given areas of legislation.

[7]

WHY IS THE COMMON LAW EFFICIENT?

*PAUL H. RUBIN**

POSNER, in *Economic Analysis of Law,*[1] argues persuasively that the common law can be best understood as an attempt to achieve economic efficiency. He is less persuasive in his explanation of why this is so—his argument is essentially that judges may as well decide in terms of efficiency, since they have no other criteria to use. To an economist accustomed to invisible hand[2] explanations of efficiency in the marketplace, this justification seems weak.

Of related interest is the analysis by Landes,[3] Gould,[4] and Tullock[5] of the decision to litigate a dispute rather than settle. All have concluded that, in general, parties will settle out of court. But, for the common law to remain efficient, it must change as conditions change; changes in the common law require that some cases be litigated. Does the rationality of the common law rest on irrational behavior of litigants?

In this paper I show that these issues—the presumed efficiency of the common law and the decision to use the courts to settle a dispute—are related. In particular, this relationship will occur because resorting to court settlement is more likely in cases where the legal rules relevant to the dispute are inefficient, and less likely where the rules are efficient. Thus, efficient rules may evolve from in-court settlement, thereby reducing the incentive for future litigation and increasing the probability that efficient rules will persist. In short, the efficient rule situation noted by Posner is due to an evolutionary mechanism whose direction proceeds from the utility maximizing decisions of disputants rather than from the wisdom of judges.

Section I of this paper contains an analysis of the framework which will be used to discuss pressures for efficiency. Section II contains the actual analy-

* Associate Professor of Economics, University of Georgia. The author would like to thank Gordon Tullock, Carl Jordan, and an anonymous referee for comments on an earlier version of this paper.

[1] Richard A. Posner, Economic Analysis of Law (1972).

[2] For a general discussion of invisible hand explanations, see Robert Nozick, Anarchy, State and Utopia (1974).

[3] William M. Landes, An Economic Analysis of the Courts, 14 J. Law & Econ. 61 (1971).

[4] John P. Gould, The Economics of Legal Conflicts, 2 J. Leg. Studies 279 (1973).

[5] Gordon Tullock, The Logic of the Law (1971).

sis, in which it is shown that efficiency occurs in situations where both parties to a dispute have an ongoing interest in cases, and that efficiency need not occur if one or both parties do not have such an ongoing interest. Section III contains some complications and extensions. The last section is a summary.

I. General Framework

Throughout this paper, I use an example of accident liability to illustrate the arguments. The particular example does not matter, for, as Posner has shown, torts, property, and contract law can all be analyzed within the same framework.[6] Suppose there is a certain type of accident which costs X when it occurs. Parties of type B are the victims and parties of type A the defendants if the accident occurs. Liability may be placed on A or on B. If liability is placed on A, the optimal solution for A is to spend S_A on accident avoidance and allow N_A accidents to occur; conversely, if liability is placed on B, S_B will be spent on avoidance and N_B accidents will occur. Assume also that this is an either/or situation: the technology of avoidance in this case is such that there is no joint action which A and B could take to further reduce accident and prevention costs. For purposes of analysis, assume that it is efficient for liability to be placed on B; that is,

$$T_B = S_B + N_BX < S_A + N_AX = T_A \qquad (1)$$

where T_A and T_B represent total present value of accident costs plus prevention costs for parties A and B respectively. Equation (1) indicates that this total cost is less if B is liable than if A is liable.

Efficiency requires that A not be made liable for the accident; the most efficient solution is for B to spend S_B and for there to be N_B accidents. Whether B will spend S_B on avoidance or A will spend S_A depends on the current liability assignment—that is, on the decision which the parties expect the courts to reach if there is an accident and litigation occurs. Courts are somewhat bound by precedent. Thus, if precedents favor B, then S_A will be spent and total accident costs will be T_A; conversely if precedents favor A. (Because we have eliminated the possibility of joint action, one situation or the other will occur.)

Define R as the probability that B will win the suit if an accident occurs and the parties litigate. The value of R is defined by precedent: if $R > .5$, precedents favor B and B is likely to win if the case is litigated. If $R < .5$ precedents favor A. We assume throughout the paper that both parties agree on the value of R. The current liability assignment is then efficient if $R < .5$. It is assumed throughout that judges are likely but not certain to decide on

[6] Richard A. Posner, *supra* note 1, at 98-102.

the basis of precedent. As shown below, it is the possibility of changing current precedents which sometimes makes litigation worthwhile and which will in some circumstances lead to efficiency.

The Coase theorem[7] indicates that placement of liability does not matter: if A were made liable, he would simply pay a bribe to B in order to induce B to avoid accidents; as indicated by (1), this would be the efficient solution. This will in fact occur if the costs of paying the bribe are sufficiently low; however, it is possible that the transactions costs will be greater than (T_A-T_B), the saving from shifting liability to the efficient bearer. In this case, if he is liable, A will accept liability rather than paying B. Even if it is feasible for A to bribe B, there will be some transactions costs involved in paying the bribe. In Section II, it is assumed that paying a bribe is not feasible; in Section III the case of feasible bribery is examined.

II. Analysis

Given the basic situation discussed above, there are some cases in which there will be pressure for the law to evolve towards efficiency. The crucial point is the interest which the parties have in decisions as precedents. Thus, some legal cases involve individuals with a one-time interest in the outcome, while other cases involve corporate bodies of some sort—government agencies, labor unions, firms, insurance companies. Such organizations would have an interest in legal cases as precedents as well as interests as litigants.[8] Insurance companies, for example, would be concerned with future liability cases as well as with a particular case. In analyzing the relation between efficiency and litigation, there are three basic situations which must be considered. In part A, the situation in which both parties have a substantial interest in the case as precedent will be considered. Part B discusses the situation in which only one party is interested in the case as precedent. Part C considers the situation where neither party is interested in the case as precedent.

A. *Both Parties Interested in Precedent*

If both parties to a certain type of legal dispute have a substantial interest in future cases of this sort, then precedents will evolve towards efficiency, the common law situation posited by Posner. If rules are inefficient, there will be an incentive for the party held liable to force litigation; if rules are efficient, there will be no such incentive. Thus, efficient rules will be maintained, and inefficient rules litigated until overturned.

[7] R. H. Coase, The Problem of Social Cost, 3 J. Law & Econ. 1 (1960).

[8] Richard A. Posner, The Behavior of Administrative Agencies, 1 J. Leg. Studies 305 (1972), discusses the interest of agencies in settling cases for use as precedents.

Substantial interest in precedent refers to a situation in which the party is likely to be in many such cases in the future. In effect, such parties are concerned with the entire stream of costs, T_A or T_B, rather than with X, the damages from one particular accident. Start with an inefficient rule—A is held liable if accidents occur, so that A is now spending S_A on accident avoidance and N_AX on damage payments for those accidents which still occur. An accident has just occurred; the parties must decide whether to settle or litigate.

If the case is litigated and B wins, he is paid X; if A wins, he does not pay X in this case, and, in addition, A saves T_A in the future, but B must begin to pay T_B. Court costs for each party are C. The value to A of a court settlement is

$$V_A = R(-X) + (1-R)T_A - C \quad (2)$$

and to B:

$$V_B = R(X) + (1-R)(-T_B) - C \quad (3)$$

The parties can settle out of court if

$$-V_A > V_B \quad (4)$$

which simply says that a settlement can be reached if the expected loss to A of going to court is greater than the expected gain to B. If this is so, there is room for negotiation. Conversely, if (4) is not satisfied, the parties will litigate. In this example, litigation will occur if

$$(1-R)(T_A-T_B) > 2C \quad (5)$$

Here, T_A-T_B is the cost of the inefficient legal rule. As this becomes larger, litigation is more likely. Conversely, as R becomes larger (that is, as the inefficient rule is more entrenched) litigation is less likely. As court costs are higher, litigation is less likely. Finally, if the current rule were efficient (that is, if T_B were greater than T_A), (5) would never be satisfied, so that there would be no litigation.

What will happen? If the parties go to court, B will probably win, since both parties agree that $R > .5$. However, whenever this stituation arises in the future A will again go to court. At some point, some court will find in favor of A; at this point, the law has been changed and is now efficient. From that time on, precedents will favor A in comparable cases. Since there is no deadweight loss to party B when he is forced to bear liability (i.e., no term comparable to T_A-T_B), B will not find it worthwhile to go to court when such an accident occurs; instead, B will spend S_B on avoiding such accidents and bear the cost N_BX of those which do occur.

It is now possible to define precisely the meaning of substantial interest.

A's interest in this sort of case is substantial precisely if T_A is large enough so that (5) is satisfied. As this problem has been defined, it is not relevant whether B has a substantial interest or not; however, as we will see in the next section, both parties must have a substantial interest if efficiency is to be guaranteed.

What if both parties are insurance companies with ongoing interests as either defendants or plaintiffs? Then both A and B become interested in $T_A - T_B$, the efficiency savings from future cases. It can easily be shown that, if both parties are equally likely to be on either side of such cases in the future, (5) is unchanged so that the pressure for efficiency will be maintained.

We have thus shown that if rules are inefficient, parties will use the courts until the rules are changed; conversely, if rules are efficient, the courts will not be used and the efficient rule will remain in force. An outside observer coming upon this legal rule would observe that the rule is efficient; but this efficiency occurs because of an evolutionary process, not because of any particular wisdom on the part of judges. If judges decide independently of efficiency, we would still find efficient rules. Intelligent judges may speed up the process of attaining efficiency; they do not drive the process.

B. *Only One Party Interested in Precedent*

If only one party to a dispute is interested in future cases of this sort, there will be pressure for precedents to evolve in favor of that party which does have a stake in future cases, whether or not this is the efficient solution. This is because a party with a stake in future decision will find it worthwhile to litigate as long as liability rests with him; conversely, a party with no stake in future decisions will not find litigation worthwhile.

Let us continue our example: an accident has happened to a certain B. As the law now stands A is likely to win the case—that is, $R < .5$, and both parties agree on the value of R. However, B has a stake in the result of this decision; A has no such stake. That is, this type of case is an ongoing case for B, but a one time case for A. If B goes to court and wins, then in the future he will save S_B per period. T_B is the present value of the stream of accident costs to B as long as he is liable. Thus, if the courts are used and B wins, he receives X from A as a result of this accident; in addition, he saves T_B in the future. On the other hand, if A wins, he does not pay X; A is, by assumption, not interested in future decision. The value to A of a court case is:

$$V_A = R(-X) - C \tag{6}$$

and the value to B is:

$$V_B = R(X) + R(T_B) - C \tag{7}$$

In this case, A will be willing to pay R(X) + C to avoid a court settlement; B will be willing to accept $R(X) + R(T_B) - C$. Therefore, there will be no settlement if

$$R(T_B) > 2C \tag{8}$$

From (8), we see that, unless R is very small (that is, unless precedents are extremely clear and unfavorable to B), or unless court costs are large, B will find litigation worthwhile. Moreover, each time such an accident occurs, B will again go to court rather than settling. As such behavior continues, at some point some court may rule in B's favor. At this point the rule favors B, and B will therefore cease taking precautions to avoid accidents. Rather, party A will begin spending S_A on accident avoidance. When such accidents again occur, the A who is involved will pay X to B, rather than litigate, since A has no future interest in the case.

This same argument could be turned around: if A has an ongoing interest in this type of case and B does not, then A will go to court until a favorable ruling is obtained; from this time on, precedents will favor A, and this rule will persist, since no B will find litigation worthwhile. Thus, when one party has an ongoing interest in a type of case there is a tendency for cases to be litigated until a precedent is established which favors this party. There is no tendency for efficiency in this situation.

This case appears to describe the evolution of nuisance law in the nineteenth century.[9] By the end of this century, those causing nuisances were largely factories, which would have ongoing interests in liability rulings; conversely, those suffering from nuisances were largely individuals with no such interest. (That is, factories were concerned with T_B, but individuals were indifferent to T_A.) The evidence indicates that nuisance law did in fact largely favor factories and firms, rather than individuals.

C. *No Interest in Precedent*

If neither party is interested in precedents, the current rule will persist, whether it is efficient or inefficient. That is, if neither party has an ongoing interest in cases of this sort, then neither will force use of the courts. All such cases will be settled on the basis of the current rule, whatever it might be. Since cases will not go to court, there will be no pressure to change this rule.

Again begin with the situation in which an accident has occurred. A certain party of type B has lost X and is considering suing the party A who is liable. Both parties agree that the probability of B winning is R. If there is no

[9] See Joel Franklin Brenner, Nuisance Law and the Industrial Revolution, 3 J. Leg. Studies 403 (1974), for a discussion which is consistent with this argument.

interest in precedent, then the exact value of R is irrelevant for our purposes. We assume risk neutrality since, as we shall indicate below, risk aversion would complicate the analysis without changing the results.

Clearly, if this is the entire problem, the parties should settle. To A the expected value of a court settlement is

$$V_A = -RX - C \tag{9}$$

and to B it is

$$V_B = RX - C. \tag{10}$$

The parties can settle out of court if (4) is satisfied; this becomes

$$RX + C > RX - C \tag{11}$$

which is obviously met. Thus rather than going to court, A can pay some amount L to B, where

$$RX - C < L < RX + C \tag{12}$$

and this will be better than a court settlement for both parties. This is the essence of the arguments as to why most cases may be expected to be settled out of court. If the parties are risk averse, we replace terms in (9) and (10) with their utility equivalents. For risk averse individuals, the utility of a lottery is less than the utility of the expected value of the lottery; thus, in (4) the left side becomes relatively larger and the right side relatively smaller. Risk aversion makes out of court settlements relatively more likely.

In this situation, the courts will be used only if the parties disagree about the value of R. However, there is no reason to assume that such disagreement is related to the efficiency of current rules. Thus, as long as there is agreement about the probability of decisions, the legal rule will not change; and if there is disagreement and consequent pressure for rule change, there is no presumption that changes would be in the direction of increased efficiency. This situation is presumably that which exists when disputants are individuals with little ongoing interest in solutions. Furthermore, disputes would ordinarily be settled in accordance with current legal rules; it would be unusual for such cases to go to court, and there is no presumption that rules in such cases would be efficient. However, to the extent that the types of legal cases involving individuals are the same types of cases as those involving corporate bodies, this conclusion must be modified for, as we have seen, there is pressure for efficiency in the latter type of case, whereas individual disputants will accept the existing rule, whether it is efficient or not.[10]

[10] See Section III, C.

III. Some Complications

In this section I consider in turn: situations in which bribery is feasible; costs of out-of-court settlements; public good problems; situations in which different types of parties are interested in the same type of case; and some applications to statute law.

A. *Bribery*

Assume again that liability is currently inefficiently assigned—that, A is liable. As mentioned in Section I, it may be possible in this case for A to bribe B to take precautions, rather than taking precautions himself. As before, define T_A and T_B as the present value of the stream of costs if liability is placed, respectively, on A or B; from (1) we know that

$$T_B < T_A. \tag{13}$$

Define T_N as the present value of costs to A of bribing B to take precautions. T_N would include normal aspects of transactions costs—costs of finding the relevant B, of actually making the payments, of monitoring B's behavior, etc. A will find it worthwhile to bribe B if

$$T_N < T_A - T_B \tag{14}$$

that is, if the cost of paying the bribe is less than the saving from taking efficient precautions. Even in this case, however, there is a deadweight loss—an efficiency loss caused by the actual cost of paying the bribe, T_N.

Even with the bribe, there will still be N_A accidents per period. One of these accidents has occurred. A is now liable to pay X to the injured B. As above, A must decide whether to pay or to litigate. If A settles out of court or loses the case in court, he must then spend $T_N + T_B$; he must continue to negotiate with parties B and pay the accident costs of these parties. If B loses, then he must pay T_B—that is, in the future A will not be liable if this type of accident occurs, so that B will spend S_B on avoiding such accidents. In addition, if B loses, he will not be paid X, damages in the accident which has already occurred. Thus, there is a $(1-R)$ chance of B losing T_B. For A, the expected value of going to court becomes

$$V_A = R(-X) + (1-R)(T_B + T_N) - C \tag{15}$$

and for B

$$V_B = R(X) + (1-R)(-T_B) - C. \tag{16}$$

This occurs because, once A has won a case, the law is changed—precedents now favor A, rather than B. This is the essence of judge made common law.

The parties will again settle out of court if (4) is satisfied; but this now becomes

$$(1-R)T_N < 2C. \tag{17}$$

They will go to court if (17) is reveresed:

$$(1-R)T_N > 2C \tag{18}$$

The parties will go to court if the expected present value of the costs to A of negotiating with B in the future to have B take precautions is greater than the total court costs. What has happened is that T_N, the present value of these negotiation costs, is a cost to A but not a gain to B. The stakes in the case are asymmetrical, so that there is less possibility of a settlement between the parties. Notice also that T_N is in this situation the present cost of the inefficient legal rule.

The situation described above is again that in which both parties have an ongoing interst in decisions. It is likely that this will be the only relevant situation for bribes; if B does not have such an interest, then it is likely that B will be unidentifiable in advance. In this case, it is likely that the cost of A of bribing B would be prohibitive, and the analysis used in Section II B would be relevant.

Notice also that there is no relationship between court costs and bribery (transactions) costs. The decision as to whether or not to bribe B is made before the accident occurs; the decision as to whether to go to court is made after an accident has happened. Our argument is that A is likely to go to court to save *future* transactions costs. Of course, as shown in (18), if court costs are high enough relative to the present value of transactions costs, the case will be settled; but this simply says that if court costs are greater than the costs of the inefficiency imbedded in the current rule it is not worth changing the rule.

B. *Settlement Costs*

Throughout, we have ignored the costs of settling the dispute out of court. This action will have some costs, and as these costs increase, the probability of going to court increases. Formally, such costs can be included in our analysis simply by redefining C everywhere as net court costs—the difference between court costs and settlement costs. The level of net court costs is itself an important parameter in our models. As can be seen from (5) and (18) the courts are more likely to be used in overturning inefficient rules as court costs are smaller. Gould[11] has argued that high court costs have the desirable effect of reducing inefficient litigation; but it must be pointed out that such

11. John P. Gould, *supra* note 4, at 296.

costs also have the undesirable effect of reducing efficient litigation—litigation aimed at overturning inefficient rules.

C. *Different Types of Parties, Same Type of Case*

In Section II we saw that when only one party has an ongoing interest in a type of case, precedents could be expected to evolve in favor of that party. Conversely, when both parties have an interest, precedents should evolve toward efficiency. However, it is possible that some cases of a certain type will involve only one party with an ongoing interest, while other cases of the same sort will involve two such parties. In this situation, there could easily arise a conflict—when only one party has an ongoing interest, the inefficient solution may be favored, while when both have such an interest the efficient solution will be favored.

It is possible that cases of this sort would be continually litigated. However, if this were to happen, parties would observe that precedents would not be binding, and this would reduce the incentive for litigation. A more likely solution is for parties to differentiate the cases, so that one sort of precedent would govern cases with one corporate body and a different set of precedents would govern cases with two corporate bodies. The law would then be inconsistent; but no litigant would have an incentive to capitalize on this inconsistency, and therefore it would continue to exist.[12] This explanation for legal inconsistency would seem to be a fruitful area of research for scholars trained in the law.

D. *Public Good Problems*

Once a decision is reached in a case, the decision is a public good.[13] It affects all parties of type A and B. Thus, a party of type A may decide not to litigate a case, even if such litigation would be efficient, in the hope that some other A may do the litigating and save the original A court costs. However, Equations (5) or (18) are not particularly stringent: In many cases, court costs are not prohibitively high. Nonetheless, we might expect some free rider problems. Our model would predict, for example, that large companies would be involved relatively more in litigation than would small companies.

[12] It might appear that the inconsistency would lead some disputants to litigate in the hope of capitalizing on the inconsistency. However, both parties would be aware of this possibility, and thus there would be no asymmetry. Our analysis rests on assuming that litigation occurs only when there is an asymmetry between parties.

[13] See Gordon Tullock, Public Decisions as Public Goods, 99 J. Pol. Econ. 913 (1971).

E. *Application to Statute Law*

Statute law is often inefficient.[14] However, in some cases lobbying for passage of statute law can take the place of deciding to litigate in our model.[15] Thus, if some law were proposed benefitting one well defined small group at the expense of another well defined small group, and if the group which would lose would lose more than the gaining group would gain (*i.e.*, if the law were inefficient), then the potential losers would be able to outspend the potential gainers, so that we would not expect the law to be passed. Thus, we would expect that inefficient statute laws would correspond to our analysis of the situation in which only one party has an interest in precedent; that is, such laws would be passed at the expense of large groups which would not be able to effectively lobby against their passage because of free rider problems.

IV. Summary

We have shown that the efficiency of the common law, to the extent that it exists, can be explained by an evolutionary model—a model in which it is more likely that parties will litigate inefficient rules than efficient rules. If decisions are made randomly, there will be a movement in the direction of efficient laws. The same model provides an explanation for using the courts to settle some disputes, rather than relying on out of court settlements.

The evolutionary pressure comes from behavior of litigants, rather than judges. We therefore found it useful to study behavior of potential litigants, classified according to their interest in cases as precedents. We found that when neither party is interested in precedent, there is no incentive to litigate, and hence, no pressure on the law to change. When only one party is interested in precedent, that party will litigate until a favorable decision is obtained; the law in such cases will favor parties with such an ongoing interest. When both parties have an ongoing interest in a type of case, there will be pressure toward efficiency. When different types of parties have an interest in the same type of case, we would expect inconsistencies to exist in the law.

Finally, we would predict that the evolution toward efficiency, in those cases where there would be such an evolution, would be faster as current rules are more inefficient, as net courts costs (court costs less settlement costs) are lower, and as inefficient rules are less soundly entrenched.

[14] Paul H. Rubin, On the Form of Special Interest Legislation, 21 Public Choice 79 (1975).

[15] This point is due to Gordon Tullock.

ADDENDUM: COMMENT ON "THE COMMON LAW PROCESS AND THE SELECTION OF EFFICIENT RULES"

Professor George L. Priest in his comment[16] has provided a valuable extension of my results. However, this extension is purchased at some cost, and this cost is perhaps greater than Priest himself realizes. It appears that his relatively informal discussion in fact hides some of his assumptions. He is of necessity assuming something more than ". . . that transactions costs in the real world are positive."[17]

I assume throughout my paper that both parties agree on the probabilities of victory for each of them. Priest claims that he avoids this assumption, and that I make the assumption for "expositional convenience."[18] This is not so: the assumption is made for substantive, not expositional, reasons. One must make some assumption about probability estimates of the parties; it is my feeling that the assumption of equal probability assessments is more easily justified than Priest's implicit assumption of differing estimates. Specifically, rational informed individuals (or their attorneys) will have the same estimates about probabilities of any given judicial decision. To assume otherwise is tantamount to assuming ignorance by one or both parties, and as a methodological principle I prefer to avoid assuming any such ignorance wherever possible. Once ignorance is assumed, it is very easy to prove anything, and thus to derive tautological models. Priest's form of the ignorance assumptions—that each party is as likely as the other to misjudge probabilities of victory—is perhaps more innocuous than most such assumptions, but it is nonetheless an assumption I prefer to avoid.

(Priest does not explicitly make any assumption about probability estimates. However, it is a well known result that rational, risk neutral or risk averse individuals with symmetric stakes in a case will not go to law. Thus, cases will be litigated only if one of these assumptions is violated. I assume asymmetric stakes to motivate my litigants. Priest denies this assumption; therefore, he must be assuming different probability estimates. He claims to be concerned only with the number of cases which will be litigated under alternative rules and not with the motives for such litigation. But it is dangerous to make assumptions about aggregate behavior without considering the behavior of the individuals which make up the aggregate.)

In this paper I desired to show how litigation would occur in a world with no ignorance, and how efficiency would be achieved in such a world. Specifically, I desired to show how rational behavior of litigants would lead to

[16] George L. Priest, The Common Law Process and the Selection of Efficient Rules, 6 J. Legal Studies 65 (1977).

[17] *Ibid.*

[18] *Id.* at 73, n. 18.

efficiency of legal decisions. I succeeded in this. Of course, to the extent that parties to disputes do in fact disagree about probabilities, Priest's mechanism would obtain, and his comment is to this extent a valuable extension of the model. However, I feel that the process described in this paper would be empirically more important in driving rules to efficiency than would Priest's process, for litigation will invariably occur if stakes are asymmetrical in my model, while Priest's mechanism is driven by random errors in perception by the parties.

I agree fully with Priest's point about judges. As stated in various places in my paper, the evolutionary model which I develop focuses attention on decisions of potential and actual litigants rather than on judges in driving the model.

[8]

THE COMMON LAW PROCESS AND THE SELECTION OF EFFICIENT RULES

*GEORGE L. PRIEST**

THIS comment simplifies and extends the important insight of the preceding paper by Paul H. Rubin.[1] I shall argue that the tendency of the set of all legal rules to become dominated by rules achieving efficient as opposed to inefficient allocative effects is substantially more pervasive than might be thought. It will be shown that efficient rules will be more likely to endure as controlling precedents regardless of the attitudes of individual judges toward efficiency, the ability of judges to distinguish efficient from inefficient outcomes, or the interest or uninterest of litigants in the allocative effects of the rules. Furthermore, it will be shown that this tendency toward efficiency is a characteristic of the common law process so that the content not only of the common law itself, but also of the legal interpretation of statutes or of the Constitution, is subject to forces pressing toward efficiency. The only assumption necessary for the hypothesis is that transaction costs in the real world are positive. It follows from this assumption that inefficient legal rules will impose greater costs than efficient rules on the parties subject to them. Since litigation is more likely than settlement where, *ceteris paribus*, the stakes of a case are greater, disputes arising under inefficient rules will be more likely to be relitigated than disputes arising under efficient rules.[2] It will be shown that, as a consequence, judges will be unable to influence the content of the law to fully reflect their attitudes toward efficiency. The set of legal rules will always contain a greater proportion of efficient rules than judges themselves would prefer.

* Fellow in Law and Economics, University of Chicago Law School; Associate Professor of Law (on leave), University of Puget Sound.

I am grateful to Gary S. Becker, Edmund W. Kitch, Anthony T. Kronman, William M. Landes, B. Peter Pashigian, Wallace M. Rudolph, Robert Sherwin, Kenneth I. Wolpin and to the participants of the Law and Economics Workshop of the University of Chicago Law School for helpful comments on an earlier draft.

[1] Paul H. Rubin, Why is the Common Law Efficient?, 6 J. Leg. Studies 51 (1977) [hereinafter cited as Rubin].

[2] For this conclusion it is necessary in addition to abstract from wealth effects on the "consumption" of litigation. See note 20 *infra*.

The hypothesis builds on a model of litigation and an assumption about transaction costs that are simple and realistic. It is unnecessary to assume, as might have been implied by Professor Rubin's discussion, for example, that the parties agree on the probability of a given verdict, that transaction costs are greater than the savings from voluntary shifts in liability, or, as was crucial to Professor Rubin's results, that both parties to the dispute have a continuing interest in the legal outcome.[3]

My analysis provides a foundation for the more general theory that common law decision making facilitates over time the efficient allocation of resources. This theory has been developed in recent years in a growing literature on the apparently efficient consequences of the common law system.[4] This literature has been less successful, however, in explaining *why* the common law has developed in this manner. The most persuasive explanation has been that common law rules of evidence and procedure tend to emphasize those characteristics of legal disputes important to a determination of efficiency,[5] but to conclude that the rules that are promulgated will, in fact, achieve efficiency has required two additional (often implicit) assumptions: that judges prefer efficient outcomes, and that judges can devise with at least some success legal rules to achieve such outcomes.[6] These assumptions have been criticized as fragile reeds on which to build a theory, because the intent and motivations of judges are difficult to infer and are frequently ambiguous and because the consistent and accurate determination of efficient results is a very difficult task.[7] The analysis in this paper, however, shows that even if judges prefer *inefficiency* or prefer efficiency but are unable to achieve it, the common law process will restrain and channel judicial discretion so that the legal rules in force will consist of a larger proportion of efficient rules than the bias or the incapacity of judges might otherwise permit.

I.

Various recent articles have developed a model in which the major determinants of the decision of two parties either to settle their dispute

[3] Rubin §§ I-II. Professor Rubin necessarily assumes that legal rules possess some precedential influence on future judicial decisions, for otherwise, legal rules would have no allocative effects whatever.

[4] Ronald H. Coase, The Problem of Social Cost, 3 J. Law & Econ. 1 (1960); Richard A. Posner, Killing or Wounding to Protect a Property Interest, 14 J. Law & Econ. 201 (1971); *id.*, A Theory of Negligence, 1 J. Leg. Studies 29 (1972), and *id.*, Economic Analysis of Law (1973) [hereinafter cited as Posner, Economic Analysis].

[5] Posner, Economic Analysis 321-27.

[6] For specific discussion of Posner's various explanations of judicial behavior see text surrounding notes 43-49, *infra*.

[7] For a discussion of criticisms of the efficiency theory of the common law see text surrounding note 49 *infra*. For an illustration of the ambiguity of inferences of judicial intent see Morton J. Horwitz, The Transformation of American Law, 1780-1860, at 61 (1977).

out of court or to litigate are the difference between the parties' attitudes toward risk, the combined expenses of litigation versus settlement, and the stakes of the case, that is, the gain or loss to the parties from a particular judgment. An implication of this model is that, if all other factors are held constant, those cases in which the stakes are higher are more likely than those in which the stakes are lower to be litigated rather than settled.[8]

For the set of all legal disputes, the stakes will be greater for disputes arising under inefficient rules than under efficient rules. Inefficient assignments of liability by definition impose greater costs on the parties subject to them than efficient assignments. For example, where the marginal cost of reducing the likelihood of an accident by a given amount is greater for one party than for the other, to place liability on the party whose cost is greater will lead in general to more accidents or more severe accidents than if the assignment were reversed. Where the cost of avoidance is made greater, the amount invested in avoidance generally will be lower. Even where it is possible for the party legally liable to pay the other party to assume the burden of prevention, it will be necessary to invest resources to achieve this reallocation. Thus the costs imposed by inefficient rules will always be higher than the costs imposed by efficient rules.[9]

It follows, therefore, that other factors held equal, litigation will be more likely for disputes arising under inefficient rules than for those arising under efficient rules. Once promulgated, inefficient rules are more likely than efficient rules to be reexamined by courts because they will come up in litigation more often. This conclusion follows directly from the fact that inefficient rules impose higher costs than efficient rules on the parties subject to them, and thus that the value to the parties from overturning the judgments that result—which is what I call the stakes of the litigation—is higher.[10]

Other characteristics besides the stakes that influence the litigation-settlement ratio—such as differences between the parties' expectations of success, aversion to risk, litigation costs, settlement costs, and even characteristics ignored by the economic model of litigation such as differences in the

[8] William M. Landes, An Economic Analysis of the Courts, 14 J. Law & Econ. 61 (1971); Richard A. Posner, An Economic Approach to Legal Procedure and Judicial Administration, 2 J. Leg. Studies 399 (1973). Greater litigation follows because for a given distribution of the parties' subjective probabilities of winning, greater stakes lead to greater differences between plaintiffs' minimum settlement offers and defendants' maximum settlement offers.

[9] If this were not true, then the rules would not be inefficient. Where there are no transaction costs, there are no inefficiencies.

[10] This conclusion does not follow where the parties subjected to the costs of a given rule, including the higher costs of the rule's inefficiency, are denied legal standing or where the parties have no continuing interest in the class of disputes and the optimal response to the liability rule is to reduce the scope of the activity so that the level of disputes weighted by intensity declines.

"litigiousness" of the particular individuals or differences in the "litigation skill" of the respective attorneys—can be ignored because they are unlikely to differ systematically between disputes arising under inefficient and those arising under efficient rules. The parties' expectations of success may be affected by the clarity of given legal rules, but there is no reason to believe that inefficient rules are any more or less clear in general than efficient rules. If these empirical judgments are correct, then regardless of the distribution within society of the various characteristics—ability to predict, aversion to risk, even litigiousness—inefficient rules as a class will be more likely than efficient rules to generate litigation and thus to be subjected to judicial reexamination.

It follows, therefore, that if the disputes that proceed to judgment consist of a disproportionately large share which contest the appropriateness of inefficient rules, then the set of rules not contested, those remaining in force, will consist of a disproportionately large share of efficient rules. It is this consequence that limits the power of the judiciary to influence the character of the law. The set of all legal rules in force at a given time will consist of the sum of the rules not contested and the rules newly promulgated by the judiciary. The newly promulgated rules, of course, will reflect judicial preference for or hostility to efficiency. But since the effects of the rules not contested will be predominantly efficient, the allocative effects of the total set of rules will be systematically more efficient than the allocative effects of the subset of newly promulgated rules. Even where the judiciary exercises a strong hostility to efficient outcomes, it will be unable to fully impose its bias on the total set of legal rules in force.[11] In fact, as we shall see, it is possible for the total set of rules to be predominantly efficient, despite a preference of the judges promulgating the rules for inefficient outcomes.

An arithmetical example will illustrate the point. Imagine that judges decide cases on some basis unrelated to efficiency of outcome, so that, with respect to allocative effects, judicial decisionmaking may be described as random. Assume for simplicity that all rules can be characterized as (equally) efficient or inefficient.[12] The likelihood in any given case of the rule being efficient or inefficient then will be .5. Imagine that 100 disputes go to judgment. By definition, the rules announced for 50 of these cases will be inefficient and for 50 will be efficient. Now assume that further litigation ensues concerning some of these rules. It is unnecessary to place any restrictions on the distribution of the other characteristics that determine the litigation-settlement ratio, but imagine that they are distributed so that 30 of the initial 50 inefficient rules are relitigated. By our previous finding (and

[11] For a consideration of those most implausible conditions when no newly promulgated rules are efficient see text following note 14 *infra*.

[12] This assumption is not essential and is relaxed in text following note 13 *infra*.

this is essential to the theory), it follows that a smaller proportion of efficient rules will be relitigated, say 20 of the initial 50.[13] By assumption, the judges will decide the 50 relitigated cases again randomly with respect to allocative effects. Thus 25 of the new rules will be inefficient and other 25 efficient. But when the new rules are added to the uncontested rules, it is clear that the stock of legal rules has become in sum more efficient. The number of inefficient rules has declined from 50 to 45, and the number of efficient rules has increased from 50 to 55. (See Table 1.)

TABLE 1
TENDENCY TOWARD EFFICIENCY WITH RANDOM DECISIONS
(.5 inefficient)

	inefficient				efficient				
	in litigation		in force		in litigation		in force		
period 1	30	(.6)	20	50	20	(.4)	30	50	50 in lit.
50 in lit.	25		25		25		25		
period 2			45	total			55	total	

N.B.: Equilibrium = 60 rules.

The tendency of the proportion of efficient rules to increase does not depend on the assumption of decision making that is random with respect to allocative effects. The proportion of efficient rules may increase over time even where each judge has a strong bias against efficient outcomes. Amend the previous example by assuming that judges promulgate inefficient rules in 90 percent of all cases, so that at period 1, 90 of the rules are inefficient, 10 efficient. Assume even greater relitigation: 80 of the 90 inefficient rules are relitigated and 7 (again a smaller proportion) of the 10 efficient rules, so that 10 inefficient and 3 efficient rules remain in force unchallenged. Of the 80 relitigated inefficient rules, 72 of the new rules will remain inefficient while 8 will be changed to become efficient. Of the 7 relitigated efficient rules, 6.3 will become inefficient and .7 remain efficient. Again the totals following relitigation favor efficiency: at the subsequent period, 88.3 as opposed to 90 rules are inefficient but 11.7 as opposed to the previous 10 are now efficient.

In this simple model the proportion of efficient rules in force at any period is a function of the stock of efficient and inefficient rules in force at the previous period, the respective rates of relitigation of efficient and inefficient rules, and the proportion of efficient rules announced by judges (the judicial bias toward efficiency). If the rates of relitigation and the judicial bias re-

[13] The difference in the rate of litigation between disputes arising under efficient rules and those arising under inefficient rules will be a function of the extent of the inefficiency.

main constant over time, the share of efficient rules will reach an equilibrium level. The proportion of efficient rules at equilibrium will be greater than the proportion of efficient rules promulgated by judges in any given period, regardless of the relitigation rates or the level of the judicial bias.

Let X_t and Y_t represent respectively the proportion of efficient and inefficient rules in force at period t. Let *a* be the proportion of efficient rules announced by the judiciary, *b* the rate of relitigation of efficient rules, and *c* the rate of relitigation of inefficient rules, each of which is assumed to remain constant through all periods. By definition $X_t + Y_t = 1$, and $c > b$. The proportion of efficient rules in force at any period is represented as follows:

$$X_t = X_{t-1}(1 - b) + a(bX_{t-1} + cY_{t-1}) \tag{1}$$

Substituting $(1 - X_{t-1})$ for Y_{t-1},

$$X_t = X_{t-1}(1 - b + ab - ac) + ac \tag{2}$$

It can be shown that in the limit (as t approaches infinity) X will converge to an equilibrium value. To show this, rewrite X_t as

$$X_t = X_0(1 - b + ab - ac)^t + ac\,[(1 - b + ab - ac)^{t-1} + (1 - b + ab - ac)^{t-2} \ldots + (1 - b + ab - ac) + 1] \tag{3}$$

where X_0 equals the proportion of efficient rules in the base period 0. Letting $Z = (1 - b + ab - ac)$, we know that $Z < 1$, since $o > b$ and $(1 - b) < 1 + a(c - b)$. We can write X_t as

$$X_t = X_0 Z^t + ac\,(Z^{t-1} + Z^{t-2} \ldots + Z + 1). \tag{4}$$

As t goes to infinity, we have

$$X_t = ac/b - ab + ac. \tag{5}$$

As expected the proportion of efficient rules in equilibrium will increase with increases in the judicial bias toward efficiency and with increases in the relitigation rate of inefficient rules. It will decline with increases in the relitigation rate of efficient rules:

$$\frac{\partial X_t}{\partial a} \geqslant 0 \quad \frac{\partial X_t}{\partial c} \geqslant 0 \quad \frac{\partial X_t}{\partial b} \leqslant 0 \tag{6}$$

It is important to appreciate the implications of this model on the exercise of judicial authority. It is true, of course, that greater judicial hostility to efficiency will lead to a lower equilibrium level of efficient rules. But the difference in the rates of relitigation between efficient and inefficient rules places an important restriction on the extent to which judges who prefer inefficiency can implement their preferences. Table 2 shows equilibrium levels of efficient rules, holding the rate of relitigation of efficient rules

TABLE 2
EQUILIBRIUM PROPORTION OF EFFICIENT RULES (%)
RELITIGATION RATE OF EFFICIENT RULES HELD CONSTANT (.02%)

		Relitigation Rate, Inefficient Rules			
		.04	.06	.08	.09
	.7	82.4%	87.5%	90.3%	91.3%
Judicial	.6	75.0	81.8	85.7	87.1
Bias	.5	66.7	75.0	80.0	81.8
(% Efficient)	.4	57.1	66.7	72.7	75.0
	.3	46.2	56.3	63.2	65.9

constant, for plausible values of judicial attitudes toward efficiency (within a range of 40 percent of the mean) and for selected relitigation rates of inefficient rules. Note that "judicial bias" represents the proportion efficient of all rules promulgated by all of the judges within a given jurisdiction over a long period of time. Thus a .3 judicial bias measure could not be achieved if only a small set of judges were hostile to efficiency or if judges were to exercise their hostility in only a selected set of cases. Rather such a measure would require deep and systematic hostility.

Table 2 shows that where judges are relatively indifferent to the allocative effects of their decisions or where the number of decisions hostile to efficiency is roughly equal to the number of decisions sympathetic to efficiency (bias = .5), the equilibrium level of efficient rules will be predominantly efficient. Where judges on the whole prefer efficient outcomes (bias = .6 or .7), the preference is strengthened and the number of efficient rules that survive becomes very large. But efficient rules will comprise a substantial and in most cases a predominating component of legal rules in force even where judicial hostility to efficiency is high (bias = .4 or .3). For example, where judges promulgate efficient rules only 30 percent of the time and the relitigation rate of inefficient rules is .06, efficient rules will dominate at equilibrium, comprising 56 percent of total rules in force.

Table 2 confirms a second limitation on judicial discretion. Regardless of judicial bias, an increase in the relitigation rate of *inefficient* rules will lead to an increase in the equilibrium share of *efficient* rules. The relitigation rate is an indirect measure of the extent of the inefficiency of individual rules. As rules become more inefficient and impose greater costs on the parties subject to them, the stakes of the disputes will increase and the litigation rate will rise. Although it may initially seem paradoxical, as judges promulgate rules imposing greater inefficiencies on society, judicial influence on the proportion of efficient rules in force will decline because each of the rules individually will be less likely to avoid challenge. The proportion of inefficient rules will be maximized where the rules themselves are only negligibly inefficient.

The tendency of legal rules to become efficient over time is independent of judicial bias or the method of judicial decisionmaking. It follows rather from the limitations on the opportunity set of cases available for judicial decision, limitations imposed by independent economic variables that determine the cases that are litigated.[14] Efficient rules "survive" in an evolutionary sense because they are less likely to be relitigated and thus less likely to be changed, regardless of the method of decision. Inefficient rules "perish" because they are more likely to be reviewed and review implies the chance of change whatever the method of judicial decision. In a state of dichotomous rules (assumed for the previous examples), this tendency toward efficiency could be thwarted only if judges could choose an inefficient rule in every case, without exception or error. If judges were to occasionally err then the tendency toward efficiency could not be reversed.[15] If judges were able only to choose rules achieving partial inefficiency, even if they could do so infallibly, the set of legal rules still would tend over time to contain more efficient rules than judges desired, because rules that imposed greater inefficiency would be more likely to be relitigated.[16] It is evident, furthermore, that the tendency of the common law over time to favor efficient rules does not depend on the ability of judges to distinguish efficient from inefficient outcomes. Even where judges are ignorant of the allocative effects of their judgments, they will be led by the litigation decisions of individual parties to promulgate rules that increase the relative proportion of efficient rules.

The tendency toward efficiency is a function of the common law process according to which legal rules are generated from the investment in litigation by individual parties and the parties' investment is systematically determined by the allocative effects of prior legal rules. This suggests, therefore, that efficient outcomes will tend to dominate for all disputes resolved by this process including not only rules derived from the common law itself but also

[14] This analysis is derived from Gary S. Becker, Irrational Behavior and Economic Theory in the Economic Approach to Human Behavior 153 (1976).

[15] The tendency will exist no matter how low the rate of error. But note that these examples assume (unrealistically) that the proportion of inefficient rules promulgated will remain constant over a long period of time, and that the probability of a particular allocative outcome in a dispute regarding any given legal rule will be unrelated to the allocative outcome in any previous dispute regarding that rule (this qualification does not deny precedential influence). If judges, however, are able to selectively reverse rules that are efficient, the proportion of inefficient rules promulgated may rise. Furthermore, where the judicial bias has shifted, there may be a greater tendency in the short run to litigate specific rules that appear inconsistent with the judiciary's new attitude so that the effective judicial bias might appear quite extreme.

Although efficient rules may remain unchallenged where judges clearly have manifested hostility to efficient rules, the settlement of disputes arising under such rules may approximate inefficient outcomes. As with Holmes, the model in this paper construes the law to mean "The prophecies of what the courts will do in fact . . ."

[16] This suggests that where legal rules have been designed to achieve a redistribution of wealth the rules will evolve so that the redistribution will occur efficiently.

rules interpreting legislation and construing provisions of the Constitution. To the extent that a statute or an interpretation of a statute imposes inefficiencies, it will be more likely to be overturned because of the greater likelihood of relitigation. Similarly, within the class of possible constructions of a given constitutional provision, those constructions with relatively more efficient allocative effects will tend over time to survive. It is immaterial to this result that one of the parties to a dispute regarding a statute or a constitutional provision may itself be the government (such as the Justice Department or an administrative agency) whose investment in litigation may be determined by the maximization of something other than dollar returns. Where government suits are brought under legal rules that are inefficient, the stakes will be higher and defendants will be more likely to resist the suits and force litigation.

It is important to appreciate the generality of the hypothesis. Professor Rubin explains that the tendency toward efficiency will be realized only where both parties have a continuing interest in the particular class of disputes so that they will take directly into account more of the costs of the inefficiency of a given rule. This view, however, is not correct. The greater costs imposed by inefficient rules will generate greater litigation whether the particular parties to a dispute bear all of the costs of the rules or not.[17] Professor Rubin argues that where both litigants are indifferent to the future allocative effects of a rule, the judgment with respect to these litigants will have distributive effects only. He infers that each party's decision to litigate, as a result, will be based on the size of the potential judgment alone.[18] But to understand the effects on litigation of the inefficiency or efficiency of rules, it is important to ignore the individual case and to consider the effects on the set of all disputes.[19] It should be apparent that of that set of disputes where neither party possesses a continuing interest in the legal rule, there is likely to be more litigation among those arising under inefficient rules (because the stakes are higher or the number of disputes greater) than among those arising under efficient rules.

With respect to the probability of litigation, a legal rule is like any commodity. A change in relative prices (here, as between efficient and inefficient rules) will change the distribution of consumption choices toward relatively

[17] See Rubin § II B-C and my note 10 *supra,* for a qualifying comment. Professor Rubin must accept this point since he acknowledges that a given rule may impose costs on parties other than the parties to the dispute that generated the rule. See Rubin § II-C.

[18] Rubin's analysis confused the allocative effects of given rules with other determinants of litigation or settlement. Rubin's assumption, for expositional convenience, that the parties possessed identical expectations of the outcome of the case, suggested that all disputes for which neither party had a continuing interest in the dispute would be settled rather than litigated. See Rubin § II-C.

[19] Emphasized in Gary S. Becker, *supra* note 14, at 167-68.

cheaper and away from more expensive commodities.[20] It is unnecessary to assume that consumers possess continuing consumption interests in a particular commodity in order to predict their responses to relative shifts in prices, although such interests may influence to speed of consumer adjustment to such shifts. Similarly, it is unnecessary to assume that individual litigants possess continuing interest in a particular class of disputes in order to predict the response in the litigation rate to an increase in the proportion of inefficient legal rules.

A relative shift from efficient to inefficient legal rules will influence both the number and intensity of disputes regardless of the characteristics of the parties to the disputes. Inefficient rules impose excessive costs, and excessive costs can be predicted to lead to nonoptimal consumption, whether of accident avoidance, contract compliance, or solicitude for another's property. Where the total costs of accidents and accident avoidance under a particular legal rule are higher, there will be nonoptimal investment in avoidance. The accidents that occur may be more severe or may be greater in number or the investment in avoidance may be greater than if the rule were changed. As a result, the litigation rate for inefficient rules will be higher.

Similarly, for the set of disputes in which only one party has a continuing interest in the allocative effects of a given rule, disputes arising under inefficient rules are more likely to be litigated than those arising under efficient rules. Professor Rubin concludes as to such cases that the tendency with respect to efficiency is indeterminate.[21] But again he fails to distinguish the decision to litigate the individual dispute from decisions for the set of all disputes. Professor Rubin notes correctly that where one party alone possesses continuing interest, the stakes of the case to that party relative to his opponent will be greater[22] and the party may be willing to invest more in the

[20] This analysis is well known. See Gary S. Becker, Economic Theory 19-24 (1971). For commodities it is assumed that the price changes are compensated; in the context of litigation, that the wealth effects on the consumption of litigation from a shift between inefficient and efficient rules is negligible, a reasonable assumption. The wealth effects of a particular decision on the rate of litigation within the society are likely to be small since the costs of litigation typically constitute a tiny fraction of an individual's purchases. Where wealth effects, to the contrary, are large, this conclusion does not follow.

[21] Rubin § II-C. Rubin supports his hypothesis by the description of 19th century nuisance law in Joel Franklin Brenner, Nuisance Law and the Industrial Revolution, 3 J. Leg. Studies 403 (1974). According to Brenner, the common law applied different (stricter) standards of proof in suits against factories by inhabitants of industrial towns than in suits by inhabitants of the country. This distinction may be quite consistent with economic efficiency. Brenner did not study whether the wage structure compensated workers coming to industrial cities for the disagreeable conditions. Regardless of inefficiency, both legal standards appear to have been derived from disputes between landowners (and especially wealthy landowners) and factories, both of which, one would imagine, had continuing interests in the dispute. *Id.* at 415-20.

[22] We must assume that there are other parties absent from the dispute whose interests are similar to the party without continuing interest; otherwise it would be efficient for the party with the continuing interest to spend more and dominate more.

litigation. The common law has attempted to deal with this problem of malrepresentation by various means such as equitable bills of peace, exceptions to collateral estoppel, the statutory class action, and more generally by adopting a style of decisionmaking that appears to take the interests of the absent parties into account.[23] The larger investment of one party to a dispute may in fact influence the allocative effect of a rule in a given case, but even if the rule favors the party with the continuing interest, if it is inefficient, it will generate more future disputes (because it generates more accidents or accident avoidance) and consequently it will be more likely to be overturned.

II.

The analysis in this paper can be distinguished from other attempts to explain and predict judicial behavior by its disregard of individual holdings and its focus on systematic changes in the aggregate set of legal rules in force. The set of legal rules can be analogized to the set of consumer decisions in a market. Like consumers, judges are restrained by a budget, derived from the aggregate budget of litigants, which determines the cases that proceed to judgment. As mentioned above, where the opportunity set of commodity choices changes, legal rules in the aggregate, like consumer decisions in the aggregate, can be expected to be shifted toward the relatively cheaper commodities (efficient rules).

Previous efforts of lawyers and political scientists to predict the content of the law have concentrated, to the contrary, on the conscious or unconscious motivations of judges that lead to particular holdings in individual cases. Such efforts, however, are as heroic as predicting the market response to a change in price by analyzing the specific motivations of individual consumers. Just as it is unnecessary for the prediction of market responses to explain the psychological processes that have led individual consumers to choose or to reject particular products,[24] it is unnecessary for the prediction of the course of the law to explain the mental processes that have led individual judges to particular holdings.

This section reviews some of the more prominent theories of judicial behavior to suggest how their predictive power can be enhanced by analysis of the variables that determine the survival of legal rules. The study of the law since Langdell has focused on the published opinions of judges. These

[23] For a discussion of equitable bills of peace see Yuba Consolidated v. Kilkeary, 206 F. 2d 884 (9th Cir. 1953); 1 John Norton Pomeroy, Equity Jurisprudence §269 (5th ed. Spencer W. Symons 1941). For a discussion of rules of estoppel see Richard A. Posner, Economic Analysis of Law § 21.9 (2d ed. forthcoming 1977). For an example of tacit consideration of the interests of individuals not parties to the litigation, see Benjamin N. Cardozo, The Nature of the Judicial Process 21 (1921); Boomer v. Atlantic Cement Co., 26 N.Y. 2d 870 (1970).

[24] Gary S. Becker, *supra* note 14.

opinions constitute, of course, the most recent and authoritative statements of the principles that will control particular disputes, and the tendency to emphasize them is encouraged by the demand for predictions of decisions that will be immediately forthcoming rather than of more substantial long-term changes in the character of legal rules. Excessively narrow attention to current decisions, however, neglects two aspects of the common law that are essential for understanding it. First, such attention ignores the broader corpus of rules and principles which remain effective as controlling precedents but which are infrequently litigated. Second, concentration on judicial opinions creates the hazard of losing sight of the processes that cause certain disputes and not others to be litigated. Every student of the law appreciates, of course, that a judge can decide only cases that come before him, but it has been a universal although implicit assumption of studies of judicial output that the cases that proceed to judgment represent an unbiased sample of the society's disputes.

An early and now notorious explanation of judicial behavior is that of Jerome Frank who, building on his understanding of modern psychology,[25] argued that the factors determining legal rules were the innumerable unconscious personal biases of judges.[26] He concluded that except to the extent that published opinions and announced rules of law were autobiographical, they provided no predictive ability for future decisions. "The law var[ies] . . .", Frank explained, "with the personality of the judge."[27]

Although his view retains currency,[28] Frank was criticized in his own time on grounds that presage in some respects the analysis in this comment. Dean Pound reproached Frank for insisting on the unique, single case which Pound thought may or may not actually be significant, rather than attempting to understand "the uniform course of judicial behavior." According to Pound, Frank and other realists ignored aspects of the common law process

[25] Frank was criticized for giving insufficient attention to the scope of contemporaneous psychological studies. Mortimer J. Adler, Legal Certainty in Law and the Modern Mind: A Symposium, 31 Colum. L. Rev. 91, 92 (1931).

[26] Jerome Frank, Law and the Modern Mind 106, 362 (1931). Frank argued that "the judge's sympathies and antipathies are likely to be active with respect to the persons of the witness, the attorneys and the parties to the suit. His own past may have created plus or minus reactions to women, or blonde women, or men with beards, or Southerners, or Italians, or Englishmen, or plumbers, or ministers, or college graduates, or Democrats. A certain twang or cough or gesture may start up memories painful or pleasant in the main. Those memories of the judge, while he is listening to a witness with such a twang or cough or gesture, may affect the judge's initial hearing of, or subsequent recollection of, what the witness said, or the weight or credibility which the judge will attach to the witness's testimony." *Id.* at 106.

[27] *Id.* at 111-16, 150.

[28] See Sheldon Goldman, Behavioral Approaches to Judicial Decision-Making: Toward a Theory of Judicial Voting Behavior, 11 Jurimetrics J. 142 (1971). For another modern evaluation of Frank see Bruce A. Ackerman, Law and the Modern Mind by Jerome Frank, Daedalus, Winter 1974, at 119.

that render nonrational judicial action unimportant. "[T]he logical and rational element and the traditional technique of application, or art of the common-law lawyer's craft . . . tends to stability and uniformity of judicial action in spite of the disturbing factors."[29] In a similar vein, Mortimer Adler criticized Frank for neglecting the restraints of the common law process on judicial discretion. Although a judge's "psychological prejudices and his hunches . . . are undoubtedly large factors in determining his disposition of the case, . . . [a judge] must nevertheless operate within the range of possible alternatives defined by an exhaustive analysis of the plurality of legal doctrines."[30]

Pound's first criticism is that Frank wrongly emphasized idiosyncratic judicial behavior, and it is true that the evidence that Frank summoned to support his theory consisted of anecdotes and confessions by various judges unable to explain some of their more difficult decisions.[31] Erratic decisions, as Pound indicates, would appear less significant if one were to consider—as a theorist must—a large sample of decisions. The second aspect of Pound's and Adler's criticism, however, is that there are characteristics inherent to the common law process that suppress irrational variations by encouraging their correction. This paper has argued that individual judges may be irrational, just as individual consumers may be irrational, yet the rules in force, like reactions in the market, may in sum exhibit strong rational characteristics. Economic variables, not psychological attributes of judges, will lead to regularities in the cases that come before judges. As a result, Frank's finding that the decision in any individual case was unpredictable was not sufficient to support his conclusion that the law itself was unpredictable.

A sophisticated variant of Frank's approach is that of modern political scientists who attempt to predict the character of the law chiefly from the ideological attitudes of judges.[32] This work has attempted to increase predictive ability by aggregating data of the backgrounds and perceptions of judges, and by selecting and narrowing the range of judicial response by

[29] Roscoe Pound, The Call for a Realist Jurisprudence, 44 Harv. L. Rev. 697, 706-07 (1931). Note that Pound's was not a consistent criticism. Elsewhere Pound criticizes the realists for "faith in masses of figures." *Id.* at 701. Pound suggested as a substitute theory that the course of the law could be explained by what he called the "ideal element," that judges do what they ought to do. See, for example, *id.* at 700.

[30] Mortimer J. Adler, *supra* note 25, at 105. Adler's view is similar to Edward H. Levi's. See text following note 37 *infra*. The constraints of the common law process that Adler perceived were doctrinal limitations as opposed to economic limitations leading to greater survival of efficient rules.

[31] Jerome Frank, *supra* note 26, at 102-17, 137, 143-45.

[32] Glendon A. Schubert, The Judicial Mind Revisited (1974); *id.*, Judicial Policy-Making (rev. ed. 1974); Sheldon Goldman & Thomas P. Jahnige, The Federal Courts as a Political System (2d ed. 1976). For an earlier review of this work see Glendon Schubert, Judicial Process and Behavior, 1963-1971 in 3 Political Science Annual, 73, 94-103 (James A. Robinson ed. 1972).

abstracting certain characteristic legal issues with respect to which it is most plausible that ideology will influence judicial decisions.[33] These studies, however, have weaknesses similar to those of Frank. First, they ignore except in an extremely narrow sense forces that lead certain cases to be brought to judgment.[34] Second, they tend to measure the "law" of a given period or the influence of the judiciary by the content of current decisions.[35] By neglecting those decisions that fail to generate continuing litigation, which are likely to comprise the predominating component of legal rules in force, these studies attribute excessive influence to measurements of the background of the current judiciary.

Various legal scholars have responded to Frank's characterization of judicial decisionmaking by emphasizing the limitations on judicial discretion imposed by the common law process. Their analysis is similar in many respects to the model in this paper.[36] A prominent example is Edward H. Levi's *An Introduction to Legal Reasoning*.[37] Levi explains that the common law process develops legal rules from reasoning by example. For a given decision a judge surveys the set of rules of law announced in earlier similar cases and applies one of the rules to decide the case at hand. The law changes as the similarities perceived between current cases and certain former cases increase. A new legal category or similarity can be proposed by one of the litigants and if the idea is accepted it will displace an earlier legal concept.[38]

[33] See Sheldon Goldman, Voting Behavior on the United States Courts of Appeals Revisited, 69 Am. Pol. Sci. Rev. 491 (1975). Goldman for example classifies cases in categories such as "Criminal Procedures", "Private Economic", "Injured Persons" and identifies judicial outcomes such as "For the injured in federal torts cases" and "For the injured or the fatally injured's estate in automobile accidents."

[34] Goldman and Jahnige mention that subsequent litigation provides "feedback" that influences judicial decision, but their only examples of "feedback" are test cases, too narrow a set. Sheldon Goldman & Thomas P. Jahnige, *supra* note 32, at 238-42. See, as further examples of studies of the judicial process that neglect the determinants of litigation, those debating the influence of the Supreme Court: Robert A. Dahl, Decision-Making in a Democracy: The Supreme Court as a National Policy-Maker, 6 J. Pub. Law 279 (1957); and Jonathan D. Casper, The Supreme Court and National Policy Making, 70 Am. Pol. Sci. Rev. 50 (1976). But see another contribution to this debate, William M. Landes & Richard A. Posner, The Independent Judiciary in an Interest-Group Perspective, 18 J. Law & Econ. 875, 895 & n.41, 896-901 (1975).

[35] Sheldon Goldman, *supra* note 33; Robert A. Dahl, *supra* note 34.

[36] *E.g.*, Henry M. Hart, Jr. and Albert M. Sacks, The Legal Process: Basic Problems in the Making and Application of Law (mimeo. class materials Harv. U., 2 vols. 1958); Edward H. Levi, An Introduction to Legal Reasoning (1948); Herbert Weschler, Toward Neutral Principles of Constitutional Law, 73 Harv. L. Rev. 1 (1959). For further references see the sources cited in Bruce A. Ackerman, *supra* note 28, at 123, 128 n. 26. Ackerman has designated these scholars the "Legal Process" school.

[37] Edward H. Levi, *supra* note 36.

[38] *Id.* at 1-8. For an earlier formulation of a similar model of the common law see Benjamin Cardozo, *supra* note 23, at 41-44, 47-49.

The similarity to the model in this paper lies in Levi's view that judicial discretion is constrained by the set of available socially acceptable legal categories. According to Levi, even though an idea may at one time have been rejected by a court, once it achieves standing in the society it will be suggested again in a subsequent case. The court thus will be offered the opportunity to reinterpret the prior decision and adopt the rejected idea. When adopted, the idea will be extended in later cases and further defined, as it is applied more generally and related to other accepted ideas.[39] The scope of judicial influence, therefore, is restricted by the tendency of decisions that conflict with controlling social concepts to be relitigated and, thus, redefined and reinterpreted.

The chief limitation of Levi's theory is its ability to predict the content of the legal rules that will develop from the common law process. The theory predicts that legal decisions will be controlled by ideas that have won acceptance in the society,[40] but it offers no means of determining which ideas are likely to prevail. Levi, for example, describes in some detail the gradual adoption and extension of different standards of liability for injuries caused by "inherently dangerous" products, but his theory explains this development only as "a reflection of a period in which increasing governmental control and responsibility for the individual were thought to be proper. No one economic or social theory was responsible . . . [A]s changes came about in the manner of living, the social theory moved ahead to explain and persuade."[41]

Levi's model of the judicial process, however, generates empirical propositions similar to those offered in this paper. A social idea or legal category is more likely to be replaced by a different idea, according to Levi, the more often alternative concepts are proposed. Similarly, a new legal category is more likely to be accepted by a court, the more often it is suggested to the court as the appropriate ground for judicial decision. Levi relates the frequency of such proposals, that is of relitigation, to the set of controlling ideas in the society. But, presumably, regardless of the content of the social consciousness, predictable differences in the rate of relitigation of certain legal rules will generate the same result. This is not to suggest that prevailing social concepts have no influence on legal doctrines. But until theories are devised relating social welfare policies or other ideas to litigation rates, one can increase predictive power by concentrating on more narrow characteristics of legal rules that can be shown with greater confidence to affect litigation.

A more recent explanation of judicial behavior is that of Richard A.

[39] Edward H. Levi, *supra* note 36, at 5-8, 33, 61, 73.

[40] *Id.* at 6.

[41] *Id.* at 102 See also pp. 8-27.

Posner in *Economic Analysis of Law*. Earlier in the paper I criticized Posner's explanation of the stimuli that might lead judges to choose efficient outcomes.[42] Posner's hypotheses, however, have generated substantial dispute among legal scholars. It is worthwhile reviewing some of the differences between Posner and his critics because the theory proposed in this paper, I believe, renders many of them moot.

Posner's explanation of judicial behavior attempts to predict various means by which a judge can increase his individual welfare by altering the content of his decisions. Posner initially comments that the common law system appears designed to both suppress and make insignificant the personal pecuniary gains to a judge from a particular decision. Rules of judicial ethics prohibit judges from deciding cases in which they have personal interests. Rules of evidence and procedure tend to conceal the distributive consequences of particular decisions.[43] Posner adds that the wealth effects to a judge from any single decision are likely to be small.[44] This contention has been forcefully contested by Arthur Leff and Morton Horwitz, who argue that the wealth effects of a judicial decision on certain social classes of which the judge may be a member can be quite large—in some cases, according to Horwitz, "enormous."[45] Since it is virtually impossible to measure empirically the wealth effects of a given decision, this dispute is irresolvable. Yet the theory in this paper suggests that even where judges are able in individual cases to directly enhance their own pecuniary welfare, they will remain unable to systematically alter the character of the law. The wealth effects of a particular decision on the rate of litigation are likely to be small,[46] and thus the principal determinants of the allocative effects of legal rules remain beyond judicial control.

Posner's theory of judicial motivation argues that since judges will be typically unable to achieve direct pecuniary gain, they will turn to other decision rules that will enhance their welfare, albeit less directly. Posner initially believed that many judges aspire to higher judicial or political office, so that if efficiency were valued by society, a judge might attempt to improve his chances of advancement by announcing efficient legal rules. In the second edition of *Economic Analysis of Law* Posner suggests that ambition to advance is less important than judges' more general desires to "impose

[42] See text surrounding notes 5-7.

[43] Posner, Economic Analysis 322. Note that the efficient character of these rules supports the hypothesis of this paper. The litigation rate is likely to be higher for procedural disputes than for other disputes since the costs are lower of litigating issues developed by argument rather than by trial. As the litigation rate increases, the tendency toward efficient rules increases.

[44] Posner, Economic Analysis 325-27.

[45] Arthur Allen Leff, Economic Analysis of Law: Some Realism about Nominalism, 60 Va. L. Rev. 451, 471 (1974); Morton J. Horwitz, *supra* note 7, at 100.

[46] See note 20 *supra*.

their preferences, tastes, values, etc. on society."[47] Much of Posner's work has shown that many common law doctrines crystallized in the 19th century, a period, he argues, in which efficiency may have been more highly valued by the society and by common law judges.[48] This description of common law decisionmaking, however, has been assailed by Arthur Leff and by James E. Krier. Leff criticized Posner for failing to explain why the judicial process is systematically less sensitive to distributive consideration than the legislative process, and Krier argued that judges themselves may prefer distributive to allocative consequences.[49]

A reformulation that bases the content of the common law on the preferences and values of judges only pushes the inquiry one step farther back. Since there are no theories for the prediction of judicial tastes, there is no increase in our understanding of the law. This paper has attempted to set forth an alternative theory that does not rely on determination of the preferences or ideology of individual judges. According to this theory, the dispute over judicial preferences becomes less important because although the ideology of individual judges may influence the rate of adoption of common law rules as well as the equilibrium level of efficient values, it cannot affect the process that leads to the survival of efficient or inefficient rules.

III.

It is important to appreciate that this paper has not shown that the rules of the common law are or ever will be completely efficient. It has suggested only that the common law process incorporates a strong tendency toward efficient outcomes. It is an implication of this theory that the rate at which efficient outcomes will be achieved will be a function of the nature of the judicial bias for or against efficiency,[50] the frequency of relitigation of inefficient rules (itself determined by the costs of litigation versus settlement, the precedential effect of the rules, and the extent of their inefficiency), the rate of change of the social conditions that underlie various disputes, and the adaptability of earlier surviving precedents to the efficient resolution of new disputes. It is a further implication that areas of the law within which characteristic disputes have remained relatively consistent over time, such as admiralty, sales, or procedure, are more likely today to be dominated by

[47] Posner, Economic Analysis 325. Richard A. Posner, Economic Analysis of Law § 19.7 (2d ed. forthcoming).

[48] Posner, Economic Analysis 327. Richard A. Posner, A Theory of Negligence, *supra* note 4.

[49] Arthur Allen Leff, *supra* note 45, at 471-73. James E. Krier, Book Review, 122 U. Pa. L. Rev. 1664, 1696 (1974).

[50] The effect of judicial bias on the rate of change toward efficiency and the ultimate equilibrium level suggests that the attention of Richard Posner and his critics to preferences of judges is not irrelevant. It is my own view that efforts to develop theories of judicial preferences will be no more successful than efforts to develop theories of consumer preferences.

efficient rules; and there is evidence supporting this hypothesis.[51] Perhaps a more important suggestion of the paper, however, is that the predictive ability of attempts to explain the character of common law decision making is likely to be enhanced by more careful attention to the forces that systematically affect the amount of litigation.

[51] For a discussion of the evolution of common law rules of admiralty see William M. Landes & Richard A. Posner, Salvors, Finders, Good Samaritans, and Other Rescuers: An Economic Study of Law and Altruism (forthcoming); of rules of sales see K. N. Llewellyn, On Warranty of Quality and Society: II 37 Colum. L. Rev. 341, 392-93 (1937); Grant Gilmore & Charles L. Black, Jr., The Law of Admiralty §§ 3.7-3.8 (2d ed. 1975); of procedure see Posner, Economic Analysis 322.

[9]

Journal of Economic Literature
Vol. XXVII (September 1989), pp. 1067–1097

Economic Analysis of Legal Disputes and Their Resolution

By ROBERT D. COOTER *and* DANIEL L. RUBINFELD
University of California, Berkeley

The authors are professor of law and professor of law and economics, respectively, University of California, Berkeley. The latter acknowledges financial support from the National Science Foundation programs in economics and law and social science. A. Mitchell Polinsky, Steve Shavell, and an anonymous referee provided comments and guidance throughout the editorial process.

Introduction

ECONOMIC THOUGHT ABOUT LAW is old, but the economic analysis of law, which relies on formal models, is new.[1] A little over 30 years ago, economics was relegated by lawyers to the technical role of providing expert advice on a relatively narrow set of laws in such fields as antitrust and labor. There were no journals devoted to the economic analysis of law, it had no place in the first-year curriculum at American law schools, and few American law schools allocated a full-time faculty position to a pure economist.[2]

From its modest beginnings in the 1960s, the economic analysis of law became an intellectual fad in the 1970s. The fad is over, but the continuing progress of the subject remains impressive. There are now four journals devoted to the economic analysis of law,[3] articles using this

[1] One conventional date for marking the beginning of the new economic analysis of law is the publication of Ronald Coase's "The Problem of Social Cost" in 1960. Of course, law and economics at Chicago had begun substantially earlier (George Stigler 1983).

[2] We know of no study documenting the role of economists in law schools prior to 1960. Our impression is that economists were absent or peripheral in major law schools thirty years ago with the exception of Chicago and possibly Yale. Among the first to teach at law schools were Henry Simons (Chicago), Aaron Director (Chicago), Ronald Coase (Chicago), Walton Hamilton (Yale), Ward Bowman (Yale), Robert Lee Hale (Columbia), Wesley Mitchell (Columbia), John Maurice Clark (Columbia), Edwin Seligman (Columbia), John R. Commons (Wisconsin), and Richard Musgrave (Harvard). The percentage of time these people spent teaching law and the centrality of their position within their law faculty varies greatly. We are grateful to Ed Kitch and Henry Hansmann for discussing these points.

Robert Ellickson (1960) has gathered some quantitative data on the extent of law and economics scholarship and influence since 1960. His data show that the economic analysis of law expanded rapidly in influence in the late 1960s and 1970s, but has not continued to expand in the 1980s. He attributes this loss of momentum to increased professionalization, which confines the subject to specialists with advanced economics degrees. He suggests that the subject's future vitality in law schools, as opposed to business schools, depends upon expanding the "rational actor model to encompass insights from psychology and sociology."

[3] *International Review of Law and Economics, Journal of Law and Economics, Journal of Legal Studies,* and *Journal of Law, Economics, and Organization. Research in Law and Economics* publishes refereed articles in book form.

approach appear frequently in the major law reviews, economic arguments and perspectives are often developed in the first-year law courses, and each of the major law schools has at least one economics PhD on its faculty.

Like the rabbit in Australia, the economic analysis of law found a vacant niche in the intellectual ecology, and filled it rapidly. The vacancy was created in part by the inability of legal theory to provide sufficient guidance for American courts that were increasingly involved with policy questions. Policy-making courts need a behavioral theory to predict responses to changes in law and to evaluate these responses systematically according to a normative standard. Economics was able to provide both the behavioral theory and a normative standard that legal theory lacked. The behavioral theory treats laws, like prices, as incentives for behavior. It has been well received, although controversy continues concerning the responsiveness (or lack of it) of poorly informed and possibly irrational actors. The normative theory of efficiency is relatively uncontroversial (Who favors wasting money?) as a broad guide to policy. But, controversy is abundant when efficiency is seen as dominating other norms of fairness and justice. The economic analysis of law, having secured a place in mainstream North American institutions of legal education, is influential but controversial,[4] which is the most a body of ideas can attain in a profession of advocates.

It seems that the acceptance of economic theory into law has been eased by structural similarities between economics and law. For example, the "reasonable man" of the law is not very different from the "rational man" of economics. The law's search for a fair division of the burdens of accidents is not very different from the economist's concern for the efficient allocation of risk.

All substantive areas of law have a common concern with the processes by which legal disputes get resolved, which is the subject of this article. The existing corpus of economic literature on courts is modest, but understanding the litigation process has become important, even urgent, as courts intrude more forcefully upon resource allocation. The number of trials, their cost, and the size of awards are unprecedented. To illustrate, civil cases tried in federal courts tripled between 1975 and 1985,[5] and an $11 billion judgment against Texaco forced one of America's largest corporations to file for reorganization through bankruptcy.[6] The related costs of litigation are known to be large, although difficult to quantify.[7]

This review consists of four parts. Part I focuses on the application of economic tools to the study of courts and outlines the chronology of a legal dispute. In our framework, legal disputes are resolved at various stages of a sequential decision-making process in which parties have limited information and act in their own self-interest. Part II reviews the predic-

[4] Part of the identity of the "critical legal studies" movement, whose members include faculty in many law schools, is its hostility to the economic analysis of law.

[5] "Lawsuits Since 1970 Triple in Federal Courts," *The New York Times*, 16 July 1987, p. Y11. See also Kathleen Engelmann and Bradford Cornell (1988).

[6] Reorganization was averted by a last-minute settlement with the plaintiff, Penzoil. For a game-theoretic analysis, see Robert Mnookin and Robert Wilson (1989). A. H. Robins Co. was also forced into bankruptcy because of tort claims resulting from its intrauterine contraceptive devices. The Manville Corporation, a producer of asbestos that caused cancer and other health problems, filed for Chapter 11 protection on 26 August 1982 in the face of massive tort claims. U.S. Bankruptcy Court gave final approval to a reorganization plan and Manville emerged from bankruptcy in October of 1988. The company will allegedly pay more than $1.5 billion in claims.

[7] The element of public subsidy is part of the difficulty. For some empirical evidence, see James Kakalik and Abby Robyn (1982), Peter Pashigian (1982), David Trubek et al. (1983), and Andrew Schotter and Janusz Ordover (1986).

tions obtained from modeling these decisions, and Part III discusses their normative significance. Part IV contains a conclusion that assesses the progress and promises of the subject.

I. *Chronology of a Legal Dispute*

Legal scholarship has long concerned itself with how the rules and practices controlling adjudication affect the quality of court decisions. Much of the existing economic literature on courts concerns a variety of microeconomic models involving perfect competition, bargaining, principal-agent relationships, and collective choice. There are special attributes of legal disputes that must be taken into account when adapting any of these models to the study of courts. We develop such a list by briefly describing the chronology of a typical legal dispute.

Initially, in the first stage, there is an underlying event, such as an accident or crime, in which one person (the injurer) allegedly harms another (the victim). The frequency of harm is affected by decisions that people make concerning activities and precaution. To illustrate, the probability of an automobile accident increases with the amount that a person drives and decreases with the amount of precaution taken when driving. High levels of certain types of activities and little precaution in doing them increase the frequency with which one person harms another.

Curtailing the activity or taking greater precaution to lower the social cost of the harm is costly in itself. As a result, economic efficiency requires balancing the cost of harm against the cost of avoiding it. If the parties are able to bargain together, the balance is struck by the market. This observation is the source of the best-known proposition in the economic analysis of law, the Coase theorem (Coase 1960), which states that, in the absence of impediments to exchange, legal entitlements will be allocated efficiently in the market regardless of their initial allocation by law.[8]

In many situations, however, bargaining is inhibited or blocked, and the social costs of harm are externalized. For example, drivers and pedestrians do not negotiate agreements in advance to allocate accident costs. For these accidents, the balance between harm and the cost of avoiding it must be struck by law, not the market. The initial allocation of legal entitlements is therefore essential to providing efficient incentives for activity levels and precaution against external harm.

In the second stage of a dispute the party that allegedly suffered harm decides whether or not to assert a legal claim. A rationally self-interested person makes this decision by solving a sequential game that balances immediate costs (hiring a lawyer, filing the claim) against benefits expected in the future (the proceeds from settlement or victory at trial).

The third stage occurs after a legal claim is asserted, but before trial. During this stage the parties reply to complaints, attend preliminary hearings with the judge, engage in pretrial discovery, and set trial dates. The overall objective of the court at this stage is to encourage plaintiffs (the victims) and defendants (the injurers) to bargain together and settle their disputes. The attributes of litigation bargaining—rivalry, communication, side payments, interdependency, and uncertainty—characterize bargaining games as analyzed in microeconomics. The third stage of the litigation process can be viewed, then, as a bargaining game whose cooperative solution corresponds to a settlement out of court, and whose noncooperative solution corresponds to an adversarial trial.

[8] Robert Cooter (1987a) presents an analytical treatment of the Coase theorem.

In settlement negotiations, as in any bargaining game, the interests of the two parties diverge with respect to division of the surplus, but converge with respect to an efficient resolution of the dispute. A legal dispute is resolved efficiently when legal entitlements are allocated to the parties who value them the most, legal liabilities are allocated to the parties who can bear them at least cost, and the transaction costs of dispute resolution are minimized.

A complicating feature of litigation bargaining is that the parties in most legal disputes are represented by lawyers, whose interests are not identical to their clients'. Designing contracts between lawyers and their clients so that incentives favor good representation is an agency (principal-agent) problem superimposed upon the basic bargaining game.[9]

The law prods disputants to resolve their differences by private bargaining, and when negotiations fail, the courts dictate a resolution in the fourth and final stage of a legal dispute. From the perspective of settlement bargaining, the expected outcome of a trial defines the threat points of the parties. Unlike settlement bargaining, the adversarial element dominates in trials, with each party trying to win as much of the stakes as possible. Litigants, as represented by their lawyers, view trials as negative-sum games.

Adjudication by the courts has two distinct products: dispute resolution and rule making. From the private viewpoint, trials are a method of resolving disputes between rational self-interested plaintiffs and defendants. But, from a social viewpoint, trials are a mechanism of collective choice for interpreting and creating laws to regulate and govern society. The decision makers in appeals courts, where laws are made and interpreted, are judges whose interests differ substantially from those of plaintiffs and defendants.

In our chronology of a legal dispute we distinguish among initial harm, the assertion of a legal claim, settlement bargaining, and trial. The initial harm can be analyzed by market models or externality models of the kind economists apply to conventional economic goods. The decision to assert a claim is a decision under uncertainty to be solved recursively by computing the expected values of subsequent stages in the dispute. Microeconomic models of bargaining are applicable to settlement bargaining. The limitations of bargaining theory, however, are not as severe as the absence of an economic theory of disinterested behavior that is needed to explain how judges interpret statutes and make laws.

The match-up between stages in a legal dispute and the economic modeling of them is summarized in Table 1.

A chart depicting the frequency with which disputes go from prior to subsequent stages, with "harm" at the bottom and "appeals court trial" at the top, looks like a broad-based pyramid. A typical finding is that ten disputes settle out of court for every one that is tried.[10] Generally speaking, the further along the litigation process the dispute has gone, the better the available empirical evidence. The steep slope of the "dispute pyramid" and the relative superiority of data describing the top as opposed to the bottom

[9] Recent examples of principal-agent relationships appear in John Coffee (1986), Patricia Danzon (1983), and Thomas Rowe (1984).

[10] Marc Galanter (1983, p. 44, note 1). Disaggregation of data shows a more complicated picture. Erhard Blankenberg (1981–82) found the ratio of settlement to court judgments in Germany to be 10 to 1 for traffic accidents, but only 2.1 to 1 for debt collection, 2.4 to 1 for disputes over service contracts, and 1.7 to 1 for disputes over rental contracts. Donald Coursey (1982) found a settlement rate of 20 to 30 percent in an experimental setting.

TABLE 1

MATCHING STAGES OF A LEGAL DISPUTE TO ECONOMIC MODELS

Stage 1: Harm—market models or externality models
Stage 2: Assertion of legal claim—decision under uncertainty to be solved recursively
Stage 3: Bargaining—strategic bargaining model with principal-agent overlay
Stage 4: Trial—negative-sum game for disputants, grafted onto collective choice by impartial court.

make the empirical study of the litigation process especially difficult.

II. *Resolving Disputes Through the Litigation Process*

What incentives do litigants face as they proceed through the litigation process? We answer this question in this section in the context of a formal model that is a hybrid of the models of suit, settlement, and trial that have been developed by William Landes (1971), Richard Posner (1973), Steven Shavell (1982a), and others. In Part III we go on to treat a number of related normative questions.

Our hybrid model of the litigation process stylizes facts to direct the reader's attention to fundamental causal relations. We assume that all accidents occur between strangers and, therefore, outside a market context. This rules out "Coasian" bargaining and the possibility that prices will convey information to the parties. There is a single injurer, who becomes a defendant, and a single victim, who becomes a plaintiff, when a suit is filed.[11] Both parties can affect the probability of an accident occurring. Initially, it is assumed that each party bears its own litigation costs. This assumption will be relaxed when we analyze alternative rules for allocating litigation costs.

We will forgo chronology and discuss the four stages of the litigation process in reverse order. This allows us to emphasize their interdependence, and in particular the fact that a decision at each point in the process depends crucially on the parties' expectations about the future. The variables in Table 2 will be used in the analysis.

A. *Behavior at Trial*

1. *Trial Effort of Plaintiffs and Defendants.* The plaintiff goes forward with the trial because she expects to win something from the defendant. The value of this transfer depends on the intrinsic merits of the case, which are determined in part by the relevant laws and in part by the particulars of the case. The pertinent laws might describe the burden of proof, the legal standard of evidence, the scope of damages (including a possible augmentation of compensatory damages reflecting punitive damages in tort cases or treble damages in antitrust cases), and the rules of procedure. The relevant facts might describe the past actions of plaintiff and defendant, and the particular circumstances that determine the applicability of legal rules. These actions would include the levels of precaution in a tort suit, promises in a contract suit, facts of ownership in a trespass suit, etc.[12]

The amount that the plaintiff expects to win is determined, not by the merits of the case alone, but also by the efforts the parties devote to winning. The efforts

[11] When the suit is filed by a regulatory agency, or by lawyers on behalf of a class of victims, the analysis becomes more complex because the objectives of the active plaintiff may diverge from the victim's. See Lewis Kornhauser (1983).

[12] The parties' perceptions about the law and the facts of the case may differ from each other and may be inaccurate as well.

TABLE 2
DEFINITION OF VARIABLES

c_{cp}	= cost to plaintiff of asserting a legal complaint
c_{sp} (c_{sd})	= cost to plaintiff (defendant) if the case is settled
c_{tp} (c_{td})	= cost to plaintiff (defendant) if the case is tried
D_P (D_d)	= plaintiff's (defendant's) estimate of the compensatory damage to be awarded if the plaintiff wins at trial
H_p	= victim's subjective value of the harm he suffers
L_p (L_d)	= potential plantiff's subjective expected value of a legal claim
p_{tp} (p_{td})	= plaintiff's (defendant's) subjective probability that a complaint that is asserted will be tried rather than settled
p_{vp} (p_{vd})	= plaintiff's (defendant's) subjective probability of plaintiff's victory win at trial
q_p (q_d)	= victim's (injurer's) subjective probability that an accident will occur and the victim will assert a claim
S_p (S_d)	= subjective value to plaintiff (defendant) of settling the case rather than going to trial
T_p (T_d)	= subjective value to plaintiff (defendant) of possible damage award by court
x_p (x_d)	= plaintiff's (defendant's) precaution against harm that gives rise to legal disputes

of the parties can be measured by expenditures on the trial, denoted c_{tp} and c_{td} for plaintiff and defendant, respectively. The subjective expected trial payoff to the plaintiff is thus given by the function

$$T_p\,(c_{tp},\, c_{td}).$$

The plaintiff's cost of proceeding with the trial must be set against her expected winnings. The plaintiff's expected gain from bringing suit, prior to trial and net of trial costs, is thus given by

$$T_p\,(c_{tp},\, c_{td}) - c_{tp}. \qquad (1)$$

Similarly, defendant's subjective expected loss, including trial costs, is given by

$$T_d\,(c_{tp},\, c_{td}) + c_{td}. \qquad (2)$$

The derivative $\partial T_p/\partial c_{tp}$ can be thought of as the marginal productivity of plaintiff's effort at trial. If effort is productive, then $\partial T_p/\partial c_{tp} > 0$ and $\partial T_p/\partial c_{td} < 0$, and similarly for defendant.

The expenditure of effort at trial can serve an important signaling function. The court must decide cases in which the defendant's liability in civil suits or guilt in criminal suits is uncertain, because information about the law or the facts is incomplete. The parties to the dispute usually know more than the court about crucial facts, and transmitting the information to the court is costly. Thus the effort that a party puts into trial provides a signal for the court. A stronger signal increases the probability that the judge or jury will favor the facts as represented by its sender.[13]

While effort is typically productive for both parties, the relative productivity depends on the merits of the case in a complex way. For example, if the defendant is negligent, effort by the plaintiff to discover and prove the facts can be very productive. But, on the other hand, effort by the defendant to represent the facts differently could also be productive.

The variables c_{tp} and c_{td} are chosen by litigants as part of their trial strategy. The plaintiff chooses c_{tp} to maximize her expected gain, while the defendant chooses c_{td} to minimize his expected loss. The first-order condition for the plaintiff is:

$$(\partial T_p/\partial c_{tp}) + (\partial T_p/\partial c_{td})i_p = 1, \qquad (3)$$

where $i_p = dc_{td}/dc_{tp}$ is the plaintiff's conjectural variation—a measure of how the defendant's costs will change in response to a change in plaintiff's costs. Equation

[13] This model is developed in Rubinfeld and David Sappington (1987) in the criminal context in which there is a single defendant.

(3) tells us that the plaintiff will expend money at trial so that the marginal benefit from more effort is equal to the marginal cost. The decision about how much money to spend during trial thus depends on strategic considerations related to i_p. A similar condition applies to the defendant.

A number of legal variables that can influence trial effort have been explored in the literature. Consider, for example, the effect of an upward adjustment to compensatory damages on the effort of both parties. To make such an evaluation consider a game in which plaintiff and defendant take each others' effort as fixed (as in a Nash game). Then $i_p = 0$, so that equation (3) reduces to $(\partial T_p/\partial c_{tp}) = (-1)$. An upward adjustment to compensatory damages should increase the marginal productivity of plaintiff's effort $(\partial T_p/\partial c_{tp})$. It follows that c_{tp} will increase (as will c_{td} under comparable assumptions). Thus, as the stakes increase, both parties will increase their trial expenditure.

If strategic behavior occurs, so that $i_p \neq 0$ and/or $i_d \neq 0$, the analysis is more complicated. Even when conjectural variations are not zero, we would expect a positive relationship between the upward adjustment to compensatory damages and the effort of both parties. But, without further structure, we cannot rule out the possibility that strategic behavior will lead to a contrary effect. Suppose, for example, that the game is sequential and only three levels of effort are possible—high, middle, and low. Initially, when only compensatory damages are given by the court, both parties choose a middle level of effort. Subsequently, when damages are increased, the plaintiff chooses first and opts for a high level of effort. Now, it may be in defendant's interest to opt for a low effort level, realizing that he is unlikely to win the case whatever his choice. In this example, augmenting compensatory damages lead one party to make more effort and the other party to make less.

The rule for allocating legal costs is another variable whose effect upon trial effort has been explored. In the American legal system, the parties to a dispute usually bear their own legal costs. In Britain, however, the loser in a trial bears the legal costs of the winner. Theoreticians have compared the effects of these two rules. John Hause (1989) uses a model in which the probability that plaintiff prevails at trial is a function of the legal expenditures of both parties. He concludes that a switch from the system in which both parties pay their own legal fees to a system in which the loser pays the winner's costs would increase trial expenditures for those suits that go to trial. Avery Katz (1989) also takes interactions and strategic considerations into account when he models trial effort. He reaches essentially the same conclusion as Hause, arguing that higher stakes raise the marginal value of additional expenditures to both parties. At the same time, the possibility that the losing side will pay part of the winner's litigation expenses lowers the expected marginal cost of litigating the case.[14]

2. *The Outcome of the Trial*

The outcome at trial (a win for plaintiff or defendant) is the result of a complex interaction between the efforts that both parties put into the trial and the underlying facts and law of the case. If both parties are only interested in winning the stakes in this trial, rather than being interested in the law or reputation or future disputes, then the levels of effort chosen and trial outcomes will depend on the relative productivities of both parties.

In many cases, however, parties are likely to engage in similar litigation in

[14] Other trial effort papers include Ronald Braeutigam, Bruce Owen, and John Panzar (1984).

the future—so that a repeated game framework becomes more appropriate. When one or both parties is concerned about the future, the probability that the plaintiff will win may increase or decrease. Typically the probability of winning will increase for the party with a future interest in victory. To see why, consider a Nash game in which the parties initially have a 50 percent chance of winning. Now suppose the defendant acquires a future interest in victory, so the cost of a trial judgment increases by a multiple *m*, where $m > 1$. It follows from equation (3) that the defendant's expenditures on trial, which were formerly determined by $(\partial T_p/\partial c_{td}) = -1$, are now given by $(\partial T_p/\partial c_{td}) = (-1/m)$. The defendant's trial effort will consequently grow, and the probability of defendant's victory will increase to a level above 50 percent.[15]

Jeffrey Perloff and Rubinfeld (1987) have suggested that defendants typically have more at stake than plaintiffs because defendants are likely to be involved in future litigation of the same type.[16] In this situation, the loss to the defendant is greater than the plaintiff's gain. The defendant will, consequently, choose to spend more on trial than the plaintiff, and will therefore have a greater than .5 probability of winning. Using an antitrust data set, Perloff and Rubinfeld find support for this view, because approximately 70 percent of all antitrust cases in their data set are won by defendants. This percentage is a substantially higher number than the rate of defendant victories in the cases studied by Priest and Benjamin Klein.

Settlement bargaining is a filter and the small percentage of cases that pass through it and go on to trial are not a random selection of all suits. Consequently, the frequency with which plaintiffs win at trial depends on the nature of the selection process. Hypotheses about the selection process and the frequency of plaintiff victory have been advanced and studied empirically. These hypotheses all build on the view that cases fail to settle as a consequence of a mistaken prediction about the outcome of a trial made by one of the parties. If, for example, the predictions of defendants and plaintiffs are normally distributed about the true mean, each party is equally likely to make a mistake. Priest and Klein (1984) use such an argument, supported by data, to conclude that cases go to trial in which defendants and plaintiffs have a 50 percent probability of winning (see also Priest 1980).

Donald Wittman (1985, 1988) replies that when the parties disagree about the expected trial award the 50 percent rule of Priest and Klein can be seriously biased. Disagreement concerns in part the meaning of "winning," which is ambiguous in the context of trials. The plaintiff "wins" a civil suit, in one sense of the word, if the court awards damages or provides injunctive relief. Many civil suits, however, concern not the fact of defendant's liability but its extent. From this perspective, the plaintiff "wins" at trial only if the damage award is larger than the defendant's settlement offer.

A further ambiguity arises when one of the parties to a dispute has a future interest in the trial's outcome. An interest in reputation or precedent by one of the parties makes the stakes asymmetrical. Even if the 50 percent rule is true

[15] See Rubinfeld (1984). This is not an equilibrium argument, because the plaintiff will respond to the defendant's increase in effort, but the direction of change should be the same in equilibrium as in the first round of responses, provided that the reaction functions have the expected shape.

[16] Econometric evidence also confirms that juries will award greater damages when there are corporate defendants, all else equal (James Hammitt, Steve Carroll, and Daniel Relles 1985). Jury awards are discussed more generally in Mark Peterson (1982), Peterson and George Priest (1982), and Mark Shanley and Peterson (1983).

when the parties are symmetrically situated, it will not be when there are asymmetries. To illustrate, a defendant who wants to cultivate a reputation for tough bargaining will contest cases that he has little chance of winning. Conversely, a defendant who wants to avoid the publicity of a trial will settle cases that he has a high probability of winning.

B. *Settlement Versus Trial*

The economic issues surrounding whether suits are settled or brought to trial have a long history in the law and economics literature. The early literature, including work by Landes (1971), John Gould (1973), Posner (1973), and William Baxter (1980), treated the private incentives of the parties, while Shavell (1982b) went further by distinguishing private from social incentives. Most of the more recent literature on the economics of settlements has moved toward a game-theoretic framework in which there are information asymmetries and a variety of sequences by which settlement offers are made by one or both parties. In this section we treat the parties' incentives, and then briefly survey the theoretical results concerning the effect of changes in policy instruments when the parties behave strategically.

1. *The Incentives of Plaintiffs and Defendants.* In some legal disputes there is scope for settlement, whereas in others trials may be inevitable. To distinguish between them, consider a civil dispute in which the parties have no future interest, so the bottom line is how much defendant pays plaintiff. The parties have expectations about the size of the transfer that would result from a trial and its cost. Plaintiff's expected gain from going to trial, net of trial costs, is given in equation (1) above, while defendant's expected loss, including trial costs, is given in equation (2) above. These expected gains and losses represent the subjective threat values of the parties. Any change that strengthens one player's threat value should increase his gains from the bargain. For example, Hugh Gravelle (1989) shows that plaintiffs with smaller risk aversion will receive larger settlements in a model in which courts have imperfect information.

The sum of the subjective threat values equals the players' assessment of the game's noncooperative value:

$$\text{Noncooperative value} = (T_p - c_{tp}) - (T_d + c_{td}) = (T_p - T_d) - (c_{tp} + c_{td}).$$

If a trial can be avoided, the parties must still bear the transaction costs associated with settlement, which are denoted c_{sp} and c_{sd} for plaintiff and defendant, respectively. In a settlement, the net transfer necessarily equals zero. The cooperative value of the game thus equals the actual net transfer (zero) less the transactions costs incurred:

$$\text{Cooperative value} = -(c_{sp} + c_{sd}).$$

The difference between the cooperative and noncooperative values of the game equals the surplus:

$$\text{Surplus} = \{(c_{tp} + c_{td}) - (c_{sp} + c_{sd})\} + [T_d - T_p]. \quad (4)$$

The surplus from cooperation equals the sum of the term in braces, representing the difference in the costs of trial and settlement, and the term in brackets, representing the difference in subjective expectations about the damages awarded at trial.

Transaction costs are less when a case is settled rather than tried:

$$(c_{tp} + c_{td}) - (c_{sp} + c_{sd}) > 0.$$

Indeed, trial costs are so much greater than settlement costs that many authors choose the simplifying assumption that settlement costs are nil, that is, $c_{sp} = c_{sd} = 0$. In this case, the surplus reduces to the gap in the expectations of the parties concerning the value of trial:

$$\text{Surplus} = (c_{td} + c_{tp}) + (T_d - T_p) = (T_d + c_{td}) - (T_p - c_{tp}).$$

For a risk-neutral plaintiff, the subjective value of the possible damage award at trial, denoted T_p, equals the money value of expected damages, D_p, times the subjective probability of their award, denoted p_{vp}, that is, $T_p = p_{vp}D_p$. Similarly, for a risk-neutral defendant, $T_d = p_{vd}D_d$. When plaintiff and defendant have the same expectations about trial ($p_{vp} = p_{vd}$ and $D_p = D_d$), they concur about its expected value, so that $T_p = T_d$. If the parties are relatively pessimistic about the prospects at trial ($p_{vp} < p_{vd}$ and $D_p < D_d$), plaintiff will expect to win less than defendant expects to lose, so that $T_p < T_d$. If they are relatively optimistic about their own prospects at trial ($p_{vp} > p_{vd}$ and $D_p > D_d$), plaintiff expects to win more than defendant expects to lose, so that $T_p > T_d$.

If the surplus is negative, the disputants prefer a trial to any possible settlement, so trial is inevitable. If the surplus is positive, however, there is scope for settlement out of court. The frequency of settlements presumably increases with the magnitude of the surplus. There is more scope for settlement when litigation is costly (c_{tp} and c_{td} are large), negotiations are inexpensive (c_{sp} and c_{sd} are small), and the disputants are pessimistic about trial outcomes ($p_{vp} < p_{vd}$, $D_p < D_d$). As a result, any policy that increases litigation costs, lowers settlement costs, or makes disputants pessimistic about their trial prospects, will increase settlements.

Now consider the effect of risk aversion upon litigants with the same information about possible outcomes of trials. A trial represents a gamble, so the subjective value of trial to risk-averse disputants will diverge from its expected value. For example, when the parties are both risk averse and they have the same expectations about trial, their subjective values of trial diverge:

$$T_p < p_{vp}D_p = p_{vd}D_d < T_d.$$

Risk aversion thus increases the surplus as given in equation (4), which presumably increases the probability of a settlement. Notice that risk aversion increases the surplus in the same way as pessimism—by increasing the difference between the subjective values of plaintiff's trial gains and defendant's trial losses.

2. *The Effects of Legal Rules.* Most models have assumed that settlement occurs automatically whenever the surplus in equation (4) is positive. This assumption has the effect of ruling out strategic behavior. Its main justification is pragmatic—predictions can be derived readily from nonstrategic bargaining models, whereas strategic models are often intractable. Given the fact that the term in braces $\{(c_{tp} + c_{td}) - (c_{sp} + c_{sd})\}$ is positive, and assuming nonstrategic bargaining, the trial/settlement split falls into two zones determined by the sign of the surplus, with one intermediate point:

$$[T_d - T_p] > -\{(c_{tp} + c_{td}) - (c_{sp} + c_{sd})\} \Rightarrow \text{settlement}$$
$$[T_d - T_p] = -\{(c_{tp} + c_{td}) - (c_{sp} + c_{sd})\} \Rightarrow \text{tipping point}$$
$$[T_d - T_p] < -\{(c_{tp} + c_{td}) - (c_{sp} + c_{sd})\} \Rightarrow \text{trial.}$$

These relationships help to generate a prediction about the effect of treble damages and punitive damages upon the frequency of trials. Consider how augmenting damages affects a case at the tipping point between settlement and trial. The fact that the term in braces is positive implies that $[T_d - T_p] < 0$ at the tipping point. Augmenting damages increases the absolute value of this negative number, which tips the case into the trial zone, so there are more trials and fewer settlements. Augmenting damages in a nonstrategic bargaining model thus strengthens the tendency of optimism to cause trials.

This conclusion must be modified once account is taken of the resulting change in trial effort. Augmenting damages increases the stakes in the trial, which typically elicits more effort at trial by the parties, as explained above. With more effort, the term in braces $\{(c_{tp} + c_{td}) - (c_{sp} + c_{sd})\}$ increases in value. The resulting increase in the surplus from cooperation presumably makes settlement more likely.

Risk aversion also affects the comparison. Augmenting damages, by increasing the stakes in trial, makes trial more risky, which makes trial less attractive to risk-averse disputants. Risk-averse disputants at the tipping point under a regime of compensatory damages may be nudged into settlement by a change to a regime of augmented damages because trial has become too risky.

In sum, augmenting damages increases the stakes in trial, which has opposing effects upon the ability to settle out of court in a nonstrategic model. On one hand, more weight is given to the parties' optimism, which tends to increase the frequency of trials. On the other hand, trials become more costly and more risky, which tends to decrease their frequency.

Similarly, changing the legal rule for distributing trial costs has opposing effects upon the ability to settle out of court. Under the American rule each party pays his own costs, and under the British rule the loser pays all. With the American rule, the parties know with certainty that they will pay their costs, while under the British rule the plaintiff expects to bear trial costs, $c_{tp} + c_{td}$, only if he loses, which occurs with probability $(1 - p_{vp})$. The same is, of course, true for the defendant. Assuming risk neutrality, we can modify equation (4) to contrast the two rules:[17]

Surplus under U.S. and British trial cost distributions:

$$\text{U.S.} = \{(c_{tp} + c_{td}) - (c_{sp} + c_{sd})\} + [p_{vd}D_d - p_{vp}D_p] \quad (4')$$

$$\text{British} = \{(1 - p_{vp} + p_{vd})(c_{tp} + c_{td}) - (c_{sp} + c_{sd})\} + [p_{vd}D_d - p_{vp}D_p] \quad (4'')$$

Equation (4″) reduces to (4′) when the parties have the same subjective beliefs about the probability of plaintiff's victory, $p_{vp} = p_{vd}$, but not otherwise.

Consider the effect of the change in rules on a case at the tipping point between settlement and trial under the American rule. The surplus is zero at the tipping point, so (4′) = 0 by assumption. The term in braces in equation (4′) is positive by assumption. Hence $p_{vp}D_p > p_{vd}D_d$, which indicates that the parties are optimistic about trial. Assume that this optimism extends to expectations about the probability of plaintiff's victory, so that $p_{vp} > p_{vd}$. $p_{vp} > p_{vd}$ implies (4′) > (4″). This fact and the fact that (4′) = 0 imply that (4″) < 0. Thus, a switch to the British rule causes the surplus at the tipping point to turn negative, resulting in more trials.

This conclusion must be modified when trial effort and risk aversion are considered. The switch in cost distribution rules from American to British increases the stakes at trial by including trial costs in the gamble. The effect of higher stakes upon trial effort and risk aversion has already been discussed—the effects of a switch in the distribution rule for trial costs parallels the effects of aug-

[17] Equation (4″) is derived as follows. The threat positions of defendant and plaintiff under the British rule are $-[p_{vd}D_d + p_{vd}(c_{tp} + c_{td})]$ and $p_{vp}D_p - [(1 - p_{vp})(c_{tp} + c_{td})]$. The cooperative surplus, given by equation (4″), equals the cooperative value of the game, $-c_{sp} - c_{sd}$, minus the sum of the threat points.

menting damages.[18] Theory tells us, therefore, that a switch from the rule of each pays his own (American), to the rule of loser pays all (British), tends to increase the frequency of trials by giving more weight to the parties' optimism, and to increase the frequency of trials by making them more costly and more risky.

The direction of the overall effect upon the frequency of trials of changing the rule for distributing legal costs cannot be determined from theory alone. The common belief among lawyers that fewer suits will occur when the loser pays more of the legal costs enjoys some support from experimental economics.[19] This belief has motivated a modification of the American rule to more closely resemble the British rule. Geoffrey Miller (1986) considers one prominent example. Suppose plaintiff rejects the defendant's final offer to settle for a specified sum of money and that, after a trial, plaintiff is awarded less than the final settlement offer. Under these circumstances the plaintiff can be said to have lost in court relative to the settlement offer. Rule 68 of the code governing procedure in federal courts, which is similar to procedural rules in a variety of states, specifies that a plaintiff who loses in court relative to the defendant's settlement offer must pay some of the winner's court costs, including such items as the cost of depositions and filings, and excluding attorney fees.[20]

[18] Katz (1988) compares trial efforts of the parties under the British and American rules. See also Braeutigam, Owen, and Panzar (1984), Shavell (1982b), and Posner (1986, ch. 21).

[19] Donald Coursey and Linda Stanley (1988) found a higher settlement rate when their experimental subjects decided disputes under Rule 68 than under the British rule, and the higher under the British rule than under the American rule.

[20] The Supreme Court recently extended Rule 68 to cover attorney's fees in cases where the statute under which the action is brought allows recovery of attorney's fees. See *Merrick v. Chesney*, 473 U.S.1, 105 S. Ct. 3012.

Whatever effect this rule has on the frequency of trials, it strengthens the bargaining position of defendants.

3. *Strategic Aspects of Settlement Behavior*. The nonstrategic bargaining model in the preceding section assumes that disputes will always settle out of court when the cooperative surplus, as perceived by the players, is positive, whereas trials will occur when it is perceived as negative. There is, however, another cause of trials—the distribution problem itself. The problem of dividing the surplus created by settlement is a source of instability that can lead to bargaining breakdowns.

Attempts by theorists to model the distribution problem in bargaining games in general have produced, not a consensus among economists, but a variety of predictive and normative theories that are rivals to each other. The unsatisfactory state of bargaining theory is reflected in strategic models of the litigation process. One approach to settlement bargaining generates definitive predictions by making restrictive assumptions about the scope of bargaining, the timing of offers, and the ability of the parties to transmit information. Thus, in Janusz Ordover and Ariel Rubinstein (1986) and Ivan P'ng (1983), the settlement amount is fixed and not open to bargaining. In P'ng the defendant knows whether he is negligent and uses this information to decide whether to make a settlement offer, whereas plaintiff responds without knowing for certain whether defendant was negligent.[21] In Lucian Bebchuk (1984), the settlement amount is endogenous, but the plaintiff knows the actual harm and the defendant knows only the probability distribution of possible

[21] For additional strategic models of bargaining, see Rayner Cheung (1988), Daniel Spulber (1985), Robert Thomas (1986). For an analysis of settlement behavior in a criminal law setting, see Gene Grossman and Michael Katz (1983).

harms. In Bebchuk's model, the relatively uninformed plaintiff makes the first and only settlement demand, which the defendant must either accept or reject in favor of a trial. The response of defendant to plaintiff's offer conveys some information about the defendant, but uncertainty persists, so cases can go to trial.

The models discussed so far do not face the distribution problem squarely. When bargaining over distribution of the cooperative surplus, the players are uncertain about the extent to which other parties will concede. A rational player will gauge his demands such that the gain from settling on slightly more favorable terms is offset by the increased risk of negotiations breaking down. The optimal strategy in settlement bargaining thus balances a larger share of the stakes against a higher probability of trial. When these considerations are balanced at the margin, expected utility is maximized relative to the distribution of an opponent's possible strategies. A bargaining equilibrium can thus be characterized as a situation in which everyone maximizes expected utility given complete knowledge about the distribution of strategies followed by others.[22] This equilibrium concept has the advantage of permitting strategic behavior to cause trials.

While the optimal strategy as characterized above is best relative to the distribution of the other party's possible strategies, it is not necessarily best against the actual strategy that will be chosen. A party may overestimate a particular opponent's willingness to make concessions, which can cause a breakdown in settlement negotiations and a trial. To illustrate, suppose that the parties must choose between a hard strategy (make no concessions) and a soft strategy (concede). Each party knows the frequency with which these strategies are chosen by others, but no one finds out his particular opponent's strategy in a specific dispute until after it is resolved. Trials occur under these circumstances when both parties commit to hard strategies, and settlements occur otherwise. To illustrate, suppose that in equilibrium 30 percent of plaintiffs and 30 percent of defendants are pursuing hard strategies. Then, 9 percent of disputes end in trial and 91 percent settle out of court, and no one is surprised by these proportions.

This equilibrium concept presupposes some means by which the parties generate their expectations about the probability that other players will concede. A full account of the genesis of concessionary expectations would go beyond the legal process into psychology and sociology. For the purposes of economic analysis, however, it is usually sufficient to assume that disputants have expectations prior to beginning a legal dispute, and then to predict how the legal process modifies them. An earlier example of this approach by Cooter, Stephen Marks, and Mnookin (1982) sought for conditions under which the predictions of the nonstrategic models could be extended to strategic bargaining. The specification of the information structure of the game is not adequate in this early work, but this has been corrected in subsequent work. In William Samuelson (1983) both parties make settlement offers simultaneously, so uncertainty persists and bargaining can fail. Stephen Salant (1984) assumes that plaintiffs come in two types, slightly injured and badly injured, and defendants cannot tell them apart in pretrial bargaining.

Several papers have applied the concept of sequential equilibria (David Kreps and Robert Wilson 1982) to settlement bargaining, notably Urs Schweizer (1986), Thomas (1986), Jennifer Reinga-

[22] For an analysis of this Bayesian-Nash equilibrium, see John Harsanyi (1968), especially part 2. See also Kenneth Binmore, Ariel Rubinstein, and Asher Wolinsky (1986).

num and Louis Wilde (1986), and Barry Nalebuff (1987) for civil suits, and Reinganum (1988) for criminal cases. At each node or state of the game, each party chooses the strategy that is optimal for the remainder of the game, given uncertainties about other players and their future actions. Parties update their beliefs in light of information provided at each stage of the game. To generate definite predictions, these approaches must exploit facts about the litigation process that prescribe sequences of moves and generate asymmetric information. Thus, plaintiff must make the first move to assert a legal claim. In settlement bargaining for civil disputes, the defendant often has more information concerning the existence of liability (e.g., whether negligence can be proved), and the plaintiff often has more information about the extent of liability (e.g., how severe was the injury).[23]

If enough structure is imposed to generate sequential moves with asymmetric information, some predictions can be derived that may contradict the nonstrategic models. To illustrate, an important topic in strategic bargaining is the information transmitted by the exchange of offers. Signaling in settlement bargaining was studied by Nalebuff (1987), who relied upon information asymmetries to generate predictions about equilibria in a sequential subgame. In the first step, plaintiff makes a single demand; next the defendant either rejects the demand or settles the case; finally, if the demand is rejected, the plaintiff decides whether to proceed to trial. Plaintiff's demand in the first stage conveys information to defendant about the probability that plaintiff is prepared to proceed to trial. Defendant's rejection of plaintiff's demand in the second stage conveys information to plaintiff about the strength of defendant's case. In equilibrium, plaintiffs know the distribution over the strength of the case of defendants who settle, and defendants know the proportion of cases that plaintiffs litigate.

A comparison of Bebchuk, Nalebuff, and our hybrid model illustrates that different specifications of the game affect important predictions about the litigation process. Consider the effect of an increase in plaintiff's trial costs on the terms of settlement. An increase in plaintiff's trial costs weakens plaintiff's threat position, which leads to lower settlement offers in Bebchuk's model and our hybrid model. While agreeing with this general argument, Nalebuff points to an alternative possibility. He argues that when trial costs increase, plaintiff will not be prepared to go to trial unless she expects to win a larger judgment. To make the threat of going to trial credible, she will demand a larger settlement. A full specification of the information structure in settlement bargaining, including the signal contained in the offers they make, may thus lead to predictions that contradict the nonstrategic model.[24]

4. *Empirical Studies of Trial/Settlement Split.* Courts have been studied by sociologists and other social scientists from both a longitudinal and a cross-sectional point of view. However, it is only recently that economists have begun the task of specifying and estimating structural models of the behavior of the parties during the dispute resolution process. The greatest attention has focused on the settlement decision. A satisfactory structural model of settlement must take ac-

[23] Shavell (1989) focuses on the incentives that the parties have to communicate and share information during the settlement bargaining process.

[24] To illustrate more contradictory predictions, Nalebuff predicts that a shift toward larger damage awards on the part of the court will increase the likelihood of settlement, which contradicts Bebchuk's prediction. Reinganum and Wilde conclude that the probability of settlement is independent of the allocation of litigation costs, which again contradicts P'ng (1983), Samuelson (1983), and Bebchuk (1984).

count of uncertainty in settlement bargaining, which results in specification errors, and the possibility that bargaining breaks down due to strategic behavior.

A structural model for empirical research on the trial/settlement split can be developed from our hybrid model. Suppose we posit that the plaintiff's expected gain from trial consists of the systematic component T_p and a randomly distributed error. Similarly, defendant's expected loss from trial consists of a systematic component T_d and a randomly distributed error. Trial costs may be random as well. Combining all of these terms, the cooperative surplus from settlement becomes

$$\text{Surplus} = (T_d - T_p) + (c_{td} + c_{tp}) + e = G + e, \quad (5)$$

where G is the systematic component and e is a random disturbance term. In this framework, a dispute may fail to settle even though the systematic component of the cooperative surplus is positive, provided that the error is large and negative.

A reduced-form model can be obtained from equation (5) in which the probability of trial, denoted p_t, is determined by evaluating the probability distribution function of the systematic component of the settlement surplus:

$$p_t = p_t\,(G). \quad (6)$$

A question investigated empirically by using equation (6) is whether augmenting compensatory damages will result in more or fewer trials. Recall our previous discussion in which we concluded that when damages are augmented, the tendency of optimism to cause trial is strengthened, the tendency of risk aversion to discourage trials is strengthened, and more costly effort is elicited to win trials that occur, which further discourages trials. Perloff and Rubinfeld (1987) found evidence suggesting that in antitrust cases, where reputational effects are important, and where the parties tend to be pessimistic ($T_d - T_p > 0$), treble damages lead to a decrease in the proportion of cases resolved by trial and an increase in the number of settlements.

Other studies, however, have suggested a contrary result, including Danzon and Lee Lillard (1983). They applied a model of the settlement process to medical malpractice claims.[25] Their model consists of two trial equations that explain the probability of plaintiff winning ($p_{vp} = p_{vd} = p$) and the amount of verdict ($T_p = T_d = T$), and two settlement equations that explain the minimum demand of the plaintiff ($T_p - c_{tp}$) and the maximum offer ($T_d + C_{td}$) of the defendant. Both the minimum demand and maximum offer depend positively on the perceived probability of winning and the perceived verdict. As in our hybrid model, the authors assume that cases will settle when the minimum asking price of the plaintiff is greater than zero, but less than maximum offer of the defendant. When the minimum asking price is greater than the maximum offer, the case will go to trial.

Danzon and Lillard assume that an increase in the stakes involved in the case (brought about when damages are augmented) will increase the random errors proportionally. The costs of litigation, however, increase less than proportionately. So G in equation (5) increases less than proportionately. As a result of the random error term's greater influence, the surplus given in equation (5) is negative in more cases, and more cases will be litigated.[26]

[25] The study uses a sample of 5,832 claims files that were closed in 1974 and 1976.

[26] Posner (1973) comes to the same conclusion as Danzon and Lillard, but makes the special assumptions that the costs of litigation are fixed, and that the parties disagree only about the probability that the plaintiff will win at trial.

Among the interesting results of this study are the following: (1) The higher the award at trial, the greater the probability that the case will go to trial; (2) the higher the plaintiff's probability of winning at trial (as perceived equally by both parties), the lower the probability that the case will go to trial; and (3) plaintiffs win only 28 percent of the cases that go to trial.

C. *Assertion of a Legal Claim*

A dispute is initiated when a party with a complaint asserts it, either officially by filing the required legal document, or informally by private communications between the parties. Some legal disputes are settled privately and never come to the court's attention. In other cases, such as tortious injuries to minors, the resolution of the dispute is not legally binding until approved by the court. In the disputes that are best documented, however, an official complaint is filed by the plaintiff against the defendant.

The decision to assert a legal claim is difficult to investigate empirically because cases that do not come to the attention of legal authorities never enter official records. Danzon and Lillard partly avoided this problem by studying insurance records. In two data sets on medical malpractice, they found that 50 percent of cases were resolved before a suit was filed, 40 percent were settled before a verdict, and 10 percent were tried to a verdict.

Asserting a complaint, whether informal or official, uses plaintiff's time or money. The expected benefit of asserting a legal claim consists of the possibility of settlement or a favorable court judgment. Shavell (1982a) and Posner (1986, chapter 21), among others, have assumed that rational decision makers assert a complaint because the cost of doing so is less than the expected benefit. Let c_{cp} denote the cost to plaintiff of asserting a legal claim, and let L_p denote the plaintiff's subjective expected benefit.

The expected benefit of asserting a legal claim can be determined explicitly from preceding sections of this article. The plaintiff's subjective value of a possible court judgment, conditional upon a trial occurring, has been written as $T_p(c_{tp}, c_{td})$. Let p_{tp} denote the plaintiff's subjective probability that a complaint will eventually lead to a trial. The plaintiff's (unconditional) subjective value of a court judgment that could result from asserting a complaint, net of litigation costs, is thus $p_{tp}[T_p(_{tp}, c_{td}) - c_{tp}]$. Similarly, let S_p denote the subjective expected value of settlement for plaintiff, conditional upon a settlement being reached, which occurs with probability $1 - p_{tp}$. The plaintiff's subjective expected value of the legal claim, L_p, is thus

$$L_p = p_{tp}[T_p(c_{tp}, c_{td}) - c_{tp}] + (1 - p_{tp})(S_p - c_{sp}) \quad (7)$$

Equation (7) implies that claims are more valuable to a victim when litigation costs and bargaining are inexpensive (low c_{tp} and c_{sp}), and plaintiff is optimistic about her prospects at trial or settlement (high T_p and S_p). Further, the plaintiff knows that a settlement will occur only if it makes her better off than going to trial. As a result, L_p must be decreasing in p_{tp}.

The decision rule for the rational plaintiff balances the subjective value of a legal claim against the cost of asserting it:

$c_{cp} < L_p$ Assert legal claim
$c_{cp} = L_p$ Tipping point
$c_{cp} > L_p$ Do not assert legal claim.

The literature is divided, however, on the appropriate measure of L_p for the rational plaintiff. Suppose that both parties have complete information about trial costs and outcomes and certain other conditions in dispute are met. Then suits will be brought only when the plaintiff's expected benefit from trial net of trial costs is positive. Settlement costs, probabilities, and amounts are irrelevant under these conditions. This can most easily be seen in a model of repeated litigation in which both parties know the plaintiff's expected net benefit from trial to be negative. Then it will be in defendant's interest not to agree to settle such a case, and consequently, plaintiff will not choose to bring the case in the first place. Thus, when both parties have complete information, the settlement probability is zero, and L_p is equal to the plaintiff's expected net benefit from trial.

Bebchuk (1988) has shown, however, that under a different assumption involving asymmetric information, the victim's decision to sue may depend on the likelihood and/or the magnitude of a settlement. In this framework the more general definition of L_p applies.

To analyze the relationship between legal costs and legal disputes, consider a person at the tipping point of asserting a legal claim, where $c_{cp} = L_p$. A change in the law that increases trial costs will immediately lower the value of L_p. The equation will thus tip in the direction $c_{cp} > L_p$, where the claim will not be asserted. More generally, laws that increase the costs of resolving disputes are likely to decrease the frequency with which legal claims are asserted and increase the cost of settling those that are asserted.

These conclusions have been applied to the explanation of nuisance suits. A nuisance suit can be defined as a suit that both sides recognize as having no merit, in which case the expected damage award is nil: $T_p = T_d = 0$. Thus the plaintiff's benefit from asserting a nuisance complaint from equation (7) reduces to:

$$L_p = (1 - p_{tp})(S_p - c_{sp}) - p_{tp}c_{tp}. \quad (8)$$

The value of equation (8) obviously cannot be positive unless S_p is positive. It is irrational to file a nuisance suit unless the expected value of a possible settlement is positive. In general, the decision rule allows the possibility of asserting claims whose expected trial value is nil only if their settlement value is positive.[27]

Why would a defendant pay damages to a plaintiff to settle a suit without merit? The answer offered in several models turns upon asymmetric costs. The central role of cost asymmetries can be illustrated by applying the Nash bargaining solution to our hybrid model. The Nash bargaining solution gives each player his threat value plus half the surplus from cooperation. Assuming risk neutrality, the general solution for plaintiff (for all suits) can be written:

$$\underbrace{p_{vp}D - c_{tp}}_{\text{Threat value}} + \underbrace{(1/2)[\{(c_{tp} + c_{td}) - (c_{sp} + c_{sd})\} + (p_{vd}D_d - p_{vp}D_p)]}_{\text{Half of surplus}} \quad (4')$$

Consider the effect of asymmetric trial costs on equation (4′). Assume that defendant's trial costs are greater than plaintiff's, $c_{td} > c_{tp}$, and assume the players are symmetric with respect to settlement costs and information about trial, so that $c_s = c_{sp} = c_{sd}$, $p_v = p_{vp} = p_{vd}$, and $D = D_p = D_d$. Under these assumptions, equation (4′) reduces to

$$p_vD + (1/2)(c_{td} - c_{tp}) - c_s/2. \quad (4'')$$

The Nash bargaining solution under these assumptions requires that plaintiff's payoff, net of all costs, equal expres-

[27] See also Bradford Cornell (1989), who uses an option pricing model to suggest that victims will file some suits for which the net present value is negative.

sion (4″). The plaintiff pays his own settlement costs, so (4″) will be satisfied if defendant pays to plaintiff a settlement amount, S, equal to the expected value of the trial judgment plus half the difference in trial costs:

$$S = p_v D + (1/2)(c_{td} - c_{tp}). \qquad (9)$$

An important conclusion follows from equation (9): Assuming strict symmetry in information and costs (including $c_{td} = c_{tp}$), the Nash solution to settlement bargaining requires the defendant to pay the plaintiff the expected judgment from trial. Furthermore, assuming asymmetry in costs, the Nash solution to settlement bargaining requires the party who saves relatively more from avoiding trial to share these gains with the party who saves relatively less.

A precise prediction about nuisance suits follows from equation (9). For nuisance suits, $p_v D = 0$ by definition, so $S = (1/2)(c_{td} - c_{tp})$. Thus the bargaining solution between risk-neutral players requires that defendant refuse to settle nuisance suits in which trial costs are symmetric ($S = 0$ when $c_{td} = c_{tp}$), and to settle for a positive amount when the trial costs the plaintiff less than the defendant ($S > 0$ when $c_{td} > c_{tp}$).

The preceding model explains nuisance suits by asymmetries in the costs of defendant and plaintiff. An alternative explanation rests upon asymmetries in the timing of costs. For example, David Rosenberg and Shavell (1985) propose a sequential game in which plaintiff files a suit at a negligible cost. Following this, the defendant must either settle or incur litigation costs. Only after the defendant's action must the plaintiff either withdraw or incur costly litigation. So long as the defendant must expend effort on litigation prior to the plaintiff, the defendant might find a small settlement cheaper than litigation.

Bebchuk (1988) uses a slightly different model that focuses on the settlement process itself. He shows that nuisance suits can lead to settlement when the defendant cannot be sure whether the plaintiff will go to trial or withdraw if there is no settlement. Finally, Thomas (1986) develops a sophisticated model of strategic bargaining and shows that asymmetric information, not asymmetric costs, can lead to settlement of nuisance suits for a positive sum of money.

The condition under which the victim will assert a claim is also sensitive to fee arrangements that the victim makes with his lawyer. Under a contingent fee arrangement, the incentive to assert a claim is different from what it would be under an hourly fee arrangement. Under the former, the lawyer bears some of the client's risk in exchange for a portion of the proceeds if the victim receives an award at settlement or trial. Under the latter the fee paid to the lawyer is independent of the victim's recovery. Danzon (1983) analyzes the effect of these two fee arrangements on the assertion of claims. She shows, for example, that a risk-preferring contingent fee attorney will accept a case that a risk-neutral hourly fee attorney would not take. However, it is also true that some claims that would be filed by a risk-neutral client using an hourly fee attorney would not be taken by a contingent fee lawyer.[28]

D. *Precaution Against Harm*

Our analysis has proceeded through three stages in a legal dispute in reverse chronological order, beginning with trial, followed by settlement bargaining, and then turning to assertion of legal claims. The fourth and final stage to consider is the harm that one person does to another. Harm can take many forms, such as tortious injury, breach of contract,

[28] Other contingent fee studies include Herbert Kritzer et al. (1984) and Danzon (1986).

trespass upon property. Injuries and victims usually have access to forms of precaution that reduce the probability and magnitude of harm.

By far the greatest focus of economists who study common law rules has been on incentives created for precaution by injurers and victims. Coverage ranges from the article by John Brown (1973) in which alternative liability rules (e.g., strict liability, negligence, and comparative negligence) are compared in a model in which accidents are treated as externalities, to the article by Coase (1960) in which similar rules are analyzed in a framework in which injurers and victims bargain over the level of precaution that both parties take. The level of precaution is determined in these models by a profit-maximizing or utility-maximizing calculus in which the cost of precaution is traded off against its benefits, often in the form of reduced liability.

Only in a few instances, however, has the analysis taken explicit account of the relationship that is the subject of this section—incentives for precaution created by the litigation process itself (see, for example, Jerry Green 1978 and P'ng 1987). Because litigation is expensive, expenditures on precaution will be made to reduce the probability and extent of litigation.

In extending our hybrid model to cover the relationship between litigation costs and incentives for precaution against harm, we proceed on the assumption that harm is an externality that cannot be cured in the market. In an externality model, harm done by the injurer affects the victim, and the victim's assertion of a legal claim affects the injurer. However, there is no bargaining between the parties to allocate the costs of harm before it occurs. As a consequence, levels of precaution by the parties are determined by the legal assignment of liability.

In an externality model, the injurer trades off the cost of additional precaution against the resulting reduction in legal claims. To formalize this optimization problem, the injurer's subjective probability that the victim will assert a legal claim, q_d, is assumed to be a decreasing, concave function of the injurer's precaution, denoted x_d, and other variables not made explicit: $q_d = q_d(x_d)$, where $q_d' < 0$, $q_d'' > 0$.

Let L_d denote the subjective expected cost to defendant of plaintiff's assertion of a legal claim. Analogous to equation (7), this expected cost is given by:

$$L_d = \{p_{td}[T_d\,(c_{tp}, c_{td}) + c_{td}] + (1 - p_{td})(S_d + c_{sd})\}. \quad (10)$$

From equation (10) it follows that more precaution by the injurer typically decreases the expected cost of legal claims.[29] This relationship is assumed to be concave: $L_d = L_d\,(x_d)$, where $L_d' < 0$ and $L_d'' > 0$. The injurer thus chooses precaution to minimize the sum of the costs of precaution and legal claims:

$$\text{Min } x_d + q_d(x_d)L_d(x_d). \quad (11)$$

Turning from injuries to victims, let x_p denote victim's expenditure on precaution against harm caused by injurer,

[29] Under every rule of law known to us, additional precaution by the injurer (weakly) decreases injurer's liability. To illustrate, under a negligence rule, more precaution by injurer increases the probability that the court will find injurer not liable because she satisfied the legal standard of care. Similarly, under a rule of strict liability, more precaution by injurer reduces the magnitude of the expected damage award. Additional precaution by the injurer thus tends to reduce her expected cost of trial, T_d. Furthermore, lowering her expected cost of trial, T_d, strengthens her threat position in settlement bargaining, so expected settlement, S_d, tends to fall as well. More precaution may even reduce the probability, p_t, that disputes will end in trial. (More precaution tends to reduce the severity of accidents, which reduces the stakes, and our previous analysis reached the tentative conclusion that larger stakes cause more trials.) Thus L_d is a nonincreasing function of x. (Strategic effects of larger x_d on plaintiff's choice variables are not discussed here.)

and let q_p and L_p indicate the probability and value, respectively, of the victim's subjective expectation concerning the assertion of a legal claim. To keep the analysis simple, assume that the victim asserts a claim if an accident occurs, but not otherwise.[30] Thus q_p can be interpreted as victim's subjective probability of an accident. q_p is assumed to be a decreasing, concave function of victim's precaution (and other implicit variables): $q_p = q_p(x_p)$, where $q_p' < 0$ and $q_p'' > 0$.

The potential victim who suffers harm equal to H_p receives a legal claim whose value is denoted L_p. The loss H_p is a concave, nonincreasing function of the victim's precaution (and other variables): $H_p = H_p(x_p)$, where $H_p' \leq 0$ and $H_p'' \geq 0$. The expected value of the legal claim L_p is also a function of x_p: $L_p = L_p(x_p)$. The sign of the derivative is not generally determinate, as can be seen from equation (7).[31] The difference in value between the harm H_p and the legal claim L_p measures the victim's net loss. The potential victim thus chooses x_p to minimize the sum of his precaution costs and his net loss from harm:

$$\text{Min } x_p + q_p(x_p)[H_p(x_p) - L_p(x_p)]. \quad (12)$$

A change in law that shifts the function $L_d(x_d)$ up, or increases its marginal value L_d', will, according to equation (11), induce more precaution from injurers. Conversely, a change in law that shifts $L_p(x_p)$ up, or increases its marginal value L_p', will, according to equation (12), induce less precaution from victims.

As an example, consider the effect of augmenting compensatory damages. This will simultaneously shift $L_d(x_d)$ and $L_p(x_p)$ up. Assuming independence, this will lead to more precaution by injurers and less by victims. This illustrates the contrast between distribution and efficiency in courts. In general, therefore, compensation rules that effectuate transfers increase incentives for precaution by one party, but they reduce incentives for the other party.

Alternatively, consider a change in the law that increases the defendant's subjective probability that a given case will go to trial. An injurer will settle a case only if the cost of settling is less than the expected cost of trial, that is, $s_d + c_{sd} < T_d + c_{td}$. It follows from equation (10) that L_d is an increasing function of the settlement probability. Consequently, as A. Mitchell Polinsky and Rubinfeld (1988b) suggest, the change in the law will shift $L_d(x_d)$ up, thereby generating more injurer precaution, and greater deterrence.

Finally, suppose another change in law increases the plaintiff's costs of litigation. The value of legal claims, L_p, to plaintiffs, will decrease, thereby causing potential victims to take more precaution. In addition, higher costs of trials will cause plaintiffs to assert fewer claims. The cost of legal claims, L_d, to defendants can either increase or decrease as a consequence, depending upon whether the effect of fewer claims or more costly claims dominates. In general, legal rules that increase the cost of resolving disputes increase incentives for precaution by victims and may either increase or decrease incentives for precaution by injurers.

III. *Normative Issues*

Legal policy has traditionally been evaluated by standards of fairness,

[30] Thus we are assuming that $c_{cp} < L_p$ for all accidents under consideration—the cost of asserting a claim is less than the plaintiff's expected benefit L_p.

[31] The plaintiff's subjective expected value of asserting a legal claim, L_p, equals the expected benefit, given by equation (7), less the cost of asserting the claim. The sign of the derivative of L_p with respect to x_p is indeterminate because more precaution by the victim generally reduces the magnitude of harm and increases the proportion of the costs of harm borne by the injurer. The magnitude of these effects, which go in opposite directions, depends upon the particulars of law and fact.

whereas the normative standard in most economic models is efficiency. Although efficiency is more controversial as a goal for law as opposed to markets, claims about efficiency have had a significant impact on legal scholarship, teaching, and, possibly, on courts (see Jerome Culp 1987). In this part of the paper we will discuss some normative concerns that can be treated within an efficiency framework. The first issue deals with the fourth stage of litigation, but the remaining issues combine several stages. The last section goes further by examining the behavior of judges as lawmakers.

A. *Trial Effort of Litigants—A Normative Analysis*

Courts and other lawmakers have several policy instruments to affect trial effort, including (1) the legal standard of care,[32] (2) the magnitude of damages (Rubinfeld and Sappington 1987), (3) the burden of evidence production (Joel Sobel 1989), (4) the standard of proof (Rubinfeld 1985), and (5) court costs (Rubinfeld and Sappington 1987). Each of these policy instruments directly affects the expenditure of parties at trial, and indirectly influences decisions at each stage of a legal dispute—trial, settlement, assertion of claims, and precaution. This section considers the direct effect of policy instruments on effort at trial and the outcomes of trials.

First consider the effect of trial effort on the accuracy of court decisions. Define a court decision as correct if it would be reached by applying the law under conditions of full information.[33] Instead of having full information, however, courts must make their decisions based on information provided largely by the disputants themselves. Effort by plaintiffs and defendants, and the rules governing evidence and procedure, determine a probability distribution of errors of Type I (finding violations where conformity occurred) and Type II (finding conformity where violations occurred).

It can be argued that more effort by both parties will disclose more information to the court, so its decision will come closer to the full information decision. More information can thus reduce errors of both types. Furthermore, cases with large stakes induce more effort by both parties. This view leads to the conclusion that bigger cases are more likely to be decided correctly (see Posner 1986, sect. 21.8).

One policy tool that typically induces greater trial effort by both parties is augmenting compensatory damages. The question of whether the increase in litigation effort from increasing damages has social value comparable to its cost has been investigated in several studies of treble damages in antitrust law (William Breit and Kenneth Elzinga 1974; Steven Salop and Lawrence White 1986). Polinsky and Rubinfeld (1988a) show how the optimal damage level changes when costly litigation is taken into account.

A different perspective is provided by considering incentives that cause more effort by one party and less by the other. If effort is productive, then more effort by the party that deserves to win increases the accuracy of court decisions, whereas more effort by the party that deserves to lose has the opposite effect. In the context of criminal trials, Rubinfeld and Sappington (1987) argue that more effort by innocent parties decreases the probability of Type I errors (convicting the innocent), and more effort by guilty parties increases the probability of Type II errors (not convicting the guilty).

Some legal rules, such as "loser pays all," may increase the accuracy of court

[32] To our knowledge, the complex relationship between the standard of care and trial effort by plaintiffs and defendants has not been formally studied.

[33] Notice that a "correct" decision gives everyone their due under law. This is Plato's first definition of justice in the *Republic*. Hobbes takes the view in *Leviathan* that there is no other concept of justice (no justice in nature).

decisions by providing incentives for more effort by parties that deserve to win than parties that deserve to lose. This point was already discussed in connection with nuisance suits, where the British and American rules for allocating litigation costs were discussed. Thus Marilyn Simon (1989) shows, assuming risk neutrality (but not otherwise), that a change from the American to the British rule reduces the probability of court error.

Instead of reducing both types of errors, some policy variables decrease one type while increasing the other. Thus a shift in the burden of proof from defendant to plaintiff might reduce Type I errors while increasing Type II errors. Identifying the "best" point on the frontier between the two types of errors involves perplexing normative issues.

Insight into these normative issues can be obtained from a game-theoretic framework. Suppose, as Sobel (1989) suggests, that both parties are bargaining with private information, but cannot publicly misrepresent that information. The judge has a prior distribution about the claims of the parties, but does not know their accuracy with certainty. In one equilibrium, each party has a positive probability of winning even if he does not provide evidence. In another equilibrium, a party wins only by presenting substantial evidence. In general the rules of the game, and in particular, which party has the burden of production of the evidence, will determine the equilibrium outcome.

Sobel shows, for example, with respect to this second equilibrium, that the overall cost of obtaining evidence is lowest if the burden of production is placed on the party that has the lowest cost of proving his claim. If the objective is to maximize the social value of the trial process, it is often better to place the burden of production on the party with the higher cost of providing evidence. If that party has a relatively weak claim, it will not present a case. But, if it has a relatively strong claim, the presentation will be worthwhile, despite the higher cost of evidence production.[34]

A central normative issue in discussions of legal procedure is balancing the cost of additional information against the benefit of reducing court errors. There is reason to wonder whether disputants value cumbersome procedural rules designed to produce accuracy as highly as do courts. Private systems of dispute resolution in which the parties choose their own rules, such as Visa corporation's system of arbitration among member banks, typically employ far cheaper procedures than those adopted by public courts.[35] Random inaccuracies are not too serious when the stakes are small relative to the disputants' wealth.

Unlike random inaccuracies in trial outcomes, which are unavoidable when information is costly, systematic inaccuracies have the appearance of bias. An alleged source of bias is defendant's identity. Econometric evidence has confirmed the belief among lawyers that juries will award greater damages when defendants are corporations rather than individuals, all else equal (see Hammitt, Carroll, and Relles 1985; and more generally Peterson 1984; Peterson and Priest

[34] Sobel's results are sensitive to the nature of the game, and the assumptions concerning asymmetry of information. Ordover and Rubinstein (1986) and Samuelson (1983) describe some alternative game-theoretic perspectives that could lead to different conclusions.

[35] We know of no systematic empirical investigations of this issue. Focusing on public decision makers, however, Alvin Klevorick and Michael Rothschild (1979) investigated whether streamlining juries would influence outcomes. They found that if the rule of unanimity on 12 person juries in criminal trials were replaced with a rule requiring at least 10 affirmative votes to convict, there would be little effect on the decision concerning guilt or innocence, but the time required to reach the decision would be reduced substantially.

1982; Shanley and Peterson 1983. Perhaps courts impose rules that are too cumbersome in an effort to reduce random inaccuracy, whereas bias is the serious concern.

B. *Private Versus Social Incentives to Bring Suit*

Many disputes involve claims for damages, which can be resolved by transfers of income. In general, the rules for making these transfers affect the incentives of the parties subject to current and future disputes. It is not surprising, therefore, that the private and social value of suits may diverge.

Our hybrid model can be used to trace this divergence with respect to incentives to assert legal claims. Recall that plaintiff decides whether to assert a legal claim by balancing the subjective expected benefit from trial with the cost of filing the claim, which yields the tipping point $C_{cp} = L_p$, where

$$L_p = p_{tp}[T_p(c_{tp}, c_{td}) - c_{tp}] + (1 - p_{tp})(S_p - c_{sp}). \quad (7)$$

Notice that defendant's litigation costs c_{td}, which are triggered by the assertion of a legal claim, are not borne by plaintiff and do not figure directly in her decision to assert a legal claim. Shavell (1982b) suggested that the private costs of asserting a legal claim are less than social costs under the American system because the plaintiff does not bear the defendant's litigation costs. Thus a plaintiff who runs the gamble of asserting a legal claim externalizes part of the cost of finding out whether it is worthless or valuable. Shavell also noted, however, a consideration pointing in the opposite direction. When trial costs are substantial, the private net benefit from trial may be negative (see also Shavell 1987, p. 267, example 11.2), even though the social gain from deterring injurers is large.

Peter Menell (1983) countered Shavell's argument that the private costs of suit are less than the social costs by pointing out that when victims do not pay injurer's costs of resolving disputes, injurers may respond by taking additional precaution. The additional precaution may or may not be socially efficient. Louis Kaplow (1986) refined this argument by distinguishing between the effect of precaution on the extent of harm and its probability. Arguments about the divergence of private and social incentives to sue were subsequently synthesized by Susan Rose-Ackerman and Mark Geistfeld (1987).

C. *Deterrence with a Costly, Uncertain Litigation Process*

Pioneering work on incentives for precaution, such as Brown (1973), compared the efficiency of alternative rules such as strict liability versus negligence for allocating the cost of harm. These studies assumed that all harm is pecuniary,[36] disputes can be resolved without cost, and courts apply clear legal standards without error. Our hybrid model will be extended to modify the conclusions when dispute resolution is costly and courts apply obscure standards or make errors.

A full extension would compare incentives for precaution by injurers and victims under alternative liability rules. For this review, however, the discussion will be restricted to the incentives for precaution by the injurer first under the rule of strict liability and then under a negligence rule. A basic conclusion of the early studies is that, assuming costless dispute resolution, the injurer's incentives for precaution under strict liability are efficient when the defendant must

[36] Nonpecuniary injuries, such as pain and suffering in tortious accidents, can affect total utility without affecting the marginal utility of money. In this situation, costly compensation is inefficient (see Philip Cook and Daniel Graham 1977).

fully compensate plaintiff. Full compensation is achieved when the victim is indifferent between avoiding the harm or suffering it and receiving compensation.

When this result is extended to the context of costly litigation, full compensation must include the cost of resolving the dispute, not just the harm that gave rise to it. Suppose disputes are resolved by trials. To achieve full compensation in our hybrid model under this assumption, a victim who is certain to win at trial must be compensated, not just for harm H_p caused by the accident, but for her trial costs c_{tp} plus her costs of asserting a claim c_{cp}. If, in addition, the court sometimes makes errors, so that the injured plaintiff wins at trial with probability p_{vp}, full compensation requires setting the damage award D_p so that

$$D_p = (H_p + c_{cp} + c_{tp})/p_{vp}. \quad (13)$$

A rule requiring full compensation of victims by injurers causes the latter to internalize costs, which induces efficient precaution by them. American law, however, typically requires the injurer to compensate the victim for the harm that gave rise to the legal claim, but not for the victim's cost of resolving the dispute. The injurer who expects accidents to result in trials will, consequently, choose a level of precaution knowing that he must pay for his precaution, the expected harm, and *his* litigation costs.

The resulting externality will distort injurer's precaution. It might appear that this element of externalized cost will always cause injurers to take too little precaution relative to the socially efficient level. In fact, this will be true if litigation is relatively costly and precaution is relatively inexpensive. (In this case the efficient level of precaution will be higher with costly litigation than without, because additional precaution reduces the expense of litigation substantially.)

However, Polinsky and Rubinfeld (1988a) have shown that this element of externalized cost may result in a greater than efficient level of injurer precaution in cases when litigation is relatively inexpensive and precaution is quite costly. This surprising result occurs when additional injurer precaution substantially reduces the number of suits that victims bring, and thereby reduces the injurer's liability and his litigation cost. (Recall that victims bring suit only when their expected benefit is greater than their litigation cost. Additional precaution by the injurer can tip many victims from the region in which they bring suit to the region in which they do not.)

A further qualification of the efficient standard is required when the outcome of litigation is uncertain and the rule of strict liability is replaced by a negligence rule. Early models showed that if courts set the legal standard of care equal to the efficient level of precaution, and if they apply this standard without error, injurers will exactly conform to the legal standard, as required for efficient precaution. Suppose, however, that courts make errors in applying a negligence rule, as a consequence of which some negligent defendants escape liability and some non-negligent defendants are found liable. It may be advantageous for injurers to depart from the legal standard under these circumstances. Whether they exceed it or fall short is indeterminate in principle, although it seems likely that injurers will want to exceed the legal standard to allow a margin of error by courts within which liability is avoided.[37] Efficiency can be achieved by appropriate adjustment in the legal standard to offset the departure of injurers from it. For further discussion, see John Calfee

[37] Calfee and Craswell (1984) show that a reduced standard may be preferred, because increased precaution by the injurer reduces the probability that a suit will be successful and that the victim will recover damages.

and Richard Craswell (1984), Craswell and Calfee (1986), and Mark Grady (1983).[38]

Errors by the court need not be symmetric, and damage rules other than compensatory damages are possible. P'ng (1986) has pursued this line of thought by focusing on the deterrent effects of Type I and Type II errors. He points out (in the context of a rule of strict liability) that Type II errors, in which penalties are mistakenly assessed against nonviolators, lower the relative cost of violating the law, rather than conforming to it. To insure that the appropriate incentives are created, P'ng proposes a positive adjustment to compensatory damages so that violators must pay more, along with a subsidy for those who engage in the activity that runs the risk of being found in violation of the law by mistake.

D. *Lawmaking By Courts*

Most analyses relating to the courts have focused on the behavior of the parties prior to and during the litigation process. An important area of study that has received less attention is the role of courts in the lawmaking process. This section briefly summarizes the state of the lawmaking literature, and speculates about some fruitful avenues of research.

Some economically oriented scholars of the common law accept the positive and normative efficiency thesis, according to which judge-made law tends toward efficiency and reinforcing this tendency is good public policy (Posner 1986). The positive thesis is testable, at least in principle, but there has been little quantitative research on how the common law changes.[39] The normative thesis, while not a statistically demonstrable conclusion, is rather a conviction that some people reach by reading many cases.

How might lawmaking by courts lead to efficient outcomes? Two different explanations correspond to two different conceptions of the common law. One conception, which regards litigation as a market, views the common law process as driven by competition among rationally self-interested actors. The other conception, which regards judging as an exercise in public reason, views the common law process as driven by the theories of law embraced by judges. We review the hypothesis that law is market-driven here, but omit a discussion of the hypothesis that it is idea-driven because of the limited economic work that has been done.

Several ingenious attempts have been made to explain how competition among litigants, like market competition among businesses, can produce efficiency without anyone consciously aiming for it.[40] One such mechanism is selective litigation. Suppose that inefficient laws are more likely to be litigated than efficient laws. If inefficient laws are repeatedly challenged in court, they may be over-

[38] Polinsky (1987) treated a different, but related, case in which the injurer has imperfect information about the victim's loss. The injurer balances his gain from acting against his perception of the victim's loss. Polinsky shows that under strict liability and a negligence rule it is optimal to adjust compensatory damages upward when the average gains of injurers are less the average losses of victims. A corresponding downward adjustment is optimal when the opposite is true.

[39] In a recent paper Priest tried to test whether changes in doctrine by judges, which increase uncertainty, cause an increase in the scope of disagreement among litigants. His data apparently show that doctrinal change and increased disagreement occur in the same year, but not which occurs first. This fact is consistent with his hypothesis or with the rival hypothesis that changes in doctrine resolve uncertainties that cause litigants to disagree. See Priest (1987) and Cooter (1987b).

[40] This possibility was first raised by Paul Rubin (1977). See also Priest (1977) and John Goodman (1978). For a discussion of dynamic efficiency, see Landes and Posner (1979) and Lawrence Blume and Rubinfeld (1982).

turned, whereas if efficient laws are less frequently challenged, they are more likely to persist unchanged. Selective litigation could work like a strainer that catches inefficient laws while allowing efficient laws to slip past. The product, being repeatedly sieved, becomes more efficient with the passage of time. Two assumptions are enough to cause the law to evolve toward efficiency, at least weakly: (i) A rule's efficiency is negatively correlated to the probability that litigants will test it in court, and (ii) efficiency is not negatively correlated to the probability of a rule surviving such a test before a judge.[41] For the process to operate, judges need not favor efficiency, but they must not disfavor it.

Does litigation tend to select inefficient laws? Theory suggests a weak "Yes." The more someone values a contested legal entitlement, the more that party will be prepared to spend on litigation to obtain it. Larger litigation expenditures increase the frequency of court challenges and improve their quality, which, in turn, increases the probability of winning. Thus the value that a person places upon a legal entitlement should correlate with the probability of winning it through litigation. By transferring legal entitlements from parties who value them less to parties who value them more, the common law tends toward efficiency.

This process can be redescribed as a contrast between distribution and efficiency. The allocation of legal entitlements affects both the quantity of wealth and its distribution. When legal entitlements are allocated inefficiently, the plaintiff who overturns the misallocation stands to gain from both the increase in wealth and from its redistribution. In contrast, when legal entitlements are already allocated efficiently, the plaintiff who overturns the allocation stands to gain from the redistribution of wealth and to lose from the decrease in its quantity. Because the value of overturning inefficient laws exceeds the value of overturning efficient laws, the frequency and quality of challenges to inefficient laws should be higher than for efficient laws.

Selective litigation is similar to the "invisible hand" in markets, but, unfortunately, the grip of the invisible hand on courts is far weaker than on markets. A law is, by its nature, general in the scope of its application, so challenging a law affects everyone who is, or will be, subject of it. Most plaintiffs appropriate no more than a fraction of the value that new precedent creates and redistributes. The effects of a new, more efficient precedent spill far beyond the litigants in the case where it is set. Litigants, however, may have little regard for the social costs that an inefficient rule imposes on others. The bias toward efficiency may be overwhelmed by the inclination of plaintiffs to challenge laws when they can capture a large share of the precedent's value. Plaintiffs may thus bring suit when they expect the redistributive gains of a successful suit to be large, regardless of the law's efficiency or inefficiency. The problem with viewing litigation as a market is that redistributive gains are frequently more important than inefficiencies in channeling litigation.[42]

An exception to this pessimistic conclusion concerns laws that are vague. Bargaining games are hard to settle when the parties do not know each others' threat points. (See Elizabeth Hoffman and Matthew Spitzer 1982.) An implication is that vague laws cause litigation.

[41] A precise statement of the conditions for such evolution is found in Cooter and Lewis Kornhauser (1980).

[42] This problem is not solved by class action suits where the plaintiff represents a whole class of people whose legal rights will be extinguished by resolution of the dispute. See Kenneth Dam (1975), Andrew Rosenfield (1976), and Kornhauser (1983).

Laws whose inefficiency derives from their vagueness will tend to be litigated until the courts achieve a clear allocation of the underlying entitlements.

Our view is that, so far as common law tends toward efficiency, it must be driven by the ideas of judges, not by competitive pressures in the market for litigation. There is some evidence that the judiciary is giving a larger role to economic reasoning in its decisions (Frank Easterbrook 1984), but there is also evidence that the judiciary tends to expand its own powers, much as a bureaucracy engorges itself, without regard to benefits and costs. In addition, the fact that important legal cases are decided by majority vote of panels of judges raises the possibility that courts are afflicted by the same voting paradoxes as legislatures (Easterbrook 1982; Kornhauser and Lawrence Sager 1986; Matthew Spitzer 1979, 1980).

The ideal of an independent judiciary implies creating circumstances under which judges decide cases that do not affect their private interests. The salary and tenure of federal judges are independent of their performance, and their performance is apparently unrelated to promotion to a higher court (Richard Higgins and Paul Rubin 1980). These facts raise an issue about whether disinterestedness provides the best incentive structure, or whether competition among adjudicators might improve the efficiency of dispute resolution. The service of resolving disputes is supplied privately by arbitrators. In some states, notably California, disputants can avoid long delays in trial by hiring a retired judge to decide their case.[43]

Economists have compared the incentives of public and private judges (Landes and Posner 1979; Robert Cooter 1983; Christopher Bruce 1988). Private judges maximize their own incomes by deciding disputes so as to maximize the demand for their services. If a judge's decisions were not on the Pareto frontier, a rival judge could lure away the former's customers by offering decisions that both parties prefer. There is, then, a strong incentive for private judges to achieve Pareto efficiency with respect to the disputants. However, the parties to a dispute who hire a private adjudicator do not internalize all the benefits of improving the law. Better rules will benefit future cases to which current disputants are not a party. Thus the incentives of private judges for creating new laws may be deficient.

Besides making common law, judges interpret statutes. Interpreting statutes involves supplying operational definitions for statutory language and applying these definitions to decide cases. Economists tend to conceive of legislation as the product of bargaining among the representatives of various interests. This view suggests that statutes should be interpreted according to the understandings and purposes of the underlying legislative bargain, much like the interpretation of business contracts (Easterbrook 1982). The purpose of legislative bargains, like business bargains, is to maximize the surplus from exchange. If this view is persuasive, then efficiency considerations should enter directly into the interpretation of statutes.[44]

Unlike the collective choice literature, which is replete with impossibility theorems, the efficiency thesis sounds an optimistic note: Courts are efficient. This

[43] California's "rent-a-judge" is bound by the substantive laws of the state, but not by its procedural rules, so decision making can be streamlined. The decision of the rented judge acquires the force of law after it is filed with the court.

[44] An alternative view is that courts lack the information to enforce the underlying bargain, and instead they should interpret statutes exclusively on the basis of the language in which they are written (Jonathan Macey 1986; Rose-Ackerman 1988).

thesis, when combined with the impossibility theorems, implies that courts are better than elected officials at shaping efficient laws. This proposition, if true, has important implications for judicial review: Instead of deferring to elected officials, courts should vigorously review legislation and regulations (William Riker and Barry Weingast 1986).

IV. *Conclusion*

The economic models of legal disputes and their resolution by courts described in this article represent a substantial improvement along some dimensions over traditional legal scholarship. Explaining the process of dispute resolution as an equilibrium in the interaction of self-interested decision makers draws upon a well-developed behavioral model that permits a comparison of the efficiency of alternative legal rules. Indeed, the greatest strength of this literature is its careful working out of the inexorable logic of self-interest. The models consequently provide a point of reference that legal theory needs for an understanding of courts and for deliberation over proposed changes in rules.

There are, however, significant obstacles and resistances that leave scope for development and, possibly, breakthroughs in the future. First, the literature suffers from the unsatisfactory state of bargaining theory. Improvements in the general theory of strategic bargaining will strengthen the economic theory of legal disputes and courts. Indeed, the insights needed to improve strategic bargaining theory may be inspired partly by law's institutional detail. Second, as long as disinterested decision making remains a mystery to economics, the motives of judges cannot be endogenous in economic models. A better model of judicial decision making will force economics into the mainstream of jurisprudential debate about the motivation of judges. Third, the law and economics literature have yet to pursue adequately the modern economic theory of organizations, and to apply that theory to the operation of courts and to other institutions (such as corporations) whose governance rules are primarily legal. Finally, and most important, empirical research has lagged woefully behind theoretical advances. Improved data collection and additional econometric studies are needed to improve the empirical grounding of the economic analysis of law.

We would be remiss if we failed to mention the gain to economics from the interaction with law. The courts, like the stock market, respond quickly to shocks in ways that economists cannot seem to anticipate. In fact, the legal institutions that have evolved to deal with the externalities created by injurers are more varied and subtle than the traditional taxing institutions that are the focal point of many economists. For example, a decade of effort by economists to develop theories of tort law succeeded on its own scholarly terms, but economists all too often provided efficiency proofs for institutions that most lawyers now view as inefficient. The proposals for reform that the "tort crisis" has put on the agenda of legislatures and courts raise issues of institutional design that economists have just begun to consider. Economists can learn from lawyers how to make our policy science more deft, flexible, and responsive to a living institution.

References

Baxter, William. "The Political Economy of Antitrust," in *The political economy of antitrust*. Ed.: Robert Tollison. Lexington, MA: Lexington Press, 1980, pp. 3–49.

Bebchuk, Lucian Arye. "Litigation and Settlement Under Imperfect Information," *Rand J. Econ.*, Autumn 1984, *15*(3), pp. 404–15.

———. "Suing Solely to Extract a Settlement Offer," *J. Legal Stud.*, June 1988, *17*(2), pp. 437–50.

BINMORE, KEN; RUBINSTEIN, ARIEL AND WOLINSKY, ASHER. "The Nash Bargaining Solution in Economic Modelling," *Rand J. Econ.*, Summer 1986, *17*(2), pp. 176–88.

BLANKENBERG, ERHARD. "Legal Insurance, Litigant Decision, and the Rising Caseloads of Courts: A West German Study," *Law Soc. Rev.*, 1981–82, *16*, pp. 601–24.

BLUME, LAWRENCE E. AND RUBINFELD, DANIEL L. "The Dynamics of the Legal Process," *J. Legal Stud.*, June 1982, *11*(2), pp. 405–19.

BRAEUTIGAM, RONALD; OWEN, BRUCE M. AND PANZAR, JOHN. "An Economic Analysis of Alternative Fee Shifting Systems," *Law Contemp. Probl.*, Winter 1984, *47*(1), pp. 173–85.

BREIT, WILLIAM AND ELZINGA, KENNETH G. "Antitrust Enforcement and Economic Efficiency: The Uneasy Case for Treble Damages," *J. Law Econ.*, Oct. 1974, *17*(2), pp. 329–56.

BROWN, JOHN P. "Toward an Economic Theory of Liability," *J. Legal Stud.*, June 1973, *2*(2), pp. 323–50.

BRUCE, CHRISTOPHER. "The Adjudication of Labor Disputes as a Private Good," *Int. Rev. Law Econ.*, June 1988, *8*(1), pp. 3–19.

CALFEE, JOHN E. AND CRASWELL, RICHARD. "Some Effects of Uncertainty on Compliance with Legal Standards," *Virginia Law Rev.*, June 1984, *70*(5), pp. 965–1003.

CHEUNG, RAYNER. "A Bargaining Model of Pre-Trial Negotiation." Working Paper No. 49, Stanford Law School, John M. Olin Program in Law and Economics, Nov. 1988.

COASE, RONALD. "The Nature of the Firm," *Economica, N.S.*, Nov. 1937, *4*, pp. 386–405.

———. "The Problem of Social Cost," *J. Law Econ.*, Oct. 1960, *3*, pp. 1–44.

COFFEE, JOHN. "Understanding the Plaintiff's Attorney: The Implications of Economic Theory for Private Enforcement of the Law Through Class and Derivative Actions," *Columbia Law Rev.*, May 1986, *86*(4), pp. 669–727.

COMMONS, JOHN R. "Law and Economics," *Yale Law J.*, Feb. 1925, *34*(4), pp. 371–82.

COOK, PHILIP J. AND GRAHAM, DANIEL A. "The Demand for Insurance and Protection: The Case of Irreplaceable Commodities," *Quart. J. Econ.*, Feb. 1977, *91*(1), pp. 143–56.

COOTER, ROBERT D. "The Objectives of Private and Public Judges," *Public Choice*, 1983, *41*(1), pp. 107–32.

———. "The Coase Theorem," *The new Palgrave: A dictionary of economics*, Vol. 1. Eds.: JOHN EATWELL, MURRAY MILGATE AND PETER NEWMAN. 1987a, pp. 457–60.

———. "Why Litigants Disagree: Comment on George Priest's Measuring Legal Change'," *J. Law Econ. Organ.*, Fall 1987b, *3*(2), pp. 227–34.

COOTER, ROBERT AND KORNHAUSER LEWIS. "Can Litigation Improve the Law Without the Help of Judges?" *J. Legal Stud.*, Jan. 1980, *9*, pp. 139–63.

COOTER, ROBERT; MARKS, STEPHEN AND MNOOKIN, ROBERT. "Bargaining in the Shadow of the Law: A Testable Model of Strategic Behavior," *J. Legal Stud.*, June 1982, *11*(2), pp. 225–51.

CORNELL, BRADFORD. "The Incentive to Sue: An Option Pricing Approach." Working Paper 3–89, Anderson Graduate School of Management, UCLA, Jan. 1989.

COURSEY, DONALD L. "Bilateral Bargaining, Pareto Optimality, and the Empirical Frequency of Impasse," *J. Econ. Behav. Organ.*, June/Sept. 1982, *3*(2–3), pp. 243–59.

COURSEY, DONALD L. AND STANLEY, LINDA R. "Pretrial Bargaining Behavior Within the Shadow of the Law: Theory and Experimental Evidence," *Int. Rev. Law Econ.*, Dec. 1988, *8*, pp. 161–79.

CRASWELL, RICHARD AND CALFEE, JOHN E. "Deterrence and Uncertain Legal Standards," *J. Law Econ. Organ.*, Fall 1986, *2*(2), pp. 279–303.

CULP, JEROME, ed. "Symposium: Economists on the Bench," *Law Contemp. Probl.*, Autumn 1987, *50*(4).

DAM, KENNETH. "Class Actions: Efficiency, Compensation Deterrence, and Conflict of Interest," *J. Legal Stud.*, Jan. 1975, *4*(1), pp. 47–73.

DANZON, PATRICIA MUNCH. "Contingent Fees for Personal Injury Litigation," *Bell J. Econ.*, Spring 1983, *14*(1), pp. 213–24.

———. "The Frequency and Severity of Medical Malpractice Claims: New Evidence," *Law Contemp. Probl.*, Spring 1986, *49*(2), pp. 57–84.

DANZON, PATRICIA MUNCH AND LILLARD, LEE A. "Settlement Out of Court: The Disposition of Medical Malpractice Claims," *J. Legal Stud.*, June 1983, *12*(2), pp. 345–77.

EASTERBROOK, FRANK H. "Ways of Criticizing the Court," *Harvard Law Rev.*, Feb. 1982, *95*(4), pp. 802–32.

———. "The Supreme Court, 1983 Term—Foreword: The Court and the Economic System," *Harvard Law Rev.*, Nov. 1984, *98*(1), pp. 4–60.

ELLICKSON, ROBERT C. "Bringing Culture and Human Frailty to Rational Actors: A Critique of Classical Law-and-Economics." Prepared for Chicago-Kent Law Review Symposium on Post-Chicago Law-and-Economics, Feb., 1989.

ENGELMANN, KATHLEEN AND CORNELL, BRADFORD. "Measuring the Cost of Corporate Litigation: Five Case Studies," *J. Legal Stud.*, June 1988, *17*(2), pp. 377–99.

GALANTER, MARC. "Reading the Landscape of Disputes: What We Know and Don't Know (And Think We Know) About Our Allegedly Contentious and Litigious Society," *UCLA Law Rev.*, Oct. 1983, *31*, pp. 4–71.

GOODMAN, JOHN. "An Economic Theory of the Evolution of the Common Law," *J. Legal Stud.*, June 1978, *7*(2), p. 393–406.

GOULD, JOHN. "The Economics of Legal Conflicts," *J. Legal Stud.*, June 1973, *2*(2), pp. 279–300.

GRADY, MARK F. "A New Positive Economic Theory of Negligence," *Yale Law J.*, Apr. 1983, *92*(5), pp. 799–829.

GRAVELLE, HUGH. "Accidents and the Allocation of Legal Costs with an Uninformed Court," *The Ge-*

neva Papers on Risk and Insurance, Jan. 1989, *14*, pp. 11–26.

GREEN, JERRY. "Medical Malpractice and the Propensity to Litigate," in *The economics of medical malpractice*. Ed.: SIMON ROTTENBERG. Washington, DC: American Enterprise Institute for Public Policy Research, 1978, pp. 193–201.

GROSSMAN, GENE M. AND KATZ, MICHAEL L. "Plea Bargaining and Social Welfare," *Amer. Econ. Rev.*, Sept. 1983, *7*(4), pp. 749–57.

HAMMITT, JAMES; CARROLL, STEVE AND RELLES, DANIEL. "Tort Standards and Jury Decisions," *J. Legal Stud.*, Dec. 1985, *14*, pp. 751–62.

HARSANYI, JOHN. "Games with Incomplete Information Played by 'Bayesian Players'," *Manage. Sci.*, Jan. 1968, *41*(5), pp. 320–34.

HAUSE, JOHN C. "Indemnity, Settlement, and Litigation, or, I'll Be Suing You," *J. Legal Stud.*, Jan. 1989, *18*(1) pp. 157–79

HIGGINS, RICHARD S. AND RUBIN, PAUL H. "Judicial Discretion," *J. Legal Stud.*, Jan. 1980, *9*(1), pp. 129–38.

HOFFMAN, ELIZABETH AND SPITZER, MATTHEW L. "The Coase Theorem: Some Experimental Tests," *J. Law Econ.*, Apr. 1982, *25*(1), pp. 73–98.

KAKALIK, JAMES S. AND ROBYN, ABBY E. "Costs of the Civil Justice System." Report R-2888-ICJ, Rand Corporation, 1982.

KAPLOW, LOUIS. "Private Versus Social Costs in Bringing Suit," *J. Legal Stud.*, June 1986, *15*(2), pp. 371–85.

KATZ, AVERY. "Measuring the Demand for Litigation: Is the English Rule Really Cheaper?" *J. Law Econ. Organ.*, Fall 1987, *3*(2), pp. 143–76.

———. "Judicial Decisionmaking and Litigation Expenditure," *Int. Rev. Law Econ.*, Dec. 1988, *8*, pp. 127–43.

KLEVORICK, ALVIN AND ROTHSCHILD, MICHAEL. "A Model of the Jury Decision Process," *J. Legal Stud.*, Jan. 1979, *8*, p. 141–64.

KORNHAUSER, LEWIS A. "Control of Conflicts of Interest in Class-Action Suits," *Public Choice*, 1983, 41(1), p. 145.

KORNHAUSER, LEWIS AND SAGER, LAWRENCE. "Unpacking the Court," *Yale Law J.*, Jan. 1986, *96*(1), pp. 82–117.

KREPS, DAVID M. AND WILSON, ROBERT. "Reputation and Imperfect Information," *J. Econ. Theory*, Aug. 1982, *27*(2), pp. 253–79.

KRITZER, HERBERT ET AL. "Understanding the Costs of Litigation: The Case of the Hourly-Fee Lawyer," *Amer. Bar Foundation Res. J.*, Spring 1984, pp. 559–604.

LANDES, WILLIAM M. "An Economic Analysis of the Courts," *J. Law Econ.*, Apr. 1971, *14*(1), pp. 61–107.

LANDES, WILLIAM M. AND POSNER, RICHARD A. "Adjudication as a Private Good," *J. Legal Stud.*, Mar. 1979, *8*(2), pp. 235–84.

MACEY, JONATHAN. "Promoting Public-Regarding Legislation Through Statutory Interpretation: An Interest Group Model," *Columbia Law Rev.*, Mar. 1986, *86*(2), pp. 223–68.

MENELL, PETER. "A Note on Private Versus Social Incentives to Sue in a Costly Legal System," *J. Legal Stud.*, Jan. 1983, *12*(1), pp. 41–52.

MILLER, GEOFFREY P. "An Economic Analysis of Rule 68," *J. Legal Stud.*, Jan. 1986, *15*(1), pp. 93–125.

MNOOKIN, ROBERT AND WILSON, ROBERT. "Rational Bargaining and Market Efficiency: Understanding Pennzoil v. Texaco," *Virginia Law Rev.*, Mar. 1989, *75*(2), pp. 295–334.

NALEBUFF, BARRY. "Credible Pretrial Negotiation," *Rand J. Econ.*, Summer 1987, *18*(2), pp. 198–210.

ORDOVER, JANUSZ A. AND RUBINSTEIN, ARIEL. "A Sequential Concession Game with Asymmetric Information," *Quart. J. Econ.*, Nov. 1986, *101*(4), pp. 879–88.

PASHIGIAN, B. PETER. "A Theory of Prevention and Legal Defense with an Application to the Legal Costs of Companies," *J. Law Econ.*, Oct. 1982, *25*(2), pp. 247–70.

PERLOFF, JEFFREY M. AND RUBINFELD, DANIEL L. "Settlements in Private Antitrust Litigation," in *Private antitrust litigation*. Eds.: STEVEN SALOP AND LAWRENCE WHITE. Cambridge: MIT Press, 1987, pp. 149–84.

PETERSON, MARK A. "Compensation of Injuries: Civil Jury Verdicts in Cook County." Report R-3011-ICJ, Rand Corporation, 1984.

PETERSON, MARK A. AND PRIEST, GEORGE L. "The Civil Jury: Trends in Trials and Verdicts, Cook County, Illinois, 1960–1979," *Federation of Insurance Counsel Quarterly*, Summer 1982, *32*, pp. 361–72.

P'NG, IVAN PAAK LIANG. "Strategic Behavior in Suit, Settlement, and Trial," *Bell J. Econ.*, Autumn 1983, *14*(2), pp. 539–50.

———. "Optimal Subsidies and Damages in the Presence of Judicial Error," *Int. Rev. Law Econ.*, June 1986, *6*(1), pp. 101–05.

———. "Litigation, Liability, and Incentives for Care," *J. Public Econ.*, Oct. 1987, *34*(1), pp. 61–86.

POLINSKY, A. MITCHELL. "Optimal Liability When the Injurer's Information About the Victim's Loss is Imperfect," *Int. Rev. Law Econ.*, Dec. 1987, *7*(2), pp. 139–47.

POLINSKY, A. MITCHELL AND RUBINFELD, DANIEL L. "The Welfare Implications of Costly Litigation for the Theory of Liability," *J. Legal Stud.*, Jan. 1988a, *17*(1), 151–64.

———. "The Deterrent Effects of Settlements and Trials," *Int. Rev. Law Econ.*, June 1988b, *8*(1), pp. 109–16.

POSNER, RICHARD A. "An Economic Approach to Legal Procedure and Judicial Administration," *J. Legal Stud.*, June 1973, *2*(2), pp. 399–458.

———. *Economic analysis of law*. 3rd ed. Boston: Little-Brown, 1986.

PRIEST, GEORGE L. "The Common Law Process and the Selection of Efficient Rules," *J. Legal Stud.*, Jan. 1977, *6*(1), pp. 65–82.

———. "Selective Characteristics of Litigation," *J. Legal Stud.*, Mar. 1980, 9, pp. 399–421.

———. "Reexamining the Selection Hypothesis," *J. Legal Stud.*, Jan. 1985, *14*(1), pp. 215–43.

_____. "Measuring Legal Change," *J. Law Econ. Organ.*, Fall 1987, *3*(2), pp. 193–225.

PRIEST, GEORGE L. AND KLEIN, BENJAMIN. "The Selection of Disputes for Litigation," *J. Legal Stud.*, Jan. 1984, *13*(1), pp. 1–55.

REINGANUM, JENNIFER F. "Plea Bargaining and Prosecutorial Discretion," *Amer. Econ. Rev.*, Sept. 1988, *78*(4), 713–28.

REINGANUM, JENNIFER F. AND WILDE, LOUIS. "Settlement, Litigation and the Allocation of Litigation Costs," *Rand J. Econ.*, Winter 1986, *17*, pp. 557–66.

RIKER, WILLIAM H. AND WEINGAST, BARRY. "The Political and Economic Consequences of Judicial Deference to Legislatures." Mimeo., Mar. 1986.

ROSE-ACKERMAN, SUSAN. "Progressive Law and Economics—and the New Administrative Law," *Yale Law J.*, Dec. 1988, *98*, pp. 341–68.

ROSE-ACKERMAN, SUSAN AND GEISTFELD, MARK. "The Divergence Between Social and Private Incentives to Sue: A Comment on Shavell, Menell and Kaplow," *J. Legal Stud.*, June 1987, *16*(2), pp. 483–91.

ROSENBERG, DAVID AND SHAVELL, STEPHEN. "A Model in Which Suits Are Brought for Their Nuisance Value," *Int. Rev. Law Econ.*, June 1985, *5*(1), pp. 3–13.

ROSENFIELD, ANDREW. "An Empirical Test of Class Action Settlement," *J. Legal Stud.*, Jan. 1976, *5*(1), pp. 113–20.

ROWE, THOMAS D., JR. "Predicting the Effects of Attorney Fee Shifting," *Law Contemp. Probl.*, Winter 1984, *47*, pp. 139–71.

RUBIN, PAUL. "Why Is the Common Law Efficient?" *J. Legal Stud.*, Jan. 1977, *6*(1), pp. 51–63.

RUBINFELD, DANIEL L. "On Determining the Optimal Magnitude and Length of Liability in Torts," *J. Legal Stud.*, June 1984, *13*(3), pp. 551–63.

_____. "Econometrics in the Courtroom," *Columbia Law Rev.*, June 1985, *85*(5), pp. 1048–97.

RUBINFELD, DANIEL L. AND SAPPINGTON, DAVID. "Efficient Awards and Standards of Proof in Judicial Proceedings," *Rand J. Econ.*, 1987, *18*, pp. 308–15.

SALANT, STEPHEN W. "Litigation of Settlement Demands Questioned by Bayesian Defendants." Social Science Working Paper No. 516, Calif. Inst. of Tech., Mar. 1984.

SALOP, STEVEN C. AND WHITE, LAWRENCE. "Economic Analysis of Private Antitrust Litigation," *Georgetown Law J.*, Apr. 1986, *74*(4), pp. 1001–64.

SAMUELSON, WILLIAM. "Negotiation vs. Litigation." Discussion Paper, Boston U. School of Management, Apr. 1983.

SCHOTTER, ANDREW AND ORDOVER, JANUSZ. "The Cost of the Tort System." C. V. Starr Center for Applied Economics, NYU, Mar. 1986.

SCHWEIZER, URS. "Litigation and Settlement in Sequential Equilibrium." Discussion Paper A-52, U. of Bonn, Apr. 1986.

SHANLEY, MARK AND PETERSON, MARK A. "Comparative Justice: Civil Jury Verdicts in San Francisco and Cook Counties, 1959–1980," *Rand Institute for Civil Justice*, Report R-3006-ICJ, 1983.

SHAVELL, STEVEN. "Suit, Settlement, and Trial: A Theoretical Analysis Under Alternative Methods for the Allocation of Legal Costs," *J. Legal Stud.*, Jan. 1982a, *11*(1), pp. 55–81.

_____. "The Social Versus Private Incentive to Bring Suit in a Costly Legal System," *J. Legal Stud.*, June 1982b, *11*(2), pp. 333–39.

_____. *Economic analysis of accidents*, Cambridge: Harvard U. Press, 1987.

_____. "Sharing of Information Prior to Settlement or Litigation," *Rand J.*, under review, 1989.

SIMON, MARILYN. "Product Quality and the Allocation of Legal Costs." U.S. Dept. of Justice, Jan. 1989.

SOBEL, JOEL. "An Analysis of Discovery Rules," *Law Contemp. Probl.*, Winter 1989, *52*(1).

SPITZER, MATTHEW. "Multicriteria Choice Process: An Application of Public Choice Theory to Bakke, the FCC, and the Courts," *Yale Law J.*, 1979, *88*(4), pp. 717–79.

_____. "Radio Formats by Administrative Choice," *U. Chicago Law Rev.*, Summer 1980, *47*(4), pp. 647–87.

SPULBER, DANIEL. "Contingent Damages and Settlement Bargaining." Working paper, U. of Southern California, Dept. of Economics, 1988.

STIGLER, GEORGE. "The Fire of Truth: A Remembrance of Law and Economics at Chicago, 1932–1970," *J. Law Econ.*, Apr. 1983, *26*, pp. 163–234.

THOMAS, ROBERT E. "Two-Stage Litigation with Two-Sided Asymmetric Information." Graduate School of Business, Stanford U., Draft, June 1986.

TRUBEK, DAVID M. ET AL. "The Costs of Ordinary Litigation," *UCLA Law Rev.*, Oct. 31, 1983, pp. 72–127.

WILLIAMSON, OLIVER. *Markets and hierarchies: Analysis and antitrust implications*. NY: Free Press, 1975.

WITTMAN, DONALD. "Is the Selection of Cases for Trial Biased?" *J. Legal Stud.*, 1985, *14*(1), pp. 185–214.

_____. "Dispute Resolution, Bargaining, and the Selection of Cases for Trial: A Study of the Generation of Biased and Unbiased Data," *J. Legal Stud.*, June 1988, *17*(2), pp. 313–52.

Part III
The Coase Theorem and the Economics of Property Rights

[10]

The Journal of

LAW & ECONOMICS

VOLUME III OCTOBER 1960

THE PROBLEM OF SOCIAL COST

R. H. COASE
University of Virginia

I. The Problem To Be Examined[1]

This paper is concerned with those actions of business firms which have harmful effects on others. The standard example is that of a factory the smoke from which has harmful effects on those occupying neighbouring properties. The economic analysis of such a situation has usually proceeded in terms of a divergence between the private and social product of the factory, in which economists have largely followed the treatment of Pigou in *The Economics of Welfare*. The conclusions to which this kind of analysis seems to have led most economists is that it would be desirable to make the owner of the factory liable for the damage caused to those injured by the smoke, or alternatively, to place a tax on the factory owner varying with the amount of smoke produced and equivalent in money terms to the damage it would cause, or finally, to exclude the factory from residential districts (and presumably from other

[1] This article, although concerned with a technical problem of economic analysis, arose out of the study of the Political Economy of Broadcasting which I am now conducting. The argument of the present article was implicit in a previous article dealing with the problem of allocating radio and television frequencies (The Federal Communications Commission, 2 J. Law & Econ. [1959]) but comments which I have received seemed to suggest that it would be desirable to deal with the question in a more explicit way and without reference to the original problem for the solution of which the analysis was developed.

areas in which the emission of smoke would have harmful effects on others). It is my contention that the suggested courses of action are inappropriate, in that they lead to results which are not necessarily, or even usually, desirable.

II. The Reciprocal Nature of the Problem

The traditional approach has tended to obscure the nature of the choice that has to be made. The question is commonly thought of as one in which A inflicts harm on B and what has to be decided is: how should we restrain A? But this is wrong. We are dealing with a problem of a reciprocal nature. To avoid the harm to B would inflict harm on A. The real question that has to be decided is: should A be allowed to harm B or should B be allowed to harm A? The problem is to avoid the more serious harm. I instanced in my previous article[2] the case of a confectioner the noise and vibrations from whose machinery disturbed a doctor in his work. To avoid harming the doctor would inflict harm on the confectioner. The problem posed by this case was essentially whether it was worth while, as a result of restricting the methods of production which could be used by the confectioner, to secure more doctoring at the cost of a reduced supply of confectionery products. Another example is afforded by the problem of straying cattle which destroy crops on neighbouring land. If it is inevitable that some cattle will stray, an increase in the supply of meat can only be obtained at the expense of a decrease in the supply of crops. The nature of the choice is clear: meat or crops. What answer should be given is, of course, not clear unless we know the value of what is obtained as well as the value of what is sacrificed to obtain it. To give another example, Professor George J. Stigler instances the contamination of a stream.[3] If we assume that the harmful effect of the pollution is that it kills the fish, the question to be decided is: is the value of the fish lost greater or less than the value of the product which the contamination of the stream makes possible. It goes almost without saying that this problem has to be looked at in total *and* at the margin.

III. The Pricing System with Liability for Damage

I propose to start my analysis by examining a case in which most economists would presumably agree that the problem would be solved in a completely satisfactory manner: when the damaging business has to pay for all damage caused *and* the pricing system works smoothly (strictly this means that the operation of a pricing system is without cost).

A good example of the problem under discussion is afforded by the case of straying cattle which destroy crops growing on neighbouring land. Let us suppose that a farmer and a cattle-raiser are operating on neighbouring proper-

[2] Coase, The Federal Communications Commission, 2 J. Law & Econ. 26–27 (1959).

[3] G. J. Stigler, The Theory of Price 105 (1952).

ties. Let us further suppose that, without any fencing between the properties, an increase in the size of the cattle-raiser's herd increases the total damage to the farmer's crops. What happens to the marginal damage as the size of the herd increases is another matter. This depends on whether the cattle tend to follow one another or to roam side by side, on whether they tend to be more or less restless as the size of the herd increases and on other similar factors. For my immediate purpose, it is immaterial what assumption is made about marginal damage as the size of the herd increases.

To simplify the argument, I propose to use an arithmetical example. I shall assume that the annual cost of fencing the farmer's property is $9 and that the price of the crop is $1 per ton. Also, I assume that the relation between the number of cattle in the herd and the annual crop loss is as follows:

Number in Herd (Steers)	Annual Crop Loss (Tons)	Crop Loss per Additional Steer (Tons)
1	1	1
2	3	2
3	6	3
4	10	4

Given that the cattle-raiser is liable for the damage caused, the additional annual cost imposed on the cattle-raiser if he increased his herd from, say, 2 to 3 steers is $3 and in deciding on the size of the herd, he will take this into account along with his other costs. That is, he will not increase the size of the herd unless the value of the additional meat produced (assuming that the cattle-raiser slaughters the cattle), is greater than the additional costs that this will entail, including the value of the additional crops destroyed. Of course, if, by the employment of dogs, herdsmen, aeroplanes, mobile radio and other means, the amount of damage can be reduced, these means will be adopted when their cost is less than the value of the crop which they prevent being lost. Given that the annual cost of fencing is $9, the cattle-raiser who wished to have a herd with 4 steers or more would pay for fencing to be erected and maintained, assuming that other means of attaining the same end would not do so more cheaply. When the fence is erected, the marginal cost due to the liability for damage becomes zero, except to the extent that an increase in the size of the herd necessitates a stronger and therefore more expensive fence because more steers are liable to lean against it at the same time. But, of course, it may be cheaper for the cattle-raiser not to fence and to pay for the damaged crops, as in my arithmetical example, with 3 or fewer steers.

It might be thought that the fact that the cattle-raiser would pay for all crops damaged would lead the farmer to increase his planting if a cattle-raiser came to occupy the neighbouring property. But this is not so. If the crop was previously sold in conditions of perfect competition, marginal cost was equal to price for the amount of planting undertaken and any expansion would have reduced the profits of the farmer. In the new situation, the existence of crop damage would mean that the farmer would sell less on the open market but his receipts for a given production would remain the same, since the cattle-raiser would pay the market price for any crop damaged. Of course, if cattle-raising commonly involved the destruction of crops, the coming into existence of a cattle-raising industry might raise the price of the crops involved and farmers would then extend their planting. But I wish to confine my attention to the individual farmer.

I have said that the occupation of a neighbouring property by a cattle-raiser would not cause the amount of production, or perhaps more exactly the amount of planting, by the farmer to increase. In fact, if the cattle-raising has any effect, it will be to decrease the amount of planting. The reason for this is that, for any given tract of land, if the value of the crop damaged is so great that the receipts from the sale of the undamaged crop are less than the total costs of cultivating that tract of land, it will be profitable for the farmer and the cattle-raiser to make a bargain whereby that tract of land is left uncultivated. This can be made clear by means of an arithmetical example. Assume initially that the value of the crop obtained from cultivating a given tract of land is $12 and that the cost incurred in cultivating this tract of land is $10, the net gain from cultivating the land being $2. I assume for purposes of simplicity that the farmer owns the land. Now assume that the cattle-raiser starts operations on the neighbouring property and that the value of the crops damaged is $1. In this case $11 is obtained by the farmer from sale on the market and $1 is obtained from the cattle-raiser for damage suffered and the net gain remains $2. Now suppose that the cattle-raiser finds it profitable to increase the size of his herd, even though the amount of damage rises to $3; which means that the value of the additional meat production is greater than the additional costs, including the additional $2 payment for damage. But the total payment for damage is now $3. The net gain to the farmer from cultivating the land is still $2. The cattle-raiser would be better off if the farmer would agree not to cultivate his land for any payment less than $3. The farmer would be agreeable to not cultivating the land for any payment greater than $2. There is clearly room for a mutually satisfactory bargain which would lead to the abandonment of cultivation.[4] But the same argument applies not only to the whole tract cultivated by the farmer but also to any

[4] The argument in the text has proceeded on the assumption that the alternative to cultivation of the crop is abandonment of cultivation altogether. But this need not be so. There may be crops which are less liable to damage by cattle but which would not be as profitable as the crop grown in the absence of damage. Thus, if the cultivation of a new crop would yield a return to the farmer of $1 instead of $2, and the size of the herd which would cause $3 damage with the old crop would cause $1 damage with the new crop, it would be profitable to the cattle-raiser to pay any sum less than $2 to induce the farmer

subdivision of it. Suppose, for example, that the cattle have a well-defined route, say, to a brook or to a shady area. In these circumstances, the amount of damage to the crop along the route may well be great and if so, it could be that the farmer and the cattle-raiser would find it profitable to make a bargain whereby the farmer would agree not to cultivate this strip of land.

But this raises a further possibility. Suppose that there is such a well-defined route. Suppose further that the value of the crop that would be obtained by cultivating this strip of land is $10 but that the cost of cultivation is $11. In the absence of the cattle-raiser, the land would not be cultivated. However, given the presence of the cattle-raiser, it could well be that if the strip was cultivated, the whole crop would be destroyed by the cattle. In which case, the cattle-raiser would be forced to pay $10 to the farmer. It is true that the farmer would lose $1. But the cattle-raiser would lose $10. Clearly this is a situation which is not likely to last indefinitely since neither party would want this to happen. The aim of the farmer would be to induce the cattle-raiser to make a payment in return for an agreement to leave this land uncultivated. The farmer would not be able to obtain a payment greater than the cost of fencing off this piece of land nor so high as to lead the cattle-raiser to abandon the use of the neighbouring property. What payment would in fact be made would depend on the shrewdness of the farmer and the cattle-raiser as bargainers. But as the payment would not be so high as to cause the cattle-raiser to abandon this location and as it would not vary with the size of the herd, such an agreement would not affect the allocation of resources but would merely alter the distribution of income and wealth as between the cattle-raiser and the farmer.

I think it is clear that if the cattle-raiser is liable for damage caused and the pricing system works smoothly, the reduction in the value of production elsewhere will be taken into account in computing the additional cost involved in increasing the size of the herd. This cost will be weighed against the value of the additional meat production and, given perfect competition in the cattle industry, the allocation of resources in cattle-raising will be optimal. What needs to be emphasized is that the fall in the value of production elsewhere which would be taken into account in the costs of the cattle-raiser may well be less than the damage which the cattle would cause to the crops in the ordinary course of events. This is because it is possible, as a result of market transactions, to discontinue cultivation of the land. This is desirable in all

to change his crop (since this would reduce damage liability from $3 to $1) and it would be profitable for the farmer to do so if the amount received was more than $1 (the reduction in his return caused by switching crops). In fact, there would be room for a mutually satisfactory bargain in all cases in which a change of crop would reduce the amount of damage by more than it reduces the value of the crop (excluding damage)—in all cases, that is, in which a change in the crop cultivated would lead to an increase in the value of production.

cases in which the damage that the cattle would cause, and for which the cattle-raiser would be willing to pay, exceeds the amount which the farmer would pay for use of the land. In conditions of perfect competition, the amount which the farmer would pay for the use of the land is equal to the difference between the value of the total production when the factors are employed on this land and the value of the additional product yielded in their next best use (which would be what the farmer would have to pay for the factors). If damage exceeds the amount the farmer would pay for the use of the land, the value of the additional product of the factors employed elsewhere would exceed the value of the total product in this use after damage is taken into account. It follows that it would be desirable to abandon cultivation of the land and to release the factors employed for production elsewhere. A procedure which merely provided for payment for damage to the crop caused by the cattle but which did not allow for the possibility of cultivation being discontinued would result in too small an employment of factors of production in cattle-raising and too large an employment of factors in cultivation of the crop. But given the possibility of market transactions, a situation in which damage to crops exceeded the rent of the land would not endure. Whether the cattle-raiser pays the farmer to leave the land uncultivated or himself rents the land by paying the land-owner an amount slightly greater than the farmer would pay (if the farmer was himself renting the land), the final result would be the same and would maximise the value of production. Even when the farmer is induced to plant crops which it would not be profitable to cultivate for sale on the market, this will be a purely short-term phenomenon and may be expected to lead to an agreement under which the planting will cease. The cattle-raiser will remain in that location and the marginal cost of meat production will be the same as before, thus having no long-run effect on the allocation of resources.

IV. The Pricing System with No Liability for Damage

I now turn to the case in which, although the pricing system is assumed to work smoothly (that is, costlessly), the damaging business is not liable for any of the damage which it causes. This business does not have to make a payment to those damaged by its actions. I propose to show that the allocation of resources will be the same in this case as it was when the damaging business was liable for damage caused. As I showed in the previous case that the allocation of resources was optimal, it will not be necessary to repeat this part of the argument.

I return to the case of the farmer and the cattle-raiser. The farmer would suffer increased damage to his crop as the size of the herd increased. Suppose that the size of the cattle-raiser's herd is 3 steers (and that this is the size of the herd that would be maintained if crop damage was not taken into account). Then the farmer would be willing to pay up to $3 if the cattle-raiser would reduce his herd to 2 steers, up to $5 if the herd were reduced to 1 steer and would pay up to $6 if cattle-raising was abandoned. The cattle-raiser would therefore receive $3 from the farmer if he kept 2 steers instead of 3. This $3 foregone is therefore part of the cost incurred in keeping the third steer. Whether the $3 is a payment which the cattle-raiser has to make if he adds the third steer to his herd (which it would be if the cattle-raiser was liable to the farmer for damage caused to the crop) or whether it is a sum of money which he would have received if he did not keep a third steer (which it would be if the cattle-raiser was not liable to the farmer for damage caused to the crop) does not affect the final result. In both cases $3 is part of the cost of adding a third steer, to be included along with the other costs. If the increase in the value of production in cattle-raising through increasing the size of the herd from 2 to 3 is greater than the additional costs that have to be incurred (including the $3 damage to crops), the size of the herd will be increased. Otherwise, it will not. The size of the herd will be the same whether the cattle-raiser is liable for damage caused to the crop or not.

It may be argued that the assumed starting point—a herd of 3 steers—was arbitrary. And this is true. But the farmer would not wish to pay to avoid crop damage which the cattle-raiser would not be able to cause. For example, the maximum annual payment which the farmer could be induced to pay could not exceed $9, the annual cost of fencing. And the farmer would only be willing to pay this sum if it did not reduce his earnings to a level that would cause him to abandon cultivation of this particular tract of land. Furthermore, the farmer would only be willing to pay this amount if he believed that, in the absence of any payment by him, the size of the herd maintained by the cattle raiser would be 4 or more steers. Let us assume that this is the case. Then the farmer would be willing to pay up to $3 if the cattle raiser would reduce his herd to 3 steers, up to $6 if the herd were reduced to 2 steers, up to $8 if one steer only were kept and up to $9 if cattle-raising were abandoned. It will be noticed that the change in the starting point has not altered the amount which would accrue to the cattle-raiser if he reduced the size of his herd by any given amount. It is still true that the cattle-raiser could receive an additional $3 from the farmer if he agreed to reduce his herd from 3 steers to 2 and that the $3 represents the value of the crop that would be destroyed by adding the third steer to the herd. Although a different belief on the part of the farmer (whether justified or not) about the size of the herd that the cattle-raiser would maintain in the absence of payments from him may affect the total payment he can be induced to pay, it is not true that this different belief would have any effect on the size of the herd that the cattle-raiser will actually keep. This will be the same as it would be if the cattle-raiser had to pay for damage caused by his cattle, since a receipt foregone of a given amount is the equivalent of a payment of the same amount.

It might be thought that it would pay the cattle-raiser to increase his herd above the size that he would wish to maintain once a bargain had been made, in order to induce the farmer to make a larger total payment. And this may be true. It is similar in nature to the action of the farmer (when the cattle-raiser was liable for damage) in cultivating land on which, as a result of an agreement with the cattle-raiser, planting would subsequently be abandoned (including land which would not be cultivated at all in the absence of cattle-raising). But such manoeuvres are preliminaries to an agreement and do not affect the long-run equilibrium position, which is the same whether or not the cattle-raiser is held responsible for the crop damage brought about by his cattle.

It is necessary to know whether the damaging business is liable or not for damage caused since without the establishment of this initial delimitation of rights there can be no market transactions to transfer and recombine them. But the ultimate result (which maximises the value of production) is independent of the legal position if the pricing system is assumed to work without cost.

V. The Problem Illustrated Anew

The harmful effects of the activities of a business can assume a wide variety of forms. An early English case concerned a building which, by obstructing currents of air, hindered the operation of a windmill.[5] A recent case in Florida concerned a building which cast a shadow on the cabana, swimming pool and sunbathing areas of a neighbouring hotel.[6] The problem of straying cattle and the damaging of crops which was the subject of detailed examination in the two preceding sections, although it may have appeared to be rather a special case, is in fact but one example of a problem which arises in many different guises. To clarify the nature of my argument and to demonstrate its general applicability, I propose to illustrate it anew by reference to four actual cases.

Let us first reconsider the case of *Sturges v. Bridgman*[7] which I used as an illustration of the general problem in my article on "The Federal Communications Commission." In this case, a confectioner (in Wigmore Street) used two mortars and pestles in connection with his business (one had been in operation in the same position for more than 60 years and the other for more than 26 years). A doctor then came to occupy neighbouring premises (in Wimpole Street). The confectioner's machinery caused the doctor no harm until, eight years after he had first occupied the premises, he built a consulting room at the end of his garden right against the confectioner's kitchen. It was then found that the noise and vibration caused by the confectioner's machin-

[5] See Gale on Easements 237–39 (13th ed. M. Bowles 1959).

[6] See Fontainebleu Hotel Corp. v. Forty-Five Twenty-Five, Inc., 114 So. 2d 357 (1959).

[7] 11 Ch. D. 852 (1879).

ery made it difficult for the doctor to use his new consulting room. "In particular . . . the noise prevented him from examining his patients by auscultation[8] for diseases of the chest. He also found it impossible to engage with effect in any occupation which required thought and attention." The doctor therefore brought a legal action to force the confectioner to stop using his machinery. The courts had little difficulty in granting the doctor the injunction he sought. "Individual cases of hardship may occur in the strict carrying out of the principle upon which we found our judgment, but the negation of the principle would lead even more to individual hardship, and would at the same time produce a prejudicial effect upon the development of land for residential purposes."

The court's decision established that the doctor had the right to prevent the confectioner from using his machinery. But, of course, it would have been possible to modify the arrangements envisaged in the legal ruling by means of a bargain between the parties. The doctor would have been willing to waive his right and allow the machinery to continue in operation if the confectioner would have paid him a sum of money which was greater than the loss of income which he would suffer from having to move to a more costly or less convenient location or from having to curtail his activities at this location or, as was suggested as a possibility, from having to build a separate wall which would deaden the noise and vibration. The confectioner would have been willing to do this if the amount he would have to pay the doctor was less than the fall in income he would suffer if he had to change his mode of operation at this location, abandon his operation or move his confectionery business to some other location. The solution of the problem depends essentially on whether the continued use of the machinery adds more to the confectioner's income than it subtracts from the doctor's.[9] But now consider the situation if the confectioner had won the case. The confectioner would then have had the right to continue operating his noise and vibration-generating machinery without having to pay anything to the doctor. The boot would have been on the other foot: the doctor would have had to pay the confectioner to induce him to stop using the machinery. If the doctor's income would have fallen more through continuance of the use of this machinery than it added to the income of the confectioner, there would clearly be room for a bargain whereby the doctor paid the confectioner to stop using the machinery. That is to say, the circumstances in which it would not pay the confectioner to continue to use the machinery and to compensate the doctor for the losses that this would bring (if the doctor had the right to prevent the confectioner's using his

[8] Auscultation is the act of listening by ear or stethoscope in order to judge by sound the condition of the body.

[9] Note that what is taken into account is the change in income after allowing for alterations in methods of production, location, character of product, etc.

machinery) would be those in which it would be in the interest of the doctor to make a payment to the confectioner which would induce him to discontinue the use of the machinery (if the confectioner had the right to operate the machinery). The basic conditions are exactly the same in this case as they were in the example of the cattle which destroyed crops. With costless market transactions, the decision of the courts concerning liability for damage would be without effect on the allocation of resources. It was of course the view of the judges that they were affecting the working of the economic system—and in a desirable direction. Any other decision would have had "a prejudicial effect upon the development of land for residential purposes," an argument which was elaborated by examining the example of a forge operating on a barren moor, which was later developed for residual purposes. The judges' view that they were settling how the land was to be used would be true only in the case in which the costs of carrying out the necessary market transactions exceeded the gain which might be achieved by any rearrangement of rights. And it would be desirable to preserve the areas (Wimpole Street or the moor) for residential or professional use (by giving non-industrial users the right to stop the noise, vibration, smoke, etc., by injunction) only if the value of the additional residential facilities obtained was greater than the value of cakes or iron lost. But of this the judges seem to have been unaware.

Another example of the same problem is furnished by the case of *Cooke v. Forbes*.[10] One process in the weaving of cocoa-nut fibre matting was to immerse it in bleaching liquids after which it was hung out to dry. Fumes from a manufacturer of sulphate of ammonia had the effect of turning the matting from a bright to a dull and blackish colour. The reason for this was that the bleaching liquid contained chloride of tin, which, when affected by sulphuretted hydrogen, is turned to a darker colour. An injunction was sought to stop the manufacturer from emitting the fumes. The lawyers for the defendant argued that if the plaintiff "were not to use . . . a particular bleaching liquid, their fibre would not be affected; that their process is unusual, not according to the custom of the trade, and even damaging to their own fabrics." The judge commented: ". . . it appears to me quite plain that a person has a right to carry on upon his own property a manufacturing process in which he uses chloride of tin, or any sort of metallic dye, and that his neighbour is not at liberty to pour in gas which will interfere with his manufacture. If it can be traced to the neighbour, then, I apprehend, clearly he will have a right to come here and ask for relief." But in view of the fact that the damage was accidental and occasional, that careful precautions were taken and that there was no exceptional risk, an injunction was refused, leaving the plaintiff to bring an action for damages if he wished. What the subsequent developments

[10] L. R. 5 Eq. 166 (1867–1868).

were I do not know. But it is clear that the situation is essentially the same as that found in *Sturges v. Bridgman*, except that the cocoa-nut fibre matting manufacturer could not secure an injunction but would have to seek damages from the sulphate of ammonia manufacturer. The economic analysis of the situation is exactly the same as with the cattle which destroyed crops. To avoid the damage, the sulphate of ammonia manufacturer could increase his precautions or move to another location. Either course would presumably increase his costs. Alternatively he could pay for the damage. This he would do if the payments for damage were less than the additional costs that would have to be incurred to avoid the damage. The payments for damage would then become part of the cost of production of sulphate of ammonia. Of course, if, as was suggested in the legal proceedings, the amount of damage could be eliminated by changing the bleaching agent (which would presumably increase the costs of the matting manufacturer) and if the additional cost was less than the damage that would otherwise occur, it should be possible for the two manufacturers to make a mutually satisfactory bargain whereby the new bleaching agent was used. Had the court decided against the matting manufacturer, as a consequence of which he would have had to suffer the damage without compensation, the allocation of resources would not have been affected. It would pay the matting manufacturer to change his bleaching agent if the additional cost involved was less than the reduction in damage. And since the matting manufacturer would be willing to pay the sulphate of ammonia manufacturer an amount up to his loss of income (the increase in costs or the damage suffered) if he would cease his activities, this loss of income would remain a cost of production for the manufacturer of sulphate of ammonia. This case is indeed analytically exactly the same as the cattle example.

Bryant v. Lefever[11] raised the problem of the smoke nuisance in a novel form. The plaintiff and the defendants were occupiers of adjoining houses, which were of about the same height.

> Before 1876 the plaintiff was able to light a fire in any room of his house without the chimneys smoking; the two houses had remained in the same condition some thirty or forty years. In 1876 the defendants took down their house, and began to rebuild it. They carried up a wall by the side of the plaintiff's chimneys much beyond its original height, and stacked timber on the roof of their house, and thereby caused the plaintiff's chimneys to smoke whenever he lighted fires.

The reason, of course, why the chimneys smoked was that the erection of the wall and the stacking of the timber prevented the free circulation of air. In a trial before a jury, the plaintiff was awarded damages of £40. The case then went to the Court of Appeals where the judgment was reversed. Bramwell, L.J., argued:

[11] 4 C.P.D. 172 (1878–1879).

. . . it is said, and the jury have found, that the defendants have done that which caused a nuisance to the plaintiff's house. We think there is no evidence of this. No doubt there is a nuisance, but it is not of the defendant's causing. They have done nothing in causing the nuisance. Their house and their timber are harmless enough. It is the plaintiff who causes the nuisance by lighting a coal fire in a place the chimney of which is placed so near the defendants' wall, that the smoke does not escape, but comes into the house. Let the plaintiff cease to light his fire, let him move his chimney, let him carry it higher, and there would be no nuisance. Who then, causes it? It would be very clear that the plaintiff did, if he had built his house or chimney after the defendants had put up the timber on theirs, and it is really the same though he did so before the timber was there. But (what is in truth the same answer), if the defendants cause the nuisance, they have a right to do so. If the plaintiff has not the right to the passage of air, except subject to the defendants' right to build or put timber on their house, then his right is subject to their right, and though a nuisance follows from the exercise of their right, they are not liable.

And Cotton, L.J., said:

Here it is found that the erection of the defendants' wall has sensibly and materially interfered with the comfort of human existence in the plaintiff's house, and it is said this is a nuisance for which the defendants are liable. Ordinarily this is so, but the defendants have done so, not by sending on to the plaintiff's property any smoke or noxious vapour, but by interrupting the egress of smoke from the plaintiff's house in a way to which . . . the plaintiff has no legal right. The plaintiff creates the smoke, which interferes with his comfort. Unless he has . . . a right to get rid of this in a particular way which has been interfered with by the defendants, he cannot sue the defendants, because the smoke made by himself, for which he has not provided any effectual means of escape, causes him annoyance. It is as if a man tried to get rid of liquid filth arising on his own land by a drain into his neighbour's land. Until a right had been acquired by user, the neighbour might stop the drain without incurring liability by so doing. No doubt great inconvenience would be caused to the owner of the property on which the liquid filth arises. But the act of his neighbour would be a lawful act, and he would not be liable for the consequences attributable to the fact that the man had accumulated filth without providing any effectual means of getting rid of it.

I do not propose to show that any subsequent modification of the situation, as a result of bargains between the parties (conditioned by the cost of stacking the timber elsewhere, the cost of extending the chimney higher, etc.), would have exactly the same result whatever decision the courts had come to since this point has already been adequately dealt with in the discussion of the cattle example and the two previous cases. What I shall discuss is the argument of the judges in the Court of Appeals that the smoke nuisance was not caused by the man who erected the wall but by the man who lit the fires. The novelty of the situation is that the smoke nuisance was suffered by the man who lit the fires and not by some third person. The question is not a trivial one since it lies at the heart of the problem under discussion. Who caused the smoke nuisance? The answer seems fairly clear. The smoke nuisance was caused both by the man who built the wall *and* by the man who lit the fires. Given the fires, there would have been no smoke nuisance without the wall; given the wall, there would have been no smoke nuisance without the fires. Eliminate the wall *or* the fires and the smoke nuisance would disappear. On the marginal principle it is clear that *both* were responsible and *both* should be forced to include the loss of amenity due to the smoke as a cost in deciding whether to continue the activity which gives rise to the smoke. And given the possibility of market transactions, this is what would in fact happen. Although the wall-builder was not liable legally for the nuisance, as the man with the smoking chimneys would presumably be willing to pay a sum equal to the monetary worth to him of eliminating the smoke, this sum would therefore become for the wall-builder, a cost of continuing to have the high wall with the timber stacked on the roof.

The judges' contention that it was the man who lit the fires who alone caused the smoke nuisance is true only if we assume that the wall is the given factor. This is what the judges did by deciding that the man who erected the higher wall had a legal right to do so. The case would have been even more interesting if the smoke from the chimneys had injured the timber. Then it would have been the wall-builder who suffered the damage. The case would then have closely paralleled *Sturges v. Bridgman* and there can be little doubt that the man who lit the fires would have been liable for the ensuing damage to the timber, in spite of the fact that no damage had occurred until the high wall was built by the man who owned the timber.

Judges have to decide on legal liability but this should not confuse economists about the nature of the economic problem involved. In the case of the cattle and the crops, it is true that there would be no crop damage without the cattle. It is equally true that there would be no crop damage without the crops. The doctor's work would not have been disturbed if the confectioner had not worked his machinery; but the machinery would have disturbed no one if the doctor had not set up his consulting room in that particular place. The matting was blackened by the fumes from the sulphate of ammonia manufacturer; but no damage would have occurred if the matting manufacturer had not chosen to hang out his matting in a particular place and to use a particular bleaching agent. If we are to discuss the problem in terms of causation, both parties cause the damage. If we are to attain an optimum allocation of resources, it is therefore desirable that both parties should take the harmful effect (the nuisance) into account in deciding on their course of action. It is one of the beauties of a smoothly operating pricing system that, as has already been explained, the fall in the value of production due to the harmful effect would be a cost for both parties.

Bass v. Gregory[12] will serve as an excellent final illustration of the problem. The plaintiffs were the owners and tenant of a public house called the Jolly Anglers. The defendant was the owner of some cottages and a yard adjoining the Jolly Anglers. Under the public house was a cellar excavated in the rock. From the cellar, a hole or shaft had been cut into an old well situated in the defendant's yard. The well therefore became the ventilating shaft for the cellar. The cellar "had been used for a particular purpose in the process of brewing, which, without ventilation, could not be carried on." The cause of the action was that the defendant removed a grating from the mouth of the well, "so as to stop or prevent the free passage of air from [the] cellar upwards through the well. . . ." What caused the defendant to take this step is not clear from the report of the case. Perhaps "the air . . . impregnated by the brewing operations" which "passed up the well and out into the open air" was offensive to him. At any rate, he preferred to have the well in his yard stopped up. The court had first to determine whether the owners of the public house could have a legal right to a current of air. If they were to have such a right, this case would have to be distinguished from *Bryant v. Lefever* (already considered). This, however, presented no difficulty. In this case, the current of air was confined to "a strictly defined channel." In the case of *Bryant v. Lefever,* what was involved was "the general current of air common to all mankind." The judge therefore held that the owners of the public house could have the right to a current of air whereas the owner of the private house in *Bryant v. Lefever* could not. An economist might be tempted to add "but the air moved all the same." However, all that had been decided at this stage of the argument was that there could be a legal right, not that the owners of the public house possessed it. But evidence showed that the shaft from the cellar to the well had existed for over forty years and that the use of the well as a ventilating shaft must have been known to the owners of the yard since the air, when it emerged, smelt of the brewing operations. The judge therefore held that the public house had such a right by the "doctrine of lost grant." This doctrine states "that if a legal right is proved to have existed and been exercised for a number of years the law ought to presume that it had a legal origin."[13] So the owner of the cottages and yard had to unstop the well and endure the smell.

[12] 25 Q.B.D. 481 (1890).

[13] It may be asked why a lost grant could not also be presumed in the case of the confectioner who had operated one mortar for more than 60 years. The answer is that until the doctor built the consulting room at the end of his garden there was no nuisance. So the nuisance had not continued for many years. It is true that the confectioner in his affidavit referred to "an invalid lady who occupied the house upon one occasion, about thirty years before" who "requested him if possible to discontinue the use of the mortars before eight o'clock in the morning" and that there was some evidence that the garden wall had been subjected to vibration. But the court had little difficulty in disposing of this line of argument: ". . . this vibration, even if it existed at all, was so slight, and the com-

The reasoning employed by the courts in determining legal rights will often seem strange to an economist because many of the factors on which the decision turns are, to an economist, irrelevant. Because of this, situations which are, from an economic point of view, identical will be treated quite differently by the courts. The economic problem in all cases of harmful effects is how to maximise the value of production. In the case of *Bass v. Gregory* fresh air was drawn in through the well which facilitated the production of beer but foul air was expelled through the well which made life in the adjoining houses less pleasant. The economic problem was to decide which to choose: a lower cost of beer and worsened amenities in adjoining houses or a higher cost of beer and improved amenities. In deciding this question, the "doctrine of lost grant" is about as relevant as the colour of the judge's eyes. But it has to be remembered that the immediate question faced by the courts is *not* what shall be done by whom *but* who has the legal right to do what. It is always possible to modify by transactions on the market the initial legal delimitation of rights. And, of course, if such market transactions are costless, such a rearrangement of rights will always take place if it would lead to an increase in the value of production.

VI. The Cost of Market Transactions Taken into Account

The argument has proceeded up to this point on the assumption (explicit in Sections III and IV and tacit in Section V) that there were no costs involved in carrying out market transactions. This is, of course, a very unrealistic assumption. In order to carry out a market transaction it is necessary to discover who it is that one wishes to deal with, to inform people that one wishes to deal and on what terms, to conduct negotiations leading up to a bargain, to draw up the contract, to undertake the inspection needed to make sure that the terms of the contract are being observed, and so on. These operations are often extremely costly, sufficiently costly at any rate to prevent many transactions that would be carried out in a world in which the pricing system worked without cost.

In earlier sections, when dealing with the problem of the rearrangement of legal rights through the market, it was argued that such a rearrangement would be made through the market whenever this would lead to an increase in the value of production. But this assumed costless market transactions. Once the costs of carrying out market transactions are taken into account it is clear that such a rearrangement of rights will only be undertaken when the increase in the value of production consequent upon the rearrangement

plaint, if it can be called a complaint, of the invalid lady . . . was of so trifling a character, that . . . the Defendant's acts would not have given rise to any proceeding either at law or in equity" (11 Ch.D. 863). That is, the confectioner had not committed a nuisance until the doctor built his consulting room.

is greater than the costs which would be involved in bringing it about. When it is less, the granting of an injunction (or the knowledge that it would be granted) or the liability to pay damages may result in an activity being discontinued (or may prevent its being started) which would be undertaken if market transactions were costless. In these conditions the initial delimitation of legal rights does have an effect on the efficiency with which the economic system operates. One arrangement of rights may bring about a greater value of production than any other. But unless this is the arrangement of rights established by the legal system, the costs of reaching the same result by altering and combining rights through the market may be so great that this optimal arrangement of rights, and the greater value of production which it would bring, may never be achieved. The part played by economic considerations in the process of delimiting legal rights will be discussed in the next section. In this section, I will take the initial delimitation of rights and the costs of carrying out market transactions as given.

It is clear that an alternative form of economic organisation which could achieve the same result at less cost than would be incurred by using the market would enable the value of production to be raised. As I explained many years ago, the firm represents such an alternative to organising production through market transactions.[14] Within the firm individual bargains between the various cooperating factors of production are eliminated and for a market transaction is substituted an administrative decision. The rearrangement of production then takes place without the need for bargains between the owners of the factors of production. A landowner who has control of a large tract of land may devote his land to various uses taking into account the effect that the interrelations of the various activities will have on the net return of the land, thus rendering unnecessary bargains between those undertaking the various activities. Owners of a large building or of several adjoining properties in a given area may act in much the same way. In effect, using our earlier terminology, the firm would acquire the legal rights of all the parties and the rearrangement of activities would not follow on a rearrangement of rights by contract, but as a result of an administrative decision as to how the rights should be used.

It does not, of course, follow that the administrative costs of organising a transaction through a firm are inevitably less than the costs of the market transactions which are superseded. But where contracts are peculiarly difficult to draw up and an attempt to describe what the parties have agreed to do or not to do (e.g. the amount and kind of a smell or noise that they may make or will not make) would necessitate a lengthy and highly involved document, and, where, as is probable, a long-term contract would be desir-

[14] See Coase, The Nature of the Firm, 4 Economica, New Series, 386 (1937). Reprinted in Readings in Price Theory, 331 (1952).

able;[15] it would be hardly surprising if the emergence of a firm or the extension of the activities of an existing firm was not the solution adopted on many occasions to deal with the problem of harmful effects. This solution would be adopted whenever the administrative costs of the firm were less than the costs of the market transactions that it supersedes and the gains which would result from the rearrangement of activities greater than the firm's costs of organising them. I do not need to examine in great detail the character of this solution since I have explained what is involved in my earlier article.

But the firm is not the only possible answer to this problem. The administrative costs of organising transactions within the firm may also be high, and particularly so when many diverse activities are brought within the control of a single organisation. In the standard case of a smoke nuisance, which may affect a vast number of people engaged in a wide variety of activities, the administrative costs might well be so high as to make any attempt to deal with the problem within the confines of a single firm impossible. An alternative solution is direct Government regulation. Instead of instituting a legal system of rights which can be modified by transactions on the market, the government may impose regulations which state what people must or must not do and which have to be obeyed. Thus, the government (by statute or perhaps more likely through an administrative agency) may, to deal with the problem of smoke nuisance, decree that certain methods of production should or should not be used (e.g. that smoke preventing devices should be installed or that coal or oil should not be burned) or may confine certain types of business to certain districts (zoning regulations).

The government is, in a sense, a super-firm (but of a very special kind) since it is able to influence the use of factors of production by administrative decision. But the ordinary firm is subject to checks in its operations because of the competition of other firms, which might administer the same activities at lower cost and also because there is always the alternative of market transactions as against organisation within the firm if the administrative costs become too great. The government is able, if it wishes, to avoid the market altogether, which a firm can never do. The firm has to make market agreements with the owners of the factors of production that it uses. Just as the government can conscript or seize property, so it can decree that factors of production should only be used in such-and-such a way. Such authoritarian methods save a lot of trouble (for those doing the organising). Furthermore, the government has at its disposal the police and the other law enforcement agencies to make sure that its regulations are carried out.

It is clear that the government has powers which might enable it to get some things done at a lower cost than could a private organisation (or at any

[15] For reasons explained in my earlier article, see Readings in Price Theory, n. 14 at 337.

rate one without special governmental powers). But the governmental administrative machine is not itself costless. It can, in fact, on occasion be extremely costly. Furthermore, there is no reason to suppose that the restrictive and zoning regulations, made by a fallible administration subject to political pressures and operating without any competitive check, will necessarily always be those which increase the efficiency with which the economic system operates. Furthermore, such general regulations which must apply to a wide variety of cases will be enforced in some cases in which they are clearly inappropriate. From these considerations it follows that direct governmental regulation will not necessarily give better results than leaving the problem to be solved by the market or the firm. But equally there is no reason why, on occasion, such governmental administrative regulation should not lead to an improvement in economic efficiency. This would seem particularly likely when, as is normally the case with the smoke nuisance, a large number of people are involved and in which therefore the costs of handling the problem through the market or the firm may be high.

There is, of course, a further alternative, which is to do nothing about the problem at all. And given that the costs involved in solving the problem by regulations issued by the governmental administrative machine will often be heavy (particularly if the costs are interpreted to include all the consequences which follow from the Government engaging in this kind of activity), it will no doubt be commonly the case that the gain which would come from regulating the actions which give rise to the harmful effects will be less than the costs involved in Government regulation.

The discussion of the problem of harmful effects in this section (when the costs of market transactions are taken into account) is extremely inadequate. But at least it has made clear that the problem is one of choosing the appropriate social arrangement for dealing with the harmful effects. All solutions have costs and there is no reason to suppose that government regulation is called for simply because the problem is not well handled by the market or the firm. Satisfactory views on policy can only come from a patient study of how, in practice, the market, firms and governments handle the problem of harmful effects. Economists need to study the work of the broker in bringing parties together, the effectiveness of restrictive covenants, the problems of the large-scale real-estate development company, the operation of Government zoning and other regulating activities. It is my belief that economists, and policy-makers generally, have tended to over-estimate the advantages which come from governmental regulation. But this belief, even if justified, does not do more than suggest that government regulation should be curtailed. It does not tell us where the boundary line should be drawn. This, it seems to me, has to come from a detailed investigation of the actual results of handling the problem in different ways. But it would be unfortunate if this investigation were undertaken with the aid of a faulty economic analysis. The aim of this article is to indicate what the economic approach to the problem should be.

VII. The Legal Delimitation of Rights and the Economic Problem

The discussion in Section V not only served to illustrate the argument but also afforded a glimpse at the legal approach to the problem of harmful effects. The cases considered were all English but a similar selection of American cases could easily be made and the character of the reasoning would have been the same. Of course, if market transactions were costless, all that matters (questions of equity apart) is that the rights of the various parties should be well-defined and the results of legal actions easy to forecast. But as we have seen, the situation is quite different when market transactions are so costly as to make it difficult to change the arrangement of rights established by the law. In such cases, the courts directly influence economic activity. It would therefore seem desirable that the courts should understand the economic consequences of their decisions and should, insofar as this is possible without creating too much uncertainty about the legal position itself, take these consequences into account when making their decisions. Even when it is possible to change the legal delimitation of rights through market transactions, it is obviously desirable to reduce the need for such transactions and thus reduce the employment of resources in carrying them out.

A thorough examination of the presuppositions of the courts in trying such cases would be of great interest but I have not been able to attempt it. Nevertheless it is clear from a cursory study that the courts have often recognized the economic implications of their decisions and are aware (as many economists are not) of the reciprocal nature of the problem. Furthermore, from time to time, they take these economic implications into account, along with other factors, in arriving at their decisions. The American writers on this subject refer to the question in a more explicit fashion than do the British. Thus, to quote Prosser on Torts, a person may

> make use of his own property or . . . conduct his own affairs at the expense of some harm to his neighbors. He may operate a factory whose noise and smoke cause some discomfort to others, so long as he keeps within reasonable bounds. It is only when his conduct is unreasonable, *in the light of its utility and the harm which results* [italics added], that it becomes a nuisance. . . . . As it was said in an ancient case in regard to candle-making in a town, "Le utility del chose excusera le noisomeness del stink."
>
> The world must have factories, smelters, oil refineries, noisy machinery and blasting, even at the expense of some inconvenience to those in the vicinity and the

plaintiff may be required to accept some not unreasonable discomfort for the general good.[16]

The standard British writers do not state as explicitly as this that a comparison between the utility and harm produced is an element in deciding whether a harmful effect should be considered a nuisance. But similar views, if less strongly expressed, are to be found.[17] The doctrine that the harmful effect must be substantial before the court will act is, no doubt, in part a reflection of the fact that there will almost always be some gain to offset the harm. And in the reports of individual cases, it is clear that the judges have had in mind what would be lost as well as what would be gained in deciding whether to grant an injunction or award damages. Thus, in refusing to prevent the destruction of a prospect by a new building, the judge stated:

> I know no general rule of common law, which . . . says, that building so as to stop another's prospect is a nuisance. Was that the case, there could be no great towns; and I must grant injunctions to all the new buildings in this town. . . .[18]

In *Webb v. Bird*[19] it was decided that it was not a nuisance to build a schoolhouse so near a windmill as to obstruct currents of air and hinder the working of the mill. An early case seems to have been decided in an opposite direction. Gale commented:

> In old maps of London a row of windmills appears on the heights to the north of London. Probably in the time of King James it was thought an alarming circumstance, as affecting the supply of food to the city, that anyone should build so near them as to take the wind out from their sails.[20]

In one of the cases discussed in section V, *Sturges v. Bridgman*, it seems clear that the judges were thinking of the economic consequences of alternative decisions. To the argument that if the principle that they seemed to be following

[16] See W. L. Prosser, The Law of Torts 398–99, 412 (2d ed. 1955). The quotation about the ancient case concerning candle-making is taken from Sir James Fitzjames Stephen, A General View of the Criminal Law of England 106 (1890). Sir James Stephen gives no reference. He perhaps had in mind *Rex. v. Ronkett*, included in Seavey, Keeton and Thurston, Cases on Torts 604 (1950). A similar view to that expressed by Prosser is to be found in F. V. Harper and F. James, The Law of Torts 67–74 (1956); Restatement, Torts §§826, 827 and 828.

[17] See Winfield on Torts 541–48 (6th ed. T. E. Lewis 1954); Salmond on the Law of Torts 181–90 (12th ed. R.F.V. Heuston 1957); H. Street, The Law of Torts 221–29 (1959).

[18] Attorney General v. Doughty, 2 Ves. Sen. 453, 28 Eng. Rep. 290 (Ch. 1752). Compare in this connection the statement of an American judge, quoted in Prosser, op. cit. supra n. 16 at 413 n. 54: "Without smoke, Pittsburgh would have remained a very pretty village," Musmanno, J., in Versailles Borough v. McKeesport Coal & Coke Co., 1935, 83 Pitts. Leg. J. 379, 385.

[19] 10 C.B. (N.S.) 268, 142 Eng. Rep. 445 (1861); 13 C.B. (N.S.) 841, 143 Eng. Rep. 332 (1863).

[20] See Gale on Easements 238, n. 6 (13th ed. M. Bowles 1959).

were carried out to its logical consequences, it would result in the most serious practical inconveniences, for a man might go—say into the midst of the tanneries of *Bermondsey*, or into any other locality devoted to any particular trade or manufacture of a noisy or unsavoury character, and by building a private residence upon a vacant piece of land put a stop to such trade or manufacture altogether,

the judges answered that

whether anything is a nuisance or not is a question to be determined, not merely by an abstract consideration of the thing itself, but in reference to its circumstances; What would be a nuisance in *Belgrave Square* would not necessarily be so in *Bermondsey;* and where a locality is devoted to a particular trade or manufacture carried on by the traders or manufacturers in a particular and established manner not constituting a public nuisance, Judges and juries would be justified in finding, and may be trusted to find, that the trade or manufacture so carried on in that locality is not a private or actionable wrong.[21]

That the character of the neighborhood is relevant in deciding whether something is, or is not, a nuisance, is definitely established.

He who dislikes the noise of traffic must not set up his abode in the heart of a great city. He who loves peace and quiet must not live in a locality devoted to the business of making boilers or steamships.[22]

What has emerged has been described as "planning and zoning by the judiciary."[23] Of course there are sometimes considerable difficulties in applying the criteria.[24]

An interesting example of the problem is found in *Adams v. Ursell*[25] in which a fried fish shop in a predominantly working-class district was set up near houses of "a much better character." England without fish-and-chips is a contradiction in terms and the case was clearly one of high importance. The judge commented:

It was urged that an injunction would cause great hardship to the defendant and to the poor people who get food at his shop. The answer to that is that it does not follow that the defendant cannot carry on his business in another more suitable place somewhere in the neighbourhood. It by no means follows that because a fried fish shop is a nuisance in one place it is a nuisance in another.

In fact, the injunction which restrained Mr. Ursell from running his shop did not even extend to the whole street. So he was presumably able to move to other premises near houses of "a much worse character," the inhabitants

[21] 11 Ch.D. 865 (1879).

[22] Salmond on the Law of Torts 182 (12th ed. R.F.V. Heuston 1957).

[23] C. M. Haar, Land-Use Planning, A Casebook on the Use, Misuse, and Re-use of Urban Land 95 (1959).

[24] See, for example, Rushmer v. Polsue and Alfieri, Ltd. [1906] 1 Ch. 234, which deals with the case of a house in a quiet situation in a noisy district.

[25] [1913] 1 Ch. 269.

of which would no doubt consider the availability of fish-and-chips to outweigh the pervading odour and "fog or mist" so graphically described by the plaintiff. Had there been no other "more suitable place in the neighbourhood," the case would have been more difficult and the decision might have been different. What would "the poor people" have had for food? No English judge would have said: "Let them eat cake."

The courts do not always refer very clearly to the economic problem posed by the cases brought before them but it seems probable that in the interpretation of words and phrases like "reasonable" or "common or ordinary use" there is some recognition, perhaps largely unconscious and certainly not very explicit, of the economic aspects of the questions at issue. A good example of this would seem to be the judgment in the Court of Appeals in *Andreae v. Selfridge and Company Ltd.*[26] In this case, a hotel (in Wigmore Street) was situated on part of an island site. The remainder of the site was acquired by Selfridges which demolished the existing buildings in order to erect another in their place. The hotel suffered a loss of custom in consequence of the noise and dust caused by the demolition. The owner of the hotel brought an action against Selfridges for damages. In the lower court, the hotel was awarded £4,500 damages. The case was then taken on appeal.

The judge who had found for the hotel proprietor in the lower court said:

> I cannot regard what the defendants did on the site of the first operation as having been commonly done in the ordinary use and occupation of land or houses. It is neither usual nor common, in this country, for people to excavate a site to a depth of 60 feet and then to erect upon that site a steel framework and fasten the steel frames together with rivets. . . . Nor is it, I think, a common or ordinary use of land, in this country, to act as the defendants did when they were dealing with the site of their second operation—namely, to demolish all the houses that they had to demolish, five or six of them I think, if not more, and to use for the purpose of demolishing them pneumatic hammers.

Sir Wilfred Greene, M.R., speaking for the Court of Appeals, first noted that when one is dealing with temporary operations, such as demolition and re-building, everybody has to put up with a certain amount of discomfort, because operations of that kind cannot be carried on at all without a certain amount of noise and a certain amount of dust. Therefore, the rule with regard to interference must be read subject to this qualification. . . .

He then referred to the previous judgment:

> With great respect to the learned judge, I take the view that he has not approached this matter from the correct angle. It seems to me that it is not possible to say . . . that the type of demolition, excavation and construction in which the defendant company was engaged in the course of these operations was of such an abnormal and unusual nature as to prevent the qualification to which I have referred coming

[26] [1938] 1 Ch. 1.

into operation. It seems to me that, when the rule speaks of the common or ordinary use of land, it does not mean that the methods of using land and building on it are in some way to be stabilised for ever. As time goes on new inventions or new methods enable land to be more profitably used, either by digging down into the earth or by mounting up into the skies. Whether, from other points of view, that is a matter which is desirable for humanity is neither here nor there; but it is part of the normal use of land, to make use upon your land, in the matter of construction, of what particular type and what particular depth of foundations and particular height of building may be reasonable, in the circumstances, and in view of the developments of the day. . . . Guests at hotels are very easily upset. People coming to this hotel, who were accustomed to a quiet outlook at the back, coming back and finding demolition and building going on, may very well have taken the view that the particular merit of this hotel no longer existed. That would be a misfortune for the plaintiff; but assuming that there was nothing wrong in the defendant company's works, assuming the defendant company was carrying on the demolition and its building, productive of noise though it might be, with all reasonable skill, and taking all reasonable precautions not to cause annoyance to its neighbors, then the planitiff might lose all her clients in the hotel because they have lost the amenities of an open and quiet place behind, but she would have no cause of complaint. . . . [But those] who say that their interference with the comfort of their neighbors is justified because their operations are normal and usual and conducted with proper care and skill are under a specific duty . . . to use that reasonable and proper care and skill. It is not a correct attitude to take to say: 'We will go on and do what we like until somebody complains!' . . . Their duty is to take proper precautions and to see that the nuisance is reduced to a minimum. It is no answer for them to say: 'But this would mean that we should have to do the work more slowly than we would like to do it, or it would involve putting us to some extra expense.' All these questions are matters of common sense and degree, and quite clearly it would be unreasonable to expect people to conduct their work so slowly or so expensively, for the purpose of preventing a transient inconvenience, that the cost and trouble would be prohibitive. . . . In this case, the defendant company's attitude seems to have been to go on until somebody complained, and, further, that its desire to hurry its work and conduct it according to its own ideas and its own convenience was to prevail if there was a real conflict between it and the comfort of its neighbors. That . . . is not carrying out the obligation of using reasonable care and skill. . . . The effect comes to this . . . the plaintiff suffered an actionable nuisance; . . . she is entitled, not to a nominal sum, but to a substantial sum, based upon those principles . . . but in arriving at the sum . . . I have discounted any loss of custom . . . which might be due to the general loss of amenities owing to what was going on at the back. . . .

The upshot was that the damages awarded were reduced from £4,500 to £1,000.

The discussion in this section has, up to this point, been concerned with court decisions arising out of the common law relating to nuisance. Delimitation of rights in this area also comes about because of statutory enactments. Most economists would appear to assume that the aim of governmental action in this field is to extend the scope of the law of nuisance by designating as nuisances activities which would not be recognized as such by the common law. And there can be no doubt that some statutes, for example, the Public Health Acts, have had this effect. But not all Government enactments are of this kind. The effect of much of the legislation in this area is to protect businesses from the claims of those they have harmed by their actions. There is a long list of legalized nuisances.

The position has been summarized in *Halsbury's Laws of England* as follows:

> Where the legislature directs that a thing shall in all events be done or authorises certain works at a particular place for a specific purposes or grants powers with the intention that they shall be exercised, although leaving some discretion as to the mode of exercise, no action will lie at common law for nuisance or damage which is the inevitable result of carrying out the statutory powers so conferred. This is so whether the act causing the damage is authorised for public purposes or private profit. Acts done under powers granted by persons to whom Parliament has delegated authority to grant such powers, for example, under provisional orders of the Board of Trade, are regarded as having been done under statutory authority. In the absence of negligence it seems that a body exercising statutory powers will not be liable to an action merely because it might, by acting in a different way, have minimised an injury.

Instances are next given of freedom from liability for acts authorized:

> An action has been held not to be against a body exercising its statutory powers without negligence in respect of the flooding of land by water escaping from watercourses, from water pipes, from drains, or from a canal; the escape of fumes from sewers; the escape of sewage: the subsidence of a road over a sewer; vibration or noise caused by a railway; fires caused by authorised acts; the pollution of a stream where statutory requirements to use the best known method of purifying before discharging the effluent have been satisfied; interference with a telephone or telegraph system by an elctric tramway; the insertion of poles for tramways in the subsoil; annoyance caused by things reasonably necessary for the excavation of authorised works; accidental damage caused by the placing of a grating in a roadway; the escape of tar acid; or interference with the access of a frontager by a street shelter or safety railings on the edge of a pavement.[27]

The legal position in the United States would seem to be essentially the same as in England, except that the power of the legislatures to authorize what would otherwise be nuisances under the common law, at least without giving compensation to the person harmed, is somewhat more limited, as it is subject to constitutional restrictions.[28] Nonetheless, the power is there and cases more or less identical with the English cases can be found. The

[27] See 30 Halsbury, Law of England 690–91 (3d ed. 1960), Article on Public Authorities and Public Officers.

[28] See Prosser, op. cit. supra n. 16 at 421; Harper and James, op. cit. supra n. 16 at 86–87.

question has arisen in an acute form in connection with airports and the operation of aeroplanes. The case of *Delta Air Corporation v. Kersey, Kersey v. City of Atlanta*[29] is a good example. Mr. Kersey bought land and built a house on it. Some years later the City of Atlanta constructed an airport on land immediately adjoining that of Mr. Kersey. It was explained that his property was "a quiet, peaceful and proper location for a home before the airport was built, but dust, noises and low flying of airplanes caused by the operation of the airport have rendered his property unsuitable as a home," a state of affairs which was described in the report of the case with a wealth of distressing detail. The judge first referred to an earlier case, *Thrasher v. City of Atlanta*[30] in which it was noted that the City of Atlanta had been expressly authorized to operate an airport.

> By this franchise aviation was recognised as a lawful business and also as an enterprise affected with a public interest . . . all persons using [the airport] in the manner contemplated by law are within the protection and immunity of the franchise granted by the municipality. An airport is not a nuisance per se, although it might become such from the manner of its construction or operation.

Since aviation was a lawful business affected with a public interest and the construction of the airport was autorized by statute, the judge next referred to *Georgia Railroad and Banking Co. v. Maddox*[31] in which it was said:

> Where a railroad terminal yard is located and its construction authorized, under statutory powers, if it be constructed and operated in a proper manner, it cannot be adjudged a nuisance. Accordingly, injuries and inconveniences to persons residing near such a yard, from noises of locomotives, rumbling of cars, vibrations produced thereby, and smoke, cinders, soot and the like, which result from the ordinary and necessary, therefore proper, use and operation of such a yard, are not nuisances, but are the necessary concomitants of the franchise granted.

In view of this, the judge decided that the noise and dust complained of by Mr. Kersey "may be deemed to be incidental to the proper operation of an airport, and as such they cannot be said to constitute a nuisance." But the complaint against low flying was different:

> . . . can it be said that flights . . . at such a low height [25 to 50 feet above Mr. Kersey's house] as to be imminently dangerous to . . . life and health . . . are a necessary concomitant of an airport? We do not think this question can be answered in the affirmative. No reason appears why the city could not obtain lands of an area [sufficiently large] . . . as not to require such low flights. . . . For the sake of public convenience adjoining-property owners must suffer such inconvenience from noise and dust as result from the usual and proper operation of an airport, but their private rights are entitled to preference in the eyes of the law where the inconvenience is not one demanded by a properly constructed and operated airport.

[29] Supreme Court of Georgia. 193 Ga. 862, 20 S.E. 2d 245 (1942).

[30] 178 Ga. 514, 173 S.E. 817 (1934).

[31] 116 Ga. 64, 42 S.E. 315 (1902).

Of course this assumed that the City of Atlanta could prevent the low flying and continue to operate the airport. The judge therefore added:

From all that appears, the conditions causing the low flying may be remedied; but if on the trial it should appear that it is indispensable to the public interest that the airport should continue to be operated in its present condition, it may be said that the petitioner should be denied injunctive relief.

In the course of another aviation case, *Smith v. New England Aircraft Co.*,[32] the court surveyed the law in the United States regarding the legalizing of nuisances and it is apparent that, in the broad, it is very similar to that found in England:

It is the proper function of the legislative department of government in the exercise of the police power to consider the problems and risks that arise from the use of new inventions and endeavor to adjust private rights and harmonize conflicting interests by comprehensive statutes for the public welfare. . . . There are . . . analogies where the invasion of the airspace over underlying land by noise, smoke, vibration, dust and disagreeable odors, having been authorized by the legislative department of government and not being in effect a condemnation of the property although in some measure depreciating its market value, must be borne by the landowner without compensation or remedy. Legislative sanction makes that lawful which otherwise might be a nuisance. Examples of this are damages to adjacent land arising from smoke, vibration and noise in the operation of a railroad . . . ; the noise of ringing factory bells . . . ; the abatement of nuisances . . . ; the erection of steam engines and furnaces . . . ; unpleasant odors connected with sewers, oil refining and storage of naphtha. . . .

Most economists seem to be unaware of all this. When they are prevented from sleeping at night by the roar of jet planes overhead (publicly authorized and perhaps publicly operated), are unable to think (or rest) in the day because of the noise and vibration from passing trains (publicly authorized and perhaps publicly operated), find it difficult to breathe because of the odour from a local sewage farm (publicly authorized and perhaps publicly operated) and are unable to escape because their driveways are blocked by a road obstruction (without any doubt, publicly devised), their nerves frayed and mental balance disturbed, they proceed to declaim about the disadvantages of private enterprise and the need for Government regulation.

While most economists seem to be under a misapprehension concerning the character of the situation with which they are dealing, it is also the case that the activities which they would like to see stopped or curtailed may well be socially justified. It is all a question of weighing up the gains that would accrue from eliminating these harmful effects against the gains that accrue from allowing them to continue. Of course, it is likely that an extension of Government economic activity will often lead to this protection against

[32] 270 Mass. 511, 523, 170 N.E. 385, 390 (1930).

action for nuisance being pushed further than is desirable. For one thing, the Government is likely to look with a benevolent eye on enterprises which it is itself promoting. For another, it is possible to describe the committing of a nuisance by public enterprise in a much more pleasant way than when the same thing is done by private enterprise. In the words of Lord Justice Sir Alfred Denning:

> . . . the significance of the social revolution of today is that, whereas in the past the balance was much too heavily in favor of the rights of property and freedom of contract, Parliament has repeatedly intervened so as to give the public good its proper place.[83]

There can be little doubt that the Welfare State is likely to bring an extension of that immunity from liability for damage, which economists have been in the habit of condemning (although they have tended to assume that this immunity was a sign of too little Government intervention in the economic system). For example, in Britain, the powers of local authorities are regarded as being either absolute or conditional. In the first category, the local authority has no discretion in exercising the power conferred on it. "The absolute power may be said to cover all the necessary consequences of its direct operation even if such consequences amount to nuisance." On the other hand, a conditional power may only be exercised in such a way that the consequences do not constitute a nuisance.

> It is the intention of the legislature which determines whether a power is absolute or conditional. . . . [As] there is the possibility that the social policy of the legislature may change from time to time, a power which in one era would be construed as being conditional, might in another era be interpreted as being absolute in order to further the policy of the Welfare State. This point is one which should be borne in mind when considering some of the older cases upon this aspect of the law of nuisance.[84]

It would seem desirable to summarize the burden of this long section. The problem which we face in dealing with actions which have harmful effects is not simply one of restraining those responsible for them. What has to be decided is whether the gain from preventing the harm is greater than the loss which would be suffered elsewhere as a result of stopping the action which produces the harm. In a world in which there are costs of rearranging the rights established by the legal system, the courts, in cases relating to nuisance, are, in effect, making a decision on the economic problem and determining how resources are to be employed. It was argued that the courts are conscious of this and that they often make, although not always in a very explicit fashion, a comparison between what would be gained and what lost by preventing

[83] See Sir Alfred Denning, Freedom Under the Law 71 (1949).

[84] M. B. Cairns, The Law of Tort in Local Government 28–32 (1954).

actions which have harmful effects. But the delimitation of rights is also the result of statutory enactments. Here we also find evidence of an appreciation of the reciprocal nature of the problem. While statutory enactments add to the list of nuisances, action is also taken to legalize what would otherwise be nuisances under the common law. The kind of situation which economists are prone to consider as requiring corrective Government action is, in fact, often the result of Government action. Such action is not necessarily unwise. But there is a real danger that extensive Government intervention in the economic system may lead to the protection of those responsible for harmful effects being carried too far.

VIII. Pigou's Treatment in "The Economics of Welfare"

The fountainhead for the modern economic analysis of the problem discussed in this article is Pigou's *Economics of Welfare* and, in particular, that section of Part II which deals with divergences between social and private net products which come about because

> one person A, in the course of rendering some service, for which payment is made, to a second person B, incidentally also renders services or disservices to other persons (not producers of like services), of such a sort that payment cannot be exacted from the benefited parties or compensation enforced on behalf of the injured parties.[35]

Pigou tells us that his aim in Part II of *The Economics of Welfare* is

> to ascertain how far the free play of self-interest, acting under the existing legal system, tends to distribute the country's resources in the way most favorable to the production of a large national dividend, and how far it is feasible for State action to improve upon 'natural' tendencies.[36]

To judge from the first part of this statement, Pigou's purpose is to discover whether any improvements could be made in the existing arrangements which determine the use of resources. Since Pigou's conclusion is that improvements could be made, one might have expected him to continue by saying that he proposed to set out the changes required to bring them about. Instead, Pigou adds a phrase which contrasts "natural" tendencies with State action, which seems in some sense to equate the present arrangements with "natural" tendencies and to imply that what is required to bring about these improvements is State action (if feasible). That this is more or less Pigou's position is evident from Chapter I of Part II.[37] Pigou starts by referring to "optimistic

[35] A. C. Pigou, The Economics of Welfare 183 (4th ed. 1932). My references will all be to the fourth edition but the argument and examples examined in this article remained substantially unchanged from the first edition in 1920 to the fourth in 1932. A large part (but not all) of this analysis had appeared previously in Wealth and Welfare (1912).

[36] *Id.* at xii.

[37] *Id.* at 127–30.

followers of the classical economists"[38] who have argued that the value of production would be maximised if the Government refrained from any interference in the economic system and the economic arrangements were those which came about "naturally." Pigou goes on to say that if self-interest does promote economic welfare, it is because human institutions have been devised to make it so. (This part of Pigou's argument, which he develops with the aid of a quotation from Cannan, seems to me to be essentially correct.) Pigou concludes:

> But even in the most advanced States there are failures and imperfections. . . . there are many obstacles that prevent a community's resources from being distributed . . . in the most efficient way. The study of these constitutes our present problem. . . . its purpose is essentially practical. It seeks to bring into clearer light some of the ways in which it now is, or eventually may become, feasible for governments to control the play of economic forces in such wise as to promote the economic welfare, and through that, the total welfare, of their citizens as a whole.[39]

Pigou's underlying thought would appear to be: Some have argued that no State action is needed. But the system has performed as well as it has because of State action. Nonetheless, there are still imperfections. What additional State action is required?

If this is a correct summary of Pigou's position, its inadequacy can be demonstrated by examining the first example he gives of a divergence between private and social products.

> It might happen . . . that costs are thrown upon people not directly concerned, through, say, uncompensated damage done to surrounding woods by sparks from railway engines. All such effects must be included—some of them will be positive, others negative elements—in reckoning up the social net product of the marginal increment of any volume of resources turned into any use or place.[40]

The example used by Pigou refers to a real situation. In Britain, a railway does not normally have to compensate those who suffer damage by fire caused by sparks from an engine. Taken in conjunction with what he says in Chapter 9 of Part II, I take Pigou's policy recommendations to be, first, that there should be State action to correct this "natural" situation and, second, that the railways should be forced to compensate those whose woods are burnt. If this is a correct interpretation of Pigou's position, I would argue that the first recommendation is based on a misapprehension of the facts and that the second is not necessarily desirable.

[38] In Wealth and Welfare, Pigou attributes the "optimism" to Adam Smith himself and not to his followers. He there refers to the "highly optimistic theory of Adam Smith that the national dividend, in given circumstances of demand and supply, tends 'naturally' to a maximum" (p. 104).

[39] Pigou, op. cit. supra n. 35 at 129–30.

[40] *Id.* at 134.

Let us consider the legal position. Under the heading "Sparks from engines," we find the following in Halsbury's Laws of England:

> If railway undertakers use steam engines on their railway without express statutory authority to do so, they are liable, irrespective of any negligence on their part, for fires caused by sparks from engines. Railway undertakers are, however, generally given statutory authority to use steam engines on their railway; accordingly, if an engine is constructed with the precautions which science suggests against fire and is used without negligence, they are not responsible at common law for any damage which may be done by sparks. . . . In the construction of an engine the undertaker is bound to use all the discoveries which science has put within its reach in order to avoid doing harm, provided they are such as it is reasonable to require the company to adopt, having proper regard to the likelihood of the damage and to the cost and convenience of the remedy; but it is not negligence on the part of an undertaker if it refuses to use an apparatus the efficiency of which is open to bona fide doubt.

To this general rule, there is a statutory exception arising from the Railway (Fires) Act, 1905, as amended in 1923. This concerns agricultural land or agricultural crops.

> In such a case the fact that the engine was used under statutory powers does not affect the liability of the company in an action for the damage. . . . These provisions, however, only apply where the claim for damage . . . does not exceed £ 200, [£ 100 in the 1905 Act] and where written notice of the occurrence of the fire and the intention to claim has been sent to the company within seven days of the occurrence of the damage and particulars of the damage in writing showing the amount of the claim in money not exceeding £200 have been sent to the company within twenty-one days.

Agricultural land does not include moorland or buildings and agricultural crops do not include those led away or stacked.[41] I have not made a close study of the parliamentary history of this statutory exception, but to judge from debates in the House of Commons in 1922 and 1923, this exception was probably designed to help the smallholder.[42]

Let us return to Pigou's example of uncompensated damage to surrounding woods caused by sparks from railway engines. This is presumably intended to show how it is possible "for State action to improve on 'natural' tendencies." If we treat Pigou's example as referring to the position before 1905, or as being an arbitrary example (in that he might just as well have written "surrounding buildings" instead of "surrounding woods"), then it is clear that the reason why compensation was not paid must have been that the railway had statutory authority to run steam engines (which relieved it of liability for fires caused by sparks). That this was the legal position was

[41] See 31 Halsbury, Laws of England 474–75 (3d ed. 1960), Article on Railways and Canals, from which this summary of the legal position, and all quotations, are taken.

[42] See 152 H.C. Deb. 2622–63 (1922); 161 H.C. Deb. 2935–55 (1923).

established in 1860, in a case, oddly enough, which concerned the burning of surrounding woods by a railway,[43] and the law on this point has not been changed (apart from the one exception) by a century of railway legislation, including nationalisation. If we treat Pigou's example of "uncompensated damage done to surrounding woods by sparks from railway engines" literally, and assume that it refers to the period after 1905, then it is clear that the reason why compensation was not paid must have been that the damage was more than £100 (in the first edition of *The Economics of Welfare*) or more than £200 (in later editions) or that the owner of the wood failed to notify the railway in writing within seven days of the fire or did not send particulars of the damage, in writing, within twenty-one days. In the real world, Pigou's example could only exist as a result of a deliberate choice of the legislature. It is not, of course, easy to imagine the construction of a railway in a state of nature. The nearest one can get to this is presumably a railway which uses steam engines "without express statutory authority." However, in this case the railway would be obliged to compensate those whose woods it burnt down. That is to say, compensation would be paid in the absence of Government action. The only circumstances in which compensation would not be paid would be those in which there had been Government action. It is strange that Pigou, who clearly thought it desirable that compensation should be paid, should have chosen this particular example to demonstrate how it is possible "for State action to improve on 'natural' tendencies."

Pigou seems to have had a faulty view of the facts of the situation. But it also seems likely that he was mistaken in his economic analysis. It is not necessarily desirable that the railway should be required to compensate those who suffer damage by fires caused by railway engines. I need not show here that, if the railway could make a bargain with everyone having property adjoining the railway line and there were no costs involved in making such bargains, it would not matter whether the railway was liable for damage caused by fires or not. This question has been treated at length in earlier sections. The problem is whether it would be desirable to make the railway liable in conditions in which it is too expensive for such bargains to be made. Pigou clearly thought it was desirable to force the railway to pay compensation and it is easy to see the kind of argument that would have led him to this conclusion. Suppose a railway is considering whether to run an additional train or to increase the speed of an existing train or to install spark-preventing devices on its engines. If the railway were not liable for fire damage, then, when making these decisions, it would not take into account as a cost the increase in damage resulting from the additional train or the faster train or the failure to install spark-preventing devices. This is the source of the di-

[43] Vaughan v. Taff Vale Railway Co., 3 H. and N. 743 (Ex. 1858) and 5 H. and N. 679 (Ex. 1860).

vergence between private and social net products. It results in the railway performing acts which will lower the value of total production—and which it would not do if it were liable for the damage. This can be shown by means of an arithmetical example.

Consider a railway, which is *not* liable for damage by fires caused by sparks from its engines, which runs two trains per day on a certain line. Suppose that running one train per day would enable the railway to perform services worth $150 per annum and running two trains a day would enable the railway to perform services worth $250 per annum. Suppose further that the cost of running one train is $50 per annum and two trains $100 per annum. Assuming perfect competition, the cost equals the fall in the value of production elsewhere due to the employment of additional factors of production by the railway. Clearly the railway would find it profitable to run two trains per day. But suppose that running one train per day would destroy by fire crops worth (on an average over the year) $60 and two trains a day would result in the destruction of crops worth $120. In these circumstances running one train per day would raise the value of total production but the running of a second train would reduce the value of total production. The second train would enable additional railway services worth $100 per annum to be performed. But the fall in the value of production elsewhere would be $110 per annum; $50 as a result of the employment of additional factors of production and $60 as a result of the destruction of crops. Since it would be better if the second train were not run and since it would not run if the railway were liable for damage caused to crops, the conclusion that the railway should be made liable for the damage seems irresistable. Undoubtedly it is this kind of reasoning which underlies the Pigovian position.

The conclusion that it would be better if the second train did not run is correct. The conclusion that it is desirable that the railway should be made liable for the damage it causes is wrong. Let us change our assumption concerning the rule of liability. Suppose that the railway is liable for damage from fires caused by sparks from the engine. A farmer on lands adjoining the railway is then in the position that, if his crop is destroyed by fires caused by the railway, he will receive the market price from the railway; but if his crop is not damaged, he will receive the market price by sale. It therefore becomes a matter of indifference to him whether his crop is damaged by fire or not. The position is very different when the railway is *not* liable. Any crop destruction through railway-caused fires would then reduce the receipts of the farmer. He would therefore take out of cultivation any land for which the damage is likely to be greater than the net return of the land (for reasons explained at length in Section III). A change from a regime in which the railway is *not* liable for damage to one in which it *is* liable is likely therefore to lead to an increase in the amount of cultivation on lands adjoining the railway. It will also, of course, lead to an increase in the amount of crop destruction due to railway-caused fires.

Let us return to our arithmetical example. Assume that, with the changed rule of liability, there is a doubling in the amount of crop destruction due to railway-caused fires. With one train per day, crops worth $120 would be destroyed each year and two trains per day would lead to the destruction of crops worth $240. We saw previously that it would not be profitable to run the second train if the railway had to pay $60 per annum as compensation for damage. With damage at $120 per annum the loss from running the second train would be $60 greater. But now let us consider the first train. The value of the transport services furnished by the first train is $150. The cost of running the train is $50. The amount that the railway would have to pay out as compensation for damage is $120. It follows that it would not be profitable to run any trains. With the figures in our example we reach the following result: if the railway is not liable for fire-damage, two trains per day would be run; if the railway is liable for fire-damage, it would cease operations altogether. Does this mean that it is better that there should be no railway? This question can be resolved by considering what would happen to the value of total production if it were decided to exempt the railway from liability for fire-damage, thus bringing it into operation (with two trains per day).

The operation of the railway would enable transport services worth $250 to be performed. It would also mean the employment of factors of production which would reduce the value of production elsewhere by $100. Furthermore it would mean the destruction of crops worth $120. The coming of the railway will also have led to the abandonment of cultivation of some land. Since we know that, had this land been cultivated, the value of the crops destroyed by fire would have been $120, and since it is unlikely that the total crop on this land would have been destroyed, it seems reasonable to suppose that the value of the crop yield on this land would have been higher than this. Assume it would have been $160. But the abandonment of cultivation would have released factors of production for employment elsewhere. All we know is that the amount by which the value of production elsewhere will increase will be less than $160. Suppose that it is $150. Then the gain from operating the railway would be $250 (the value of the transport services) minus $100 (the cost of the factors of production) minus $120 (the value of crops destroyed by fire) minus $160 (the fall in the value of crop production due to the abandonment of cultivation) plus $150 (the value of production elsewhere of the released factors of production). Overall, operating the railway will increase the value of total production by $20. With these figures it is clear that it is better that the railway should not be liable for the damage it causes, thus enabling it to operate profitably. Of course, by altering the figures, it could be shown that there are other cases in which it would be desirable that the railway should be liable for the damage it causes. It is enough for my purpose to show that, from an economic point of view, a situation in which there is "uncompensated damage done to surrounding woods by sparks from railway engines" is not necessarily undesirable. Whether it is desirable or not depends on the particular circumstances.

How is it that the Pigovian analysis seems to give the wrong answer? The reason is that Pigou does not seem to have noticed that his analysis is dealing with an entirely different question. The analysis as such is correct. But it is quite illegitimate for Pigou to draw the particular conclusion he does. The question at issue is not whether it is desirable to run an additional train or a faster train or to install smoke-preventing devices; the question at issue is whether it is desirable to have a system in which the railway has to compensate those who suffer damage from the fires which it causes or one in which the railway does not have to compensate them. When an economist is comparing alternative social arrangements, the proper procedure is to compare the total social product yielded by these different arrangements. The comparison of private and social products is neither here nor there. A simple example will demonstrate this. Imagine a town in which there are traffic lights. A motorist approaches an intersection and stops because the light is red. There are no cars approaching the intersection on the other street. If the motorist ignored the red signal, no accident would occur and the total product would increase because the motorist would arrive earlier at his destination. Why does he not do this? The reason is that if he ignored the light he would be fined. The private product from crossing the street is less than the social product. Should we conclude from this that the total product would be greater if there were no fines for failing to obey traffic signals? The Pigovian analysis shows us that it is possible to conceive of better worlds than the one in which we live. But the problem is to devise practical arrangements which will correct defects in one part of the system without causing more serious harm in other parts.

I have examined in considerable detail one example of a divergence between private and social products and I do not propose to make any further examination of Pigou's analytical system. But the main discussion of the problem considered in this article is to be found in that part of Chapter 9 in Part II which deals with Pigou's second class of divergence and it is of interest to see how Pigou develops his argument. Pigou's own description of this second class of divergence was quoted at the beginning of this section. Pigou distinguishes between the case in which a person renders services for which he receives no payment and the case in which a person renders disservices and compensation is not given to the injured parties. Our main attention has, of course, centred on this second case. It is therefore rather astonishing to find, as was pointed out to me by Professor Francesco Forte, that the problem of the smoking chimney—the "stock instance"[44] or "classroom example"[45] of the second case—is used by Pigou as an example of the first case (services rendered without payment) and is never mentioned, at any rate explicitly, in connection with the second case.[46] Pigou points out that factory owners who devote resources to preventing their chimneys from smoking render services for which they receive no payment. The implication, in the light of Pigou's discussion later in the chapter, is that a factory owner with a smokey chimney should be given a bounty to induce him to install smoke-preventing devices. Most modern economists would suggest that the owner of the factory with the smokey chimney should be taxed. It seems a pity that economists (apart from Professor Forte) do not seem to have noticed this feature of Pigou's treatment since a realisation that the problem could be tackled in either of these two ways would probably have led to an explicit recognition of its reciprocal nature.

In discussing the second case (disservices without compensation to those damaged), Pigou says that they are rendered "when the owner of a site in a residential quarter of a city builds a factory there and so destroys a great part of the amenities of neighbouring sites; or, in a less degree, when he uses his site in such a way as to spoil the lighting of the house opposite; or when he invests resources in erecting buildings in a crowded centre, which by contracting the air-space and the playing room of the neighbourhood, tend to injure the health and efficiency of the families living there."[47] Pigou is, of course, quite right to describe such actions as "uncharged disservices." But he is wrong when he describes these actions as "anti-social."[48] They may or may not be. It is necessary to weigh the harm against the good that will result. Nothing could be more "anti-social" than to oppose any action which causes any harm to anyone.

The example with which Pigou opens his discussion of "uncharged disservices" is not, as I have indicated, the case of the smokey chimney but the case of the overrunning rabbits: ". . . incidental uncharged disservices are rendered to third parties when the game-preserving activities of one occupier involve the overrunning of a neighbouring occupier's land by rabbits. . . ." This example is of extraordinary interest, not so much because the economic

[44] Sir Dennis Robertson, I Lectures on Economic Principles 162 (1957).

[45] E. J. Mishan, The Meaning of Efficiency in Economics, 189 The Bankers' Magazine 482 (June 1960).

[46] Pigou, op. cit. supra n. 35 at 184.

[47] *Id.* at 185–86.

[48] *Id.* at 186 n.1. For similar unqualified statements see Pigou's lecture "Some Aspects of the Housing Problem" in B. S. Rowntree and A. C. Pigou, Lectures on Housing, in 18 Manchester Univ. Lectures (1914).

analysis of the case is essentially any different from that of the other examples, but because of the peculiarities of the legal position and the light it throws on the part which economics can play in what is apparently the purely legal question of the delimitation of rights.

The problem of legal liability for the actions of rabbits is part of the general subject of liability for animals.[49] I will, although with reluctance, confine my discussion to rabbits. The early cases relating to rabbits concerned the relations between the lord of the manor and commoners, since, from the thirteenth century on, it became usual for the lord of the manor to stock the commons with conies (rabbits), both for the sake of the meat and the fur. But in 1597, in *Boulston*'s case, an action was brought by one landowner against a neighbouring landowner, alleging that the defendant had made coney-burrows and that the conies had increased and had destroyed the plaintiff's corn. The action failed for the reason that

> . . . so soon as the coneys come on his neighbor's land he may kill them, for they are ferae naturae, and he who makes the coney-boroughs has no property in them, and he shall not be punished for the damage which the coneys do in which he has no property, and which the other may lawfully kill.[50]

As *Boulston*'s case has been treated as binding—Bray, J., in 1919, said that he was not aware that *Boulston*'s case has ever been overruled or questioned[51]—Pigou's rabbit example undoubtedly represented the legal position at the time *The Economics of Welfare* was written.[52] And in this case, it is not far from the truth to say that the state of affairs which Pigou describes came about because of an absence of Government action (at any rate in the form of statutory enactments) and was the result of "natural" tendencies.

Nonetheless, *Boulston*'s case is something of a legal curiousity and Professor Williams makes no secret of his distaste for this decision:

[49] See G. L. Williams, Liability for Animals—An Account of the Development and Present Law of Tortious Liability for Animals, Distress Damage Feasant and the Duty to Fence, in Great Britain, Northern Ireland and the Common Law Dominions (1939). Part Four, "The Action of Nuisance, in Relation to Liability for Animals," 236–62, is especially relevant to our discussion. The problem of liability for rabbits is discussed in this part, 238–47. I do not know how far the common law in the United State regarding liability for animals has diverged from that in Britain. In some Western States of the United States, the English common law regarding the duty to fence has not been followed, in part because "the considerable amount of open, uncleared land made it a matter of public policy to allow cattle to run at large" (Williams, *op. cit. supra* 227). This affords a good example of how a different set of circumstances may make it economically desirable to change the legal rule regarding the delimitation of rights.

[50] 5 Coke (Vol. 3) 104 b. 77 Eng. Rep., 216, 217.

[51] See Stearn v. Prentice Bros. Ltd., (1919) 1 K.B., 395, 397.

[52] I have not looked into recent cases. The legal position has also been modified by statutory enactments.

> The conception of liability in nuisance as being based upon ownership is the result, apparently, of a confusion with the action of cattle-trespass, and runs counter both to principle and to the medieval authorities on the escape of water, smoke and filth. . . . The prerequisite of any satisfactory treatment of the subject is the final abandonment of the pernicious doctrine in *Boulston*'s case. . . . Once *Boulston*'s case disappears, the way will be clear for a rational restatement of the whole subject, on lines that will harmonize with the principles prevailing in the rest of the law of nuisance.[53]

The judges in *Boulston*'s case were, of course, aware that their view of the matter depended on distinguishing this case from one involving nuisance:

> This cause is not like to the cases put, on the other side, of erecting a lime-kiln, dye-house, or the like; for there the annoyance is by the act of the parties who make them; but it is not so here, for the conies of themselves went into the plaintiff's land, and he might take them when they came upon his land, and make profit of them.[54]

Professor Williams comments:

> Once more the atavistic idea is emerging that the animals are guilty and not the landowner. It is not, of course, a satisfactory principle to introduce into a modern law of nuisance. If A. erects a house or plants a tree so that the rain runs or drips from it on to B.'s land, this is A.'s act for which he is liable; but if A. introduces rabbits into his land so that they escape from it into B.'s, this is the act of the rabbits for which A. is not liable—such is the specious distinction resulting from *Boulston*'s case.[55]

It has to be admitted that the decision in *Boulston*'s case seems a little odd. A man may be liable for damage caused by smoke or unpleasant smells, without it being necessary to determine whether he owns the smoke or the smell. And the rule in *Boulston*'s case has not always been followed in cases dealing with other animals. For example, in *Bland v. Yates*,[56] it was decided that an injunction could be granted to prevent someone from keeping an *unusual and excessive* collection of manure in which flies bred and which infested a neighbour's house. The question of who owned the flies was not raised. An economist would not wish to object because legal reasoning sometimes appears a little odd. But there is a sound economic reason for supporting Professor Williams' view that the problem of liability for animals (and particularly rabbits) should be brought within the ordinary law of nuisance. The reason is not that the man who harbours rabbits is solely responsible for the damage; the man whose crops are eaten is equally responsible. And given that the costs of market transactions make a rearrange-

[53] Williams, op. cit. supra n. 49 at 242, 258.

[54] Boulston v. Hardy, Cro. Eliz., 547, 548, 77 Eng. Rep. 216.

[55] Williams, op. cit. supra n. 49 at 243.

[56] 58 Sol.J. 612 (1913–1914).

ment of rights impossible, unless we know the particular circumstances, we cannot say whether it is desirable or not to make the man who harbours rabbits responsible for the damage committed by the rabbits on neighbouring properties. The objection to the rule in *Boulston's* case is that, under it, the harbourer of rabbits can *never* be liable. It fixes the rule of liability at one pole: and this is as undesirable, from an economic point of view, as fixing the rule at the other pole and making the harbourer of rabbits always liable. But, as we saw in Section VII, the law of nuisance, as it is in fact handled by the courts, is flexible and allows for a comparison of the utility of an act with the harm it produces. As Professor Williams says: "The whole law of nuisance is an attempt to reconcile and compromise between conflicting interests. . . ."[57] To bring the problem of rabbits within the ordinary law of nuisance would not mean *inevitably* making the harbourer of rabbits liable for damage committed by the rabbits. This is not to say that the sole task of the courts in such cases is to make a comparison between the harm and the utility of an act. Nor is it to be expected that the courts will always decide correctly after making such a comparison. But unless the courts act very foolishly, the ordinary law of nuisance would seem likely to give economically more satisfactory results than adopting a rigid rule. Pigou's case of the overrunning rabbits affords an excellent example of how problems of law and economics are interrelated, even though the correct policy to follow would seem to be different from that envisioned by Pigou.

Pigou allows one exception to his conclusion that there is a divergence between private and social products in the rabbit example. He adds: ". . . unless . . . the two occupiers stand in the relation of landlord and tenant, so that compensation is given in an adjustment of the rent."[58] This qualification is rather surprising since Pigou's first class of divergence is largely concerned with the difficulties of drawing up satisfactory contracts between landlords and tenants. In fact, all the recent cases on the problem of rabbits cited by Professor Williams involved disputes between landlords and tenants concerning sporting rights.[59] Pigou seems to make a distinction between the case in which no contract is possible (the second class) and that in which the contract is unsatisfactory (the first class). Thus he says that the second class of divergences between private and social net product

> cannot, like divergences due to tenancy laws, be mitigated by a modification of the contractual relation between any two contracting parties, because the divergence arises out of a service or disservice rendered to persons other than the contracting parties.[60]

[57] Williams, op. cit. supra n. 49 at 259.

[58] Pigou, op. cit. supra n. 35 at 185.

[59] Williams, op. cit. supra n. 49 at 244–47.

[60] Pigou, op. cit. supra n. 35 at 192.

But the reason why some activities are not the subject of contracts is exactly the same as the reason why some contracts are commonly unsatisfactory—it would cost too much to put the matter right. Indeed, the two cases are really the same since the contracts are unsatisfactory because they do not cover certain activities. The exact bearing of the discussion of the first class of divergence on Pigou's main argument is difficult to discover. He shows that in some circumstances contractual relations between landlord and tenant may result in a divergence between private and social products.[61] But he also goes on to show that Government-enforced compensation schemes and rent-controls will also produce divergences.[62] Furthermore, he shows that, when the Government is in a similar position to a private landlord, e.g. when granting a franchise to a public utility, exactly the same difficulties arise as when private individuals are involved.[63] The discussion is interesting but I have been unable to discover what general conclusions about economic policy, if any, Pigou expects us to draw from it.

Indeed, Pigou's treatment of the problems considered in this article is extremely elusive and the discussion of his views raises almost insuperable difficulties of interpretation. Consequently it is impossible to be sure that one has understood what Pigou really meant. Nevertheless, it is difficult to resist the conclusion, extroardinary though this may be in an economist of Pigou's stature, that the main source of this obscurity is that Pigou had not thought his position through.

IX. The Pigovian Tradition

It is strange that a doctrine as faulty as that developed by Pigou should have been so influential, although part of its success has probably been due to the lack of clarity in the exposition. Not being clear, it was never clearly wrong. Curiously enough, this obscurity in the source has not prevented the emergence of a fairly well-defined oral tradition. What economists think they learn from Pigou, and what they tell their students, which I term the Pigovian tradition, is reasonably clear. I propose to show the inadequacy of this Pigovian tradition by demonstrating that both the analysis and the policy conclusions which it supports are incorrect.

I do not propose to justify my view as to the prevailing opinion by copious references to the literature. I do this partly because the treatment in the literature is usually so fragmentary, often involving little more than a reference to Pigou plus some explanatory comment, that detailed examination would be inappropriate. But the main reason for this lack of reference is that the doctrine, although based on Pigou, must have been largely the product of an oral tradition. Certainly economists with whom I have discussed these problems have shown a unanimity of opinion which is quite

[61] *Id.* 174–75. [62] *Id.* 177–83. [63] *Id.* 175–77.

remarkable considering the meagre treatment accorded this subject in the literature. No doubt there are some economists who do not share the usual view but they must represent a small minority of the profession.

The approach to the problems under discussion is through an examination of the value of physical production. The private product is the value of the additional product resulting from a particular activity of a business. The social product equals the private product minus the fall in the value of production elsewhere for which no compensation is paid by the business. Thus, if 10 units of a factor (and no other factors) are used by a business to make a certain product with a value of $105; and the owner of this factor is not compensated for their use, which he is unable to prevent; and these 10 units of the factor would yield products in their best alternative use worth $100; then, the social product is $105 minus $100 or $5. If the business now pays for one unit of the factor and its price equals the value of its marginal product, then the social product rises to $15. If two units are paid for, the social product rises to $25 and so on until it reaches $105 when all units of the factor are paid for. It is not difficult to see why economists have so readily accepted this rather odd procedure. The analysis focusses on the individual business decision and since the use of certain resources is not allowed for in costs, receipts are reduced by the same amount. But, of course, this means that the value of the social product has no social significance whatsoever. It seems to me preferable to use the opportunity cost concept and to approach these problems by comparing the value of the product yielded by factors in alternative uses or by alternative arrangements. The main advantage of a pricing system is that it leads to the employment of factors in places where the value of the product yielded is greatest and does so at less cost than alternative systems (I leave aside that a pricing system also eases the problem of the redistribution of income). But if through some God-given natural harmony factors flowed to the places where the value of the product yielded was greatest without any use of the pricing system and consequently there was no compensation, I would find it a source of surprise rather than a cause for dismay.

The definition of the social product is queer but this does not mean that the conclusions for policy drawn from the analysis are necessarily wrong. However, there are bound to be dangers in an approach which diverts attention from the basic issues and there can be little doubt that it has been responsible for some of the errors in current doctrine. The belief that it is desirable that the business which causes harmful effects should be forced to compensate those who suffer damage (which was exhaustively discussed in section VIII in connection with Pigou's railway sparks example) is undoubtedly the result of not comparing the total product obtainable with alternative social arrangements.

The same fault is to be found in proposals for solving the problem of harmful effects by the use of taxes or bounties. Pigou lays considerable stress on this solution although he is, as usual, lacking in detail and qualified in his support.[64] Modern economists tend to think exclusively in terms of taxes and in a very precise way. The tax should be equal to the damage done and should therefore vary with the amount of the harmful effect. As it is not proposed that the proceeds of the tax should be paid to those suffering the damage, this solution is not the same as that which would force a business to pay compensation to those damaged by its actions, although economists generally do not seem to have noticed this and tend to treat the two solutions as being identical.

Assume that a factory which emits smoke is set up in a district previously free from smoke pollution, causing damage valued at $100 per annum. Assume that the taxation solution is adopted and that the factory owner is taxed $100 per annum as long as the factory emits the smoke. Assume further that a smoke-preventing device costing $90 per annum to run is available. In these circumstances, the smoke-preventing device would be installed. Damage of $100 would have been avoided at an expenditure of $90 and the factory-owner would be better off by $10 per annum. Yet the position achieved may not be optimal. Suppose that those who suffer the damage could avoid it by moving to other locations or by taking various precautions which would cost them, or be equivalent to a loss in income of, $40 per annum. Then there would be a gain in the value of production of $50 if the factory continued to emit its smoke and those now in the district moved elesewhere or made other adjustments to avoid the damage. If the factory owner is to be made to pay a tax equal to the damage caused, it would clearly be desirable to institute a double tax system and to make residents of the district pay an amount equal to the additional cost incurred by the factory owner (or the consumers of his products) in order to avoid the damage. In these conditions, people would not stay in the district or would take other measures to prevent the damage from occurring, when the costs of doing so were less than the costs that would be incurred by the producer to reduce the damage (the producer's object, of course, being not so much to reduce the damage as to reduce the tax payments). A tax system which was confined to a tax on the producer for damage caused would tend to lead to unduly high costs being incurred for the prevention of damage. Of course this could be avoided if it were possible to base the tax, not on the damage caused, but on the fall in the value of production (in its widest sense) resulting from the emission of smoke. But to do so would require a detailed knowledge of individual preferences and I am unable to imagine how the data needed for such a taxation system could be assembled. Indeed,

[64] *Id.* 192–4, 381 and Public Finance 94–100 (3d ed. 1947).

the proposal to solve the smoke-pollution and similar problems by the use of taxes bristles with difficulties: the problem of calculation, the difference between average and marginal damage, the interrelations between the damage suffered on different properties, etc. But it is unnecessary to examine these problems here. It is enough for my purpose to show that, even if the tax is exactly adjusted to equal the damage that would be done to neighboring properties as a result of the emission of each additional puff of smoke, the tax would not necessarily bring about optimal conditions. An increase in the number of people living or of business operating in the vicinity of the smoke-emitting factory will increase the amount of harm produced by a given emission of smoke. The tax that would be imposed would therefore increase with an increase in the number of those in the vicinity. This will tend to lead to a decrease in the value of production of the factors employed by the factory, either because a reduction in production due to the tax will result in factors being used elsewhere in ways which are less valuable, or because factors will be diverted to produce means for reducing the amount of smoke emitted. But people deciding to establish themselves in the vicinity of the factory will not take into account this fall in the value of production which results from their presence. This failure to take into account costs imposed on others is comparable to the action of a factory-owner in not taking into account the harm resulting from his emission of smoke. Without the tax, there may be too much smoke and too few people in the vicinity of the factory; but with the tax there may be too little smoke and too many people in the vicinity of the factory. There is no reason to suppose that one of these results is necessarily preferable.

I need not devote much space to discussing the similar error involved in the suggestion that smoke producing factories should, by means of zoning regulations, be removed from the districts in which the smoke causes harmful effects. When the change in the location of the factory results in a reduction in production, this obviously needs to be taken into account and weighed against the harm which would result from the factory remaining in that location. The aim of such regulation should not be to eliminate smoke pollution but rather to secure the optimum amount of smoke pollution, this being the amount which will maximise the value of production.

X. A Change of Approach

It is my belief that the failure of economists to reach correct conclusions about the treatment of harmful effects cannot be ascribed simply to a few slips in analysis. It stems from basic defects in the current approach to problems of welfare economics. What is needed is a change of approach.

Analysis in terms of divergencies between private and social products concentrates attention on particular deficiencies in the system and tends to nourish the belief that any measure which will remove the deficiency is necessarily desirable. It diverts attention from those other changes in the system which are inevitably associated with the corrective measure, changes which may well produce more harm than the original deficiency. In the preceding sections of this article, we have seen many examples of this. But it is not necessary to approach the problem in this way. Economists who study problems of the firm habitually use an opportunity cost approach and compare the receipts obtained from a given combination of factors with alternative business arrangements. It would seem desirable to use a similar approach when dealing with questions of economic policy and to compare the total product yielded by alternative social arrangements. In this article, the analysis has been confined, as is usual in this part of economics, to comparisons of the value of production, as measured by the market. But it is, of course, desirable that the choice between different social arrangements for the solution of economic problems should be carried out in broader terms than this and that the total effect of these arrangements in all spheres of life should be taken into account. As Frank H. Knight has so often emphasized, problems of welfare economics must ultimately dissolve into a study of aesthetics and morals.

A second feature of the usual treatment of the problems discussed in this article is that the analysis proceeds in terms of a comparison between a state of laissez faire and some kind of ideal world. This approach inevitably leads to a looseness of thought since the nature of the alternatives being compared is never clear. In a state of laissez faire, is there a monetary, a legal or a political system and if so, what are they? In an ideal world, would there be a monetary, a legal or a political system and if so, what would they be? The answers to all these questions are shrouded in mystery and every man is free to draw whatever conclusions he likes. Actually very little analysis is required to show that an ideal world is better than a state of laissez faire, unless the definitions of a state of laissez faire and an ideal world happen to be the same. But the whole discussion is largely irrelevant for questions of economic policy since whatever we may have in mind as our ideal world, it is clear that we have not yet discovered how to get to it from where we are. A better approach would seem to be to start our analysis with a situation approximating that which actually exists, to examine the effects of a proposed policy change and to attempt to decide whether the new situation would be, in total, better or worse than the original one. In this way, conclusions for policy would have some relevance to the actual situation.

A final reason for the failure to develop a theory adequate to handle the problem of harmful effects stems from a faulty concept of a factor of production. This is usually thought of as a physical entity which the businessman acquires and uses (an acre of land, a ton of fertiliser) instead of as a right to perform certain (physical) actions. We may speak of a person owning land and using it as a factor of production but what the land-owner in fact possesses is the right to carry out a circumscribed list of actions. The rights of a land-owner are not unlimited. It is not even always possible for him to remove the land to another place, for instance, by quarrying it. And although it may be possible for him to exclude some people from using "his" land, this may not be true of others. For example, some people may have the right to cross the land. Furthermore, it may or may not be possible to erect certain types of buildings or to grow certain crops or to use particular drainage systems on the land. This does not come about simply because of Government regulation. It would be equally true under the common law. In fact it would be true under any system of law. A system in which the rights of individuals were unlimited would be one in which there were no rights to acquire.

If factors of production are thought of as rights, it becomes easier to understand that the right to do something which has a harmful effect (such as the creation of smoke, noise, smells, etc.) is also a factor of production. Just as we may use a piece of land in such a way as to prevent someone else from crossing it, or parking his car, or building his house upon it, so we may use it in such a way as to deny him a view or quiet or unpolluted air. The cost of exercising a right (of using a factor of production) is always the loss which is suffered elsewhere in consequence of the exercise of that right—the inability to cross land, to park a car, to build a house, to enjoy a view, to have peace and quiet or to breathe clean air.

It would clearly be desirable if the only actions performed were those in which what was gained was worth more than what was lost. But in choosing between social arrangements within the context of which individual decisions are made, we have to bear in mind that a change in the existing system which will lead to an improvement in some decisions may well lead to a worsening of others. Furthermore we have to take into account the costs involved in operating the various social arrangements (whether it be the working of a market or of a government department), as well as the costs involved in moving to a new system. In devising and choosing between social arrangements we should have regard for the total effect. This, above all, is the change in approach which I am advocating.

[11]

WHEN DOES THE RULE OF LIABILITY MATTER?

*HAROLD DEMSETZ**

THE active interface between law and economics has been limited largely to antitrust and regulation, but recent work, primarily in economics, has revealed a much wider area of common interest. The new development, which deals with the definition and structure of property rights, has implications for central areas of the law, such as real property, torts, and contracts, although it originated in an economic analysis of the divergence between private and social cost. While still in its embryonic stage, the analysis has proceeded far enough for it to be called to the attention of a wider audience.

The questions with which we shall be concerned are whether and under what conditions a legal decision about liability affects the uses to which resources will be put and the distribution of wealth between owners of resources. If ranchers are held liable for the damage done by their cattle to corn fields, how will the outputs of meat and corn be affected? If drivers or pedestrians, alternatively, are held liable for automobile-pedestrian accidents, how will the accident rate be affected? What implications for extortion (an extreme form of wealth redistribution) are found in the decision about who is liable for damages?

I.

Recent developments in this area began with an article by Professor R. H. Coase.[1] Coase's work presented a penetrating criticism of the conventional treatment by economists of divergences between private and social cost. The social cost of furthering an economic activity is the resulting reduction in the value of production that is obtainable from other activities. Such reductions occur because the resources required to further an activity are scarce and must be diverted from other possible uses. According to the view that Coase challenged, social cost, being the sum total of the costs incurred to carry on any activity, might very well differ from private cost. For example, the so-

* Professor of Business Economics, Law School and Graduate School of Business, University of Chicago. The author wishes to thank the Charles R. Walgreen Foundation for financial aid through its grant to the University of Chicago, and, also, the Lilly Endowment through its grant to the University of California.

[1] R. H. Coase, The Problem of Social Cost, 3 J. Law & Econ. 1 (1960).

cial cost of running steam locomotives properly includes the fire damage done to surrounding farm crops by sparks from the locomotive. If the railroad is not required to pay for these damages, perhaps through a tax per train, then, according to the conventional analysis, the railroad would not take account of crop damage costs in deciding how many trains to run. In the absence of a specific public policy to intervene, the rate at which an activity is carried forth, which is determined solely by private cost, would diverge from the optimum rate, which is determined by social cost. In the present example, the private cost of running additional trains, being less than the social cost because crop damage is not taken into account, would encourage the railroad to run too many trains per day. The conventional economic analysis called for the levy of a tax per train, equivalent to the damages, in order to bring social cost and private cost into equality.

Coase demonstrated that the imposition of such a tax could, in some circumstances, aggravate the difficulty, but two other aspects of his work are of more concern to us. Coase (1) showed that powerful market forces exist that tend to bring private and social cost into equality without the use of a tax, and (2) discussed the conditions under which the legal position toward liability for damages would and would not alter the allocation of resources. Coase discusses an interaction between two productive activities, ranching and farming, in the context of a competitive regime in which the cost of transacting (or negotiating) is assumed to be zero.[2] His analysis concludes that social cost and private cost will be brought into equality through market negotiations—and this regardless of which party is assigned the responsibility for bearing the cost that results from the proximity of ranching and farming.

The law, reasoning that crops *stand in the way* of a neighbor's cattle, can leave the farmer to bear the cost of crop damage; alternatively, reasoning that cattle *stray errantly* across farm fields, the law can assign liability for crop damages to ranchers. Coase's work demonstrates that either legal position will result in the same resource allocation—*i.e.*, in the same quantities of corn and meat—and, also, that negotiations between the parties to the damage will, with either legal position, eliminate any divergence between private and social cost. If the law favors ranchers by leaving farmers to bear the cost of crop damage, then there exist incentives for farmers to pay ranchers to reduce the sizes of the herds, or to take other measures that will reduce the amount of damage. A summary arithmetic example reveals how such market transactions lead to Coase's results.

Suppose that the net return to an owner of ranchland would be increased by $50 if herd size were increased by one head of cattle but that the additional

[2] *Id.* at 2-8.

head of cattle would impose corn damage on the owner of neighboring farmland that reduced his net return by $60. If the law did ***not*** require the rancher to compensate the farmer, the farmer would offer to pay the rancher a sum up to $60, the damage he would suffer if the rancher increased his herd by one head. The rancher would accept the offer since any amount above $50 would be more than ample compensation for the reduction in net returns associated with the smaller herd size.

Negotiations would continue until the net return to the rancher of a head of cattle exceeded the reduction in net return to the farmer associated with the damage done by that head of cattle. Such negotiations would bring the total value of corn and beef produced to a maximum since herd size would be reduced only when the consequent increase in the net value of corn output ($60 in the above example) exceeded the decrease in the net value of beef output ($50 in the example) required to reduce crop damage.

If the rule of liability were the reverse, requiring the owner of ranchland to compensate the farmer for the crop damage, the same equilibrium would be reached. Since the rancher earns a net return of only $50 and must pay damages of $60 if he raises an additional head of cattle, he would find it in his interest not to increase the size of his herd. Moreover, he would reduce the size of his herd as long as the net return forgone was smaller than the resulting increase in the net return to farming since this would be the liability to him if he did not reduce herd size by another unit. He would be led to settle upon the same herd size, with the same consequence for crop size, as he would have chosen in the absence of liability. The mix of output is not changed[8] because negotiations between the parties eliminate all divergence between private and social cost.

The resulting equality between social and private cost is important enough to warrant a few more words. The conventional analysis of the farmer-rancher interaction would have concluded that in the absence of liability for damage (or of an appropriate tax per head of cattle) the social cost of increasing herd size would have exceeded the rancher's private cost by the $60 damage done to the neighboring farmer's crops. The rancher, if he were neither held liable nor taxed, would have no reason to take account of this damage and would

[8] I ignore other possibilities such as building a fence. These are discussed by Coase (*id.* at 3). Consideration of them changes the exposition but not the results.

One further assumption is required for the mix of output to remain unchanged. Any redistribution of wealth resulting from a change in the rule of liability is assumed to have no consequences for the demands for the products produced. Owners of farmland and ranchland should be vegetarians in equal proportions, for otherwise a redistribution of wealth between these two groups would alter the market demands for corn and beef and thereby indirectly alter the mix of output produced. The wealth redistribution problem will be discussed later when we turn to the subject of extortion.

therefore be led to raise too many cattle and impose too much damage on farm crops. It is the supposed existence of this gap between private and social cost that seems to call for a tax per head of cattle or for an assignment of liability to the rancher. Coase's reasoning shows this logic to be in error. Even in the absence of a tax or liability for damage, the harmful effects of his activities on surrounding crops would be brought to bear on the private calculations of the owner of ranchland, for he must reckon as a true (but implicit) cost of increasing herd size the payment from the farmer that he must forgo if he refuses to agree to the farmer's request for a reduction in herd size. Market negotiations bring the full cost of his decision to bear on him through the offers made by the farmer and thereby eliminate any difference between private and social cost. This, as Coase recognized, would not be true if the cost of negotiating could not be assumed to be negligible. We shall return to this problem later.

It is not generally appreciated that Coase's reasoning has legal applications that extend beyond problems of the divergence between social and private cost as these typically are conceived. What is at issue in the farmer-rancher case is which party has a particular property right. In the one case the farmer has the right to allow or prohibit cattle grazing on certain specified lands, while in the other case it is the rancher who has the right. Private property takes the form of a bundle of rights, of which different components may be held by different persons. In the absence of significant negotiating cost, the use to which these property rights is put is independent of the identities of the owners since each owner will be given market incentives to use his property right in the most valuable way. Just what is the most valuable way depends on market conditions and not owner identities.

The analysis can be extended to many types of property right problems. One that is of current interest to lawyers is the continuing litigation about the legal status of the reserve clause in organized baseball. An important defense of the reserve clause has been the assertion that it prevents wealthy baseball clubs from acquiring too large a share of the good players. By applying the above analysis to this problem it is possible to refute the assertion, especially since the cost of negotiations would seem to be negligible in this case. For what is at issue is whether the identity of the owner of a player's baseball services will alter the location of his playing activities. An application of Coase's analysis to this problem suggests that the reserve clause should have no effect on the identity of the team for which a player plays.

When signing initially with a major league organization, a player owns his baseball talent in the sense that he has the right to offer his services for sale to any ball club. But once he signs with a major league club, he can no longer negotiate with other clubs for the sale of his services, although he retains the right to refuse to play. The reserve clause, which is written into every major league contract, requires major league clubs who wish to acquire the services of a player who is already under contract to purchase his contract from the club currently owning it. Thus, once a player signs with a major league organization, part of the bundle of property rights to his services are transferred from the player to the club with which he signs. The right to play on various teams passes via the reserve clause from the player to the club owning his contract, and this club can reserve the player for its own use even though other teams might be willing to pay the player more than he is receiving.

The question considered here is *not* whether there exists a correlation between the wealth of a club and the quality of its players. The relevant question is whether the distribution of players among teams would change were the reserve clause to be declared illegal. Would wealthier clubs acquire more good players if the right to negotiate with other teams always resided with the player?[4]

In the absence of the reserve clause, a player would change clubs only if he found it in his interest to do so. With the reserve clause, a player will change clubs only if the club that owns his contract finds it in its interest. It appears that a different pattern of player migration between clubs might exist with the reserve clause than without it. But the appearance is deceptive. No matter who owns the right to sell the contract for the services of a baseball player, the distribution of players among teams will remain the same.

To see why this is so, assume that a player *not* subject to the reserve clause receives a $15,000 per annum wage from club A for which he currently plays. Club B offers him $16,000 to play for them. If this amount exceeds the value of the player to club A, the club will not find it in its interest to make a counteroffer large enough to retain the player's services and he will join club B. However, if his services are worth more than $16,000 to club A, the club will find it in its interest to make a counteroffer large enough to retain his services. With no reserve clause the player plays for the club that most highly values[5] his services.

Let us now suppose that the reserve clause is effective and, as before, that

[4] The reserve clause and other aspects of organized baseball are discussed in Simon Rottenberg, The Baseball Players' Labor Market, 64 J. Pol. Econ. 242 (1956). The reasoning employed by Rottenberg is similar but not identical to the above argument. Rottenberg's argument is based partly on the premise, not used here, that it takes two fairly well matched teams to produce a good game.

[5] Nonpecuniary aspects of his employment are discussed later, but it should be noted that the argument for retention of the reserve clause is not based on nonpecuniary job amenities.

the player is currently paid $15,000 by club A. Club B now offers club A $1,000 per annum (or its present value equivalent) for the player's contract, so that if the negotiations succeed club B will pay $16,000 for the player's services of which $15,000 is paid to the player under the terms of the purchased contract and $1,000 is paid to club A. If $1,000 per annum exceeds the player's net value to club A after it pays his $15,000 annual salary, then it will be in club A's interest to sell his contract to club B, but if the player is worth more to club A than $16,000 (equal to the $1,000 offer from club B plus the player's $15,000 salary), it will refuse to sell his contract.

The condition under which the player is transferred to club B when he is subject to the reserve clause is precisely the condition under which he will elect to transfer to club B when he is not subject to the reserve clause. He transfers to club B if club B finds his services more valuable than does club A whether or not the reserve clause is in effect. The reserve clause, therefore, cannot be expected to result in a different distribution of players among teams than would prevail in its absence.

The reader may object, suggesting that nonpecuniary considerations might make the distribution of players different depending on the legal status of the reserve clause. But this objection also would be in error. Suppose that the player, presently owned by a California club, has developed a preference for working in California. If there were no reserve clause, his preference would lead him to ask at least $1,000 more to play ball with a Chicago club than he earns playing for a California club; and, in the absence of a reserve clause, a Chicago club would need to bid $1,000 more than a California club to obtain his services. But this is also true with the reserve clause. Under reserve clause arrangements, suppose that the Chicago club offers the California club only $500 more than the player's net value to the California club. The California club, indeed, will be tempted to sell the player's contract to Chicago. It appears that the $500 increment, which would be too small to move the player were there no reserve clause, is large enough to move him if there is a reserve clause. This is incorrect because the player, when working under the reserve clause arrangement, would be willing to offer a sum of up to $1,000 (the value of the nonpecuniary amenities to him of California) to the California club to induce it to refuse to sell his contract to Chicago. Any amount above $500 would be sufficient to make the California club reject Chicago's offer since Chicago is offering only $500 more than the player is worth to the California club. (The player can "offer" such an amount by accepting a pay reduction.) With or without the reserve clause, then, the player will locate where the value he places on amenities plus the value of his baseball talent is greatest.

II

The significance of Coase's work quickly led to critical responses by Wellisz,[6] Calabresi,[7] and others, although Calabresi withdrew his criticism in a later paper.[8] The criticism centered around two allegations—that the Coase theorem neglects long-run considerations that negate it and that the spirit of the work endorses the use of resources for the undesirable purpose of "extortion." The long-run issue is discussed here and the "extortion" problem in Part III. In Part IV, I discuss the problems introduced when the assumption of negligible transaction cost is dropped.

The question of long-run considerations has been raised because it would seem that different liability rules would alter the profitability of remaining inside or outside each industry. It is alleged that if farmers are left to bear the cost that arises from proximity to cattle, the rate of return to farming will fall and resources will therefore leave the farming industry. Alternatively, if ranchers are left to bear the cost, the resulting reduction in rate of return to ranching will lead to the exit of resources from that industry. Hence, even if transaction cost is zero, the market will allocate resources differently in the long run depending upon which rule of liability is chosen.

But short-run versus long-run considerations should have no bearing on the Coase theorem, which is based on the proposition that an implicit cost (the forgone payment from the farmer) is just as much a cost as is an explicit cost (the liability damage), and this proposition surely must hold in the long run as well as in the short run. One way of demonstrating this is by allowing the two activities to be merged under a common owner. A detailed example of this is given by G. Warren Nutter.[9] If there is no special cost to operating a multiproduct firm, the costly interaction between farming and ranching will be fully brought to the owner's attention in his operation of a farming-ranching enterprise. The mix of output that he produces will be that which maximizes his earnings. The rule of liability that is chosen can have no effect on his decisions because the owner of such a firm must bear the interaction cost whichever legal rule is adopted. The cost interdependence is a technical-economic interdependence, not a legal one. Since such merged operations are possible, the rule of liability is rendered irrelevant to the

[6] Stanislaw Wellisz, On External Diseconomies and the Government Assisted Invisible Hand, 31 Economica (N.S.) 345 (1964).

[7] Guido Calabresi, The Decision for Accidents: An Approach to Nonfault Allocation of Costs, 78 Harv. L. Rev. 713 (1965).

[8] Guido Calabresi, Transaction Costs, Resource Allocation and Liability Rules—A Comment, 11 J. Law & Econ. 67 (1968).

[9] G. Warren Nutter, The Coase Theorem on Social Cost: A Footnote, 11 J. Law & Econ. 503 (1968).

choice of output mix. But a refutation of the criticism that is based on the use of the joint product enterprise gives rise to the (incorrect) suspicion that the basic problem has been begged, since the rule of liability that is chosen cannot in this case alter the wealth of the owner of a farming-ranching enterprise. The spirit of the argument can be preserved, while the suspicion is allayed, by assuming that the advantages offered by specialization of ownership are so great that it is uneconomic to merge the two activities into a single ranching-farming firm.

If owners of farmland bear the cost of crop damage, what must be the cost conditions that are associated with an equilibrium allocation of land to farming, ranching, and other uses? For such damage to arise there must be a sufficient scarcity of land to force farms and ranches into proximity. Marginal farm acreage (acreage that just "breaks even") must earn revenue sufficient to cover all cost, including the cost of crop damage done by straying cattle. Suppose the proximity of ranching and farming reduces the net return to the owner of farmland by $100 as compared with what could be earned were there no neighboring ranch. If ranching continues on the neighboring acres, it must be true that the net return to the owner of the ranchland exceeds $100, for otherwise the farmer would have been able to purchase the removal of cattle from neighboring land by offering $100 to the neighboring ranchers. The reduction in net return to farming brought about because of crop damage is thus implicitly taken into account by the owner of the ranchland when he refuses the offer of the owner of the neighboring farmland. The money offered by the farmer is refused by the rancher precisely because the continued use of the land for grazing brings in additional net revenue in excess of $100.

Land that is submarginal as farm or ranchland (land that cannot be profitably farmed or ranched) is unable to earn revenue sufficient to cover the explicit $100 damage cost if it is put to the plough or the $100 implicit cost if it is employed in ranching. Were this land to be employed in farming, its owner would suffer losses attributable in part to the damage done to his crops by straying cattle, whereas if it were employed in ranching its owner would suffer the implicit loss of forgoing a $100 payment from the neighboring farmer (the owners of farmland bearing the cost of crop damage). Submarginal land by definition can be neither farmed nor ranched profitably.

Now let the rule of liability be changed so that ranchers become liable for crop damage. If there is to be a long-run effect, it must be true that the cost interrelationships change in a manner that causes either the conversion of ranchland to farmland or submarginal land to farmland. But neither conversion can be made profitable by the change in liability.

Acreage that was marginally profitable in ranching must remain ranchland because it had been earning net revenues in excess of the $100 damages done by cattle to surrounding farmland. If a producing ranch were to be switched from ranching to farming to avoid the new liability its owner would forgo revenues (in excess of $100) that exceeded the resulting reduction in liability ($100). The owner of what was marginal ranchland, therefore, will continue to employ his land in ranching under the new liability rule.

The land that previously was submarginal must remain submarginal. The changed liability rule will not attract this land into farming. Submarginal lands under the original rule of liability earned insufficient revenues in farming to cover the $100 cost of crop damage. Under the new rule of liability, neighboring ranchers will succeed in negotiating with the owners of this land to keep it out of farming. Operating ranches, under the old rule of liability, had been yielding net revenues in excess of $100; therefore it will be possible and profitable for ranchers, in order to avoid the $100 crop damage that otherwise would result, to offer an amount to the owners of submarginal land that is sufficient to keep the land out of farming.

There is a temptation at this point in the argument to believe that an error has been made. Suppose that the farmer suffers damages equal to $100 and the rancher enjoys a net return equal to $110. If the rancher is not liable he will choose to continue ranching and to refuse a payment from a neighboring farmer of $100 to stop ranching. But if the rule of liability is reversed, he will continue ranching only if his $110 net return is sufficient to cover the cost imposed on the farmer ($100) *plus* the payment required to keep submarginal land (which can be assumed to border on another boundary of the ranch) out of farming. There has been no error in the argument, but there is an error in introducing the second neighbor halfway through the analysis. With the rancher not liable, he would have elected to remain in ranching only if the net return to ranching exceeded the payments to leave ranching offered to him by *both* his neighbors. If the rancher finds it remunerative to remain in ranching in the face of both these offers he must earn a sufficient net return from ranching, after the rule of liability is changed and he is held liable, to be able to pay damages to his neighboring farmer *and* to pay the owner of neighboring submarginal land to keep that land out of production.

The change in the rule of liability does not lead to a conversion of ranchland or submarginal land to farming. The use of land that maximized returns before the change in liability rule continues to maximize returns after the new rule is adopted, and the mix of output is unaffected by the choice of liability rule even when long-run considerations are analyzed. To understand the effect of altering the rule of liability it is important to recognize that the owner of a resource who finds it in his interest to employ that resource in a particular way when he bears the cost of an interaction will be paid to employ that resource ***in the same way*** when the rule of liability is reversed. What can happen, and in this case does happen, when the rule of liability is changed is that present owners of land having a comparative advantage in ranching suffer a ***windfall*** loss in the value of their land while owners of farmland enjoy a ***windfall*** gain. But this redistribution of wealth cannot alter the uses of these lands.

III

The problem of "extortion" is part of the larger problem of wealth redistribution that may accompany a change in the rule of liability. Our concern here is with situations in which such a redistribution takes place. However, it should be noted that, when there is no restriction on contracting, a change in the rule of liability need not be accompanied by wealth redistribution. If owners of firms are made liable for industrial accidents, for example, then the equilibrium wage will move downward to reflect the shifting of this explicit cost from workers to employers. Employers no longer will need to cover the cost of industrial accidents in the wages they pay since this cost will be paid by them in the form of industrial accident insurance or self-insurance required by the new rule of liability. The general effect of shifting accident liability directly to firms will be merely to change the classification, not the amount, of remuneration. What under no employer liability were simply wages become under employer liability wages plus accident benefits. No redistribution of wealth accompanies the change in liability. Workers who, when they had to bear the cost of accidents directly, received $X in wages will, under the new rule of liability, receive part of the $X in the form of accident compensation and the remainder in wages, but there will be no change in their total income after taking account of expected accident costs under the two systems.

This holds strictly only if workers and employers are allowed to enter into voluntary contractual arrangements for reshifting the explicit cost back to workers, a matter that need not be discussed in detail here. If such agreements are disallowed by the law—*i.e.*, if the costs of making such agreements is prohibitively high because of their illegality—then some wealth may be redistributed from those workers who would have found it advantageous to self-insure to workers who find it advantageous to buy insurance; such a law would force workers, in the wage reductions they must accept, to purchase insurance for industrial accidents from their employers.

The problem of "extortion" arises when a change in liability gives rise to a redistribution in wealth. In the farmer-rancher case, the relative values of nearby farm and ranchlands will be changed when the rule of liability is altered. Under one rule of liability, with farmers required to bear the cost of crop damage, farmers will need to pay ranchers to reduce herd size; under the other rule ranchers will have to pay farmers for damages or for any alteration in the quantity of corn grown nearby. The change in the direction of payments must affect the rents that can be collected by owners of these lands and thus the market values of these lands.

In these cases the owner of the specialized resource, ranchland or farmland, that is not required to bear the cost of the interaction may threaten to increase the intensity of the interaction in an attempt to get his neighbor to pay him a larger sum than would ordinarily be required to obtain his cooperation in adjusting the intensity of the interaction downward. The owner of ranchland, if he is not liable for crop damage done by straying cattle, might, in the absence of a neighboring farmer, raise only 1,000 head of cattle. With proximity between farming and ranching, a neighboring owner of farmland might be willing to pay the rancher the sum required to finance a 200-head reduction in herd size. However, if the owner of ranchland *threatens* to raise 1,500 head, he may be able to secure more than this sum from the farmer because of the additional crop damage that would be caused by the larger herd size. With or without this "extortion" threat, the size of the herd will be reduced to 800 because that is the size, by assumption, that maximizes the total value of both activities. Given the interrelationship between the two activities, that is the herd size that will maximize the return to the farmer and, indirectly, the sum available for possible transfer to the rancher. What is at issue is the sharing of this maximum return.

To the extent that there exist alternative farm sites, the ability of the owner of ranchland to make such a threat credible is compromised. Competition among such owners will reduce the payment that farmers make to ranchers to that sum which is just sufficient to offset the revenue forgone by ranchers when herd size is reduced. No rancher could succeed in a threat to increase herd size above normal numbers because other ranchers would be willing to compete to zero the price that farmers are asked to pay to avoid abnormally large herd sizes. Abnormally large herd size, in itself, will generate losses to owners of ranchland and, for this reason, competition among such owners will reduce the price that owners of farmland must pay to avoid such excessive herd sizes to zero.

But if a ranchland owner has a locational monopoly, in the sense that there are no alternative sites available to farmers, then the rancher may succeed in acquiring a larger sum from his neighboring farmer in order to avoid abnormally large herd sizes. The acquisition of a larger sum by the owner of ranchland generally will require him to incur some cost to make his threat credible, perhaps by actually beginning to increase herd size beyond normal levels. If the cost of making this threat credible is low relative to the sum available for transfer from the owner of farmland, the rancher will be in a good position to accomplish the transfer. The sum available for transfer will be the amount by which the value of the neighboring land when used as farmland exceeds its value in the next best use. If the rancher were to demand a larger payment from his neighbor, the neighboring land would be switched to some other use.

The temptation to label such threats extortion or blackmail must be resisted by economists for these are legal and not economic distinctions. The rancher merely attempts to maximize profits. If his agreements with neighboring farmers are marketed in competition with other ranchers, profit maximization constrained by competition implies that an agreement to reduce herd size can be purchased for a smaller payment than if effective competition in such agreements is absent. The appropriate economic label for this problem is nothing more nor less than monopoly. It takes on the cast of such legal classifications as extortion only because the context seems to be one where the monopoly return is received by threatening to produce something that is not wanted—excessively large herds. The conventional monopoly problem involves a reduction or a threat to reduce the output of a desired good. In the unconventional monopoly problem presented here, there is a threat to increase herd size beyond desirable levels. But this difference is superficial. The conventional monopoly problem can be viewed as one in which the monopolist produces more scarcity than is desired, and the unconventional monopoly problem discussed here can be considered one in which the monopolist threatens to produce too small a reduction in crop damage. Any additional sum that the rancher succeeds in transferring to himself from the farmer is correctly identified as a monopoly return.

The temptation to resolve this monopoly problem merely by reversing the rule of liability must be resisted. Should the liability rule be reversed and the owner of ranchland now be held liable for damage done by his cattle to surrounding crops, the specific monopoly problem that we have been discussing would be resolved. But if the farmer enjoys a locational monopoly such that the rancher has nowhere else to locate, the shoe will now be on the other foot. The farmer can threaten to increase the number of bushels of corn planted, and hence the damage for which the rancher will be liable, unless the rancher pays the farmer a sum greater than would be required under competitive conditions. The potential for monopoly and the wealth redistribution implied by monopoly is present in principle whether or not the owner of ranchland is held liable for damages. Both the symmetry of the problem and its disappearance under competitive conditions refute the allegation that Coase's analysis implicitly endorses the use of resources in undesirable activities.

Should the law treat such classes of monopoly problem as "extortion" or "blackmail"? It may not be useful for the law to take this step because the threat is made credible by increasing the output of an economic good—cattle if the rancher is not liable, corn if he is. Because it is difficult to sort desirable from undesirable increases in herd or crop size, there is a real danger of penalizing desirable increases in herd or crop size by mistake if such wealth transfers are treated as extortion. Activities to which anti-extortion laws normally apply typically involve the use of violence or the threat to take some action that falls within a general class of actions considered socially undesirable. The application of anti-extortion legal measures in such cases is less likely to penalize socially desirable actions by mistake. In other cases, it may be possible for the courts to limit the amount of payments to levels that are reasonable compensations for costs incurred (or profits forgone), although it is not clear how easily such determinations can be made by courts. Alternatively, it is possible to attempt to eliminate the source of the problem—monopoly—but the wisdom of relying on antitrust in this context is a matter on which the author is unprepared to speak.

IV

The costly interaction between farming and ranching is not properly attributed to the actions of either party individually, being "caused," instead, by resource scarcity, the scarcity of land and fencing materials. If transaction cost is negligible, it would seem that the choice of liability rule cannot depend on who "causes" the damage since both jointly do, or on how resource allocation will be altered, since no such alteration will take place, but largely on judicial or legislative preferences with regard to wealth distribution.

Once significant transacting or negotiating cost is admitted into the analysis, the choice of liability rule will have effects on resource allocation, and it no longer follows that wealth distribution is the main or even an important consideration in choosing the liability rule. The assumption of negligible transacting cost can be only a beginning to understanding the economic consequences of the legal arrangements that underlie the operations of the economy, but little more can be done here than to illustrate the nature of the considerations.[10]

The most obvious effect of introducing significant transacting cost is that

[10] Other considerations that arise when the cost of transacting is positive are discussed in Harold Demsetz, Some Aspects of Property Rights, 9 J. Law & Econ. 61 (1966).

negotiations will not be consummated in those situations where the expected benefits from exchange are less than the expected cost of exchanging. Exchange opportunities will be exploited only up to the point where the marginal gain from trade equals the marginal cost of trade. Of course, there is nothing necessarily inefficient in halting exchange at this point. If this were all that could be said on the subject, there would be little more to do than call the reader's attention to the similar analytical roles of transport cost in international trade and transacting cost in exchange generally. But there is more to say.

Significant transacting cost implies that the rule of liability generally will have allocative effects (as Coase recognizes). Consider the problem of liability for automobile-pedestrian accidents. To the extent that "accident" has any economic meaning it must mean that circumstances are such that voluntary negotiations between the driver and the pedestrian are prohibitively costly in many driving situations. The parties to an accident, either because of the speed with which the accident occurs or because of a failure to notice the presence of a competing claimant for the right-of-way, cannot conclude an agreement over the use of the right-of-way at costs that are low enough, *ex ante*, to make the effort worthwhile.

Partly as a consequence of the costliness of such negotiations, rules of the road are developed. Speed limits, traffic signals, and legal constraints on passing are substituted for the development of saleable private rights. In a specific case it may be possible to assign private rights to use the road in a way that makes the exchange of these rights feasible, but, in general, if these rules make economic sense it is precisely because the cost of transacting is expected to be too high in most cases to warrant the development of saleable private rights to the use of roads.

The practicality of such rules is not an argument for or against government action, but a rationale for the substitution of rules for negotiation. The use of rules to eliminate costly negotiations can be found in the management of privately owned parking lots and toll roads as well as in those that are publicly owned.

Such rules notwithstanding, accidents do take place. Assuming that the cost of transacting is too high to make negotiated agreements practical in such cases, we can compare the effect on resource allocation of the rule of liability that is chosen. If drivers are held liable in automobile-pedestrian accidents, the incentives for pedestrians to be careful about how and where they cross streets will be reduced. The incentives for drivers to be careful will be increased. Indeed, if each pedestrian could be guaranteed *full* compensation for all financial, physical, and psychological costs suffered in an accident, then pedestrians would become indifferent between being struck by an auto and not being struck. Drivers, however, would actively seek to avoid accidents since they would always be liable, whereas if it were possible to have a system of complete and full pedestrian liability it would be the drivers who became indifferent between accidents and no accidents and it would be the pedestrians who actively sought to avoid accidents.

In a regime in which transacting cost was zero, either system of liability would generate the same accident-avoiding behavior, as the Coase analysis suggests. With driver liability, drivers would themselves avoid accidents or, if such avoidance could be purchased at lower cost from pedestrians, drivers would pay pedestrians to avoid accidents. Under a scheme of pedestrian liability it would be the pedestrians who took direct action to avoid accidents or indirect action by paying drivers to avoid accidents. Under either rule of liability those accidents are avoided for which the accident cost exceeds the least cost method of avoiding accidents, where the least cost is the lesser of either the driver or pedestrian cost of avoiding accidents. Both rules of liability, assuming zero transacting cost, yield the same accident rate and the same accident-avoiding behavior. The effect of switching from one rule of liability to another is limited to wealth redistribution.

In a situation in which transacting cost is prohibitively high, driver liability leads to the avoidance only of those accidents for which the cost of avoidance to the *driver* is less than the expected accident cost, and pedestrian liability leads to the avoidance of only those accidents for which the cost of avoidance to the *pedestrian* is less than the expected accident cost. In general, the accident rate that results will differ under these two systems since the cost of avoiding accidents will not be the same for drivers and pedestrians. Both systems will lead to higher accident rates than would be true if transacting costs were zero. The effect of positive transacting cost is to raise the cost of avoiding accidents through the foreclosure of the use of possibly cheaper cost-avoidance techniques when these can be employed only by the other party to the accident. A similar conclusion can be reached for all liability problems when transacting cost is prohibitive and when the law cannot particularize the rule of liability to take account of who is the least-cost damage avoider in every instance.

One liability rule may be superior to another if transacting costs are more than negligible precisely because the difficulty of avoiding costly interactions is not generally the same for the interacting parties. It may be less costly for pedestrians to avoid accidents or for farmers to relocate their crops than it is for drivers to avoid accidents or ranchers to reduce the number of cattle they raise. If information about this were known, it would be possible for the legal system to improve the allocation of resources by placing liability on that party who in the usual situation could be expected to avoid the costly interaction most cheaply.

The use of words such as "blame," "responsible," and "fault" must be treated with care by the economist because they have no useful meanings in an economic analysis of these problems other than as synonyms for the party who could have most easily avoided the costly interaction. Whether the interaction problem involves crop damage, accidents, soot, or water pollution, the qualitative relationship between the interacting parties is symmetrical. It is the *joint* use of a resource, be it geographic location, air, or water that leads to these interactions. It is the demand for scarce resources that leads to conflicting interests.

The legal system does produce rules for determining *prima facie* "fault," but in this context "fault" means only according to some acceptable and applicable legal precedent. In an accident involving a rear-end collision, the court generally will place the burden for proving the absence of negligence on the party driving the following car. If a car strikes a person running across a fenced expressway at night the burden of proving the absence of negligence is likely to be placed on the pedestrian. In treating such cases differently, the law bases its decisions on acceptable and appropriate precedents, but the acceptability of these precedents should not be confused with the morality of the interacting parties. A deeper analysis of these precedents may reveal that they generally make sense from the economic viewpoint of placing the liability on that party who can, at least cost, reduce the probability of a costly interaction happening. Less care need be taken by the driver of the following car in a rear-end collision than would need to be taken by the lead driver to avoid the accident, and less care is needed by a pedestrian to refrain from running across an expressway than is needed by a driver to avoid striking the pedestrian. Nor need the acceptability of such precedents be based on restitution since, as these precedents become known, their long-run effect is to deter accidents at least cost. If courts are to ignore wealth, religion, or family in deciding such conflicts, if persons before the courts are to be treated with regard only to the cause of action and available proof, then, as a normative proposition, it is difficult to suggest any criterion for deciding liability other than placing it on the party able to avoid the costly interaction most easily.

[12]

TOWARD A THEORY OF PROPERTY RIGHTS

By HAROLD DEMSETZ
University of Chicago

When a transaction is concluded in the marketplace, two bundles of property rights are exchanged. A bundle of rights often attaches to a physical commodity or service, but it is the value of the rights that determines the value of what is exchanged. Questions addressed to the emergence and mix of the components of the bundle of rights are prior to those commonly asked by economists. Economists usually take the bundle of property rights as a datum and ask for an explanation of the forces determining the price and the number of units of a good to which these rights attach.

In this paper, I seek to fashion some of the elements of an economic theory of property rights. The paper is organized into three parts. The first part discusses briefly the concept and role of property rights in social systems. The second part offers some guidance for investigating the emergence of property rights. The third part sets forth some principles relevant to the coalescing of property rights into particular bundles and to the determination of the ownership structure that will be associated with these bundles.

The Concept and Role of Property Rights

In the world of Robinson Crusoe property rights play no role. Property rights are an instrument of society and derive their significance from the fact that they help a man form those expectations which he can reasonably hold in his dealings with others. These expectations find expression in the laws, customs, and mores of a society. An owner of property rights possesses the consent of fellowmen to allow him to act in particular ways. An owner expects the community to prevent others from interfering with his actions, provided that these actions are not prohibited in the specifications of his rights.

It is important to note that property rights convey the right to benefit or harm oneself or others. Harming a competitor by producing superior products may be permitted, while shooting him may not. A man may be permitted to benefit himself by shooting an intruder but be prohibited from selling below a price floor. It is clear, then, that property rights specify how persons may be benefited and harmed, and, therefore, who must pay whom to modify the actions taken by persons. The recognition of this leads easily to the close relationship between property rights and externalities.

Externality is an ambiguous concept. For the purposes of this paper, the concept includes external costs, external benefits, and pecuniary as well as nonpecuniary externalities. No harmful or beneficial effect is external to the world. Some person or persons always suffer or enjoy these effects. What converts a harmful or beneficial effect into an externality is that the cost of bringing the effect to bear on the decisions of one or more of the interacting persons is too high to make it worthwhile, and this is what the term shall mean here. "Internalizing" such effects refers to a process, usually a change in property rights, that enables these effects to bear (in greater degree) on all interacting persons.

A primary function of property rights is that of guiding incentives to achieve a greater internalization of externalities. Every cost and benefit associated with social interdependencies is a potential externality. One condition is necessary to make costs and benefits externalities. The cost of a transaction in the rights between the parties (internalization) must exceed the gains from internalization. In general, transacting cost can be large relative to gains because of "natural" difficulties in trading or they can be large because of legal reasons. In a lawful society the prohibition of voluntary negotiations makes the cost of transacting infinite. Some costs and benefits are not taken into account by users of resources whenever externalities exist, but allowing transactions increases the degree to which internalization takes place. For example, it might be thought that a firm which uses slave labor will not recognize all the costs of its activities, since it can have its slave labor by paying subsistence wages only. This will not be true if negotiations are permitted, for the slaves can offer to the firm a payment for their freedom based on the expected return to them of being free men. The cost of slavery can thus be internalized in the calculations of the firm. The transition from serf to free man in feudal Europe is an example of this process.

Perhaps one of the most significant cases of externalities is the extensive use of the military draft. The taxpayer benefits by not paying the full cost of staffing the armed services. The costs which he escapes are the additional sums that would be needed to acquire men voluntarily for the services or those sums that would be offered as payment by draftees to taxpayers in order to be exempted. With either voluntary recruitment, the "buy-him-in" system, or with a "let-him-buy-his-way-out" system, the full cost of recruitment would be brought to bear on taxpayers. It has always seemed incredible to me that so many economists can recognize an externality when they see smoke but not when they see the draft. The familiar smoke example is one in which negotiation costs may be too high (because of the large number of interacting parties) to make it worthwhile to internalize all the effects of smoke. The draft is an externality caused by forbidding negotiation.

The role of property rights in the internalization of externalities can be made clear within the context of the above examples. A law which establishes the right of a person to his freedom would necessitate a payment on the part of a firm or of the taxpayer sufficient to cover the cost of using that person's labor if his services are to be obtained. The costs of labor thus become internalized in the firm's or taxpayer's decisions. Alternatively, a law which gives the firm or the taxpayer clear title to slave labor would necessitate that the slaveowners take into account the sums that slaves are willing to pay for their freedom. These costs thus become internalized in decisions although wealth is distributed differently in the two cases. All that is needed for internalization in either case is ownership which includes the right of sale. It is the prohibition of a property right adjustment, the prohibition of the establishment of an ownership title that can thenceforth be exchanged, that precludes the internalization of external costs and benefits.

There are two striking implications of this process that are true in a world of zero transaction costs. The output mix that results when the exchange of property rights is allowed is efficient and the mix is independent of who is assigned ownership (except that different wealth distributions may result in different demands).[1] For example, the efficient mix of civilians and military will result from transferable ownership no matter whether taxpayers must hire military volunteers or whether draftees must pay taxpayers to be excused from service. For taxpayers will hire only those military (under the "buy-him-in" property right system) who would not pay to be exempted (under the "let-him-buy-his-way-out" system). The highest bidder under the "let-him-buy-his-way-out" property right system would be precisely the last to volunteer under a "buy-him-in" system.[2]

We will refer back to some of these points later. But for now,

[1] These implications are derived by R. H. Coase, "The Problem of Social Cost," *J. of Law and Econ.*, Oct., 1960, pp. 1-44.

[2] If the demand for civilian life is unaffected by wealth redistribution, the assertion made is correct as it stands. However, when a change is made from a "buy-him-in" system to a "let-him-buy-his-way-out" system, the resulting redistribution of wealth away from draftees may significantly affect their demand for civilian life; the validity of the assertion then requires a compensating wealth change. A compensating wealth change will not be required in the ordinary case of profit maximizing firms. Consider the farmer-rancher example mentioned by Coase. Society may give the farmer the right to grow corn unmolested by cattle or it may give the rancher the right to allow his cattle to stray. Contrary to the Coase example, let us suppose that if the farmer is given the right, he just breaks even; i.e., with the right to be compensated for corn damage, the farmer's land is marginal. If the right is transferred to the rancher, the farmer, not enjoying any economic rent, will not have the wherewithal to pay the rancher to reduce the number of head of cattle raised. In this case, however, it will be profitable for the rancher to buy the farm, thus merging cattle raising with farming. His self-interest will then lead him to take account of the effect of cattle on corn.

enough groundwork has been laid to facilitate the discussion of the next two parts of this paper.

The Emergence of Property Rights

If the main allocative function of property rights is the internalization of beneficial and harmful effects, then the emergence of property rights can be understood best by their association with the emergence of new or different beneficial and harmful effects.

Changes in knowledge result in changes in production functions, market values, and aspirations. New techniques, new ways of doing the same things, and doing new things—all invoke harmful and beneficial effects to which society has not been accustomed. It is my thesis in this part of the paper that the emergence of new property rights takes place in response to the desires of the interacting persons for adjustment to new benefit-cost possibilities.

The thesis can be restated in a slightly different fashion: property rights develop to internalize externalities when the gains of internalization become larger than the cost of internalization. Increased internalization, in the main, results from changes in economic values, changes which stem from the development of new technology and the opening of new markets, changes to which old property rights are poorly attuned. A proper interpretation of this assertion requires that account be taken of a community's preferences for private ownership. Some communities will have less well-developed private ownership systems and more highly developed state ownership systems. But, given a community's tastes in this regard, the emergence of new private or state-owned property rights will be in response to changes in technology and relative prices.

I do not mean to assert or to deny that the adjustments in property rights which take place need be the result of a conscious endeavor to cope with new externality problems. These adjustments have arisen in Western societies largely as a result of gradual changes in social mores and in common law precedents. At each step of this adjustment process, it is unlikely that externalities per se were consciously related to the issue being resolved. These legal and moral experiments may be hit-and-miss procedures to some extent but in a society that weights the achievement of efficiency heavily, their viability in the long run will depend on how well they modify behavior to accommodate to the externalities associated with important changes in technology or market values.

A rigorous test of this assertion will require extensive and detailed empirical work. A broad range of examples can be cited that are consistent with it: the development of air rights, renters' rights, rules for liability in automobile accidents, etc. In this part of the discussion, I shall present one group of such examples in some detail. They deal with the development of private property rights in land among American Indians. These examples are broad ranging and come fairly close to what can be called convincing evidence in the field of anthropology.

The question of private ownership of land among aboriginals has held a fascination for anthropologists. It has been one of the intellectual battlegrounds in the attempt to assess the "true nature" of man unconstrained by the "artificialities" of civilization. In the process of carrying on this debate, information has been uncovered that bears directly on the thesis with which we are now concerned. What appears to be accepted as a classic treatment and a high point of this debate is Eleanor Leacock's memoir on *The Montagnes "Hunting Territory" and the Fur Trade.*[3] Leacock's research followed that of Frank G. Speck[4] who had discovered that the Indians of the Labrador Peninsula had a long-established tradition of property in land. This finding was at odds with what was known about the Indians of the American Southwest and it prompted Leacock's study of the Montagnes who inhabited large regions around Quebec.

Leacock clearly established the fact that a close relationship existed, both historically and geographically, between the development of private rights in land and the development of the commercial fur trade. The factual basis of this correlation has gone unchallenged. However, to my knowledge, no theory relating privacy of land to the fur trade has yet been articulated. The factual material uncovered by Speck and Leacock fits the thesis of this paper well, and in doing so, it reveals clearly the role played by property right adjustments in taking account of what economists have often cited as an example of an externality—the overhunting of game.

Because of the lack of control over hunting by others, it is in no person's interest to invest in increasing or maintaing the stock of game. Overly intensive hunting takes place. Thus a successful hunt is viewed as imposing external costs on subsequent hunters—costs that are not taken into account fully in the determination of the extent of hunting and of animal husbandry.

Before the fur trade became established, hunting was carried on primarily for purposes of food and the relatively few furs that were required for the hunter's family. The externality was clearly present. Hunting could be practiced freely and was carried on without assessing its impact on other hunters. But these external effects were of such

[3] Eleanor Leacock, *American Anthropologist* (American Anthropological Asso.), Vol. 56, No. 5, Part 2, Memoir No. 78.

[4] Cf., Frank G. Speck, "The Basis of American Indian Ownership of Land," *Old Penn Weekly Rev.* (Univ. of Pennsylvania), Jan. 16, 1915, pp. 491-95.

small significance that it did not pay for anyone to take them into account. There did not exist anything resembling private ownership in land. And in the *Jesuit Relations*, particularly Le Jeune's record of the winter he spent with the Montagnes in 1633-34 and in the brief account given by Father Druilletes in 1647-48, Leacock finds no evidence of private land holdings. Both accounts indicate a socioeconomic organization in which private rights to land are not well developed.

We may safely surmise that the advent of the fur trade had two immediate consequences. First, the value of furs to the Indians was increased considerably. Second, and as a result, the scale of hunting activity rose sharply. Both consequences must have increased considerably the importance of the externalities associated with free hunting. The property right system began to change, and it changed specifically in the direction required to take account of the economic effects made important by the fur trade. The geographical or distributional evidence collected by Leacock indicates an unmistakable correlation between early centers of fur trade and the oldest and most complete development of the private hunting territory.

> By the beginning of the eighteenth century, we begin to have clear evidence that territorial hunting and trapping arrangements by individual families were developing in the area around Quebec. . . . The earliest references to such arrangements in this region indicates a purely temporary allotment of hunting territories. They [Algonkians and Iroquois] divide themselves into several bands in order to hunt more efficiently. It was their custom . . . to appropriate pieces of land about two leagues square for each group to hunt exclusively. Ownership of beaver houses, however, had already become established, and when discovered, they were marked. A starving Indian could kill and eat another's beaver if he left the fur and the tail.[5]

The next step toward the hunting territory was probably a seasonal allotment system. An anonymous account written in 1723 states that the "principle of the Indians is to mark off the hunting ground selected by them by blazing the trees with their crests so that they may never encroach on each other. . . . By the middle of the century these allotted territories were relatively stabilized."[6]

The principle that associates property right changes with the emergence of new and reevaluation of old harmful and beneficial effects suggests in this instance that the fur trade made it economic to encourage the husbanding of fur-bearing animals. Husbanding requires the ability to prevent poaching and this, in turn, suggests that socioeconomic changes in property in hunting land will take place. The chain of reasoning is consistent with the evidence cited above. Is it inconsistent with the absence of similar rights in property among the southwestern Indians?

Two factors suggest that the thesis is consistent with the absence of

[5] Eleanor Leacock, *op. cit.*, p. 15.
[6] Eleanor Leacock, *op. cit.*, p. 15.

similar rights among the Indians of the southwestern plains. The first of these is that there were no plains animals of commercial importance comparable to the fur-bearing animals of the forest, at least not until cattle arrived with Europeans. The second factor is that animals of the plains are primarily grazing species whose habit is to wander over wide tracts of land. The value of establishing boundaries to private hunting territories is thus reduced by the relatively high cost of preventing the animals from moving to adjacent parcels. Hence both the value and cost of establishing private hunting lands in the Southwest are such that we would expect little development along these lines. The externality was just not worth taking into account.

The lands of the Labrador Peninsula shelter forest animals whose habits are considerably different from those of the plains. Forest animals confine their territories to relatively small areas, so that the cost of internalizing the effects of husbanding these animals is considerably reduced. This reduced cost, together with the higher commercial value of fur-bearing forest animals, made it productive to establish private hunting lands. Frank G. Speck finds that family proprietorship among the Indians of the Peninsula included retaliation against trespass. Animal resources were husbanded. Sometimes conservation practices were carried on extensively. Family hunting territories were divided into quarters. Each year the family hunted in a different quarter in rotation, leaving a tract in the center as a sort of bank, not to be hunted over unless forced to do so by a shortage in the regular tract.

To conclude our excursion into the phenomenon of private rights in land among the American Indians, we note one further piece of corroborating evidence. Among the Indians of the Northwest, highly developed private family rights to hunting lands had also emerged—rights which went so far as to include inheritance. Here again we find that forest animals predominate and that the West Coast was frequently visited by sailing schooners whose primary purpose was trading in furs.[7]

[7] The thesis is consistent with the development of other types of private rights. Among wandering primitive peoples the cost of policing property is relatively low for highly portable objects. The owning family can protect such objects while carrying on its daily activities. If these objects are also very useful, property rights should appear frequently, so as to internalize the benefits and costs of their use. It is generally true among most primitive communities that weapons and household utensils, such as pottery, are regarded as private property. Both types of articles are portable and both require an investment of time to produce. Among agriculturally-oriented peoples, because of the relative fixity of their location, portability has a smaller role to play in the determination of property. The distinction is most clearly seen by comparing property in land among the most primitive of these societies, where crop rotation and simple fertilization techniques are unknown, or where land fertility is extremely poor, with property in land among primitive peoples who are more knowledgeable in these matters or who possess very superior land. Once a crop is grown by the more primitive agricultural societies, it is necessary for them to abandon the land for several years to restore productivity. Property rights in land among such people would require policing cost for several years during which no sizable output is obtained. Since to provide for

The Coalescence and Ownership of Property Rights

I have argued that property rights arise when it becomes economic for those affected by externalities to internalize benefits and costs. But I have not yet examined the forces which will govern the particular form of right ownership. Several idealized forms of ownership must be distinguished at the outset. These are communal ownership, private ownership, and state ownership.

By communal ownership, I shall mean a right which can be exercised by all members of the community. Frequently the rights to till and to hunt the land have been communally owned. The right to walk a city sidewalk is communally owned. Communal ownership means that the community denies to the state or to individual citizens the right to interfere with any person's exercise of communally-owned rights. Private ownership implies that the community recognizes the right of the owner to exclude others from exercising the owner's private rights. State ownership implies that the state may exclude anyone from the use of a right as long as the state follows accepted political procedures for determining who may not use state-owned property. I shall not examine in detail the alternative of state ownership. The object of the analysis which follows is to discern some broad principles governing the development of property rights in communities oriented to private property.

It will be best to begin by considering a particularly useful example that focuses our attention on the problem of land ownership. Suppose that land is communally owned. Every person has the right to hunt, till, or mine the land. This form of ownership fails to concentrate the cost associated with any person's exercise of his communal right on that person. If a person seeks to maximize the value of his communal rights, he will tend to overhunt and overwork the land because some of the costs of his doing so are borne by others. The stock of game and the richness of the soil will be diminished too quickly. It is conceivable that those who own these rights, i.e., every member of the community, can agree to curtail the rate at which they work the lands if negotiating and policing costs are zero. Each can agree to abridge his rights. It is obvious that the costs of reaching such an agreement will not be zero. What is not obvious is just how large these costs may be.

Negotiating costs will be large because it is difficult for many per-

sustenance these people must move to new land, a property right to be of value to them must be associated with a portable object. Among these people it is common to find property rights to the crops, which, after harvest, are portable, but not to the land. The more advanced agriculturally based primitive societies are able to remain with particular land for longer periods, and here we generally observe property rights to the land as well as to the crops.

sons to reach a mutually satisfactory agreement, especially when each hold-out has the right to work the land as fast as he pleases. But, even if an agreement among all can be reached, we must yet take account of the costs of policing the agreement, and these may be large, also. After such an agreement is reached, no one will privately own the right to work the land; all can work the land but at an agreed upon shorter workweek. Negotiating costs are increased even further because it is not possible under this system to bring the full expected benefits and expected costs of future generations to bear on current users.

If a single person owns land, he will attempt to maximize its present value by taking into account alternative future time streams of benefits and costs and selecting that one which he believes will maximize the present value of his privately-owned land rights. We all know that this means that he will attempt to take into account the supply and demand conditions that he thinks will exist after his death. It is very difficult to see how the existing communal owners can reach an agreement that takes account of these costs.

In effect, an owner of a private right to use land acts as a broker whose wealth depends on how well he takes into account the competing claims of the present and the future. But with communal rights there is no broker, and the claims of the present generation will be given an uneconomically large weight in determining the intensity with which the land is worked. Future generations might desire to pay present generations enough to change the present intensity of land usage. But they have no living agent to place their claims on the market. Under a communal property system, should a living person pay others to reduce the rate at which they work the land, he would not gain anything of value for his efforts. Communal property means that future generations must speak for themselves. No one has yet estimated the costs of carrying on such a conversation.

The land ownership example confronts us immediately with a great disadvantage of communal property. The effects of a person's activities on his neighbors and on subsequent generations will not be taken into account fully. Communal property results in great externalities. The full costs of the activities of an owner of a communal property right are not borne directly by him, nor can they be called to his attention easily by the willingness of others to pay him an appropriate sum. Communal property rules out a "pay-to-use-the-property" system and high negotiation and policing costs make ineffective a "pay-him-not-to-use-the-property" system.

The state, the courts, or the leaders of the community could attempt to internalize the external costs resulting from communal property by allowing private parcels owned by small groups of person with similar interests. The logical groups in terms of similar interests, are, of course, the family and the individual. Continuing with our use of the land ownership example, let us initially distribute private titles to land randomly among existing individuals and, further, let the extent of land included in each title be randomly determined.

The resulting private ownership of land will internalize many of the external costs associated with communal ownership, for now an owner, by virtue of his power to exclude others, can generally count on realizing the rewards associated with husbanding the game and increasing the fertility of his land. This concentration of benefits and costs on owners creates incentives to utilize resources more efficiently.

But we have yet to contend with externalities. Under the communal property system the maximization of the value of communal property rights will take place without regard to many costs, because the owner of a communal right cannot exclude others from enjoying the fruits of his efforts and because negotiation costs are too high for all to agree jointly on optimal behavior. The development of private rights permits the owner to economize on the use of those resources from which he has the right to exclude others. Much internalization is accomplished in this way. But the owner of private rights to one parcel does not himself own the rights to the parcel of another private sector. Since he cannot exclude others from their private rights to land, he has no direct incentive (in the absence of negotiations) to economize in the use of his land in a way that takes into account the effects he produces on the land rights of others. If he constructs a dam on his land, he has no direct incentive to take into account the lower water levels produced on his neighbor's land.

This is exactly the same kind of externality that we encountered with communal property rights, but it is present to a lesser degree. Whereas no one had an incentive to store water on any land under the communal system, private owners now can take into account directly those benefits and costs to their land that accompany water storage. But the effects on the land of others will not be taken into account directly.

The partial concentration of benefits and costs that accompany private ownership is only part of the advantage this system offers. The other part, and perhaps the most important, has escaped our notice. The cost of negotiating over the remaining externalities will be reduced greatly. Communal property rights allow anyone to use the land. Under this system it becomes necessary for all to reach an agreement on land use. But the externalities that accompany private ownership of property do not affect all owners, and, generally speaking, it will be necessary for only a few to reach an agreement that takes these effects into account. The cost of negotiating an internalization of these effects is thereby reduced considerably. The point is important enough to elucidate.

Suppose an owner of a communal land right, in the process of plowing a parcel of land, observes a second communal owner constructing a dam on adjacent land. The farmer prefers to have the stream as it is, and so he asks the engineer to stop his construction. The engineer says, "Pay me to stop." The farmer replies, "I will be happy to pay you, but what can you guarantee in return?" The engineer answers, "I can guarantee you that I will not continue constructing the dam, but I cannot guarantee that another engineer will not take up the task because this is communal property; I have no right to exclude him." What would be a simple negotiation between two persons under a private property arrangement turns out to be a rather complex negotiation between the farmer and everyone else. This is the basic explanation, I believe, for the preponderance of single rather than multiple owners of property. Indeed, an increase in the number of owners is an increase in the communality of property and leads, generally, to an increase in the cost of internalizing.

The reduction in negotiating cost that accompanies the private right to exclude others allows most externalities to be internalized at rather low cost. Those that are not are associated with activities that generate external effects impinging upon many people. The soot from smoke affects many homeowners, none of whom is willing to pay enough to the factory to get its owner to reduce smoke output. All homeowners together might be willing to pay enough, but the cost of their getting together may be enough to discourage effective market bargaining. The negotiating problem is compounded even more if the smoke comes not from a single smoke stack but from an industrial district. In such cases, it may be too costly to internalize effects through the marketplace.

Returning to our land ownership paradigm, we recall that land was distributed in randomly sized parcels to randomly selected owners. These owners now negotiate among themselves to internalize any remaining externalities. Two market options are open to the negotiators. The first is simply to try to reach a contractual agreement among owners that directly deals with the external effects at issue. The second option is for some owners to buy out others, thus changing the parcel size owned. Which option is selected will depend on which is cheaper. We have here a standard economic problem of optimal scale. If there exist constant returns to scale in the ownership of different sized parcels, it will be largely a matter of indifference between outright purchase and contractual agreement if only a single, easy-to-police, contractual agreement will internalize the externality. But, if there are several externalities, so that several such contracts will need to be negotiated, or if the contractual agreements should be difficult to police, then outright purchase will be the preferred course of action.

The greater are diseconomies of scale to land ownership the more will contractual arrangement be used by the interacting neighbors to settle these differences. Negotiating and policing costs will be compared to costs that depend on the scale of ownership, and parcels of land will tend to be owned in sizes which minimize the sum of these costs.[8]

The interplay of scale economies, negotiating cost, externalities, and the modification of property rights can be seen in the most notable "exception" to the assertion that ownership tends to be an individual affair: the publicly-held corporation. I assume that significant economies of scale in the operation of large corporations is a fact and, also, that large requirements for equity capital can be satisfied more cheaply by acquiring the capital from many purchasers of equity shares. While economies of scale in operating these enterprises exist, economies of scale in the provision of capital do not. Hence, it becomes desirable for many "owners" to form a joint-stock company.

But if all owners participate in each decision that needs to be made by such a company, the scale economies of operating the company will be overcome quickly by high negotiating cost. Hence a delegation of authority for most decisions takes place and, for most of these, a small management group becomes the *de facto* owners. Effective ownership, i.e., effective control of property, is thus legally concentrated in management's hands. This is the first legal modification, and it takes place in recognition of the high negotiating costs that would otherwise obtain.

The structure of ownership, however, creates some externality difficulties under the law of partnership. If the corporation should fail, partnership law commits each shareholder to meet the debts of the corporation up to the limits of his financial ability. Thus, managerial *de facto* ownership can have considerable external effects on shareholders. Should property rights remain unmodified, this externality would make it exceedingly difficult for entrepreneurs to acquire equity capital from wealthy individuals. (Although these individuals have recourse to reimbursements from other shareholders, litigation costs will be high.) A second legal modification, limited liability, has taken place to reduce the effect of this externality.[9] *De facto* management ownership and limited liability combine to minimize the overall cost of operating large enterprises. Shareholders are essentially lenders of equity capital and not owners, although they do participate in such infrequent decisions as

[8] Compare this with the similar rationale given by R. H. Coase to explain the firm in "The Nature of the Firm," *Economica*, New Series, 1937, pp. 386–405.

[9] Henry G. Manne discusses this point in a forthcoming book about the American corporate system.

those involving mergers. What shareholders really own are their shares and not the corporation. Ownership in the sense of control again becomes a largely individual affair. The shareholders own their shares, and the president of the corporation and possibly a few other top executives control the corporation.

To further ease the impact of management decisions on shareholders, that is, to minimize the impact of externalities under this ownership form, a further legal modification of rights is required. Unlike partnership law, a shareholder may sell his interest without first obtaining the permission of fellow shareholders or without dissolving the corporation. It thus becomes easy for him to get out if his preferences and those of the management are no longer in harmony. This "escape hatch" is extremely important and has given rise to the organized trading of securities. The increase in harmony between managers and shareholders brought about by exchange and by competing managerial groups helps to minimize the external effects associated with the corporate ownership structure. Finally, limited liability considerably reduces the cost of exchanging shares by making it unnecessary for a purchaser of shares to examine in great detail the liabilities of the corporation and the assets of other shareholders; these liabilities can adversely affect a purchaser only up to the extent of the price per share.

The dual tendencies for ownership to rest with individuals and for the extent of an individual's ownership to accord with the minimization of all costs is clear in the land ownership paradigm. The applicability of this paradigm has been extended to the corporation. But it may not be clear yet how widely applicable this paradigm is. Consider the problems of copyright and patents. If a new idea is freely appropriable by all, if there exist communal rights to new ideas, incentives for developing such ideas will be lacking. The benefits derivable from these ideas will not be concentrated on their originators. If we extend some degree of private rights to the originators, these ideas will come forth at a more rapid pace. But the existence of the private rights does not mean that their effects on the property of others will be directly taken into account. A new idea makes an old one obsolete and another old one more valuable. These effects will not be directly taken into account, but they can be called to the attention of the originator of the new idea through market negotiations. All problems of externalities are closely analogous to those which arise in the land ownership example. The relevant variables are identical.

What I have suggested in this paper is an approach to problems in property rights. But it is more than that. It is also a different way of viewing traditional problems. An elaboration of this approach will, I hope, illuminate a great number of social-economic problems.

[13]

PROPERTY RULES, LIABILITY RULES, AND INALIENABILITY: ONE VIEW OF THE CATHEDRAL

Guido Calabresi * *and A. Douglas Melamed* **

Professor Calabresi and Mr. Melamed develop a framework for legal analysis which they believe serves to integrate various legal relationships which are traditionally analyzed in separate subject areas such as Property and Torts. By using their model to suggest solutions to the pollution problem that have been overlooked by writers in the field, and by applying the model to the question of criminal sanctions, they demonstrate the utility of such an integrated approach.

I. Introduction

ONLY rarely are Property and Torts approached from a unified perspective. Recent writings by lawyers concerned with economics and by economists concerned with law suggest, however, that an attempt at integrating the various legal relationships treated by these subjects would be useful both for the beginning student and the sophisticated scholar.[1] By articulating a concept of "entitlements" which are protected by property, liability, or inalienability rules, we present one framework for such an approach.[2] We then analyze aspects of the pollution problem and of

* John Thomas Smith Professor of Law, Yale University. B.S. Yale, 1953; B.A. Oxford, 1955; LL.B. Yale, 1958; M.A. Oxford, 1959.

** Member of the District of Columbia Bar. B.A. Yale University, 1967; J.D. Harvard University, 1970.

[1] *See, e.g.*, Michelman, *Pollution as a Tort: A Non-Accidental Perspective on Calabresi's* Costs, 80 Yale L.J. 647 (1971) (analysis of three alternative rules in pollution problems); Demsetz, *Toward a Theory of Property Rights*, 57 Am. Econ. Rev. 347 (1967) (Vol. 2 — Papers and Proceedings) (analysis of property as a means of cost internalization which ignores liability rule alternatives).

[2] Since a fully integrated approach is probably impossible, it should be emphasized that this article concerns only one possible way of looking at and analyzing legal problems. Thus we shall not address ourselves to those fundamental legal questions which center on what institutions and what procedures are most suitable for making what decisions, except insofar as these relate directly to the problems of selecting the initial entitlements and the modes of protecting these entitlements. While we do not underrate the importance, indeed perhaps the primacy, of legal process considerations, *see* pp. 1116–17 *infra*, we are merely interested in the light

criminal sanctions in order to demonstrate how the model enables us to perceive relationships which have been ignored by writers in those fields.

The first issue which must be faced by any legal system is one we call the problem of "entitlement." Whenever a state is presented with the conflicting interests of two or more people, or two or more groups of people, it must decide which side to favor. Absent such a decision, access to goods, services, and life itself will be decided on the basis of "might makes right" — whoever is stronger or shrewder will win.[3] Hence the fundamental thing that law does is to decide which of the conflicting parties will be entitled to prevail. The entitlement to make noise versus the entitlement to have silence, the entitlement to pollute versus the entitlement to breathe clean air, the entitlement to have children versus the entitlement to forbid them — these are the first order of legal decisions.

Having made its initial choice, society must enforce that choice. Simply setting the entitlement does not avoid the problem of "might makes right"; a minimum of state intervention is always necessary.[4] Our conventional notions make this easy to compre-

---

that a rather different approach may shed on problems frequently looked at primarily from a legal process point of view.

As Professor Harry Wellington is fond of saying about many discussions of law, this article is meant to be only *one* of Monet's paintings of the Cathedral at Rouen. To understand the Cathedral one must see all of them. *See* G. Hamilton, Claude Monet's Paintings of Rouen Cathedral 4–5, 19–20, 27 (1960).

[3] One could of course look at the state as simply a larger coalition of friends designed to enforce rules which merely accomplish the dominant coalition's desires. Rules of law would then be no more than "might makes right" writ large. Such a view does not strike us as plausible if for no other reason than that the state decides too many issues in response to too many different coalitions. This fact, by itself, would require a different form of analysis from that which would suffice to explain entitlements resulting from more direct and decentralized uses of "might makes right."

[4] For an excellent presentation of this general point by an economist, see Samuels, *Interrelations Between Legal and Economic Processes*, 14 J. Law & Econ. 435 (1971).

We do not intend to imply that the state relies on force to enforce all or most entitlements. Nor do we imply that absent state intervention only force would win. The use by the state of feelings of obligation and rules of morality as means of enforcing most entitlements is not only crucial but terribly efficient. Conversely, absent the state, individuals would probably agree on rules of behavior which would govern entitlements in whole series of situations on the basis of criteria other than "might makes right." That these rules might themselves reflect the same types of considerations we will analyze as bases for legal entitlements is, of course, neither here nor there. What is important is that these "social compacts" would, no less than legal entitlements, give rise to what may be called obligations. These obligations in turn would cause people to behave in accordance with the compact in particular cases regardless of the existence of a predominant force. In this article

hend with respect to private property. If Taney owns a cabbage patch and Marshall, who is bigger, wants a cabbage, he will get it unless the state intervenes.[5] But it is not so obvious that the state must also intervene if it chooses the opposite entitlement, communal property. If large Marshall has grown some communal cabbages and chooses to deny them to small Taney, it will take state action to enforce Taney's entitlement to the communal cabbages. The same symmetry applies with respect to bodily integrity. Consider the plight of the unwilling ninety-eight-pound weakling in a state which nominally entitles him to bodily integrity but will not intervene to enforce the entitlement against a lustful Juno. Consider then the plight — absent state intervention — of the ninety-eight-pounder who desires an unwilling Juno in a state which nominally entitles everyone to use everyone else's body. The need for intervention applies in a slightly more complicated way to injuries. When a loss is left where it falls in an auto accident, it is not because God so ordained it. Rather it is because the state has granted the injurer an entitlement to be free of liability and will intervene to prevent the victim's friends, if they are stronger, from taking compensation from the injurer.[6] The loss is shifted in other cases because the state has granted an entitlement to compensation and will intervene to prevent the stronger injurer from rebuffing the victim's requests for compensation.

we are not concerned as much with the workings of such obligations as with the reasons which may explain the rules which themselves give rise to the obligations.

[5] "Bigger" obviously does not refer simply to size, but to the sum of an individual's resources. If Marshall's gang possesses superior brain and brawn to that of Taney, Marshall's gang will get the cabbages.

[6] Different cultures deal with the problem in different ways. Witness the following account:

> "Life Insurance" Fee is 4 Bulls and $1200. Port Moresby, New Guinea. Peter Howard proved that he values his life more than four bulls and $1200. But he wants $24 and one pig in change.
>
> Mr. Howard gave the money and livestock to members of the Jiga tribe, which had threatened to kill him because he killed a tribe member in an auto accident last October 29.
>
> The police approved the extortion agreement after telling the 38 year old Mr. Howard they could not protect him from the sworn vengeance of the tribe, which lives at Mt. Hagen, about 350 miles Northeast of Port Moresby.
>
> Mr. Howard, of Cambridge, England, was attacked and badly beaten by the tribesmen after the accident.
>
> They said he would be killed unless the payment of money and bulls was made according to the tribal traditions. It was the first time a white man in New Guinea had been forced to bow to tribal laws.
>
> After making the payment, Mr. Howard demanded to be compensated for the assault on him by the tribesmen. He said he wanted $24 and one pig. A Jiga spokesman told him the tribe would "think about it." New York Times, Feb. 16, 1972, at 17, col. 6.

The state not only has to decide whom to entitle, but it must also simultaneously make a series of equally difficult second order decisions. These decisions go to the manner in which entitlements are protected and to whether an individual is allowed to sell or trade the entitlement. In any given dispute, for example, the state must decide not only which side wins but also the kind of protection to grant. It is with the latter decisions, decisions which shape the subsequent relationship between the winner and the loser, that this article is primarily concerned. We shall consider three types of entitlements — entitlements protected by property rules, entitlements protected by liability rules, and inalienable entitlements. The categories are not, of course, absolutely distinct; but the categorization is useful since it reveals some of the reasons which lead us to protect certain entitlements in certain ways.

An entitlement is protected by a property rule to the extent that someone who wishes to remove the entitlement from its holder must buy it from him in a voluntary transaction in which the value of the entitlement is agreed upon by the seller. It is the form of entitlement which gives rise to the least amount of state intervention: once the original entitlement is decided upon, the state does not try to decide its value.[7] It lets each of the parties say how much the entitlement is worth to him, and gives the seller a veto if the buyer does not offer enough. Property rules involve a collective decision as to who is to be given an initial entitlement but not as to the value of the entitlement.

Whenever someone may destroy the initial entitlement if he is willing to pay an objectively determined value for it, an entitlement is protected by a liability rule. This value may be what it is thought the original holder of the entitlement would have sold it for. But the holder's complaint that he would have demanded more will not avail him once the objectively determined value is set. Obviously, liability rules involve an additional stage of state intervention: not only are entitlements protected, but their transfer or destruction is allowed on the basis of a value determined by some organ of the state rather than by the parties themselves.

An entitlement is inalienable to the extent that its transfer is not permitted between a willing buyer and a willing seller. The state intervenes not only to determine who is initially entitled and to determine the compensation that must be paid if the en-

[7] A property rule requires less state intervention only in the sense that intervention is needed to decide upon and enforce the initial entitlement but not for the separate problem of determining the value of the entitlement. Thus, if a particular property entitlement is especially difficult to enforce — for example, the right to personal security in urban areas — the actual amount of state intervention can be very high and could, perhaps, exceed that needed for some entitlements protected by easily administered liability rules.

titlement is taken or destroyed, but also to forbid its sale under some or all circumstances. Inalienability rules are thus quite different from property and liability rules. Unlike those rules, rules of inalienability not only "protect" the entitlement; they may also be viewed as limiting or regulating the grant of the entitlement itself.

It should be clear that most entitlements to most goods are mixed. Taney's house may be protected by a property rule in situations where Marshall wishes to purchase it, by a liability rule where the government decides to take it by eminent domain, and by a rule of inalienability in situations where Taney is drunk or incompetent. This article will explore two primary questions: (1) In what circumstances should we grant a particular entitlement? and (2) In what circumstances should we decide to protect that entitlement by using a property, liability, or inalienability rule?

II. The Setting of Entitlements

What are the reasons for deciding to entitle people to pollute or to entitle people to forbid pollution, to have children freely or to limit procreation, to own property or to share property? They can be grouped under three headings: economic efficiency, distributional preferences, and other justice considerations.[8]

A. Economic Efficiency

Perhaps the simplest reason for a particular entitlement is to minimize the administrative costs of enforcement. This was the reason Holmes gave for letting the costs lie where they fall in accidents unless some clear societal benefit is achieved by shifting them.[9] By itself this reason will never justify any result except that of letting the stronger win, for obviously that result minimizes enforcement costs. Nevertheless, administrative efficiency may be relevant to choosing entitlements when other reasons are taken into account. This may occur when the reasons accepted are indifferent between conflicting entitlements and one entitlement is cheaper to enforce than the others. It may also occur when the reasons are not indifferent but lead us only slightly to prefer one over another and the first is considerably more expensive to enforce than the second.

But administrative efficiency is just one aspect of the broader concept of economic efficiency. Economic efficiency asks that we

---

[8] *See generally* G. Calabresi, The Costs of Accidents 24–33 (1970) [hereinafter cited as Costs].

[9] *See* O.W. Holmes, Jr., The Common Law 76–77 (Howe ed. 1963). For a criticism of the justification as applied to accidents today, see Costs 261–63. *But cf.* Posner, *A Theory of Negligence*, 1 J. Legal Stud. 29 (1972).

choose the set of entitlements which would lead to that allocation of resources which could not be improved in the sense that a further change would not so improve the condition of those who gained by it that they could compensate those who lost from it and still be better off than before. This is often called Pareto optimality.[10] To give two examples, economic efficiency asks for that combination of entitlements to engage in risky activities and to be free from harm from risky activities which will most likely lead to the lowest sum of accident costs and of costs of avoiding accidents.[11] It asks for that form of property, private or communal, which leads to the highest product for the effort of producing.

Recently it has been argued that on certain assumptions, usually termed the absence of transaction costs, Pareto optimality or economic efficiency will occur regardless of the initial entitlement.[12] For this to hold, "no transaction costs" must be under-

---

[10] We are not here concerned with the many definitional variations which encircle the concept of Pareto optimality. Many of these variations stem from the fact that unless compensation actually occurs after a change (and this itself assumes a preexisting set of entitlements from which one makes a change to a Pareto optimal arrangement), the redistribution of wealth implicit in the change may well make a return to the prior position also seem Pareto optimal. There are any number of variations on this theme which economists have studied at length. Since in the world in which lawyers must live, anything close to Pareto efficiency, even if desirable, is not attainable, these refinements need not detain us even though they are crucial to a full understanding of the concept.

Most versions of Pareto optimality are based on the premise that individuals know best what is best for them. Hence they assume that to determine whether those who gain from a change could compensate those who lose, one must look to the values the individuals themselves give to the gains and losses. Economic efficiency may, however, present a broader notion which does not depend upon this individualistic premise. It may be that the state, for paternalistic reasons, *see* pp. 1113–14 *infra*, is better able to determine whether the total gain of the winners is greater than the total loss of the losers.

[11] The word "costs" is here used in a broad way to include all the disutilities resulting from an accident and its avoidance. As such it is not limited to monetary costs, or even to those which could in some sense be "monetizable," but rather includes disutilities or "costs" — for instance, the loss to an individual of his leg — the very expression of which in monetary terms would seem callous. One of the consequences of not being able to put monetary values on some disutilities or "costs" is that the market is of little use in gauging their worth, and this in turn gives rise to one of the reasons why liability, or inalienability rules, rather than property rules may be used.

[12] This proposition was first established in Coase's classic article, *The Problem of Social Cost*, 3 J. LAW & ECON. 1 (1960), and has been refined in subsequent literature. *See, e.g.*, Calabresi, *Transaction Costs, Resource Allocation and Liability Rules — A Comment*, 11 J. LAW & ECON. 67 (1968); Nutter, *The Coase Theorem on Social Cost: A Footnote*, 11 J. LAW & ECON. 503 (1968). *See also* G. STIGLER, THE THEORY OF PRICE 113 (3d ed. 1966); Mishan, *Pareto Optimality and the Law*, 19 OXFORD ECON. PAPERS 255 (1967).

stood extremely broadly as involving both perfect knowledge and the absence of any impediments or costs of negotiating. Negotiation costs include, for example, the cost of excluding would-be freeloaders from the fruits of market bargains.[13] In such a frictionless society, transactions would occur until no one could be made better off as a result of further transactions without making someone else worse off. This, we would suggest, is a necessary, indeed a tautological, result of the definitions of Pareto optimality and of transaction costs which we have given.

Such a result would not mean, however, that the *same* allocation of resources would exist regardless of the initial set of entitlements. Taney's willingness to pay for the right to make noise may depend on how rich he is; Marshall's willingness to pay for silence may depend on his wealth. In a society which entitles Taney to make noise and which forces Marshall to buy silence from Taney, Taney is wealthier and Marshall poorer than each would be in a society which had the converse set of entitlements. Depending on how Marshall's desire for silence and Taney's for noise vary with their wealth, an entitlement to noise will result in negotiations which will lead to a different quantum of noise than would an entitlement to silence.[14] This variation in the quantity

[13] The freeloader is the person who refuses to be inoculated against smallpox because, given the fact that almost everyone else is inoculated, the risk of smallpox to him is less than the risk of harm from the inoculation. He is the person who refuses to pay for a common park, though he wants it, because he believes that others will put in enough money to make the park available to him. *See* COSTS 137 n.4. The costs of excluding the freeloader from the benefits for which he refused to pay may well be considerable as the two above examples should suggest. This is especially so since these costs may include the inefficiency of pricing a good, like the park once it exists, above its marginal cost in order to force the freeloader to disclose his true desire to use it — thus enabling us to charge him part of the cost of establishing it initially.

It is the capacity of the market to induce disclosure of individual preferences which makes it theoretically possible for the market to bring about exchanges leading to Pareto optimality. But the freeloader situation is just one of many where no such disclosure is achieved by the market. If we assume perfect knowledge, defined more broadly than is normally done to include knowledge of individual preferences, then such situations pose no problem. This definition of perfect knowledge, though perhaps implicit in the concept of no transaction costs, would not only make reaching Pareto optimality easy through the market, it would make it equally easy to establish a similar result by collective fiat.

For a further discussion of what is implied by a broad definition of no transaction costs, see note 59 *infra*. For a discussion of other devices which may induce individuals to disclose their preferences, see note 38 *infra*.

[14] *See* Mishan, *Pareto Optimality and the Law*, 19 OXFORD ECON. PAPERS 255 (1967). Unless Taney's and Marshall's desires for noise and silence are totally unaffected by their wealth, that is, their desires are totally income inelastic, a change in their wealth will alter the value each places on noise and silence and hence will alter the outcome of their negotiations.

of noise and silence can be viewed as no more than an instance of the well accepted proposition that what is a Pareto optimal, or economically efficient, solution varies with the starting distribution of wealth. Pareto optimality is optimal *given* a distribution of wealth, but different distributions of wealth imply their own Pareto optimal allocation of resources.[15]

All this suggests why distributions of wealth may affect a society's choice of entitlements. It does not suggest why *economic efficiency* should affect the choice, if we assume an absence of any transaction costs. But no one makes an assumption of no transaction costs in practice. Like the physicist's assumption of no friction or Say's law in macro-economics, the assumption of no transaction costs may be a useful starting point, a device which helps us see how, as different elements which may be termed transaction costs become important, the goal of economic efficiency starts to prefer one allocation of entitlements over another.[16]

Since one of us has written at length on how in the presence of various types of transaction costs a society would go about deciding on a set of entitlements in the field of accident law,[17] it is enough to say here: (1) that economic efficiency standing alone would dictate that set of entitlements which favors knowledgeable choices between social benefits and the social costs of obtaining them, and between social costs and the social costs of avoiding them; (2) that this implies, in the absence of certainty as to whether a benefit is worth its costs to society, that the cost should be put on the party or activity best located to make such a cost-benefit analysis; (3) that in particular contexts like accidents or pollution this suggests putting costs on the party or activity which

[15] There should be no implication that a Pareto optimal solution is in some sense better than a non-Pareto optimal solution which results in a different wealth distribution. The implication is only that given the *same* wealth distribution Pareto optimal is in some meaningful sense preferable to non-Pareto optimal.

[16] *See* Demsetz, *When Does the Rule of Liability Matter?*, 1 J. LEGAL STUD. 13, 25–28 (1972); Stigler, *The Law and Economics of Public Policy: A Plea to the Scholars*, 1 J. LEGAL STUD. 1, 11–12 (1972).

The trouble with a term like "no transaction costs" is that it covers a multitude of market failures. The appropriate collective response, if the aim is to approach Pareto optimality, will vary depending on what the actual impediments to full bargaining are in any given cases. Occasionally the appropriate response may be to ignore the impediments. If the impediments are merely the administrative costs of establishing a market, it may be that doing nothing is preferable to attempting to correct for these costs because the administrative costs of collective action may be even greater. Similarly, if the impediments are due to a failure of the market to cause an accurate disclosure of freeloaders' preferences it may be that the collective can do no better.

[17] *See* COSTS 135–97.

can most cheaply avoid them; (4) that in the absence of certainty as to who that party or activity is, the costs should be put on the party or activity which can with the lowest transaction costs act in the market to correct an error in entitlements by inducing the party who can avoid social costs most cheaply to do so;[18] and (5) that since we are in an area where by hypothesis markets do not work perfectly — there are transaction costs — a decision will often have to be made on whether market transactions or collective fiat is most likely to bring us closer to the Pareto optimal result the "perfect" market would reach.[19]

Complex though this summary may suggest the entitlement choice to be, in practice the criteria it represents will frequently indicate which allocations of entitlements are most likely to lead to optimal market judgments between having an extra car or taking a train, getting an extra cabbage and spending less time working in the hot sun, and having more widgets and breathing the pollution that widget production implies. Economic efficiency is not, however, the sole reason which induces a society to select a

[18] In *The Costs of Accidents*, the criteria here summarized are discussed at length and broken down into subcriteria which deal with the avoidance of different types of externalization and with the finding of the "best briber." Such detailed analysis is necessary to the application of the criteria to any specific area of law. At the level of generality of this article it did not seem to us necessary.

[19] In accident law this election takes the form of a choice between general or market deterrence and specific deterrence, in which the permitted level and manner of accident causing activities is determined collectively. For example, society may decide to grant an entitlement to drive and an entitlement to be compensated for accidents resulting from driving, and allow decisions by individual parties to determine the level and manner of driving. But a greater degree of specific deterrence could be achieved by selecting a different set of initial entitlements in order to accord with a collective cost-benefit analysis — by, for example, prohibiting cars of more than a certain horsepower.

The primary disadvantage of specific deterrence, as compared with general deterrence, is that it requires the central decisionmaker not only to determine the costs of any given activity, but also to measure its benefits, in order to determine the optimum level of activity. It is exceedingly difficult and exceedingly costly for any centralized decisionmaker to be fully informed of the costs and benefits of a wide range of activities. The irony is that collective fiat functions best in a world of costless perfect information; yet in a world of costless transactions, including costless information, the optimum allocation would be reached by market transactions, and the need to consider the alternative of collective fiat would not arise. One could, however, view the irony conversely, and say that the market works best under assumptions of perfect knowledge where collective fiat would work perfectly, rendering the market unnecessary. The fact that both market and collective determinations face difficulties in achieving the Pareto optimal result which perfect knowledge and no transaction costs would permit does not mean that the same difficulties are always as great for the two approaches. Thus, there are many situations in which we can assume fairly confidently that the market will do better than a collective decider, and there are situations where we can assume the opposite to be true. *See* COSTS 103–13.

set of entitlements. Wealth distribution preferences are another, and thus it is to distributional grounds for different entitlements to which we must now turn.

B. Distributional Goals

There are, we would suggest, at least two types of distributional concerns which may affect the choice of entitlements. These involve distribution of wealth itself and distribution of certain specific goods, which have sometimes been called merit goods.

All societies have wealth distribution preferences. They are, nonetheless, harder to talk about than are efficiency goals. For efficiency goals can be discussed in terms of a general concept like Pareto optimality to which exceptions — like paternalism — can be noted.[20] Distributional preferences, on the other hand, cannot usefully be discussed in a single conceptual framework. There are some fairly broadly accepted preferences — caste preferences in one society, more rather than less equality in another society. There are also preferences which are linked to dynamic efficiency concepts — producers ought to be rewarded since they will cause everyone to be better off in the end. Finally, there are a myriad of highly individualized preferences as to who should be richer and who poorer which need not have anything to do with either equality or efficiency — silence lovers should be richer than noise lovers because they are worthier.[21]

Difficult as wealth distribution preferences are to analyze, it should be obvious that they play a crucial role in the setting of entitlements. For the placement of entitlements has a fundamental effect on a society's distribution of wealth. It is not enough, if a society wishes absolute equality, to start everyone off with the same amount of money. A financially egalitarian society which gives individuals the right to make noise immediately makes the would-be noisemaker richer than the silence

[20] For a discussion of paternalism, see pp. 1113–14 *infra*.

[21] The first group of preferences roughly coincides with those notions which writers like Fletcher, following Aristotle, term distributive justice. The second and third groups, instead, presumably deal with Fletcher's "corrective" justice — rewards based on what people do rather than what they are. *See* Fletcher, *Fairness and Utility in Tort Theory*, 85 HARV. L. REV. 537, 547 n.40 (1972).

Within the "corrective" justice category our second and third groupings distinguish those preferences which are transparently linked to efficiency notions from those whose roots are less obvious. If there were a generally accepted theory of desserts, one could speak in general terms about the role the third group plays just as one tends to speak about the role of either the first or second group. We do not believe that an adequate theory of desserts — even if possible — is currently available. *See also* pp. 1102–05 *infra*.

loving hermit.[22] Similarly, a society which entitles the person with brains to keep what his shrewdness gains him implies a different distribution of wealth from a society which demands from each according to his relative ability but gives to each according to his relative desire. One can go further and consider that a beautiful woman or handsome man is better off in a society which entitles individuals to bodily integrity than in one which gives everybody use of all the beauty available.

The consequence of this is that it is very difficult to imagine a society in which there is complete equality of wealth. Such a society either would have to consist of people who were all precisely the same, or it would have to compensate for differences in wealth caused by a given set of entitlements. The former is, of course, ridiculous, even granting cloning. And the latter would be very difficult; it would involve knowing what everyone's tastes were and taxing every holder of an entitlement at a rate sufficient to make up for the benefits the entitlement gave him. For example, it would involve taxing everyone with an entitlement to private use of his beauty or brains sufficiently to compensate those less favorably endowed but who nonetheless desired what beauty or brains could get.

If perfect equality is impossible, a society must choose what entitlements it wishes to have on the basis of criteria other than perfect equality. In doing this, a society often has a choice of methods, and the method chosen will have important distributional implications. Society can, for instance, give an entitlement away free and then, by paying the holders of the entitlement to limit their use of it, protect those who are injured by the free entitlement. Conversely, it can allow people to do a given thing only if they buy the right from the government. Thus a society can decide whether to entitle people to have children and then induce them to exercise control in procreating, or to require people to buy the right to have children in the first place. A society can also decide whether to entitle people to be free of military service and then induce them to join up, or to require all to serve but enable each to buy his way out. Which entitlement a society decides to sell, and which it decides to give away, will likely depend in part on which determination promotes the wealth distribution that society favors.[23]

[22] This assumes that there is not enough space for the noisemaker and the silence lover to coexist without intruding upon one another. In other words, this assumes that we are dealing with a problem of allocation of scarce resources; if we were not, there would be no need to set the initial entitlement. *See generally* Mishan, *supra* note 12.

[23] Any entitlement given away free implies a converse which must be paid for. For all those who like children, there are those who are disturbed by children;

If the choice of entitlements affects wealth distribution generally, it also affects the chances that people will obtain what have sometimes been called merit goods.[24] Whenever a society wishes to maximize the chances that individuals will have at least a minimum endowment of certain particular goods — education, clothes, bodily integrity — the society is likely to begin by giving the individuals an entitlement to them. If the society deems such an endowment to be essential regardless of individual desires, it will, of course, make the entitlement inalienable.[25] Why, however, would a society entitle individuals to specific goods rather than to money with which they can buy what they wish, unless it deems that it can decide better than the individuals what benefits them and society; unless, in other words, it wishes to make the entitlement inalienable?

We have seen that an entitlement to a good or to its converse is essentially inevitable.[26] We either are entitled to have silence or entitled to make noise in a given set of circumstances. We either have the right to our own property or body or the right to share others' property or bodies. We may buy or sell our-

for all those who detest armies, there are those who want what armies accomplish. Otherwise, we would have no scarce resource problem and hence no entitlement problem. Therefore, one cannot simply say that giving away an entitlement free is progressive while selling it is regressive. It is true that the more "free" goods there are the less inequality of wealth there is, if everything else has stayed the same. But if a free entitlement implies a costly converse, entitlements are *not* in this sense free goods. And the issue of their progressivity and regressivity must depend on the relative desire for the entitlement as against its converse on the part of the rich and the poor.

Strictly speaking, even this is true only if the money needed to finance the alternative plans, or made available to the government as a result of the plans, is raised and spent in a way that is precisely neutral with respect to wealth distribution. The point is simply this: even a highly regressive tax will aid wealth equality if the money it raises is all spent to benefit the poorest citizens. And even a system of outdoor relief for the idle rich aids wealth equality if the funds it requires are raised by taxing only the wealthiest of the wealthy. Thus whenever one speaks of a taxing program, spending program, or a system of entitlements as progressive or regressive, one must be assuming that the way the money is spent (if it is a tax) or the way it is raised (if it is a spending program) does not counter the distributive effect of the program itself.

[24] *Cf.* R. Musgrave, The Theory of Public Finance 13–14 (1959).

[25] The commonly given reasons why a society may choose to do this are discussed *infra* at pp. 1111–15. All of them are, of course, reasons which explain why such goods are often categorized as merit goods. When a society subsidizes a good it makes a similar decision based on similar grounds. Presumably, however, in such cases the grounds only justify making possession of the good less costly than would be the case without government intervention, rather than making possession of the good inevitable.

[26] This is true unless we are prepared to let the parties settle the matter on the basis of might makes right, which itself may also be viewed as a form of entitlement.

selves into the opposite position, but we must start somewhere. Under these circumstances, a society which prefers people to have silence, or own property, or have bodily integrity, but which does not hold the grounds for its preference to be sufficiently strong to justify overriding contrary preferences by individuals, will give such entitlements according to the collective preference, even though it will allow them to be sold thereafter.

Whenever transactions to sell or buy entitlements are very expensive, such an initial entitlement decision will be nearly as effective in assuring that individuals will have the merit good as would be making the entitlement inalienable. Since coercion is inherent because of the fact that a good cannot practically be bought or sold, a society can choose only whether to make an individual have the good, by giving it to him, or to prevent him from getting it by giving him money instead.[27] In such circumstances society will pick the entitlement it deems favorable to the general welfare and not worry about coercion or alienability; it has increased the chances that individuals will have a particular good without increasing the degree of coercion imposed on individuals.[28] A common example of this may occur where the good involved is the present certainty of being able to buy a future benefit and where a futures market in that good is too expensive to be feasible.[29]

[27] For a discussion of this inevitable, and therefore irrelevant degree of coercion in the accident context, see COSTS 50–55, 161–73.

[28] The situation is analogous to that which involves choosing between systems of allocation of accident costs which minimize rapid changes in wealth, through spreading, and those that do not. Indeed, if the avoidance of rapid changes in wealth is, itself, viewed as a merit good, the analogy is complete. In the accident field a great deal of attention has been devoted to the problem of rapid changes in wealth. *See, e.g.*, Morris & Paul, *The Financial Impact of Automobile Accidents*, 110 U. PA. L. REV. 913, 924 (1962). *But see* W. BLUM & H. KALVEN, PUBLIC LAW PERSPECTIVES ON A PRIVATE LAW PROBLEM — AUTO COMPENSATION PLANS (1965).

[29] A full discussion of this justification for the giving of goods in "kind" is well beyond the scope of this article. An indication of what is involved may be in order, however. One of the many reasons why the right to vote is given in kind instead of giving individuals that amount of money which would assure them, in a voteless society, of all the benefits which having the vote gives them, is that at any given time the price of those benefits in the future is totally uncertain and, therefore, virtually no amount of money would assure individuals of having those future benefits. This would not be the case if an entrepreneur could be counted on to guarantee those future benefits in exchange for a present money payment. That is what happens in a futures market for, say, sow's bellies. The degree of uncertainty in the cost of the future benefits of the vote is such, however, that a futures market is either not feasible, or, what is the same thing, much too costly to be worthwhile. In such circumstances the nonmarket alternative of giving of the good in kind seems more efficient. Many of the merit goods which are, in fact, given in kind in our society — for example, education — share this character-

C. Other Justice Reasons

The final reasons for a society's choice of initial entitlements we termed other justice reasons, and we may as well admit that it is hard to know what content can be poured into that term, at least given the very broad definitions of economic efficiency and distributional goals that we have used. Is there, in other words, a reason which would influence a society's choice of initial entitlements that cannot be comprehended in terms of efficiency and distribution? A couple of examples will indicate the problem.

Taney likes noise; Marshall likes silence. They are, let us assume, inevitably neighbors. Let us also assume there are no transaction costs which may impede negotiations between them. Let us assume finally that we do not know Taney's and Marshall's wealth or, indeed, anything else about them. Under these circumstances we know that Pareto optimality — economic efficiency — will be reached whether we choose an entitlement to make noise or to have silence. We also are indifferent, from a general wealth distribution point of view, as to what the initial entitlement is because we do not know whether it will lead to greater equality or inequality. This leaves us with only two reasons on which to base our choice of entitlement. The first is the relative worthiness of silence lovers and noise lovers. The second is the consistency of the choice, or its apparent consistency, with other entitlements in the society.

The first sounds appealing, and it sounds like justice. But it is hard to deal with. Why, unless our choice affects other people, should we prefer one to another?[30] To say that we wish, for

istic of involving present rights to future benefits in circumstances where a futures market does not exist and at first glance seems very difficult to organize cheaply. We do not suggest that this is the sole explanation for the way voting is handled in our society. For instance, it does not explain why the vote cannot be sold. (An explanation for that may be found in the fact that Taney's benefit from the vote may depend on Marshall's not having more of it than he.) It does, however, add another, not frequently given, explanation for the occasional allocation of goods rather than money to individuals.

[30] The usual answer is religious or transcendental reasons. But this answer presents problems. If it means that Chase, a third party, suffers if the noise-maker is preferred, because Chase's faith deems silence worthier than noise, then third parties *are* affected by the choice. Chase suffers; there is an external effect. But that possibility was excluded in our hypothetical. In practice such external effects, often called moralisms, are extremely common and greatly complicate the reaching of Pareto optimality. *See* pp. 1112–13 *infra*.

Religious or transcendental reasons may, however, be of another kind. Chase may prefer silence not because he himself cares, not because he suffers if noise-makers get the best of it when his faith deems silence lovers to be worthier, but because he believes God suffers if such a choice is made. No amount of compensation will help Chase in this situation since he suffers nothing which can be

instance, to make the silence lover relatively wealthier because we prefer silence is no answer, for that is simply a restatement of the question. Of course, if the choice does affect people other than Marshall and Taney, then we have a valid basis for decision. But the fact that such external effects are extremely common and greatly influence our choices does not help us much. It does suggest that the reaching of Pareto optimality is, in practice, a very complex matter precisely because of the existence of many external effects which markets find hard to deal with. And it also suggests that there often are general distributional considerations between Taney-Marshall and the rest of the world which affect the choice of entitlement. It in no way suggests, however, that there is more to the choice between Taney-Marshall than Pareto optimality and distributional concerns. In other words, if the assumptions of no transaction costs and indifference as to distributional considerations, made as between Taney and Marshall (where they are unlikely), could be made as to the world as a whole (where they are impossible), the fact that the choice between Taney's noise or Marshall's silence might affect other people would give us no guidance. Thus what sounds like a justice standard is simply a handy way of importing efficiency and distributional notions too diverse and general in their effect to be analyzed fully in the decision of a specific case.

The second sounds appealing in a different way since it sounds like "treating like cases alike." If the entitlement to make noise in other people's ears for one's pleasure is viewed by society as closely akin to the entitlement to beat up people for one's pleasure, and if good efficiency and distributional reasons exist for not allowing people to beat up others for sheer pleasure, then there may be a good reason for preferring an entitlement to silence rather than noise in the Taney-Marshall case. Because the two entitlements are apparently consistent, the entitlement to silence strengthens the entitlement to be free from gratuitous beatings which we assumed was based on good efficiency and distributional reasons.[31] It does so by lowering the enforcement costs of the entitlement to be free from gratuitous beatings; the entitlement to silence reiterates and reinforces the values protected by the entitlement to be free from gratuitous beatings and reduces the number of discriminations people must make between one activity and another, thus simplifying the task of obedience.

compensated, and compensating God for the wrong choice is not feasible. Such a reason for a choice is, we would suggest, a true nonefficiency, nondistribution reason. Whether it actually ever plays a role may well be another matter.

[31] The opposite would be true if noisemaking were thought to be akin to industry, and drive and silence to lethargy and laziness, and we had good efficiency or distributional reasons for preferring industry to lethargy.

The problem with this rationale for the choice is that it too comes down to efficiency and distributional reasons. We prefer the silence maker because *that* entitlement, even though it does not of itself affect the desired wealth distribution or lead us away from efficiency in the Taney-Marshall case, helps us to reach those goals in other situations where there are transaction costs or where we do have distributional preferences. It does this because people do not realize that the consistency is only apparent. If we could explain to them, both rationally and emotionally, the efficiency and distributional reasons why gratuitous beating up of people was inefficient or led to undesirable wealth distribution, and if we could also explain to them why an entitlement to noise rather than silence in the Taney-Marshall case would not lead to either inefficiency or maldistribution, then the secondary undermining of the entitlement to bodily integrity would not occur. It is only because it is expensive, even if feasible, to point out the difference between the two situations that the apparent similarity between them remains. And avoiding this kind of needless expense, while a very good reason for making choices, is clearly no more than a part of the economic efficiency goal.[32]

Still we should admit that explaining entitlements solely in terms of efficiency and distribution, in even their broadest terms, does not seem wholly satisfactory. The reasons for this are worth at least passing mention. The reason that we have so far explained entitlements simply in terms of efficiency and distribution is ultimately tautological. We defined distribution as covering *all* the reasons, other than efficiency, on the basis of which we might prefer to make Taney *wealthier* than Marshall. So defined, there obviously was no room for any other reasons. Distributional grounds covered broadly accepted ideas like "equality" or, in some societies, "caste preference," and highly specific ones like "favoring the silence lover." We used this definition because there is a utility in lumping together all those reasons for preferring Taney to Marshall which cannot be explained in terms of a desire to make everyone better off, and in contrasting them with efficiency reasons, whether Paretian or not, which can be so explained.

Lumping them together, however, has some analytical dis-

---

[32] We do not mean to underestimate the importance of apparent consistency as a ground for entitlements. Far from it, it is likely that a society often prefers an entitlement which even leads to mild inefficiencies or maldistribution of wealth between, say, Taney and Marshall, because that entitlement tends to support other entitlements which are crucial in terms of efficiency or wealth distribution in the society at large and because the cost of convincing people that the situations are, in fact, different is not worth the gain which would be obtained in the Taney-Marshall case.

advantages. It seems to assume that we cannot say any more about the reasons for some distributional preferences than about others. For instance, it seems to assume a similar universality of support for recognizing silence lovers as relatively worthier as there is for recognizing the relative desirability of equality. And that, surely, is a dangerous assumption. To avoid this danger the term "distribution" is often limited to relatively few broad reasons, like equality. And those preferences which cannot be easily explained in terms of these relatively few broadly accepted distributional preferences, or in terms of efficiency, are termed justice reasons. The difficulty with this locution is that it sometimes is taken to imply that the moral gloss of justice is reserved for these residual preferences and does not apply to the broader distributional preferences or to efficiency based preferences. And surely this is wrong, for many entitlements that properly are described as based on justice in our society can easily be explained in terms either of broad distributional preferences like equality or of efficiency or of both.

By using the term "*other* justice reasons" we hope to avoid this difficulty and emphasize that justice notions adhere to efficiency and broad distributional preferences as well as to other more idiosyncratic ones. To the extent that one is concerned with contrasting the difference between efficiency and other reasons for certain entitlements, the bipolar efficiency-distribution locution is all that is needed. To the extent that one wishes to delve either into reasons which, though possibly originally linked to efficiency, have now a life of their own, or into reasons which, though distributional, cannot be described in terms of broad principles like equality, then a locution which allows for "other justice reasons" seems more useful.[33]

III. Rules For Protecting and Regulating Entitlements

Whenever society chooses an initial entitlement it must also determine whether to protect the entitlement by property rules, by liability rules, or by rules of inalienability. In our framework, much of what is generally called private property can be viewed as an entitlement which is protected by a property rule. No one can take the entitlement to private property from the holder unless the holder sells it willingly and at the price at which he subjectively values the property. Yet a nuisance with sufficient public utility to avoid injunction has, in effect, the right to take property with compensation. In such a circumstance the entitlement to the property is protected only by what we call a liability rule:

[33] *But see* Fletcher, *supra* note 21, at 547 n.40.

an external, objective standard of value is used to facilitate the transfer of the entitlement from the holder to the nuisance.[34] Finally, in some instances we will not allow the sale of the property at all, that is, we will occasionally make the entitlement inalienable.

This section will consider the circumstances in which society will employ these three rules to solve situations of conflict. Because the property rule and the liability rule are closely related and depend for their application on the shortcomings of each other, we treat them together. We discuss inalienability separately.

A. *Property and Liability Rules*

Why cannot a society simply decide on the basis of the already mentioned criteria who should receive any given entitlement, and then let its transfer occur only through a voluntary negotiation? Why, in other words, cannot society limit itself to the property rule? To do this it would need only to protect and enforce the initial entitlements from all attacks, perhaps through criminal sanctions,[35] and to enforce voluntary contracts for their transfer. Why do we need liability rules at all?

In terms of economic efficiency the reason is easy enough to see. Often the cost of establishing the value of an initial entitlement by negotiation is so great that even though a transfer of the entitlement would benefit all concerned, such a transfer will not occur. If a collective determination of the value were available instead, the beneficial transfer would quickly come about.

Eminent domain is a good example. A park where Guidacres, a tract of land owned by 1,000 owners in 1,000 parcels, now sits would, let us assume, benefit a neighboring town enough so that the 100,000 citizens of the town would each be willing to pay an average of $100 to have it. The park is Pareto desirable if the owners of the tracts of land in Guidacres actually value their entitlements at less than $10,000,000 or an average of $10,000 a tract. Let us assume that in fact the parcels are all the same and all the owners value them at $8,000. On this assumption, the park is, in economic efficiency terms, desirable — in values foregone it costs $8,000,000 and is worth $10,000,000 to the buyers. And yet it may well not be established. If enough of the owners hold-out for more than $10,000 in order to get a share of the $2,000,000 that they guess the buyers are willing to pay over the

[34] *See, e.g.*, Boomer v. Atlantic Cement Co., 26 N.Y.2d 219, 309 N.Y.S.2d 312, 257 N.E.2d 870 (1970) (avoidance of injunction conditioned on payment of permanent damages to plaintiffs).

[35] The relationship between criminal sanctions and property entitlements will be examined *infra* pp. 1124–27.

value which the sellers in actuality attach, the price demanded will be more than $10,000,000 and no park will result. The sellers have an incentive to hide their true valuation and the market will not succeed in establishing it.

An equally valid example could be made on the buying side. Suppose the sellers of Guidacres have agreed to a sales price of $8,000,000 (they are all relatives and at a family banquet decided that trying to hold-out would leave them all losers). It does not follow that the buyers can raise that much even though each of 100,000 citizens *in fact* values the park at $100. Some citizens may try to free-load and say the park is only worth $50 or even nothing to them, hoping that enough others will admit to a higher desire and make up the $8,000,000 price. Again there is no reason to believe that a market, a decentralized system of valuing, will cause people to express their true valuations and hence yield results which all would *in fact* agree are desirable.

Whenever this is the case an argument can readily be made for moving from a property rule to a liability rule. If society can remove from the market the valuation of each tract of land, decide the value collectively, and impose it, then the holdout problem is gone. Similarly, if society can value collectively each individual citizen's desire to have a park and charge him a "benefits" tax based upon it, the freeloader problem is gone. If the sum of the taxes is greater than the sum of the compensation awards, the park will result.

Of course, one can conceive of situations where it might be cheap to exclude all the freeloaders from the park, or to ration the park's use in accordance with original willingness to pay. In such cases the incentive to free-load might be eliminated. But such exclusions, even if possible, are usually not cheap. And the same may be the case for market methods which might avoid the holdout problem on the seller side.

Moreover, even if holdout and freeloader problems can be met feasibly by the market, an argument may remain for employing a liability rule. Assume that in our hypothetical, freeloaders can be excluded at the cost of $1,000,000 and that all owners of tracts in Guidacres can be convinced, by the use of $500,000 worth of advertising and cocktail parties, that a sale will only occur if they reveal their true land valuations. Since $8,000,000 plus $1,500,000 is less than $10,000,000, the park will be established. But if collective valuation of the tracts and of the benefits of the prospective park would have cost less than $1,500,000, it would have been inefficient to establish the park through the market — a market which was not worth having would have been paid for.[36]

[36] It may be argued that, given imperfect knowledge, the market is preferable because it places a limit — the cost of establishing a market — on the size of the

Of course, the problems with liability rules are equally real. We cannot be at all sure that landowner Taney is lying or holding out when he says his land is worth $12,000 to him. The fact that several neighbors sold identical tracts for $10,000 does not help us very much; Taney may be sentimentally attached to his land. As a result, eminent domain may grossly undervalue what Taney would actually sell for, even if it sought to give him his true valuation of his tract. In practice, it is so hard to determine Taney's true valuation that eminent domain simply gives him what the land is worth "objectively," in the full knowledge that this may result in over or under compensation. The same is true on the buyer side. "Benefits" taxes rarely attempt, let alone succeed, in gauging the individual citizen's relative desire for the alleged benefit. They are justified because, even if they do not accurately measure each individual's desire for the benefit, the market alternative seems worse. For example, fifty different households may place different values on a new sidewalk that is to abut all the properties. Nevertheless, because it is too difficult, even if possible, to gauge each household's valuation, we usually tax each household an equal amount.

The example of eminent domain is simply one of numerous instances in which society uses liability rules. Accidents is another. If we were to give victims a property entitlement not to be accidentally injured we would have to require all who engage in activities that may injure individuals to negotiate with them before an accident, and to buy the right to knock off an arm or a leg.[37] Such pre-accident negotiations would be extremely ex-

possible loss, while the costs of coercion cannot be defined and may be infinite. This may be true in some situations but need not always be the case. If, for example, we know that the holdouts would sell for $500,000 more than is offered, because they recently offered the land at that higher price, coercing them to sell at an objectively determined price between the seller's offer and the purchaser's offer cannot result in more than $500,000 in harm. Thus, the costs of coercion would also not be infinite. Nor is it an answer to say that the man who would sell for a higher price but is coerced for a lower one suffers an indefinite nonmonetary cost in addition to the price differential simply because he is coerced and resents it. For while this may well be true, the same nonmonetary resentment may also exist in those who desire the park and do not get it because the market is unable to pay off those who are holding out for a greater than actual value. In other words, unascertainable resentment costs may exist as a result of either coercion or market failure.

[37] Even if it were possible, it should be clear that the good which would be sold would not be the same as the good actually taken. If Taney waives for $1,000 the right to recover for the loss of a leg, should he ever lose it, he is negotiating for a joint product which can be described as his "desire or aversion to gamble" and "his desire to have a leg." The product actually taken, however, is the leg. That the two goods are different can be seen from the fact that a man who demands $1,000 for a 1 in a 1,000 chance of losing a leg may well demand more

pensive, often prohibitively so.[38] To require them would thus preclude many activities that might, in fact, be worth having. And, after an accident, the loser of the arm or leg can always very plausibly deny that he would have sold it at the price the buyer would have offered. Indeed, where negotiations after an accident do occur — for instance pretrial settlements — it is largely because the alternative is the collective valuation of the damages.

It is not our object here to outline all the theoretical, let alone the practical, situations where markets may be too expensive or fail and where collective valuations seem more desirable. Economic literature has many times surrounded the issue if it has not

---

than $100,000 for a 1 in 10 chance of losing it, and more than $1,000,000 for the sale of his leg to someone who needs it for a transplant. *See generally* COSTS 88–94. This does not mean that the result of such transactions, if feasible, would *necessarily* be worse than the result of collective valuations. It simply means that the situation, even if feasible, is different from the one in which Taney sells his house for a given price.

[38] Such preaccident negotiations between potential injurers and victims are at times not too costly. Thus in a typical products liability situation the cost of negotiation over a potential injury need not be prohibitive. The seller of a rotary lawn mower may offer to sell at a reduced price if the buyer agrees not to sue should he be injured. Nevertheless, society often forbids such negotiations because it deems them undesirable. This may occur because of the reasons suggested in note 37 *supra*, or for any of the other reasons which cause us to make some entitlements wholly or partly inalienable, *see infra* pp. 1111–15.

Attempts have been made to deal with situations where ex ante negotiations are not feasible by fiscal devices designed to cause people to reveal their preferences. One of these contemplates requiring individuals to declare a value on their properties, or even limbs, and paying a tax on the self assessed value. That value would be the value of the good if it were taken in an accident or by eminent domain. *See generally* N. Tideman, Three Approaches to Improving Urban Land Use, ch. III (1969) (unpublished Ph.D. dissertation submitted to U. of Chicago Economics Department, on file in Yale Law Library). Of course, if the good is only taken as a result of an accident or eminent domain, the problem of gambling described in note 37 *supra* would remain. If, instead, the property or limb could be taken at will at the self assessed value, serious problems would arise from the fact that there are enormous nonmonetizable, as well as monetizable, costs involved in making people put money values on all their belongings and limbs.

An additional, though perhaps solvable, problem with self assessed taxes is the fact that the taking price would exclude any consumer surplus. This may have no significance in terms of economic efficiency, but if the existence of consumer surplus in many market transactions is thought to have, on the whole, a favorable wealth distribution effect, it might well be a reason why self assessed taxes are viewed with skepticism. *Cf.* Little, Self-Assessed Valuations: A Critique (1972) (unpublished paper, on file in Harvard Law School Library). The reader might reasonably wonder why many individuals who view self assessed taxes with skepticism show no similar concerns for what may be a very similar device, optional first party insurance covering pain and suffering damages in automobile injuries. *See, e.g.*, Calabresi, *The New York Plan: A Free Choice Modification*, 71 COLUM. L. REV. 267, 268 n.6 (1971).

always zeroed in on it in ways intelligible to lawyers.[39] It is enough for our purposes to note that a very common reason, perhaps the most common one, for employing a liability rule rather than a property rule to protect an entitlement is that market valuation of the entitlement is deemed inefficient, that is, it is either unavailable or too expensive compared to a collective valuation.

We should also recognize that efficiency is not the sole ground for employing liability rules rather than property rules. Just as the initial entitlement is often decided upon for distributional reasons, so too the choice of a liability rule is often made because it facilitates a combination of efficiency and distributive results which would be difficult to achieve under a property rule. As we shall see in the pollution context, use of a liability rule may allow us to accomplish a measure of redistribution that could only be attained at a prohibitive sacrifice of efficiency if we employed a corresponding property rule.

More often, once a liability rule is decided upon, perhaps for efficiency reasons, it is then employed to favor distributive goals as well. Again accidents and eminent domain are good examples. In both of these areas the compensation given has clearly varied with society's distributive goals, and cannot be readily explained in terms of giving the victim, as nearly as possible, an objectively determined equivalent of the price at which he would have sold what was taken from him.

It should not be surprising that this is often so, even if the original reason for a liability rule is an efficiency one. For distributional goals are expensive and difficult to achieve, and the collective valuation involved in liability rules readily lends itself to promoting distributional goals.[40] This does not mean that distributional goals are always well served in this way. Ad hoc decision-making is always troublesome, and the difficulties are especially acute when the settlement of conflicts between parties is used as a vehicle for the solution of more widespread distributional problems. Nevertheless, distributional objectives may be better attained in this way than otherwise.[41]

---

[39] For a good discussion of market failure which is intelligible to lawyers, see Bator, *The Anatomy of Market Failure*, 72 Q. J. Econ. 351 (1958).

[40] Collective valuation of costs also makes it easier to value the costs at what the society thinks they should be valued by the victim instead of at what the victim would value them in a free market if such a market were feasible. The former kind of valuation is, of course, paternalism. This does not mean it is undesirable; the danger is that paternalism which is not desirable will enter mindlessly into the cost valuation because the valuation is necessarily done collectively. *See* pp. 1113–14 *infra*.

[41] For suggestions that at times systematic distributional programs may cause

B. Inalienable Entitlements

Thus far we have focused on the questions of when society should protect an entitlement by property or liability rules. However, there remain many entitlements which involve a still greater degree of societal intervention: the law not only decides who is to own something and what price is to be paid for it if it is taken or destroyed, but also regulates its sale — by, for example, prescribing preconditions for a valid sale or forbidding a sale altogether. Although these rules of inalienability are substantially different from the property and liability rules, their use can be analyzed in terms of the same efficiency and distributional goals that underlie the use of the other two rules.

While at first glance efficiency objectives may seem undermined by limitations on the ability to engage in transactions, closer analysis suggests that there are instances, perhaps many, in which economic efficiency is more closely approximated by such limitations. This might occur when a transaction would create significant externalities — costs to third parties.

For instance, if Taney were allowed to sell his land to Chase, a polluter, he would injure his neighbor Marshall by lowering the value of Marshall's land. Conceivably, Marshall could pay Taney not to sell his land; but, because there are many injured Marshalls, freeloader and information costs make such transactions practically impossible. The state could protect the Marshalls and yet facilitate the sale of the land by giving the Marshalls an entitlement to prevent Taney's sale to Chase but only protecting the entitlement by a liability rule. It might, for instance, charge an excise tax on all sales of land to polluters equal to its estimate of the external cost to the Marshalls of the sale. But where there are so many injured Marshalls that the price required under the liability rule is likely to be high enough so that no one would be willing to pay it, then setting up the machinery for collective valuation will be wasteful. Barring the sale to polluters will be the most efficient result because it is clear that avoiding pollution is cheaper than paying its costs — including its costs to the Marshalls.

Another instance in which external costs may justify inalienability occurs when external costs do not lend themselves to collective measurement which is acceptably objective and nonarbitrary. This nonmonetizability is characteristic of one category of external costs which, as a practical matter, seems frequently to

greater misallocation of resources than ad hoc decisions, see Ackerman, *Regulating Slum Housing Markets on Behalf of the Poor: Of Housing Codes, Housing Subsidies and Income Redistribution Policy*, 80 YALE L.J. 1093, 1157–97 (1971); Calabresi, *supra* note 12.

lead us to rules of inalienability. Such external costs are often called moralisms.

If Taney is allowed to sell himself into slavery, or to take undue risks of becoming penniless, or to sell a kidney, Marshall may be harmed, simply because Marshall is a sensitive man who is made unhappy by seeing slaves, paupers, or persons who die because they have sold a kidney. Again Marshall could pay Taney not to sell his freedom to Chase the slaveowner; but again, because Marshall is not one but many individuals, freeloader and information costs make such transactions practically impossible. Again, it might seem that the state could intervene by objectively valuing the external cost to Marshall and requiring Chase to pay that cost. But since the external cost to Marshall does not lend itself to an acceptable objective measurement, such liability rules are not appropriate.

In the case of Taney selling land to Chase, the polluter, they were inappropriate because we *knew* that the costs to Taney and the Marshalls exceeded the benefits to Chase. Here, though we are not certain of how a cost-benefit analysis would come out, liability rules are inappropriate because any monetization is, by hypothesis, out of the question. The state must, therefore, either ignore the external costs to Marshall, or if it judges them great enough, forbid the transaction that gave rise to them by making Taney's freedom inalienable.[42]

Obviously we will not always value the external harm of a moralism enough to prohibit the sale.[43] And obviously also, external costs other than moralisms may be sufficiently hard to value to make rules of inalienability appropriate in certain circumstances; this reason for rules of inalienability, however, does seem most often germane in situations where moralisms are involved.[44]

---

[42] Granting Taney an inalienable right to be free is in many respects the same as granting most of the people a property entitlement to keep Taney free. The people may bargain and decide to surrender their entitlement, *i.e.*, to change the law, but there are limits on the feasibility of transactions of this sort which make the public's entitlements virtually inalienable.

[43] For example, I am allowed to buy and read whatever books I like, or to sell my house to whomever I choose, regardless of whether my doing so makes my neighbors unhappy. These entitlements could be a form of self paternalism on the part of the neighbors who fear a different rule would harm them more in the long run, or they could be selected because they strengthen seemingly similar entitlements. *See* pp. 1103–04 *supra*. But they may also reflect a judgment that the injury suffered by my neighbors results from a moralism shared by them but not so widespread as to make more efficient their being given an entitlement to prevent my transaction. In other words, people who are hurt by my transaction are the cheapest cost avoiders, *i.e.*, the cost to them of my being allowed to transact freely is less than the cost to me and others similarly situated of a converse entitlement.

[44] The fact that society may make an entitlement inalienable does not, of

There are two other efficiency reasons for forbidding the sale of entitlements under certain circumstances: self paternalism and true paternalism. Examples of the first are Ulysses tying himself to the mast or individuals passing a bill of rights so that they will be prevented from yielding to momentary temptations which they deem harmful to themselves. This type of limitation is not in any real sense paternalism. It is fully consistent with Pareto efficiency criteria, based on the notion that over the mass of cases no one knows better than the individual what is best for him or her. It merely allows the individual to choose what is best in the long run rather than in the short run, even though that choice entails giving up some short run freedom of choice. Self paternalism may cause us to require certain conditions to exist before we allow a sale of an entitlement; and it may help explain many situations of inalienability, like the invalidity of contracts entered into when drunk, or under undue influence or coercion. But it probably does not fully explain even these.[45]

True paternalism brings us a step further toward explaining such prohibitions and those of broader kinds — for example the prohibitions on a whole range of activities by minors. Paternalism is based on the notion that at least in some situations the Marshalls know better than Taney what will make Taney better off.[46] Here we are not talking about the offense to Marshall from Taney's choosing to read pornography, or selling himself into slavery, but rather the judgment that Taney was not in the position to choose best for himself when he made the choice for erotica or servitude.[47]

---

course, mean that there will be no compensation to the holder of the entitlement if it is taken from him. Thus even if a society forbids the sale of one's kidneys it will still probably compensate the person whose kidney is destroyed in an auto accident. The situations are distinct and the kidney is protected by different rules according to which situation we are speaking of.

[45] As a practical matter, since it is frequently impossible to limit the effect of an inalienable rule to those who desire it for self paternalistic reasons, self paternalism would lead to some restraints on those who would desire to sell their entitlements. This does not make self paternalism any less consistent with the premises of Pareto optimality; it is only another recognition that in an imperfect world, Pareto optimality can be approached more closely by systems which involve some coercion than by a system of totally free bargains.

[46] This locution leaves open the question whether Taney's future well-being will ultimately be decided by Taney himself or the many Marshalls. The latter implies a further departure from Paretian premises. The former, which may be typical of paternalism towards minors, implies simply that the minors do not know enough to exercise self paternalism.

[47] Sometimes the term paternalism is used to explain use of a rule of inalienability in situations where inalienability will not make the many Marshalls or the coerced Taney any better off. Inalienability is said to be imposed because the many Marshalls believe that making the entitlement inalienable is doing God's

The first concept we called a moralism and is a frequent and important ground for inalienability. But it is consistent with the premises of Pareto optimality. The second, paternalism, is also an important economic efficiency reason for inalienability, but it is not consistent with the premises of Pareto optimality: the most efficient pie is no longer that which costless bargains would achieve, because a person may be better off if he is prohibited from bargaining.

Finally, just as efficiency goals sometimes dictate the use of rules of inalienability, so, of course, do distributional goals. Whether an entitlement may be sold or not often affects directly who is richer and who is poorer. Prohibiting the sale of babies makes poorer those who can cheaply produce babies and richer those who through some nonmarket device get free an "unwanted" baby.[48] Prohibiting exculpatory clauses in product sales makes richer those who were injured by a product defect and poorer those who were not injured and who paid more for the product because the exulpatory clause was forbidden.[49] Favoring the specific group that has benefited may or may not have been the reason for the prohibition on bargaining. What is important is that, regardless of the reason for barring a contract, a group did gain from the prohibition.

This should suffice to put us on guard, for it suggests that direct distributional motives may lie behind asserted nondistributional grounds for inalienability, whether they be paternalism, self paternalism, or externalities.[50] This does not mean that giving

will, that is, that a sale or transfer of the entitlement would injure God. Assuming this situation exists in practice, we would not term it paternalism, because that word implies looking after the interests of the coerced party. *See* note 30 *supra*.

[48] This assumes that a prohibition on the sale of unwanted babies can be effectively enforced. If it can, then those unwanted babies which are produced are of no financial benefit to their natural parents and bring an increase in well-being to those who are allowed to adopt them free and as a result of a nonmarket allocation. Should the prohibition on sales of babies be only partially enforceable, the distributional result would be more complex. It would be unchanged for those who could obtain babies for adoption legally, *i.e.*, for those who received them without paying bribes, as it would for the natural parents who obeyed the law, since they would still receive no compensation. On the other hand, the illegal purchaser would probably pay, and the illegal seller receive, a higher price than if the sale of babies were legal. This would cause a greater distributive effect within the group of illegal sellers and buyers than would exist if such sales were permitted.

[49] *See* note 37 *supra*.

[50] As a practical matter, it is often impossible to tell whether an entitlement has been made partially inalienable for any of the several efficiency grounds mentioned or for distributional grounds. Do we bar people from selling their bodies for paternalistic, self paternalistic, or moralistic cost reasons? On what basis do we prohibit an individual from taking, for a high price, one chance in three of having

weight to distributional goals is undesirable. It clearly is desirable where on efficiency grounds society is indifferent between an alienable and an inalienable entitlement and distributional goals favor one approach or the other. It may well be desirable even when distributional goals are achieved at some efficiency costs. The danger may be, however, that what is justified on, for example, paternalism grounds is really a hidden way of accruing distributional benefits for a group whom we would not otherwise wish to benefit. For example, we may use certain types of zoning to preserve open spaces on the grounds that the poor will be happier, though they do not know it now. And open spaces may indeed make the poor happier in the long run. But the zoning that preserves open space also makes housing in the suburbs more expensive and it may be that the whole plan is aimed at securing distributional benefits to the suburban dweller regardless of the poor's happiness.[51]

IV. The Framework and Pollution Control Rules

Nuisance or pollution is one of the most interesting areas where the question of who will be given an entitlement, and how it will be protected, is in frequent issue.[52] Traditionally, and very ably in the recent article by Professor Michelman, the nuisance-pollution problem is viewed in terms of three rules.[53] First, Taney

to give his heart to a wealthy man who needs a transplant? Do we try to avoid a market in scarce medical resources for distributional or for some or all of the efficiency reasons discussed?

[51] There is another set of reasons which causes us to prohibit sales of some entitlements and which is sometimes termed distributional; this set of reasons causes us to prohibit sales of some entitlements because the underlying distribution of wealth seems to us undesirable. These reasons, we would suggest, are not true distributional grounds. They are, rather, efficiency grounds which become valid because of the original maldistribution. As such they can once again be categorized as due to externalities, self paternalism, and pure paternalism: (1) Marshall is offended because Taney, due to poverty, sells a kidney, and therefore Marshall votes to bar such sales (a moralism); (2) Taney, seeking to avoid temporary temptation due to his poverty, votes to bar such sales (self paternalism); and (3) the law prohibits Taney from the same sale because, regardless of what Taney believes, a majority thinks Taney will be better off later if he is barred from selling than if he is free to do so while influenced by his own poverty (pure paternalism). We do not mean to minimize these reasons by noting that they are not strictly distributional. We call them nondistributional simply to distinguish them from the more direct way in which distributional considerations affect the alienability of entitlements.

[52] It should be clear that the pollution problem we discuss here is really only a part of a broader problem, that of land use planning in general. Much of this analysis may therefore be relevant to other land use issues, for example exclusionary zoning, restrictive covenants, and ecological easements. *See* note 58 *infra*.

[53] Michelman, *supra* note 1, at 670. *See also* Restatement (Second) of Torts

may not pollute unless his neighbor (his only neighbor let us assume), Marshall, allows it (Marshall may enjoin Taney's nuisance).[54] Second, Taney may pollute but must compensate Marshall for damages caused (nuisance is found but the remedy is limited to damages).[55] Third, Taney may pollute at will and can only be stopped by Marshall if Marshall pays him off (Taney's pollution is not held to be a nuisance to Marshall).[56] In our terminology rules one and two (nuisance with injunction, and with damages only) are entitlements to Marshall. The first is an entitlement to be free from pollution and is protected by a property rule; the second is also an entitlement to be free from pollution but is protected only by a liability rule. Rule three (no nuisance) is instead an entitlement to Taney protected by a property rule, for only by buying Taney out at Taney's price can Marshall end the pollution.

The very statement of these rules in the context of our framework suggests that something is missing. Missing is a fourth rule representing an entitlement in Taney to pollute, but an entitlement which is protected only by a liability rule. The fourth rule, really a kind of partial eminent domain coupled with a benefits tax, can be stated as follows: Marshall may stop Taney from polluting, but if he does he must compensate Taney.

As a practical matter it will be easy to see why even legal writers as astute as Professor Michelman have ignored this rule. Unlike the first three it does not often lend itself to judicial imposition for a number of good legal process reasons. For example, even if Taney's injuries could practicably be measured, apportionment of the duty of compensation among many Marshalls would present problems for which courts are not well suited. If only those Marshalls who voluntarily asserted the right to enjoin Taney's pollution were required to pay the compensation, there would be insuperable freeloader problems. If, on the other

§§ 157–215 (1965). Michelman also discusses the possibility of inalienability. Michelman, *supra*, at 684. For a discussion of the use of rules of inalienability in the pollution context, see pp. 1123–24 *infra*.

[54] *See, e.g.*, Department of Health & Mental Hygiene v. Galaxy Chem. Co., 1 Envir. Rep. 1660 (Md. Cir. Ct. 1970) (chemical smells enjoined); Ensign v. Walls, 323 Mich. 49, 34 N.W. 2d 549 (1948) (dog raising in residential neighborhood enjoined).

[55] *See, e.g.*, Boomer v. Atlantic Cement Co., 26 N.Y. 2d 219, 309 N.Y.S. 2d 312, 257 N.E.2d 870 (1970) (avoidance of injunction conditioned on payment of permanent damages to plaintiffs).

[56] *See, e.g.*, Francisco v. Department of Institutions & Agencies, 13 N.J. Misc. 663, 180 A. 843 (Ct. Ch. 1935) (plaintiffs not entitled to enjoin noise and odors of adjacent sanitarium); Rose v. Socony-Vacuum Corp., 54 R.I. 411, 173 A. 627 (1934) (pollution of percolating waters not enjoinable in absence of negligence).

hand, the liability rule entitled one of the Marshalls alone to enjoin the pollution and required all the benefited Marshalls to pay their share of the compensation, the courts would be faced with the immensely difficult task of determining who was benefited how much and imposing a benefits tax accordingly, all the while observing procedural limits within which courts are expected to function.[57]

The fourth rule is thus not part of the cases legal scholars read when they study nuisance law, and is therefore easily ignored by them. But it is available, and may sometimes make more sense than any of the three competing approaches. Indeed, in one form or another, it may well be the most frequent device employed.[58] To appreciate the utility of the fourth rule and to com-

---

[57] This task is much more difficult than that which arises under rule two, in which the many Marshalls would be compensated for their pollution injuries. Under rule two, each victim may act as an individual, either in seeking compensation in the first instance or in electing whether to be a part of a class seeking compensation. If he wishes to and is able to convince the court (by some accepted objective standard) that he has been injured, he may be compensated. Such individual action is expensive, and thus may be wasteful, but it presents no special problems in terms of the traditional workings of the courts. But where the class in question consists, not of those with a right to enjoin, but of those who must pay to enjoin, freeloader problems require the court to determine that an unwilling Marshall has been benefited and should be required to pay. The basic difficulty is that if we begin with the premise which usually underlies our notion of efficiency — namely, that individuals know what is best for them — we are faced with the anomaly of compelling compensation from one who denies he has incurred a benefit but whom we require to pay because *the court* thinks he has been benefited.

This problem is analogous to the difficulties presented by quasi-contracts. In terms of the theory of our economic efficiency goal, the case for requiring compensation for unbargained for (often accidental) benefits is similar to the argument for compensating tort victims. Yet courts as a general rule require compensation in quasi-contract only where there is both an indisputable benefit (usually of a pecuniary or economic nature) and some affirmative acknowledgment of subjective benefit (usually a subsequent promise to pay). *See* A. CORBIN, CONTRACTS §§ 231–34 (1963). This hesitancy suggests that courts lack confidence in their ability to distinguish real benefits from illusions. Perhaps even more importantly, it suggests that the courts recognize that what may clearly be an objective "benefit" may, to the putative beneficiary, not be a subjective benefit — if for no other reason than that unintended changes from the status quo often exact psychological costs. If that is the case, there has been no benefit at all in terms of our efficiency criterion.

[58] *See* A. KNEESE & B. BOWER, MANAGING WATER QUALITY: ECONOMICS, TECHNOLOGY, INSTITUTIONS 98–109 (1968); Krier, *The Pollution Problem and Legal Institutions: A Conceptual Overview*, 18 U.C.L.A.L. REV. 429, 467–75 (1971).

Virtually all eminent domain takings of a nonconforming use seem to be examples of this approach. Ecological easements may be another prime example. A local zoning ordinance may require a developer to contribute a portion of his land for purposes of parkland or school construction. In compensation for taking

pare it with the other three rules, we will examine why we might choose any of the given rules.

We would employ rule one (entitlement to be free from pollution protected by a property rule) from an economic efficiency point of view if we believed that the polluter, Taney, could avoid or reduce the costs of pollution more cheaply than the pollutee, Marshall. Or to put it another way, Taney would be enjoinable if he were in a better position to balance the costs of polluting against the costs of not polluting. We would employ rule three (entitlement to pollute protected by a property rule) again solely from an economic efficiency standpoint, if we made the converse judgment on who could best balance the harm of pollution against its avoidance costs. If we were wrong in our judgments and if transactions between Marshall and Taney were costless or even very cheap, the entitlement under rules one or three would be traded and an economically efficient result would occur in either case.[59] If we entitled Taney to pollute and Marshall valued clean air more than Taney valued the pollution, Marshall would pay Taney to stop polluting even though no nuisance was found. If we entitled Marshall to enjoin the pollution and the right to pollute was worth more to Taney than freedom from pollution was to Marshall, Taney would pay Marshall not to seek an injunction or would buy Marshall's land and sell it to someone who would agree not to seek an injunction. As we have assumed no one else was hurt by the pollution, Taney could now pollute even though the initial entitlement, based on a wrong guess of who was the cheapest avoider of the costs involved, allowed the pollution to be enjoined. Wherever transactions between Taney and Marshall are easy, and wherever economic efficiency is our goal, we could employ entitlements protected by property rules even though we would not be sure that the entitlement chosen was the right one. Transactions as described above would cure the error. While the entitlement might have important distributional effects, it would not substantially undercut economic efficiency.

the developer's entitlement, the locality will pay the developer "damages": it will allow him to increase the normal rate of density in his remaining property. The question of damage assessment involved in ecological easements raises similar problems to those raised in the benefit assessment involved in the question of quasi-contract. *See* note 57 *supra*.

[59] For a discussion of whether efficiency would be achieved in the long, as well as the short, run, see Coase, *supra* note 12; Calabresi, *supra* note 12 (pointing out that if "no transaction costs" means no impediments to bargaining in the short or long run, and if Pareto optimality means an allocation of resources which cannot be improved by bargains, assumptions of no transaction costs and rationality necessarily imply Pareto optimality); Nutter, *supra* note 12 (a technical demonstration of the applicability of the Coase theorem to long run problems). *See also* Demsetz, *supra* note 16, at 19–22.

The moment we assume, however, that transactions are not cheap, the situation changes dramatically. Assume we enjoin Taney and there are 10,000 injured Marshalls. Now *even if* the right to pollute is worth more to Taney than the right to be free from pollution is to the sum of the Marshalls, the injunction will probably stand. The cost of buying out all the Marshalls, given holdout problems, is likely to be too great, and an equivalent of eminent domain in Taney would be needed to alter the initial injunction. Conversely, if we denied a nuisance remedy, the 10,000 Marshalls could only with enormous difficulty, given freeloader problems, get together to buy out even one Taney and prevent the pollution. This would be so even if the pollution harm was greater than the value to Taney of the right to pollute.

If, however, transaction costs are not symmetrical, we may still be able to use the property rule. Assume that Taney can buy the Marshalls' entitlements easily because holdouts are for some reason absent, but that the Marshalls have great freeloader problems in buying out Taney. In this situation the entitlement should be granted to the Marshalls unless we are sure the Marshalls are the cheapest avoiders of pollution costs. Where we do not know the identity of the cheapest cost avoider it is better to entitle the Marshalls to be free of pollution because, even if we are wrong in our initial placement of the entitlement, that is, even if the Marshalls are the cheapest cost avoiders, Taney will buy out the Marshalls and economic efficiency will be achieved. Had we chosen the converse entitlement and been wrong, the Marshalls could not have bought out Taney. Unfortunately, transaction costs are often high on both sides and an initial entitlement, though incorrect in terms of economic efficiency, will not be altered in the market place.

Under these circumstances — and they are normal ones in the pollution area — we are likely to turn to liability rules whenever we are uncertain whether the polluter or the pollutees can most cheaply avoid the cost of pollution. We are only likely to use liability rules where we are uncertain because, if we are certain, the costs of liability rules — essentially the costs of collectively valuing the damages to all concerned plus the cost in coercion to those who would not sell at the collectively determined figure — are unnecessary. They are unnecessary because transaction costs and bargaining barriers become irrelevant when we are certain who is the cheapest cost avoider; economic efficiency will be attained without transactions by making the correct initial entitlement.

As a practical matter we often are uncertain who the cheapest cost avoider is. In such cases, traditional legal doctrine tends to find a nuisance but imposes only damages on Taney payable to the Marshalls.[60] This way, if the amount of damages Taney is made to pay is close to the injury caused, economic efficiency will have had its due; if he cannot make a go of it, the nuisance was not worth its costs. The entitlement to the Marshalls to be free from pollution unless compensated, however, will have been given *not* because it was thought that polluting was probably worth less to Taney than freedom from pollution was worth to the Marshalls, nor even because on some distributional basis we preferred to charge the cost to Taney rather than to the Marshalls. It was so placed *simply because we did not know* whether Taney desired to pollute more than the Marshalls desired to be free from pollution, and the only way we thought we could test out the value of the pollution was by the only liability rule we thought we had. This was rule two, the imposition of nuisance damages on Taney. At least this would be the position of a court concerned with economic efficiency which believed itself limited to rules one, two, and three.

Rule four gives at least the possibility that the opposite entitlement may also lead to economic efficiency in a situation of unçertainty. Suppose for the moment that a mechanism exists for collectively assessing the damage resulting to Taney from being stopped from polluting by the Marshalls, and a mechanism also exists for collectively assessing the benefit to each of the Marshalls from such cessation. Then — assuming the same degree of accuracy in collective valuation as exists in rule two (the nuisance damage rule) — the Marshalls would stop the pollution if it harmed them more than it benefited Taney. If this is possible, then even if we thought it necessary to use a liability rule, we would still be free to give the entitlement to Taney or Marshall for whatever reasons, efficiency or distributional, we desired.

Actually, the issue is still somewhat more complicated. For just as transaction costs are not necessarily symmetrical under the two converse property rule entitlements, so also the liability rule equivalents of transaction costs — the cost of valuing collectively and of coercing compliance with that valuation — may not be symmetrical under the two converse liability rules. Nuisance damages may be very hard to value, and the costs of informing all the injured of their rights and getting them into court may be prohibitive. Instead, the assessment of the objective damage to Taney from foregoing his pollution may be cheap and so might the as-

[60] *See, e.g.*, City of Harrisonville v. W.S. Dickey Clay Mfg. Co., 289 U.S. 334 (1933) (damages appropriate remedy where injunction would prejudice important public interest); Madison v. Ducktown Sulphur, Copper & Iron Co., 113 Tenn. 331, 83 S.W. 658 (1904) (damages appropriate because of plaintiff's ten year delay in seeking to enjoin fumes).

sessment of the relative benefits to all Marshalls of such freedom from pollution. But the opposite may also be the case. As a result, just as the choice of which property entitlement may be based on the asymmetry of transaction costs and hence on the greater amenability of one property entitlement to market corrections, so might the choice between liability entitlements be based on the asymmetry of the costs of collective determination.

The introduction of distributional considerations makes the existence of the fourth possibility even more significant. One does not need to go into all the permutations of the possible tradeoffs between efficiency and distributional goals under the four rules to show this. A simple example should suffice. Assume a factory which, by using cheap coal, pollutes a very wealthy section of town and employs many low income workers to produce a product purchased primarily by the poor; assume also a distributional goal that favors equality of wealth. Rule one — enjoin the nuisance — would possibly have desirable economic efficiency results (if the pollution hurt the homeowners more than it saved the factory in coal costs), but it would have disastrous distribution effects. It would also have undesirable efficiency effects if the initial judgment on costs of avoidance had been wrong and transaction costs were high. Rule two — nuisance damages — would allow a testing of the economic efficiency of eliminating the pollution, even in the presence of high transaction costs, but would quite possibly put the factory out of business or diminish output and thus have the same income distribution effects as rule one. Rule three — no nuisance — would have favorable distributional effects since it might protect the income of the workers. But if the pollution harm was greater to the homeowners than the cost of avoiding it by using a better coal, and if transaction costs — holdout problems — were such that homeowners could not unite to pay the factory to use better coal, rule three would have unsatisfactory efficiency effects. Rule four — payment of damages to the factory after allowing the homeowners to compel it to use better coal, and assessment of the cost of these damages to the homeowners — would be the only one which would accomplish both the distributional and efficiency goals.[61]

An equally good hypothetical for any of the rules can be constructed. Moreover, the problems of coercion may as a

[61] Either of the liability rules may also be used in another manner to achieve distributional goals. For example, if victims of pollution were poor, and if society desired a more equal distribution of wealth, it might intentionally increase "objective" damage awards if rule two were used; conversely, it might decrease the compensation to the factory owners, without any regard for economic efficiency if rule four were chosen. There are obvious disadvantages to this ad hoc method of achieving distributional goals. *See* p. 1110 *supra*.

practical matter be extremely severe under rule four. How do the homeowners decide to stop the factory's use of low grade coal? How do we assess the damages and their proportional allocation in terms of benefits to the homeowners? But equivalent problems may often be as great for rule two. How do we value the damages to each of the many homeowners? How do we inform the homeowners of their rights to damages? How do we evaluate and limit the administrative expenses of the court actions this solution implies?

The seriousness of the problem depends under each of the liability rules on the number of people whose "benefits" or "damages" one is assessing and the expense and likelihood of error in such assessment. A judgment on these questions is necessary to an evaluation of the possible economic efficiency benefits of employing one rule rather than another. The relative ease of making such assessments through different institutions may explain why we often employ the courts for rule two and get to rule four — when we do get there — only through political bodies which may, for example, prohibit pollution, or "take" the entitlement to build a supersonic plane by a kind of eminent domain, paying compensation to those injured by these decisions.[62] But

---

[62] Of course, variants of the other rules may be administered through political institutions as well. Rule three, granting a property entitlement to a polluter, may be effectuated by tax credits or other incentives such as subsidization of nonpolluting fuels offered for voluntary pollution abatement. In such schemes, as with rule four, political institutions are used to effect comprehensive benefit assessment and overcome freeloader problems which would be encountered in a more decentralized market solution. However, this centralization — to the extent that it replaces voluntary payments by individual pollution victims with collective payments not unanimously agreed upon — is a hybrid solution. The polluter must assent to the sale of his entitlement, but the amount of pollution abatement sought and the price paid by each pollution victim is not subjectively determined and voluntarily assented to by each.

The relationship of hybrids like the above to the four basic rules can be stated more generally. The buyer of an entitlement, whether the entitlement is protected by property or liability rules, may be viewed as owning what is in effect a property right not to buy the entitlement. But when freeloader problems abound, that property right may instead be given to a class of potential buyers. This "class" may be a municipality, a sewer authority, or any other body which can decide to buy an entitlement and compel those benefited to pay an objective price. When this is done, the individuals within the class have themselves only an entitlement not to purchase the seller's entitlement protected by a liability rule.

As we have already seen, the holder of an entitlement may be permitted to sell it at his own price or be compelled to sell it at an objective price: he may have an entitlement protected by a property or liability rule. Since, therefore, in any transaction the buyer may have a property or liability entitlement not to buy and the seller may have a property or a liability entitlement not to sell, there are, in effect, four combinations of rules for each possible original location of the en-all this does not, in any sense, diminish the importance of the fact that an awareness of the possibility of an entitlement to pollute, but one protected only by a liability rule, may in some instances allow us best to combine our distributional and efficiency goals.

We have said that we would say little about justice, and so we shall. But it should be clear that if rule four might enable us best to combine efficiency goals with distributional goals, it might also enable us best to combine those same efficiency goals with other goals that are often described in justice language. For example, assume that the factory in our hypothetical was using cheap coal *before* any of the wealthy houses were built. In these circumstances, rule four will not only achieve the desirable efficiency and distributional results mentioned above, but it will also accord with any "justice" significance which is attached to being there first. And this is so whether we view this justice significance as part of a distributional goal, as part of a long run efficiency goal based on protecting expectancies, or as part of an independent concept of justice.

Thus far in this section we have ignored the possibility of employing rules of inalienability to solve pollution problems. A general policy of barring pollution does seem unrealistic.[63] But rules of inalienability can appropriately be used to limit the levels of pollution and to control the levels of activities which cause pollution.[64]

One argument for inalienability may be the widespread exist-

---

titlement: voluntary seller and voluntary buyer; voluntary seller and compelled buyer; compelled seller and voluntary buyer; compelled seller and compelled buyer. Moreover, since the entitlement to that which is being bought or sold could have been originally given to the opposite party, there are, in effect, eight possible rules rather than four.

We do not mean by the above to suggest that political institutions are used only to allocate collectively held property rights. Quite the contrary, rule two, for instance, gives pollution victims an entitlement protected by a liability rule to be free from pollution. This rule could be administered by decentralized damage assessment as in litigation, or it could be effected by techniques like effluent fees charged to polluters. The latter type of collective intervention may be preferred where large numbers are involved and the costs of decentralized injury valuation are high. Still, under either system the "sale price" is collectively determined, so the basic character of the victims' entitlement is not changed.

[63] *See* Michelman, *supra* note 1, at 667.

[64] This is the exact analogue of specific deterrence of accident causing activities. *See* COSTS at 95–129.

Although it may seem fanciful to us, there is of course the possibility that a state might wish to grant a converse entitlement — an inalienable entitlement to pollute in some instances. This might happen where the state believed that in the long run everyone would be better off by allowing the polluting producers to make their products, regardless of whether the polluter thought it advantageous to accept compensation for stopping his pollution.

ence of moralisms against pollution. Thus it may hurt the Marshalls — gentleman farmers — to see Taney, a smoke-choked city dweller, sell his entitlement to be free of pollution. A different kind of externality or moralism may be even more important. The Marshalls may be hurt by the expectation that, while the present generation might withstand present pollution levels with no serious health dangers, future generations may well face a despoiled, hazardous environmental condition which they are powerless to reverse.[65] And this ground for inalienability might be strengthened if a similar conclusion were reached on grounds of self paternalism. Finally, society might restrict alienability on paternalistic grounds. The Marshalls might feel that although Taney himself does not know it, Taney will be better off if he really can see the stars at night, or if he can breathe smogless air.

Whatever the grounds for inalienability, we should reemphasize that distributional effects should be carefully evaluated in making the choice for or against inalienability. Thus the citizens of a town may be granted an entitlement to be free of water pollution caused by the waste discharges of a chemical factory; and the entitlement might be made inalienable on the grounds that the town's citizens really would be better off in the long run to have access to clean beaches. But the entitlement might also be made inalienable to assure the maintenance of a beautiful resort area for the very wealthy, at the same time putting the town's citizens out of work.[66]

V. The Framework and Criminal Sanctions

Obviously we cannot canvass the relevance of our approach through many areas of the law. But we do think it beneficial to examine one further area, that of crimes against property and bodily integrity. The application of the framework to the use of criminal sanctions in cases of theft or violations of bodily integrity is useful in that it may aid in understanding the previous material, especially as it helps us to distinguish different kinds of legal problems and to identify the different modes of resolving those problems.

Beginning students, when first acquainted with economic efficiency notions, sometimes ask why ought not a robber be simply charged with the value of the thing robbed. And the same question

[65] *See* Michelman, *supra* note 1, at 684.

[66] *Cf.* Frady, *The View from Hilton Head*, Harper's, May, 1970, at 103–112 (conflict over proposed establishment of chemical factory that would pollute the area's beaches in economically depressed South Carolina community; environmental groups that opposed factory backed by developers of wealthy resorts in the area, proponents of factory supported by representatives of unemployed town citizens).

is sometimes posed by legal philosophers.[67] If it is worth more to the robber than to the owner, is not economic efficiency served by such a penalty? Our answers to such a question tend to move quickly into very high sounding and undoubtedly relevant moral considerations. But these considerations are often not very helpful to the questioner because they depend on the existence of obligations on individuals not to rob for a fixed price and the original question was why we should impose such obligations at all.

One simple answer to the question would be that thieves do not get caught every time they rob and therefore the costs to the thief must at least take the unlikelihood of capture into account.[68] But that would not fully answer the problem, for even if thieves were caught every time, the penalty we would wish to impose would be greater than the objective damages to the person robbed.

A possible broader explanation lies in a consideration of the difference between property entitlements and liability entitlements. For us to charge the thief with a penalty equal to an objectively determined value of the property stolen would be to convert all property rule entitlements into liability rule entitlements.

The question remains, however, why *not* convert all property rules into liability rules? The answer is, of course, obvious. Liability rules represent only an approximation of the value of the object to its original owner and willingness to pay such an approximate value is no indication that it is worth more to the thief than to the owner. In other words, quite apart from the expense of arriving collectively at such an objective valuation, it is no guarantee of the economic efficiency of the transfer.[69] If this is so with property, it is all the more so with bodily integrity, and we would not presume collectively and objectively to value the cost of a rape to the victim against the benefit to the rapist even if economic efficiency is our sole motive. Indeed when we approach bodily integrity we are getting close to areas where we do not let the entitlement be sold at all and where economic efficiency enters

---

[67] One of the last articles by Professor Giorgio Del Vecchio came close to asking this question. *See* Del Vecchio, *Equality and Inequality in Relation to Justice*, 11 NAT. LAW FORUM 36, 43–45 (1966).

[68] *See, e.g.*, Becker, *Crime and Punishment: An Economic Approach*, 76 J. POL. ECON. 169 (1968).

[69] One might also point out that very often a thief will not have the money to meet the objectively determined price of the stolen object; indeed, his lack of resources is probably his main motivation for the theft. In such cases society, if it insists on a liability rule, will have to compensate the initial entitlement holder from the general societal coffers. When this happens the thief will not feel the impact of the liability rule and hence will not be sufficiently deterred from engaging in similar activity in the future. *Cf.* COSTS at 147–48.

in, if at all, in a more complex way. But even where the items taken or destroyed are things we do allow to be sold, we will not without special reasons impose an objective selling price on the vendor.

Once we reach the conclusion that we will not simply have liability rules, but that often, even just on economic efficiency grounds, property rules are desirable, an answer to the beginning student's question becomes clear. The thief not only harms the victim, he undermines rules and distinctions of significance beyond the specific case. Thus even if in a given case we can be sure that the value of the item stolen was no more than X dollars, and even if the thief has been caught and is prepared to compensate, we would not be content simply to charge the thief X dollars. Since in the majority of cases we cannot be sure of the economic efficiency of the transfer by theft, we must add to each case an undefinable kicker which represents society's need to keep all property rules from being changed at will into liability rules.[70] In other words, we impose criminal sanctions as a means of deterring future attempts to convert property rules into liability rules.[71]

The first year student might push on, however, and ask why we treat the thief or the rapist differently from the injurer in an auto

[70] If we were not interested in the integrity of property rules and hence we were not using an indefinable kicker, we would still presumably try to adjust the amount of damages charged to the thief in order to reflect the fact that only a percentage of thieves are caught; that is, we would fix a price-penalty which reflected the value of the good and the risk of capture.

[71] A problem related to criminal sanctions is that of punitive damages in intentional torts. If Taney sets a spring gun with the purpose of killing or maiming anyone who trespasses on his property, Taney has knowledge of what he is doing and of the risks involved which is more akin to the criminal than the negligent driver. But because Taney does not know precisely which one of many Marshalls will be the victim of his actions, ex ante negotiations seem difficult. How then do we justify the use of criminal sanctions and of more than compensatory damages? Probably the answer lies in the fact that we assume that the benefits of Taney's act are not worth the harm they entail if that harm were fully valued. Believing that this fact, in contrast with what is involved in a simple negligence case, should be, and in a sense can be, made known to the actor at the time he acts, we pile on extra damages. Our judgment is that most would act differently if a true cost-benefit burden could be placed. Given that judgment and given the impossibility of imposing a true cost-benefit burden by collective valuations — because of inadequate knowledge — we make sure that if we err we will err on the side of overestimating the cost.

There may be an additional dimension. Unlike fines or other criminal sanctions, punitive damages provide an extra compensation for the victim. This may not be pure windfall. Once the judgment is made that injuries classified as intentional torts are less desirable than nonintentional harms — either because they are expected to be less efficient or because there is less justification for the tortfeasor's not having purchased the entitlement in an ex ante bargain — then it may be that the actual, subjective injury to the victim from the tort is enhanced. One

accident or the polluter in a nuisance case. Why do we allow liability rules there? In a sense, we have already answered the question. The only level at which, before the accident, the driver can negotiate for the value of what he might take from his potential victim is one at which transactions are too costly. The thief or rapist, on the other hand, could have negotiated without undue expense (at least if the good was one which we allowed to be sold at all) because we assume he knew what he was going to do and to whom he would do it. The case of the accident is different because knowledge exists only at the level of deciding to drive or perhaps to drive fast, and at that level negotiations with potential victims are usually not feasible.

The case of nuisance seems different, however. There the polluter knows what he will do and, often, whom it will hurt. But as we have already pointed out, freeloader or holdout problems may often preclude any successful negotiations between the polluter and the victims of pollution; additionally, we are often uncertain who is the cheapest avoider of pollution costs. In these circumstances a liability rule, which at least allowed the economic efficiency of a proposed transfer of entitlements to be tested, seemed appropriate, even though it permitted the nonaccidental and unconsented taking of an entitlement. It should be emphasized, however, that where transaction costs do not bar negotiations between polluter and victim, or where we are sufficiently certain who the cheapest cost avoider is, there are no efficiency reasons for allowing intentional takings, and property rules, supported by injunctions or criminal sanctions, are appropriate.[72]

VI. Conclusion

This article has attempted to demonstrate how a wide variety of legal problems can usefully be approached in terms of a specific framework. Framework or model building has two shortcomings.

---

whose automobile is destroyed accidentally suffers from the loss of his car; one whose automobile is destroyed intentionally suffers from the loss of the car, and his injury is made greater by the knowledge that the loss was intentional, wilful, or otherwise avoidable.

[72] *Cf.* pp 1111–13.

We have not discussed distributional goals as they relate to criminal sanctions. In part this is because we have assumed the location of the initial entitlement — we have assumed the victim of a crime was entitled to the good stolen or to his bodily integrity. There is, however, another aspect of distributional goals which relates to the particular rule we choose to protect the initial entitlement. For example, one might raise the question of linking the severity of criminal sanctions to the wealth of the criminal or the victim. While this aspect of distributional goals would certainly be a fruitful area of discussion, it is beyond the scope of the present article.

The first is that models can be mistaken for the total view of phenomena, like legal relationships, which are too complex to be painted in any one picture. The second is that models generate boxes into which one then feels compelled to force situations which do not truly fit. There are, however, compensating advantages. Legal scholars, precisely because they have tended to eschew model building, have often proceeded in an ad hoc way, looking at cases and seeing what categories emerged. But this approach also affords only one view of the Cathedral. It may neglect some relationships among the problems involved in the cases which model building can perceive, precisely because it does generate boxes, or categories. The framework we have employed may be applied in many different areas of the law. We think its application facilitated perceiving and defining an additional resolution of the problem of pollution. As such we believe the painting to be well worth the oils.

Part IV
The Economics of Contract Law

[14]

THE ECONOMIC BASIS OF DAMAGES FOR BREACH OF CONTRACT

*JOHN H. BARTON**

In many respects, the common law of contract failed to survive the industrial revolution. It is now applied only in the interstices among specialized statutory and judge-made rules dealing with specific contract types.[1] And business now often prefers informal understandings to formal contracts.[2]

Perhaps the decline is the result of increases in the variousness of commercial transactions or in the costs and delays of judicial procedure. Nonetheless one is tempted first to examine the body of law itself. If that law has become ambiguous or economically irrational it must accept some of the blame for its own demise.

This paper is an attempt to carry out such an examination for one part of contract law, that of damages for breach of contract, by examining the possible economic theory which can be argued to underlie such damages. This theory will be developed in terms of models, one for a transaction involving a future sale of goods for which a market exists and one, which will be embellished variously, for a transaction involving a sale of custom-made goods for which no ready market exists. In the process, the meaning attributable to the concept of economically optimum damages will be examined, ways to test the actual workings of the laws of damages suggested, and a modification of the law of damages proposed.

I. The Market Transaction

The paradigm that might have been chosen for this paper, had it been written in the formative years of contract law, is a market contract: a contract to sell a specified quantity of a commodity at a specified date in the

* Assistant Professor of Law, Stanford University. The author wishes to thank the many who have helped him with this paper, including particularly Dr. Richard Venti, Professors Wayne G. Barnett, William F. Baxter, and Richard S. Markovits, the participants in the Seminar on Microeconomics and Public Policy at Stanford University, and the participants in the Industrial Organization Workshop at the University of Chicago.

1 See E. Allan Farnsworth, The Past of Promise: An Historical Introduction to Contract, 69 Colum. L. Rev. 576 (1969).

2 See Stewart Macaulay, Non-Contractual Relations in Business: A Preliminary Study, 28 Am. Soc. Rev. 55 (1963).

future, under conditions in which all damages can be determined by hypothetical or actual purchase or liquidation of the commodity in a market that is always available. The contract is then essentially a bet against the future course of the market. Each party enters the contract in the hope that he is guessing the market more accurately than the other, or, if the parties differ in their willingness to bear risks, in the judgment that the certain price set by the contract is more desirable than the uncertainty of the market price.

There are two goals that might guide the determination of damages for breach of such a contract: *expectation protection* (the plaintiff should be put in as good a position as if the promise had been honored), and *incentive maintenance* (the defendant should honor his promises). It is appropriate to begin with the goal of expectation protection, since that is the one usually expressed by common law courts. The goal is to give the offended party a sum of money damages that places him in as good a position as he would have been in had the contract been honored. Thus, suppose a contract is made to sell grain at price p on a specified date. In fact, grain turns out to be selling at market price s on the specified date. Assuming for the moment that $s > p$, the buyer will want to enforce the contract against the seller, and the seller will want to avoid the contract. If the seller breaches, the buyer must purchase the grain on the open market at price s, so he should obtain an additional payment d sufficient to compensate him for not obtaining the grain at price p. Clearly, one is led to the damage measure $d \geqslant s - p$.

The incentive-maintenance analysis leads to the same results. Aside from financial incapacity—in which event a rather different body of law may be brought into play—the primary reason a party to a market-oriented contract might fail to keep the contract is that the other party's prediction of future price was better than his. If parties are to be prevented from dishonoring contracts on this ground, the law must impose a penalty that is as great as the cost of compliance.[3] Assuming that the case is one of seller's breach (so that $s > p$) the problem is to define a penalty d that makes it more desirable for the seller to honor the contract than to dishonor it. If he honors the contract he gains p; if he violates it, as by selling the grain on the market, he gains s, but loses the penalty d. The condition for making the penalty effective is then

$$p \geqslant s - d \text{ or } d \geqslant s - p.$$

These equivalent results are the classical measures of contract recovery in an economy of organized markets, and are telescoped in the term "expectation damages."[4] The distinction between the two possible supporting theories

[3] I am ignoring litigation costs.

[4] The Uniform Commercial Code modifies the result slightly by substituting the price at the time the buyer learns of breach for that at the contractual delivery date. This is

must be noted, however. One seeks to penalize the potential contract violator in such a way that he normally prefers not to violate, and is thus defined by the alternatives he faces in carrying out the contract or not. Common law courts are seldom explicit about this policy of preventing default. Yet they are concerned that the damage doctrines not *encourage* default. Moreover, to the extent that contract law's ordinary role is as a threat to prevent breach, the incentive maintenance policy is implicit. The other theory seeks to place the innocent party in as good a position as he would have been in had the contract been carried out, and is thus defined by his expectations in receiving the desired performance.

The above analysis may be restated in terms of game theory. The market contract is essentially a bet that the market price will behave in a certain way, and the gain of one party will be the loss of the other. The game can be described as follows:

		Seller: Honor	Seller: Dishonor
Buyer	Honor	$(s-p, p-s)$	$(0, 0)$
	Dishonor	$(0, 0)$	$(0, 0)$

This is a zero-sum game, whose equilibrium solution will be the dishonor-dishonor point, so long as the losing party has an incentive to avoid the contract.

The law of damages changes this result by modifying the off-diagonal blocks, interpreted as those in which a party seeks to dishonor the contract but is subject to suit by the other party:

		Seller: Honor	Seller: Dishonor
Buyer	Honor	$(s-p, p-s)$	$(0, 0)$
	Dishonor	$(d, -d)$	$(d, -d)$

(Buyer's and seller's damages are both encompassed here by allowing d to be negative.) This is again a zero-sum game, but one in which at $d = s - p$, the conventional measure of damages, the equilibrium solution becomes the honor-honor point. Thus, this measure of damages serves to make it possible to contract with the expectation that the contract will be binding.[5]

---

on the assumption that the buyer will "cover" by buying alternate goods. See Uniform Commercial Code § 2-713, comment.

[5] Certain of the concepts underlying this analysis of the enforcement role of contract derive from Robert L. Birmingham, Legal and Moral Duty in Game Theory: Common Law Contract and Chinese Analogies, 18 Buffalo L. Rev. 99 (1969). His analysis is ex-

II. The Non-Market Transaction

Although the model described above may have been the norm at the time when contract law began its development, and may still account for a large proportion of actual transactions, it does not exhibit the characteristic problems of contemporary contract law. To expose those problems requires only a slight increase in complexity. Our example will be that of a contract of purchase and sale of a product manufactured to order. It will be assumed that there is no market in which the product could be readily bought or sold and that the buyer expects to use the purchased product in his business in the hope of making a profit. These assumptions correspond to those underlying many actual contracts in the world of business today.

The problems immediately raised are: (a) there is no market by which a measure of damages can be defined or by which the injured party can protect himself; (b) the costs and benefits to the parties do not provide an unequivocal basis for estimation of damages, since the cost incurred by the injured party is generally different from the benefit bestowed on the breaching party; and (c), less obviously, completion of the transaction can no longer be assumed desirable, since the overall benefit to the parties may be less than the overall costs to them.

The character of these difficulties can be elucidated by considering the details of the transaction. The buyer negotiates to obtain a custom-made good from the seller. If the transaction is completed without difficulty, the seller will normally receive a profit above his costs, since he would not otherwise enter the contract. Similarly, the buyer will expect to conduct further operations on the goods or combine them with other goods and sell the whole at a profit, here called an enterprise expectation. If the transaction fails during performance, each party may be stuck with unrecoverable costs. The seller's partly completed goods may be valueless except as scrap.[6] This possible loss

---

pressed in terms of the use of contract damages to make solvable the Prisoner's Dilemma, a non-zero-sum game of the form:

(1, 1)	(−2, 2)
(2, − 2)	(−1, −1)

By cooperating, both players could get the payoff 1 of the upper left hand corner. But each is tempted to cheat by shifting to the off-diagonal box where he can receive 2. When both do this (and both are forced to do so by the −2 cost of not seeking the double payoff when the other does seek it), they end up each losing one unit, an unfortunate kind of equilibrium. Birmingham shows how damages serve to shift this equilibrium to the honor-honor point.

I believe, however, that the model outlined in text which shows the market contract as a zero-sum game is more appropriate. First, it corresponds to the actual win-lose character of the market bet. Second, it allows more explicit contrast with the clearly non-zero sum features of the "non-market" transaction, discussed in the next part.

[6] A complete definition of the sunk costs would consider the alternative markets for

is seller's reliance, or, in Fuller's vocabulary, essential reliance.[7] Similarly, the buyer may have incurred expenditures—such as printing of packages—that become losses now that the contract has failed. These are buyer's reliance, or, in Fuller's vocabulary, incidental reliance.

This description leads to the following game pattern for the non-market transaction (in the absence of any legal remedies):

		Seller/Manufacturer: Honor	Seller/Manufacturer: Dishonor
Buyer/Entrepreneur	Honor	(buyer's profit or enterprise expectation, seller's profit)	(—buyer's or incidental reliance, 0)
	Dishonor	(0, —seller's or essential reliance)	(0, 0)

A complete model would have to consider various alternative strategies of partial performance. Nevertheless, the model is qualitatively correct, and it does display the problems already mentioned. First, the expectations are not explicit in the contract and cannot be estimated easily from a market. Thus, losses become difficult to evaluate, and normal bookkeeping data often may not be very helpful. Moreover, some of the expectations may be relatively subjective; for example, the parties may have been interested in obtaining gainful employment (or institutional stability) as well as in obtaining the entrepreneurial profits associated with the transaction.[8] Second, since the gains and losses to each party are now quite different, the policies of incentive maintenance and of expectation protection diverge.

---

the material on hand, *e.g.*, sale for scrap or (possibly) completion of the contract, etc., and evaluate for each of these possible uses or markets the difference between the additional necessary cost to prepare the materials for that market and the price available in that market. If there is no market such that there would be a positive return on such additional expenditures, then the costs already expended represent the sunk cost or reliance. Otherwise, these costs should be adjusted by an amount equal to the return from preparing the materials for the alternative market offering the greatest return. In fact, this is the definition adopted by the courts, although allowance is made for the problems of uncertainty and error in choosing the alternate performance. See, *e.g.*, Uniform Commercial Code § 2-704(2). Throughout this article, it will be assumed for simplicity's sake that there is no such economically desirable alternative performance.

[7] Lon L. Fuller and William R. Perdue, Jr., The Reliance Interest in Contract Damages, 46 Yale L.J. 52, 78 (1936).

[8] Thus, complex doctrine has been developed to deal with the question whether the seller is a "lost-volume manufacturer." See Robert J. Harris, A Radical Restatement of the Law of Seller's Damages: Sales Act and Commercial Code Results Compared, 18 Stan. L. Rev. 66, 80-87 (1965).

The third point is somewhat more difficult, and requires consideration of the character of the equilibrium solution of the game as shown above. This is a non-zero sum game, whose normal equilibrium solution is the honor-honor point. It follows that in the ordinary course of business, businessmen will feel no need for contract law. The cases in which default is likely are those in which, through some casualty or change of circumstances, expected profit is converted into an expected loss. In the situation of changed circumstances, it may well be economically inefficient to complete the transaction. The changes may make the total costs of the transaction greater than the total benefits. Consequently one is properly chary about requiring the enforcement of what I have called the "non-market" contract, through injunction or through damages of a form that always induces performance. This is the point hidden in Justice Holmes' aphorism that the obligation imposed by a contract is not to comply, but either to comply or to pay damages.[9]

There is a further point. It is clear by now that the defaults likely to arise in the non-market transaction are the result of specific problems—a casualty loss or a market change, for example. If so, why cannot the parties arrange a set of damage rules for themselves? The answer is that parties do this in many transactions, although, for reasons to be discussed in part IV, they do not do it for all transactions.

Whether the parties create such rules, or whether the law does so in a more general way, the rules will affect resource allocation by influencing the probability that parties will continue a performance that is not economically justifiable, and by changing the way that parties will allocate the costs of covering various risks. These allocative effects can be illuminated by an economic analysis. Such an analysis will usually not show which party should bear a risk in the "normal-form" contract (one adopted by trade practice or made for the parties by a court facing a silent or ambiguous risk allocation), but it can show whether or not enforcement of a risk-bearing arrangement through the award of damages will produce non-optimal results, and it can provide an understanding of the relationship between damage theory and the pattern of contract negotiation.

A number of simplifying assumptions are made in this discussion. All markets are assumed to be competitive except that for the goods manufactured to order and sold under the contract. Differences between parties as to risk aversion are ignored. The negotiation model used is a very simple one, and assumes a rather complete knowledge by the parties of each other's utilities. Since this assumption is seldom warranted in practice, the model's applicability to the problems of mistake and misunderstanding, and to consumer problems (where rather complex market forces combine with mystifyingly subtle and

[9] O. W. Holmes, The Path of the Law, 10 Harv. L. Rev. 457, 462 (1897).

abbreviated negotiations), is limited. But it seems better to proceed with a limited model than not to proceed at all.[10]

III. The Economics of the Fully-Negotiated Transaction

It has been suggested that parties (at least so long as the bargaining is fair) ought to be free to distribute risks as they choose and that economics has nothing to say about a bargained risk allocation.[11] This statement is true, but can easily be taken to mean too much, so it is worthwhile to attempt to elucidate its limitations.

A. *Contracting in the Absence of Uncertainty*

A fundamental postulate is needed: the character of contract law should be such that the allocation of resources is the same when a productive venture is conducted under one management as when the venture is conducted by

[10] The alternative would be to adopt a more sophisticated model of negotiation. Such models exist, but are generally either unsatisfactory or extremely complex. See generally Alan Coddington, Theories of the Bargaining Process (1968); John G. Cross, The Economics of Bargaining (1969); Lawrence E. Fouraker and Sidney Siegel, Bargaining Behavior (1963); Sidney Siegel and Lawrence E. Fouraker, Bargaining and Group Decision Making (1960). The technique adopted here, that of attempting to use damages to shift utility curves and consequently relocate the contract curve, is perhaps immune to some of the difficulties of typical negotiation models which generally attempt to define that point on the contract curve at which agreement is reached. However, there remains the difficulty that utility curves usually are not really understood by negotiators except for small regions as to which knowledge is acquired during the course of the negotiation. Given this fact, and given the dependence of the later development of this paper on the differences between the knowledge of the different parties, one is tempted towards the sequential negotiation models of Appendix 8 of Robert D. Luce and Howard Raiffa, Games and Decisions: Introduction and Critical Survey (1957). Such a model could be cast in the form of a game in which an offer may provoke acceptance, counter-offer or termination of negotiations. In turn, the counter-offer is followed by a new game, etc. One could, with this model, consider the pressures on a negotiator to avoid raising the question of certain risks. The mathematics, however, are nearly intractable.

There is another pervasive difficulty associated with the negotiation model. Economic optimality is normally defined with respect to a market, and negotiation will not occur except as a substitute for a market or in a situation in which the market is imperfect. How then, without invoking rather complex doctrines of the second best, can one ever refer to a negotiated result as optimal? My response to this problem has been to ignore it. This response can be justified by the observation that the difficulties which lead to a negotiated contract structure rather than a market structure are often not incompatible with reasonably competitive market-oriented behavior. Thus, negotiated contracts for growth and sale of foodstuffs exist alongside competitive markets in both grain and farmland. Likewise, whatever may be the non-optimal features of the housing market, the negotiation of leases or sale contracts does not disrupt the market. One may doubt, of course, that there is competitive (as opposed to oligopolistic) behavior with respect to many contract terms, but this does not invalidate the model described in text. It is clear that there is an important need for research in why the different patterns of negotiation, unilateral price setting, and auction predominate in different markets.

[11] Cf. R. H. Coase, The Problem of Social Cost, 3 J. Law & Econ. 1 (1960).

several contract-linked managements facing the same underlying cost functions. Put differently, the institution of contract law should not bias the choice that would otherwise be made between one's own productive efficiency and that of a contractor.

To examine this postulate, we may begin by considering output determination—the critical allocative decision—for the integrated manufacturer.

Assume that the manufacturer will face an average cost curve $c_a(n)$, describing the average cost of producing n items. If s is the market price, he will gain ns from selling n items, which he can produce at a cost $nc_a(n)$. The difference, the value of the venture to him, will be described here as profit, P, although the difficulties posed by that term are recognized. Thus

$$P = ns - nc_a(n).$$

The optimum n, which maximizes P, can now be determined in any of several ways. The normal mathematical technique is to differentiate, and to choose the point at which the derivative is equal to zero.[12] The method yields:

$$\frac{\partial P}{\partial n} = s - \frac{\partial}{\partial n}[nc_a(n)] = 0.$$

Define $n = u(s)$ as the solution of this implicit equation. For this n it is clear from the equation that marginal cost, $\frac{\partial}{\partial n}[nc_a(n)]$, equals marginal revenue, s. This allocation is optimal both for society as a whole and for the firm.

Alternatively, the entrepreneur can buy the products at a negotiated price p (which may vary, depending on the quantity produced) from a manufacturer who faces the same cost curves.[13] Profits can then be defined for the entrepreneur, P_e, and for the manufacturer, P_m, as follows:

$$P_e = n(s - p), \text{ and}$$
$$P_m = np - nc_a(n).$$

The parties' behavior during negotiations can now be estimated from their indifference curves (*i.e.*, utility curves) in the p, n plane (the variables that are subject to negotiation). These curves, which are by definition the curves of constant profit, are given by $P_e =$ constant for the entrepreneur and by $P_m =$ constant for the manufacturer. They are shown in figure 1.

The parties can negotiate about two variables, p and q. Hence each point

[12] Different mathematical techniques are necessary if the continuity conditions required for the calculation are not satisfied, but the results of this paper would still hold.

[13] To the extent that the process of negotiation and dealing with outsiders poses costs, those costs are not reflected in the model. They need not be substantial and will not change greatly with contract size or negotiation outcome. Hence, they can be ignored without serious effect on the analysis.

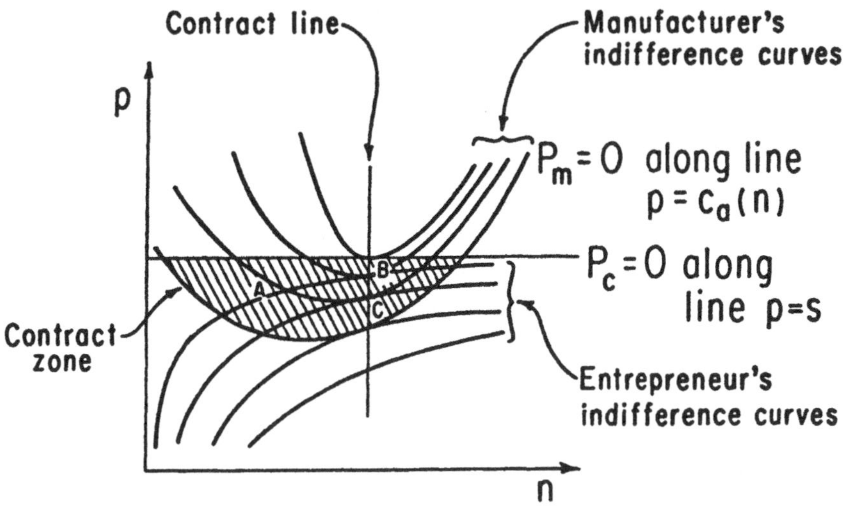

FIGURE 1

in the space is an imaginable negotiation outcome. Since, however, neither party will normally enter a losing contract, the entrepreneur will not enter a contract above the line $P_e = 0$, and the manufacturer will not enter one below the line $P_m = 0$. This restricts the outcome to the shaded "contract zone."[14]

But if the parties are good negotiators, more can be said. Consider the point A as a possible outcome and compare it with any point on the line segment BC. All the latter points are preferable to each party (except that the manufacturer is indifferent between A and C and the entrepreneur indifferent between A and B), because, except for the end points, they allow higher profits to *both* parties. It can be concluded then that the parties will negotiate to the "contract line," defined mathematically as the line of common tangency, and defined economically as the line along which joint profits are maximized. This construction tells nothing about how the parties will split those joint profits (where they will be along the contract line) but it does tell how they can negotiate together to make their joint profits as large as possible.

What is not so obvious is the form of the contract line, shown as a vertical line. This form is intuitively clear from the assumption that the parties will seek to maximize their joint profits:

$$P_e + P_m = n(s - p) + np - nc_a(n) = ns - nc_a(n),$$

[14] The presence of some competition could be represented in the model by noting for example that a price p_0 offered by an alternative supplier creates a horizontal line $p = p_0$ above which the entrepreneur would prefer to deal with the alternative. Thus, the contract zone would be shrunk.

exactly the function which the single firm sought to maximize. It is clear from the form of this function that this maximization is independent of the actual price p chosen and does in fact occur at $n = u(s)$. Hence the contract line will be the vertical one $n = u(s)$. The pressures of bargaining lead the contract negotiations towards the allocative optimum that would be reached were the manufacturing performed by the entrepreneur rather than contracted out. If the parties are bargaining well, they will be forced into an optimum allocative decision, regardless of how they split the profits among themselves.

Now suppose there are risks that the contract will become unprofitable for the entrepreneur so that he may wish to terminate it, or that there will be casualties to the goods during their production. Suppose that these risks and their probabilities of occurrence are fully understood by both parties, and that the parties agree upon a set of releases and of cross-payments (or damages) to be invoked in the event that any of the risks are realized. Suppose further that the parties are equally willing and able to bear risks and that the character of the cross-payments does not affect either party's incentive to perform or to protect the goods. It is clear, then, that the integrated entrepreneur will optimize in a manner that allows for all the expected risks. Moreover, if the entrepreneur and the manufacturer are now separated and work through contract, they will negotiate to the same production level, with the price parameter now appearing as a combination of price and damages. All of the cross-payments that the parties decide should be invoked in particular situations would drop out of the joint profit-maximization function in the same way that price dropped out in the example of the preceding paragraph. It is a matter of indifference whether a party protects itself against a risk by negotiating for "damages" or by negotiating a price adjustment, based on the same damages discounted by the probability of their occurrence, in the event that the loss occurs. So long as the understandings of the parties do indeed coincide, the results are indifferent in any allocative sense. The negotiated damages are very much like bets, and may have to be judicially enforceable in order to be paid, just as did market bets.

Hypothesis 1: Between parties with equivalent and substantial knowledge of the risks involved in the transaction as a whole, any bargained-for allocation of risks (whether in the form of a liquidated-damage clause or of any other foreseen and agreed-upon method of determining damages) should be enforced in a commercial contract.[15] This suggests, in particular, that in evaluating the enforceability of a liquidated damages clause a court should inquire not into the uncertainty of estimating damages beforehand or the consistency of the clause with the traditional law of damages, but only

[15] See Robert L. Birmingham, Breach of Contract, Damage Measures, and Economic Efficiency, 24 Rutgers L. Rev. 273 (1970).

whether the provision was knowledgeably and fairly bargained-for. I do not deny that the tests classically used to distinguish an imposed "penal damage" clause (which will not be enforced) from a negotiated "liquidated damage" clause (which will be enforced) may be useful evidence of the fairness of the bargaining. It is clear, however, that courts are acting improperly in ignoring a liquidated damage clause if their ground is that the parties are setting their own law. Liquidated damage clauses can reasonably be rejected only on a basis that the negotiation (or its reduction to writing) was unfair in some way.

B. *Contracting in the Presence of Market Uncertainty (Buyer's Breach)*

The fact that a negotiated allocation will, under appropriate bargaining conditions, be optimal does not mean that the contract institution may not be misallocative due to its frictional effect in the presence of changing conditions. Under certain conditions, an integrated firm confronted with a time-varying demand curve may find it appropriate to begin work on a certain number of units and then to discontinue efforts and write off the loss on some of these units if the market changes unfavorably. Since this behavior maximizes profits in a competitive market, it must be assumed optimal. If, however, the production effort is contracted out and, because of the method by which damages are computed, the contractual arrangement effectively prevents cancellation under appropriate conditions, performance is continued—a non-optimal result.

This result can be examined with a simple model. Suppose that production, in this model the cultivation of an agricultural commodity, requires one growing season, can be started only in May, and once started cannot be stopped. Raw materials, or seeds, costing b per unit of output, can be bought only in March. They are perishable, and can be used only in the one season. The crop is always sold in September, and, also being perishable, cannot be held over. Finally, the September price is learned in April, too late to affect the decision to purchase seeds, but early enough to affect the decision to commit land, plant, and cultivate. For simplicity, the price per unit of the crop will be assumed to be either s, with a probability π, or zero, the bottom dropping out of the market $(1-\pi)$ proportion of the seasons. Although grossly simplified, this model does permit analysis of the problems arising when improved price information becomes available at a time when some costs are already incurred but others can still be avoided.[16]

The critical allocation decision is then to define the production level (here,

[16] A related and interesting problem is presented in Karl H. Borch, The Economics of Uncertainty 143-49 (1968), which discusses the maneuvering, but not the contracting, between wholesaler and retailer over inventory size.

perhaps in the form of a choice of the number of acres of land to plant). The profit function for an integrated entrepreneur or farmer is

$$P = \pi\,[ns - c_t(n)] - bn,$$

where $c_t(n)$ is the total cost curve for the production process. He has to pay for n units of raw material each season, but incurs production costs and gains sales for only a proportion π of the seasons. The remaining seasons he avoids production costs and realizes no sales. Using standard techniques to establish the optimum n

$$\frac{\partial P}{\partial n} = \pi s - b - \pi\frac{\partial c_t(n)}{\partial n} \text{ or } \frac{\partial c_t(n)}{\partial n} = s - \frac{b}{\pi}$$

it can be shown that $n = u\,(s - \frac{b}{\pi})$. The good-season market price must, in effect, be discounted to allow for the loss in bad seasons.

Suppose now that the production is carried out by a separate supplier who contracts to buy seed, plant and cultivate the land, and sell the crop to an agricultural entrepreneur at a pre-negotiated price. In this case, simple contract enforcement would be non-optimal if it required the buyer to honor the contract even after the market falls. The profit functions of the entrepreneur buyer (P_e) and the manufacturer or cultivator-seller (P_m) are then as follows:

$$P_e = \pi sn - pn;$$
$$P_m = pn - c_t(n) - bn.$$

Assuming as before that the contract curve is the line $P_e + P_m = \max$, the parties will negotiate to maximize

$$P = P_e + P_m = \pi sn - c_t(n) - bn,$$

again a function of n alone. Since

$$\frac{\partial P}{\partial n} = \pi s - b - \frac{\partial c_t(n)}{\partial n} = 0,$$

it appears that $n = u(\pi s - b) = u[\pi(s - \frac{b}{\pi})]$. The fact that the entrepreneur buyer must honor the contract, even when it is a losing contract, cuts back acreage to that corresponding to a price π times the actual price. This is the way the parties react to being "locked-in" to complete performance once the contract is signed.[17]

[17] The extreme version of this effect is exemplified by an entrepreneur who enters into a long-term contract to buy stated quantities from a supplier. To the extent that the

Fortunately, contract law does not go this far. Unless the buyer has negotiated a special clause permitting termination of the contract when the market drops, he indeed cannot cancel without being in breach of contract. (Unprofitability of performance is not adequate grounds for rescission, and, as a ground for breach, may lead the court to view the offender with some disfavor.) Consequently, the buyer in this case is subject to damages. But the damages are limited to seller's expectation as of the time of cancellation, usually his expected profit, here $pn - c_t(n) - bn$, plus the costs *already* incurred, here bn. In that case, assuming that each party has complete knowledge of the risks, the profit functions can be written

$$P_e = \pi sn - \pi pn - (1 - \pi)[pn - c_t(n)];$$
$$P_m = \pi[pn - c_t(n)] + (1 - \pi)[pn - c_t(n)] - bn.$$

Through the same calculation as before,

$$P = P_e + P_m = \pi sn - \pi c_t(n) - bn$$
$$\frac{\partial P}{\partial n} = \pi s - b - \pi \frac{\partial c_t(n)}{\partial n} = 0;$$

it appears that $n = u(s - \frac{b}{\pi})$. Production is now at the correct level.

This definition of seller's expectation, which seems to correct for the rigidity of automatic contract performance, is based on a principle that contract law will not reward the seller for unwanted performance. The principle is illustrated by *Clark* v. *Marsiglia*.[18] Plaintiff had a contract to clean and repair paintings. Half-way through, defendant told him to stop. Plaintiff continued performance and sought the entire contract price. Defendant argued that he should be liable for only the portion of the price corresponding to the work done at the time of the stop-order. Hence the question posed was: under color of the contract-enforcement policy, could the seller continue work on the contract, thus forcing the buyer to pay for additional work which he did not desire?

---

supplier insists on a fixed quantity per year, the buyer will negotiate to keep that quantity low, out of fear of bad years.

The requirements contract, in which the volume is flexible, avoids this problem, but, because it fixes prices for the future, may produce a different form of misallocation, by limiting the extent to which production reacts to price changes. The effect may be in either direction, depending on whether prices rise or fall. Whether or not the effect is thoroughly random depends on whether those market situations most likely to produce requirements contracts are also associated with a probable secular trend in prices. Moreover, this problem of lag in responsiveness may be minor compared with the intimate relationship between market structure and the use of requirements contracts and with the possibility that requirements contracts are a response to differential ability to bear risk.

[18] 1 Denio 317, 43 Am. Dec. 670 (N.Y. Sup. Ct. 1845).

The conventional judicial answer, which is no, can be justified in either of two ways. A first way is to make the choice between the incentive maintenance and the expectation protection policies in favor of the latter. The seller can achieve his expectation interest by recovering an amount equal to the reliance together with an amount equal to the "profit" expected from the contract. This is normally a cost to the buyer lower than that which would be incurred if the seller were to complete the contract. It would be unduly harmful to defendant to allow plaintiff to build up damages without conferring any benefit. Alternatively, if the buyer no longer wants the product, perhaps because *his* sales volume has fallen, it would be wasteful to require the seller to finish the unwanted performance. It is socially better that he not waste his resources on an unnecessary activity.

It is clear that the seller should recover his sunk costs and need recover no more costs. What about his profits? They are typically given, if not too speculative, often under a formulation of the damage measure as "contract price less cost to complete." This can mean that full profits are due, even if the contract is cancelled the day it is made and there is no reliance whatever. Such a result is unsatisfying, and can lead to rather formalistic disputes over whether or not a contract was ever made. The problem is slight in the market transaction, where the market will usually change slowly so damages for early breach are quite small, but acute in the non-market transaction.

In fact, all that is necessary to permit optimality, when both parties have complete and accurate information, is to allow termination upon the market's drop with a pre-established settlement payment to be made at that time. The parties can either negotiate a special clause providing for damages or price adjustments or rely on a judicially defined measure of damages. (In practice, specific clauses will be found in only the most sophisticated contracts, although extra-legal business custom often permits termination under the necessary circumstances, achieving the same result as if the clause were included.)[19] If such a payment is established to allow termination after purchase of the raw materials in the event that the price drops, the profit functions become

$$P_e = \pi sn - p\pi n - d(1 - \pi)\, n, \text{ and}$$
$$P_m = p\,\pi n + d(1 - \pi)\, n - \pi\, c_t(n) - nb,$$

where the assumption is made that the entrepreneur pays p for completed items and d for items on which production is stopped. On adding these profits, it can be seen that the joint profit maximum is indeed achieved at the optimum production start level. No matter how the parties split their profits by negotiating over p and d, they will still negotiate to the optimum

[19] See Stewart Macaulay, *supra* note 2.

production levels. This is possible at any predictable level, and the damage measure chosen can be that which the courts will use. Its predictability (not at all clear) must be assumed along with that of the risk, and the parties must both have this information.

Hypothesis 2: Completion of a contract according to its terms is often not optimal. This is, of course, the economic-waste point that underlies *Clark* v. *Marsiglia*, but it goes even further. Even if work under the contract is not completed, an expectation upon entering the contract that the contract may have to be completed may lead to non-optimality. Hence courts should be hesitant to place very substantial weight upon a role of "enforcing" contracts.

Indeed, one might conclude that the fact that one party wants to get out of a production contract should be reason enough to excuse further performance (although not to excuse payment of damages). After all, if the parties are in court at all, it is likely to mean that there is no settlement payment such that further performance can be made profitable to the combined parties. If a party wishes to default, it normally means that he expects to lose money by going ahead. Presumably, we want him to go ahead anyway if there exists a positive bribe that can be paid to the defaulter such that both parties end up with a profit.

The entire discussion must be qualified by the point that there are times when contracts have to be enforced by their own terms (*e.g.*, to carry out the terms of an agreed-upon resolution of a risk or to prevent extortion of the bribe of the preceding paragraph in situations when it is sought without economic reason) as well as times when, averaged over many transactions, simplicity and certainty are more valuable than allocative perfection in the individual transaction.

Hypothesis 3: Since risks and the settlements to be made in the event of their realization can be allowed for in negotiating a price, *economic allocation theory provides no basis for prescribing measures of damages, so long as the risks involved are understood and projected correctly by each party in the negotiation.* This conclusion assumes, of course, that no effort need be made to influence incentives to perform or to avoid the risk.

IV. Behavioral Sources of Contract Law

The above analysis shows that, when parties with equal bargaining power negotiate about an equally understood risk or uncertainty, the court can do no better from an economic viewpoint than to enforce their understanding, much the way it enforced the contract where damages could be ascertained automatically by reference to an organized market. The typical problem in what I have called "non-market" contract law, however, is that the parties often have not negotiated such a way to handle the risk, but the risk still materializes. They either did not consider the risk at all or, while considering it, negotiated on the basis of different understandings as to its magnitude or who would assume it.

The practical problem of contract damages is thus conceptually reducible to that of mistake or misunderstanding. When the judicial system imposes damages, it can, for economic purposes, be said to be adding an unstated term to the contract. The court is saying: "You parties didn't negotiate about this risk or didn't reach any understanding about it. Now the risk has materialized, and I have to figure out what terms should be implied to cover the risk." The role for economics, then, in the law of damages is to make the additional terms consistent insofar as possible with (a) the allocation assumptions likely to have been implicitly negotiated into the contract and (b) the economic desirability or undesirability of continued performance. Goal (a) is most closely related to misunderstanding about the meaning of the negotiation while goal (b) is most closely related to failure to predict future contingencies (*e.g.*, contract frustration). And the law should meet these goals in a way that minimizes transaction costs, the element of cost that is ultimately at stake when the parties can, by special negotiations, undo most general damage rules.

Goal (b), the incentive to continue performance, might appeal to courts more than goal (a) (allocative efficiency) because it does not require the court to make an allocation of risks. Unfortunately, it turns out that pursuit of this goal often leads to a measure of damages inconsistent with that defined on allocation grounds. For the reasons developed in the preceding section, this goal would normally seem less important than the allocative goal, and, except for the proof of inconsistency, will be ignored here.

With respect to goal (a), there is a reciprocal dependence between the judicial system and the contract-makers in defining who should bear the risk. Insofar as the judicial system consistently places an undiscussed risk on a particular party, that party will, if responsive to the system, tend to protect himself against the risk by either shifting it explicitly to the other party by negotiation or making his allocational decisions as if he faced the risk. Likewise, if commercial practice makes "normal" assumptions as to the location of the risk parties will accept these assumptions when they make their allocational decisions and the judicial system will achieve proper allocation by accepting them too.

Nevertheless, courts will sometimes have to allocate the risk without having any form of practice to rely upon. Unless transaction costs are considered, economics has nothing to say to this question, at least so long as there can be bargaining about the risk. (There may, of course, be risk-spreading or social policy reasons for one party to bear the risk, even if the other can be induced to accept it.) An answer may be definable directly in terms of transaction costs.[20] If, for example, it would be very unusual for the buyer to bear a particular risk, then, unless the parties explicitly agreed otherwise, the seller should bear it.[21] There are also reasons that can be related only to a sense of bargaining justice—this is particularly the case with questions like "did A's statement mean that he was taking the risk?" No general analysis of these problems will be presented here.

What will be attempted is a more general task, based on the locations of information about the risks and about possible countermeasures. In the real-world case, contracting parties are not in symmetrical positions. There may be one party who is abler to appreciate the magnitude of the risk or to negotiate about it. There may also be a party, not necessarily the same one, who is abler to understand the effects of the law and to take in response those corrective actions that will establish optimal allocation. The problem for the law of damages is then to encourage the party able to appreciate the risk to conduct his negotiations toward optimality even though the other party negotiates in naive ignorance of the risk. The costs of exchanging full knowledge of the risk can then be avoided. If this is to be successful, the details must vary somewhat from contract type to contract type, since the typical expectations (or indifference functions) of the parties will vary also. This variance may be one of the reasons why the unity of contract law is breaking down. In this paper, two examples will be considered, one in which the party appreciating the risk magnitude and the party better situated to effect an optimal allocation are different and one in which they are the same. It will appear that the mathematics, and indeed the existing law, are drastically different in the two cases.

A. *Buyer's Damages: Allocation of Casualty Risk*

How contract damages can be tailored to promote efficient allocation is demonstrated most clearly in the case of buyer's damages, which often result from a situation in which the supplier suffers a casualty loss, such as a fire or machine failure.[22]

[20] See Steven N. S. Cheung, Transaction Cost, Risk Aversion and the Choice of Contractual Arrangement, 12 J. Law & Econ. 23 (1969).

[21] Note that the way risks are allocated in the case of a silent contract will often affect negotiated allocations. A party on whom a risk will fall in such a case can certainly negotiate to transfer the risk to the other party. But he may be deterred by the effect of even raising the issue on whether the negotiation will be successfully completed and on how profits will be divided. Thus, one can speak of a "burden of negotiation" that is very similar to a burden of proof.

[22] The problem of late or defective performance is not dealt with explicitly in this paper, but, as a "quality" of performance, can perhaps be assimilated theoretically to the manufacturer's problem of ensuring an adequate safety margin in number of production starts.

Assume that the entrepreneur markets with a known technology against a competitive market with a known constant price level. At the last step of the production effort, a fraction $(1 - \pi)$ of the products blow up, without creating further costs or leaving any recoverable value.[23] For the single firm,

$$P = \pi sn - nc_a(n).$$

Efforts will be made to produce n, but only πn of these will be marketable. It is evident that the optimal number to be started is $n = u(\pi s)$.

Suppose instead that production is contracted out and that only the manufacturer knows the details of the production problems, so that the manufacturer negotiates with knowledge of π while the entrepreneur lacks this knowledge and naively expects full performance. Suppose negotiation is over q (quantity sold) and p, the only variables known to the entrepreneur, and suppose further that the price p will be paid only for delivered items. The manufacturer knows of the casualties, however, and may start more than q in production (m). He also knows of a *legal* duty to pay damages d per unit for any shortfall. Thus, the two parties will enter negotiations with anticipated profit functions based on different understandings of the risk.

The question then becomes whether there is a way of establishing d—defined not by negotiation but as a matter of law—which leads the negotiations towards the optimal result.

$$P_e = sq - qp \text{ (as anticipated)};$$
$$P_m = \pi mp - d(q - \pi m) - mc_a(m).$$

It is clear that d and p will be present in the sum of these; hence the contract curve negotiated under the anticipated profit functions may not be vertical. Depending on the way the parties split the profits, they may then negotiate to a non-optimal level of production starts. It turns out, however, as shown in Appendix A to this paper, that, by setting $d = s - p$, an optimal production on the manufacturer's part is achieved, but the negotiations become indeterminate. Whatever the price, p, and quantity, q (within the contract zone), when this damage function is used, the optimal activity for the manufacturer is to start m items, where $m = u(\pi p + \pi d) = u(\pi s)$. The negotiations are indeterminate in the sense that the utility curves of manufacturer and entrepreneur become parallel. For any profit split, there is a curve of prices and quantities of equal appeal to each side. Different curves correspond to different profit splits. Through the dependence of damages on s, however, the manufacturer's expected profits depend on s and he is led to the optimum production start point for any p and q within the contract zone.[24]

[23] If a more realistic example is needed, one could have a predictable fraction $(1 - \pi)$ be rejected by quality inspectors.

[24] This is somewhat like the typical tort law products liability situation in which the

An alternative approach to casualty damages is to seek to use these damages as a tool to optimize the allocation of efforts to avoid casualties. It can be shown that this problem is solved by the same definition of damages

$$d = s - p.$$

The allocation of production efforts is optimized as well, and the negotiation is again indeterminate.

The measure of damages developed here is exactly the normal (buyer's expectation) legal measure of damages. It suffers—and the difficulty is fundamental as can be seen from the derivation—from the fact that damages involve s, a quantity which may not be known by the manufacturer. Because the negotiation has become indeterminate, it does not lead the manufacturer to the optimum automatically; to optimize properly, he must instead obtain additional information, here s, as a separate part of the negotiation.

Again, the common law has come close, although in part for rather different reasons. Seller's default raises several problems for courts. The failure of the contract may cause the failure of the buyer's enterprise, which was expected to cover the costs of the reliance and of the contract and to yield additional returns besides. Measurement of this enterprise expectation and of the associated reliance is difficult. There are questions of causality, as in the classical case of the horseshoe nail and the kingdom. Perhaps most seriously, the expectation doctrine, if not modified, may imply that large potential damages arise from a small contract. This seems inequitable to courts; the development of doctrines (such as that of certainty of damages) to limit these damages has been a recurrent judicial theme.

Of these doctrines, the most relevant one is that of *Hadley* v. *Baxendale*.[25] Defendant railroad had lost a mill shaft that it was shipping to the plaintiff's mill. Because of the loss, the mill was closed down for some days. Plaintiff sought to recover lost profits under the contract of carriage. The dilemmas are clear—to impose liability for these damages may require other railroad customers to bear costs that the mill could have prevented by holding an extra shaft in inventory; not to impose liability may require the mill to bear costs that the railroad could have prevented by using additional care.

The court's resolution is an ingenious one. The mill will receive these damages only if, at the time of contracting, it explained to the railroad the magnitude of risk that was at stake. This result effectively avoids the question of allocating a realized risk and replaces it by one of allocating efforts to

---

damages imposed on the manufacturer can lead him to an optimum level of effort to avoid the liability, even though the individual buyer is unaware of the risk involved and does not allow for it in his negotiation.

[25] 9 Exch. 341 (1854).

avoid the realization of the risk. More explicitly, the resolution assumes that certain risks are borne by each party as a "normal form" of the transaction. If any other risks are to be transferred, they must be considered explicitly during the negotiation. It can be assumed—if the negotiation operates as the rule anticipates—that the party undertaking to bear such atypical risks will charge an appropriate insurance premium and exercise appropriate extraordinary care in the execution of the transaction.

What is most interesting about this resolution is that in effect it rejects both the incentive-maintenance and the expectation-protection policies. It says, "If you are *really* concerned that the other party may dishonor the contract, you may have to pay him extra!" And it reaches that position in part on the basis of an assumption that default is no longer willful and in part on the basis of an underlying concern with what is ultimately an economic allocation issue. Its result is exactly the duty to inform required to give the seller guidance when the negotiation is indeterminate.

Hypothesis 4: Assuming that the seller knows of the risk at the time of entering upon the contract, damages in the event of casualty loss should be measured by full buyer's expectation, but disclosure of the magnitude of this expectation must be made to seller at the time of negotiation. Thus, the rule of *Hadley* v. *Baxendale* is economically correct in its reliance upon notice and information. Such notice is the only way that economic optima can be achieved, since the negotiation itself cannot serve as a mechanism for transmitting information with respect to the magnitude of the risk to be transferred. To the extent that reliance or other similar measures are often used in this situation, they are economically invalid, except as evidence of what the seller might reasonably have thought was at stake—but, if his thought is different from reality, his performance may still be suboptimal.

B. *Seller's Damages: Allocation of Market Risk*

The typical example of seller's damages arises when, most likely because of a market shift, the entrepreneur finds the enterprise unprofitable and seeks to rescind the contract.

The entrepreneur would normally bear the market risk, while the manufacturer would normally assume that the contract is firm. If the parties negotiate with these differing assumptions, the contract curve will be non-vertical, implying that the contract will sometimes be for a non-optimal quantity. The damage theory of this paper then asks whether there is a measure of damages that shifts the utility curves of the entrepreneur (who knows the size of the risk and can consider it in his optimization) in such a way that the contract curve is made vertical at the optimal point in spite of the manufacturer's continued ignorance. Then, the parties cannot help negotiating properly. For the example of the uncertain farmer described above, it is shown in Appendix B that this can be done by setting[26]

$$d = \frac{p\pi b}{\pi s - (1-\pi)b} = \frac{pb}{b + \frac{\partial c_t(n)}{\partial n}}.$$

This function will usually be a little greater than b, the classic measure of seller's reliance. Moreover, given the form of the expression, the question of the liability of the entrepreneur for seller's "lost profits" is avoided. For a very early stop (b near zero) damages are near zero also, so that lost profits are not paid. For a very late stop (b near p) damages become nearly equal to p, which would include profits.[27] These results are appealing.

The alternative approach is to use damages as a way of influencing the incentive to go on with the contract or to stop work where economically appropriate. A somewhat different model is necessary because the focus must be on changes in expectations during the course of performance, and on the conditions determining the time at which performance "should" (in an economic sense) be halted.

If activity is conducted by a single firm, that firm's anticipated profit, as defined at any time during the course of performance, can be stated:

$$P_c = s_c - (c_i + c_c) - (r_i + r_c),$$

where s, c, and r refer to market prices, cost, and reliance expenditures respectively, and where subscript i refers to costs already incurred and subscript c to market price at completion time as projected at any point and to costs or expenditures that must still be incurred in order to complete. Hence all of these amounts are considered to be variable functions of time.[28] If the firm stops work at any time, its profit (loss) is given by

$$-c_i - r_i.$$

Economic optimality requires that the firm go on to complete if and only if

[26] More than mathematical vagary underlies the substantial differences between this solution and that of the preceding section. Not only is the formula different, but the topology of what happens to the utility curves is different. The reason is that in the preceding section the optimization burden (which must go on the party conscious that he may default and be liable to pay damages) is being placed on a party without knowledge of the size of the losses to optimize against, while in this section that burden rests on the party who does have this knowledge.

[27] Note that under the model, $\partial c_t(n)/\partial n$ represents the marginal cost of the operations remaining at the time of possible default. Hence, the sum of $\partial c_t(n)/\partial n$ and b will be approximately constant as b varies, and will normally be less than p.

[28] They can also be considered to be already discounted at an appropriate interest rate.

its profit will be increased (or loss decreased) by completing. Assuming that all costs already incurred are irretrievably sunk, so that no mitigation is possible,[29] the condition for completing can be stated in terms of the difference between the two expressions:

$$s_e - c_e - r_e \geqslant 0 \qquad \text{Inequality 1}$$

If this inequality is satisfied, production should continue; if not, it should stop.

If the operation is now divided among two firms linked by contract, the same considerations still define whether it is optimal to complete performance or to terminate the contract. The question then becomes whether damage measures, d_m paid by manufacturer if he defaults and d_e paid by entrepreneur if he defaults, can be defined in such a way that they create an incentive to go ahead when the inequality is satisfied and to stop when it is not.

Each party will follow an analogous incentive pattern: he will go ahead if there is an increase in profits (or decrease in loss) compared with stopping, making allowance for damages. The inequalities, which hold when performance is to continue, are, for the manufacturer and entrepreneur respectively:

$$p - (c_l + c_e) \geqslant -(c_l + d_m) \text{ or } p - c_e \geqslant -d_m; \qquad \text{Inequality 2}$$

$$s_e - p - (r_l + r_e) \geqslant -(r_l + d_e) \text{ or } s_e - p - r_e \geqslant -d_e. \qquad \text{Inequality 3}$$

Treating the inequalities as equations and solving simultaneously, one is led to the following plausible measures, which do indeed solve the requirements just posed:

$$d_m = s_e - r_e - p$$

and

$$d_e = p - c_e.$$

The seller's damages are the traditional "sales price less cost to complete." The buyer's damages are lost profits from which expenditures already made in reliance are not deducted—in classical contract terms, both lost profits and lost reliance. This result is perhaps to be expected—an incentive-maintenance policy, being itself forward-looking, can consider only future expenditures and hence cannot consider sunk expenditures.[30]

Applying the second equation to the price change cases analyzed in the

[29] Presumably, the case in which mitigation is possible can be handled by considering the mitigation as an alternative performance to be compared with the planned performance on either a profit or a return-to-capital basis.

[30] Note that in the commodity sales case, $r_e = 0$, $c_e = s =$ market price of the commodity, and our equations yield the traditional measures of damage: $d_m = p - s$, $d_e = s - p$.

earlier part of this section, one can see the differences between the optimum-allocation and the incentive-maintenance approaches. The cost to complete is $c_a(n)$ (per unit). Hence, the damages under the incentive approach are $p - c_a(n)$. This bears no similarity to the formula for damages computed under the allocative approach. In fact, without assuming a form for the cost function, one cannot even say which measure is larger. Nevertheless, plausible situations can be described in which damages determined under the allocative rule are inadequate to provide an incentive to complete performance, and these situations are probably the most typical ones.[31] The existence of this situation may be one reason why business so strongly dislikes expectation damages (which may often be even bigger than incentive-maintenance damages).

Hypothesis 5: The two policies are inconsistent. ***It is impossible to define a single damage measure such that (a) optimal initial decisions are made while the ignorance of one party to the contract is accepted and (b) incentives to contract performance are appropriate.*** It is sometimes possible, however, to distinguish situations in which one of the damage approaches is better than another. For example, where initial planning is not feasible and where business custom does not support contract performance, the incentive approach might be better. Where planning is feasible and where contractual ethics are high, the allocative approach would be better. For contracts among businessmen, the latter situation probably is more common, so that the optimum-

[31] For example, assuming, as is normal, that marginal cost $\frac{\partial c_t(n)}{\partial n}$ is positive, one can assert that the incentive measure is greater than the allocative measure:

$$p - c_a(n) > \frac{pb}{\frac{\partial c_t(n)}{\partial n} + b}$$

provided

$$p\frac{\partial c_t(n)}{\partial n} - \left(\frac{\partial c_t(n)}{\partial n} + b\right) c_a(n) > 0.$$

(The assumption is needed to ensure that the inequality is not reversed through multiplication by a negative number.) If the original price p was set to cover all costs for the last unit produced (so $p > \frac{\partial c_t(n)}{\partial n} + b$) and marginal cost is greater than average cost (so $\partial c_t(n)/\partial n > c_a(n)$), this latter inequality will be satisfied. Thus under these restrictive but plausible assumptions, the level of seller's damages necessary to ensure correct incentives to the buyer to perform is greater than the level necessary to obtain correct allocation. Note that the restrictions as stated here are stronger than necessary to support the conclusion; hence the judgment is made in text that this situation is a typical one.

allocation approach should normally be adopted.[32] Reliance is placed on business ethics rather than on damage-law incentives.

Hence, one has finally:

Hypothesis 6: If a court concludes that the buyer should bear a particular risk, *the seller's damages should include his reliance costs plus a portion of expected profits varying from none to all depending on how far along seller is in performing the contract at the time of breach.*

IV. Conclusion

The policy of contract damages changes substantially as contract law makes the transition from market transactions to non-market transactions. In particular, the contract-enforcement policy becomes almost irrelevant as does the expectation policy. Instead, one is led to view damages as a substitute for negotiated liquidated-damages clauses that can be used when only one party is likely to be aware of the risks and to be able to make allocative decisions in view of the risks.

If damages in the non-market transaction are calculated in accordance with this policy, one is led to specific measures which are remarkably similar to those developed intuitively by courts but which also avoid the conceptual difficulties associated with the concept of expectation.

A. *Areas of Empirical Interest*

Nevertheless, two areas of possible deviation are suggested, each of which may be fertile for empirical research. The first is that of definition of the "normal" form of a contract—how to allocate the risks about which the contract is silent. There are problems when no custom is established or when different categories of contractors have different normal patterns. Poor performance by the courts here would be marked by increased transaction costs as shown by either lengthier forms and negotiations or price adjustments to cover the uncertain possibilities of adverse judgments. These effects might be observable through tracing contract forms and prices in particular markets, especially as new risks arise. For example, as courts place new consumer-oriented risks of tort liability on enterprises, how quickly is a clear-cut ultimate allocation of these costs worked out among the responsible entrepreneurs through contractually or judicially developed decisions for or against in-

[32] Skilled use of specific performance techniques might sometimes serve to accomplish the goals of the incentive approach while awarding damages under the allocation approach. There is no reason why damages cannot be used as a loss-allocating method at the same time that criteria based on factors other than the presence or absence of "damages" are used to make decisions as to whether further performance is to be imposed or excused.

demnification? Can prices or negotiating costs be shown to be affected by the uncertainties?

The second problem area derives more centrally from this paper. What does business do when caught in the bind suggested here between incentive-based and allocation-based damages? The clearest examples would be where a buyer and a seller possessed comparable bargaining power and financial responsibility, and where the seller faced a highly variable market. Certain supplier-manufacturer relationships and certain distribution relationships (such as a manufacturer dealing with a chain retailer) may meet these criteria. In such cases, legal damages, being closer to incentive-based damages, are probably too large for allocation purposes. One would then expect relatively unusual contractual phenomena such as efforts by the seller to obtain data about the ultimate market or elaborate excuse clauses. It may be that these are precisely the situations in which requirements contracts are common. Such contracts, which allow one party almost at will to define a quantity over a broad range, amount to flexible excuse clauses.

B. *Proposed Alternative Judicial Process*

The analysis of this paper also suggests a scheme for judicial decision-making in the commercial contract damages area:

(1) If the contract defines the relevant allocation of risks or measure of damages, the judge should enforce the contract as written.

(2) The judge should choose between allocative and incentive goals for the law of damages applicable to the particular kind of risk in the particular contract type. If incentive goals are paramount, the damage measure can be readily applied.

(3) If allocative goals are chosen, the judge should determine whether there is a reasonably established custom in the area. If there is, and if the custom does not unfairly impose a risk on a class of parties, the judge should accept the custom.

(4) If there is no custom, the judge should choose that party most able to manipulate the risk and to allocate in response to it, and place the burden of the risk on him.

(5) If the party bearing the risk will normally negotiate with access to data on the magnitude of the risk, he should be required to pay the other party's reliance costs plus a portion of profit depending on the portion of the contract completed at time of breach.

(6) If the party bearing the risk will not normally negotiate with access to data on the magnitude of the risk, he should be required to pay the other party's total losses resulting from those risks as to whose magnitude he was informed at the time of negotiating.

APPENDIX A

Optimal Allocation of Production Starting Level Under Casualty Risk

Use the model in text at page 294. Also, for completeness, include a reliance expenditure by the entrepreneur of r per unit sold. Assuming that it is evident that the integrated entrepreneur should incur this expense only for units expected to survive explosion, his profit function is

$$P = \pi sn - \pi rn - c_t(n). \tag{1}$$

It is evident that the optimal number to be started is

$$n = u(\pi s - \pi r).$$

Shifting now to the dual enterprises with reliance, the profit functions are

$$P_e = sq - qp - qr, \text{ and} \tag{2}$$

$$P_m = \pi mp - d(q - \pi m) - c_t(m). \tag{3}$$

The manufacturer will optimize on m in determining the best course of action vis-à-vis a particular p, q, and d:

$$\frac{\partial P_m}{\partial m} = \pi p + \pi d - \frac{\partial}{\partial m}[c_t(m)].$$

Hence, $m = u(\pi p + \pi d)$. (4)

Now, this must yield the same number of starts as the integrated operation, *i.e.*, d must be chosen so that $m = n$:

$$u(\pi p + \pi d) = u(\pi s - \pi r).$$

Assuming that u has appropriate and reasonable properties, equality of the functions can be obtained by equality of their arguments, yielding

$$d = s - p - r.$$

Thus

$$P_m = \pi mp - sq + pq + rq + \pi ms - \pi mp - \pi mr - c_t(m),$$

and

$$P_m + P_e = \pi ms - \pi mr - c_t(m),$$

which is exactly (1) with m substituted for n. From this equation, also, it can be seen that m can then be determined independently of p and q.

The negotiation becomes indeterminate, however:

$$P_m = -P_e + f(m, r, s, \pi).$$

Since m is independent of p and q, there is no unique contract curve. Through any point p, q, there is an entrepreneur's indifference curve, P_e. This curve is also a manufacturer's indifference curve $-P_e + f(m)$. Hence all points along the curve are equally acceptable to both parties. The damage measure relates p, s, and d and therefore m and q in such a way that values of p and q become irrelevant, except as a way to split the profit. Whatever values of p and q are negotiated, it is optimal for the manufacturer to start m items and then either receive the payments or pay damages under the contract. Thus, this measure of damages incorporates the market's behavior (and therefore requires the manufacturer to know s and r in order to optimize) in such a way that the market optimization problem is fully transferred to the manufacturer.

APPENDIX B

Market Risk Under Assumptions of Negotiation Misunderstanding

The model on page 288 of the text can be modified to reflect the anticipation on the entrepreneur-buyer's part that he will have to pay damages (instead of the price) in the event of contract cancellation, which will occur $(1-\pi)$ portion of the time:

$$P_e = \pi sn - \pi pn - d(1-\pi)n \tag{1}$$

$$P_m = pn - c_t(n) - nb. \tag{2}$$

The contract curve is the locus of all points p, n such that the slopes $\partial p/\partial n$ of the curves $P =$ constant and $P_m =$ constant are the same for the members of each family of curves passing through the point. There is no negotiation over d, which is set by law, but the fact that d may depend on p must be remembered in the differentiation. The first equation is solved for n, and differentiated with respect to p, yielding:

$$\frac{\partial n}{\partial p} = \frac{P_e}{[\pi s - \pi p - d(1-\pi)]^2}\left[\pi + (1-\pi)\frac{\partial d}{\partial p}\right].$$

The second equation is solved for p and differentiated with respect to n. By setting $\partial p/\partial n$ from it equal to the reciprocal of $\partial n/\partial p$ for the first equation, one obtains the locus of all points for which the slopes of the two sets of utility curves are equal. Substitution is also made for P_e and P_m, to ensure that slopes are compared for the particular curves passing through a point. The result,

$$\left[\pi b + \pi\frac{\partial c_t(n)}{\partial n} - \pi s\right] + (1-\pi)\,d + \left(b - p + \frac{\partial c_t(n)}{\partial n}\right)(1-\pi)\frac{\partial d}{\partial p} = 0, \tag{3}$$

is the equation of the contract line. For it to direct negotiations to the optimum, it must at the very least be vertical, *i.e.*, the coefficient of p must be zero:

$$d(1-\pi) - p(1-\pi)\frac{\partial d}{\partial p} = 0.$$

This is now an elementary differential equation whose general solution is $d = kp$, where k is an arbitrary number. For any damage function of this form, the contract curve will be vertical.

The next step is to choose that k which selects the optimum vertical contract curve, *i.e.*, the one for which

$$\frac{\partial c_t(n)}{\partial n} = \frac{\pi s - b}{\pi}. \tag{3a}$$

(This is taken from the text at page 288.) To do so, this equation and $d = kp$ are substituted into equation (3) to yield

$$k = \frac{b}{b + \dfrac{\pi s - b}{\pi}} = \frac{\pi b}{\pi s - (1 - \pi)b}.$$

Hence, by choosing as a measure of damages

$$d = kp = \frac{\pi p b}{\pi s - (1 - \pi)b},$$

selection of the optimum vertical contract curve is ensured. The intuitive meaning of this expression is not immediately clear. Under practical conditions, π will be quite near 1, and $s > b$. Hence $\pi s - (1 - \pi)b$ will be slightly less than s. Since p is also likely to be slightly less than s, d is approximately equal to b, the normal reliance measure of damages.

Note also that π can be eliminated, using equation (3a), to yield

$$d = \frac{pb}{\dfrac{\partial c_t(n)}{\partial n} + b}.$$

Since the manufacturer will normally not enter the contract unless $p > \dfrac{\partial c_t(n)}{\partial n} + b$, this form suggests further that the defined damage measure is likely to be greater than reliance damages.

[15]

MISTAKE, DISCLOSURE, INFORMATION, AND THE LAW OF CONTRACTS*

*ANTHONY T. KRONMAN***

"[The greater part of the writers on natural law] are of opinion, that the good faith which ought to govern the contract of sale, only requires that the vendor should represent the thing sold as it is, without dissimulating its defects, and not to sell it above the price which it bears at the time of the contract; that he commits no injustice in selling it at this price, although he knows that the price must soon fall; that he is not obliged to disclose to the vendee a knowledge which he may have of the circumstances that may produce a depression of the price; the vendee having no more right to demand that the vendor should impart this knowledge than that he should give away his property. . ."

Pothier, *Traité du Contract de Vente****

Introduction

THIS paper attempts to explain an apparent inconsistency in the law of contracts. On the one hand, there are many contract cases—generally classified under the rubric of unilateral mistake—which hold that a promisor is excused from his obligation to either perform or pay damages when he is mistaken about some important fact and his error is known (or should be known) to the other party. On the other hand, cases may also be found which state that in some circumstances one party to a contract is entitled to withhold information he knows the other party lacks. These latter cases typically rest upon the proposition that the party with knowledge does not owe the other party a "duty of disclosure."

Although these two lines of cases employ different doctrinal techniques, they both address essentially the same question: if one party to a contract knows or has reason to know that the other party is mistaken about a

* I would like to thank Gerhard Casper, Richard Epstein, Walter Hellerstein, Thomas Jackson, Edmund Kitch, William Landes, Richard Posner, George Priest, and George Stigler for their helpful comments on an earlier draft of this paper. Work on this paper was made possible by a grant from the Charles R. Walgreen Foundation.

** Assistant Professor of Law, University of Chicago Law School.

*** As quoted in Laidlaw v. Organ, 15 U.S. (2 Wheat.) 187-88, note b.

particular fact, does the knowledgeable party have a duty to speak up or may he remain silent and capitalize on the other party's error? The aim of this paper is to provide a theory which will explain why some contract cases impose such a duty and others do not.

The paper is divided into three parts. In the first part, I discuss the problem of unilateral mistake and offer an economic justification for the rule that a unilaterally mistaken promisor is excused when his error is known or should be known to the other party. In the second part of the paper, I propose a distinction between two kinds of information—information which is the result of a deliberate search and information which has been casually acquired. I argue that a legal privilege of nondisclosure is in effect a property right and attempt to show that where special knowledge or information is the fruit of a deliberate search the assignment of a property right of this sort is required in order to insure production of the information at a socially desirable level. I then attempt to show that a distinction between deliberately and casually accquired information is useful in explaining why disclosure is required in some contract cases but not in others.

In the third, and concluding, part of the paper, I return briefly to the problem of unilateral mistake, in order to reconcile the apparent conflict between the two lines of cases described above. I argue that this apparent conflict disappears when the unilateral mistake cases are viewed from the perspective developed in the second part of the paper.

I. Mistake and the Allocation of Risk.

Every contractual agreement is predicated upon a number of factual assumptions about the world. Some of these assumptions are shared by the parties to the contract and some are not. It is always possible that a particular factual assumption is mistaken.[1] From an economic point of view, the risk of such a mistake (whether it be the mistake of only one party or both) represents a cost.[2] It is a cost to the contracting parties themselves and to

[1] In a strictly economic sense, not all predictive errors are mistakes. An individual may fail to correctly predict a particular outcome merely because his knowledge of the world is incomplete. But unless it would be cost-justified for him to reduce the incompleteness of his knowledge by acquiring new information about the world, it would be incorrect—from an economic point of view—to regard a predictive error of this sort as a genuine mistake. An economist would be likely to define a mistake as an error in prediction resulting from a state of uncertainty which the mistaken party himself would agree could have been cured at a reasonable cost (by augmenting his knowledge of the world). In ordinary parlance, however, the term "mistake" is often used in a much broader sense to mean simply an error which would not have been made if the mistaken party's knowledge of the world had been more complete. It is in this ordinary sense that I use the term here.

[2] Traditionally, academic writers have urged that a variety of different factors be considered in deciding when to excuse a mistaken promisor. The following have been thought especially important: 1) the "nature" of the mistake: Samuel Williston, 13 A Treatise on the Law of

society as a whole since the actual occurrence of a mistake always (potentially) increases the resources which must be devoted to the process of allocating goods to their highest-valuing users.

There are basically two ways in which this particular cost can be reduced to an optimal level. First, one or both of the parties can take steps to prevent the mistake from occurring. Second, to the extent a mistake cannot be prevented, either party (or both) can insure against the risk of its occurrence

Contracts §§ 1544, 1569, 1570 (3d ed. 1970 [hereinafter cited as Williston]; Arthur Linton Corbin, 3 Corbin on Contracts § 597 (1960) [hereinafter cited as Corbin]; Restatement of Restitution § 9, comment c, § 16, comment c (1937); Restatement of Contracts § 502 (1932); 2) the likelihood of unjust enrichment if the promise is enforced: James Bradley Thayer, Unilateral Mistake and Unjust Enrichment as a Ground for the Avoidance of Legal Transactions, in Harvard Legal Essays 467-99 (1934); George E. Palmer, Mistake and Unjust Enrichment 8, 53, 96 (1962) [hereinafter cited as Palmer]; 3) the magnitude of the promisor's potential loss: Warren A. Seavey, Problems in Restitution, 7 Okla. L. Rev. 257, 267 (1954); Edward H. Rabin, A Proposed Black-Letter Rule Concerning Mistaken Assumptions in Bargaining Transactions, 45 Tex. L. Rev. 1273, 1288-91 (1967) [hereinafter cited as Rabin]; 4) the difficulty of compensating the promisee for any costs he may have incurred in reliance on the promise: Annot., 59 A.L.R. 809 (1929); Rabin at 1299; and 5) the allocation—to one party or the other—of the risk of the mistake: Rabin at 1292-94; Richard A. Posner, Economic Analysis of Law, 73-74 (2d ed. 1977) [hereinafter cited as Posner].

It has usually been assumed that each of these factors ought to be given some unspecifiable weight in deciding when to excuse a mistaken promisor. See Rabin at 1275. Recent treatments of mistake, however, particularly emphasize the importance of determining which party to the contract bears the risk of the mistake in question. This tendency to emphasize the importance of risk-allocation is quite apparent, for example, in the proposed chapter on mistake in the Second Restatement of Contracts. See Restatement (Second) of Contracts §§ 294-96 and Introductory Note (Tent. Draft No. 10, 1975).

The idea that the law often performs a risk-allocating function is of course not a new one. See Edwin W. Patterson, The Apportionment of Business Risks Through Legal Devices, 24 Colum. L. Rev. 335 (1924). But a growing and increasingly sophisticated literature on the subject has deepened our understanding of the concept of risk and has refined its use as an analytical tool. See, for example, Richard A. Posner & Andrew M. Rosenfield, Impossibility and Related Doctrines in Contract Law: An Economic Analysis, 6 J. Leg. Studies 83 (1977); Stephen S. Ashley, The Economic Implications of the Doctrine of Impossibility, 26 Hastings L. J. 1251 (1975); Paul L. Joskow, Commercial Impossibility, The Uranium Market and the Westinghouse Case, 6 J. Leg. Studies 119 (1977); Posner at 73-74; John P. Brown, Product Liability: The Case of an Asset with a Random Life, 64 Am. Econ. Rev. 149 (1974); Alan Schwartz, Sales Law and Inflations, 50 S. Cal. L. Rev. 1 (1976); Kenneth J. Arrow, Insurance, Risk and Resource Allocation, in Theory of Risk-Bearing (1971). An older, but useful, book is Charles O. Hardy, Risk and Risk-Bearing (1923).

As yet, no one has employed the idea of risk-allocation to give a systematic account of the law of mistake as a whole. Posner and Rosenfield, however, offer such an account of the closely allied problems of impossibility and frustration. A theory of mistake based upon the notion of risk-allocation may easily be constructed by generalizing from what has already been said about these related subjects.

Since it rests upon the principle of efficiency and is inspired by the work of scholars writing in the so-called "law and economics" field, I often characterize the point of view adopted in this paper as the "economic" point of view. There is, of course, much more to the economic theory of law in general and contract law in particular than the notion of risk-allocation. See, for example, Posner at 65-69, and Richard A. Posner, Gratuitous Promises in Economics and Law, 6 J. Leg. Studies 411 (1977).

by purchasing insurance from a professional insurer or by self-insuring.[3]

In what follows, I shall be concerned exclusively with the prevention of mistakes. Although this limitation might appear arbitrary, it is warranted by the fact that most mistake cases involve errors which can be prevented at a reasonable cost. Where a risk cannot be prevented at a reasonable cost—which is true of many of the risks associated with what the law calls "supervening impossibilities"—insurance is the only effective means of risk reduction. (This is why the concept of insurance unavoidably plays a more prominent role in the treatment of impossibility than it does in the analysis of mistake.)[4]

Information is the antidote to mistake. Although information is costly to produce,[5] one individual may be able to obtain relevant information more cheaply than another. If the parties to a contract are acting rationally, they will minimize the joint costs of a potential mistake by assigning the risk of its occurrence to the party who is the better (cheaper) information-gatherer. Where the parties have actually assigned the risk—whether explicitly, or implicitly through their adherence to trade custom and past patterns of dealing—their own allocation must be respected.[6] Where they have not—and there is a resulting gap in the contract[7]—a court concerned with economic efficiency should impose the risk on the better information-gatherer. This is so for familiar reasons: by allocating the risk in this way, an

[3] Posner, *supra* note 2, at 74-79; Richard A. Posner & Andrew M. Rosenfield, *supra* note 2.

[4] Many of the events which constitute supervening impossibilities cannot be prevented at a reasonable cost by either contracting party. For example, it is impossible to prevent the outbreak of war (Paradine v. Jane, 82 Eng. Rep. 897 (K.B., 1647), Société Franco Tunisienne d'Armement v. Sidermar S.P.A., [1961] 2 Q.B. 278), a crop failure (Howell v. Coupland, [1874] 9 Q.B. 462, Anderson v. May, 50 Minn. 280, 52 N.W. 530 (1892)), the establishment of a government regulation (Lloyd v. Murphy, 25 Cal. 2d 48, 153 P.2d 47 (1944)), or the cancellation of a coronation parade (Krell v. Henry, [1903] 2 K.B. 740 (C.A.)). Where an event cannot be prevented from occurring, the risk of its occurrence can be effectively reduced only through insurance. This is the principal reason why insurance plays a more important role in impossibility cases than it does in dealing with mistake. Richard A. Posner & Andrew M. Rosenfield, *supra* note 2, at 91.

[5] George J. Stigler, The Economics of Information, 69 J. Pol. Econ. 213 (1961), reprinted in The Organization of Industry 171 (1968).

[6] For a discussion of the way in which trade customs may affect the allocation of risk, see Harold J. Berman, Excuse for Nonperformance in the Light of Contract Practices in International Trade, 63 Colum. L. Rev. 1413 (1963), and Note, Custom and Trade Usages: Its Application to Commercial Dealings and the Common Law, 55 Colum. L. Rev. 1192 (1955).

[7] Whether such a gap exists will depend upon the intentions of the parties as reconstructed by a process of judicial interpretation. The fact that a contract does not cover a particular point explicitly does not mean that the parties failed to reach an understanding with respect to the point in question. Only if no such understanding exists can the contract be said to contain a genuine gap or lacuna. The difficult problems of interpretation which are involved in identifying and then filling gaps are explored in two articles by Professor Farnsworth. See E. Allen Farnsworth, "Meaning" in the Law of Contracts, 76 Yale L.J. 939 (1967), and *id.*, Disputes Over Omissions in Contracts, 68 Colum. L. Rev. 860 (1968).

efficiency-minded court reduces the transaction costs of the contracting process itself.[8]

The most important doctrinal distinction in the law of mistake is the one drawn between "mutual" and "unilateral" mistakes. Traditionally, courts have been more reluctant to excuse a mistaken promisor where he alone is mistaken than where the other party is mistaken as to the same fact.[9] Although relief for unilateral mistake has been liberalized during the last half-century[10] (to the point where some commentators have questioned the utility of the distinction between unilateral and mutual mistake and a few have even urged its abolition),[11] it is still "black-letter" law that a promisor whose mistake is not shared by the other party is less likely to be relieved of his duty to perform than a promisor whose mistake happens to be mutual.[12]

Viewed broadly, the distinction between mutual and unilateral mistake makes sense from an economic point of view. Where both parties to a contract are mistaken about the same fact or state of affairs, deciding which of them would have been better able to prevent the mistake may well require a detailed inquiry regarding the nature of the mistake and the (economic) role or position of each of the parties involved.[13] But where only one party is mistaken, it is reasonable to assume that he is in a better position than the other party to prevent his own error. As we shall see, this is not true in every case, but it provides a useful beginning point for analysis and helps to explain the generic difference between mutual and unilateral mistakes.

The case of *Bowser v. Hamilton Glass Co.*[14] provides a simple illustration. In *Bowser*, the plaintiff was a contractor working on a government project. He solicited bids from subcontractors for the production, among other things, of "variable reflector glasses." In response to the solicitation, the defendant submitted a bid of $.22 each for 1,400 glasses. The plaintiff sent the defendant a formal "purchase order," which constituted his offer to enter a binding contract. Detailed specifications and blueprints were attached to the purchase order. The defendant acknowledged receipt of the purchase

[8] Posner, *supra* note 2, at 74-79; Richard A. Posner & Andrew M. Rosenfield, *supra* note 2, at 88-89.

[9] Restatement (Second) of Contracts, § 295, Comment A (Tent. Draft No. 10, 1975).

[10] *Id.*

[11] 3 Corbin, *supra* note 2, at § 608; Palmer, *supra* note 2, at 67, 96-98; Rabin, *supra* note 2, at 1277-79.

[12] Although it liberalizes relief for unilateral mistake, the Second Restatement of Contracts preserves the basic doctrinal distinction between unilateral and mutual mistake, and makes relief less freely available in the former case than in the latter. In this regard, compare Restatement (Second) of Contracts, §§ 294-95 (Tent. Draft No. 10, 1975) with Restatement of Contracts §§ 502-03 (1932).

[13] Professor Posner's discussion of Sherwood v. Walker illustrates this point. See Posner, *supra* note 2.

[14] 207 F.2d 341 (7th Cir. 1953).

order and produced the glasses. Upon learning that the finished glasses did not conform to the contract specifications, the defendant informed the plaintiff that it would "cancel" the agreement. The plaintiff obtained the glasses from another manufacturer and sued to recover the difference between what it eventually had to pay for them and what it had agreed to pay the defendant. The defendant asserted that it had been mistaken as to the nature of the goods to be produced. The court, in holding for the plaintiff, said that the defendant's mistake did not justify relief, asserting that a unilateral mistake will excuse only where it is known to the other party.

Clearly, the result in *Bowser* makes economic sense. The defendant was in the best position to guard against his own mistake by carefully reading the specifications and examining the blueprints. Although the plaintiff could have prevented the mistake by acquiring the necessary expertise himself, by supervising the defendant's own initial reading of the proposed contract, and by periodically checking to make sure that the produced goods conformed to the contract specifications, it would have been very expensive for him to do so. The joint costs of an error of this sort are minimized by putting the risk of the mistake on the mistaken party. This is the solution the parties themselves would have agreed to if they had been made aware of the risk at the time the contract was formed. It is also the solution which is optimal from a social point of view.

In the past, it was often asserted that, absent fraud or misrepresentation, a unilateral mistake never justifies excusing the mistaken party from his duty to perform or pay damages.[15] This is certainly no longer the law, and Corbin has demonstrated that in all probability it never was.[16] One well-established exception protects the unilaterally mistaken promisor whose error is known or reasonably should be known to the other party.[17] Relief has long been available in this case despite the fact that the promisor's mistake is not shared by the other party to the contract.

For example, if a bidder submits a bid containing a clerical error or miscalculation, and the mistake is either evident on the face of the bid or may reasonably be inferred from a discrepancy between it and other bids, the bidder will typically be permitted to withdraw the bid without having to

[15] 3 Corbin, *supra* note 2, at § 608; Restatement of Contracts § 503 (1932).

[16] 3 Corbin, *supra* note 2, at § 608; "Statements are exceedingly common, both in texts and in court opinions, that relief will not be given on the ground of mistake unless the mistake is 'mutual'. Such a broad generalization is untrue. Seldom is it accompanied by either definition or analysis . . . Cases do not always submit to be classified with either 'mutual mistake' or 'unilateral mistake'. And even when they do submit, the solution does not mechanically follow in accordance with a separate set of rules for each class. Very often relief has been and will be granted where the mistake is unilateral."

[17] 3 Corbin, *supra* note 2, at § 610; Benedict I. Lubell, Unilateral Palpable and Impalpable Mistake in Construction Contracts, 16 Minn. L. Rev. 137 (1932) [hereinafter cited as Lubell]; Rabin, *supra* note 2, at 1279-81.

pay damages (even after the bid has been accepted and in some cases relied upon by the other party).[18] Or, to take another example, suppose that *A* submits a proposed contract in writing to *B* and knows that *B* has misread the document. If *B* accepts the proposed contract, upon discovering his error, he may avoid his obligations under the contract and has no duty to compensate *A* for *A*'s lost expectation.[19] A closely related situation involves the offer which is "too good to be true." One receiving such an offer cannot "snap it up"; if he does so, the offeror may withdraw the offer despite the fact that it has been accepted.[20]

In each of the cases just described, one party is mistaken and the other has actual knowledge or reason to know of his mistake. The mistaken party in each case is excused from meeting any contractual obligations owed to the party with knowledge.

A rule of this sort is a sensible one. While it is true that in each of the cases just described the mistaken party is likely to be the one best able to prevent the mistake from occurring in the first place (by exercising care in preparing his bid or in reading the proposed contract which has been submitted to him), the other party may be able to rectify the mistake more cheaply in the interim between its occurrence and the formation of the contract. At one moment in time the mistaken party is the better mistake-preventer (information-gatherer). At some subsequent moment, however, the other

[18] "Suppose, first, a case in which a bidding contractor makes an offer to supply specified goods or to do specified work for a definitely named price, and that he was caused to name this price by an antecedent error of computation. If, before acceptance, the offeree knows, or has reason to know, that a material error has been made, he is seldom mean enough to accept; and if he does accept, the courts have no difficulty in throwing him out. He is not permitted 'to snap up' such an offer and profit thereby." 3 Corbin, *supra* note 2, at § 609. For a case in which a bidding contractor was permitted to withdraw his bid despite acceptance *and reliance* by the party to whom it was submitted, see Union Tank Car Co. v. Wheat Brothers, 15 Utah 2d 101, 387 P.2d 1000 (1964).

It would be irrational from an economic point of view to permit the party with knowledge (or reason to know) of the mistake to enforce the other party's promise on reliance grounds. A rule of this sort would encourage reliance precisely where it ought to be discouraged.

If the non-mistaken party has *no reason to know* of the error, however, the extent of his reliance is often a factor in determining the damages to which he is entitled. If he has substantially relied on the mistaken party's promise, the non-mistaken party will usually be given the right to enforce the contract (by suing to recover his lost expectation). If, on the other hand, the non-mistaken party has not substantially relied on the promise before the error is discovered, courts will often allow the mistaken party to withdraw from the contract on the condition that he compensate the non-mistaken party for any reliance expenses or incidental costs he has incurred (such as having to solicit new bids).

[19] 3 Corbin, *supra* note 2, at § 607; Williston, *supra* note 2, at § 1577. See also Restatement of Contracts § 505, Comment A (1932) (dealing with the mistaken party's right to have the contract reformed).

[20] 1 Williston, *supra* note 2, at § 94. See Bell v. Carroll, 212 Ky. 231, 278 S.W. 541 (1925), Germain Fruit Co. v. Western Union Tel Co., 137 Cal. 598, 70 P. 658 (1902), United States v. Braunstein, 75 F. Supp. 137 (S.D.N.Y. 1947).

party may be the better preventer because of his superior access to relevant information that will disclose the mistake and thus allow its correction. This may be so, for example, if he has other bids to compare with the mistaken one since this will provide him with information which the bidder himself lacks.[21] Of course, if the mistake is one which cannot reasonably be known by the non-mistaken party (that is, if he would have to incur substantial costs in order to discover it), there is no reason to assume that the non-mistaken party is the better (more efficient) mistake-preventer at the time the contract is executed. But if the mistake is actually known or could be discovered at a very slight cost, the principle of efficiency is best served by a compound liability rule which imposes initial responsibility for the mistake on the mistaken party but shifts liability to the other party if he has actual knowledge or reason to know of the error. Compound liability rules of this sort are familiar in other areas of the law: the tort doctrine of "last clear chance" is one example.[22]

The cases in which relief is granted to a unilaterally mistaken promisor on the grounds that his mistake was known or reasonably knowable by the other party appear, however, to conflict sharply with another line of cases. These cases deal with the related problems of fraud and disclosure: if one party to a contract knows that the other is mistaken as to some material fact, is it fraud for the party with knowledge to fail to disclose the error and may the mistaken party avoid the contract on the theory that he was owed a duty of disclosure?[23] This question is not always answered in the same way. In some cases, courts typically find a duty to disclose and in others they do not.[24] It is the latter group of cases—those not requiring disclosure—which

[21] See Lubell, *supra* note 17, at 147-54.

[22] See Richard A. Posner, A Theory of Negligence, 1 J. Leg. Studies 29, 58 (1972); Charles O. Gregory, Harry Kalven, Jr., & Richard A. Epstein, Cases and Materials on Torts, 400-06 (3d ed. 1977). It might be argued that a compound liability rule of this sort will encourage the mistaken party to reduce his own initial investment in mistake prevention. This may be true to a limited extent. But since the (potentially) mistaken party has no way of knowing whether any mistake he might make would be known or reasonably knowable by the other party, he takes a substantial risk in reducing the level of his own efforts at mistake prevention. The larger this risk, the smaller his reduction will be. For a general discussion of how liability rules affect individual behavior and accident prevention in the context of a single activity, see Peter A. Diamond, Single Activity Accidents, 3 J. Leg. Studies 107 (1974).

[23] Although the nondisclosure cases are often discussed in connection with the problem of unilateral mistake, the relation between the doctrines of nondisclosure and mistake has frequently puzzled commentators. Thus, in a classic article one commentator writes: "A case of some difficulty arises where the unilateral mistake is known to the other party and he joins in the formation of the contract with the mistake uncorrected. The question of how far he is under a duty to disclose his superior knowledge is determined by principles of the law other than those we have under discussion [that is, the principles of mistake], and where there is such a duty to disclose and failure to observe it, there is generally a case of fraud." Roland R. Foulke, Mistake in the Formation and Performance of a Contract, 11 Colum. L. Rev. 197, 229 (1911). See also Rabin, *supra* note 2, at 1279; Palmer, *supra* note 2, at 80-89.

[24] 12 Williston, *supra* note 2, at §§ 1497-99. See text at notes 49-76 *infra*.

appear to conflict with the rule that a unilateral mistake will excuse if the other party knows or has reason to know of its existence.

In the cases not requiring disclosure, one party is mistaken and the other party knows or has reason to know it. Can these cases be reconciled with those which stand for the proposition that a unilateral mistake plus knowledge or reason to know will excuse the mistaken party? More particularly, can the apparent divergence between these two lines of cases be explained on economic grounds?

The rest of this paper is devoted to answering these two questions. In brief, the answer I propose is as follows. Where nondisclosure is permitted (or put differently, where the knowledgeable party's contract rights are enforced despite his failure to disclose a known mistake), the knowledge involved is typically the product of a costly search. A rule permitting nondisclosure is the only effective way of providing an incentive to invest in the production of such knowledge. By contrast, in the cases requiring disclosure,[25] and in those excusing a unilaterally mistaken promisor because the other party knew or had reason to know of his error, the knowledgeable party's special information is typically not the fruit of a deliberate search. Although information of this sort is socially useful as well, a disclosure requirement will not cause a sharp reduction in the amount of such information which is actually produced. If one takes into account the investment costs incurred in the deliberate production of information, the two apparently divergent lines of cases described above may both be seen as conforming (roughly) to the principle of efficiency, which requires that the risk of a unilateral mistake be placed on the most effective risk-preventer.

II. The Production of Information and the Duty to Disclose

A. *General Considerations*

It is appropriate to begin a discussion of fraud and nondisclosure in contract law with the celebrated case of *Laidlaw v. Organ*.[26] Organ was a New Orleans commission merchant engaged in the purchase and sale of tobacco.

[25] Although throughout the paper I use the expression "duty to disclose," the duty involved is typically not a true legal obligation. If the party with knowledge fails to disclose the other party's error, his failure to do so will give the mistaken party grounds for avoiding any contract which has been concluded between them. In the absence of such a contract, however, the knowing party has no positive duty to disclose—that is, nondisclosure will not by itself give the mistaken party the right to sue him for damages. Of course, in some cases—for example, where there is a fiduciary relation between the parties—a positive duty of this latter sort may exist. Where it does, a failure to disclose is not simply a defense to the knowing party's suit to enforce the other party's contractual obligations; it also provides the mistaken party with an independent cause of action for damages.

[26] Laidlaw v. Organ, 15 U.S. (2 Wheat.) 178.

Early on the morning of February 19, 1815, he was informed by a Mr. Shepherd that a peace treaty had been signed at Ghent by American and British officers, formally ending the War of 1812. Mr. Shepherd (who was himself interested in the profits of the transaction involved in *Laidlaw v. Organ*) had obtained information regarding the treaty from his brother who, along with two other gentlemen, brought the news from the British Fleet. (What Shepherd's brother and his companions were doing with the British Fleet is not disclosed.)

Knowledge of the treaty was made public in a handbill circulated around eight o'clock on the morning of the nineteenth. However, before the treaty's existence had been publicized ("soon after sunrise" according to the reported version of the case), Organ, knowing of the treaty, called on a representative of the Laidlaw firm and entered into a contract for the purchase of 111 hogsheads of tobacco. Before agreeing to sell the tobacco, the Laidlaw representative "asked if there was any news which was calculated to enhance the price or value of the article about to be purchased." It is unclear what response, if any, Organ made to this inquiry.[27]

As a result of the news of the treaty—which signalled an end to the naval blockade of New Orleans—the market price of tobacco quickly rose by 30 to 50 percent. Laidlaw refused to deliver the tobacco as he had originally promised. Organ subsequently brought suit to recover damages and to block Laidlaw from otherwise disposing of the goods in controversy. Although the report of the case is unclear, it appears that the trial judge directed a verdict in Organ's favor. The case was appealed to the United States Supreme Court which in an opinion by Chief Justice Marshall remanded with directions for a new trial. The Court concluded that the question "whether any imposition was practiced by the vendee upon the vendor ought to have been submitted to the jury" and that as a result "the absolute instruction of the judge was erroneous." Marshall's opinion is more famous, however, for its dictum than for its holding:

> The question in this case is, whether the intelligence of extrinsic circumstances, which might influence the price of the commodity, and which was exclusively within the knowledge of the vendee, ought to have been communicated by him to the vendor? The court is of opinion that he was not bound to communicate it. It would be difficult to circumscribe the contrary doctrine within proper limits, where the means of intelligence are equally accessible to both parties. But at the same time, each party must take care not to say or do anything tending to impose upon the other.

[27] If Organ denied that he had heard any news of this sort, he would have committed a fraud. It may even be, in light of Laidlaw's direct question, that silence on Organ's part was fraudulent. William W. Story, A Treatise on the Law of Contracts 444 n.2 (2d ed. 1847). In my discussion of the case, and of the general rule which Marshall lays down in his famous dictum, I have put aside any question of fraud on Organ's part. See note 49 *infra*.

Although Marshall's dictum in *Laidlaw v. Organ* has been sharply criticized,[28] it is still generally regarded as an accurate statement of the law (when properly interpreted).[29] The broad rule which Marshall endorses has usually been justified on three related grounds: that it conforms to the legitimate expectations of commercial parties and thus accurately reflects the (harsh) morality of the marketplace;[30] that in a contract for the sale of goods each party takes the risk that his own evaluation of the worth of the goods may be erroneous;[31] or finally, that it justly rewards the intelligence and industry of the party with special knowledge (in this case, the buyer).[32] This last idea may be elaborated in the following way.

News of the treaty of Ghent affected the price of tobacco in New Orleans. Price measures the relative value of commodities: information regarding the treaty revealed a new state of affairs in which the value of tobacco—relative to other goods and to tobacco-substitutes in particular—had altered.[33] An alteration of this sort is almost certain to affect the allocation of social resources.[34] If the price of tobacco to suppliers rises, for example, farmers will be encouraged to plant more tobacco and tobacco merchants may be prepared to pay more to get their goods to and from market. In this way, the

[28] See, for example, Palmer, *supra* note 2, at 84.

[29] 12 Williston, *supra* note 2, at § 1497; Restatement of Contracts § 472, Comment B (1932); Rabin, *supra* note 2, at 1279; W. Page Keeton, Fraud—Concealment and Non-Disclosure, 15 Tex. L. Rev. 1, 21-23 (1936) [hereinafter cited as Keeton]; Edwin W. Patterson, Essentials of Insurance Law 447 (1957).

[30] Classic statements of this idea may be found in William W. Story, *supra* note 27, at 442-43, and James Kent, 2 Commentaries §§ 484, 485 (12th ed. 1873).

[31] "If in an arm's-length bargaining transaction A has assumed the risk concerning the existence or nonexistence of certain facts, and he is mistaken concerning these facts, and there has been no fraud or imposition, A will not be able to rescind his contract, regardless of B's knowledge of A's mistake" [citing Laidlaw v. Organ, 15 U.S. (2 Wheat.) 178 (1817)]. Rabin, *supra* note 2, at 1279.

[32] In his excellent law review article on fraud and nondisclosure, Professor Keeton draws attention to the fact that courts, in deciding when to impose a duty to disclose special information, have been influenced by the way in which the information was acquired. At one point, for example, he states that "the way in which the buyer acquires the information which he conceals from the vendor should be a material circumstance. The information might have been acquired as a result of his bringing to bear a superior knowledge, intelligence, skill or technical judgment; it might have been acquired by mere chance; or it might have been acquired by means of some tortious action on his part." Keeton, *supra* note 29, at 25. The main purpose of the present article is to develop this distinction between different kinds of information in a more rigorous fashion, to justify the distinction on economic grounds, and to demonstrate its explanatory power as a principle for ordering the disclosure cases.

[33] See generally Jack Hirshleifer, The Private and Social Value of Information and the Reward to Inventive Activity, 61 Am. Econ. Rev. 561 (1977) [hereinafter cited as Hirshleifer].

[34] This will not be true in a regime of "pure exchange," that is, in a regime where goods are only exchanged and not produced (the pool of exchanged goods remaining constant). In "the more realistic regime in which production and exchange both take place," however, information of the sort involved in Laidlaw v. Organ will have allocative consequences. Hirshleifer, *supra* note 33, at 566-67.

proportion of society's (limited) resources devoted to the production and transportation of tobacco will be increased. Information revealing a change in circumstances which alters the relative value of a particular commodity will always have some (perhaps unmeasurable) allocative impact. (In addition, of course, information of this sort will have distributive consequences: the owners of tobacco or of rights to tobacco will be relatively wealthier after the price rise, assuming that other prices have not risen or have not risen as fast.)

From a social point of view, it is desirable that information which reveals a change in circumstances affecting the relative value of commodities reach the market as quickly as possible (or put differently, that the time between the change itself and its comprehension and assessment be minimized).[35] If a farmer who would have planted tobacco had he known of the change plants peanuts instead, he will have to choose between either uprooting one crop and substituting another (which may be prohibitively expensive and will in any case be costly), or devoting his land to a nonoptimal use. In either case, both the individual farmer and society as a whole will be worse off than if he had planted tobacco to begin with. The sooner information of the change reaches the farmer, the less likely it is that social resources will be wasted.

Consider another (and perhaps more realistic) illustration of the same point. *A* is a shipowner who normally transports goods between New Orleans and various other ports. However, because of the naval blockade, he is unable to enter the New Orleans harbor. Some time after the treaty is signed, but before its existence is publicized, *A* enters a contract to ship cotton from Savannah to New York City. After news of the treaty reaches New Orleans, a tobacco merchant in that city offers *A* a "bonus" if he will agree to deliver a shipment of tobacco to Baltimore. If we assume that the offer is sufficiently attractive to induce *A* to breach his first contract and pay damages,[36] although his ship will be properly allocated to its highest-valuing

[35] "To gain an advantage from better knowledge of facilities of communication or transport is sometimes regarded as almost dishonest, although it is quite as important that society make use of the best opportunities in this respect as in using the latest scientific discoveries. This prejudice has in a considerable measure affected the attitude toward commerce in general compared with that toward production. Even economists who regard themselves as definitely above the crude materialist fallacies of the past constantly commit the same mistake where activities directed toward the acquisition of such practical knowledge are concerned—apparently because in their scheme of things all such knowledge is supposed to be 'given'. The common idea now seems to be that all such knowledge should as a matter of course be readily at the command of everybody, and the reproach of irrationality leveled against the existing economic order is frequently based on the fact that it is not so available. This view disregards the fact that the method by which such knowledge can be made as widely available as possible is precisely the problem to which we have to find an answer." F. A. Hayek, The Use of Knowledge in Society, 35 Am. Econ. Rev. 519, 522 (1945).

[36] Which it will be if the new offer is for an amount greater than the old contract plus whatever damages *A* will have to pay *B* for breach of his original promise to carry *B*'s cotton to

user, the cost of allocating it will be greater than it would have been had information of the treaty reached *A* before he entered his first contract. Resources will be consumed by *A* in transacting out of the first contract; from a social point of view, their consumption represents a pure waste.

Allocative efficiency is promoted by getting information of changed circumstances to the market as quickly as possible. Of course, the information doesn't just "get" there. Like everything else, it is supplied by individuals (either directly, by being publicized, or indirectly, when it is signalled by an individual's market behavior).

In some cases, the individuals who supply information have obtained it by a deliberate search; in other cases, their information has been acquired casually.[37] A securities analyst, for example, acquires information about a particular corporation in a deliberate fashion—by carefully studying evidence of its economic performance. By contrast, a businessman who acquires a valuable piece of information when he accidentally overhears a conversation on a bus acquires the information casually.[38]

As it is used here, the term "deliberately acquired information" means information whose acquisition entails costs which would not have been incurred but for the likelihood, however great, that the information in question would actually be produced. These costs may include, of course, not only direct search costs (the cost of examining the corporation's annual statement) but the costs of developing an initial expertise as well (for example, the cost of attending business school). If the costs incurred in acquiring the information (the cost of the bus ticket in the second example) would have been incurred in any case—that is, whether or not the information was forthcoming—the information may be said to have been casually acquired. The distinction between deliberately and casually acquired information is a shorthand way of expressing this economic difference. Although in reality it may be difficult to determine whether any particular item of information has been acquired in one way or the other, the distinction between these two types of information has—as I hope to show—considerable analytical usefulness.

If information has been deliberately acquired (in the sense defined above), and its possessor is denied the benefits of having and using it, he will have an

---

New York. See John H. Barton, The Economic Basis of Damages for Breach of Contract, 1 J. Leg. Studies 277 (1972); Posner, *supra* note 2, at 88-93.

[37] Compare the distinction between "professional" and "altruistic" rescuers drawn by William M. Landes & Richard A. Posner in Salvors, Finders, Good Samaritans, and Other Rescuers: An Economic Study of Law and Altruism, 7 J. Leg. Studies 83 (1978). The costs of searching for information are analyzed in Stigler, The Economics of Information in the Organization of Industry (1968).

[38] Unless, of course, he rides buses for this very purpose. In this improbable case, he would acquire his information deliberately.

incentive to reduce (or curtail entirely) his production of such information in the future. This is in fact merely a consequence of defining deliberately acquired information in the way that I have, since one who acquires information of this sort will by definition have incurred costs which he would have avoided had it not been for the prospect of the benefits he has now been denied. By being denied the same benefits, one who has casually acquired information will not be discouraged from doing what—for independent reasons—he would have done in any case.

It might be claimed that whenever the benefits of possessing any kind of information are either increased or decreased, one would expect to find *some* overall adjustment in the level of investment in the production of such information. If he is not permitted to benefit from the information he acquires, even the bus rider will in the future pay less attention to the conversations going on around him (although it would certainly be strange if he stopped riding buses altogether). But while it is true that in reality every adjustment (upwards or downwards) in the benefits of possessing a particular kind of information will have an incentive effect of some sort, the effect may vary in magnitude—it may be greater or lesser. Strictly speaking, casually acquired information (as I have used the term up to this point) represents the ideal limit of a continuum—the case in which the change in magnitude that results from eliminating one of the benefits of possessing certain information is zero. In any real case there will be incentive effects which fall somewhere along the continuum. However, where the decline in the production of a certain kind of information which is caused by denying its possessor the right to appropriate the information for his own benefit is small, it is likely to be more than offset by the corresponding social gain that results from the avoidance of mistakes. In the argument that follows, I shall use the term "casually acquired information" in a somewhat looser sense than I have used it so far to refer to information of this sort.

One effective way of insuring that an individual will benefit from the possession of information (or anything else for that matter) is to assign him a property right in the information itself—a right or entitlement to invoke the coercive machinery of the state in order to exclude others from its use and enjoyment.[39] The benefits of possession become secure only when the state transforms the possessor of information into an owner by investing him with a legally enforceable property right of some sort or other. The assignment of property rights in information is a familiar feature of our legal system. The legal protection accorded patented inventions and certain trade secrets are two obvious examples.[40]

[39] See Harold Demsetz, Toward a Theory of Property Rights, 57 Am. Econ. Rev. 347 (Papers & Proceedings 1967).

[40] See Arnold Plant, The Economic Theory Concerning Patents for Inventions, in Selected Economic Essays and Addresses 35 (1974).

One (seldom noticed) way in which the legal system can establish property rights in information is by permitting an informed party to enter—and enforce—contracts which his information suggests are profitable, without disclosing the information to the other party.[41] Imposing a duty to disclose upon the knowledgeable party deprives him of a private advantage which the information would otherwise afford. A duty to disclose is tantamount to a requirement that the benefit of the information be publicly shared and is thus antithetical to the notion of a property right which—whatever else it may entail—always requires the legal protection of private appropriation.[42]

Of course, different sorts of property rights may be better suited for protecting possessory interests in different sorts of information.[43] It is unlikely, for example, that information of the kind involved in *Laidlaw v. Organ* could be effectively protected by a patent system.[44] The only feasible way of assigning property rights in short-lived market information is to permit those with such information to contract freely without disclosing what they know.

It is unclear, from the report of the case, whether the buyer in *Laidlaw* casually acquired his information or made a deliberate investment in seeking it out (for example, by cultivating a network of valuable commercial "friendships"). If we assume the buyer casually acquired his knowledge of the treaty, requiring him to disclose the information to his seller (that is, denying him a property right in the information) will have no significant effect on his future behavior. Since one who casually acquires information makes no investment in its acquisition, subjecting him to a duty to disclose is not likely

[41] This notion is suggested—but not developed—by Hirshleifer. In discussing the fate of Eli Whitney, who "invested considerable resources in the attempt to protect his patent and prosecute infringements" (to no avail), Hirshleifer has this to say:

> "But what seems to have been overlooked is that there were other routes to profit for Whitney. The cotton gin had obvious speculative implications for the price of cotton, the value of slaves and of cotton-bearing land, the business prospects of firms engaged in cotton ware-housing and shipping, the site values of key points in the transportation network that sprang up. There were also predictable implications for competitor industries (wool) and complementary ones (textiles, machinery). It seems very likely that some forethoughted individuals reaped speculative gains on these developments, though apparently Whitney did not. And yet, he was the first in the know, the possessor of an unparalleled opportunity for speculative profit. Alternatively, of course, Whitney could have attempted to keep his process secret except to those who bought the information from him."

Hirshleifer, *supra* note 33, at 571.

[42] If one party to a contract is under a duty to disclose, he must speak up whether or not the other party to the contract asks him what he knows. The fact that the knowledgeable party is *not* under a duty of disclosure does not mean, however, that he can lie when asked a question of this sort. That would be fraud. However, the knowledgeable party who is not under such a duty may refuse to respond to the other party's inquiries, and put the other party to the risk of deciding whether to go ahead with the contract or not. (The knowledgeable party may, of course, simply sell his information to the other party if he wishes.)

[43] On the general costs of establishing property rights in information, see Harold Demsetz, Information and Efficiency: Another Viewpoint, 12 J. Law & Econ. 1, 10-11 (1969).

[44] See Arnold Plant, *supra* note 40 for a discussion of the costs of the patent system, as compared with other legal devices for the assignment of property rights in information.

to reduce the amount of socially useful information which he actually generates. Of course, if the buyer in *Laidlaw* acquired his knowledge of the treaty as the result of a deliberate and costly search, a disclosure requirement will deprive him of any private benefit which he might otherwise realize from possession of the information and should discourage him from making similar investments in the future.

In addition, since it would enable the seller to appropriate the buyer's information without cost and would eliminate the danger of his being lured unwittingly into a losing contract by one possessing superior knowledge, a disclosure requirement will also reduce the seller's incentive to search. Denying the buyer a property right in deliberately acquired information will therefore discourage both buyers and sellers from investing in the development of expertise and in the actual search for information. The assignment of such a right will not only protect the investment of the party possessing the special knowledge, it will also impose an opportunity cost on the other party and thus give him an incentive to undertake a (cost-justified) search of his own.

If we assume that courts can easily discriminate between those who have acquired information casually and those who have acquired it deliberately, plausible economic considerations might well justify imposing a duty to disclose on a case-by-case basis (imposing it where the information has been casually acquired, refusing to impose it where the information is the fruit of a deliberate search). A party who has casually acquired information is, at the time of the transaction, likely to be a better (cheaper) mistake-preventer than the mistaken party with whom he deals—regardless of the fact that both parties initially had equal access to the information in question. One who has deliberately acquired information is also in a position to prevent the other party's error. But in determining the cost to the knowledgeable party of preventing the mistake (by disclosure), we must include whatever investment he has made in acquiring the information in the first place. This investment will represent a loss to him if the other party can avoid the contract on the grounds that the party with the information owes him a duty of disclosure.

If we take this cost into account, it is no longer clear that the party with knowledge is the cheaper mistake-preventer when his knowledge has been deliberately acquired. Indeed, the opposite conclusion seems more plausible. In this case, therefore, a rule permitting nondisclosure (which has the effect of imposing the risk of a mistake on the mistaken party) corresponds to the arrangement the parties themselves would have been likely to adopt if they had negotiated an explicit allocation of the risk at the time they entered the contract. The parties to a contract are always free to allocate this particular risk by including an appropriate disclaimer in the terms of their agreement. Where they have failed to do so, however, the object of the law of contracts should be (as it is elsewhere) to reduce transaction costs by providing a legal rule which approximates the arrangement the parties would have chosen for themselves if they had deliberately addressed the problem.[45] This consideration, coupled with the reduction in the production of socially useful information which is likely to follow from subjecting him to a disclosure requirement, suggests that allocative efficiency is best served by permitting one who possesses deliberately acquired information to enter and enforce favorable bargains without disclosing what he knows.[46]

A rule which calls for case-by-case application of a disclosure requirement is likely, however, to involve factual issues that will be difficult (and expensive) to resolve. *Laidlaw* itself illustrates this point nicely. On the facts of the case, as we have them, it is impossible to determine whether the buyer actually made a deliberate investment in acquiring information regarding the treaty. The cost of administering a disclosure requirement on a case-by-case basis is likely to be substantial.[47]

As an alternative, one might uniformly apply a blanket rule (of disclosure or nondisclosure) across each class of cases involving the same sort of information (for example, information about market conditions or about defects in property held for sale). In determining the appropriate blanket rule for a particular class of cases, it would first be necessary to decide whether the

[45] Posner, *supra* note 2, at 65-69; Richard A. Posner & Andrew M. Rosenfield, *supra* note 2, at 88-89.

[46] In recent years, there has been considerable disagreement among economists regarding the optimal level of private investment in the production of information. This problem has been discussed in Kenneth J. Arrow, Higher Education as a Filter, 2 J. Pub. Econ. 193 (1973); Harold Demsetz, Information and Efficiency: Another Viewpoint, 12 J. Law & Econ. 1 (1969): John M. Marshall, Private Incentives and Public Information, 64 Am. Econ. Rev. 373 (1974); Eugene F. Fama & Arthur B. Laffer, Information and Capital Markets, 44 J. Bus. 289 (1971); Hirshleifer, *supra* note 33; and Yoram Barzel, Some Fallacies in the Interpretation of Information Costs, 20 J. Law & Econ. 291 (1977).

The economists who have discussed the problem agree that under a legal system which recognized no property rights in information, too little information would be produced. Several economists, however, have expressed a concern that a system of property rights in information may, under some circumstances, induce an overinvestment in the production of information. See, for example, Hirshleifer, *supra* note 33, at 573. Assuming that our legal rules cannot be more finely tuned, in deciding whether to permit the nondisclosure of certain information (that is, grant a property right in the information), we may be forced to make a practical choice between over- and underinvestment—between two less-than-optimal alternatives. However, since it is certain that the elimination of property rights will result in underproduction, and merely a danger that the recognition of such rights will lead to overproduction, there is a strong (but not conclusive) economic case for recognizing property rights in information, at least where the information is deliberately acquired. From an economic point of view, this may not be an optimal solution, but it is more attractive than the other (practical) alternative.

[47] For a general discussion of the costs (and benefits) of specificity in the formulation of legal rules, see Isaac Ehrlich & Richard A. Posner, An Economic Analysis of Legal Rulemaking, 3 J. Leg. Studies 257 (1974). One of the disadvantages of a case-by-case approach is that it may encourage information seekers to invest more than they would otherwise invest merely in order to "stake" their proprietary claims. For a discussion of this problem, in the context of water rights, see Jack Hirshleifer, James C. DeHaven, & Jerome W. Milliman, Water Supply: Economics, Technology, and Policy 59-66 (1960).

kind of information involved is (on the whole) more likely to be generated by chance or by deliberate searching. The greater the likelihood that such information will be deliberately produced rather than casually discovered, the more plausible the assumption becomes that a blanket rule permitting nondisclosure will have benefits that outweigh its costs.

In *Laidlaw*, for example, the information involved concerned changing market conditions. The results in that case may be justified (from the more general perspective just described) on the grounds that information regarding the state of the market is typically (although not in every case) the product of a deliberate search. The large number of individuals who are actually engaged in the production of such information lends some empirical support to this proposition.[48]

B. *The Case Law*

The distinction between deliberately and casually acquired information helps us to understand the pattern exhibited by the cases in which a duty to disclose is asserted by one party or the other. By and large, the cases requiring disclosure involve information which is likely to have been casually acquired (in the sense defined above). The cases permitting nondisclosure, on the other hand, involve information which, on the whole, is likely to have been deliberately produced. Taken as a group, the disclosure cases give at least the appearance of promoting allocative efficiency by limiting the assignment of property rights to those types of information which are likely to be the fruit of a deliberate investment (either in the development of expertise or in actual searching).[49]

[48] In its 42nd annual report for the fiscal year ending June 30, 1976, the Securities and Exchange Commission states that at the end of fiscal year 1976 total broker-dealer registrations numbered 5,308 and total investment adviser registrations numbered 3,857; 42 S.E.C. Ann. Rep. 182 (1976). The number of individuals actually engaged in the deliberate collection and dissemination of market information is, of course, much larger than these figures would indicate since a single broker-dealer or investment adviser may well be a large firm with many employees.

[49] I note, before turning to disclosure cases themselves, that many of the cases raise two problems which are not addressed in this paper. The first problem involves the existence or nonexistence of a confidential or fiduciary relation between the parties to the contract. Where such a relation exists, courts are more likely to require disclosure than they would otherwise be. "Where a fiduciary relationship exists between the parties, such as attorney and client, guardian and ward, trustee and *cestui que trust*, executor and legatee, principal and agent, partner and copartners, joint venturer and fellow joint venturers, there is a positive duty to disclose material facts; a failure to do so is constructively fraudulent. As mentioned earlier, a similar obligation exists where a broker dealing in securities or real estate represents a principal.

Also, the nature of the transaction or the relation of the parties may be such that as to the particular transaction in question, the duties of a fiduciary are imposed upon one or the other party, and such a relation involves a duty of disclosure." 12 Williston, *supra* note 2, at § 1499. See

The economic rationale for permitting nondisclosure is nicely illustrated by several cases involving the purchase of real estate where the buyer had reason to believe in the existence of a subsurface oil or mineral deposit unknown to the seller.[50] For example, in *Neill v. Shamburg,*[51] the parties were cotenants[52] of an oil lease on a 200-acre tract. The buyer (Shamburg) bought his cotenant's interest in the tract for $550 (with a provision for an additional $100 in case a well producing six or more barrels of oil a day should be found). At the time of the sale, Shamburg was operating several wells on an adjacent tract of land. One of the wells was quite valuable. Shamburg "directed his employees not to give information on this subject" and said nothing to his cotenant regarding the well when he purchased her interest in the 200-acre tract. The court held that Shamburg did not owe Neill any duty of disclosure and refused to set aside the sale of her half-interest in the oil lease. The court supported its conclusion with the following argument:

> The plaintiff [the seller] had no interest in the 50-acre lease, but we may concede that, when she was about to sell her part of the other lease to her co-tenant, she became entitled to know such facts with regards to its production as would bear upon the value of the other. [In light of what follows, the meaning of this sentence is not entirely clear.] But, unless there is some exceptional circumstance to put on him the duty to speak, it is the right of every man to keep his business to himself. Possibly,

also William W. Kerr, Kerr on the Law of Fraud and Mistake 185-86 (7th ed. 1952); George Spencer Bower, Actionable Non-Disclosure 273-74 (1915).

The second problem concerns the line between nondisclosure, on the one hand, and fraud or positive misrepresentation, on the other. Even if a party to a contract is owed no duty of disclosure, fraud or misrepresentation by the other party will almost invariably give him a legal basis for avoiding the contract. 12 Williston, *supra* note 2, at §§ 1487, 1488; Keeton, *supra* note 29, at 1-6 (note especially the distinction drawn between nondisclosure and "active concealment").

Each of these two general rules or principles makes sense from an economic point of view: a fiduciary relation can be viewed as a deliberate form of risk sharing (the beneficiary in effect purchases the other party's information), and fraud is economically undesirable because it positively increases the amount of misinformation in the market and is therefore likely to reduce the efficiency of the market as a mechanism for allocating resources. See generally Michael R. Darby & Edi Karni, Free Competition and the Optimal Amount of Fraud, 16 J. Law & Econ. 67 (1973).

I have chosen not to discuss these two problems because they are centered on difficult questions of fact (when does a fiduciary relation exist? where do we draw the line between nondisclosure and fraud?) about which it is difficult to generalize in a way that is theoretically interesting. The cases selected for discussion have been chosen, in part, because they do not raise questions of this sort.

[50] Fox v. Mackreth, 2 Bro. Ch. 400, 420, 30 Eng. Rep. 148 (1788) (dictum); Smith v. Beatty, 2 Ired. Eq. 456 (N.C. 1843); Harris v. Tyson, 24 Pa. 347 (1855); Stackpole v. Hancock, 40 Fla. 362, 24 So. 914 (1898); Holly Hill Lumber Co. v. McCoy, 201 S.C. 427, 23 S.E. 2d 372 (1942); William W. Story, *supra* note 27, at 442; 12 Williston, *supra* note 2, at § 1498.

[51] Neill v. Shamburg, 158 Pa. 263, 27 Atl. 992 (1893).

[52] The court held, *inter alia,* that their cotenancy did not create a fiduciary relation between the parties.

Shamburg was unduly suspicious on this point, but the nature and position of his business suggested caution. Fogle testifies that Shamburg was the only person operating in that neighborhood, *and James says that Shamburg told him he had spent near $150,000 in developing that territory, "and now all these fellows are anxious to pry into my business."* We do not find in the acts of Shamburg, under the circumstances, anything more than *a positive intention and effort to reap the benefit of his enterprise, by keeping the knowledge of its results to himself,* and we agree with the master that this "falls far short of establishing fraud."[53]

A more recent—and certainly a more dramatic—case of this sort arose in connection with Texas Gulf Sulphur's discovery of the fabulously rich Kidd Creek mine near Timmins, Ontario.[54] After conducting extensive aerial surveys which revealed a geological anomaly indicating the presence of massive sulphide deposits, Texas Gulf Sulphur purchased options covering mineral and surface rights from the owners of several adjacent lots on which the anomaly was located. One of these options covered a parcel of land owned by the estate of Murray Hendrie. The Hendrie option (which was obtained for $500) provided that Texas Gulf Sulphur could acquire mining rights to the property by the payment of $18,000 at any time during the two years immediately following execution of the option.[55] The option also provided that in case a commercial deposit of ore were discovered, the Hendrie estate would be given 10 percent of any profits. After the existence of the deposit became publicly known, representatives of the Hendrie estate protested that Texas Gulf Sulphur had intentionally misled the seller by failing to disclose that it had "an unusually promising indication of economic mineralization on the Hendrie property." A lawsuit, brought by the representatives, was eventually settled out of court.[56]

Both Shamburg and Texas Gulf Sulphur had reason to think that the land they were purchasing was far more valuable than the owner of the land believed it to be. In each case, the buyer's information regarding the value of

[53] Neill v. Shamburg, 27 Atl. 993 (1893). Italics added.

[54] For an account of the discovery, and subsequent events, see Morton Shulman, The Billion Dollar Windfall (1969).

[55] *Id.* at 82.

[56] As part of the settlement, Texas Gulf Sulphur agreed to purchase Hendrie's 10% share in the profits of the mine. The value of Hendrie's share has been estimated to be about $100,000,000. This fact, of course, considerably weakened his misrepresentation claim; in addition, the 10% provision should probably be regarded as a device for deliberately allocating the risk in question.

It is interesting to note that in a litigated case arising out of a related transaction, the Ontario High Court of Justice remarked that Texas Gulf Sulphur was only doing "What any prudent mining company would have done to acquire property in which it knew a very promising anomaly lay" when it purchased property "without causing the prospective vendors to suspect that a discovery had been made." Leitch Gold Mines, Ltd. v. Texas Gulf Sulphur, 1 Ontario Reports 469, 492-93 (1969).

the property was the product of a deliberate search, in which the buyer had invested a substantial sum of money. (In the four years before its discovery of the Kidd Creek deposit, Texas Gulf Sulphur spent nearly $3 million exploring other anomalies—with no results.)[57] The information, in both cases, revealed characteristics of the property which increased the efficiency of its utilization and, therefore, its value to society as a whole.

Information pertaining to the likelihood of a subsurface oil or mineral deposit will often be the fruit of a deliberate investment either in actual exploration or in the development of geological expertise. In order to encourage the production of such information, our legal system generally permits its possessor to take advantage of the ignorance of others by trading without disclosure.

A similar result is usually reached where the information concerns an anticipated development of some sort which will make the property more valuable.[58] In *Guaranty Safe Deposit & Trust Co. v. Liebold,*[59] for example, the trust company purchased an option on Liebold's property. It subsequently exercised the option and purchased the property for $15,000. Liebold sought to avoid the sale on the grounds "that at the time the option was secured, a company known as the Standard Steel Car Company contemplated coming to Butler [Pa.] to establish a large manufacturing plant; that Mr. Reiber [an agent of the trust co.] had knowledge of this matter, and while defendant had heard of the coming of some contemplated company, his knowledge was indistinct and indefinite, and the certainty of its coming was known to the plaintiff, who withheld his knowledge from defendant." The trial court found that both parties had known of the "rumor" that a manufacturing plant would be established in Butler, and that they had adjusted the price of the option accordingly. The Pennsylvania Supreme Court, in affirming a judgment for the trust company, had this to say:

[57] Morton Shulman, *supra* note 54, at 7. It is unlikely that Texas Gulf Sulphur could have benefited from its information in any other way than by purchasing the property on which the anomaly was located. If it had attempted to sell its information to the landowners, Texas Gulf Sulphur would have encountered two difficulties. It would first have had to convince the landowners of the value of the information without actually disclosing it. Second, it would have had to persuade all of the landowners involved to purchase the information jointly—since, in all likelihood, no single owner could pay a price that would compensate the corporation for the costs it had incurred in obtaining it. A multi-party transaction of this sort would involve obvious free-rider problems, and would be made especially difficult by the fact that disclosure of the information to one party would make it nearly impossible to conceal it from the others. If one owner obtains the information and begins mining, this will tip the others off and they will have no reason to buy the information themselves. Since it is reasonable to assume that the only effective way in which Texas Gulf Sulphur could profit from its information was by purchasing the rights to the property itself, a disclosure rule would have frustrated its only real hope of recovering the costs incurred in acquiring the information in the first place.

[58] See, for example, Burt v. Mason, 97 Mich. 127, 56 N.W. 365 (1893), and Furman v. Brown, 227 Mich. 629, 199 N.W. 703 (1924). See also 12 Williston, *supra* note 2, at § 1498 n.6.

[59] Guaranty Safe Deposit and Trust Co. v. Liebold, 207 Pa. 399, 56 A. 951 (1904).

Suppose Reiber had known definitely that the plant was to be established in Butler, and Liebold had been ignorant of this, was it the duty of the former to disclose such information to the latter, and can it be that, without such disclosure, his contract with Liebold is not enforceable in equity? In this commercial age, options are daily procured by those in possession of information from which they expect to profit, simply because those from whom the options are sought are ignorant of it. When the prospective seller knows as much as the prospective buyer, options can rarely, if ever, be procured, and the rule that counsel for appellant would have us apply would practically abolish them.[60]

Courts frequently have stated that in the absence of a confidential or fiduciary relation between buyer and seller, "a purchaser [of real estate], though having superior judgment of values, does not commit fraud merely by purchasing without disclosing his knowledge of value."[61] A rule of this sort makes economic sense where the buyer's judgment is based upon his prediction of the likelihood of various future uses to which the property might be put. Although a buyer's "knowledge of value" is not always based upon deliberately acquired information, the number of entrepreneurs involved in professional real estate speculation makes it plausible to assume that such knowledge is often (if not typically) acquired in a deliberate manner. (Real estate speculators, by matching buyers and sellers, facilitate the movement of real property to its most efficient use. The information on which their predictions of future use are based should therefore be regarded as a social asset.)

A third line of cases permitting nondisclosure appears, at first glance, to be inconsistent with the thesis argued here. These cases involve the sale of property which is *patently* defective in some way; courts regularly have found that the seller of such property has no duty to bring the defect to the buyer's attention.[62]

In *Gutelius v. Sisemore*,[63] for example, the plaintiff bought a house and subsequently discovered that rain water accumulated under the floors causing the residence "to become permeated with noxious and offensive odors." The buyer asserted that the tendency of water to accumulate was a latent defect, and that the defendant-seller had a duty to warn him of its existence. In finding for the defendant, the court said that an inspection of the premises (which the plaintiff had in fact made) should have acquainted the plaintiff with the conditions responsible for the accumulation of water. (The conditions cited included the placement of air vents, the slope of the ground surrounding the house, and the composition of soil in the yard.) "Where the means of knowledge are at hand and equally available to both parties," the

[60] *Id.* at 405, 56 A., at 953.

[61] Pratt Land & Improvement Co. v. McClain, 135 Ala. 452, 33 So. 185 (1902).

[62] See 37 Am. Jur. 2d § 157, and cases cited there.

[63] Gutelius v. Sisemore, 365 P.2d 732 (Okla. 1961).

court concluded, "and the subject of purchase is alike open to their inspection, if the purchaser does not avail himself of these means and opportunities, he will not be heard to say that he had been deceived by the vendor's misrepresentations."

If we assume that the seller in the *Gutelius* case knew or had reason to know that the buyer was unaware of the defect (despite the fact that the buyer had inspected the premises), he would be in much the same position as the recipient of a palpably mistaken bid, and if his knowledge of the buyer's error were not the fruit of a deliberate search, it would be reasonable to assume that the seller was the cheaper mistake-preventer—at least at the time of contracting. For reasons that will be considered in a moment, it is implausible to think that a seller's knowledge of defects in his own property is typically the result of a deliberate search in which he would not have invested had he known he would be required to disclose the existence of the defects in question. This being the case, on the assumption that the seller in *Gutelius* had reason to know of his buyer's error, it would seem to make sense, from an economic point of view, to require the seller to eliminate the error by bringing the defect to the buyer's attention. This is so despite the fact that both parties initially had an equal opportunity to discover the defect themselves—just as it is efficient to impose the risk of a mistaken bid on the party receiving it where he has reason to know of the mistake, despite the fact that the bidder was the party best able to prevent occurrence of the mistake in the first place.

But if a seller has no reason to know that his buyer is mistaken, it would be uneconomical to require him to notify the buyer of patent defects, since in all likelihood he would only be telling the buyer what the buyer already knows. Communications of this sort needlessly increase transaction costs. The critical issue in a case like *Gutelius*, therefore, is not whether knowledge of the defect was "equally available to the parties" at some previous moment in time, but whether the seller, at the time the contract is executed, actually knows or has reason to know that the buyer is mistaken. The rule that a seller of real property has no duty to disclose patent defects makes economic sense where—as is often the case—the seller has no reason to know that the buyer is mistaken. These cases (of which *Gutelius* is an example) appear to conflict with the interpretation offered here only because of their failure to explicitly discuss this key issue, focusing instead on the parties' initial parity of access to information concerning the defect.

With regard to *latent* defects, the older authorities are equivocal. Some cases state that a seller who is aware of such a defect must disclose it to his buyer or forgo the bargain.[64] Others state that the seller is privileged to

[64] See generally, William W. Story, *supra* note 27, at 444-45; James Kent, 2 Commentaries § 482 n.1 (12th ed. 1873).

remain silent if he wishes.[65] In the last twenty-five years, however, there has been a marked expansion of the duty to disclose latent defects.[66] One particularly dramatic illustration involves the sale of a home infested with termites. A seller of a house in Massachusetts in 1942 was held to have no legal duty to disclose the existence of a termite infestation of which the buyer was ignorant.[67] If it were to impose such a duty, the Massachusetts Supreme Court declared, it would make every seller liable "who fails to disclose any nonapparent defect known to him in the subject of the sale which materially reduces its value and which the buyer fails to discover." Similarly, the court went on to say, "it would seem that every buyer would be liable who fails to disclose any nonapparent virtue known to him in the subject of the purchase which materially enhances its value and of which the seller is ignorant."

Eighteen years later, in *Obde v. Schlemeyer,*[68] a Washington seller was held to have a duty to disclose under identical circumstances. The Washington court concluded that the seller had a duty to speak up, "regardless of the [buyer's] failure to ask any questions relative to the possibility of termites," since the condition was "clearly latent—not readily observable upon reasonable inspection." The court bolstered its argument with a long quotation from an article by Professor Keeton:

> It is of course apparent that the content of the maxim "caveat emptor", used in its broader meaning of imposing risks on both parties to a transaction, has been greatly limited since its origin. When Lord Cairns stated in Peek v. Gurney that there was no duty to disclose facts, however morally censurable their non-disclosure may be, he was stating the law as shaped by an individualistic philosophy based upon freedom of contract. It was not concerned with morals. In the present state of the law, the decisions show a drawing away from this idea, and there can be seen an attempt by many courts to reach a just result in so far as possible, but yet maintaining the degree of certainty which the law must have. The statement may often be found that if either party to a contract of sale conceals or suppresses a material fact which he is in good faith bound to disclose then his silence is fraudulent.
>
> The attitude of the courts toward non-disclosure is undergoing a change and contrary to Lord Cairns' famous remark it would seem that the object of the law in

[65] Swinton v. Whitinsville Sav. Bank, 311 Mass. 677, 42 N.E.2d 808 (1942). See also Perin v. Mardine Realty Co., 5 App. Div. 2d 685, 168 N.Y.S. 2d 647 (1957).

[66] William B. Goldfarb, Fraud and Nondisclosure in the Vendor-Purchaser Relation, 8 W. Res. L. Rev. 5 (1956); Leo Bearman, Jr., Caveat Emptor in Sales of Realty—Recent Assaults Upon the Rule, 14 Vand. L. Rev. 541 (1961). Two illustrative cases are Kaze v. Compton, 283 S.W.2d 204 (Ky. 1955), and Cohen v. Vivian, 141 Colo. 443, 349 P.2d 366 (1960).

[67] Swinton v. Whitinsville Sav. Bank, 311 Mass. 677, 42 N.E.2d 808 (1942). See also Perin v. Mardine Realty Co., 5 App. Div. 2d 685, 168 N.Y.S.2d 647 (1957).

[68] Obde v. Schlemeyer, 56 Wash. 2d 449, 353 P.2d 672 (1960). See also Williams v. Benson, 3 Mich. App. 9, 141 N.W.2d 650 (1966); Cohen v. Blessing, 259 S.C. 400, 192 S.E.2d 204 (1972), Annot., 22 A.L.R.3d 972.

these cases should be to impose on parties to the transaction a duty to speak whenever justice, equity, and fair dealing demand it.[69]

However one feels about Professor Keeton's moral claim, requiring the disclosure of latent defects makes good sense from the more limited perspective offered here. In the first place, it is likely to be expensive for the buyer to discover such defects; the discovery of a latent defect will almost always require something more than an ordinary search. Even where neither party has knowledge of the defect, it may be efficient to allocate to the seller the risk of a mistaken belief that no defect exists, on the grounds that of the two parties he is likely to be the cheapest mistake-preventer.[70]

Where the seller actually knows of the defect, and the buyer does not, the seller is clearly the party best able to avoid the buyer's mistake at least cost—unless the seller has made a deliberate investment in acquiring his knowledge which he would not have made had he known he would be required to disclose to purchasers of the property any defects he discovered. A seller, of course, may make a substantial investment in acquiring information concerning a particular defect: for example, he may hire exterminators to check his property for termites. But even so, it is unlikely that his principal aim in acquiring such information is to obtain an advantage over potential purchasers. Typically, homeowners conduct investigations of this sort in order to protect their own investments. In most cases, a homeowner will have an adequate incentive to check for termites even if the law requires him to disclose what he discovers;[71] furthermore, many termite infestations are discovered by simply living in the house—something the owner will do in any event. A disclosure requirement is unlikely to have a substantial effect on the level of investment by homeowners in the detection of termites: the point is not that information regarding termites is costless (it isn't), but that a disclosure requirement would not be likely to reduce the production of such information. This represents an important distinction between cases like *Obde,* on the one hand, and those like *Laidlaw, Shamburg,* and *Guaranty Safe,* on the other.

A seller of goods might argue that a rule requiring him to disclose latent defects will discourage him from developing (socially useful) expertise regarding the qualities or attributes of the goods he is selling: if he cannot enjoy its fruits by selling without disclosure, what incentive will he have to acquire

[69] Keeton, *supra* note 29, at 31.

[70] Because of his superior access to the relevant information. See Posner, *supra* note 2, at 74-75.

[71] This will not be true in every case. It may not be true, for example, if the homeowner plans to sell his home in the immediate future.

such expertise in the first place? This argument is rather unconvincing. A seller benefits in many different ways from his knowledge of the various attributes which his goods possess. For example, expertise of this sort enables him to be more efficient in purchasing materials, and reduces the likelihood that he will fail to identify any special advantage his goods enjoy (and therefore undersell them). Because the benefits which he derives from such knowledge are many and varied, it is unlikely that a duty to disclose latent defects will by itself seriously impair a seller's incentive to invest in acquiring knowledge regarding the attributes of what he sells.

By contrast, the usefulness of market information (as distinct from information regarding the attributes of goods held for sale) is substantially reduced by imposing a duty to disclose on its possessor. It is doubtful whether the benefits of market information which are not eliminated by a disclosure requirement are sufficient by themselves to justify a deliberate investment in its production. Consequently, even if we regard these two kinds of information—market information and product information—as equally useful from a social point of view, a legal rule requiring disclosure is likely to have a different impact upon the production of each. It follows from what I have just said that a rule permitting nondisclosure of market information is sensible whether the party possessing the information is a buyer or a seller.[72] Thus, if the seller in *Laidlaw* had known the treaty would have a depressing effect on the price of cotton and had sold to the buyer without disclosing this fact, the economic considerations favoring enforcement would be the same as where the buyer had acquired special information. Although economic considerations would appear to support similar treatment for buyers and sellers possessing market information, these same considerations may justify different treatment where product information is involved. It should be clear, from what I have already said, that there is no inconsistency in requiring sellers to disclose latent defects, while not requiring buyers to disclose latent advantages.

The latent defect cases have an interesting analogue in the insurance field. An applicant for a life insurance policy is usually held to have a duty to disclose known "defects" in his own constitution.[73] For example, if an appli-

[72] This point has long been recognized. See William W. Story, *supra* note 27, at 444-45. See also the classic discussion of the problem in Book 3 of Marcus Tullius Cicero's, De Officiis (Loeb Classical Library 1975).

[73] For a thorough discussion of the duty to disclose in the context of insurance contracts, see Edwin W. Patterson, Essentials of Insurance Law 444-73 (1957). At one point in his discussion, Professor Patterson makes an "economic" point similar to the one developed in this paper:

"The doctrine of concealment in relation to insurance contracts is, and long has been, an exceptional rule. In commercial contracts, and in all others between persons dealing at arm's length, A, one party, is not required to *volunteer*, at the time of negotiating the contract, disclosure to the other, B, of A's knowledge of fact X, which he knows that B does not know and which A knows B would deem material to the making of the contract. For example, if A

cant has a history of heart trouble which the insurance company's own medical examination fails to reveal, and he does not disclose the problem himself, the insurance company will usually be permitted to set the contract of insurance aside.[74] In many cases, of course, an applicant's failure to disclose will constitute actual fraud (this will be so, for example, if a question on the application asks him whether he has a history of heart trouble and he answers that he does not).[75] But even in the absence of fraud, an applicant is usually held to have a positive duty to speak up even where he has not been asked a specific question.[76] In this respect, the same disclosure is required of one who purchases an insurance policy as is required of a seller who sells a house with a latent defect (such as a termite infestation). From an economic point of view, these two cases are quite similar and it is therefore understandable that the same disclosure requirement should be applied to each. Because of his intimate familiarity with his own medical history and symptoms, an applicant for an insurance policy will typically be in a better position than the insurance company itself to prevent a mistake by the company regarding some latent defect in the applicant's constitution. More importantly, an applicant will have a strong incentive to acquire information concerning his own health whether or not we impose a disclosure requirement on him.[77] In this sense, he resembles the homeowner who will have an incentive to protect his home from destruction by termites whether we require him to disclose the existence of a termite infestation or not. Both the homeowner and the insurance applicant have an independent reason for producing information of this sort, and the value to them of the information will in most cases be unimpaired by a disclosure requirement.

---

offers to sell B a large quantity of coffee beans, knowing, as B does not, that the report of a prospective coffee-crop failure in Brazil was false, B, contracting to buy in ignorance of this fact, cannot avoid the contract on the ground of A's silence. [Citing *Laidlaw v. Organ.*] The policy supporting this rule is based on the economic function of 'the market,' as a process whereby the best-informed traders provide a medium for the selling and buying of property at the 'best' prices obtainable, and for this public service they are rewarded by being allowed to profit by their special knowledge. The bargaining process on a 'free market' would become tedious and unstable if each bargainer had to tell the other all his reasons for the price he asks or bids."

Id. at 446-47.

[74] See Equitable Life Assurance Soc'y of United States v. McElroy, 83 Fed. 631 (8th Cir. 1897) (nondisclosure of an operation for appendicitis in the interim period between signing the application for insurance and completion of the contract); Stipcich v. Metropolitan Life Ins. Co., 277 U.S. 311 (9th Cir. 1928) (dictum).

[75] Edwin W. Patterson, Essentials of Insurance Law 458 (1957).

[76] Assuming that he has reason to believe the nondisclosed fact is materially relevant to the risk the insurer is assuming. *Id.* at 456.

[77] This will not be true in every case. If he knows that he must disclose whatever he discovers, an applicant with disturbing symptoms may forgo a medical examination for fear of what it will reveal (just as a disclosure requirement may in some circumstances discourage a homeowner contemplating sale from inspecting for termites).

C. *The Duty to Disclose and the Restatements*

In addition to generating a substantial case law, the problem of disclosure in bargain transactions has also been addressed by the draftsmen of three different Restatements. It is instructive to compare the treatment which the problem of disclosure has received at the hands of the restaters. The analysis developed in this paper suggests that the different restaters were closer in their thinking about disclosure than might appear to be the case.

Section 472(1)(b) of the Restatement of Contracts (First) provides that "there is no duty of disclosure, by a party who knows that the other party is acting under a mistake as to undisclosed material facts, and the mistake if mutual would render voidable a transaction caused by relying thereon. . ." Like many of the Restatement's black-letter principles, this one is rather shapeless, and acquires content only by the examples which are offered to illustrate its meaning. Two of the five illustrations appended to Section 472 involve situations which appear to be within the contemplated scope of Section 472(1)(b). The two examples are these.

> A owns two tracts of land, Blackacre and Whiteacre. B makes a written offer to buy Blackacre for $10,000. A knows that B is under a mistake as to the names of the tracts and that the more valuable tract, Whiteacre, is the one that B has in mind. A accepts B's offer without disclosing B's mistake to him. Though A is in no way the cause of B's original mistake, the lack of disclosure is fraud.
>
> A learns that the business of C, a corporation, has suffered a serious loss. He knows that B is ignorant of the loss, and without disclosing it to B, contracts to sell to B shares in the corporation. A has no fiduciary relation to B. A's non-disclosure is not fraud. If the mistake had been mutual it would not have made the contract voidable.[78]

In each case, one party is mistaken and the other party knows it. In both cases the party with knowledge is the seller. What distinguishes the two cases is the *kind* of knowledge they involve. Only the knowledge involved in the second case (a species of market information) is likely to be the fruit of a search in which the knowledgeable party has made a deliberate investment. The seller's special knowledge in the first case comes to him—in the most literal sense—by accident. Requiring him to disclose the other party's error will not give the seller in the first case a disincentive to do anything he would not have done anyway; imposing a similar requirement on the seller in the second case may very well have a disincentive effect of this sort. Although today the result in the second case would undoubtedly be affected by our complex securities laws, it does suggest that in framing an appropriate disclosure rule, the draftsmen of the First Restatement of Contracts intuitively

[78] Restatement of Contracts § 472, Illustrations 2 & 4 (1932).

attached great importance to the distinction drawn here between two different kinds of knowledge or information.

The treatment of disclosure in the Second Restatement of Torts also accords with the analysis offered here. Section 551(2)(e) states that "one party to a business transaction is under a duty to disclose to the other before the transaction is consummated facts basic to the transaction, if he knows that the other is about to enter into the transaction under a mistake as to such facts, and that the other, because of the relationship between them, the customs in the trade, or other objective circumstances, would reasonably expect a disclosure of such facts."[79] In an explanatory comment accompanying Section 551, the draftsmen note that

> to a considerable extent, fully sanctioned by the customs and mores of the community, superior information and better business acumen are legitimate advantages, which lead to no liability. The defendant may reasonably expect the plaintiff to make his own investigation, draw his own conclusions, and to protect himself; and if the plaintiff is indolent, inexperienced or ignorant, or his judgment is bad, or he does not have access to adequate information, the defendant is under no obligation to make good his deficiencies. This is true in general, where it is the buyer of land or chattels who has the better information and fails to disclose it; somewhat less frequently, it may be true of the seller.[80]

Section 551(2)(e) is illustrated with the following example.

> A is a violin expert. He pays a casual visit to B's shop where second-hand musical instruments are sold. He finds a violin which, by reason of his expert knowledge and experience, he immediately recognizes as a genuine Stradivarius, in good condition, and worth at least $50,000. The violin is priced for sale at $100. Without disclosing his information or his identity, A buys the violin from B for $100. A is not liable to B.[81]

Although *A*'s visit to *B*'s shop is described as "casual," *A* has certainly incurred costs in building up his knowledge of musical instruments and one of his anticipated benefits may have been the discovery of an undervalued masterpiece. (Whether this is true will depend, in part, upon what it means to be a "violin expert." Is a "violin expert" someone who plays the instrument, or who collects them? If the latter, then the discovery of an unrecognized Stradivarius is more likely to be one of the important benefits which the expert anticipates from his special knowledge.) Regardless of *A*'s particular motives for becoming an expert, it is plausible to think that many discoveries of the sort described in the example are the result of a deliberate search in the sense defined above.

[79] Restatement (Second) of Torts § 551(2)(e) (Tent. Draft No. 11, 1965).

[80] *Id.* Comment e, at 50.

[81] *Id.*

Locating valuable instruments which have been incorrectly identified by their owners serves a useful social purpose: after the Stradivarius has been discovered, it will undoubtedly find its way into the hands of a higher-valuing user (for example, a concert violinist or a university with a collection of rare instruments). An undiscovered Stradivarius is almost certainly misallocated. By bringing it to light, a bargain-hunting expert in musical instruments promotes the efficiency with which society's scarce resources are allocated. If he has incurred costs in doing so (and the development of expertise is one—perhaps the most important—of these costs), the bargain hunter will be discouraged from future searching if he is not given a property right in whatever information he acquires (in the form of a privilege to deal without disclosing).

By the same token, since it enables him to benefit (costlessly) from the other party's special information and eliminates the risk that he will be unable to recover an undervalued masterpiece which he sells by mistake, a disclosure requirement also reduces the owner's incentive to search (that is, to correctly identify the attributes of his own property). Because it reduces the incentive of both the owner and the bargain-hunter to undertake a deliberate search, a disclosure requirement increases the likelihood that the instrument will remain undiscovered and therefore misallocated.

The draftsmen of the Second Restatement of Torts offer four examples to illustrate the circumstances in which Section 551(2)(e) would require a party with special information to disclose what he knows. In the first case, a seller sells a house "without disclosing the fact that the drain tile under the house is so constructed that at periodic intervals it accumulates water under the house"; in the second case, the owner of a business sells it to someone without disclosing that he has been ordered by the United States Government to discontinue his principal activity; in the third case, the owner of an amusement center sells it "without disclosing the fact that it has just been raided by the police, and that [the seller] is being prosecuted for maintaining prostitution and the sale of marijuana on the premises"; and in the last case, one party sells a summer resort to another without disclosing that a substantial portion of the resort encroaches on a public highway. The special knowledge involved in each of these four examples is unlikely to be the intended product of a deliberate search for information in which the knowing party has made an investment he would not otherwise have made. They may all be distinguished, in this regard, from the violin hypothetical. The line which the draftsmen of the Second Restatement of Torts draw between the duty to disclose and the privilege to remain silent is drawn where the analysis developed in this paper would suggest it should be.

The Restatement of Restitution treats the problem of disclosure in Section 12: "A person who confers a benefit upon another, manifesting that he does so as an offer of a bargain which the other accepts or as the acceptance of an offer which the other has made, is not entitled to restitution because of a mistake which the other does not share and the existence of which the other does not know or suspect." In Comment *c* to Section 12 the draftsmen state: "Where the transferee knows or suspects the mistake of the transferor, restitution is granted if, and only if, the fact as to which the mistake is made is one which is at the basis of the transaction unless there is a special relation between the parties." Comment *c* is illustrated by two examples.

A, looking at cheap jewelry in a store which sells both very cheap and expensive jewelry, discovers what he at once recognizes as being a valuable jewel worth not less than $100 which he correctly believes to have been placed there by mistake. He asks the clerk for the jewel and gives 10¢ for it. The clerk puts the 10¢ in the cash drawer and hands the jewel to A. The shopkeeper is entitled to restitution because the shopkeeper did not, as A knew, intend to bargain except with reference to cheap jewelry.

A enters a second-hand bookstore where, among books offered for sale at one dollar each, he discovers a rare book having, as A knows, a market value of not less than $50. He hands this to the proprietor with one dollar. The proprietor, reading the name of the book and the price tag, keeps the dollar and hands the book to A. The bookdealer is not entitled to restitution since there was no mistake as to the identity of the book and both parties intended to bargain with reference to the ability of each to value the book.[82]

The second example closely resembles the violin hypothetical in the Second Restatement of Torts and makes economic sense for the same reasons. The first example is more puzzling. The one important factual difference between the first example and the second one is that while the latter involves a secondhand store, the former involves a store which sells new, high quality merchandise as well as inferior goods. Why should this make a difference so far as the knowledgeable party's duty to disclose is concerned? The restaters distinguish the two situations in terms of the parties' intentions to bargain. This explanation is unsatisfactory, however, since it fails to indicate why their intentions should be different in the two cases. An alternative way of reconciling the two apparently contradictory examples might be the following.

One can easily imagine an expert (in violins or books) browsing in secondhand stores in the hope of finding an undervalued masterpiece. It seems less likely, however, that a bargain hunter would spend time searching the display cases of a fine jewelry store that also sells inferior goods in the hope of finding a gem which has been misclassified.

The owner of a fine jewelry store is almost certain to be an expert in discriminating between valuable jewels and paste. Since he is an expert, and typically takes great care in sorting his own goods, it is unlikely that he will

[82] Restatement of Restitution § 12, Comment c, Illustrations 8 & 9 (1936).

make an error of classification. If similar errors occur more frequently in secondhand bookstores (either because their owners, generally speaking, lack expertise or are careless in sorting), a bargain-hunting expert will be more likely to discover an undervalued item there than he would in a jewelry store which sells both fine gems and junk. Assuming this to be true, one would expect to find more deliberate searches in the one case than in the other. It would follow that a disclosure requirement is more appropriate in the jewelry store setting than in the sale of secondhand books.

This explanation is admittedly a rather tenuous one which rests upon an undemonstrable assumption regarding the incidence of errors of classification in the two cases. If the explanation is unsatisfactory, however, this may itself be a reason for rejecting the view of the restaters or for believing that it does not accurately restate the law.

III. Unilateral Mistake and the Duty to Disclose

The rule that a unilaterally mistaken promisor will be excused when his mistake is known or should be known to the other party is typified by the mistaken bid cases and by those in which the mistaken party's error is the result of his having misread a particular document (usually, the proposed contract itself). In both instances, the special knowledge of the non-mistaken party (his knowledge of the other party's error) is unlikely to be the fruit of a deliberate search. Put differently, a rule requiring him to disclose what he knows will not cause him to alter his behavior in such a way that the production of information of this sort will be reduced.

A contractor receiving a mistaken bid, for example, usually becomes aware of the mistake (if he does at all) by comparing the mistaken bid with others that have been submitted, or by noting an error which is evident on the face of the bid itself. In either case, his knowledge of the mistake arises in the course of a routine examination of the bids which he would undertake in any event. The party receiving the bid has an independent incentive to scrutinize carefully each of the bids which are submitted to him: the profitability of his own enterprise requires that he do so. It is of course true that the recipient's expertise may make it easier for him to identify certain sorts of errors in bids that have been submitted. But the detection of clerical mistakes and errors in calculation is not likely to be one of the principal reasons for his becoming an expert in the first place. A rule requiring the disclosure of mistakes of this kind is almost certain not to discourage investment in developing the sort of general expertise which facilitates the detection of such mistakes.

In the first part of the paper, I argued that a rule requiring disclosure where a unilateral mistake is known or reasonably knowable by the other party makes economic sense because the party with knowledge is—at the time the contract is executed—the cheaper mistake-preventer. If the party possessing special information has deliberately invested in its production—and if the information is socially useful (so that we regard its production as desirable in the first place)—the costs of his search must be considered in determining whether he is in fact the cheaper mistake-preventer. In the cases which are most often cited to support the proposition that a unilateral mistake will excuse where it is known or reasonably knowable by the other party (*i.e.*, the mistaken bid and misread document cases), it is unlikely that the special information in question is the fruit of a deliberate investment. This being so, the conclusion reached in the first part of the paper is confirmed.

The unilateral mistake cases are indistinguishable, in principle, from the other contract cases, discussed in the second part of the paper, which impose a duty to disclose. These cases are distinguished as a group by the fact that in each of them the social interest in efficiency is best served by allocating the risk of a unilateral mistake to the party with knowledge (since this is unlikely to discourage him from investing in the production of socially useful information). In the cases permitting nondisclosure, a similar allocation of risk would—as I have attempted to show—eliminate the private incentive for producing such information and would therefore work to the disadvantage of society as a whole. When viewed in this way, both the cases requiring disclosure (including the unilateral mistake cases) and those permitting nondisclosure appear to conform to (or at least to be consistent with) the principle of efficiency.

Conclusion

In this paper, I have emphasized the way in which one branch of the law of contracts promotes efficiency by encouraging the deliberate search for socially useful information. It does so, I have argued, by giving the possessor of such information the right to deal with others without disclosing what he knows. This right is in essence a property right, and I have tried to show that the law tends to recognize a right of this sort where the information is the result of a deliberate and costly search and not to recognize it where the information has been casually acquired. This basic distinction between two kinds of information (and the theory of property rights which is based upon it) introduces order into the disclosure cases and eliminates the apparent conflict between those cases which permit nondisclosure and the well-established rule that a unilaterally mistaken promisor will be excused if his error is or reasonably should be known by the other party.

Although I have confined my discussion to contract law—indeed, to one rather small part of it—the theoretical approach developed in the second part of the paper may prove to be useful in analyzing related problems in other areas of the law. For example, to what extent can the disclosure requirements in our securities laws which are aimed at frustrating insider-trading be said to rest upon (and to be justified by) the idea that inside information is more likely to be casually discovered rather than deliberately produced?[83] If this is in fact one of the principal assumptions underlying the various disclosure requirements imposed by our securities laws, what conclusions—if any—can be drawn regarding the proper scope of these requirements? For example, how much should a tender offeror have to publicly disclose concerning his plans for the corporation he hopes to acquire? Does the analysis offered in this paper throw any light on the requirement of "non-obviousness" in patent law?[84] (Is this perhaps a legal device for discriminating between information which is the result of a deliberate search and information which is not?) Do the distinctions suggested here help us to understand the proliferation of disclosure requirements in the consumer products field and to form a more considered judgment as to their desirability? A legal theory which provided a common framework for the analysis of these and other questions would have considerable appeal.

[83] Useful discussions of the economics of disclosure requirements in the securities field may be found in Henry G. Manne, Insider Trading and the Stock Market (1966), and Eugene F. Fama & Arthur B. Laffer, Information and Capital Markets, 44 J. Bus. 289, 297-98 (1971).

[84] See Edmund W. Kitch, Graham v. John Deere Co: New Standards for Patents, 1966 Sup. Ct. Rev. 293.

[16]

The Case for Specific Performance

Alan Schwartz†

The purpose of contract remedies is to place a disappointed promisee in as good a position as he would have enjoyed had his promisor performed.[1] Contract law has two methods of achieving this "compensation goal": requiring the breaching party to pay damages, either to enable the promisee to purchase a substitute performance, or to replace the net gains that the promised performance would have generated; or requiring the breaching party to render the promised performance. Although the damages remedy is always available to a disappointed promisee under current law, the remedy of specific performance is available only at the discretion of the court. Moreover, courts seldom enforce contract clauses that explicitly provide for specific performance in the event of breach.

This Article argues that the remedy of specific performance should be as routinely available as the damages remedy. Part I reviews the current doctrine governing specific performance. Part II argues that the damage remedy is undercompensatory more often than is generally supposed and establishes that promisees have economic incentives not to elect specific performance unless the damage remedy is likely not to provide adequate compensation. Thus, expanding the availability of specific performance would not give promisees an incentive to exploit breaching promisors. Part III goes on to show that making specific performance generally available is unlikely to result in the efficiency losses predicted by other commentators.[2] Part IV argues that expand-

† Professor of Law, University of Southern California Law Center. This Article benefited greatly from comments received at faculty workshops held at U.S.C. and Hebrew University, Jerusalem, and at a graduate economics seminar at the California Institute of Technology. David W. Carroll, Melvin A. Eisenberg, Robert C. Ellickson, Julius G. Getman, Stephen J. Morse, Richard A. Posner, Margaret Jane Radin, Robert E. Scott, and Louis L. Wilde also made helpful comments on prior drafts.

1. *See, e.g.*, U.C.C. § 1-106(1) (1972 version) ("remedies . . . shall be liberally administered to the end that the aggrieved party may be put in as good a position as if the other party had fully performed. . . ."); RESTATEMENT OF CONTRACTS § 329 (1932) (same) [hereinafter cited as RESTATEMENT].

2. *See, e.g.*, R. POSNER, ECONOMIC ANALYSIS OF LAW 88-89 (2d ed. 1977) (defending current law on efficiency grounds); Kronman, *Specific Performance*, 45 U. CHI. L. REV. 351 (1978) (same); Farnsworth, *Damages and Specific Relief*, 27 AM. J. COMP. L. 247 (1979). The only modern commentator to criticize specific performance law seriously is Professor Dawson, who has called for the specific performance of all contracts to deliver chattels. *See* Dawson, *Specific Performance in France and Germany*, 57 MICH. L. REV. 495, 532 (1959). Professor Dawson, however, did not deal with efficiency objections to the wider availability of specific performance.

ing the availability of specific performance would not unduly restrict the liberty interests of promisors. Finally, Part V argues that defenses not available in an action for damages should be eliminated or severely restricted in their application to actions for specific performance.[3]

I. The Current Law Regarding Specific Performance

Under current law, courts grant specific performance when they perceive that damages will be inadequate compensation. Specific performance is deemed an extraordinary remedy, awarded at the court's discretion:

> [I]t must be remembered that specific performance is not a matter of right, even when the plaintiff's evidence establishes a contract valid at law and sufficient for the recovery of damages. Ordering specific enforcement of a contract is a matter within the sound judicial discretion of the court. . . . [T]he plaintiff was required to show the good faith and equities of its own position, and the trial chancellor, in weighing the equities, was entitled to consider whether a decree of specific performance would work an unconscionable advantage to the plaintiff or would result in injustice.[4]

The paradigm cases in which the specific performance remedy is currently granted include sales of "unique goods,"[5] in which substitutional damages are difficult to compute; sales of land, because land is

3. This Article omits consideration of several interesting facets of the specific performance question. First, a personal services contract is enforced by an injunction preventing the promisor from performing elsewhere rather than by an injunction requiring the promisor to perform. *See* Restatement § 379. This rule rests partly on the difficulty of supervising the promisor's performance, but primarily on the promisor's liberty interest in not being compelled to work at a particular job. *See* pp. 296-97 *infra*. Second, contracts in a family context, such as separation agreements, are sometimes specifically enforceable. Third, a seller usually cannot obtain specific performance of the price if the buyer has not accepted the goods, whereas vendors of land can sue for the price of unaccepted property. This Article does not analyze sellers' remedies; its concern is with cases in which the purchasers of goods, realty or services sue for specific performance. Fourth, expanding specific performance may raise questions concerning the availability of jury trials because suits for specific performance may be regarded as actions in equity.

4. Public Water Supply Dist. v. Fowlkes, 407 S.W.2d 642, 647 (Mo. App. 1966); *accord*, Green, Inc. v. Smith, 40 Ohio App. 2d 30, 39, 317 N.E.2d 227, 233 (1974). The current Restatement retains this rule. *See* Restatement (Second) of Contracts § 371(1) (Tent. Draft No. 14, 1979) ("[S]pecific performance of a contract duty will be granted in the discretion of the court against a party who has committed or is threatening to commit a breach of the duty") [hereinafter cited as Restatement (Second)].

5. *See, e.g.*, Leasco Corp. v. Taussig, 473 F.2d 777, 786 (2d Cir. 1972) (specifically enforcing contract for sale of business as each business is deemed unique); U.C.C. § 2-716(1) ("[s]pecific performance may be decreed where the goods are unique or in other proper circumstances").

Specific Performance

presumed unique;[6] and, more recently, long-term requirements contracts, for which damages from breach are hard to calculate.[7]

A disappointed promisee who is able to show that he has no adequate remedy at law nevertheless is not assured of obtaining specific performance. Promisors can raise a number of defenses against specific performance that are not available against a damages award: inadequacy of consideration;[8] lack of security for the promisee's performance;[9] the promisor's unilateral mistake;[10] and the difficulty a court would have in supervising a specific performance decree.[11] These defenses serve to restrict further the availability of the specific performance remedy.

Further, courts currently refuse to enforce contracts providing for remedies different from those that they would grant. Liquidated damage clauses with sufficiently high damage provisions would in effect guarantee performance by the promisor because the costs to him of breach would always exceed the costs of performance. However, courts will not enforce such clauses; liquidated damage clauses are enforced only if they reflect a "reasonable" forecast of "actual" damages—the damages courts would grant if there were no liquidated damage clauses in the contracts.[12] In addition, courts seldom enforce contract

6. *See, e.g.*, Henderson v. Fisher, 236 Cal. App. 2d 468, 473, 46 Cal. Rptr. 173, 177 (1965); Gethsemane Lutheran Church v. Zacho, 258 Minn. 438, 443, 104 N.W.2d 645, 648 (1960).

7. *See, e.g.*, Laclede Gas Co. v. Amoco Oil Co., 522 F.2d 33, 40 (8th Cir. 1975); Eastern Air Lines, Inc. v. Gulf Oil Corp., 415 F. Supp. 429, 442-43 (S.D. Fla. 1975); *cf.* U.C.C. § 2-716 (Comment 2) (requirements contracts considered "unique goods").

8. *See, e.g.*, Loeb v. Wilson, 253 Cal. App. 2d 383, 388, 61 Cal. Rptr. 377, 380 (1967); Schlegel v. Moorhead, 170 Mont. 391, 553 P.2d 1009 (1976); RESTATEMENT (SECOND) § 378(1)(c). *But see* note 78 *infra* (citing cases in which specific performance granted despite inadequacy of consideration). In some states, this defense is statutory. *See, e.g.*, CAL. CIV. CODE § 3391.1 (West 1970). Some state courts allow the defense only if the inadequacy is so great as to constitute fraud. *See, e.g.*, Shepard v. Dick, 203 Kan. 164, 169, 453 P.2d 134, 138 (1969); Banner v. Elm, 251 Md. 694, 697, 248 A.2d 452, 453 (1968). For a criticism of this more stringent form of the defense, see J. POMEROY, TREATISE ON THE SPECIFIC PERFORMANCE OF CONTRACTS 504-07 (3d ed. 1926) (stringent form of defense of little additional help to courts in deciding when to deny the remedy).

9. *See, e.g.*, Rego v. Decker, 482 P.2d 834, 837-38 (Alaska 1971); Handy v. Gordon, 65 Cal. 2d 578, 422 P.2d 329, 55 Cal. Rptr. 769 (1967); RESTATEMENT (SECOND) § 377.

10. *See, e.g.*, 4500 Suitland Rd. Corp. v. Ciccarello, 269 Md. 444, 452, 306 A.2d 512, 516 (1973); Public Water Supply Dist. v. Fowlkes, 407 S.W.2d 642, 649 (Mo. App. 1966).

11. *See, e.g.*, Ryan v. Ocean Twelve, Inc., 316 A.2d 573, 575 (Del. Ch. 1973); Yonan v. Oak Park Fed. Sav. & Loan Ass'n, 27 Ill. App. 3d 967, 974, 326 N.E.2d 773, 779 (1975).

12. *See, e.g.*, Wise v. United States, 249 U.S. 361 (1919) (enforcing liquidated damage clause because not disproportionate to property loss); J. Weinstein & Sons, Inc. v. City of New York, 264 App. Div. 398, 35 N.Y.S.2d 530, *aff'd*, 289 N.Y. 741, 46 N.E.2d 351 (1942) (striking down liquidated damages clause as out of proportion to probable damage); U.C.C. § 2-718(1); C. MCCORMICK, LAW OF DAMAGES § 149 (1935). Recent commentators have persuasively criticized these restrictions on the use of liquidated damage clauses. *See* Goetz & Scott, *Liquidated Damages, Penalties and the Just Compensation Principle: Some Notes on an Enforcement Model and a Theory of Efficient Breach*, 77 COLUM. L. REV. 554 (1977) (all liquidated damage clauses should be enforceable); Note, *A Critique of the Penalty Limitation on Liquidated Damages*, 50 S. CAL. L. REV. 1055 (1977) (same).

clauses that provide explicitly for specific performance in the event of breach.[13]

II. Contract Remedies and the Compensation Goal

Specific performance is the most accurate method of achieving the compensation goal of contract remedies because it gives the promisee the precise performance that he purchased.[14] The natural question, then, is why specific performance is not routinely available.[15] Three explanations of the law's restrictions on specific performance are possible. First, the law's commitment to the compensation goal may be less than complete; restricting specific performance may reflect an inarticulate reluctance to pursue the compensation goal fully. Second, damages may generally be fully compensatory. In that event, expanding the availability of specific performance would create opportunities for promisees to exploit promisors by threatening to compel, or actually compelling, performance, without furthering the compensation goal. The third explanation is that concerns of efficiency or liberty may justify restricting specific performance, despite its greater accuracy; specific performance might generate higher transaction costs than the damage remedy, or interfere more with the liberty interests of promisors. The first justification is beyond the scope of the analysis here.[16] The second and third explanations will be examined in detail.

With respect to the second justification, current doctrine authorizes

13. *See, e.g.,* Stokes v. Moore, 262 Ala. 59, 77 So. 2d 331 (1955); Snell v. Mitchell, 65 Me. 48 (1876). For criticism of this rule, see Kronman, *supra* note 2, at 371-76; Macneil *Power of Contract and Agreed Remedies,* 47 CORNELL L.Q. 495, 520-23 (1962).

14. Admittedly, the equitable remedy does not compensate for the costs of legal delay; however, such delay is also a feature of actions for damages. Also, inflation partially offsets the costs of delay for promisees because it enables them to pay in cheaper dollars.

15. One of the earliest English royal writs available to promisees in contract, the writ of covenant, routinely provided for specific performance. *See* A. SIMPSON, A HISTORY OF THE COMMON LAW OF CONTRACT 14 (1975) ("[i]n common with other early writs the writ of covenant . . . seems to be designed not so much to initiate proceedings directed towards compensating the plaintiff for wrong done, as to ensure that what was wrong should be put right. . . ."). By 1260, however, damages had become the usual remedy in covenant.

Thereafter, courts of law were authorized only to give damage awards, *id.* at 595; courts of equity issued specific performance decrees, but only if there was no adequate remedy at law, *id.* at 596. With the merging of law and equity courts into a unified judicial system, the question arises whether continued restrictions on the availability of specific performance are still justified.

16. This Article's conclusion that specific performance should be made routinely available presupposes the desirability of the compensation goal. To deal fully with the claim that courts should not pursue the compensation goal fully, it would be necessary to formulate both a descriptive theory of why contracts are breached and a normative theory assessing the reasons for breach in terms of the underlying goals of contract law. Neither theory exists at present and creating them is beyond the scope of this Article.

specific performance when courts cannot calculate compensatory damages with even a rough degree of accuracy.[17] If the class of cases in which there are difficulties in computing damages corresponds closely to the class of cases in which specific performance is now granted, expanding the availability of specific performance is obviously unnecessary. Further, such an expansion would create opportunities for promisees to exploit promisors. The class of cases in which damage awards fail to compensate promisees adequately is, however, broader than the class of cases in which specific performance is now granted. Thus the compensation goal supports removing rather than retaining present restrictions on the availability of specific performance.

It is useful to begin by examining the paradigm case for granting specific performance under current law, the case of unique goods.[18] When a promisor breaches and the promisee can make a transaction that substitutes for the performance the promisor failed to render, the promisee will be fully compensated if he receives the additional amount necessary to purchase the substitute plus the costs of making a second transaction. In some cases, however, such as those involving works of art, courts cannot identify which transactions the promisee would regard as substitutes because that information often is in the exclusive possession of the promisee. Moreover, it is difficult for a court to assess the accuracy of a promisee's claim. For example, if the promisor breaches a contract to sell a rare emerald, the promisee may claim that only the Hope Diamond would give him equal satisfaction, and thus may sue for the price difference between the emerald and the diamond. It would be difficult for a court to know whether this claim is true. If the court seeks to award money damages, it has three choices: granting the price differential, which may overcompensate the promisee; granting the dollar value of the promisee's foregone satisfaction as estimated by the court, which may overcompensate or undercompensate; or granting restitution of any sums paid, which undercompensates the promisee. The promisee is fully compensated without risk of overcompensation or undercompensation if the remedy of specific performance is available to him and its use encouraged by the doctrine that damages must be foreseeable and certain.[19]

If specific performance is the appropriate remedy in such cases, there

17. *See* pp. 272-73 and notes 5-7 *supra*.

18. *See, e.g.*, Copylease Corp. of America v. Memorex Corp., 408 F. Supp. 758, 759 (S.D.N.Y. 1976) (unique goods contracts are exception to general rule limiting availability of specific performance); U.C.C. § 2-716(1) (buyer has right to specific performance in unique goods case).

19. For a fuller exposition of this argument, see Kronman, *supra* note 2, at 355-65.

are three reasons why it should be routinely available. The first reason is that in many cases damages actually are undercompensatory. Although promisees are entitled to incidental damages,[20] such damages are difficult to monetize. They consist primarily of the costs of finding and making a second deal, which generally involve the expenditure of time rather than cash; attaching a dollar value to such opportunity costs is quite difficult. Breach can also cause frustration and anger, especially in a consumer context, but these costs also are not recoverable.[21]

Substitution damages, the court's estimate of the amount the promisee needs to purchase an adequate substitute, also may be inaccurate in many cases less dramatic than the emerald hypothetical discussed above. This is largely because of product differentiation and early obsolescence. As product differentiation becomes more common, the supply of products that will substitute precisely for the promisor's performance is reduced. For example, even during the period when there is an abundant supply of new Datsuns for sale, two-door, two-tone Datsuns with mag wheels, stereo, and air conditioning may be scarce in some local markets. Moreover, early obsolescence gives the promisee a short time in which to make a substitute purchase. If the promisor breaches late in a model year, for example, it may be difficult for the promisee to buy the exact model he wanted. For these reasons, a damage award meant to enable a promisee to purchase "another car" could be undercompensatory.

In addition, problems of prediction often make it difficult to put a promisee in the position where he would have been had his promisor performed.[22] If a breach by a contractor would significantly delay or prevent completion of a construction project and the project differs in important respects from other projects—for example, a department store in a different location than previous stores—courts may be reluctant to award "speculative" lost profits attributable to the breach.[23]

20. *E.g.*, U.C.C. § 2-715(1).

21. Emotional distress caused by a breach, which does not in itself constitute a tort, ordinarily is not recoverable in damages. *See, e.g.*, Jankowski v. Mazzotta, 7 Mich. App. 483, 486, 152 N.W.2d 49, 50-51 (1967) (damages for mental anguish limited to cases involving "reckless misconduct" or contracts "inherently personal in nature").

22. The difficulties of prediction have been recognized for some time. *See, e.g.*, RESTATEMENT § 329, Comment a (difficulties involved in awarding compensatory damages "make it impracticable to attain its purpose with any near approach to exactness"); W. WALSH, A TREATISE ON EQUITY 300 (1930) (damages at best only substitute for what plaintiff lost through loss of performance).

23. *See, e.g.*, Fredonia Broadcasting Corp. v. RCA Corp., 481 F.2d 781, 802-04 (5th Cir. 1973) (future profits of new business deemed too speculative for inclusion in damages); Atomic Fuel Extraction Corp. v. Slick's Estate, 386 S.W.2d 180, 189-90 (Tex. Civ. App. 1965) (same).

Specific Performance

Second, promisees have economic incentives to sue for damages when damages are likely to be fully compensatory. A breaching promisor is reluctant to perform and may be hostile. This makes specific performance an unattractive remedy in cases in which the promisor's performance is complex, because the promisor is more likely to render a defective performance when that performance is coerced, and the defectiveness of complex performances is sometimes difficult to establish in court. Further, when the promisor's performance must be rendered over time, as in construction or requirements contracts, it is costly for the promisee to monitor a reluctant promisor's conduct. If the damage remedy is compensatory, the promisee would prefer it to incurring these monitoring costs. Finally, given the time necessary to resolve lawsuits, promisees would commonly prefer to make substitute transactions promptly and sue later for damages rather than hold their affairs in suspension while awaiting equitable relief. The very fact that a promisee requests specific performance thus implies that damages are an inadequate remedy.[24]

The third reason why courts should permit promisees to elect routinely the remedy of specific performance is that promisees possess better information than courts as to both the adequacy of damages and the difficulties of coercing performance. Promisees know better than courts whether the damages a court is likely to award would be adequate because promisees are more familiar with the costs that breach imposes on them. In addition, promisees generally know more about their promisors than do courts; thus they are in a better position to predict whether specific performance decrees would induce their promisors to render satisfactory performances.

In sum, restrictions on the availability of specific performance cannot be justified on the basis that damage awards are usually compensatory. On the contrary, the compensation goal implies that specific performance should be routinely available. This is because damage awards actually are undercompensatory in more cases than is commonly supposed; the fact of a specific performance request is itself good evidence that damages would be inadequate; and courts should delegate to promisees the decision of which remedy best satisfies the compensation goal. Further, expanding the availability of specific per-

24. Noneconomic motives could sometimes impel a promisee to seek specific performance; the German experience, however, provides some confirmation of this point. Although specific performance is much more widely available in Germany than in the United States, promisees there seek the damage remedy "in a high percentage of cases." Dawson, *supra* note 2, at 530; *see* Treitel, *Remedies for Breach of Contract*, in VII INTERNATIONAL ENCYCLOPEDIA OF COMPARATIVE LAW 16-17 to 16-29 (1976) (claims for damages "more common" than claims for specific performance).

formance would not result in greater exploitation of promisors. Promisees would seldom abuse the power to determine when specific performance should be awarded because of the strong incentives that promisees face to seek damages when these would be even approximately compensatory.

III. Specific Performance and Efficiency

Before examining in detail the efficiency justifications that could be given for restricting specific performance, it will be useful to relate these justifications to the possible bases of the compensation goal. First, suppose that the goal rests on utilitarian or wealth maximization grounds,[25] that is, on an assumption that compensating disappointed promisees fully is less costly than not compensating them fully. If the broader availability of specific performance would generate transaction costs that exceed the costs of undercompensation the equitable remedy would avoid, then current restrictions on specific performance would be justified. On the other hand, if the compensation goal rests on a moral notion that promises should be kept,[26] that contract remedies should effectuate the state of affairs—performance—that the promisor has a duty to bring about and that the promisee has a right to have brought about, then specific performance is a preferable remedy to damages even though it might generate higher costs. These costs would be the price of achieving the moral goal of contract remedies. Under this theory, the promisee's right to an actual performance should be overridden only if the costs of its exercise would be so excessive as to constitute an interference with the rights of other persons.

Both possible bases of the compensation goal thus would support the routine availability of specific performance unless specific per-

25. Professor Posner recently argued that a nonutilitarian version of consequentialism which he calls wealth maximization underlies and justifies much current law. *See* Posner, *Utilitarianism, Economics, and Legal Theory*, 8 J. LEGAL STUD. 103 (1979). According to Posner, a legal rule (indeed, all conduct) is good if it increases society's wealth, bad if it reduces that wealth.

26. For an introduction to how a moral justification for promise-keeping can be made, see J. MACKIE, ETHICS 110-11, 116-18, 184-85 (1977). Professor Mackie's argument, derived from Hobbes and Hume, is that it is in a promisor's self-interest to keep his word. A similar argument may follow from Kantian premises. Kant uses promise-keeping as one of his four illustrations of the categorical imperative:

> For the universality of a law that everyone believing himself to be in need can make any promise he pleases with the intention not to keep it would make promising, and the very purpose of promising, itself impossible, since no one would believe he was being promised anything, but would laugh at utterances of this kind as empty shams.

I. KANT, GROUNDWORK OF THE METAPHYSIC OF MORALS 90 (H. Paton trans. 1964).

formance is a more costly remedy than damages. There are two principal ways in which efficiency might suffer as the result of expanding specific performance. First, many parties might prefer to have the specific performance remedy available only in those cases in which the law currently grants it. If the remedy's availability were greatly expanded, these parties would negotiate contract provisions restricting its use. Legal limitations on the availability of specific performance save these transaction costs. Professor Anthony Kronman has argued that limiting specific performance is justified precisely because it avoids such "pre-breach" negotiations.[27] Second, if specific performance were routinely available, promisors who wanted to breach would often be compelled to "bribe" promisees to release them from their obligations. The negotiations required might be more complex and costly than the post-breach negotiations that occur when breaching promisors have merely to pay promisees their damages. Professor Richard Posner argues, therefore, that restricting specific performance reduces "post-breach" negotiation costs.[28] Part III considers these two arguments in detail, as well as other efficiency aspects of the choice between specific performance and damages.

A. *Pre-Breach Negotiations*

"Intention justification" theories for restricting specific performance argue that the class of cases in which the parties now can get the remedy, and the class of cases in which the parties would want the remedy to be available, are coextensive. There are two difficulties with this position. First, there is no reason to assume that the parties' preferences are congruent with current law. Second, it is excessively difficult to derive from parties' preferences general legal rules respecting when either remedy should be used.

Both weaknesses are illustrated through an analysis of the most sophisticated intention justification theory, that of Professor Kronman.

27. Kronman, *supra* note 2, at 365-69.

28. R. Posner, *supra* note 2, at 88-89. Other commentators have made similar arguments. *See* Clarkson, Miller, & Muris, *Liquidated Damages v. Penalties: Sense or Nonsense?* 1978 Wis. L. Rev. 351, 360 n.32. Professor Farnsworth recently criticized the specific performance remedy on the apparently distinct ground that specific relief prevents a promisor from reallocating his resources to higher valued uses even though substitutional relief would be fully compensatory to the promisee. Farnsworth, *supra* note 2, at 250-51. This criticism is incorrect because promisors can reallocate their resources—*i.e.*, breach—by bribing promisees not to seek specific relief. Thus Farnsworth's position reduces to the claim that Posner makes, that the transaction costs entailed in these post-breach negotiations would be higher than the transaction costs that now obtain under the damage remedy.

Kronman classifies as "unique" those objects for which courts would have great difficulty identifying substitutes. Courts today generally limit specific performance to such cases. Professor Kronman argues that this limitation is consistent with the parties' intentions; if they were to contract as to remedy in the absence of a general rule, they would create a specific performance remedy only for sales of "unique" goods or services. Kronman's argument starts from the premise that the "cost of a specific performance provision to the promisor will be determined, in part, by his own estimate of the likelihood that he will want to breach the contract."[29] This likelihood is primarily a function of "the probability that he will receive a better offer for his goods or services in the interim between formation of the contract and performance."[30] This probability is low "where the subject matter of the contract is unique" because "there is by definition no developed market [and] transactions are spotty at best. . . ."[31] In situations in which the subject matter of the contract is not unique, "by contrast, the existence of a developed market increases the likelihood that the promisor will receive alternative offers before he has performed the contract."[32] The promisee in the unique goods case may doubt whether the promisor will actually perform, despite the unlikelihood that the promisor will receive a better offer. Since damage remedies could be undercompensatory, the promisee would probably prefer to have the specific performance remedy available.[33] When the goods are not unique, however, the promisee regards the "risk [of undercompensation] as slight where there is a developed market generating information about suitable substitutes."[34] Thus in the unique goods case the parties would be expected to agree to a specific performance remedy; the promisee wants the remedy, whereas the promisor is indifferent. In the nonunique goods case, on the other hand, the parties would probably negotiate for a damage remedy, because damages would adequately protect the promisee, while the promisor would want to be free to accept more favorable offers.

Analysis of the equilibria in "developed" and "undeveloped markets" and their reactions to exogenous shocks suggests, however, that the promisors of unique goods care more about retaining the option of breach than do promisors of nonunique goods. Respecting equilibria,

29. Kronman, *supra* note 2, at 367.
30. *Id.* at 368.
31. *Id.*
32. *Id.*
33. *Id.*
34. *Id.* at 369. The risk of undercompensation, however, actually may be substantial even when "developed" markets exist. *See* pp. 275-76 *supra*.

Specific Performance

Professor Kronman equates an undeveloped market with a market in which unique goods are sold. This is misleading because unique goods markets often are well organized; the antique market provides an example. Such markets have two distinguishing features. First, they are usually characterized by greater price dispersion than obtains in the market equilibria for roughly fungible goods. In addition, sellers of unique goods face a lower "rate of arrival" of potential buyers than do sellers of roughly fungible goods. These two phenomena are related; a high "buyer arrival" rate implies extensive comparison shopping among firms, whereas the degree of price dispersion a market can sustain varies inversely with the amount of comparison shopping.[35] Sellers of unique goods face a relatively low buyer arrival rate because each item they sell is highly differentiated; consequently, relatively few potential customers for such items exist. Also, search costs are comparatively higher for unique goods; locating them can be difficult, and the sellers often are geographically dispersed. Further, analyzing the quality of particular unique goods and comparing different goods usually are more time-consuming than searching for roughly fungible goods.

A promisor/seller in an "undeveloped market"—a market in which unique goods are sold—thus faces a lower arrival rate of potential buyers together with the resultant higher degree of price dispersion than a promisor in a developed market. The promisor of unique goods consequently has grounds to believe that the offers he receives are to some extent random, and that later offers could be much higher than earlier ones. This promisor thus prefers damages to specific performance because the damages remedy preserves his freedom to breach.

This conclusion is reinforced by an examination of the differing reactions of "developed" and "undeveloped" markets to exogenous shocks.[36] Exogenous shocks help to explain why promisors might receive better offers between the time they contract and the time they are supposed to render performance. This phenomenon needs explanation because a vendor of goods or services is generally assumed to sell

35. *See* Schwartz & Wilde, *Intervening In Markets on the Basis of Imperfect Information: A Legal and Economic Analysis*, 127 U. PA. L. REV. 630, 640-51 (1979).

36. Economists draw a distinction between the factors influencing market equilibria that are intrinsic to the market ("endogenous" factors) and those that are extrinsic to it ("exogenous" factors). An example of an endogenous factor is the strategies that consumers use in acquiring purchase information; market equilibria are partly a function of the information-gathering strategies of consumers. An example of an exogenous factor is an embargo; a particular equilibrium will be disturbed if an embargo reduces available supply. For a discussion of the contributions of endogenous and exogenous factors to the character of market equilibria in an information-gathering context, see Rothschild, *Models of Market Organization with Imperfect Information: A Survey*, 81 J. POL. ECON. 1283 (1973).

to all of his purchasers on the same terms. Price discrimination is often unlawful and its costs in mass transactions exceed the gains it produces.[37] Customers generally know whether a firm offers the same terms to all and are unlikely to make offers that exceed the going price. In addition, firms that negotiate contracts on an individual basis have a strong incentive not to breach, even if they receive better offers, in order to maintain goodwill.[38] In what circumstances, then, will promisors receive and accept better offers?

The most frequent situation in which these circumstances arise is when there is an unexpected and dramatic increase in demand. The increase in demand will exert an upward pressure on prices. In the case of nonunique goods, this pressure is partially relieved by the ability of sellers to increase output. Unique goods, however, are in inelastic supply; only a few Rembrandts exist, and an increase in demand will not increase their number.[39] In consequence, when buyers demand more of a unique item, the primary response of sellers is to increase the price; they can expand output only slightly, if at all.[40]

37. Schwartz & Wilde, *supra* note 35, at 638, 663-65.

38. The desire of firms to preserve goodwill is evident in the existence of two common retail practices: marking items "sold" and holding them for the original purchasers rather than reselling them to subsequent buyers at higher prices, and, in the case of firms that sell services, rationing temporary excess demand by queuing rather than by selling services to subsequent customers at increased rates.

39. For a more rigorous discussion of the theory of supply elasticity, see P. Samuelson, Economics 386-87 (10th ed. 1976).

40. The argument in text can be clarified by a diagram.

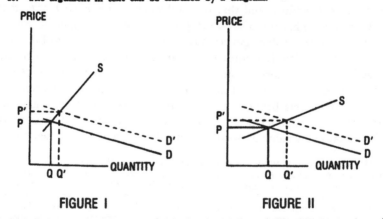

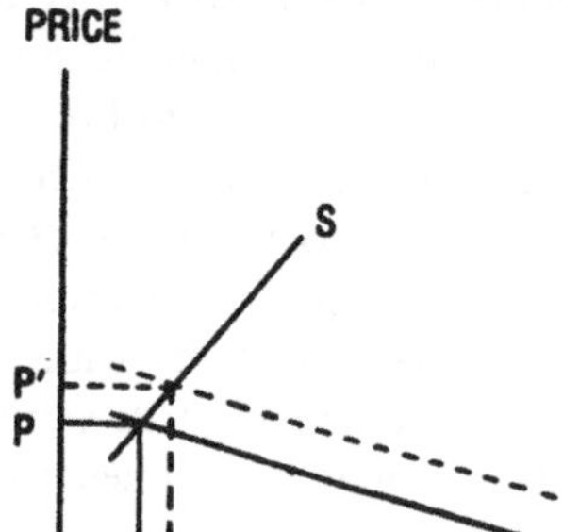

FIGURE I

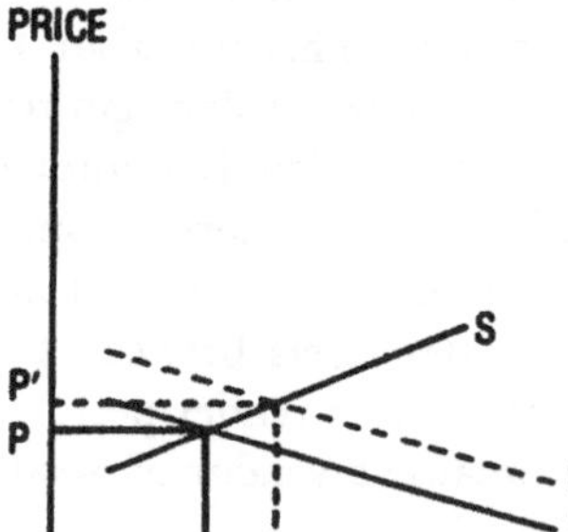

FIGURE II

In both figures, an increase in demand is represented by a similar shift in the demand curve from D to D'. In Figure 1, however, supply (S) is inelastic; no matter how great the shift in demand, little more of the good is supplied. Thus almost the full force of the demand shift is translated into the price increase. In Figure 2, supply is elastic, so that output expands considerably and the price increase is more moderate.

Specific Performance

Therefore, when demand unexpectedly increases, a promisor in a unique goods market could command higher prices than a promisor in a nonunique goods market. The seller of unique goods, when the contract is negotiated, thus has a strong incentive to preserve his freedom to breach. A seller of nonunique goods, by contrast, will probably have to compete with many other vendors for any new business that a demand increase generates, and the resultant price rise will be relatively modest. Thus he will care less about preserving his freedom to breach in response to demand shifts.[41] In sum, if the promisor's preference for specific performance or damages is assumed to be determined solely by whether the performance at issue is unique, the promisor would not choose specific performance in situations in which the law now routinely grants it.[42]

In addition, considerations exist that could lead promisees not to prefer a right to specific performance in cases in which it is currently available and to seek this right in situations in which it is not now granted.[43] Purchasers of houses or land, for example, may sometimes

41. This analysis applies not only to goods that have traditionally been considered unique but also to goods that are currently in inelastic supply. Prices also will rise if demand remains constant and supply contracts. Provided the demand curve remains constant, the suppliers of unique and nonunique goods will be similarly affected, and thus have similar incentives to preserve their freedom to breach.

42. Confirming the textual analysis that shifts in demand affect preferences for specific performance, a number of recent suits for specific performance seem to have been caused in part by shifts in demand, *e.g.*, Weathersby v. Gore, 556 F.2d 1247, 1249 (5th Cir. 1977) (cotton); Tower City Grain Co. v. Richman, 232 N.W.2d 61, 63 (N.D. 1975) (boxcar shortage suggests increased demand for grain); or combinations of shifts in demand and supply, *e.g.*, Laclede Gas Co. v. Amoco Oil Co., 522 F.2d 33, 36 (8th Cir. 1975) (propane gas); Eastern Air Lines, Inc. v. Gulf Oil Corp., 415 F. Supp. 429, 441 (S.D. Fla. 1975) (jet fuel).

43. The cheapest cost-avoider technique, *see* G. Calabresi, The Cost of Accidents 135-40 (1970), provides an alternative means of analyzing the parties' intentions respecting remedy provisions in unique goods transactions. The relevant risk is that the promisor/seller will get a better offer in the interval between contract formation and performance time. If the seller bears this risk, he must perform despite the better offer; if the buyer bears the risk, the seller is free to take the better offer and pay damages to the first buyer. The seller, this analysis assumes, is the cheapest cost-avoider of the risk of receiving a better offer because he generally has superior knowledge of market conditions. Since the parties will typically negotiate to put the risk on the cheapest cost-avoider, they would normally contract for a specific performance remedy in the unique goods case. Professor Kronman does not make this argument, and he may be right not to do so because generalizations about whether promisors or promisees have superior ability to predict the future are too difficult to make. For example, an individual selling an heirloom to a dealer would probably have less knowledge than the dealer; a dealer selling to a consumer would probably have more knowledge than the consumer; and a wholesale antique dealer selling to a retail dealer would probably have no more knowledge than this buyer. Thus it is incorrect to argue that parties commonly would negotiate for a specific performance remedy in the unique goods case; such an argument must rest on the unproven assertion that promisors have a comparative advantage at predicting the future.

prefer liquidated damage clauses to specific performance because sellers in possession during the specific performance action might cause damage that would be difficult to prove in court. Also, a purchaser of a unique good may prefer damages to specific performance if he believes that he could later persuade a court to accept his exaggerated claim as to the cost of an adequate substitute. Promisees of nonunique goods, on the other hand, may prefer specific performance because large damage judgments can be difficult to obtain or satisfy.[44]

Thus no single factor—such as the uniqueness of the performance—will determine the parties' preferences as to remedy in all cases, for the parties' preferences are context-dependent. Further analysis would probably suggest additional discrepancies between the remedies the parties desire in specific situations and those the law now provides. The costs of tailoring the law to the parties' preferences on a case-by-case basis, however, would exceed the gains. As with an attempt to draft substantive contract clauses, a great number of rules would have to be devised. Therefore, because it has not been established that restricting specific performance minimizes transaction costs of negotiating remedies, and tailoring remedies to the parties' preferences would be so costly administratively, intention justification theories should be abandoned as guides to remedy availability. Rather, specific performance should be made generally available on the ground that the compensation goal is not met adequately by making damages the sole available remedy in many cases. This recommendation presupposes, however, that the post-breach negotiation costs thereby generated would not exceed those generated under current law. This presupposition must be analyzed next.

B. *Post-Breach Negotiations*

The second efficiency argument for restricting the availability of specific performance is that making specific performance freely avail-

44. For example, some cotton purchasers unsuccessfully sought specific performance of contracts that their grower-sellers had breached when cotton prices tripled between the time the contract was negotiated and the time for performance. The buyers may have believed that local juries might be reluctant to award large damages against local farmer defendants. *See* Weathersby v. Gore, 556 F.2d 1247 (5th Cir. 1977); Duval & Co. v. Malcom, 233 Ga. 784, 214 S.E.2d 356 (1975).

The Restatement lists "the degree of probability that damages awarded cannot in fact be collected" as a factor to be considered in "determining the adequacy of the remedy in damages." RESTATEMENT § 361(d); *accord*, RESTATEMENT (SECOND) § 374(c). *See* Severson v. Elberon Elevator, Inc., 250 N.W.2d 417, 423 (Iowa 1977) (defendant's financial straits relevant to specific performance request). The unlikelihood of collecting a damage award would of course justify specific performance regardless of whether the goods were "unique."

able would generate higher post-breach negotiation costs than the damage remedy now generates. For example, suppose that a buyer (B1) contracts with a seller (S) to buy a widget for $100. Prior to delivery, demand unexpectedly increases. The widget market is temporarily in disequilibrium as buyers make offers at different prices. While the market is in disequilibrium, a second buyer (B2) makes a contract with S to purchase the same widget for $130. Subsequently, the new equilibrium price for widgets is $115. If specific performance is available in this case, B1 is likely to demand it, in order to compel S to pay him some of the profit that S will make from breaching. B1 could, for example, insist on specific performance unless S pays him $20 ($15 in substitution damages plus a $5 premium).[45] If S agrees, B1 can cover at $115,[46] and be better off by $5 than he would have been under the damage remedy, which would have given him only the difference between the cover price and the contract price ($15). Whenever S's better offer is higher than the new market price, the seller has an incentive to breach, and the first buyer has an incentive to threaten specific performance in order to capture some of the seller's gains from breach.

The post-breach negotiations between S and B1 represent a "deadweight" efficiency loss; the negotiations serve only to redistribute wealth between S and B1, without generating additional social wealth. If society is indifferent as to whether sellers or buyers as a group profit from an increase in demand, the law should seek to eliminate this efficiency loss. Limiting buyers to the damage remedy apparently does so by foreclosing post-breach negotiations.

This analysis is incomplete, however. Negotiation costs are also generated when B1 attempts to collect damages. If the negotiations by which first buyers (B1 here) capture a portion of their sellers' profits from breach are less costly than the negotiations (or lawsuits) by which first buyers recover the market contract differential, then specific performance would generate lower post-breach negotiation costs than damages. This seems unlikely, however. The difference between the contract and market prices is often easily determined, and breaching sellers have an incentive to pay it promptly so as not to have their extra profit consumed by lawyers' fees. By contrast, if buyers can threaten

45. B1 would not require S to convey the widget to him for resale to B2 at $130 because if S breached his contract with B2, B2 would then buy a widget in the open market for $115. Only S can sell to B2 at $130, because B2 has contracted only with S to purchase at that price.

46. To "cover" is to make a substitute purchase. *See* U.C.C. § 2-712(1). "Cover costs" refer not to the price paid for the substitute, but rather to the costs incurred in locating the substitute and making a second transaction.

specific performance and thereby seek to capture some of the sellers' profits from breach, sellers will bargain hard to keep as much of the profits as they can. Therefore, the damage remedy would probably result in quick payments by breaching sellers while the specific performance remedy would probably give rise to difficult negotiations.[47] Thus the post-breach negotiation costs associated with the specific performance remedy would seem to be greater than those associated with the damage remedy.[48]

This analysis makes the crucial assumption, however, that the first buyer, B1, has access to the market at a significantly lower cost than the seller;[49] though both pay the same market price for the substitute, B1 is assumed to have much lower cover costs. If this assumption is false, specific performance would not give rise to post-breach negotiations. Consider the illustration again. Suppose that B1 can obtain specific performance, but that S can cover as conveniently as B1.[50] If

47. Similarly, a liquidated damage clause with a very high payoff would also produce negotiations. This is because, if the clause is enforceable, the payoff would exceed any profit the promisor could realize from breach, but the promisee has an incentive to permit breach in return for a share of this profit. A commentator discussing the enforceability of these clauses has asserted that the transaction costs of negotiating over the profit would seem to be less than "the litigation or settlement costs of breach of contract" if the clauses were not enforceable. Note, *Liquidated Damages and Penalties Under the Uniform Commercial Code and the Common Law: An Economic Analysis of Contract Damages,* 72 Nw. U.L. Rev. 1055, 1079 (1978). This fails to take into account the promisee's incentive to settle quickly when the legal damages are easily ascertainable and less than the profit. Other recent commentary suggests that the negotiation costs that might result from a liquidated damage clause with a high payoff "may not be merely nominal" because "there are no legal guidelines to provide a certain answer as to what" the seller must pay his initial buyer. Clarkson, Miller, & Muris, *supra* note 28, at 362 n.34; *cf.* Ellickson, *Alternatives to Zoning: Covenants, Nuisance Rules, and Fines as Land Use Controls,* 40 U. Chi. L. Rev. 681, 743-44 (1973) (negotiation costs are reduced when damage rules establish clear guidelines for bargaining).

48. The sales-law rule that prohibits sellers from obtaining specific performance, *i.e.,* payment, for unaccepted goods can be explained in these terms. Under the current rule, the seller must resell the goods; otherwise, the rejecting buyer would have to resell them. Sellers are probably more efficient resellers than the rejecting buyers because selling is sometimes a specialized activity. Thus, if buyers were liable for the price, they would probably bribe sellers to resell the goods for them. Negotiation costs avoided under the current rule would thereby be generated. At present, the sellers resell the goods and proceed against the buyers to recover the market contract differential. If the resultant transaction costs are lower than those that would result from the buyers' attempts to bribe sellers to resell the goods, then the current rule is more efficient than granting sellers a price action. Because the market contract differential is easily determined while the appropriate bribe is not, it seems likely that the current rule is the more efficient one.

49. *See* R. Posner, *supra* note 2, at 89.

50. When the contract between S and B1 involves the sale of goods, S of course covers by purchasing similar goods in the market. When the contract involves services, S covers by providing a delegate to render the promised performance. Buyers are required to accept the delegate unless the promisor's performance is in some sense unique. *Compare* Corson v. Lewis, 77 Neb. 446, 449, 109 N.W. 735, 736 (1906) (attorney's service to his client held nondelegable) *with* New England Iron Co. v. Gilbert Elevated R.R. Co., 91 N.Y. 153, 167-68 (1883) (construction contract duties delegable). *See generally* J. Calamari & J. Perillo, Contracts 430-33 (1970).

B1 insists on a conveyance, S would buy another widget in the market for $115 and deliver on his contracts with both B1 and B2. A total of three transactions would result: S-B1; S-B2; S2-S (S's purchase of a second widget). None of these transactions involves post-breach negotiations. Thus if sellers can cover conveniently, the specific performance remedy does not generate post-breach negotiation costs.

The issue, then, is whether sellers and buyers generally have similar cover costs. Analysis suggests that they do. Sellers as well as buyers have incentives to learn market conditions. Because sellers have to "check the competition," they will have a good knowledge of market prices and quality ranges. Also, when a buyer needs goods or services tailored to his own needs, he will be able to find such goods or services more cheaply than sellers in general could, for they would first have to ascertain the buyer's needs before going into the market. However, in situations in which the seller and the first buyer have already negotiated a contract, the seller is likely to have as much information about the buyer's needs as the buyer has. Moreover, in some markets, such as those for complex machines and services, sellers are likely to have a comparative advantage over buyers in evaluating the probable quality of performance and thus would have lower cover costs. Therefore, no basis exists for assuming that buyers generally have significantly lower cover costs than sellers. It follows that expanding the availability of specific performance would not generate higher post-breach negotiation costs than the damage remedy.

Four serious objections may be made to this conclusion: (i) differential cover costs sometimes help induce breach, and their existence leads to higher post-breach negotiation costs under specific performance than under damages; (ii) in some cases, sellers cannot cover at all; (iii) when the first and second buyers have different uses for the subject of the sale, specific performance generates higher post-breach negotiation costs than damages; (iv) when changed circumstances occur—an important cause of breach—transaction costs are higher under specific performance than under damages.

The first objection assumes that sellers breach partly because their cover costs are higher than those of their buyers; it then argues that when cover costs do diverge, allowing specific performance seemingly is less efficient than having damages be the sole remedy. Returning to the widget hypothetical, let Cb = the first buyer's (B1's) cover costs; Cs = the seller's cover costs. Assume that S has higher cover costs than B1, *i.e.*, Cs > Cb. If specific performance were available, B1 could

Specific Performance

B1 insists on a conveyance, S would buy another widget in the market for $115 and deliver on his contracts with both B1 and B2. A total of three transactions would result: S-B1; S-B2; S2-S (S's purchase of a second widget). None of these transactions involves post-breach negotiations. Thus if sellers can cover conveniently, the specific performance remedy does not generate post-breach negotiation costs.

The issue, then, is whether sellers and buyers generally have similar cover costs. Analysis suggests that they do. Sellers as well as buyers have incentives to learn market conditions. Because sellers have to "check the competition," they will have a good knowledge of market prices and quality ranges. Also, when a buyer needs goods or services tailored to his own needs, he will be able to find such goods or services more cheaply than sellers in general could, for they would first have to ascertain the buyer's needs before going into the market. However, in situations in which the seller and the first buyer have already negotiated a contract, the seller is likely to have as much information about the buyer's needs as the buyer has. Moreover, in some markets, such as those for complex machines and services, sellers are likely to have a comparative advantage over buyers in evaluating the probable quality of performance and thus would have lower cover costs. Therefore, no basis exists for assuming that buyers generally have significantly lower cover costs than sellers. It follows that expanding the availability of specific performance would not generate higher post-breach negotiation costs than the damage remedy.

Four serious objections may be made to this conclusion: (i) differential cover costs sometimes help induce breach, and their existence leads to higher post-breach negotiation costs under specific performance than under damages; (ii) in some cases, sellers cannot cover at all; (iii) when the first and second buyers have different uses for the subject of the sale, specific performance generates higher post-breach negotiation costs than damages; (iv) when changed circumstances occur—an important cause of breach—transaction costs are higher under specific performance than under damages.

The first objection assumes that sellers breach partly because their cover costs are higher than those of their buyers; it then argues that when cover costs do diverge, allowing specific performance seemingly is less efficient than having damages be the sole remedy. Returning to the widget hypothetical, let Cb = the first buyer's (B1's) cover costs; Cs = the seller's cover costs. Assume that S has higher cover costs than B1, *i.e.*, $Cs > Cb$. If specific performance were available, B1 could

when neither party can cover—the case under discussion—buyers have a right to specific performance under current law.[51]

To summarize, if the initial buyer has access to the market at a significantly lower cost than the seller, a damages rule generates lower post-breach negotiation costs than a rule that makes specific performance routinely available. It seems likely, however, that both parties will be able to cover at similar, relatively low cost, or that neither will be able to cover at all. In either event, post-breach negotiation costs are similar under the two rules.[52]

The third objection to this conclusion concerns cases in which the first and second buyers have different uses for the good for sale. If the good is in inelastic supply in one of those uses, allowing specific performance would be less efficient than only allowing a damages remedy. For example, suppose that B1 contracts to purchase property for use as a farm. B2 discovers that the land is an ideal location for a restaurant and persuades the seller to convey it to him at a much higher price than B1 agreed to pay. Both B1 and S could probably cover respecting the first contract, for farmland is often fungible. Thus if a damage rule obtained, S would offer to convey a different parcel to B1 or pay B1 damages, and sell his own land, which is unique to B2's use, to B2. If B1 could get specific performance, however, two undesirable outcomes might occur. First, B1 may discover B2's purpose and insist on a conveyance to adopt B2's intended use. Thus B1 could freeload on the

51. *See, e.g.*, U.C.C. § 2-716(1) (authorizing specific performance "where the goods are unique or in other proper circumstances.") Comment 2 to the provision provides that "inability to cover is strong evidence of 'other proper circumstances.'" *See* Kaiser Trading Co. v. Associated Metals & Minerals Corp., 321 F. Supp. 923, 932-33 (N.D. Cal. 1970), *appeal dismissed*, 443 F.2d 1364 (9th Cir. 1971); p. 275 *supra*.

When the seller is a monopolist, there would seem to be one case in which specific performance should be denied. Suppose that a monopolist contracts to sell widgets before his factory is destroyed by fire. If specific performance would lie, the buyer might attempt to extort the seller by threatening to obtain a specific performance order, for the seller could neither cover nor perform. Negotiations would result as to the sum the seller would pay to avoid being found in contempt. These negotiations would constitute a deadweight efficiency loss. *See* R. Posner, *supra* note 2, at 96-97. This outcome would not occur, however. When goods are to be delivered from a specified source and the source is destroyed by unanticipated casualty, the seller is excused from performing. *See* U.C.C. § 2-615, Comment 5.

52. This analysis seems to overlook the buyer's duty to mitigate damages. Suppose that S has significantly higher performance costs than the market as a whole, so that B1 could purchase a substitute for less than it would cost S to perform. Should S be able to assert his unusually high costs as a defense to an action for specific performance on the ground that B1 can mitigate S's damages by making a substitute purchase? The answer should be no for two reasons. First, this situation will rarely occur because S can often cover as easily as B1, *see* p. 287 *supra*. Therefore the defense is largely unnecessary. Second, enabling S to oppose an action for specific performance on the ground that his costs are relatively high would create a defense that would be costly to adjudicate, and could be unpredictable in application.

information developed by B2, which would reduce the incentive of persons like B2 to discover new uses. Alternatively, B1 might either negotiate with S to capture some of S's profit from breach, or insist on conveyance and resell the property to B2. Both alternatives could create transaction costs without generating new social wealth. On the other hand, if B1 could only recover from S the difference between the price of a similar piece of farmland and the contract price, transaction costs would be lower, because S has strong incentives to cover or remit this sum voluntarily.[53] Therefore, the damage remedy is more efficient than the specific performance remedy where the market provides substitutes for B1's intended use of the property, but not for B2's intended use. Courts nevertheless currently allow specific performance in such cases.[54] Thus the issue is whether, if specific performance were made routinely available, an exception should be created for the different-use case. The answer is no, because the litigation and uncertainty costs that the exception would generate would probably exceed the excess bargaining costs of making specific performance available in this relatively uncommon situation.

The final objection to the conclusion that post-breach negotiation costs are no higher under specific performance than under damages applies in the context of unexpectedly rapid inflation. Suppose that a promisee would realize $3,000 profit from a construction project that he contracted to buy for $10,000. Suppose also that, at the time he made the contract, the promisor anticipated that the project would cost him $8,000, and that unanticipated inflation raised the promisor's costs to $15,000. In the event that the promisee's anticipated profits from completion of the project do not similarly increase, the promisee's best strategy would be to threaten specific performance so as to force the promisor to share part of the $7,000 cost savings that the promisor

53. *See* p. 285 *supra*.

54. The overwhelmingly popular rule is that "[s]pecific performance of a contract for the sale of land is generally granted even though the injury resulting from nonperformance is compensable in damages." Atchison v. City of Englewood, 568 P.2d 13, 22 (Colo. 1977). In a very few cases, courts have refused to grant specific performance of land contracts on the ground that money damages would adequately protect the promisee. *See, e.g.*, Watkins v. Paul, 95 Idaho 499, 511 P.2d 781 (1973). When the vendor has sold to a subsequent good faith purchaser at a price considerably above the contract price, however, courts have occasionally refused to impose a constructive trust on the proceeds of the sale, and only awarded damages. *See* Grummel v. Hollenstein, 90 Ariz. 356, 367 P.2d 960 (1962) (refusing to reopen judgment to take evidence as to proceeds of sale to third party); Cushing v. Levi, 117 Cal. App. 94, 3 P.2d 958 (1931) (awarding as damages less than one-third of profit from sale to third party). A much higher price suggests that the second buyer had a higher valued use, and the failure of some courts to impose a constructive trust shows an unwillingness to prevent sellers from conveying to subsequent buyers who have more valuable uses.

would realize from breaching. Although the promisee loses $3,000 from breach, the promisor saves $7,000. The negotiations over division of the net $4,000 savings that breach makes possible are a deadweight efficiency loss. If only the damage remedy were available to the promisee, however, the promisee could still force such negotiations because he would retain the power to impose a $7,000 loss on the promisor.

The standard damage measure for breach of a construction contract is the difference between the contract price and the new market price.[55] In the hypothetical, the new market price would be $17,000 ($15,000 cost plus the contractor's $2,000 profit), and the contract price is $10,000. Thus specific performance and the damages remedy create identical incentives for the parties to engage in costly post-breach negotiations in the event of unexpected inflation.[56]

C. *Efficiency Gains from the Routine Availability of Specific Performance*

The analysis thus far suggests that making specific performance widely available at the election of the promisee would not result in more costly pre- or post-breach negotiations than the damage remedy does at present. Further expanding the availability of specific performance would produce certain efficiency gains: it would minimize the inefficiencies of undercompensation, reduce the need for liquidated damage clauses, minimize strategic behavior, and save the costs of litigating complex damage issues.

First, if only a damage remedy is available, promisors may sometimes breach when their gains from breach exceed the damages a court will assess, though not the full costs breach imposes on the promisees. Such breaches may be inefficient for they make promisors better off but promisees worse off.

Second, under current law, parties have an incentive to create a "contractual" specific performance remedy in cases in which specific

55. *See* RESTATEMENT § 346.

56. The widget hypothetical used in text illustrates that expanding the availability of specific performance could sometimes result in overcompensation. Suppose that S actually conveyed the widget to B2, a good faith purchaser for value. B1 could not recover the widget from B2, nor could B1 get specific performance. In many jurisdictions he could, however, impose a constructive trust on the sales proceeds; thus he would recover $30 rather than the contract market differential of $15. The constructive trust remedy that a right to specific performance enables the promisee to invoke thus can overcompensate. The deterrent effect of the constructive trust, however, often is the only effective way of ensuring that a promisor will not defeat the promisee's right to specific performance by promptly conveying to a third party. The occasional overcompensation that results seems a reasonable price to pay in order to maintain the effectiveness of the specific performance remedy.

performance is now prohibited or its availability is uncertain by negotiating liquidated damage clauses.[57] This is because these clauses perform the same function as specific performance—ensuring adequate compensation or performance when damage rules provide neither. If specific performance were routinely available, much of the costs to the parties of negotiating liquidated damage clauses would be saved.[58]

Third, commentators have argued that liquidated damage clauses that require relatively high payouts would create incentives for the promisee to breach when changed circumstances cause the promisee to prefer the payout to performance.[59] Resources spent on inducing breach or on countering this conduct constitute deadweight efficiency losses. If specific performance were made widely available, however, contracting parties would have an incentive to choose it rather than liquidated damage clauses because, as we have seen, specific performance and liquidated damages often are substitutes. Since the gains to the promisee from inducing breach are greatly minimized when large damage payouts do not accompany it, such strategic behavior would rarely occur.

Finally, specific performance often is sought when damages would be difficult to establish. Granting the remedy in such cases would save the resources that would otherwise be devoted to exploring complex damage questions.[60]

D. *Administrative Cost Objections to Specific Performance*

The previous discussion has shown that certain efficiency gains can be expected as the result of expanding the availability of specific performance. One final efficiency objection remains—that the remedy increases the administrative costs of the parties and the courts because

57. *See* Goetz & Scott, *supra* note 2, at 559.

58. There would be new costs associated with parties' "contracting out" of a general specific performance rule, which would in part offset these savings. As pp. 281-84 *supra* showed, however, the general preferences of the parties respecting specific performance or damages seem impossible to ascertain; thus any demonstrated savings from expanding the availability of specific performance should be considered a net gain.

59. *See* Clarkson, Miller, & Muris, *supra* note 28, at 368-72. Liquidated damage clauses are not likely to inspire many attempts to induce breach, however, for if the penalty is high, the promisee would have to go to great lengths to get the promisor not to perform. Because any attempt to induce breach violates the promisee's duty to act in good faith and because the requisite extraordinary efforts should be relatively easy to prove, the promisee would probably be precluded from enforcing the liquidated damage clause if he engaged in such "strategic behavior." While Clarkson, Miller, and Muris recognize the relevance of the promisee's duty of good faith to their argument, they underestimate its force. *Id.* at 371. For another criticism of their argument see A. KRONMAN & R. POSNER, THE ECONOMICS OF CONTRACT 224-25 (1979).

60. *See* D. DOBBS, REMEDIES 885 (1973).

Specific Performance

of the expense entailed in creating and implementing specific performance decrees. This objection is at present the basis for a defense to a specific performance action: a court can deny the remedy on the ground of "difficulty of supervision"[61] even if a plaintiff otherwise establishes a right to specific performance. An analysis of the administrative cost objection, however, establishes that the difficulty of supervision defense should be available much less frequently than current law permits. Two arguments support this view. First, as demonstrated below, it is often difficult to know whether the costs to courts of allowing a specific performance remedy would exceed the gains resulting from increased availability of the remedy. In situations in which a cost comparison between specific performance and damages is not possible, the more accurate remedy, specific performance, should be granted. Second, the administrative costs that the specific performance remedy imposes on the parties should not count against its wider use, because those costs will be incurred only when the parties perceive them to be lower than the gains from equitable relief.

Courts, in enforcing the supervision defense, are concerned with their inability to supervise performance[62] and with the burden of further litigation.[63] Yet, as the cases of the civil rights and antitrust injunctions demonstrate, courts have effectively supervised contentious parties in complex matters over long periods.[64] Courts that refuse to award specific performance on the basis of supervision difficulties seem implicitly to assume, however, that the costs of granting equitable relief exceed any benefits from doing so.

Granting specific performance does impose costs on courts. Judges may have to devote greater time and resources to tailoring and supervising a specific performance decree than would have to be devoted to devising and enforcing a damage judgment. Thus equitable relief can be given at the expense of judicial attention to other matters.[65] Courts, however, can eliminate much of this opportunity cost by

61. *See* note 11 *supra* (citing cases in which the difficulty of supervision defense was allowed).

62. *See, e.g.*, Thayer Plymouth Center, Inc. v. Chrysler Motors Corp., 255 Cal. App. 2d 300, 304, 63 Cal. Rptr. 148, 150 (1967) (specific performance denied for contract requiring continuing supervision); Egbert v. Way, 15 Wash. App. 76, 80, 546 P.2d 1246, 1248-49 (1976) (specific performance might properly be denied if judicial supervision were unreasonably difficult).

63. *See, e.g.*, Yonan v. Oak Park Fed. Sav. & Loan Ass'n, 27 Ill. App. 3d 967, 974, 326 N.E.2d 773, 779 (1975) (specific performance denied for construction contract where there was risk of further litigation).

64. Extensive illustrations are given in O. Fiss, Injuctions 325-481 (1972). *See also* O. Fiss, The Civil Rights Injunction 36-37 (1978).

65. This conclusion seems plausible intuitively, but may be incorrect because it assumes that the supply of judicial services is inelastic. In a recent statistical study, Professor

appointing special masters.[66] This practice would also shift any additional resource costs of specific performance primarily to the parties. Masters can be used to fashion decrees, as well as to supervise performance and hear appeals respecting compliance.

As the previous section has shown, increasing the availability of specific performance actually creates substantial efficiency gains. On the basis of information currently available, it is impossible to say whether those gains would exceed the increase in administrative and judicial opportunity costs that the availability of specific performance would engender. This is particularly so if courts delegated supervisory and other administrative tasks to masters. Because the normative goal of contract remedies is compensation, specific performance should lie unless it can be shown that the costs of specific performance would exceed the gains. As such a case has not been made, the administrative cost objection should seldom support denial of specific performance.[67]

The possibility that the parties will incur greater costs as a result of the specific performance remedy if supervision of a decree is required should not count against the wider availability of the remedy. These costs will be incurred only when the benefits of specific performance

Gillespie cast doubt on the validity of this assumption. *See* Gillespie, *The Production of Court Services*, 5 J. LEGAL STUD. 243 (1976). He found that federal district courts disposed of more cases when they conducted a higher proportion of trials. He suggested two explanations for these results. First, when courts use trials as a matter of course, the parties have greater incentives to settle. Second, the evidence suggests that the supply of judicial services is fairly elastic; as he put it, "judges work harder, longer or more efficiently when there is a need to do so." *Id.* at 264.

This argument, as applied to specific performance questions, suggests that if courts issued a higher proportion of decrees that required supervision, they might not be forced to neglect other tasks, because the prospect of these decrees might induce more parties to settle or perform and because judges might expand output. Thus the opportunity cost of increased supervision might in fact be slight.

66. Masters have been used to help enforce specific performance decrees since Elizabethan times. *See* 1 G. SPENCE, EQUITABLE JURISDICTION 647 (1846). Judge Hough was an influential advocate of the use of masters in this country. *See* Kearns-Gorsuch Bottle Co. v. Hartford-Fairmont Co., 1 F.2d 318, 319-20 (S.D.N.Y. 1921) (urging use of "competent receivers" to aid judges in supervising difficult business problems). Rule 53(b), however, states that use of a master "shall be the exception and not the rule." FED. R. CIV. P. 53(b). Commentators have argued that use of a master is an abdication of judicial functions, and that it increases the cost of litigation. *See* Note, *Masters and Magistrates in the Federal Courts*, 88 HARV. L. REV. 779, 790-91, 791 n.82 (1975); Kaufman, *Masters in the Federal Courts: Rule 53*, 58 COLUM. L. REV. 452, 452-53 (1958). Neither objection is forceful in this context, however. Since a master's role would primarily be to supervise court decrees, courts would perform the major aspect of the judicial function. Furthermore, the costs of supervision do not vanish if a court performs them; they are simply externalized to the public fisc. The parties would more appropriately bear these costs because they are best able to minimize them. *See* pp. 295-96 *infra*.

67. *See* pp. 304-05 *infra* (discussing narrow circumstances in which difficulty of supervision defense should be permitted).

Specific Performance

exceed its incremental costs.[68] The question remains, however, which party should absorb supervision costs if a court appoints a master. If both parties can calculate the expected value of these costs when they contract, this question is trivial. Suppose a rule is adopted that promisees must pay the costs of a master and other court costs associated with specific performance. In the Figure, let D be the demand curve for

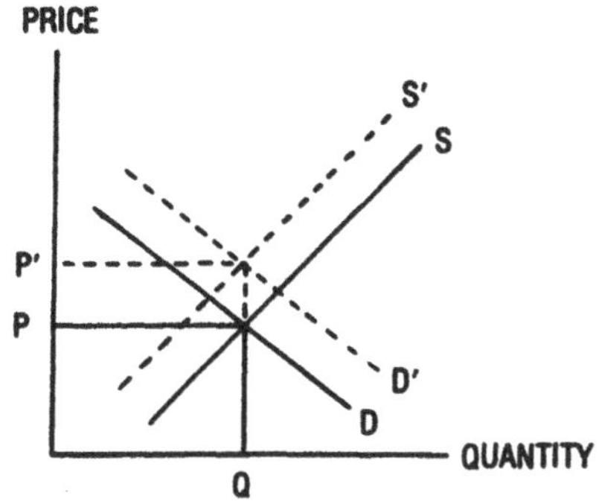

construction services, for example, and let S be the supply curve. At equilibrium, quantity Q of services are supplied at price P. If the rule were changed, and promisors were required to absorb the additional costs of specific performance, the supply curve would shift to S' because it would then be more expensive to supply construction services. The magnitude of the shift would reflect the expected value of these costs. The demand curve, however, would shift by roughly the same amount as the supply curve because construction services become more desirable to promisees: if a promisor breaches, a master's services are provided "free."[69] Whereas the market price for construction services will rise to P' when promisors bear the extra costs of specific performance, the quantity of services traded remains at Q. Therefore, no efficiency consequences result from allocating these costs to one party or the other.

This analysis assumes, however, that no information asymmetries exist. In fact, promisors may know more about the likelihood of their

68. This argument assumes certain knowledge on the part of the parties concerning the benefits and costs of equitable relief. *See* pp. 276-77 *supra*.

69. Because the costs of a master's services would be included in the contract price, the marginal cost to a promisee of using these services in the event of breach falls to zero. This could create a "moral hazard" problem because more masters' services will be consumed than if promisees had to pay for these services as they were required. The other costs of litigation that promisees would have to bear, however, seem high enough to make this problem unimportant.

own breach than do promisees. If promisees were to bear the costs of masters, they might over- or underestimate them. Either mistake reduces allocative efficiency. In the former case, too few services are purchased; in the latter case, too many. At the same time, promisees know better than promisors whether and to what extent damages might be undercompensatory. Thus if promisors are made to bear the additional costs of specific performance, they may over- or underestimate these costs. Again, allocative inefficiency is likely to result. It is difficult to predict the direction in which these information asymmetries are most pronounced.

However, in the most important practical context, that of construction contracts, it is possible to predict the direction in which the asymmetries would be most pronounced. Construction promisors seem better able to predict the likelihood that damages will be unsatisfactory to promisees than promisees are able to predict the likelihood of breach. A promisee would have difficulty in predicting breach because there are probably numerous contractor promisors, and construction firms differ widely in competence and reliability. Thus the promisee would have to obtain data about numerous firms; the promisee could not instead rely on common knowledge about the reliability of the service. In addition, consumer promisees would have even greater difficulty in predicting breach. Consumers use major construction services infrequently, and thus lack the incentive to explore market conditions in detail as well as the opportunity to obtain expertise in evaluating market data. On the other hand, construction firms in all markets often can assess the relative "uniqueness" of their own performances. Therefore, greater misallocations would probably result if promisees rather than promisors bore the costs of supervision. Thus breaching promisors should bear these costs in construction contexts.[70]

IV. Specific Performance and Liberty

The analysis thus far indicates that none of the efficiency arguments against expansion of the availability of specific performance are persuasive, except in the rare cases in which the difficulty of supervision defense properly applies. There is, however, another basis for objection to specific performance. A moral objection to expansion of the availability of this remedy can be raised on the ground that requiring per-

70. To allow for exceptional individual circumstances, parties should be permitted to contract out of this rule.

Specific Performance

formance interferes with the promisor's liberty more than requiring the payment of money. If this liberty interest takes precedence over the goals that specific performance serves, the equitable remedy should be prohibited or restricted.[71] The liberty interest objection consequently cannot be evaluated fully without a theory that would either reconcile or enable choice to be made among four arguably relevant goals of contract law: (i) to permit a promisor freely to choose the terms under which to contract, including an implied term providing for specific performance; (ii) to prevent a promisor from the possibly undue compulsion of having to perform; (iii) to minimize the costs of undercompensation; (iv) to give the promisee the performance he bought because he is morally entitled to it. Developing such a metatheory is beyond the scope of this Article, but fortunately it is not necessary to deal with most of the liberty interest arguments.

To begin, a promisor's liberty interest is not seriously compromised by a specific performance decree if the promisor sells roughly fungible goods or is in the business of selling unique goods. In either circumstance, the goods are assets to the promisor much like cash; requiring their delivery is not relevantly different from requiring the delivery of cash. Similarly, requiring a sizable corporation that renders services to perform for a given promisee does not violate the corporation's associational interests or the associational interests of its employees.

Liberty interests are affected, however, in the case of an individual promisor who performs personal services. In part for this reason, current law does not allow specific performance to be granted in this case.[72] Liberty interests might also be implicated if a promisor were required to deliver goods or realty to which he has a sentimental attachment, on the ground that his liberty comprehends the right to define himself partly in terms of the possession of tangible things.[73] The law, however, commonly awards specific performance in such cases; goods which have sentimental associations for the promisor may

71. The distinction in French law between "obligations to do and not to do" and "obligations to convey" reflects this concern. Breach of the former is compensable only in damages, whereas breach of the latter may be remedied by an order equivalent to specific performance. Different remedies apply because "[i]t was considered less onerous to owe money than to be liable to compulsion actually to perform an act or forebearance." Treitel, *supra* note 24, at 13.

72. *See* Lumley v. Wagner, 42 Eng. Rep. 687 (1852) (personal services contract enforced by enjoining performance elsewhere rather than by requiring specific performance); RESTATEMENT § 379 (same).

73. This "personality theory of property" is usually traced to Hegel. *See* G. HEGEL, PHILOSOPHY OF RIGHT §§ 41-71 (T. Knox trans. 1972); S. AVINERI, HEGEL'S THEORY OF THE MODERN STATE 88-89, 135-37 (1972).

not have close substitutes for the promisee,[74] while all realty is presumed unique.[75]

The liberty interest objection thus poses no barrier to expanding the availability of specific performance to sales of roughly fungible goods and corporate services. But it does suggest eliminating use of the remedy in some cases in which it now is available. This suggestion is premature, however. To limit specific performance with regard, say, to unique goods would first require the development of a coherent theory of the "personality aspect" of property ownership. It must then be shown that protection of the liberty interest to which the theory gives rise is more important than the goals that specific performance is thought to serve. Until this showing is made, liberty motivated exceptions to a rule of specific performance on promisee request should not be created.

V. Defenses to Specific Performance

Under current law, a promisee cannot obtain specific performance simply by showing breach and the absence of an adequate remedy at law; special defenses that apply only to requests for specific performance further limit the availability of the remedy. These defenses include inadequacy of consideration, lack of security for the promisee's performance, unilateral mistake by the promisor, and difficulty of supervising performance.[76] They can be divided into two categories, those stemming from perceived unfairness of the contract and those stemming from perceived difficulties in implementing the remedy.

A. *Unfair Contracts*

When a promisee cannot prove damages, denial of an equitable remedy constitutes a decision not to enforce the contract.[77] Because

74. For example, "[h]eirlooms, family treasures . . . , a grandfather's clock . . . , a baby's worn-out shoe, or faithful old Dobbin the faithful horse . . . ," RESTATEMENT § 361 Comment e, are goods with "sentimental associations" that may justify a grant of specific performance. *Id.* § 361(b). Such items may have sentimental associations for promisors as well as promisees.

75. For a striking example of a grant of specific performance in spite of the promisor's sentimental attachment to the property, see Hutchins v. Honeycutt, 286 N.C. 314, 210 S.E.2d 254 (1974) (conveyance of "The old Home Place").

76. *See* p. 273 and notes 8-11 *supra*.

77. This conclusion is intuitively valid and some data exists to support it. In a survey covering 150 cases in which specific performance was denied on grounds of equitable unfairness, the 56 responses showed that "[i]n every instance, an equitable defeat was a total defeat." Frank & Endicott, *Defenses in Equity and "Legal Rights,"* 14 LA. L. REV. 380, 381 (1954).

defenses to specific performance differ from defenses at law, there are in effect two doctrines regulating relief from contractual obligations, "equitable" and "legal" unconscionability. Two features distinguish the equitable version. First, courts often refuse to enforce contracts in equity—that is, deny specific performance—on the ground that particular clauses are substantively unfair, without reaching the issue of whether the contracting process itself was also unfair. Second, when equity courts do require process unfairness as a condition of nonenforcement, their version of it seems different from and easier to establish than the process unfairness required in actions at law. These two features are unjustifiable and produce confusion and unpredictability. They should thus be abolished, so that the defenses that can be asserted against a request for specific performance will be identical to those that can be asserted against a request for damages.

1. *A Too Low Price*

A promisor can defeat an action for specific performance in some jurisdictions by proving that the contract price is too low.[78] Though this defense is meant to rescue promisors from bad deals, it does the job poorly. Suppose a party contracts to sell for $5,000 property that, judging from sales of similar property, has a market value of $10,000. Both specific performance and damages would impose a $5,000 loss on the promisor in the event of breach. Now suppose instead that property similar to the subject of sale is not commonly traded in the promisor's area, but experts attest that the property at issue is "worth" much more than $5,000. In this latter case, the breaching promisor would prefer the promisee to be limited to a damage action. The difficulty of measuring damages might cause a court to order the promisor only to make restitution or to award a sum as damages that is less than the value of the property to the promisor. Thus contracts with allegedly inadequate prices are enforced when damages are provable but not when damages are not provable.

There is no normative justification for making promisor protection turn on the promisee's ability to establish damages rather than on the price that the parties set. This difficulty can be avoided by making the defense of a too low price generally available in contract law, or by

78. *See* note 8 *supra* (citing cases in which specific performance was denied due to inadequacy of consideration). Courts may grant specific performance, however, despite an apparent inadequacy of consideration. *See, e.g.*, Gross v. J & L Camping & Sports Center, Inc., 270 Md. 539, 312 A.2d 270 (1973) (price was $85,000, value apparently above $120,000); Blankenship v. Porter, 479 S.W.2d 409 (Mo. 1972) (price was $6,000, value said to be $12,000).

abolishing it. There are two principal reasons why the defense should be eliminated entirely. First, the defense leads to unpredictable outcomes. Unpredictability arises because the defense is often asserted in cases involving goods for which no recognized markets exist. In consequence, courts are often required to resolve the difficult issue of what the property is "worth," as well as the more difficult issue of what fraction of this worth justice requires the seller to receive. Because judicial outcomes on these issues are difficult for the parties to predict, promisors frequently assert the defense and thus force courts to spend time considering it.[79] Resources would be saved if the defense were eliminated.

Moreover, contracts involving low prices should be enforced because enforcing such contracts creates incentives for promisees to seek out good deals. Increased search, in turn, correlates positively with the existence of competitive prices, for the more comparison shoppers there are, the more likely it is that sellers can increase profits by offering lower prices.[80] Since competitive prices are preferable to supracompetitive prices, the defense that a too low price alone ought to bar specific performance should be eliminated.

Some courts allow the defense of inadequate consideration only if there was also unfairness in the contracting process.[81] Because some forms of process unfairness, such as misrepresentation, are inconsistent with competitive outcomes, this version of the defense seems justifiable. But the forms of process unfairness that support a denial of specific performance should be the same as those that support a finding of unconscionability at law. Otherwise, promisor protection does turn on the promisee's ability to prove damages rather than on the unfairness that actually occurred; if "equitable" unconscionability is easier for a promisor to establish than legal unconscionability, the promisee will sue at law if possible. Furthermore, since the factors that make up legal unconscionability are themselves suspect,[82] the vaguer equitable ver-

79. *See, e.g.*, Loeb v. Wilson, 253 Cal. App. 2d 383, 388, 61 Cal. Rptr. 377, 380 (1967) (two expert real estate appraisers testified as to adequacy of consideration). In at least one jurisdiction, a motion for specific performance must allege the value of the property in order to allow the court to judge the adequacy of the consideration. *See, e.g.*, Georgia Money Corp. v. Monteleone Apartments, Inc., 223 Ga. 418, 418-19, 156 S.E.2d 39, 39-40 (1967).

80. *See* Schwartz & Wilde, *supra* note 35, at 640-51.

81. *See, e.g.*, *In re* Estate of Brown, 130 Ill. App. 2d 514, 264 N.E.2d 287 (1970); Peters v. Wallach, 366 Mass. 622, 321 N.E.2d 806 (1975).

82. *See* Epstein, *Unconscionability: A Critical Reappraisal*, 18 J. L. & ECON. 293 (1975); Schwartz, *A Reexamination of Nonsubstantive Unconscionability*, 63 VA. L. REV. 1053 (1977); Trebilcock, *The Doctrine of Inequality of Bargaining Power: Post-Benthamite Economics in the House of Lords*, 26 U. TORONTO L.J. 359 (1976).

sion is even less attractive.[83] Finally, having two versions of unconscionability, both of which are unpredictable in application, generates excessive uncertainty costs. Thus, the standards of legal unconscionability should furnish the guidelines for the process unfairness version of the too low price defense.

2. *Unfair Terms*

The unfair contract terms defense is best discussed in the context of an illustration. Consider the rule used in some jurisdictions that specific performance is denied if the promisee's performance is inadequately secured.[84] This defense is often invoked in the case of installment contracts that fail to require the promisee to give a purchase money mortgage.[85]

Suppose a party contracts to sell property for $8,000 and the market price has risen to $10,000 at the time of performance. Under the contract, the price is to be paid in installments, but the promisee fails to give security. The promisor then breaches. Though it appears at first that the promisor would be indifferent between specific performance and damages, the promisor would, in fact, prefer to pay damages. Although the legal remedy deprives the promisor of the $2,000 increment in value, it permits him to sell the property to another on a secured basis and thus be relatively assured of receiving the full price. If the promisor instead were specifically required to perform, he would be forced to sell to the original promisee on an unsecured basis. Indeed, denial of the remedy in these circumstances seems to be a pareto

83. *See* Hutchins v. Honeycutt, 286 N.C. 314, 210 S.E.2d 254 (1974); II J. Pomeroy, Equity Jurisprudence § 400 (1941); Restatement (Second) § 378, Comment a, Illustrations (1) and (4).

A good example of the vacuousness of equitable unconscionability is given in Morgan v. Reasor, 204 N.W.2d 98 (S.D. 1973), in which the court refused to require specific performance of a contract to exchange a ranch for an apartment complex. The sellers had purchased a 3,362 acre ranch for $169,500, and reneged on an agreement to exchange it for an apartment complex. The buyer had claimed that the complex would operate at a profit, the chances of which were slight. The court explained:

> [T]he evidence discloses that this Pennington County rancher was without understanding of a transaction of this nature and magnitude. There is such a lack of competency on the part of the defendants as to have made it necessary that they should have had protection and advice; these facts coupled with the circumstances that the Reasors were misled as to the value of Whispering Sands, and that they, in effect, were actually giving their ranch away is sufficient in our opinion to constitute constructive fraud.

Id. at 109.

84. *See* note 9 *supra* (citing cases denying specific performance on grounds that promisee's performance was inadequately secured).

85. *Id.*

superior move;[86] the promisee is as well off with damages as with the property, while the promisor is better off if he is free to sell elsewhere on more favorable terms.

If damages are undercompensatory, however, as is commonly the case in suits for specific performance, promisors are made better off but promisees worse off by the defense. Some courts attempt to take this into account by granting specific performance if the promisee furnishes a mortgage or other adequate security.[87] This version of the unfair terms defense, however, does not produce a pareto superior outcome; instead, it inappropriately redistributes wealth from promisees to promisors and creates uncertainty. Suppose in the earlier example that the implicit price of a purchase money mortgage is $500.[88] Then making the grant of specific performance conditional on the promisee's provision of a purchase money mortgage in effect raises the price of the house, which would have been $7,500 in a secured sale. Yet courts do not reduce the price when requiring a mortgage as a precondition to specific performance. The resultant redistribution seems unjustified; the promisee in this illustration was not guilty of process unfairness in making the contract, yet the promisor receives a price increase because he balked at completing a deal to which he freely agreed.[89] Furthermore, uncertainty is created because promisees would have difficulty predicting actual transaction prices in the event of breach since the parties seldom calculate implicit prices for terms such as mortgages at the time the price is negotiated.

These arguments can be generalized to cover any contract term challenged on fairness grounds. A court can either deny specific performance altogether[90] or condition its grant on deletion of the offend-

86. For a definition of the concept of pareto superiority, see J. Hirshleifer, Price Theory and Applications 441 (1976). In brief, solution A is pareto superior to solution B if everyone is as well off under A as under B, and at least one individual is better off under A. *Id.*

87. *See, e.g.*, Rego v. Decker, 482 P.2d 834, 838 (Alaska 1971); Restatement § 373.

88. An "implicit price" is the price that would have been charged for a contract term or product feature if the parties had separately priced it. This example is more realistic than the previous example, *see* p. 301 *supra*, which inaccurately presupposed that mortgages did not have implicit prices.

89. The Restatement unpersuasively justifies making grant of specific performance conditional on the provision of security on the ground that "[t]here is no injustice to the plaintiff in requiring the reduction of that risk [of nonpayment], as the price of getting so drastic a remedy." Restatement § 373, Comment a. This argument ignores the fact that increased risk in a transaction results in a higher price. Thus a decrease in risk should result in a decrease in price.

90. *See* Campbell Soup Co. v. Wentz, 172 F.2d 80, 83 (3d Cir. 1948); Restatement (Second) § 378(1)(c) (specific performance will be denied if contract itself is unfair).

Specific Performance

ing contract term.[91] Both solutions are pareto superior to specific performance when damages are fully compensatory. When damages are not compensatory, the latter solution is preferable because the promisor would be as well off with a conditioned grant as with denial of the remedy, while the promisee in some cases would be better off. However, making grant of the remedy conditional is itself a questionable response to the problem of unfair terms because it redistributes wealth inappropriately and creates uncertainty.

The appropriate solution to the unfair terms problem in light of these difficulties is to permit the conditional grant version of the defense only if it is accompanied by unfairness in the contracting process. The existence of such unfairness largely vitiates the objections to the defense. First, any redistributions engendered by making the grant of specific performance conditional seem justifiable; the promisee has behaved inappropriately with the apparent result that the promisor was influenced to make a worse deal than he otherwise would have made. Second, while deals made on favorable terms should be enforced so as to induce promisees to search for good deals and thereby promote competitive outcomes, process unfairness often produces noncompetitive outcomes. Third, uncertainty will be reduced because a promisee not guilty of process unfairness knows that his deal will be enforced on the original terms. Also, the process unfairness necessary to trigger application of the unfair terms defense should be measured by legal rather than equitable standards.[92]

91. *See, e.g.*, Rego v. Decker, 482 P.2d 834, 839 (Alaska 1971) (grant conditional even when promisor explicitly assumed risk of nonperformance by promisee); RESTATEMENT § 373, Comment b (same).

92. None of these objections apply to the rule that specific performance will be denied if the promisee lacks "clean hands," that is, if he fails to perform in accordance with the terms of the contract. *See* Fultz v. Graven, 7 Ill. App. 3d 698, 699, 288 N.E.2d 491, 491-92 (1972); Shannon v. Gull Lake Ass'n, 11 Mich. App. 644, 645, 162 N.W.2d 111, 111 (1968). If a plaintiff fails so to perform, the contract itself bars his claim to the defendant's performance.

The defense of unilateral mistake, however, is subject to the criticisms made of the defense of unfair terms. Some courts deny specific performance if the promisor failed to understand the terms of the contract even though the promisee did not conceal those terms. *See* note 10 *supra*. If one party takes advantage of the supposed ignorance or lack of sophistication of the other party, the court may refuse to enforce the contract. *See* UNIFORM CONSUMER CREDIT CODE § 5.108(4)(e) (1974). Because this rule is itself open to attack on the ground that a person's freedom to contract is unduly restricted if it is too lightly presumed that he is incompetent, *see* Schwartz, *supra* note 82, at 1076-82, equity courts should go no further. Some support for this argument is found in the fact that some courts grant specific performance when the unilateral mistake could have been prevented by the promisor's due diligence. *See* Tayyara v. Stetson, 521 P.2d 185, 189 (Colo. App. 1974); Van Curler Dev. Corp. v. City of Schenectady, 59 Misc. 2d 621, 628, 300 N.Y.S.2d 765, 775 (1969).

B. *Difficulty of Supervision*

The difficulty of supervision defense largely rests on the assumption that specific performance unduly raises administrative costs.[93] As indicated above, the administrative cost objection is much less forceful than is commonly supposed. This defense, however, also rests on a related premise—that courts should not do ineffectual tasks.[94] When the promisor wants to avoid performing, even a specific performance decree may not cause him to render the promised performance satisfactorily. Given this possibility, three arguments can be made in support of the difficulty of supervision defense: (i) the decree would not be in the promisee's best interests; (ii) judicial prestige will suffer if court decrees are flouted; (iii) courts should not waste judicial resources. The first basis for the defense is untenable; it should be the promisee's choice whether to risk the possible defects of a coerced performance. Furthermore, the promisee is better able to assess the likelihood of compliance than a court because the promisee knows more about the promisor.

Although the second argument is based on a legitimate concern, it does not support denial of the remedy. Because the costs to a promisor of noncompliance with a court decree are likely to be high, and because business promisors seldom breach for ideological reasons, substantial compliance with most decrees can be expected. Further, the typical contract law dispute is unlikely to attract publicity; consequently, any noncompliance will not adversely affect the public perception of the courts. In the event, however, that noncompliance seems particularly likely in a given case, and the noncompliance is likely to be publicized, a court could justifiably deny specific performance under the difficulty of supervision defense.

The third argument also will rarely support denial of the remedy. Judicial resources will not be wasted because a promisee is unlikely to seek specific performance unless the gain—substantial compliance

93. For standard statements of the defense, see D. Dobbs, *supra* note 60, at 908-09; Restatement (Second) § 380. Courts in some jurisdictions grant specific performance even though it involves extensive supervision. *See, e.g.*, Laclede Gas Co. v. Amoco Oil Co., 522 F.2d 33, 39 (8th Cir. 1975); City Stores Co. v. Ammerman, 266 F. Supp. 766, 776-78 (D.D.C. 1967), *aff'd*, 394 F.2d 950, 956 (D.C. Cir. 1968); Pembroke Park Lakes, Inc. v. High Ridge Water Co., 213 So.2d 727, 728-29 (Fla. App. 1968).

94. The Restatement (Second) articulates this premise of the difficulty of supervision defense:

> Difficult questions may be raised as to the quality of the performance rendered under the decree. Supervision may be required for an extended period of time. Specific relief will not be granted if these burdens are disproportionate to the advantages to be gained from enforcement and the harm to be suffered from its denial.

Restatement (Second) § 380, Comment a.

by the promisor—exceeds the associated costs. Moreover, as suggested previously, much of the cost of supervision can and should be allocated to the parties.

Thus arguments based on the premise that courts should refuse to assume ineffectual tasks only support a quite restricted use of the difficulty of supervision defense. There are cases in which the cost of a master would be enormous in relation to the stakes at issue, in which the court is aware that publicized noncompliance is likely, or in which the plaintiff is seeking specific performance out of spiteful motives. Although such cases are rare, courts should have the power to deny specific performance when necessary. Ordinarily, however, even if a court or master would have to engage in extensive supervisory tasks, a promisee should have the option of requesting the remedy of specific enforcement.[95]

Conclusion

The compensation goal of contract law can be achieved by requiring the promisor to pay damages or by requiring the promisor to render the promised performance. Under current law, a promisee is entitled to a damage award as of right but the court retains discretion to decide whether specific performance should be granted. Because specific performance is a superior method for achieving the compensation goal, promisees should be able to obtain specific performance on request. An expanded specific performance remedy would not generate greater transaction costs than the damage remedy involves, nor would its increased use interfere unduly with the liberty interests of promisors. Making specific performance freely available also would eliminate the uncertainty costs of planning and litigation created by the difficulty of predicting whether the remedy will be available. In addition, this reform would reduce the negotiation costs incurred by parties in at-

95. A defense related to the difficulty of supervision defense is uncertainty of terms. Specific performance is denied when a contract's terms are too uncertain, even though the uncertainty might not defeat a damage action. *See, e.g.*, S. Jon Kreedman & Co. v. Meyers Bros. Parking-Western Corp., 58 Cal. App. 3d 173, 180-81, 130 Cal. Rptr. 41, 46-47 (1976); RESTATEMENT (SECOND) § 376, Comment b. If the contract's meaning is unclear, a court would have difficulty in framing a specific performance decree, but would also have difficulty in making a damage award. Thus if a contract is not too uncertain to enforce at law, it should be enforceable in equity. *See* W. WALSH, *supra* note 22, at 329-30. A more stringent standard of certainty might be required in equity on the ground that a promisor may have a greater liberty interest in not being compelled to perform acts than in not being forced to pay money. *See* pp. 296-97 *supra*. This justification is unsatisfactory, however, because the liberty interest distinction between conveying property or performing services and paying money is obscure.

tempting to create forms of contractual specific performance such as liquidated damage clauses.[96] Further, defenses to requests for specific performance that rest on unfairness of contract terms or prices and that differ from the defenses in actions at law should be eliminated; the grounds for denial of specific performance should be the same as those that now will bar a damage suit. Finally, the defense based on difficulty of supervision should be greatly restricted. If the law is committed to putting disappointed promisees in as good a position as they would have been had their promisors performed, specific performance should be available as a matter of course to those promisees who request it.

96. This conclusion is similar to the conclusion Professor Fiss reached with regard to injunctions:

> I will urge that the traditional view give way to a nonhierarchical conception of remedies, where there is no presumptive remedy, but rather a context-specific evaluation of the advantages and disadvantages of each form of relief. It should not be necessary to establish the inadequacy of alternative remedies before the injunction becomes available; at the same time, the superiority of the injunction should not be presumed, but rather dependent on an analysis of its technical advantages and the system of power allocation that it implies.
>
> My plea is not confined to the civil rights injunction, but should extend to all types of injunctions.

O. Fiss, The Civil Rights Injunction 6 (1978). Contract remedies also should be "nonhierarchical," so that promisees need not "establish the inadequacy of alternative remedies before" specific performance is available. *Id.* This Article's argument goes further toward authorizing equitable relief than does Professor Fiss's analysis, both because of the clear superiority of specific performance over damages in achieving the compensation goal and because "a context-specific evaluation of the advantages and disadvantages of each form of relief," *id.*, shows that this superiority can usually be purchased at relatively slight, if any, net cost.

[17]

The Yale Law Journal

Volume 89, Number 7, June 1980

Enforcing Promises: An Examination of the Basis of Contract*

Charles J. Goetz† and Robert E. Scott‡

The obligation to keep promises is a commonly acknowledged moral duty.[1] Yet not all promises—however solemnly vowed—are enforceable at law.[2] Why are some promises legally binding and others not? Orthodox doctrinal categories provide only modest assistance in answering this persistent question. Conventional analysis, for example, has distinguished promises made in exchange for a return promise or performance from nonreciprocal promises.[3] Indeed, common law "bar-

* We would like to thank Michael Dooley, Stanley Henderson, Arthur Leff, Douglas Leslie, Alan Schwartz, Paul Stephan, and the participants in the University of Virginia Faculty Workshop and the University of Chicago Law and Economics Workshop for their helpful comments on earlier versions of this Article.

† Professor of Law, University of Virginia School of Law.

‡ Professor of Law, University of Virginia School of Law.

1. Pound, *Promise or Bargain?* 33 TUL. L. REV. 455, 455 (1959) ("From antiquity the moral obligation to keep a promise [has] been a cardinal tenet of ethical philosophers, publicists, and philosophical jurists.") [hereinafter cited as *Promise or Bargain?*]; *see id.* at 457-63. *See generally* Pound, *Individual Interests of Substance—Promised Advantages,* 59 HARV. L. REV. 1, 3-11 (1945). In terms of moral obligation, promises have been clearly distinguished from other representations or predictions. "A promise is not, therefore, merely an assurance one gives to help another, just as it is not merely an expression of a resolution to perform an action. It is, in addition, to *underwrite* any endeavor the other party to the transaction may choose to launch. . . ." A. MELDEN, RIGHTS AND PERSONS 46, 47-54 (1977). The peculiar status of promissory representations forms the basis of the law of contract.

2. The hint of this restraint is revealed in the common definition of contract as a promise that is legally enforceable. *See, e.g.*, 1 RESTATEMENT OF CONTRACTS § 1 (1932) [hereinafter cited without cross-reference as RESTATEMENT 1ST]. This definition of contract is retained in the *Second Restatement*. RESTATEMENT (SECOND) OF CONTRACTS § 1 (Tent. Draft Nos. 1-7, 1973) [hereinafter cited without cross-reference as RESTATEMENT 2D].

3. *See* RESTATEMENT 2D § 75. The traditional distinction between bargained-for and gratuitous promises suggests that only two categories can be identified. Actually the institutional environment is more accurately described as having three distinct contexts. Explicitly bargained-for promises are only a part of a larger exchange context in which the opportunity for interactive communication remains. We define nonreciprocal promises as being limited to those contexts in which the promisee has no realistic ability to obtain adjustments in promise-making through bargaining. *See* p. 1301 & note 38 *infra*.

gain theory" is classically simple: bargained-for promises are presumptively enforceable; nonreciprocal promises are presumptively unenforceable. But this disarmingly simple theory has never mirrored reality.[4] Contract law has ventured far beyond such narrow limitations, embracing reliance and unjust enrichment as additional principles of promissory obligation.[5]

Thus, a promise may be enforceable to the extent that the promisee has incurred substantial costs, or conferred benefits, in reasonable reliance on the promise.[6] Promissory estoppel under Section 90 of the *Restatement of Contracts* is the primary enforcement mechanism when action in reliance follows the promise.[7] If the change of position by the promisee precedes the promise, its nexus with the promise is more subtle. For example, a promise is enforceable when it follows a nondonative material benefit conferred by the promisee. Unjust enrichment principles are typically invoked to enforce such "past consideration" promises.[8] Despite this expansion of liability, "gratuitous" promises of gifts or unilateral pledges to confer benefits remain legally unenforceable.[9]

4. Professor Grant Gilmore has argued provocatively that a clearly defined "bargain theory" of contract never really existed in the first place. The "theory," he argues, was simply the creature of nineteenth-century formalism. *See* G. GILMORE, THE DEATH OF CONTRACT (1974).

5. The first breach in the armor of classical bargain theory is credited to Professor Corbin. *See id.* at 62-66. *See generally* 1 A. CORBIN, CONTRACTS §§ 109, 110 (1963). Subsequently, the pioneering scholarship of Lon Fuller and Stanley Henderson has demonstrated that the environment of promissory liability differs markedly from conventional assumptions. *See, e.g.*, Fuller & Perdue, *The Reliance Interest in Contract Damages* (pt. 1), 46 YALE L.J. 52 (1936); Henderson, *Promises Grounded in the Past: The Idea of Unjust Enrichment and the Law of Contracts*, 57 VA. L. REV. 1115 (1971) [hereinafter cited as *Unjust Enrichment*]; Henderson, *Promissory Estoppel and Traditional Contract Doctrine*, 78 YALE L.J. 343 (1969) [hereinafter cited as *Promissory Estoppel*].

In addition to Professor Gilmore's essay, the development of contract theory is thoughtfully explored by Lawrence Friedman, *see* L. FRIEDMAN, CONTRACT LAW IN AMERICA (1965), and by Patrick Atiyah, *see* P. ATIYAH, THE RISE AND FALL OF FREEDOM OF CONTRACT (1979).

6. *See* pp. 1345-54 *infra*. Under classical common law doctrine, a mere promise could be elevated to a legally binding contract only by the formality of a seal or a bargained-for exchange of consideration for the promise. L. FULLER & M. EISENBERG, BASIC CONTRACT LAW 124 (1972).

7. *See* note 106 *infra*. The inclusion of section 90 in the *Restatement 1st* is generally identified as the initial doctrinal recognition of the inadequacy of the simple bargain model in explaining the enforcement of promises. Professor Gilmore suggests that Corbin's "revolutionary" attack on bargain theory predates the *Restatement* by several decades. G. GILMORE, *supra* note 4, at 58. Following the adoption of the *Restatement*, scholarly attention turned to describing the emerging principle. *See* Boyer, *Promissory Estoppel: Principle From Precedents* (pts. 1 & 2), 50 MICH. L. REV. 639, 873 (1952); *Promissory Estoppel*, *supra* note 5; Shattuck, *Gratuitous Promises—A New Writ?* 35 MICH. L. REV. 908 (1937).

8. *See* pp. 1349-54 *infra*.

9. *See* pp. 1339-45 *infra*.

Enforcing Promises

These often overlapping, yet seemingly unconnected, principles of bargain, detrimental reliance, and unjust enrichment characterize all legally enforceable promises. They, in turn, are linked with corresponding sanctions that determine the level of enforcement for a given set of promises.[10] Contract damage rules embrace a variety of remedial choices. But the principles determining this choice of remedies are largely unarticulated. In most cases *A* can seek the value of what he expected from *B*'s promise. Such standard "compensatory" recovery puts *A* in the economic position he would have occupied had *B* fulfilled his obligation.[11] There are alternatives to the compensation rule, however. Thus, *A* may seek restitution of any benefit conferred on *B* as a result of *B*'s promise.[12] Alternatively, *A* may seek to recover identifiable costs incurred in reliance on *B*'s promise.[13] Recovering conferred benefits and reliance expenditures has the stated objective of returning the parties to the same economic position they occupied before the promise was made.

How can these interlocking doctrinal patterns be explained? Damage and liability rules have both redistributive and behavior-adaptive functions. In an earlier paper we commented on the apparently random—and arguably regressive—distributive effects of the basic contract remedial options.[14] The adaptive effects of contract rules seem to offer greater explanatory possibilities.[15] A liability or damage rule induces

10. *See* Farnsworth, *Legal Remedies for Breach of Contract*, 70 Colum. L. Rev. 1145 (1970); Fuller & Perdue, *supra* note 5; Goetz & Scott, *Liquidated Damages, Penalties and the Just Compensation Principle: Some Notes on an Enforcement Model and a Theory of Efficient Breach*, 77 Colum. L. Rev. 554, 558-62, 568-77 (1977); Shattuck, *supra* note 7.

11. *See* Goetz & Scott, *supra* note 10, at 558-59. Notwithstanding the universality with which the goal is articulated, scholars have long doubted the rigor of the law's commitment to compensation. We have previously suggested that "a strong argument can be made that the theory of damages is designed to err toward undercompensation." *Id.* at 558 n.19.

12. *See* p. 1337 *infra;* Childres & Garamella, *The Law of Restitution and the Reliance Interest in Contract*, 64 Nw. U.L. Rev. 433 (1969); Dawson, *Restitution or Damages?* 20 Ohio St. L.J. 175 (1959).

13. *See* p. 1337 *infra*. The definitive work in this area remains Fuller & Perdue, *supra* note 5.

14. Goetz & Scott, *supra* note 10, at 566-68.

15. A wealth of theories has been advanced to explain the enforcement of promises. The "intuitionist" theory of the inherent moral force of promises formed the basis of obligation for the social contract theorists of the 17th and 18th centuries. Although the intuitionist perspective is appealing, it fails to explain the simple fact that no legal system attempts to enforce all promises. The 19th-century response to the morality of promising was the "will" theory of contract. The law of contract was conceived of as merely executing and protecting the will of the parties. The 19th-century formalists, typified by Langdell and Pollock, used the notion that the essence of contract is the agreement of wills—or the meeting of minds—to craft the classical bargain theory of consideration.

The obvious limitations of the will theory have produced a reaction among 20th-

contracting parties to adapt their behavior in ways that will affect social welfare. The rules of promissory liability can, therefore, be examined usefully in terms of these welfare effects. It is important to emphasize that the proper focus here is on prospective effects, that future promising is the behavior to be influenced by the rules summarized above. If only promises already made were considered, ease of measurement is a primary factor that might commend the compensation rule over any more complex damage measure.[16] With respect to past promises, choosing among reliance, compensatory, or punitive remedies involves primarily a distributional issue; the damage rule allocates the gains or losses from any particular broken promise between the promisor and promisee. But, considered prospectively, rules of promissory liability have efficiency consequences as well: they frequently alter the actual magnitude of the gains or losses to be divided between the parties. Whether a particular type of promise will be enforceable, and to what extent, are choices that may powerfully modify the nature and amount of future promising. We will evaluate these choices by separating the enforcement question into two parts:

First, which system of promissory enforcement yields the maximum net social benefits from promise making?

Second, does such an optimal enforcement scheme explain current doctrinal patterns?

Part I of this Article considers the first of these questions by developing an analytical model that examines both the function of promises and the impact of liability on the making of promises. Clarifying the function of promising is a necessary first step in deriving an optimal enforcement model. It is critically important to realize that a promise is conceptually distinct from the actual transfer that it announces. As advance information signaling a future transfer, a typical promise prospectively carries *both* benefit if kept and harm if broken. This entanglement of benefits and harms substantially complicates the en-

century contract scholars that leads toward an instrumentalist view of promissory liability: promises are enforceable because enforcement secures socially desirable ends. *See, e.g.*, Atiyah, *Contracts, Promises and the Law of Obligations*, 94 LAW Q. REV. 193, 197-98 (1978); Patterson, *An Apology for Consideration*, 58 COLUM. L. REV. 929, 941 (1958); *Promise or Bargain?*, *supra* note 1, at 463. Although evaluation of promises in terms of their welfare effects dominates current contract jurisprudence, alternative evaluations based on shared ethical norms or common moral intuitions continue to be asserted. *See* J. RAWLS, A THEORY OF JUSTICE 342-50 (1971); Havighurst, *Consideration, Ethics and Administration*, 42 COLUM. L. REV. 1, 9 (1942). Such claims have not proved very helpful, however, in explaining the observable limits that the law sets on enforcing the sanctity of promises. And if moral force is attached to promises merely because people rely upon them, the argument is subject to the claim that such reliance is dependent upon legal enforceability.

16. *See* Goetz & Scott, *supra* note 10, at 566-68.

Enforcing Promises

forcement question. Thus, the enforcement of promises may have harmful consequences by deterring socially useful future promising. Alternatively, nonenforcement encourages more promises but also reduces the reliability of the announcement; the promisor's intent to perform is not tested against a potential penalty for its nonperformance. The value of social welfare is maximized by a system of legal rules that provides the optimal balance between the beneficial and the harmful effects of promising.

In Part II, we discuss the practical compromises necessary to implement efficient regulation of promises in a world of costly legal process and imperfect information. We examine common law rules of liability as proxies for theoretically optimal rules rendered impractical by the inherent difficulties of measuring the true social effects of promising. We conclude that a substantial congruence exists between traditional contract rules and optimal promissory enforcement. Indeed, this congruence offers a persuasive explanation for the peculiar patterns of promissory liability observed in actual practice.[17]

I. Optimal Enforcement of Promises

Attempts have been made to explain the overlapping patterns of promissory liability in terms of the economic implications of promise-making. Bargained-for promises support value-enhancing exchanges. Such promises are thus seen as fully enforceable under the compensation rule in order to protect and encourage value-maximizing resource allocation.[18] Measuring damages in terms of expectation rather than reliance is said to encourage more efficient breach decisions once the contract is made.[19] A nonreciprocal promise, on the other hand, is

17. A recent scholarly debate has centered on the hypothesis that the common law can be explained in terms of principles of economic efficiency. *See, e.g.*, R. Posner, Economic Analysis of Law 404-05, 439-41 (2d ed. 1977); Rubin, *Why is the Common Law Efficient?* 6 J. Legal Stud. 51 (1977); Priest, *The Common Law Process and the Selection of Efficient Rules*, 6 J. Legal Stud. 65 (1977); Michelman, *A Comment on Some Uses and Abuses of Economics in Law*, 46 U. Chi. L. Rev. 307 (1979). We take no position on the extent to which economic efficiency is a dominant or merely subsidiary element in explaining the development of common law doctrine in general. Our intent is the more modest one of measuring a relatively narrow segment of legal doctrine against some underlying economic optimality considerations.

18. *See* Restatement 2d § 76, Comment b ("Bargains are widely believed to be beneficial to the community in the provision of opportunities for freedom of individual action and exercise of judgment and as a means by which productive energy and product are apportioned in the economy.") The assumption that enforcement of bargains promotes allocative efficiency is widespread. *See* Hays, *Formal Contracts and Consideration: A Legislative Program*, 41 Colum. L. Rev. 849, 852-53 (1941); Llewellyn, *What Price Contract?—An Essay in Perspective*, 40 Yale L.J. 704, 716-18 (1931); Patterson, *supra* note 15, at 945-48.

19. R. Posner, *supra* note 17, at 88-93.

frequently labeled as a "sterile transaction," which does not facilitate the movement of resources to more valued uses.[20] On this basis, enforcement is justified only as a deterrent to the harm caused by any detrimental reliance on the promise.[21] In sum, these lines of analysis suggest that full enforcement of bargains consolidates benefits while protection of reliance-based promissory interests minimizes harms.

But existing explanations of the legal enforcement of promises are incomplete and perhaps misleading. A principal limitation has been the failure to consider the effects of various levels of legal enforcement on the making of promises. Inquiry has generally focused instead on the effects of legal sanctions on decisions to breach or perform, assuming that the promise has already been made.[22] Yet, a decision to enforce promises, and the subsequent choice of remedy, does not merely mold the performance behavior of contracting parties; it also shapes both the nature and amount of promise-making activity.

Appropriately calibrated enforcement rules can be used to achieve the optimal number and type of promises based on the degree and form of adaptation by promisor and promisee. Thus, the effects of legal enforcement on promise-making are critical factors in evaluating the seemingly disparate liability and damage rules of contract. In Part I we examine these effects by first describing the reactions of both the promisee and promisor to the risks inherent in promising. We then specify an enforcement model that encourages the socially optimal interaction between the promising parties.

A. *The Function of Promises: Adaptation by the Promisee*

In analyzing the promisee's reactions to a promise, it is critically important to bear in mind the conceptual distinction between the promise itself and the future benefit that it foretells. By communicating a

20. *See* C. Bufnoir, Propriété et Contrat 487 (2d ed. 1924); Fuller, *Consideration and Form*, 41 Colum. L. Rev. 799, 815 (1941); *cf.* R. Posner, *supra* note 17, at 69 (gratuitous, nonreciprocal promises not part of "process by which resources are moved").

21. *See* R. Posner, *supra* note 17, at 69-70; Fuller, *supra* note 20, at 811.

22. *See generally* Shavell, *Damage measures for breach of contract*, Bell J. Econ. (forthcoming 1980); W. Rogerson, Economic Efficiency and Damage Measures in Contract Law (unpublished paper on file with *Yale Law Journal*).

In order to increase its accessibility to a legal readership, this Article uses relatively nontechnical terms to present an underlying economic model that typically would be articulated by economists in highly formal mathematical terms. The formal model developed in the economic literature by Shavell and extended by Rogerson differs conceptually from ours in some important areas. For instance, we focus upon the influence of potential remedies on the quality and quantity of promises, rather than upon the optimal enforcement of a promise, the character of which is already determined. In addition, our definition of reliance damages differs because we incorporate the notion of "reasonableness." Hence, the implicit model underlying this Article is somewhat more complex conceptually than are those cited above.

Enforcing Promises

promise, the promisor informs the promisee about the proposed future receipt of a benefit. The promise itself is merely the production of a piece of information about the future. Normally, advance knowledge of a future transfer will increase the benefit to the promisee because he can more perfectly adapt his consumption decisions to the impending change in wealth. For instance, a person informed of a $25,000 bequest to be made one year hence may revise some of the plans that he otherwise would have followed in the interim twelve months. Because of the revisions in plans, the individual can achieve a higher intertemporal level of satisfaction than if the wealth were transferred without any advance notice. Such adaptive gain from the information embodied in a promise may appropriately be termed "beneficial reliance." The problem occurs, however, when the transfer foretold by the promise is not actually performed. In this case, the information conveyed by the promise turns out to have been misleading and the promisee's induced adaptation in behavior makes him worse off than he would have been without the expectation of a future benefit. Losses incurred by ill-premised adaptive behavior are commonly termed "detrimental reliance." Because the role of promises as units of information is so fundamental to the entire analysis developed below, we will use an economic indifference curve model to give more rigorous content to such key legal concepts as reliance and the reasonableness of the promisee's adaptation process.

1. *Reliance Reactions of a Promisee*

Figure 1 will be used to develop a very simple intertemporal allocation model, one in which a person must allocate his income between two periods, present and future. *A*, the potential promisee, begins with $100, which he can divide between consumption now and consumption in the future. In Figure 1, his possible choices are represented by the straight line budget constraint indicating all combinations of present and future consumption that sum to $100. His preferences about alternative combinations of present and future consumption are summarized by the indifference curves, which define a kind of topographic map of the desirability of different present-future consumption patterns.[23] On these assumptions, the highest preference level consistent with the scarce resources is point e_1, where indifference curve I_1 is

23. Indifference curves may be thought of as a topographical map of a "preference mountain," on which higher "elevations" represent the greater preferences of outcomes. The points in any single indifference curve constitute equally preferred outcomes. An individual thus will be indifferent between any two points on an indifference curve. In the model represented by Figure 1, the higher an indifference curve lies to the northeast, the more utility the individual derives from the outcomes represented by the curves.

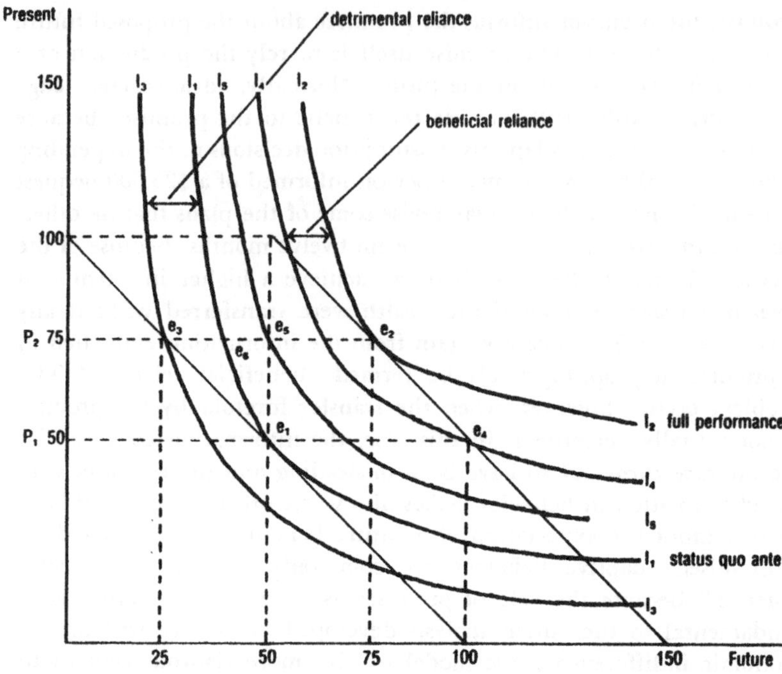

Figure 1

tangent to the budget constraint. This involves spending $50 now and a planned expenditure of $50 in the future.

Suppose now that *B* promises *A* a transfer of $50 to be made in the future period and that *A* believes the promise. Even neglecting the possibility of borrowing against his future wealth, *A*'s budget constraint will shift out to the dotted line in Figure 1.[24] The new constraint indicates that, although no more than $100 can be spent in the present, the two-period consumption levels may now total $150 rather than $100. Based on the new information, *A*'s best two-period plan would be point e_2. *A* is thus led to revise his current consumption upward to $75 and to project $75 worth of future consumption.[25] But what happens if

24. For simplicity, we assume that the interest rate on money is zero in order to produce a one-to-one tradeoff between present and future consumption. The introduction of interest is irrelevant to this analysis because it merely alters the rate of tradeoff, reflected in the slopes of the budget lines.

25. The promisee's consumption of all goods with nonzero income elasticities will be modified. His intertemporal consumption stream will be adjusted to the higher wealth level created by the gift.

Enforcing Promises

the promise is broken when the second period actually arrives? *A* has already expended $75 and has only $25, rather than the prospective $75, left to spend. In terms of Figure 1, breach of the promise pushes *A* leftward from his anticipated outcome of e_2 back to his original budget constraint at e_3. As indifference curve I_3 indicates, *A* is worse off at the post-breach result e_3 than he was at e_1, the pre-promise point on indifference curve I_1. In sum, *A* has been misled by the promise into making what is now recognizable as a mistake; the consequences of that detrimental reliance are captured in the difference between indifference curves I_1 and I_3.

Because detrimental reliance is widely regarded as a basis for damage computation, an advantage of the Figure 1 model is that it clearly illustrates why it is a mistake to use *A*'s observable action in reliance on a promise as the measure of his damages. Under the facts assumed, *A*'s observable reliance is the $25 extra he spends in period 1. If, however, he were awarded this $25 as damages for breach, his ultimate position would be at e_5 on indifference curve I_5. He would have spent $75 in the first period and, including the $25 damages, would have available $50 for the final period. But since return to the status quo ante requires only that indifference curve I_1 be achieved, the true reliance damages are equal only to the lesser amount indicated by the horizontal distance between e_3 and e_6 in Figure 1. The common-sense explanation for this, of course, is that detrimental adaptation in behavior is usually only a partial rather than a total loss. In this case, *A* did get some benefit from the excessive $25 consumption, even though not as much as he would have if the consumption had been postponed to the optimal time. Reliance is, simply, the opportunity cost of the broken promise. Thus, true damages are measured by the difference between the value of the stream of consumption choices not taken—indifference curve I_1—and those choices induced by the promise—indifference curve I_3. Because it is important to distinguish compensation based on observable reliance from true reliance damages, we shall refer to the former as "reimbursement damages" in the discussion below.

Even where the precise meaning is imperfectly captured, the notion of detrimental reliance tends to be better understood than that of beneficial reliance. This is unfortunate because the production of beneficial reliance is perhaps the principal social rationale of promising; the risk of detrimental reliance is merely the unavoidable concomitant cost. Figure 1 aptly illustrates the beneficial consequences of promising when the promise is performed. Assume, for instance, that the $50 in our hypothetical is merely transferred to *A* in period two without any advance warning. Not knowing about the wealth increase, *A* will have committed himself to plan e_1. When period two arrives, *A* will unexpectedly find himself with $100 to spend. At this point, the best available choice is at e_4, which is on a lower indifference curve than e_2, the point that would have been achievable had *A* obtained advance knowledge of the transfer. In common-sense terms, the difference between I_2 and I_4 illustrates the benefits to *A* of being able to adjust, because of the promise, to revised expectations about the future.

2. *The "Self-Protection" Reaction to Uncertain Promises*

Conceptualizing beneficial and detrimental reliance in the context of a simple model such as Figure 1 does have one major limitation. We have assumed implicitly that the promisee places total credence in the promise. Against the background of the Figure 1 model, however, it is possible to consider at least heuristically the imperfect credibility situation. When the promisee does not completely believe a promise, the results illustrated in Figure 1 can be understood as extreme or limiting cases of reliance.

What happens if the promisee knows that the probability of the promisor's performance is less than certain? In this case, the beneficial results of any adaptive behavior when the promise is performed must be weighed against the detrimental results of the same adaptive behavior if the promise is breached. A prospective gain from an adaptive action is balanced against the risk of loss.[26] Whatever the reasons for the riskiness attached to the performance prospects of any promise, the promisee can protect himself against prospective losses from detrimental reliance by limiting his behavior adjustments. In practice, the attempt to do this is frequently manifested in intermediate courses of action taken by promisees who do not completely ignore the implications of a promise in their planning but do not react as fully as if performance were certain. The price for this self-protection against the risk of detrimental reliance is, therefore, the value of the prospective beneficial reliance that would accrue from full adaptation to the advance knowledge of a promissory performance.[27]

26. In formal statements of this balancing process, the promisee is usually regarded as weighting the alternative consequences by the probabilities of performance and nonperformance. It should be noted that the promisee's central concern is whether the preannounced transfer will take place, not whether the performance is a purely voluntary one as opposed to one motivated by legal or other sanctions. Thus, because legal sanctions presumably affect the expected performance probability of many promises, the extent of the reliance experienced can be modified by the legal treatment of promises.

27. An important observation with regard to the promisee's adjustments to uncertain

Enforcing Promises

The possibility of self-protection adjustments by promisees undermines the common assumption that detrimental reliance is the only behavior modified by the enforcement choice. This assumption often leads to characterizing certain "gratuitous" promises as incapable of inducing any reasonable reliance. Once the legal rule is announced, detrimental reliance on such announcements would, it is argued, not be reasonable. But the problem is quite simply that policies that reduce the reliability of promises are likely to reduce both beneficial and detrimental reliance. Thus, legal rules that encourage self-protective adaptation by the promisee achieve desired reductions in detrimental reliance only at the cost of concomitant reductions in beneficial reliance.

B. *Making Promises: Actions of the Promisor*

Understanding the behavior of the promisor is the next important step in our analytic model. How do promisors act and how do prospective sanctions modify their behavior? The initial phase of our analysis employs some strong simplifying assumptions. First, we assume that although future events may be uncertain, retrospective information is perfectly accurate. Second, we also posit that legal process costs are negligible, so that the theoretical gains from an otherwise beneficial regulatory rule are never counterbalanced by implementation costs. These assumptions are relaxed below when we discuss the practical compromises that may be dictated in a more realistic setting.

Potential promisees view promises as beneficial actions and as desirable economic goods. One can thus consider a promisor's willingness to make promises in much the same manner as his willingness to pursue any other economic goal. To predict the level of promise-making activity, the costs of promising must be examined.

1. *The Costs of Promising: The Regret Contingency*

Derivation of the promisor's cost of promising requires consideration of a number of potentially confusing factors. Therefore, we shall begin with the simplest possible environment. First we shall assume

prospects is that even very uncertain promises may produce substantial detrimental reliance if their prospective beneficial reliance is high. The mere improbability of performance does not destroy the informational significance of the promise. Recognition of this fact suggests that the legal concept of "reasonable" reliance is more complex than is sometimes realized. For example, it is perfectly reasonable and rational to rely detrimentally, to some extent, on many promises even though there is a substantial probability of nonperformance.

that the cost of communicating the promise is negligible.[28] Second, we assume that no legal mechanism exists to enforce promises. Absent a legal compulsion, the promisor remains free to refuse performance. If he does, the making of the promise will have generated costs in the amount of the detrimental reliance imposed on the promisee.

The option of nonperformance also imposes costs on the promisor in two situations. The first case is when the promisor exhibits some welfare interdependence with the promisee; that is, he is to some extent altruistic and cares about costs incurred by the promisee.[29] Then, the detrimental reliance costs imposed by nonperformance become, to some degree, costs to the promisor himself. Intrafamilial promises and promises between close friends are most likely to exemplify this phenomenon. In addition, and closely related, guilt may accompany the promisor's imposition of harmful results on others. In any event, this class of breach-related costs, which arise out of an altruistic or ethical sense, may be termed "self-sanctions."

The second extra-legal sanction arises when nonperformance would produce some post-breach reaction, either from the promisee or others, that is costly to the promisor. The resulting costs may range from hostile, retributive behavior to a mere loss of others' esteem to foreclosure of future beneficial dealings.

What are the effects of these extra-legal sanctions for breaking promises? To the extent that such sanctions are effective, their prospect acts as a "cost" of promising and deters promises that are worth less to the promisor than the prospective cost. Thus, extra-legal sanctions are a supplement to, or substitute for, legal sanctions.[30] Given the

28. On these facts, the cost of promising may be zero. One key question to ask, of course, is whether the act of promising has foreclosed any future opportunities to the promisor or made such opportunities more expensive.

29. The economic terminology for such relationship is "interdependent utility functions." The intrafamilial promise offers an obvious illustration of how such interdependency can increase the utility of any given transfer. *See* Posner, *Gratuitous Promises in Economics and Law*, 6 J. LEGAL STUD. 411, 412, 418-19 (1977).

30. Although the existence of extra-legal sanctions may properly affect the choice of legal measures, extra-legal sanctions have several disadvantages as mechanisms for inducing optimal promise-making. First, extra-legal penalties are highly circumstantial, are difficult to calibrate, and vary widely in their efficacy from individual to individual. Second, a sanction must constitute a cost to the person on whom it is imposed; it is not necessary, however, that no one benefit from the sanction. When damages or performance are extracted from a promisor, the resources are transferred to someone else who benefits thereby. Consequently, there may be no net social cost associated with the sanction; at least, the net loss is less than the gross loss imposed on the promisor. By contrast, many forms of extra-legal sanction represent a cost to one party without counterbalancing benefit to another. Prospects of retributive reaction or guilt, for example, tend to be inefficient sanctions in the sense that they could be replaced by resource transfers from promisor to promisee so that the promisee is made better off while the promisor is made no worse off than under the extra-legal sanction.

existence of extra-legal sanctions, under what circumstances might a promisor fail to perform his promise? When a promise is made in good faith, the promisor presumably believes that he is likely to perform. Still, many good-faith promisors would acknowledge the possibility that events may arise that cause them to regret having made the promise. Thereafter, if it were costless to do so, they would indeed breach the promise. Such contingencies may involve a wide range of factors, from changes in personal conditions to disappointment about external considerations that orginally made the promise seem desirable. The term "regret contingency" will be used to denote the future occurrence of a condition that would motivate breach if breach were a costless option for the promisor. Assuming any reliance, the occurrence of a regret contingency necessarily implies that either the promisor or promisee must bear a cost.

When a regret contingency arises, the promisor's options are either to bear the loss attributable to performance, which now costs more than it is worth, or to breach and accept the cost of any corresponding sanction. Presumably the promisor would adopt the cheaper of these regret costs. In any event, someone will suffer a net loss whenever a regret contingency arises, whether in the form of regret costs to the promisor, uncompensated detrimental reliance to the promisee, or both.[31]

2. *Adaptation by the Promisor: Precautions and Reassurance*

By what means does the promisor adapt to the prospective costs of promising?[32] The promisor can substantially influence the probability of a regret contingency, and thus its prospective costs, by adjusting his behavior ex ante. One means of mitigating potential costs is by altering the form of the promise. For instance, the promisor may condition performance on the proviso that certain circumstances—potential regret contingencies—not arise. Alterations in the form of the promise will generally entail a cost to the promisor either in terms of direct resource

31. The regret contingency is a key concept because much of the discussion below will involve either how society can adjust to an optimal volume of exposure to regret contingencies or how to achieve the objective that any given volume of such risk exposure be borne in a least-cost manner.

32. The prospective cost of promising is based on a two-step estimation process by the promisor. First, what is the probability that a regret contingency will arise? Second, if one does arise, what is the magnitude of the accompanying regret costs? The promisor uses the probability of the regrettable outcome to discount the costs of that outcome. Because the future consequences of promises are frequently uncertain, it should be emphasized that the adjective "prospective" is used in a particular sense. Specifically, it indicates that a set of alternative future consequences have been weighted by their probabilities, adjusted for any risk preference, and reduced to a single-valued equivalent.

cost—time and trouble—or in the possibility that the benefit of the promise-making to the promisor will be diminished. The second means of avoiding regret costs is simply to make fewer promises. The costs of this option are forgone benefits from unmade promises.

The costs that result from restrictions in the scope or number of one's promises can be termed "precautionary costs." It is useful to distinguish these further as either quality precautions or quantity precautions. Quality precautions involve adjustments restricting the scope of promises and impose a cost of decreased reliability. Quantity precautions, which consist of reductions in the number of promises made, result in a loss of benefits from promising. A rational promisor will pursue precautionary adjustments up to the point at which marginal precautionary costs are exactly balanced by marginal reductions in regret costs.

Precautionary adjustments by the promisor decrease the value of the promise. Conversely, when the promise is worth more to the promisor than its prospective cost, the promisor may engage in "reassurance." Reassurance includes such actions as the offer of guarantees, verbal persuasions, and the development of a reliable reputation, designed to convince the promisee that the promise is valuable. Reassurances increase the value of the promise to the promisee. Indeed, promisees may regard voluntary reassurance measures as substitutes for sanctions. Reassurance usually entails some cost to the promisor and, hence, will be pursued up to the point at which marginal reassurance costs are exactly balanced by increases in resulting benefits to the promisor.

Precautionary and reassurance reactions by promisors are triggered by variations in the cost of promising. It should be apparent, therefore, that an additional legal sanction will raise prospective costs, thereby precipitating adjustments of the scope and volume of promises. The net effects of these changes can be evaluated by combining the descriptive models of promisee and promisor reaction developed above.

C. *Optimizing Promisor-Promisee Interaction*

To what extent do legal sanctions optimize the interactions between promisor and promisee? In the present context, optimization is defined as maximizing the net social benefits of promissory activity—that is, the benefits of promises minus their costs.[33] This approach is equivalent

33. The adjective "prospective" should be applied to such costs and benefits, and this sense is intended below even when the term is not explicitly used. Strictly speaking, the maximization of prospective benefits need not produce results that, viewed retrospectively, will have truly maximized the net benefits ultimately realized. This is not a serious

Enforcing Promises

to the balancing of prospective costs and benefits under the widely accepted Learned Hand test for the required duty of care in potential tort-producing activities.[34] Indeed, there are strong theoretical parallels between the production of dangerous, but useful, products and the making of promises.[35]

The role of damages or sanctions in generating socially optimal behavior can be focused more sharply by observing the distinction between internal and external effects.[36] Because self-interested maximiz-

objection, however, because the prospective benefits criterion amounts to one under which people are induced to maximize benefits to the extent possible within the limits of the information at their disposal at the time the relevant decisions are made. There is no reason to believe that, as a practical matter, any other criterion can function as well.

34. Under the Hand definition, an actor is guilty of negligence if the loss caused by the accident multiplied by the probability of its occurrence exceeds the burden of taking adequate precautions. United States v. Carroll Towing Co., 159 F.2d 169, 173 (2d Cir. 1947).

35. The optimization process can be analyzed most clearly in terms of marginal effects—that is, the incremental variations in costs and benefits associated with a proposed change in legal treatment. If the marginal benefits attributable to a rule adjustment exceed the marginal costs, then the adjustment is beneficial, and vice versa. The system is optimized when no changes exist for which the marginal net benefits are positive. It is not necessary, therefore, to know the absolute levels of costs and benefits associated with alternative legal rules as long as the increases or decreases in the levels of costs and benefits can be estimated.

Social optimization implicitly presumes that the welfare of promisors and promisees is given equal weight ex ante. In the extreme, this assumption implies that even a promise with a high prospect of net cost to the promisee is optimal if the promisee's costs are outweighed by sufficient benefits to the promisor. In particular classes of cases, such results may be quite discomforting; their possibility constitutes one of the caveats applicable to any efficiency analysis of legal policy. In situations in which such cases arise, supplemental norms may be applied. One such case may be that of the bad-faith promisor who does not intend to perform, but who seeks nevertheless to benefit by making the promise. Here, standard intentional fraud analysis, providing for damages at least equalling the amount of detrimental reliance necessary to make the victimized promisee whole, would be appropriate. Indeed, it might be socially desirable to increase the sanction and extract any unjust gains from the bad-faith promisor.

The most commonly adopted measure of damages for fraud is the "benefit of the bargain" rule. Similar to the compensation principle, the rule puts the plaintiff in the same financial position as if the fraudulent representation had in fact been true. *See* Auffenberg v. Hafley, 457 S.W.2d 929, 938-39 (Mo. App. 1970); Lawson v. Citizens & S. Nat'l Bank, 255 S.C. 517, 180 S.E.2d 206 (1971).

Punitive damages are available when the defrauder has been guilty of morally reprehensible conduct. This generally requires more aggravated conduct than a mere intentional misrepresentation of fact or intentional lie; rather, the fraud must be gross, oppressive, or violative of a position of trust and confidence. *See, e.g.*, J. Truett Payne Co. v. Jackson, 281 Ala. 426, 203 So. 2d 443 (1967); Fowler v. Benton, 245 Md. 540, 552-53, 226 A.2d 556, 564, *cert. denied*, 389 U.S. 851 (1967).

When the plaintiff has transferred property or conferred benefits upon the defendant, he is entitled to a disgorgement of the property or its value. *See* Brooks v. Conston, 364 Pa. 256, 72 A.2d 75 (1950); RESTATEMENT OF RESTITUTION § 202 (1937).

36. Internal effects are those costs and benefits felt by the individual actor. External effects are those consequences of an act that are felt only by individuals other than the actor. Only if a party makes decisions as if he were experiencing all of the consequences of his behavior, external as well as internal, will his behavior be socially optimal.

ing behavior entails consideration of only internal costs and benefits, unfettered individual behavior is incompatible with social optimization in circumstances in which significant external costs or benefits are present. Individuals will oversupply activities with external costs and undersupply those with external benefits. By imposing costs and creating incentives, the law can cause individuals to consider external effects in their decisionmaking and thus "internalize" them.

Inducing optimal promise-making therefore requires that the promisor's costs of promising be adjusted to reflect any external effects on the promisee.[37] But this adjustment process is complex. Changes in the costs and benefits of promising are highly interactive in two senses. First, an individual's adjustments may substitute one category of his costs for another. Second, the actions of one party may produce reactions by the other and, in turn, feedback responses to the first party. The role of legal damages in optimizing this interaction depends upon whether a promise is reciprocal or nonreciprocal. Nonreciprocal or gratuitous promises, which are not conditioned upon performance of a return promise, do not typically enjoy the presumption of enforceability attached to reciprocal or bargained-for promises. As the analysis below reveals, the critical variable that distinguishes these categories of promises is whether the parties can interactively influence the nature and amount of promise-making through bargaining. It is the existence of effective impediments to interaction in the case of nonreciprocal promises that seems to explain why the law treats these two types of promises in such different fashions.[38]

1. *Nonreciprocal Promises*

Consider the case of a gratuitous promisor who has adjusted his promise-making to an arbitrarily assumed level of extra-legal sanction so that he cannot further improve his situation. In addition, assume that social considerations effectively prevent the promisee from influencing the promisor's calculations through bargaining. Under these conditions, when does the intervention of the law lead to optimal

37. As long as the effects of the announcement of the promise itself are carefully distinguished from those of any actual resource transfer, the value of the performance per se to the promisee can be ignored.

38. Barriers to effective interaction between parties to promises may arise from many different sources. Ordinary transaction-costs impediments may exist as a result of the time and trouble involved in negotiating. Alternatively, there may be something inherent in the very relationship of the parties that renders interaction impractical, such as a social taboo, a status relationship, or an institutional environment that obstructs meaningful communication. *See* Leff, *Injury, Ignorance and Spite—The Dynamics of Coercive Collection*, 80 YALE L.J. 1, 41 (1970).

results? We shall first discuss the conditions under which nonenforcement of such a nonreciprocal promise will produce suboptimal reassurance and precautionary adjustments. We then derive an optimal damage formula for those cases in which some level of enforcement is suggested.

a. *Legal Enforcement and Reassurance*

Legal enforcement of a particular class of nonreciprocal promises increases the reliability of the promises. This added reassurance increases social benefits in three situations. First, legal enforcement increases the net benefits of promissory reassurance if a legal sanction such as money damages displaces existing extra-legal penalties such as guilt or social pressure. If the total level of the sanction stays the same, the promisor's costs, benefits, and behavior all remain unchanged, while the promisee's benefits are increased by the receipt of the damages. The promisee's self-protection costs also fall. Because the consequences of a regret contingency are reduced by a prospect of legal compensation, the promisee can spend less on mitigating the risk of uncompensated detrimental reliance. In the event of breach, damage payments reduce the cost of nonperformance to the promisee. Thus, his beneficial reliance on the promise will increase. In essence, the substitution of one type of sanction for the other provides the promisee with the benefits of more reassurance against the regret contingency at no additional cost to the promisor. Hence, the imposition of legal sanctions may increase net reassurance benefits, if extra-legal sanctions are replaced by legal enforcement.[39]

Second, legal enforcement may increase net reassurance benefits regardless of the degree of substitutability of sanctions. Such an opportunity arises when a gratuitous promisor assesses the risk of a regret contingency at zero, because he is certain he will perform. In this case, if the law intervenes by raising the sanction for breach, the promisor's prospective regret and precautionary costs remain at zero. The prospect of sanctions is largely irrelevant to such a promisor. If the promisee knew that the risk of a regret contingency were in fact zero, he too would be unaffected by a stronger sanction. He would be perfectly assured already and, consequently, would incur no self-protection costs. Generally, however, a promisee's subjectively perceived risk of a regret contingency will be greater than the actual zero risk known to the

39. In the case of nonreciprocal promises, no basis appears for predicting when legal enforcement will successfully replace extra-legal sanctions. To the extent that sanctions are cumulative rather than substitutable, the net reassurance benefits of legal sanctions will be reduced.

promisor. Therefore, the increased sanction provides greater reassurance and permits a promisee who was originally engaging in excessive self-protection to decrease his self-protection costs.[40]

Third, even the gratuitous promisor who is not totally certain of future performance may prefer more enforcement. This will occur, for instance, when the promisor cares about the welfare or the reaction of the promisee. Then, the net benefit of promising to the promisor may be enhanced by the provision of additional reliability to the promisee through legal enforcement. Although enforcement puts such promisors at additional risk, the greater reassurance to the promisee may generate increased benefits to the promisor that outweigh any increased costs.[41]

Under what circumstances, then, will legally induced increases in the reliability of nonreciprocal promises be socially optimal? When the mutual interests of both parties are furthered by more assured promises, the promisor will voluntarily seek legal mechanisms for providing additional reassurance. However, often it will not be in the self-interest of the promisor to undertake voluntarily a more reliable promise. Even when some benefits to the promisor are produced by additional reassurance, the external benefits from performance may be inadequately communicated to the promisor by self-sanctions. As a general empirical premise, therefore, enforcement will be more likely to optimize promissory reassurance when extra-legal sanctions are relatively ineffective. The social desirability of enforcement, however, ultimately depends upon whether those gains are offset by corresponding costs. Before proposing a sanction for particular nonreciprocal cases, therefore, we must consider the societal effect of the promisors' precautionary adjustments triggered by legal liability.

b. *Legal Enforcement and Precautionary Action*

Although legal enforcement of nonreciprocal promises will initially increase the reliability of such promises, it may induce both qualitative and quantitative precautionary action by promisors. The net societal

40. As has been noted in different terms, the value of the transfer to the promisee is enhanced because the information content of the promise is improved and the beneficial reliance is increased. *See* Posner, *supra* note 29 (discussing the enforceability of gratuitous promises). The Posner analysis, though persuasive, is limited by its pristine premises.

41. Based on essentially this line of reasoning, Posner is critical of the abandonment of the formal promise under seal as a means of permitting a promisor to opt for legal enforcement of his gratuitous promise. *Id.* at 419-20. Reintroducing measurement costs may conceivably explain the abandonment of the seal. However, as a theoretical principle, an opportunity for the promisor voluntarily to adopt an enforceable form of promise does hold out the opportunity for gains to both parties.

effect of legal enforcement of a class of promises depends on the relative social value of these interacting adjustments.

Qualitative precautionary adjustments by promisors to increased sanctions may be thought of as merely the converse of reassurance. These precautionary moves entail a lessening of the scope of the promise and a shifting of the risk of potential regret contingencies to the promisee, while reassurance enhances the value of the promise and constitutes an assumption of risk by the promisor. These qualitative dimensions of a promise encompass two conceptually distinct effects: first, risk minimization by providing the promisee with better information on which to determine his degree of reliance; and, second, risk allocation by dividing the costs of regret contingencies between promisor and promisee. Analysis of these two factors suggests that legal sanctions can be used to induce risk-minimizing precautionary adjustments by both parties, but are much less successful in directing risk-bearing choices.

By providing the promisee with information concerning regret contingencies, precautionary adjustments by the gratuitous promisor improve the accuracy of the promisee's degree of reliance. Without a legal sanction, the benefits generated by the information effect of precautionary adjustments may not be maximized. The promisor is motivated to make precautionary adjustments only to the extent that his increased precautionary costs are outweighed by decreases in his regret costs. For instance, when only minimal extra-legal sanctions are imposed on breach, the savings in regret costs are relatively trivial, and precautionary moves by the promisor are not likely to be cost-effective. Under these circumstances, the promisee will be insufficiently forewarned about the risks of breach and will consequently overrely, failing to protect himself adequately against the prospect of breach.

Thus, where the external costs of a nonreciprocal promise are unlikely to be conveyed to the promisor, legal enforcement can induce the promisor to make optimal precautionary adjustments. Alternatively, the promisee must optimize self-protection and reliance in the light of the information he now possesses about the reliability of the promise. Paradoxically, if promises are unenforceable, the promisee has the correct incentives to protect himself to the optimal level against risks. Because the promisee bears all risks of breach, in this environment, he will rely on a promise only to the extent that the prospective cost of reliance is outweighed by prospective benefits. In contrast, if a promise is legally enforceable, and the regret costs shift to the promisor, the promisee may engage in a greater than optimal level of reliance. Because the reduction of regret costs becomes an external benefit of the promisee's actions, the promisee may ignore these costs in determining the extent of his reliance. In order to discourage the promisee from overrelying, the promisor must not be held liable for damages when the promisee knew or should have known that the marginal cost of self-protection was lower than the corresponding marginal reduction in prospective regret costs. This rule gives meaning to the concept of "reasonable reliance" and avoids not only an underinvestment in self-protection by the promisee, but also an overinvestment in precautionary adjustments by the promisor. It fills essentially the same function as does the rule of contributory negligence in tort.[42]

In addition to these risk minimization effects, legally induced qualitative precautionary moves reallocate the risk of regret to the promisee. What can be said of the risk allocation implications of these qualitative adjustments? The allocation of risk to a least-cost risk bearer by the manipulation of legal liability may have efficiency consequences that justify the costs of such adjustments. However, in the case of most nonreciprocal promises, the risk of a regret contingency ultimately will be borne by the promisee in spite of the promisor's risk-bearing advantages. Initially, the imposition of a legal sanction allocates some or all of the risk of a regret contingency to the promisor. But so long as the promisor is free to make qualitative adjustments, by conditioning his promise, he can shift that risk back to the promisee. In some cases, of course, the promisee may be the least-cost risk bearer. However, because it is the enforcement of the promise that removed the risk from the promisee initially, legally induced precautionary moves to shift it back again cannot be regarded as efficiency gains attributable to the liability rule. Thus, in terms of risk allocation, qualitative adjustments have only distributional consequences; their implementation costs may be regarded as net social losses.[43]

This analysis suggests that qualitative precautionary adjustments by

42. Imposition of a legal sanction equal to full detrimental reliance would, in the absence of a mitigation limitation, encourage overinvestment in reliance by promisees. Indeed, it has been suggested that enforcement of promises under a reliance scheme would create a moral hazard in terms of the promisee's adjustments. In other words, a promisee might be tempted to extend his reliance beyond any objectively reasonable point; if the promise is kept, he reaps the benefits, while if it is broken, the promisor bears the full costs under the liability rule. *See* Shavell, *supra* note 22. Optimal legal sanctions can respond to the problem of over-investment in reliance by structuring a compound liability rule under which the behavioral adaptations of both parties are scrutinized. Of course, the implementation costs of such a rule may be substantial. *See* pp. 1289-90 *infra*.

43. If promises are unenforceable, however, promisors may also engage in qualitative reassurance adjustments. This also entails social costs of implementation. These costs will be reduced under an enforcement rule.

the gratuitous promisor have mixed effects. Increasing these adjustments by legally enforcing nonreciprocal promises is optimal, therefore, only when gains in promisee reliance from improved information exceed the net implementation costs of reallocating the risk of regret to the promisee. This implies, as an empirical generalization, that enforcing nonreciprocal promises will improve outcomes when there exists a substantial prospect of beneficial information exchanges through qualitative adjustments. Conversely, in contexts in which self-sanctions are already effective and the prospects of improved information are poor, the social gains from enforcement are negligible and may be exceeded by implementation costs. Nonenforcement of such nonreciprocal promises is thus the optimal choice.

c. *An Optimal Damage Formula*

The effect of a decision to enforce legally any particular class of nonreciprocal promises depends upon the nature of the sanction imposed for breach. Promisors will respond to higher levels of sanction by increasing their qualitative and quantitative precautions, reducing both the reliability of a given volume of promises and the number of promises actually made.

A necessary starting point in determining an optimal damage rule is to specify the external effects of a nonreciprocal promise as the supply of such promises is increased by one marginal unit. The external effects are the prospective detrimental reliance incurred if the promise is broken and the prospective beneficial reliance enjoyed if the promise is performed. Proper reflection of external effects therefore requires not only that the promisor be charged for the harm expected from broken promises, but also that he be rewarded for the prospective benefits of performance. It is helpful to state this condition symbolically. Let p be the promisor's reasonable, subjective assessment of the probability that he will perform a promise under an existing legal rule calling for damages of D in the event of breach. For the damage rule to deter all promises with net social costs and encourage those with net benefits, the amount of damages awarded must satisfy the following equation:

$$(1 - p)D = (1 - p)R - pB$$

where R and B are the values of detrimental and beneficial reliances, respectively. Assuming that all broken promises are litigated, the left-hand side of the equation represents the expected value of the prospective legal sanction. Because only broken promises are affected by the

The Yale Law Journal Vol. 89: 1261, 1980

law, the probability $(1 - p)$ of the promise being broken is used to "discount" the damages D. The values for R and B on the right-hand side of the equation should be understood as those resulting from optimal self-protection by the promisee. Thus, promisees will appropriately minimize the value of the right-hand term, which is the net social cost of the promise. In calculating this prospective net reliance, the magnitudes of the potential detrimental and beneficial reliances are each discounted by their probabilities. When the equation is satisfied through the imposition of optimal damages D, the promisor's internal cost-benefit calculus will reflect the external effects of his promise-making. If the external effects are thus accounted for, the promisor's maximization of his internal net benefits is consistent with supply of the socially optimal quantity and quality of promises. We call this damage rule the "prospective net reliance" formulation.

In some cases, the prospective beneficial reliance from a promise will exceed its prospective detrimental reliance. Because the net external effect of such a promise is beneficial, it would be optimal to reward the making of such promises. However, in the nonreciprocal setting no practical legal mechanism exists for rewarding promises. This limitation renders true optimization impossible; the situation is necessarily second-best. At minimum, promises with prospects of net beneficial reliance should not be the subject of damages if breached. Only promises with prospective net detrimental external effects should be enforceable.

The prospective net reliance formulation developed above can be used to analyze the optimal level of enforcement. By dividing both sides of the original equation by the probability of breach $(1 - p)$, the following damage rule emerges:

$$D = R - \left[\frac{p}{(1-p)}\right] B.$$

The optimal damage rule thus subtracts from the promisee's reliance cost a fraction of his potential beneficial reliance. This fraction is the ratio of the ex ante subjective probability of performance to that of nonperformance. It determines the extent to which the prospect of beneficial reliance when the promise was made is credited against the promisee's prospective detrimental reliance. Because this ratio may be thought of as an index of the promisor's good faith, we call it the "good-faith ratio." A damage offset based on the good-faith ratio and on the amount of potential beneficial reliance will encourage the optimal quantity and quality of promises by reflecting in the promisor's decision calculus both the harmful and beneficial effects of his promise-making. This optimal legal sanction is likely to be unattainable in an environment of costly legal process and imperfect information.[44] But specifying an optimal sanction permits more rigorous evaluation of the error produced by any practical adjustment attributable to process costs. In addition, the good-faith ratio and the damage offset suggest a possible explanation for the language of the *Restatement of Contracts*, which conditions both the enforceability and the magnitude of reliance-based sanctions upon the "requirements of justice."[45] This language may reflect the view that the prospective beneficial effects of a promise should be considered in effecting a remedy for nonperformance.

The rule suggested by the formula above will admittedly result in a large quantity of uncompensated damages from broken nonreciprocal promises. Although greater damages would deter many injurious transactions, a stricter standard also would deter beneficial transactions in even greater magnitudes. Viewing an already-broken promise, the affected promisee would always prefer the highest possible damage award. But from the ex ante standpoint, a promisee would not wish to discourage a promise that creates a prospect of gain outweighing the risk of uncompensated loss. Such promises are "good bets" for the promisee over the long run, even though some of the promises will result in uncompensated harm. The penalty formulation developed above awards damages both to protect promisees from "bad bet" promises and to avoid deterrence of promises that are "good bets."

Under this prospective net reliance damage formula, the gratuitous promisor also has an incentive to undertake cost-effective qualitative precautions to modify prospective reliance induced by any promise actually made. A properly calibrated legal sanction will induce the promisor to convey to the promisee socially beneficial information about the risk of regret contingencies. In essence, such a promisor is encouraged to make cost-effective adjustments in both the quality and the quantity of his promises because the legal rule converts social benefits into savings for him. If, in addition, the law recognizes only the amount of damages that constitutes a "reasonable"—*i.e.*, cost-effective—reliance by the promisee, then the promisee will also have an incentive to minimize net social costs. Thus, the rule penalizes each party for failing to take cost-effective steps to minimize the social costs of promising. Damages exceeding those described above will tend to induce the promisor to invest too much in precautionary adjustments. This phenomenon is analogous to the excessive level of prudence anticipated if tort victims were awarded a multiple of their true damages.

44. *See* pp. 1289-90 *infra*.
45. Restatement 1st § 90; Restatement 2d §§ 89B(2), 89D, 90(1), 217A(1).

2. *Reciprocal Promises*

Promising is reciprocal when the parties can adjust interactively to the nature and amount of promise-making. The prospective net reliance formulation is equally applicable to reciprocal as well as to nonreciprocal promises. But the net reliance damage rule seems in sharp conflict with accepted legal doctrine in the reciprocal promise context, in which damages for breach are typically based on the promisee's full-performance expectation rather than on his detrimental reliance. Upon analysis, the apparent conflict can be dissipated; moreover, reciprocal promises are easier than nonreciprocal promises for the law to address.

This conclusion is buttressed by two independent lines of argument. First, in the case of reciprocal promises, a plausible empirical generalization is that a promisee's acceptance of one promise frequently requires his foregoing a potential substitute promise. The forgone value of the best substitute promise available—the opportunity cost—is key in determining the promisee's detrimental reliance when an accepted promise is subsequently broken. In a well-organized market, alternative promises will be close, if not perfect, substitutes. In that case, detrimental reliance is equal to the full performance value of the breached promise.[46] Similarly, beneficial reliance will be small, because the promisor's pledge, even if performed, will not constitute a very substantial improvement over the potential beneficial reliance from substitute promises. This empirical generalization implies that, in the damage formula developed above, full performance expectation E can be substituted for detrimental reliance R because $E \approx R$. Furthermore, because $B \approx 0$, the term of $\left[\frac{1-p}{P}\right]$ B drops out. We are left with $D \approx E$; thus, expectation damages are a good proxy for the prospective net reliance damage formulation developed above.[47]

Second, a fundamental theoretical difference exists between reciprocal and nonreciprocal promises. In the case of a reciprocal promise,

46. The correlation between detrimental reliance and full performance expectation whenever there is a competitive market for the broken promise was first observed by Fuller and Perdue. *See* Fuller & Perdue, *supra* note 5, at 62-63.

47. Nothing in the logic of this argument limits its applicability to reciprocal promises. Although the argument's empirical premise tends to have greater validity with respect to bargained-for promises, classes of nonreciprocal promises may exist for which forgone substitute promises also yield a close convergence between reliance and expectation. The implications of using expectation as a proxy for reliance on reciprocal promises will become apparent when we introduce practical problems of measurement below. *See* pp. 1288-1321 *infra*.

the principal objective of a promisor is to obtain consideration in the form of a return promise. The value of the return promise elicited is the main element of the promisor's benefit. Therefore, changes in the qualitative aspects of the promise are reflected in commensurate shifts of benefits to the promisor; a higher quality promise motivates a more valuable return promise, and vice versa. In contrast to the case of nonreciprocal promises, qualitative adjustments are internalized in the promisor's cost-benefit calculus by generating a more or less valuable consideration for his promise. Hence, the bargaining process accomplishes an important part of the behavioral regulation that, for nonreciprocal promises, must be performed by the legal system.

Furthermore, the bargaining process, not available by definition in the nonreciprocal context, can facilitate the optimal allocation of risk for reciprocal promises. Precautionary action is subject to a test of the ability of the promisee to bribe the promisor to make an unconditioned promise. Within any scheme of enforcement, then, the parties can reallocate the risks of regretted promises by buying or selling protection through the terms of their agreement. The least-cost bearer of any risk will presumably agree to absorb that risk in exchange for an enhanced return promise.

For much the same reasons, the consequences of excessive damages for breaching reciprocal promises are also mitigated, as long as the rule providing for excessive damages is understood in advance. The parties can always bargain out from the rule, for instance by a limited damages agreement. Thus, when transactions costs are zero, the particular damage rule selected for reciprocal promises is irrelevant. Although the existence of transactions costs renders bargaining over damage rules costly in practice, the feedback adjustment of the return promise markedly reduces the potentially inefficient effects of legal rules. While in the nonreciprocal case, excessive damages overdeter the promisor from promissory activity, in the reciprocal relationship, the promisee will regard the excessive damages as a quality improvement and will offer an enhanced return promise. The enhanced return promise will tend to offset the deterrence effect of the damages. However, some inefficiencies remain. Legally mandated "overinsurance" induces a moral hazard because the promisee will not exercise optimal self-protection. Furthermore, there is a cheaper allocation of risk than the legally mandated level of reassurance provided to—and paid for by—the promisee.[48]

48. There is a close conceptual analogy between excessive contractual damages and specific guarantees or minimum quality requirements imposed by law on consumer

The Yale Law Journal Vol. 89: 1261, 1980

The result may be even more costly, however, when the law provides a suboptimal level of enforcement. The extreme case of a complete refusal to enforce reciprocal promises provides an instructive illustration.[49] The initial impact of the rule, which is to underdeter promisors, will be counterbalanced by reductions in the value of return promises. Promisors may then substitute extra-legal forms of reassurance for legal sanctions. Creating adequate extra-legal enforcement mechanisms is likely to be less efficient than legally sanctioned reassurance. If so, the inefficiency consequences of underenforcement may be more serious than those of overenforcement.

In sum, the theoretical damages principles developed in connection with nonreciprocal promises apply to reciprocal promises as well. The difference in their legal treatment may be due to a close empirical identity of reliance and expectation in reciprocal promises. However, modification of the return promise is a powerful additional adjustment mechanism, which exists, by definition, only for reciprocal promises. By internalizing many of the promissory interactions among contracting parties, the return promise reduces the stress placed on legal rules for optimally influencing the behavior of promisors and promisees.

D. *Summary and Implications*

The preceding analysis suggests that the function of promises can be observed more precisely by conceptually distinguishing the effects of the advance information from the actual transfer. Information from promises induces reliance whenever the promisee attaches a positive probability to performance. Reliance responses are beneficial when a promise is kept and detrimental when it is broken. The principal normative justification for permitting promises to be made freely is the belief that, on balance, promissory benefits exceed harms. Legally enforcing promises can sometimes increase this net social gain by encouraging cost-reducing behavior by both promisors and promisees.

The treatment of promises when performance or nonperformance is certain is simple: such promises can be fully enforced so as to maximize benefits or minimize costs respectively. In the sure performance case,

products. Because the product is required to be "better," it can command a higher price, which overcomes at least in part the reluctance of producers to supply a more expensive output. Nevertheless, a suboptimal result exists because consumers and producers could, if permitted, work out a mutually advantageous trade of less quality for less money.

49. In contrast to bargained-for limitations of standard damage measures, attempts to contract for supranormal remedies may run afoul of the rule against penalties. *See* Goetz & Scott, *supra* note 10, at 558-62.

enforcement, without deterring the promisor, increases the reliability of the promise to the promisee. In the certain nonperformance case, maximum deterrence of promises serves to prevent a bad-faith promisor from enriching himself at certain cost to the promisee.

The more important case of promises for which performance is potentially uncertain is more complex, because each promise carries both potential benefits and harms that must be balanced. Future contingencies may materialize rendering performance of such promises unattractive to the promisor. The risk of this regret contingency can be allocated several ways. On the one hand, nonenforcement of promises induces self-protective reductions in reliance by the promisee. These, in turn, may trigger reassurance reactions from the promisor. On the other hand, enforcement of promises increases promisee reliance, but also induces precautionary adjustments by the promisor. The social cost of the regret contingency is minimized when the optimal interactive adaptations are encouraged.

An examination of the function of legal rules in optimizing the interactions between the promisor and promisee explains the traditional distinction between nonreciprocal and reciprocal promises. In the case of reciprocal promises, the bargain mechanism provides a feedback of costs and benefits to the promisor and promisee. Thus, the liability rules for reciprocal promises do not directly influence promise-making; instead, they affect the costs of contracting between bargainers. For nonreciprocal promises, however, enforcement substantially shapes the adaptive responses of both parties.[50] For example, enforcement of nonreciprocal promises will optimize social benefits when extra-legal sanctions are minimal and the promisor can be encouraged to adapt the form of the promise to the risk of regret. Calibration of the optimal damages for such enforceable promises requires a consideration of both the beneficial and the detrimental reliance prospectively induced by the promise. Such a prospective net reliance formulation encourages promisors accurately to internalize social effects and thereby induces appropriate qualitative and quantitative adjustments.

But the practical implications of this ideal enforcement scheme must be considered. When nonenforcement is optimal, no measurement difficulties impede its implementation. When enforcement is indicated, implementation of the optimal rule is more difficult. A standard expectation-interest sanction may impose supra-optimal damages and deter socially valuable promise-making by inducing excessive precautionary behavior in promisors. The traditional reliance damage formulation—

50. *See* pp. 1307-08 *infra*.

return of the promisee to the status quo ante—most clearly approximates the optimal level of enforcement.[51] However, despite the language usually invoked, the status quo ante goal is rarely achieved by courts awarding so-called reliance damages. This systematic disparity between principle and practice isolates a central dilemma of promissory liability. True reliance damages, which include the value of opportunities forgone as well as the costs of actions taken, are extraordinarily difficult to measure accurately. Courts have generally responded to this largely unarticulated measurement conundrum by simply reimbursing the promisee for the gross value of any actions taken or actual expenditures incurred in reliance on the promise.[52] The recovery of such expenditures, which we have termed "reimbursement damages," should be distinguished from the theoretical objective of reliance damages.

We have developed the preceding model under an assumption of perfect measurement in order to evaluate the effects of legal rules on promissory behavior. Existing patterns of promissory liability often appear to produce substantial error costs in failing to regulate this conduct efficiently. Can this systematic error be explained? The complexity of the preceding analysis suggests that measurement of the true social cost of promising is likely to be itself a very costly activity. Enforcement costs increase the risk that the promisee's true reliance losses will not be fully recouped.[53] Moreover, process costs necessary to ascertain and implement the optimal level of enforcement may be so high that they exceed the error costs attributable to simpler rules of thumb such as no enforcement, full enforcement, or reimbursement. In Part II we relax the assumptions of perfect measurement and zero process costs to evaluate the efficiency of the rules of promissory obligation from a more practical standpoint.

51. *See* p. 1298 *infra*.
52. *See* pp. 1292-93 *infra*.
53. *See* Goetz & Scott, *supra* note 10, at 558 n.19; Schwartz, *The Case for Specific Performance*, 89 YALE L.J. 271, 274-78 (1979).

Conclusion

Examination of the economic implications of promising reveals a tension between ideal and practical objectives. Because uncertainty cannot be eliminated, it may be tempting to resist systematization of expanding areas of liability.[176] The suggestion that the results in individual cases can safely be predicted by employing a handful of simple economic tools is misguided. Economic concepts are useful, however, in specifying the effects of legal objectives and in observing and isolating systemic patterns of enforcement. The indeterminacy of empirical parameters necessitates the use of assumptions that only crudely approximate the true theoretical objectives. Often the effects of using estimates are unclear, as undetermined factors affect the behavior under examination.[177] Nonetheless, systematic collection and observation of data increases understanding of the regulation of behavior by legal rules.

We have assumed that the economic objective of regulating promises is to maximize the net beneficial reliance derived from promise-making activity. In general, this objective is best achieved by a scheme of

175. For a discussion of the legitimacy of using contract law to achieve distributional ends, see Kronman, *Contract Law and Distributive Justice*, 89 YALE L.J. 472 (1980).

176. *See* G. GILMORE, *supra* note 4, at 102-03.

177. *See* Leff, *Law and*, 87 YALE L.J. 989, 1005-11 (1978).

promissory enforcement that induces adaptive behavior by the party better able to minimize the risk that future contingencies may materialize and cause the promisor to regret the announcement. Optimal adaptation requires a reduction in the prospective reliance on promising whenever this investment produces a greater decrease in expected harms from nonperformance. Both legal and extra-legal sanctions impose these social costs on the promising parties. Optimal legal sanctions are, therefore, a function of both the magnitude of these extra-legal factors and the parties' relative advantage in risk avoidance. The ideal liability choice ranges from zero enforcement to liability equal to the reasonable detrimental reliance caused by breach. However, because promissory reliance is peculiarly impervious to measurement, alternative rules are often applied as proxies for true reliance.

Promissory liability rules can be examined by classifying promises in three categories along principles of reciprocity and bargain. First, reciprocal promises are distinguishable from nonreciprocal promises on the basis of the ability of bargainers to adjust the volume and form of promising by varying the price of the promise. When such adjustments are not possible, promises are not enforced. Nonenforcement of gratuitous promises is justified because in the nonreciprocal setting, self-sanctions against breach are frequently effective, and promisees are often better able than promisors to adapt to the risks of regret. Second, the narrow consideration model defined by common law delineates a subdivision within the category of reciprocating promises. Enforcement is narrowly limited by assumptions that costs of promise-making are best reduced by precautions at the core of bargaining, and by reassurances on the periphery.

However, courts have used alternate theories of liability to expand enforcement appropriately beyond the confines of the consideration model. Promises have been enforced when increased accuracy, transactional efficiency, or bad faith justified the imposition of liability. These alternative bases of liability have been recently generalized into broad grants of judicial discretion. Although discretion permits the pursuit of distributional goals, it increases the uncertainty facing future bargainers. Absent careful articulation of distributional objectives, the social cost of uncertainty requires the development of clear rules for recoveries grounded on reliance.

[18]

Damage measures for breach of contract

Steven Shavell*

This article studies rules or "damage measures" that determine how much money must be paid by a party who defaults on a contract to the other party to the contract. The theme of the article is that damage measures serve as a substitute for completely specified contracts. In particular, it is shown that under an incompletely specified contract, damage measures can induce parties to behave in a way that approximates what they would have explicitly agreed upon under a fully specified contract. Moreover, it is argued on familiar lines that because it is often costly or impossible to make contractual provisions for contingencies at a very detailed level, there is an evident need for such substitutes for well-specified contingent contracts as are afforded by damage measures.

1. Introduction

■ **General remarks.** When a contract is made, there is always a possibility that one of the parties to it will fail to perform. If this happens, the defaulting party often must pay the other party "damages," the amount being determined in any of a number of ways—by law or regulation, by trade practice or custom, by a previous and explicit agreement of the parties' own device (so called liquidated damages). We shall speak here of the amount paid as depending on a *damage measure* with the understanding that this term is to be given the broadest interpretation.[1]

In considering the nature and function of damage measures, it will first be necessary to recall the notion of a *complete contingent contract*. This is an agreement that specifies the obligations of the contracting parties and the payments to be made under each conceivable circumstance or "contingency." Such an agreement can be as well tailored as is feasible to the capacities and

---

* Harvard University.

I wish to thank R. Claman, P. Diamond, R. Ericson, J. Green, B. Greenwald, A. M. Polinsky, R. Posner, and the Editorial Board for comments and the National Science Foundation (grant SOC-76-20862) for financial support.

[1] The reader who is interested in the economic role of damage measures may wish to refer to the following articles: Barton (1972), Birmingham (1969), Diamond and Maskin (1979), Fuller and Perdue (1937), Goetz and Scott (1977), Grossfeld (1963), Kornhauser (1979), Posner (1977, pp. 88–94), Priest (1978), and Rogerson (1980). Barton's article is the most closely related to the present one (but see footnote 17 on Rogerson), and we shall comment briefly on it as well as on some of the other articles later. The reader may also find it instructive to compare the general approach taken in most of the above references with one based on "moralist" argument; for a recent and systematic analysis of breach and other issues in contract law employing the latter approach, see Fried (1980).

needs of the parties and to the particular contingency that obtains. If the agreement is so constructed, and more specifically, if there are no (prospectively viewed) mutually beneficial changes that the parties can make, then it is said to be a *Pareto efficient* complete contingent contract.

Now it is immediate from its definition that a Pareto efficient complete contingent contract is one to which the parties would find it in their mutual interest to be *bound* to adhere. In particular, they would wish for damages for failure to meet the terms of the contract to be set sufficiently high that the terms would *always* be obeyed.[2]

However, contracts are usually enforced by means of damage measures which are not so stringent that the parties would always decide to meet their terms; contracts are frequently broken. Thus, we are led to infer that contracts must not generally be Pareto efficient complete contingent contracts. And it is, of course, the case that contracts typically do not provide for many contingencies; they leave much unsaid.[3] To understand the connection between their incompleteness and damage measures for breach, it will be convenient to consider an example.

Suppose that a buyer contracts with and pays a seller at the outset to produce and deliver a machine, that the value of having the machine to the buyer would be $200, and that the relevant contingencies concern production cost, which will become apparent to the seller before he actually begins the production process. Assume first that the contract is Pareto efficient and depends on production cost. Such a contract would *specify* that the seller should proceed with production if the cost is less than the $200 value of the machine to the buyer, and that the seller should not proceed with production if the cost exceeds $200.[4] Now assume that the contract does not depend on production

[2] Yet it should be emphasized that *according to the terms* of a Pareto efficient complete contingent contract, a party will typically be released from certain "obligations" under certain contingencies. For example, such a contract might say that a seller does not have to produce and deliver a good if his factory burns down or if his workers go on strike. Therefore, the statement that a party always obeys the terms of a Pareto efficient complete contingent contract does not mean that the party always meets a named obligation, takes a particular action.

[3] A moment's reflection or a reading of cases should convince the reader of the truth of this assertion, but reference may also be made to a well-known article by Macaulay (1968).

[4] That this really characterizes the Pareto efficient, that is, the *jointly preferred*, complete contingent contract will be proved in the paper. But a calculation may make this plausible to the reader who does not find it obvious.

What we shall illustrate is that, given a contract under which the seller must always perform, we can construct an alternative contract which both he and the buyer would prefer and under which he performs only if production cost is less than or equal to $200 (which in strict logic should be interpreted as the value of the machine over that of available alternatives). Assume that the cost of production will be $100 with probability .99 and $1000 with probability .01. Suppose first that the contract requires the seller to perform regardless of production cost and that the price (recall, paid at the outset) is, say, $150. Then the expected value of the contract to the seller is $150 − (.99($100) + .01($1000)) = $150 − $109 = $41; and the value to the buyer is $200 − $150 = $50. Now suppose that the contract requires the seller to perform only if the production cost is $100 and that the contract price is lowered to, say, $145. Then the expected value of the contract to the seller is $145 − .99($100) = $46 and its expected value to the buyer is .99($200) − $145 = $53. Thus, *both the seller and the buyer strictly prefer the second contract, the one which allows the seller not to perform under a certain contingency*; letting the seller avoid producing when the cost of doing so exceeds the value of the machine to the buyer made it possible to reduce the price by enough to make the buyer better off (despite the chance he would not get the machine) but at the same time by sufficiently little as still to leave the seller better off.

cost. (Why it might not will be discussed subsequently.) Instead, the contract merely says that the seller "shall produce and deliver the machine," and it further stipulates that the seller shall pay the buyer, let us say, $200 in damages in the event of breach. Clearly, under this contract, the seller would be *induced* to behave just as he was *explicitly obligated* to behave under the terms of the complete contingent contract: if the production cost is less than $200, it would be cheaper for the seller to perform than to default and pay damages; and if the cost is greater than $200, it would be cheaper for the seller to default and pay damages than to perform.[5] (And, equally clearly, it would not be in the mutual interests of the buyer and seller to set damages for breach so high that the seller would always satisfy his contractual obligation to "produce and deliver the machine," for then he would produce it when the production cost exceeds $200.)

This example illustrates that a damage measure for breach of contract may create incentives for parties who have made a contract which does not provide for various contingencies to act in a way that is close to (and in the example is actually identical to) what they would have agreed upon under a Pareto efficient complete contingent contract.

If it is granted that damage measures for breach of contract can serve as a kind of substitute for complete contingent contracts, the question must still be asked why there is a need for such substitutes, and two frequently noted answers may be reviewed. The first is simply that because of the costs involved in enumerating and bargaining over contractual obligations under the full range of relevant contingencies, it is normally impractical to make contracts which approach completeness.[6] More precisely, if the probability of a contingency (or class of contingencies—an event) is low, then it may be less costly in the expected sense for the parties to resolve difficulties only on the chance that they arise than to bear with certainty the costs of providing for the contingency in the contract.[7]

---

[5] Recall that we have assumed that the seller received payment from the buyer at the outset; thus the seller does not lose his payment if he defaults. (But it will be seen from the analysis that our present assumption concerning timing of payment is inessential.)

[6] It should be mentioned that this reason for a need for a substitute for complete contingent contracts explains why there is often (a) resort to renegotiation as a means of "filling in" gaps in contracts and (b) reliance on the background of custom and law to recognize certain contingencies as excuses for breach.

Renegotiation, however, has two disadvantages which limit (but, of course, hardly eliminate) its usefulness relative to damage measures. The first is that renegotiation is a costly process. And the second is that there is no strong reason to believe renegotiation will result in a Pareto efficient outcome when one party cannot verify the occurrence of a contingency. In our example the seller might wish to renegotiate owing to an increase in production costs, and let us assume that the increase is such that the total costs are still below the value of the machine to the buyer. If the buyer does not know what the production costs really are and thinks the seller is bluffing, he might refuse to accommodate the seller, and thereby cause the breakdown of what would still have been a Pareto efficient contract.

Reliance on custom and law is subject to similar disadvantages; and it can act to fill in gaps in contracts only with respect to those readily observable contingencies for which the agreement that parties would have come to can be fairly confidently imputed.

It should also be noted that since reliance on custom and law (and perhaps on renegotiation as well) amounts to an actual addition of contract terms under certain contingencies, it is to be seen as having a function that is quite distinct from damage measures, for they do not add terms in a virtual sense, but rather in an implicit sense through incentive effects.

[7] This might be put as follows. Suppose that t_1 is the cost of including in the contract a Pareto efficient provision for a contingency that will occur with probability p, that e is the cost of en-

The second reason there is a need for substitutes for complete contingent contracts is that it may be difficult or impossible for a party to verify the occurrence of certain contingencies and therefore to tell whether the other party is adhering to the contract.[8] In the example we might imagine that the buyer is unable to determine what the true production cost is—perhaps this would require of him a detailed knowledge of the production process or of the prices of material inputs: thus the buyer would not know whether production cost exceeds $200; this would render meaningless a contract that depends on production costs. The importance of the problem of some party not easily being able to verify the occurrence of contingencies may be appreciated as substantial when one begins to reflect on the types of contingencies which may be pertinent in a contractual situation. There are usually many aspects of a seller's position which matter to him and which the buyer cannot observe or sometimes even recognize;[9] and the converse is true of the buyer's position.[10]

The arguments of the last two paragraphs should justify interest in the program of the paper, which is to ask how damage measures for breach of contract function and how they compare, given the assumption that contracts do not explicitly provide for *any* contingencies. This is an extreme assumption, but it is appropriate if the goal is to clarify understanding about the role of damage measures as a substitute for Pareto efficient complete contingent contracts.[11]

□ **Informal summary.** In the model to be examined,[12] a risk neutral buyer makes a contract with a risk neutral seller for the delivery of a good or the performance of a service.[13] And, as we have just explained, the contract con-

forcing the provision if the contingency occurs, that $t_2 > e$ is the cost of dispute resolution if there is no contract provision for the contingency and it occurs, and that b is the cost attributable to deviation from Pareto efficiency under the system for dispute resolution. Then there will be no provision for the contingency included in the contract if the expected cost of making a provision, $t_1 + pe$, exceeds the expected cost of not doing so, $p(t_2 + b)$, or, equivalently, if $t_1 > p(t_2 + b - e)$. *Hence, a low probability of occurrence* (or a low cost due to deviation from Pareto efficiency, etc.) *militates against including a provision for the contingency in the contract.*

[8] This point was first emphasized in the economics literature by Radner (1968).

[9] These include (a) not only determinants of the production cost for a good to be produced, but also (b) determinants of how the seller would turn out to value for his own use a good to be produced (a machine, a portrait to be painted) or one already held (a house, a car, a piece of jewelry) and also (c) bids for the seller's good from alternative buyers.

[10] These aspects include (a) determinants of how the buyer would turn out to value the good and (b) offers of the good from alternative sellers.

[11] A more complete analytical approach than ours would ask (on the basis of factors which we have just discussed) exactly when contingencies would fail to be included in a contract; and presumably, under such an approach damage measures would play the same role in relation to these contingencies as damage measures do generally under our approach.

[12] This model is similar to Barton's (1972), the first of which I am aware to be used in a formal study of damage measures. Barton asks in a series of examples how the use of different damage measures would affect contracting parties' behavior and whether it would lead to maximization of "total value." His analysis touches on several issues which we do not, but it says relatively little about reliance (to be defined shortly), and in any event it is not explicitly directed at showing that damage measures serve as a substitute for Pareto efficient complete contingent contracts.

[13] Issues concerning contract formation (encompassing how parties meet and, if so, whether they reach agreement) are not studied here. However, such issues and others (but not the one of concern to us) are emphasized in Diamond and Maskin (1979), who analyze a model of a market for exchange according to contract of an indivisible commodity (say, homes) in which buyers and sellers decide how long to engage in costly search for contracting partners.

tains no provisions for contingencies; however, the parties understand that if someone defaults, he will have to pay an amount determined by a damage measure.[14] Once the contract is made, the buyer or the seller may have to decide about his level of *reliance*, that is, actions taken before and in anticipation of contract performance.[15] In our example the buyer of the machine might make various expenditures in expectation of delivery; he might hire and train workers to operate the machine or advertise the good to be produced with it. Likewise, the seller might make certain expenditures on the assumption of the buyer's accepting delivery; he would presumably bear some costs of production or might make advance outlays for transportation. After one or the other of the parties decides on and engages in reliance, whatever uncertainty there is in the environment is resolved: the seller learns about production cost or about alternative bids and the buyer realizes how valuable performance will be or learns about alternative offers. Then the contract is either performed or is broken.[16] The possibilities of partial performance or of renegotiation[17] are not considered.

How will these decisions about reliance and about breach be made and, in particular, how will they be influenced by the damage measure? The decision about breach depends on the damage measure in the obvious way: a party will default if and only if his position, given that he does so and pays damages, will be better than that if he performs. On the other hand, the decision about reliance depends on the damage measure in a more complicated and in some respects rather subtle manner. Consider first the possibility that a party who is deciding about reliance may *himself* wish to default. In thinking about this he will take into account the fact that if he turns out to default, he would typically fail to realize the full "benefits" of reliance; in our example, the buyer's expenditures on the hiring and training of workers, etc., might be wasted in whole or in part if he defaults, and similarly with the seller's expenditures on production costs and so forth if he defaults. Since the probability that a party will wish to default is influenced by the damage measure, it follows that his decision about reliance will also be. Next, with regard to the possibility that a party who is deciding about reliance may find himself the *victim* of a breach, the damage measure must be considered for three distinct reasons. The first is analogous to what was just mentioned: the damage measure helps to determine the probability of becoming a victim of breach, and, therefore, the likelihood that the party may not realize the full benefits of his reliance. Second, the

[14] We do not ask whether the damage measure is decided on by the parties, originates in custom, or is a matter of law. We should note in the latter case that it need not be imagined that the parties would actually go to court were there a breach, for if they agree about the damages the court would award, they would generally avoid risk and save time and legal costs by reaching an out-of-court settlement.

[15] Our usage of the term reliance is standard. See Fuller and Perdue (1937) or Dawson and Harvey (1977).

[16] Our view of the sequence of events is of course overly simple—in reality, it is often true that reliance is engaged in in a continuous fashion over time and that the same is true of the resolution of uncertainty. However, our view does allow study of what seems to be the issue of interest concerning reliance, that it is to an important extent an investment made under conditions of uncertainty as to the final outcome of the contract.

[17] Rogerson (1980) employs the model introduced in this paper in an interesting study of the situation when parties renegotiate if that would be to their mutual advantage. We did not choose to study this situation (and therefore we implicitly assume "high" costs of renegotiation) just because of a desire to study the situation when a party might default, even though this would not be Pareto efficient, or when he might perform, even though that would not be Pareto efficient.

amount of damages he receives if a victim of breach may be a function of his level of reliance. Third, because the damages he receives may be a function of his level of reliance, he may in effect change the probability that the other party defaults by varying his level of reliance.

Knowing how the decisions about reliance and about breach depend on the damage measure and given also the contract price, the expected values of a contract to the buyer and to the seller can be determined. Thus, damage measures can be compared not only in a descriptive sense—in how they differentially affect reliance and breach—but also as to their mutual desirability to the contracting parties. Specifically, one damage measure is *Pareto superior* to another in a given contractual situation if both parties could assure themselves of higher expected values with a contract, quite possibly with a different price, under which the first rather than the second damage measure is to be employed.

Several commonly used damage measures are to be studied. Under the *expectation measure*, the defaulting party pays an amount that puts the other party in the position he would have been in had the contract been performed. Under the *reliance measure*, the defaulting party compensates the other party for his reliance expenditures and returns to the other party payments that he made; thus except for foregone opportunities, the victim of breach is put in the position he was in before he made a contract.[18] Under the *restitution measure* the defaulting party returns only the payments made to him;[19] he does not compensate the other party for reliance expenditures. In addition, the case of *no damages*—when a defaulting party pays nothing—is considered. We may view this measure as being employed in the many instances in which the various costs of seeking damages are large enough to make doing so impractical.[20] (Other damage measures can certainly be imagined, and something is said about them too.)

Let us now sketch our results, beginning with the description of a Pareto efficient complete contingent contract. Under the terms of such a contract a party would fail to perform when and only when, given the contingency and the level of reliance, the sum of the values to the buyer and to the seller would thereby be raised. For instance, in our example it would be Pareto efficient for the seller to default whenever his production cost would exceed the value of the machine to the buyer, given his reliance. Further, under such a contract the Pareto efficient level of reliance would reflect the probability of Pareto efficient breach (itself determined as just noted). In particular, because in the event of a breach the full benefits of reliance would not be realized, the greater the probability of breach, the lower will be the Pareto efficient

---

[18] The reliance measure is sometimes considered to include foregone opportunities: see Fuller and Perdue (1937) or Dawson and Harvey (1977). When this is so, the reliance measure may shade into the expectation measure. For instance, if the buyer could have made an identical contract with another seller, one might say that the foregone opportunity was the "expectancy." Thus, to isolate the effect of compensation for actions taken in reliance after the making of the contract from protection of the expectancy, it seems best to analyze the version of the reliance measure that we do.

[19] Readers familiar with contract law will note that because we ignore the possibility of partial performance, we shall not be concerned with restitution for benefits conferred by the seller to the buyer before a breach.

[20] This interpretation ignores the moral factors and the harm to reputation that enter into decisions about breach.

level of reliance, other things equal. In our example the greater the probability of high production costs and, consequently, of Pareto efficient breach by the seller, the lower will be the Pareto efficient amount committed by the buyer for training of workers, advertising, and so forth.

With respect to the damage measures, the following points are made. (1) The payment of damages for breach of contract tends to promote Pareto efficient breach behavior. It implicitly forces a party contemplating breach to take account of the loss that breach would impose on the other party. (2) The receipt of damages by the victim of a breach often results in his choosing a level of reliance that exceeds the Pareto efficient level. The reason is that the receipt of damages serves to insure him against losing the benefits of reliance; thus, in deciding on his level of reliance, he does not properly recognize that reliance is in fact like an investment which does not pay off in the event of breach.[21] (3) The expectation measure is generally Pareto superior to the reliance measure. Yet neither of these measures can be unambiguously compared with the restitution measure or the no damages case; their relationship depends on the nature of the contractual situation. (4) There does not exist a damage measure which leads to Pareto efficient decisions concerning both breach and reliance independent of the type of contractual situation; in other words, there is no damage measure which acts as a perfect substitute for complete contingent contracts.

These four points, however, provide only a relatively rough description of the results. Therefore, even those readers who are not interested in the details of the analysis will want to look at the formal statements of propositions in the next part of the paper; and they will probably wish to look also at the concluding comments, which are of a general nature.

2. Analysis of the model

■ **Preliminaries.** As explained above, it will be assumed that a contract is made between a risk neutral buyer and a risk neutral seller,[22] and then that reliance is chosen, that the contingency becomes known (to whom will be specified later), and that the contract is or is not performed. For simplicity, it will be supposed that only one of the parties decides about reliance and only one—possibly the same one—decides about breach. Therefore, two cases will be considered: that in which one party decides about reliance and the other party about breach and that in which the same party decides about both.

Now define

r = level of reliance;
θ = contingency;
$p(\cdot)$ = probability density over θ; and
B = breach set, that is, $\{\theta \mid \text{the contract will not be performed}\}$.

[21] The legal requirement that a victim of a breach make a reasonable effort to make his losses as small as possible is aimed at solving a different problem from the one we are pointing out, for our problem concerns the initial choice of reliance, not the "mitigation of damages" *ex post*.

[22] More precisely, each party acts so as to maximize his expected (von Neumann-Morgenstern) utility, and his utility simply equals the level of a single variable called wealth or value or, often (in this paper) "position"; thus we shall say that each party acts so as to maximize his expected wealth or expected value or expected position.

Here r is a nonnegative amount and will be endogenously determined; θ is a scalar, to be variously interpreted; $p(\cdot)$ is differentiable[23] and is given exogenously; and B will be endogenously determined.

In what follows it will be seen how, given a damage measure, each party maximizes (over r and B, as the case may be) his own expected position,[24]

$$\int_{\sim B} (\text{position given performance})p(\theta)d\theta + \int_{B} (\text{position given breach})p(\theta)d\theta, \quad (1)$$

while taking into account that the other party is doing the same. Reliance and the breach set will be determined by the resulting (Nash) equilibrium behavior of the two parties.

☐ **First case: one party decides about reliance and the other about breach.** Let us define the values enjoyed by the two contracting parties as a function of reliance, of the contingency, and of whether the contract is performed. These values are to be understood as *exclusive of any monetary transfers* between the parties; they are exclusive of payment of the contract price and of payment of damages for breach. Let

$v(r)$ = value enjoyed by the party who chooses reliance, provided that the contract is performed;

$\bar{v}(r)$ = value enjoyed by this party if the other party defaults;

$w(\theta)$ = value enjoyed by the other party if he performs and θ is the contingency; and

$\bar{w}(\theta)$ = value enjoyed by this party if he defaults and θ is the contingency.

Notice here that the party who chooses reliance does not face uncertainty in a direct way and that the other party does. This means that the party who decides about reliance is not the one who decides about breach.

If we are considering a situation in which a new party—an alternative buyer or an alternative seller—might be involved in a breach with one of the original contracting parties, then we will need to refer to $\bar{z}(\theta)$:

$\bar{z}(\theta)$ = bid made by an alternative buyer—or minus the offer made by an alternative seller—if such a new party is involved in a breach and if θ is the contingency.[25]

The bids and offers are assumed to be nonnegative.

[23] We shall also assume, without further comment, that other functions to be defined and considered here are differentiable.

[24] $\sim B$ stands for the complement of B.

[25] Note that these bids or offers are taken as exogenous to the model. This assumption seems apt if one is thinking of situations in which new parties would for some reason make their bids or offers relatively quickly, without real inquiry into the position of the original contracting party and without real negotiation. The assumption does not seem appropriate if one is considering situations in which the new parties' bids or offers would be influenced by aspects of the position of the original contracting party. (For example, if an alternative buyer met a seller who had already made a contract, this new buyer might well bid more if the seller would have to pay a large amount in damages for breach than if he would only have to pay a small amount.) However, in a previous version of this paper the assumption was relaxed, and new parties' bids and offers were endogenously determined; the qualitative nature of the results was then much the same, but since the complications which arose in the analysis were tangential to our purposes, it seemed best to make the present simplifying assumption.

It will be helpful to describe in terms of this notation several types of examples.

(a) The buyer relies and the seller faces uncertainty over production cost: If he carries out certain activities before the production cost becomes known to the seller, the gross value v of contract performance to the buyer will be enhanced; r is the level of these reliance activities, so that $v(r) - r$ is the buyer's net value, given performance. However, if the seller defaults, the buyer gets only $\bar{v}(r)$ (scrap value of reliance; or its value if the buyer can find an alternative seller of the good—who will presumably deliver it later), so that $\bar{v}(r) - r$ is his net value in this situation. The seller's production cost is influenced by random factors and is given by $c + \theta$, where c is a constant expenditure that must be made before θ becomes known and where θ is the additional amount necessary for completing production. If on learning θ the seller defaults, he gets a scrap value of s. Therefore, $w(\theta) = -c - \theta$ and $\bar{w}(\theta) = -c + s$. As there are no new parties involved, $\bar{z}(\theta) \equiv 0$.

(b) The buyer relies and the seller faces uncertainty over bids from alternative buyers: The description of the buyer is as in (a), but here the seller has the good in inventory and the uncertainty is over how much an alternative buyer would bid for the good. If θ denotes this amount, then $\bar{z}(\theta) = \theta$ and $w(\theta) \equiv \bar{w}(\theta) \equiv 0$ (since there are no production costs).

(c) The seller relies and the buyer faces uncertainty over the value of the contract: It is advantageous for the seller to begin the production process early, before the value of contract performance becomes known to the buyer. That is, up to a point, the more the seller does during this initial period, the lower will be his total production costs. Total production costs are therefore the sum of the initial costs r made in reliance plus whatever are the costs $c(r)$ that have to be borne to complete production. Since the seller's net value, given performance, is $-c(r) - r$, the interpretation is that $v(r) = -c(r)$. If the buyer defaults, the seller's unfinished good has scrap value $\bar{v}(r)$. The value of contract performance to the buyer is θ. Consequently, $w(\theta) = \theta$, and since the buyer does not get the good if he defaults, $\bar{w}(\theta) \equiv 0$. Also, because no new party is involved, $\bar{z}(\theta) \equiv 0$.

(d) The seller relies and the buyer faces uncertainty over offers from alternative sellers: The description of the seller is as in (c), but here the value of contract performance to the buyer is fixed at w. The uncertainty is over the price at which an alternative seller would offer the good to the buyer. If θ is this offer, then $\bar{z}(\theta) = -\theta$ and $w(\theta) = \bar{w}(\theta) = w$.

With these types of examples in mind, we make the following assumptions: $v'(r) > 1$ for nonnegative r sufficiently low (otherwise it would never be advantageous to engage in reliance), $v''(r) < 0$ (diminishing returns), and $\bar{v}'(r) < 1$ and $\bar{v}(r) < r$ (in keeping with the notion that reliance turns out to be unprofitable in the event of a breach).

Given these assumptions, we are almost ready to consider damage measures and how they perform as substitutes for Pareto efficient complete contingent contracts. What we wish to do first is to determine the nature of such complete contingent contracts, and to this end let k be the contract price. In the proof of the Proposition that follows and in the discussion and proofs of subsequent results of this subsection, we shall consider only situations in which the buyer relies and the seller might commit breach, for the analysis of situations in which the seller relies and the buyer might commit breach is either analogous or identical. However, to avoid the possibility of confusion, the statements of Propositions will mention any differences between the two kinds of situations (in Propositions 1 and 2, it happens that there are no differences). Moreover, occasional comments will be made in footnotes about the situations in which the seller relies and the buyer might commit breach.

Proposition 1. Under the terms of a Pareto efficient complete contingent contract, (i) the sum of the expected values of the contract to the buyer and to the seller is maximized. This implies that (ii) there is failure to perform in a contingency if and only if that would raise the sum of the values enjoyed by the buyer and the seller (plus the bid or the offer of any new party). More precisely, the Pareto efficient breach set equals $B^*(r^*)$, where

$$B^*(r) = \{\theta \,|\, \bar{v}(r) + \bar{w}(\theta) + \bar{z}(\theta) \geqq v(r) + w(\theta)\} \tag{2}$$

is the Pareto efficient breach set given r, and where (iii) r^* is the Pareto efficient level of reliance. This is determined by the condition

$$v'(r) = \frac{1 - \bar{v}'(r)\Pr(B^*(r))}{1 - \Pr(B^*(r))}. \tag{3}$$

Thus, in particular, r^* satisfies

$$v'(r^*) > 1. \tag{4}$$

Notes: Part (i) is true for familiar reasons: if the sum of expected values is not maximized, it is possible to construct a different contract with a larger sum under which both the buyer's and the seller's expected positions are higher. Part (ii) follows obviously from (i), and let us illustrate it with an example in which the buyer relies and the seller faces uncertainty over production cost. (Refer to examples of type (a) above.) If we assume for simplicity that the values $\bar{v}(r)$ and s, given failure to perform, are zero and that the seller bears no cost c before learning θ, then (2) reduces to $B^*(r) = \{\theta \,|\, \theta \geqq v(r)\}$, which says that it is Pareto efficient for the seller to default whenever he determines that production cost would exceed the value of performance to the buyer, given his reliance.[26] With regard to part (iii), observe that (4) is in keeping with our previous remarks. Inasmuch as reliance may be viewed as an investment with an uncertain payoff, maximizing the sum of expected values requires that one stop short of the point where the marginal product of reliance conditional on performance is unity. Carrying reliance to the point where $v'(r) = 1$ would be appropriate only if performance were a certainty; and to avoid discussion of uninteresting cases, we assume that $0 < \Pr(B^*(r)) < 1$.[27]

Proof: To verify (i), denote the expected value of a contract, exclusive of the price, to the buyer by $X(r,B)$. Thus, the expected value to him (inclusive of

[26] Consider one further illustration. In regard to examples of type (d), assume that the scrap value $\bar{c}(r)$ is zero. Then (2) reduces to $B^*(r) = \{\theta \,|\, c(r) \geqq \theta\}$, which says that it is Pareto efficient for the buyer to default and purchase the good for θ from an alternative seller if θ is less than $c(r)$, the cost to the contracting seller of completing production of the good.

[27] We shall, without further mention, make similar assumptions about the breach sets in the propositions that follow.

price) is $X(r,B) - k$. Similarly, denote the expected value, exclusive of price, to the seller by $Y(r,B)$, so that the expected value of the contract to him is $Y(r,B) + k$. Denote the sum of the expected values by $Z(r,B)$, that is $Z(r,B) = X(r,B) - k + Y(r,B) + k = X(r,B) + Y(r,B)$. If a contract specified by r_1, B_1, and k_1 is such that Z is not maximized, there is some r_2 and B_2 and a $\delta > 0$ such that $Z(r_2,B_2) - Z(r_1,B_1) = \delta$. Now under the contract specified by r_2, B_2, and $k_2 = k_1 + X(r_2,B_2) - X(r_1,B_1) - \delta/2$, the buyer is better off since

$$X(r_2,B_2) - k_2 = X(r_1,B_1) - k_1 + \delta/2 > X(r_1,B_1) - k_1 \tag{5}$$

and the seller is better off since

$$\begin{aligned} Y(r_2,B_2) + k_2 &= Y(r_2,B_2) + k_1 + X(r_2,B_2) - X(r_1,B_1) - \delta/2 \\ &= Z(r_2,B_2) - Z(r_1,B_1) + Y(r_1,B_1) + k_1 - \delta/2 \\ &= Y(r_1,B_1) + k_1 + \delta/2 > Y(r_1,B_1) + k_1. \end{aligned} \tag{6}$$

To confirm (ii), note now that

$$X(r,B) = \int_{\sim B} v(r)p(\theta)d\theta + \int_B \bar{v}(r)p(\theta)d\theta - r \tag{7}$$

and that

$$Y(r,B) = \int_{\sim B} w(\theta)p(\theta)d\theta + \int_B (\bar{w}(\theta) + \bar{z}(\theta))p(\theta)d\theta. \tag{8}$$

Thus

$$Z(r,B) = \int_{\sim B} (v(r) + w(\theta))p(\theta)d\theta + \int_B (\bar{v}(r) + \bar{w}(\theta) + \bar{z}(\theta))p(\theta)d\theta - r, \tag{9}$$

from which it follows immediately that the B that maximizes Z, given r, is indeed $B^*(r)$.

From (i) and (ii) it is clear that r^* is determined by maximizing $Z(r,B^*(r))$ over r. Let us assume that $B^*(r)$ is an interval of the form $[\theta(r),\infty)$. (This is the case in examples of type (a) and (b). However, our argument may be verified to hold for $B^*(r)$ of a general form.[28]) Differentiating, and using the fact that $\Pr(\sim B^*(r)) = 1 - \Pr(B^*(r))$, we obtain

$$\begin{aligned} \frac{dZ(r,B^*(r))}{dr} &= (1 - \Pr(B^*(r)))v'(r) + \Pr(B^*(r))\bar{v}'(r) - 1 + \theta'(r)[v(r) + w(\theta(r)) \\ &\quad - \bar{v}(r) - \bar{w}(\theta(r)) - \bar{z}(\theta(r))]p(\theta(r)) \\ &= (1 - \Pr(B^*(r)))v'(r) + \Pr(B^*(r))\bar{v}'(r) - 1. \end{aligned} \tag{10}$$

The term in brackets is zero because the characterization (2) of $B^*(r)$ implies $v(r) + w(\theta) = \bar{v}(r) + \bar{w}(\theta) + \bar{z}(\theta)$ at the boundary point $\theta(r)$ of $B^*(r)$. Setting the derivative equal to zero, we get (3); and (4) then follows since we assumed $\Pr(B^*(r)) > 0$ and since $\bar{v}'(r) < 1$. *Q.E.D.*

Let us proceed to consider damage measures. Define

$d(\cdot)$ = the damage measure determining damages paid by a defaulting party to the other party; d will be various functions of the variables k, r, v, and $\bar{v}$ and will be specified below.

---

[28] If $B^*(r)$ is the union of intervals with endpoints which are differentiable in r, the argument is the same, and we shall assume that $B^*(r)$ is of that form.

Notice that we do not consider damage measures that depend on the contingency θ; this is in line with the stated purpose of the paper and the assumption that the contract does not provide for contingencies.[29] Except in the case of no damages, we shall assume without loss of generality that the contract price k is paid when the contract is made.[30]

We can now describe the positions of the contracting parties and derive their behavior. We have[31]

$$\begin{aligned} v(r) - r - k &= \text{buyer's position, given contract performance;} \\ \bar{v}(r) - r - k + d &= \text{buyer's position, given breach;} \\ w(\theta) + k &= \text{seller's position, given performance; and} \\ \bar{w}(\theta) + k - d + \bar{z}(\theta) &= \text{seller's position, given breach } (\bar{z} = 0 \text{ unless an alternative buyer is involved).} \end{aligned}$$

It follows that the seller will default whenever $\bar{w}(\theta) + k - d + \bar{z}(\theta) \geqq w(\theta) + k$, that is, whenever $\bar{w}(\theta) + \bar{z}(\theta) - w(\theta) \geqq d$; equivalently, the breach set is

$$B(r) = \{\theta | \bar{w}(\theta) + \bar{z}(\theta) - w(\theta) \geqq d\}. \tag{11}$$

(The dependence on r comes about because d may be a function of r.)

The buyer will choose reliance so as to maximize his expected position, $\int_{\sim B(r)} v(r)p(\theta)d\theta + \int_{B(r)} (\bar{v}(r) + d)p(\theta)d\theta - r - k$, which reduces to

$$(1 - \Pr(B(r)))v(r) + \Pr(B(r))(\bar{v}(r) + d) - r - k. \tag{12}$$

We shall assume that for the damage measures considered, this maximization problem has a solution which is uniquely identified by setting the derivative of (12) equal to zero. Moreover, we shall assume that both the buyer and the seller are at least as well off with the contract as without it. Thus, as we shall assume that the position of each would be zero if no contract were made,[32] the contract must be such that the expected positions of the buyer and the seller are nonnegative: (12) must be nonnegative (given the buyer's optimal choice of r), and the seller's position

$$\int_{\sim B(r)} w(\theta)p(\theta)d\theta + \int_{B(r)} (\bar{w}(\theta) + \bar{z}(\theta) - d)p(\theta)d\theta + k \tag{13}$$

must also be nonnegative.

What knowledge must the parties have about each other so as to be able to act in the way just described? To decide about breach, the seller needs to know the measure of damages, and as stated above, this may depend on the buyer's reliance and on the value he attaches to performance. (Of course, the seller is presumed to observe θ in the first place.) To decide about reliance, the buyer needs to know $B(r)$ and its probability. This requires that he understand the

[29] If d depended on θ, our assumption would have to be that θ can be observed by both parties, which conflicts with the assumption that the contract itself does not provide for contingencies.

[30] The reader will easily be able to satisfy himself that for any damage measure d applying if k is paid when the contract is made, there is an equivalent damage measure which can be used if k is instead paid when the contract is performed: the equivalent measure is just $d - k$ in situations in which the seller might default and $d + k$ in situations in which the buyer might default.

[31] In situations in which the seller relies and the buyer might default, $v(r) - r + k$ is the seller's position given performance, $\bar{v}(r) - r + k - d$ is his position given breach, and so forth.

[32] In other words, here we abstract from issues concerning foregone opportunities.

nature of the seller's problem (in particular, the *functions* $w(\cdot)$, $\bar{w}(\cdot)$, $\bar{z}(\cdot)$ and the density $p(\cdot)$), but *not* that he be able to observe θ.

Let us apply the general characterization, given by (11) and (12), of the parties' behavior in examining the several damage measures of particular interest, and let us begin with the expectation measure. Recall that under this damage measure, the victim of a breach is put in the position he would have been in had the contract been performed. Thus, under the expectation measure

$$d = v(r) - \bar{v}(r); \tag{14}$$

for if there is a breach, the buyer's position is $\bar{v}(r) - r - k + (v(r) - \bar{v}(r)) = v(r) - r - k$ as claimed. We now have

Proposition 2. Under the expectation measure, (i) the breach set, given reliance, is $B^*(r)$; breach is therefore Pareto efficient given reliance.[33] However (ii), reliance, r_e, is determined by

$$v'(r) = 1 \tag{15}$$

so that

$$r_e > r^*; \tag{16}$$

reliance exceeds the Pareto efficient level.

Notes: Part (i) is easily understood. The seller will default if and only if his gain exceeds the buyer's "expectancy," $v(r)$ which is to say, if and only if the sum of the values enjoyed by both parties is increased. Referring to the example of type (a) mentioned in the notes accompanying the previous proposition, since $d = v(r)$, it is clear that the seller will default whenever his production cost θ would exceed the value of the good to the buyer; so the breach set is indeed $B^*(r) = \{\theta | \theta \geqq v(r)\}$. With regard to (ii), consider the fact that under the expectation measure the buyer is in effect guaranteed his expectancy, and hence he sees reliance as an investment with a certain payoff. Therefore, he engages in reliance up to the point where its marginal product conditional on performance is driven down to one. This exceeds Pareto efficient reliance since, as has been emphasized, that level is such that the marginal product conditional on performance is greater than one and reflects the probability that the investment in reliance will not pay off in terms of the sum of values if there is a breach.

Proof: Using (14) to substitute for d in (11), we get

$$\begin{aligned} B(r) &= \{\theta | \bar{w}(\theta) + \bar{z}(\theta) - w(\theta) \geqq v(r) - \bar{v}(r)\} \\ &= \{\theta | \bar{v}(r) + \bar{w}(\theta) + \bar{z}(\theta) \geqq v(r) + w(\theta)\} = B^*(r), \end{aligned} \tag{17}$$

establishing (i). And using (14) to substitute for d in (12), we see that r is chosen to maximize

$$\begin{aligned} &(1 - \Pr(B(r)))v(r) + \Pr(B(r))(\bar{v}(r) + v(r) - \bar{v}(r)) \\ &\qquad - r - k = v(r) - r - k, \end{aligned} \tag{18}$$

[33] The notion that the expectation measure is somehow socially desirable, because it induces a party to default whenever doing so is worth more to him than the value of performance to the other party was, as far as I can determine, first stated in the 1972 edition of Posner (1977). However, that this is an aspect of Pareto efficiency is, to my knowledge, first stated here.

so that r must satisfy (15). Also, (16) follows from (4), (15), and the assumption that v is strictly concave in r. *Q.E.D.*

Let us now examine the reliance measure. Under this measure, the party must be compensated for expenditures (net of their value, given nonperformance) made in anticipation of performance and his payment must be returned: equivalently, he must be put in the position he would have been in had he not made a contract, namely zero. Thus, under the reliance measure, the buyer must receive from a defaulting seller[34]

$$d = r - \bar{v}(r) + k; \tag{19}$$

for then the buyer's position becomes $\bar{v}(r) - r - k + (r - \bar{v}(r) + k) = 0$ as claimed. The result concerning the reliance measure is

Proposition 3. Under the reliance measure, (i) the breach set is given by[35]

$$B(r) = \{\theta | \bar{w}(\theta) + \bar{v}(r) + \bar{z}(\theta) \geqq w(\theta) + r + k\} \supset B^*(r). \tag{20}$$

(In situations in which the buyer might default, the sign preceding k is negative.) Thus breach occurs more often, given reliance, than would be Pareto efficient.[36] (ii) Reliance, r_r, is determined by

$$v'(r) = 1 + \frac{\frac{d\,\Pr(B(r))}{dr}(v(r) - r - k)}{1 - \Pr(B(r))} \tag{21}$$

(The sign preceding k is positive in situations in which the buyer might default.) Thus r_r satisfies

$$v'(r_r) \leqq 1 \tag{22}$$

so that

$$r_r \geqq r_e, \tag{23}$$

the level of reliance generally exceeds the level under the expectation measure (and therefore the Pareto efficient level).

Notes: The claim of part (i) is explained as follows. The seller will commit breach if and only if his gain exceeds the buyer's reliance, which as will be seen, must be less than his expectancy. Thus, the seller might commit breach when his gain, although larger than reliance, is less than the buyer's expectancy; this would not be Pareto efficient, since the sum of values enjoyed by both parties would be reduced. Referring again to our simple example of type (a), suppose that the buyer has paid a contract price of \$4 to the seller, that the buyer has spent \$1 in reliance, and that he will enjoy a value of \$10 if the seller delivers the good. Under the reliance measure, the seller will have to pay \$5 if he defaults (the \$4 price plus the \$1 reliance); thus, he will default whenever his production cost θ exceeds \$5, rather than only when θ exceeds \$10, which would be Pareto efficient. Notice here that the higher the price paid by the buyer, the

[34] In situations in which the buyer might default, $d = r - \bar{v}(r) - k$.

[35] In (20) it will be seen that $B(r)$ will typically properly include $B^*(r)$: and the same will be true whenever we use the set inclusion symbol elsewhere in this paper.

[36] Essentially this fact has been stated by Posner (1977).

lower the probability that the seller will default.[37] This means that the price has a role other than that of splitting the "surplus" from the transaction; the price also affects the total value of the transaction through its influence on breach behavior.

The plausibility of part (ii) follows from two considerations. First, because the buyer is compensated for his reliance in the event of a breach, he sees reliance as an investment in which at worst he will break even. This immediately suggests that he will choose a higher level of reliance than would be Pareto efficient. Second, because the buyer is made worse off if there is a breach (he gets reliance rather than the larger expectancy), he would like to reduce the probability of breach; and he can do so by increasing his reliance, for that raises the measure of damages. This second motive is absent under the expectation measure, which suggests why reliance is higher under the reliance measure.

Proof: Using (19) to substitute for d in (11), we immediately get $B(r)$ as given in (20). To prove that $B(r) \supset B^*(r)$, we need to show that $w(\theta) + r + k \leqq w(\theta) + v(r)$, or that $r + k \leqq v(r)$. But since the expected value to the buyer must have been nonnegative, we have, using (19) and (12),

$$0 \leqq (1 - \Pr(B(r))v(r) + \Pr(B(r))(\bar{v}(r) + r - \bar{v}(r) + k) - r - k$$
$$= (1 - \Pr(B(r))(v(r) - r - k), \qquad (24)$$

which implies that $0 \leqq v(r) - r - k$ or that $r + k \leqq v(r)$. To derive (21), differentiate the last expression in (24) with respect to r and set it equal to zero:

$$(1 - \Pr(B(r)))(v'(r) - 1) - \frac{d \Pr(B(r))}{dr}(v(r) - r - k) = 0. \qquad (25)$$

This gives (21). And (22) (which is generally a strict inequality) follows because $0 \leqq v(r) - r - k$ and because $d \Pr(B(r))/dr \leqq 0$. The latter is true because $B(r)$ may be rewritten as $\{\theta | \bar{w}(\theta) + \bar{z}(\theta) - w(\theta) - k \geqq r - \bar{v}(r)\}$ and $d/dr(r - \bar{v}(r)) = 1 - \bar{v}'(r) > 0$; thus the set $B(r)$ shrinks in size with increases in r. Finally, (23) follows from strict concavity of v in r and our previous results. *Q.E.D.*

Under the restitution measure the seller must return to the buyer the payment he made, so $d = k$. The results under this measure and in the case of no damages are given in

Proposition 4. If there are no damages for breach of contract, (i) the parties will agree that the price will be paid when the contract is performed. Thus, the results when there are no damages are identical with those under restitution: (ii) The breach set is given by

$$B = \{\theta | \bar{w}(\theta) + \bar{z}(\theta) - w(\theta) \geqq k\} \supset B^*(r). \qquad (26)$$

[37] It might, therefore, seem that our claim about breach's occurring too often could be contradicted. For instance, if in the example the contract price were sufficiently high, say \$9.25, breach would occur too seldom (for d would then be \$10.25 under the reliance measure). However, the proof shows (as it must) that the contract price cannot be high enough to cause this to happen; the argument is that the buyer would not have been willing to pay so high a price in the first place.

(The sign preceding k is negative in situations in which the buyer might default.) Thus, breach occurs more often, given reliance, than would be Pareto efficient.[38] (iii) Reliance, r_n, is determined by

$$v'(r) = \frac{1 - \Pr(B)\bar{v}'(r)}{1 - \Pr(B)} \tag{27}$$

so that

$$v'(r_n) > 1 \tag{28}$$

and

$$r_e > r_n; \tag{29}$$

reliance is less than under the expectation measure. Moreover, (iv) reliance is Pareto efficient, given the breach set.

Notes: In the case of no damages, if the buyer were to pay the seller when the contract was made, there would be nothing to keep the latter from defaulting and from holding on to the buyer's money, whereas if the buyer pays only at contract performance, the seller would have something to lose from a breach. (We do not consider the possibility of partial payment at the outset and the remainder at performance.) This explains part (i). The claim of part (ii), that breach occurs too often, is true because the seller defaults if and only if his gain exceeds the contract price, but this must be less than the buyer's expectancy (otherwise the buyer would not have been willing to pay the price). Notice here, as under the reliance measure, that the higher the price, the lower the probability of breach;[39] again, the price affects the total value of the transaction. With regard to part (iv), it is clear that since the buyer sees reliance as an investment which pays off if and only if the contract is performed, he will engage in reliance in a Pareto efficient way, given the probability of breach. Part (iii) is similarly explained.

Proof: The first part of the Proposition is obvious from the comment about it in the Notes. In addition, given that k is paid at performance, it follows that in the case of no damages and under the restitution measure, the seller will default if and only if his position if he defaults, $\bar{w}(\theta) + \bar{z}(\theta)$, is larger than that if he performs, $w(\theta) + k$; thus the breach set B in (26) is correct. To prove that $B \supset B^*(r)$, note that the condition that the expected value of the contract to the buyer must be nonnegative is

$$(1 - \Pr(B))(v(r) - k) + \Pr(B)\bar{v}(r) - r \geqq 0. \tag{30}$$

This and the assumption that $r > \bar{v}(r)$ imply that $v(r) - \bar{v}(r) > k$. From the latter inequality, the expression for B, and the fact that $B^*(r) = \{\theta | \bar{w}(\theta) + \bar{z}(\theta) - w(\theta) \geqq v(r) - \bar{v}(r)\}$, the result immediately follows. To get (27) set the derivative of the left-hand side of (30) equal to zero. Equation (28) follows from (27) since $\bar{v}'(r) < 1$, and (29) follows from (28), (15), and the strict concavity of r. To establish (iv), note that the Pareto efficient level of reliance, given B, is found by maximizing over r

[38] Actually, as we show later, it is also true that given r and k, $B \supset B(r)$, breach occurs more often than under the reliance measure.

[39] This raises the possibility that the buyer might actually prefer to pay (within some range) a "high" price to the seller: that would be especially likely if the surplus the buyer would derive from contract performance were large.

$$\int_{\sim B} (v(r) + w(\theta))p(\theta)d\theta + \int_{B} (\bar{v}(r) + \bar{w}(\theta) + \bar{z}(\theta))p(\theta)d\theta - r$$

$$= (1 - \Pr(B))v(r) + \Pr(B)\bar{v}(r) - r + \text{terms independent of } r, \quad (31)$$

which differs from the left-hand side of (30) by the terms that do not depend on r. Thus, r_* must equal the Pareto efficient level of reliance, given B. *Q.E.D.*

Let us next compare the four damage measures that we have studied.

Proposition 5. (i) The expectation measure is Pareto superior to the reliance measure independent of the nature of the contractual situation. Yet (ii) there is no necessary Pareto relationship between either of these measures and restitution or no damages; the relationship depends on the features of the particular contractual situation.

Notes: Recall that under the expectation measure, but not the reliance measure, breach is Pareto efficient, given reliance. Furthermore, under the expectation measure, reliance is less excessive than under the reliance measure. This indicates why part (i) is true. I am indebted to William Rogerson for a step of the proof of (i) under general conditions. With regard to part (ii), note first that it was shown that if there are no damages for breach or under the restitution measure, then reliance is Pareto efficient, given the breach set. Thus, if in a certain contractual situation the reliance decision is sufficiently more important (in terms of raising the sum of expected values) than the breach decision, restitution and no damages will be Pareto superior to the expectation and the reliance measures. On the other hand, if in a contractual situation the breach decision is sufficiently more important than the reliance decision, the expectation or the reliance measure will be Pareto superior to both no damages and restitution, because breach is more likely under the latter measures.

Proof: Note first (see (9)) that $Z(r,B^*(r))$ is the sum of expected values as a function of r, given that breach is Pareto efficient, and suppose that

$$Z(r_e,B^*(r_e)) \geqq Z(r_r,B^*(r_r)). \quad (32)$$

By Proposition 2(i), $Z(r_e,B^*(r_e))$ equals the sum of expected values under the expectation measure; and by Proposition 3(i), $Z(r_r,B^*(r_r))$ is greater than or equal to the sum of expected values under the reliance measure. From this and (32), it follows that the sum of expected values under the expectation measure is at least that under the reliance measure. Hence part (i) follows by an argument analogous to that used to show Proposition 1(i), if we can show that (32) is true. Now $Z(r,B^*(r))$ may be written $\int \max\,(v(r) - r + w(\theta),$ $\bar{v}(r) - r + \bar{w}(\theta) + \bar{z}(\theta))p(\theta)d\theta$. But since (see (18)) r_e maximizes $v(r) - r$, we have $v(r_e) - r_e \geqq v(r_r) - r_r$; and since (see (23)) $r_r \geqq r_e$ and $\bar{v}'(r) < 1$, we have $\bar{v}(r_e) - r_e \geqq \bar{v}(r_r) - r_r$. Thus for any θ, $\max\,(v(r_e) - r_e + w(\theta), \bar{v}(r_e)$ $- r_e + \bar{w}(\theta) + \bar{z}(\theta)) \geqq \max\,(v(r_r) - r_r + w(\theta),\ \bar{v}(r_r) - r_r + \bar{w}(\theta) + \bar{z}(\theta))$, so that indeed $Z(r_e,B^*(r_e)) \geqq Z(r_r,B^*(r_r))$. (It should also be noticed that since (32) holds strictly if $r_r > r_e$, the expectation measure is generally strictly Pareto superior to the reliance measure.)

Part (ii) should be obvious from our comments in the Notes, except for the assertion that the reliance measure could be Pareto superior to no damages and restitution. To justify this, it will suffice to show that breach behavior under the reliance measure is closer to Pareto efficient, given r and k, than when there are no damages for breach or under restitution. Under the reliance measure the seller's breach set is $B(r) = \{\theta | \bar{w}(\theta) + \bar{z}(\theta) - w(\theta) \geqq r - \bar{v}(r) + k\}$, and when there are no damages or under restitution, the breach set is $B = \{\theta | \bar{w}(\theta) + \bar{z}(\theta) - w(\theta) \geqq k\}$. And since $r > \bar{v}(r)$, we have $B \supset B(r)$. *Q.E.D.*

We conclude this subsection by proving a fact about the general class of damage measures.

Proposition 6. There does not exist a damage measure which always induces Pareto efficient behavior; equivalently, any damage measure will lead either to Pareto inefficient reliance or to Pareto inefficient breach in some contractual situations.[40]

Notes: The logic of the proof is, more or less, as follows. If there were a damage measure which always induced Pareto efficient behavior, then in particular it would have to induce Pareto efficient breach. But this turns out to imply that the damage measure must essentially be the expectation measure,[41] and we know from Proposition 2(ii) that this measure induces Pareto inefficient reliance. Thus, the assumption that there exists a damage measure which induces Pareto efficient behavior is seen to lead to a contradiction.

Proof: Assume such a damage measure d does exist. Then, given an arbitrary contractual situation, we must have that

$$d(k, r^*, v(r^*), \bar{v}(r^*)) = v(r^*) - \bar{v}(r^*), \tag{33}$$

because d is presumed to induce the buyer to choose r^* and to induce the seller to default in a Pareto efficient way, given r^*. That is, the chosen breach set $B(r^*)$ must equal $B^*(r^*)$. Since from (11), $B(r^*) = \{\theta | \bar{w}(\theta) + \bar{z}(\theta) - w(\theta) \geqq d(k, r^*, v(r^*), \bar{v}(r^*))\}$, and from (2), $B^*(r^*) = \{\theta | \bar{w}(\theta) + \bar{z}(\theta) - w(\theta) \geqq v(r^*) - \bar{v}(r^*)\}$, (33) follows.

What we have just shown may be restated as follows: if a 4-tuple $(k, r, v, \bar{v})$ corresponds to a Pareto efficient outcome for *some* contractual situation, then $d(k, r, v, \bar{v})$ must equal $v - \bar{v}$ (the expectation measure). Now it is clear that the set of such 4-tuples has a nonempty interior. Consider a contractual situation such that an associated Pareto efficient 4-tuple $(k, r^*, v(r^*), \bar{v}(r^*))$ is in the interior. Then, in particular, for all r in some neighborhood of r^*, we must have that $d(k, r, v(r), \bar{v}(r)) = v(r) - \bar{v}(r)$. Thus, from (12), the derivative of the buyer's expected position evaluated at r^* is $v'(r^*) - 1$. But since, from (4), $v'(r^*) - 1 > 0$, d could not have induced the buyer to choose r^*. *Q.E.D.*

[40] Lest the result be misinterpreted, it should be kept in mind that a damage measure is assumed here to depend only on the *values of variables* (other than θ—see footnote 29). Were it assumed instead that a damage measure could depend on the complete *functions* ($r(\cdot)$, $v(\cdot)$, $\bar{v}(\cdot)$, $w(\cdot)$, $\bar{w}(\cdot)$, $\bar{z}(\cdot)$, and $p(\cdot)$) that describe a contractual situation, a damage measure leading to Pareto efficient behavior could easily be designed: with its then perfect knowledge of the contractual situation, the court might simply determine Pareto efficient reliance and breach and threaten to punish severely any deviation from Pareto efficient behavior; the parties would thus be led to act in a Pareto efficient manner. Our having assumed that damage measures depend on the values of variables and not on the functions is justified to the extent that courts' knowledge of the nature of contractual situations is limited.

[41] It should be mentioned that this step of the proof implies that *there does not exist a damage measure which is always Pareto superior to the expectation measure*. The argument is that any other damage measure would be Pareto inferior to the expectation measure in contractual situations in which the breach decision is sufficiently more important than the reliance decision.

□ **Second case: the same party decides about both reliance and breach.**[42] In this subsection one party, the "active" party, decides about the level of reliance and also faces uncertainty in a direct way, which means that he decides about breach as well. The other, "passive" party makes no decisions. Let us define the values enjoyed by the two parties, where, as in the last subsection, these are to be understood as exclusive of any monetary transfers:

$v(r,\theta)$ = the value exclusive of reliance r enjoyed by the active party, given that he performs;

$\tilde{v}(r,\theta)$ = the value exclusive of reliance enjoyed by this party, given that he defaults;

w = the value enjoyed by the passive party if the contract is performed; and

$\tilde{w}$ = the value enjoyed by the passive party if the contract is not performed.

We may think of relevant examples by combining aspects of the examples of the previous subsection: the buyer might engage in reliance and also face uncertainty about the value to him of the contracted for good or about offers to be made by alternative sellers; the seller might engage in reliance and face uncertainty about production cost or about bids to be made by alternative buyers. We should also comment on a matter of interpretation concerning the passive party. Although he does not make any decision, under our definitions he might in some cases be imagined to engage in a level of reliance which is effectively fixed in the nature of things. For instance, he might be a seller who must spend exactly c_1 to set up production and, if the buyer were not to default on learning θ, exactly c_2 to complete production; thus we would have $w = -c_1 - c_2$ and $\tilde{w} = -c_1$ (assuming that scrap value is zero).

We shall also make several assumptions which are similar to those made before, namely $v_r(r,\theta) > 1$ for nonnegative r sufficiently low, $v_{rr}(r,\theta) < 0$, $\tilde{v}_r(r,\theta) < 1$, and $\tilde{v}_r(r,\theta) < v_r(r,\theta)$.

We shall now state several propositions corresponding to those of the last subsection. When a proof (or a step of a proof) would be obvious from what was done previously, it will be omitted; moreover, as before, when an argument is supplied, it will suffice that the argument apply only for one of the two possible types of situations (here for those in which the buyer is the active party).

Proposition 7. Under the terms of a Pareto efficient complete contingent contract, (i) the sum of the expected values of the contract to the buyer and to the seller is maximized. This implies that (ii) there is failure to perform in a contingency if and only if that would raise the sum of the values enjoyed by the buyer and the seller (plus the bid or the offer of any new party). More precisely, the Pareto efficient breach set equals $B^*(r^*)$, where

$$B^*(r) = \{\theta \mid \tilde{v}(r,\theta) + \tilde{w} + \tilde{z}(\theta) \geqq v(r,\theta) + w\} \quad (34)$$

is the Pareto efficient breach set given r, and where (iii) r^* is the Pareto efficient level of reliance. This is determined by the condition

[42] Unless otherwise noted, the assumptions and definitions of the last subsection will apply here as well.

$$\int_{\sim B^*(r)} v_r(r,\theta)p(\theta)d\theta = 1 - \int_{B^*(r)} \bar{v}_r(r,\theta)p(\theta)d\theta. \quad (35)$$

Thus, in particular, r^* satisfies

$$\int_{\sim B^*(r^*)} v_r(r^*,\theta)\frac{p(\theta)}{\Pr(\sim B^*(r^*))}d\theta > 1. \quad (36)$$

Notes: The explanation for this Proposition is much the same as that for Proposition 1; and in this respect, the only remark that may need to be made is that since (36) means that the expected marginal product of reliance conditional on performance exceeds one, it is indeed the analog of (4). Likewise, the proof of the result is similar to that of Proposition 1.

Given a damage measure d, the positions of the parties if the buyer is the active party are as follows:[43]

$v(r,\theta) - r - k$ = buyer's position if he performs;
$\bar{v}(r,\theta) - r - k + \bar{z}(\theta) - d$ = buyer's position if he defaults ($\bar{z}(\theta) = 0$ unless an alternative seller is involved);
$w + k$ = seller's position given performance; and
$\bar{w} + k + d$ = seller's position given breach.

Thus, the breach set is

$$B(r) = \{\theta \mid \bar{v}(r,\theta) + \bar{z}(\theta) - v(r,\theta) \geqq d\} \quad (37)$$

and the buyer chooses r so as to maximize his expected position

$$\int_{\sim B(r)} v(r,\theta)p(\theta)d\theta + \int_{B(r)} (\bar{v}(r,\theta) + \bar{z}(\theta) - d)p(\theta)d\theta - r - k. \quad (38)$$

Under the expectation measure $d = w - \bar{w}$, for this is the amount necessary to bring the passive party to the position he would have been in had the contract been performed, and we have

Proposition 8. Under the expectation measure, (i) the breach set and (ii) the level of reliance are Pareto efficient; the expectation measure is therefore a perfect substitute for a Pareto efficient complete contingent contract.

Notes: Part (i) is explained just as was part (i) of Proposition 2. Part (ii) is true because the active party sees reliance as an investment which pays off if and only if he performs. (Unlike in the previous subsection, here the party who relies does not receive damages if there is a breach, since he is the one who defaults.)

Proof: The proof of part (i) will be omitted. The argument for part (ii) is simply that from part (i) and (38). It follows that r is chosen to maximize

$$\int_{\sim B^*(r)} v(r,\theta)p(\theta)d\theta + \int_{B^*(r)} (\bar{v}(r,\theta) + \bar{z}(\theta) - w + \bar{w})p(\theta)d\theta - r - k. \quad (39)$$

[43] If the seller is the active party, then $v(r,\theta) - r + k$ is the seller's position if he performs, $\bar{v}(r,\theta) - r + k + \bar{z}(\theta) - d$ is his position if he defaults, $w - k$ is the buyer's position, given performance, and $\bar{w} - k + d$ is his position, given breach. Thus, the breach set is given by (37), and the seller's expected position is given by (38), except that the sign of k in that expression must be changed from negative to positive.

But (39) differs from

$$Z(r,B^*(r)) = \int_{\sim B^*(r)} (v(r,\theta) + w)p(\theta)d\theta + \int_{B^*(r)} (\bar{v}(r,\theta) + \bar{z}(\theta) + \bar{w})p(\theta)d\theta - r \quad (40)$$

by a term that is independent of r—by $-w - k$. Thus, as r^* is the r which maximizes (40), it must also be the r which maximizes (39). *Q.E.D.*

Under the reliance measure, $d = -\bar{w} - k$ if the buyer is the active party[44] since this is the amount necessary to restore the seller to the position he would have been in had the contract not been made, and we have

Proposition 9. Under the reliance measure, (i) the breach set is given by

$$B(r) = \{\theta | \bar{v}(r,\theta) + \bar{w} + \bar{z}(\theta) \geqq v(r,\theta) - k\} \supset B^*(r). \quad (41)$$

(The sign preceding k is positive when the seller is the active party.) Thus, breach occurs more often given reliance than would be Pareto efficient. (ii) Reliance is determined by

$$\int_{\sim B(r)} v_r(r,\theta)p(\theta)d\theta + \int_{B(r)} \bar{v}_r(r,\theta)p(\theta)d\theta = 1 \quad (42)$$

so that

$$r^* \geqq r_r; \quad (43)$$

reliance is generally less than the Pareto efficient level.

Notes: Part (i) is explained in the same way as part (i) of Proposition 3. Part (ii) follows from part (i), for the latter means that the active party's reliance pays off less often than would be Pareto efficient; and this, in turn, makes it seem reasonable that the chosen level of reliance is lower than would be Pareto efficient. However, an additional assumption (that the active party's expected payoff is strictly concave in r) is needed in the actual proof.

Proof: The proof of part (i) will be omitted. With regard to the proof of part (ii), use (38) to write the expected position of the buyer

$$\int_{\sim B(r)} v(r,\theta)p(\theta)d\theta + \int_{B(r)} (\bar{v}(r,\theta) + \bar{z}(\theta) + \bar{w} + k)p(\theta)d\theta - r - k \quad (44)$$

and differentiate with respect to r to get (by the type of logic employed in (10))

$$\int_{\sim B(r)} v_r(r,\theta)p(\theta)d\theta + \int_{B(r)} \bar{v}_r(r,\theta)p(\theta)d\theta - 1. \quad (45)$$

Setting this equal to zero gives (42). To get (43), note from (35) that

$$0 = \int_{\sim B^*(r^*)} v_r(r^*,\theta)p(\theta)d\theta + \int_{B^*(r^*)} \bar{v}_r(r^*,\theta)p(\theta)d\theta - 1$$

$$\geqq \int_{\sim B(r^*)} v_r(r^*,\theta)p(\theta)d\theta + \int_{B(r^*)} \bar{v}_r(r^*,\theta)p(\theta)d\theta - 1. \quad (46)$$

[44] If the seller is the active party, $d = -\bar{w} + k$.

The inequality (which would generally be strict) holds since $B(r^*) \supset B^*(r^*)$ and since $v_r(r^*, \theta) > \bar{v}_r(r^*, \theta)$. But this last expression is, from (45), just the derivative of (44) evaluated at r^*. Hence, assuming that (44) is strictly concave, we have $r^* \geqq r_r$. *Q.E.D.*

In the case when there are no damages for breach or under restitution, the conclusion is much the same as described in Proposition 4, and we shall refrain from formally stating its analog. With regard to a comparison of damage measures, it is true here, as in the previous subsection, that the expectation measure is Pareto superior to the reliance measure. However, unlike the result in the last subsection, the expectation measure is also Pareto superior to no damages and to restitution. Both these statements follow from the fact that the expectation measure was shown to induce both Pareto efficient reliance and Pareto efficient breach.

3. Concluding comments

■ The results of the paper should help in understanding the functioning of damage measures in situations which combine the features of the last two subsections, that is, when the buyer and the seller may each decide about both reliance and breach. For example, under the expectation measure, our results indicate that to the extent that each party believes he will be the victim of a breach, he will engage in excessive reliance (Proposition 2(ii)); but to the extent that he believes he himself will default, he will engage appropriately in reliance (Proposition 8); and however much he and the other party engage in reliance, he will decide on a correct basis whether or not to default (Propositions 2(i) and 8). However, a formal study of damage measures in the more general situations would require a more complicated type of analysis than ours, especially because of the interdependence of the two parties' decisions about reliance.

□ Although we assumed that the buyer and the seller were risk neutral, the willingness and abilities of the two parties to bear risk may, in fact, differ; and analysis allowing for this possibility would thus recognize issues of the allocation of risk as well as of the allocation of resources in determining how well damage measures for breach of contract serve as a substitute for Pareto efficient complete contingent contracts.[45]

In some instances, the allocation of risk is the principal aspect of a contractual arrangement, and when this is so, the role of damage measures should be seen in this light. Suppose that a risk averse buyer contracts with a risk neutral seller for future delivery of a fixed amount of a perishable commodity which trades on a spot market (and which is not traded on an organized futures market). If we further suppose that the seller is a middleman (not a producer), then we need think only about the issue of the allocation of risk. It is apparent that under a Pareto efficient complete contingent contract, the risk averse buyer would get the commodity at a fixed price—he would be insured by the risk

[45] In the "law and economics" literature, see a recent unpublished manuscript, Kornhauser (1979), which considers how damage measures for breach of contract allocate risk (as well as allocate resources); and see also Joskow (1977), Posner and Rosenfield (1977), and Perloff (1979), which focus on the allocation of risk in analyzing impossibility and related doctrines of excuse in contract law.

neutral seller against fluctuations in the future spot price (the contingency). It is also apparent that the expectation measure would act as a perfect substitute for the complete contingent contract, for under that measure the buyer would be effectively guaranteed the commodity at the agreed price.[46]

But in most contractual relationships, both the allocation of risk and the allocation of resources will need to be considered with respect to the role of damage measures. Were the risk neutral seller of the commodity its producer rather than a middleman, then the expectation measure would serve not only to allocate risk appropriately, but also to allocate resources, and in a way similar to that described in this paper.

☐ Two points of qualification should be made in regard to our result that the expectation measure is Pareto superior to the reliance measure (Propositions 5, 8, 9). First, as just emphasized, the allocation of risk may enter into an evaluation of damage measures; and while consideration of this factor would strengthen the case for the expectation measure if the buyer (or whoever is the likely victim of a breach) is more risk averse than the seller (or whoever is the likely defaulting party), it would work in favor of the reliance measure if the seller is more risk averse than the buyer. Second, the court's (or other authority's) information may be sufficiently limited as to make it unable to apply one or the other damage measure. Although one can imagine circumstances in which the court knows the expectancy but not reliance, circumstances in which the reverse is true are perhaps more likely to occur.[47]

☐ When the use of an incomplete contract together with a damage measure would lead to significant inefficiency—when it would induce the parties to act in a way that departs substantially from how they would act under a Pareto efficient complete contingent contract—then we would generally expect there to be some pressure for a more fully specified contract, despite the attendant costs. (As discussed in the introduction, these costs explain the tendency toward incompleteness in the first place.) To illustrate, suppose that the applicable damage measure is the reliance measure (perhaps the expectancy would be particularly hard for the court to infer), that the buyer spends virtually nothing in reliance on delivery of a good to be manufactured by the seller, and that the value of the good to the buyer would be very large. Then to prevent the seller from defaulting too often (for he would pay very little in damages for breach), it might be stipulated in the contract that the seller cannot default unless his production cost is large, even though this provision would entail certain costs (that of literal inclusion in the contract and, especially, that of buyer's verification of the magnitude of the seller's production cost, should he claim it is large).

---

[46] If the seller defaulted and the buyer bought the commodity at a higher price on the spot market, then under the expectation measure the seller would have to pay the buyer the excess of his cost over the cost at the contract price.

[47] This results because the determination of reliance (exclusive of foregone opportunities) is concerned with fact (actions actually taken), whereas the determination of the expectancy is concerned with a hypothetical (what a firm's profits would have been; what the value of having his portrait painted would have been to an individual).

□ Finally, it may be worthwhile to compare the view of this paper with the often expressed view that damage measures have a *socially advantageous* economic role.[48] Under the latter view, the role of damage measures is seen as deriving from the two direct effects of their use, namely, that parties are motivated to adhere to contracts but, at the same time, that they have the option to escape their obligations and will decide to do so in certain atypical circumstances. These two effects are recognized as having two socially beneficial roles: adherence to contracts promotes trade, both private and commercial (it would be an inconvenient and much encumbered world in which there could be little assurance of contract performance); and the option not to perform means that contracts will be broken when performance would involve "waste" or excessive expense, or when performance would prevent resources from flowing to their most valued use (as when an alternative buyer is willing to pay much more to the contract seller than would the contract buyer).

The view elaborated here is in strict logic a different but complementary one, for, as stressed, we showed that the use of damage measures is in the *mutual interest* of the particular contracting parties.[49] The utility of damage measures to contracting parties themselves is no doubt a and perhaps *the* major aspect in which the social advantage of damage measures inheres. Furthermore, it affords a more appealing explanation of the observed use of damage measures than an explanation based on the notion that they are in the diffuse social interest.

References

BARTON, J. "The Economic Basis of Damages for Breach of Contract." *Journal of Legal Studies*, Vol. 1, No. 2 (1972), pp. 277–304.

BIRMINGHAM, S. "Breach of Contract, Damage Measures, and Economic Efficiency." *Rutgers Law Review*, Vol. 24, No. 2 (1970), pp. 273–292.

DAWSON, J. AND HARVEY, W. *Contracts*, 3rd ed. Mineola, N.Y.: Foundation Press, 1977.

DIAMOND, P. AND MASKIN, E. "An Equilibrium Analysis of Search and Breach of Contract, I: Steady States." *The Bell Journal of Economics*, Vol. 10, No. 1 (Spring 1979), pp. 282–316.

FRIED C. *Contract as Promise: a Theory of Contractual Obligation*. Cambridge: Harvard University Press, forthcoming.

FULLER, L. AND PERDUE, W. "Reliance Interest in Contract Damages." *Yale Law Journal*, Vol. 46, No. 3 (1937), pp. 373–420.

GOETZ, C. AND SCOTT, R. "Liquidated Damages, Penalties, and the Just Compensation Principle: Some Notes in an Enforcement Model of Efficient Breach." *Columbia Law Review*, Vol. 77, No. 4 (1977), pp. 554–594.

GROSSFELD, B. "Money Sanctions for Breach of Contract in a Communist Economy." *Yale Law Journal*, Vol. 72, No. 7 (1963), pp. 1326–1346.

JOSKOW, P. "Commercial Impossibility, the Uranium Market, and the Westinghouse Case." *Journal of Legal Studies*, Vol. 6, No. 1 (1977), pp. 119–176.

KORNHAUSER, L. "An Essay on the Economics of the Construction and Interpretation of Contracts." New York University Law School, mimeo, 1979.

[48] This view is reflected in (but not fully or exactly expressed by), for example, Birmingham (1969) and Fuller and Perdue (1937).

[49] That adherence to a contract in typical circumstances is in the mutual interest of the parties is obvious. For an example illustrating the argument behind the claim that breach under atypical circumstances is also in their interest, readers who did not follow the details of the analysis should reconsider the example in footnote 4.

MACAULAY, S. "Noncontractual Relations in Business: A Preliminary Study." *American Sociological Review*, Vol. 28, No. 1 (1963), pp. 55–69.

PERLOFF, J. "The Forward Market Effects of the Excuse Doctrines." University of Pennsylvania, mimeo, 1979.

POSNER, R. *Economic Analysis of Law*, 2nd ed. Boston: Little Brown, 1977.

——— AND ROSENFIELD, A. "Impossibility and Related Doctrines in Contract Law: An Economic Analysis." *Journal of Legal Studies*, Vol. 6, No. 1 (1977) pp. 83–118.

PRIEST, G. "Breach and Remedy for the Tender of Nonconforming Goods under the Uniform Commercial Code: An Economic Approach." *Harvard Law Review*, Vol. 91, No. 5 (1978), pp. 960–1001.

RADNER, R. "Competitive Equilibrium under Uncertainty." *Econometrica*, Vol. 36, No. 1 (1968), pp. 31–58.

ROGERSON, W. "Economic Efficiency and Damage Measures in Contract Law." California Institute of Technology, mimeo, 1980.

WILLIAMSON, O. "Transaction-Cost Economics: The Governance of Contractual Relations." *Journal of Law and Economics*, Vol. 22 (1979), pp. 233–261.

[19]

Filling Gaps in Incomplete Contracts: An Economic Theory of Default Rules

Ian Ayres† and Robert Gertner††

INTRODUCTION

The legal rules of contracts and corporations can be divided into two distinct classes. The larger class consists of "default" rules that parties can contract around by prior agreement, while the smaller, but important, class consists of "immutable" rules that parties cannot change by contractual agreement.[1] Default rules fill the gaps in incomplete contracts; they govern unless the parties contract around them. Immutable rules cannot be contracted around; they govern even if the parties attempt to contract around them. For example, under the Uniform Commercial Code (U.C.C.) the duty to act in good faith is an immutable part of any contract,[2] while the warranty of merchantability is simply a default rule that parties can waive by agreement.[3] Similarly, most corporate statutes

---

† Assistant Professor, Northwestern University School of Law; Research Fellow, American Bar Foundation. B.A., Yale University; J.D., Yale Law School; Ph.D. (Economics), Massachusetts Institute of Technology. The support of Northwestern's Corporate Counsel Center is gratefully acknowledged.

†† Assistant Professor, University of Chicago, Graduate School of Business. A.B., Princeton University; Ph.D. (Economics), Massachusetts Institute of Technology. The authors would like to thank Douglas Baird, Randy Barnett, Richard Craswell, John Donohue, Frank Easterbrook, Mark Grady, David Haddock, Steve Harris, Oliver Hart, Ian MacNeil, Joel Rogers, Steve Salop, David Scharfstein, David Van Zandt, Robert Vishny and seminar participants at the University of Chicago, Georgetown, Michigan, Northwestern, and Illinois law schools, and at the U.S. Department of Justice for helpful comments. Rebecca Mitchells and Jerry Richman provided excellent research assistance.

1. *See* B. Black, Corporate Law As Neutral Mutation, (Nov. 1988) (unpublished manuscript on file with authors) (arguing that few corporate laws are immutable). Immutable rules are similar to what Calabresi and Melamed call "inalienable" rules, Calabresi & Melamed, *Property Rules, Liability Rules, and Inalienability: One View of the Cathedral*, 85 HARV. L. REV. 1089, 1093 (1972), except that immutable entitlements are created by and conditioned upon contract, while inalienable entitlements exist outside of contract. *See* Schwab, *A Coasean Experiment on Contract Presumptions*, 17 J. LEGAL STUD. 237, 239 n.6 (1988) (distinguishing between inalienable and immutable rules).

2. U.C.C. § 1-203 (1976); *see* Morin Bldg. Prod. Co. v. Baystone Constr., Inc., 717 F.2d 413, 414-15 (7th Cir. 1983); RESTATEMENT (SECOND) OF CONTRACTS § 205 (1979); R. POSNER, ECONOMIC ANALYSIS OF LAW 81 (3d ed. 1986).

3. U.C.C. § 2-314 (1976). U.C.C. § 1-102 (1976) distinguishes between default and immutable rules and states its preference for the former:

> (3) The effect of provisions of this Act may be varied by agreement, except as otherwise provided in this Act and except that the obligations of good faith, diligence, reasonableness and care prescribed by this Act may not be disclaimed by agreement but the parties may by agreement determine the standards by which the performance of such obligations is to be measured if such standards are not manifestly unreasonable.
>
> (4) The presence in certain provisions of this Act of the words "unless otherwise agreed" or

require that stockholders elect directors annually[4] but allow the articles of incorporation to contract around the default rule of straight voting.[5] Statutory language such as "[u]nless otherwise provided in the certificate of incorporation"[6] or "[u]nless otherwise unambiguously indicated"[7] makes it easy to identify statutory default, but common-law precedents can also be divided into the default and immutable camps. For example, the common-law holding of *Peevyhouse v. Garland Coal & Mining Co.*,[8] which limited damages to diminution in value, could be contractually reversed by prospective parties.[9] In contrast, the common law prerequisite of consideration is largely an immutable rule that parties cannot contractually abrogate.[10]

There is surprising consensus among academics at an abstract level on two normative bases for immutability. Put most simply, immutable rules are justifiable if society wants to protect (1) parties within the contract, or (2) parties outside the contract.[11] The former justification turns on parentalism; the latter on externalities. Immutable rules displace freedom of contract. Immutability is justified only if unregulated contracting would be socially deleterious because parties internal or external to the contract cannot adequately protect themselves.[12] With regard to immutable rules, the disagreement among academics is not over this abstract theory, but

---

> words of similar import does not imply that the effect of other provisions may not be varied by agreement under subsection (3).

U.C.C. § 1-102 (1976).

4. *See, e.g.*, DEL. CODE ANN. tit. 8, § 211(c) (1974).
5. *See, e.g.*, DEL. CODE ANN. tit. 8, § 214 (1974).
6. DEL. CODE ANN. tit. 8, § 223 (1974).
7. U.C.C. § 2-206 (1976).
8. 382 P.2d 109 (Okla. 1962), *cert. denied*, 375 U.S. 906 (1963).
9. Whether the *Peevyhouse* majority actually intended for prospective parties to be able to choose the "cost of performance measure" is discussed more fully *infra* text accompanying notes 151-61.
10. The consideration requirement is not immutable if written agreements "under seal" serve as a contractual substitute for consideration. *See* U.C.C. § 2-203 (1976) (making inoperative "the law with respect to sealed instruments").

This default rule/immutable rule dichotomy also pervades other areas of the law that have contractual components. In the law of divorce, for example, wealth accrued before marriage is allocated according to default rules that can be altered in pre-nuptial agreements, while income earned after marriage is immutably divided. Similarly, the repayment priorities set by state debtor-creditor law can, like default rules, be reordered through private contract. The laws of intestacy are also default rules: they fill any testamentary gap, but can be contracted around. As discussed below, *infra* text accompanying notes 83-91, one can distinguish between defaults that must be *bilaterally* contracted around and defaults that may be *unilaterally* overcome.

11. *See* I. MACNEIL, CONTRACTS: EXCHANGE TRANSACTIONS AND RELATIONS 346-47 (1978); Calabresi & Melamed, *supra* note 1; Easterbrook & Fischel, *The Economic Structure of Corporate Law*, 89 COLUM. L. REV. (forthcoming 1989) (manuscript at 21-30; on file with authors).
12. Note that even when there are negative externalities, third parties may be able to protect themselves without immutable rules. One implication of the Coase theorem is that in a world with no transaction costs, third parties will have an incentive to contract to reduce externalities to an efficient level. *See* Coase, *The Problem of Social Cost*, 3 J. LAW & ECON. 1 (1960). There are no externalities if the class of parties to the potential contract is defined broadly enough. G. Priest, Internalizing Costs (Yale Law School Program in Civil Liability 1988; working paper no. 93) (explicating pervasiveness of private incentives to internalize costs).

whether in particular contexts parentalistic concerns or externalities are sufficiently great to justify the use of immutable rules.[13]

When the preconditions for immutability are not present, the normative legal analysis devolves to the choice of a default rule. Yet academics have paid little attention about how to choose among possible default rules.[14] The law-and-economics movement has fought long and hard to convince courts to restrict the use of immutable rules,[15] but has lost most of its normative energy in constructing a theory of default choice.[16] Economists seem to believe that, even if lawmakers choose the wrong default, at worst there will be increased transaction costs of a second order of magnitude.[17]

Few academics have gone beyond one-sentence theories stipulating that default terms should be set at what the parties would have wanted.[18]

---

13. A recent conference (Dec. 9-10, 1988) on "Contractual Freedom in Corporate Law" at Columbia's Center for Law and Economic Studies focused directly on the appropriate application of immutable rules. For example, Jeffrey Gordon argued that having multiple precedents that construe a single legal standard produces positive externalities that might justify imposing an immutable rule. *See* J. Gordon, The Mandatory Structure of Corporate Law (Dec. 2, 1988) (unpublished manuscript on file with authors).

14. Courts or legislatures are inevitably forced to set defaults, because contracts with gaps need to be interpreted. Courts must do something—even if that something is non-enforcement. As discussed *infra* text accompanying notes 51-52, defaults of non-enforcement can play an important role in efficient law.

15. For instance, Anthony Kronman has written:

> [E]x ante arguments for the efficiency of a particular legal rule assume that individuals remain free to contract around that rule, and a legal system that denies private parties the right to vary rules in this way will tend to be less efficient than a system that adopts the same rules but permits contractual variation.

Kronman, *Specific Performance*, 45 U. CHI. L. REV. 351, 370 (1978). *See* Haddock, Macey & McChesney, *Property Rights in Assets and Resistance to Tender Offers*, 73 VA. L. REV. 701, 736 (1987) ("The ability of firms to contract around costly legal rules when lower-cost private alternatives are available must be a feature of any efficient standard-form contract."); *see also* Goetz & Scott, *Liquidated Damages, Penalties and the Just Compensation Principle: Some Notes on an Enforcement Model and a Theory of Efficient Breach*, 77 COLUM. L. REV. 554 (1977) (arguing that "immutable" standards for determining enforceability of liquidated damages clauses should be relaxed). *But see* Clarkson, Miller & Muris, *Liquidated Damages v. Penalties: Sense or Nonsense?*, 1978 WIS. L. REV. 351 (providing efficiency rationale for immutable liquidated-damages rules).

16. For example, Haddock and Macey have suggested that immutable rules against insider trading are inefficient but have remained agnostic about whether corporations wishing to allow their insiders to trade should be forced to "opt out" of an insider trading prohibition, or whether corporations wishing to prohibit insider trading should be forced to "opt in" to such a system. Haddock & Macey, *A Coasian Model of Insider Trading*, 80 NW. U.L. REV. 1449 (1987).

17. *See, e.g.*, Easterbrook & Fischel, *Limited Liability and the Corporation*, 52 U. CHI. L. REV. 89, 102 (1985) ("In light of the ability of firms to duplicate or at least approximate either limited or unlimited liability by contract, does the legal rule of limited liability matter? The answer is yes, but probably not much.").

18. Looking backward to what the present litigants "would have wanted" is analytically analogous to looking forward to what prospective contractors will want. It is to ask (as Lea Brilmayer often does) "who are the prospective parties rooting for?" In both cases the court examines ex ante incentives. While ex post each party will have economic incentives to shift costs to the other side, ex ante the parties have an incentive to place the risks on the least-cost avoider. Kronman, *Mistake, Disclosure, Information and the Law of Contracts*, 7 J. LEGAL STUD. 1 (1978). If a court can identify that ex ante the parties to the contract had identical interests in allocating a certain risk or duty of performance, then it can, in a sense, pierce the ex post adversarial veil. Thus, for example, even if ex post a particular tenant wants to avoid the risk of fire damage, ex ante both landlords *and* tenants may have preferred to have tenants bear this risk as the least-cost avoider. Thus, the fact that after a fire a tenant tries to avoid liability is not dispositive of what prospective tenants would contract for or,

Frank Easterbrook and Daniel Fischel have championed the "would have wanted" theory in a number of articles suggesting that "corporate law should contain the [defaults] people would have negotiated, were the costs of negotiating at arms'-length for every contingency sufficiently low."[19] Similarly, Richard Posner has argued that default rules should "economize on transaction costs by supplying standard contract terms that the parties would otherwise have to adopt by express agreement."[20] Douglas Baird and Thomas Jackson have argued that the default rules governing the debtor-creditor relationship "should provide all the parties with the type of contract that they would have agreed to if they had had the time and money to bargain over all aspects of their deal."[21] While this literature has vigorously examined what particular parties would have contracted for in particular contractual settings,[22] it has failed to question whether the "would have wanted" standard is conceptually sound.[23]

Thus, although the academy recognizes the analytic difference between

indeed, of what this particular tenant would have contracted for.

19. Easterbrook & Fischel, *supra* note 11 at 14-15; *see also id.* at 20-21 (default term should be "the term that the parties would have selected with full information and costless contracting"); Easterbrook & Fischel, *Corporate Control Transactions*, 91 YALE L.J. 698, 702 (1982) (default fiduciary duties are derived from a hypothetical contract, imagined by judges, between investors and managers dickering with each other free of bargaining costs); Easterbrook & Fischel, *The Proper Role of a Target's Management in Responding to a Tender Offer*, 94 HARV. L. REV. 1161, 1182 (1981) (corporate law should supply "standard form 'contracts' of the sort shareholders would be likely to choose . . . ."). Calabresi and Melamed's analysis may be an early antecedent of the "would have wanted" analysis. They argue that efficiency-minded law would establish default entitlements as the parties would allocate them in a world without transaction costs. Calabresi & Melamed, *supra* note 1, at 1093-98.

20. R. POSNER, *supra* note 2, at 372; *see also* Schwartz, *Proposals for Products Liability Reform: A Theoretical Synthesis*, 97 YALE L.J. 353, 361 (1988) (offering as default rule "the contract that most well-informed persons would have adopted if they were to bargain about the matter").

21. Baird & Jackson, *Fraudulent Conveyance Law and Its Proper Domain*, 38 VAND. L. REV. 829, 835-36 (1985); *see also* Goetz & Scott, *The Mitigation Principle: Toward a General Theory of Contractual Obligation*, 69 VA. L. REV. 967, 971 (1983) ("Ideally, the preformulated rules supplied by the state should mimic the agreements contracting parties would reach were they costlessly to bargain out each detail of the transaction.").

In Lewis v. Benedict Coal Corp., 361 U.S. 459 (1960), the Supreme Court applied this default-setting standard in deciding whether, in the absence of explicit contractual language, payments to a third-party beneficiary pension fund should be subject to setoff if the union breaches the underlying labor contract. The Court stated, "[i]t may be fair to assume that had the parties anticipated the possibility of a breach by the promisee they *would have provided* that the promisor might protect himself by such means as would be available against the promisee under a two-party contract." *Id.* at 468 (emphasis added). The Court later distinguished what parties to a collective bargaining agreement might have wanted and accordingly established a no-setoff default. *Id.* at 469.

22. *See, e.g.*, Craswell, *Contract Remedies, Renegotiation, and the Theory of Efficient Breach*, 61 S. CAL. L. REV. 629 (1988); *see also infra* text accompanying notes 136-39 (discussing judicial disagreement of Judges Easterbrook and Posner).

23. Charles Goetz and Robert Scott have written one of the more thoughtful examinations of default choice. Goetz & Scott, *The Limits of Expanded Choice: An Analysis of the Interactions Between Express and Implied Contract Terms*, 73 CALIF. L. REV. 261 (1985). Their theory of default rules is based on the idea that a large body of precedent will develop regarding the interpretation and application of a standard-form clause. Parties who contract around a standard-form clause will face the prospect that courts will interpret their contract in a manner that is inconsistent with the parties' initial intentions. Thus, parties who prefer an alternative to the standard-form may accept the latter for fear of misinterpretation.

default and immutable rules, a detailed theory of how defaults should be set has yet to be proposed. Indeed, the lack of agreement over even what to call the "default" concept is evidence of the underdeveloped state of default theory.[24] Default rules have alternatively been termed background, backstop, enabling, fallback, gap-filling, off-the-rack, opt-in, opt-out, preformulated, preset, presumptive, standby, standard-form and suppletory rules.[25]

This Article provides a theory of how courts and legislatures should set default rules. We suggest that efficient defaults would take a variety of forms that at times would diverge from the "what the parties would have contracted for" principle. To this end, we introduce the concept of "penalty defaults." Penalty defaults are designed to give at least one party to the contract an incentive to contract around the default rule and therefore to choose affirmatively the contract provision they prefer. In contrast to the received wisdom, penalty defaults are purposefully set at what the parties would not want—in order to encourage the parties to reveal information to each other or to third parties (especially the courts).

This Article also distinguishes between tailored and untailored defaults. A "tailored default" attempts to provide a contract's parties with precisely "what they would have contracted for." An "untailored default," true to its etymology, provides the parties to all contracts with a single, off-the-rack standard that in some sense represents what the majority of contracting parties would want. *The Restatement (Second) of Contracts'* approach to filling gaps, for example, provides tailored defaults that are "reasonable in the circumstances."[26] "Reasonable" defaults usually entail a tailored determination of what the individual contracting parties would have wanted because courts evaluate reasonableness in relation to the "cir-

24. The "default" characterization seems currently in vogue. Professor Robert Clark explains its etymology:

> For those who haven't been exposed to this jargon from the world of computers, "default rules" are the rules that a program follows in "default" of an explicit choice by the user to have some other principle apply. For example, your word processing program may set paper margins of 1 inch on all sides unless you take the trouble to learn the relevant commands and set the margins otherwise.

Clark, *Contracts, Elites, and Traditions in the Making of Corporate Law*, 89 COLUM. L. REV. (forthcoming 1989) (manuscript at 3 n.9; on file with authors).

25. *See* Bebchuk, *Limiting Contractual Freedom in Corporate Law: The Desirable Constraints on Charter Amendments*, 102 HARV. L. REV. 1820 (1989) (using "opt-out" and "opt-in"); Coffee, *The Mandatory/Enabling Balance in Corporate Law: An Essay on the Judicial Role*, 89 COLUM. L. REV. (forthcoming 1989) (using "enabling"); Easterbrook & Fischel, *supra* note 11 (using "standby," "enabling," "presets," and "fallback"); Eisenberg, *The Foundational Model of the Corporation*, 89 COLUM. L. REV. (forthcoming 1989) (using "enabling" and "suppletory" terms); Goetz & Scott, *supra* note 21, at 971 (using "preformulated"); Haddock, Macey & McChesney, *supra* note 15, at 736 (using "default" and "standard-form"); Schwab, *supra* note 1, at 237 (using "presumptive" and "off-the-rack"); Speidel, *Restatement Second: Omitted Terms and Contract Method*, 67 CORNELL L. REV. 785 n.2 (1982) (using "gap-filling").

26. RESTATEMENT (SECOND) OF CONTRACTS § 204 ("Supplying an Omitted Essential Term") (setting default for missing term to be "a term which is reasonable in the circumstances"). *See* Speidel, *supra* note 25, at 792–809.

cumstances" of the individual contracting parties.[27] In contrast, Charles Goetz and Robert Scott have proposed that courts should set untailored default rules by asking "what arrangements would *most* bargainers prefer?"[28]

This Article provides a general theory of when efficiency-minded courts or legislatures should set penalty defaults and how they should choose between tailored and untailored default rules. Some common-law and statutory defaults are flatly at odds with the "would have wanted" principle. Although this Article does not make the full-blown positivist claim that current default rules are efficient, it does offer a more complete explanation of the current diversity of defaults.

An essential component of our theory of default rules is our explicit consideration of the sources of contractual incompleteness. We distinguish between two basic reasons for incompleteness.[29] Scholars have primarily attributed incompleteness to the costs of contracting. Contracts may be incomplete because the transaction costs of explicitly contracting for a given contingency are greater than the benefits.[30] These transaction costs may

---

27. For example, U.C.C. § 2-306, governing output and requirement contracts, establishes as a default that: In the absence of a stated estimate, "no quantity unreasonably disproportionate . . . to any normal or otherwise comparable prior output or requirements may be tendered or demanded." U.C.C. § 2-306(1) (1976). In determining reasonableness, courts are expressly asked by the U.C.C. to look at specific characteristics of the contracting parties. For example, "[a] shut-down by a requirements buyer for lack of orders might be permissible when a shut-down merely to curtail losses would not." U.C.C. § 2-306(1) comment 2 (1976).

28. Goetz & Scott, *supra* note 21, at 971 (emphasis in original).

29. There are two distinct ways for a contract to be incomplete. First, a contract may fail to specify the parties' duties for specific future contingencies. For example, a contract for the construction of a third floor to a house may not state the parties' respective rights and responsibilities should the entire house burn down before construction is started. Since construction of a third floor is impossible (without the lower two floors), the contract does not cover the contingency of the house burning down.

The second form of contractual incompleteness is more subtle. A contract may also be incomplete in that it is insensitive to relevant future contingencies. Under this second form of contractual incompleteness, parties' duties are fully specified, but the contracts are incomplete because those specified duties are not tailored to economically relevant future events. *See* K. Spier, Incomplete Contracts in a Model with Adverse Selection and Exogenous Costs of Enforcement (Dec. 1988) (unpublished manuscript on file with authors) (discussing causes for such incompleteness). For example, consider a contract that simply obligates one party to construct a garage adjacent to a house. On the face this contract imposes a duty to build a garage whether or not the adjacent house burns down before construction of the garage is complete. The contract is incomplete in this second sense, however, because the duty to build a garage is not sufficiently dependent on future contingencies. If the adjacent house burns down, the parties probably would want to adjust the terms of contract. Such contracts we call insufficiently state-contingent.

Courts recognize the first form of incompleteness and know they must decide how to fill the gap. For instance, non-enforcement is one way courts can fill the gap. Courts seldomly recognize the second form of contractual incompleteness. That is, they are generally unwilling to alter (they strictly enforce) the terms of a contract that is insufficiently state-contingent. The main exception to strict enforcement is the doctrine of impossibility (or economic impracticability) with which courts sometimes refuse enforcement when performance, although literally possible, is not ex post efficient. *See* Posner & Rosenfield, *Impossibility and Related Doctrines in Contract Law: An Economic Analysis*, 6 J. LEGAL STUD. 83, 87 (1977) (discussing legal contours of impossibility doctrine).

30. *See* O. WILLIAMSON, THE ECONOMIC INSTITUTIONS OF CAPITALISM 70 (1985); MacNeil, *Contracts: Adjustment of Long-Term Economic Relations Under Classical, Neoclassical and Relational Contract Law*, 72 NW. U.L. REV. 854, 871-73 (1978); Shavell, *Damage Measures for Breach*

include legal fees, negotiation costs, drafting and printing costs, the costs of researching the effects and probability of a contingency, and the costs to the parties and the courts of verifying whether a contingency occurred. Rational parties will weigh these costs against the benefits of contractually addressing a particular contingency. If either the magnitude or the probability of a contingency is sufficiently low, a contract may be insensitive to that contingency even if transaction costs are quite low.

The "would have wanted" approach to gap filling is a natural outgrowth of the transaction cost explanation of contractual incompleteness. Lawmakers can minimize the costs of contracting by choosing the default that most parties would have wanted. If there are transaction costs of explicitly contracting on a contingency, the parties may prefer to leave the contract incomplete. Indeed, as transaction costs increase, so does the parties' willingness to accept a default that is not exactly what they would have contracted for. Scholars who attribute contractual incompleteness to transaction costs are naturally drawn toward choosing defaults that the majority of contracting parties "would have wanted" because these majoritarian defaults seem to minimize the costs of contracting.

We show, however, that this majoritarian "would have wanted" approach to default selection is, for several reasons, incomplete. First, the majoritarian approach fails to account for the possibly disparate costs of contracting and of failing to contract around different defaults.[31] For example, if the majority is more likely to contract around the minority's preferred default rule (than the minority is to contract around the majority's rule), then choosing the minority's default may lead to a larger set of efficient contracts. Second, the received wisdom provides little guidance about how tailored or particularized the "would have wanted" analysis should be.[32] Finally, the very costs of ex ante bargaining may encourage parties to inefficiently shift the process of gap filling to ex post court determination.[33] If it is costly for the courts to determine what the parties would have wanted, it may be efficient to choose a default rule that induces the parties to contract explicitly. In other words, penalty defaults are appropriate when it is cheaper for the parties to negotiate a term ex ante than for the courts to estimate ex post what the parties would have wanted. Courts, which are publicly subsidized, should give parties incentives to negotiate ex ante by penalizing them for inefficient gaps.

---

of Contract, 11 BELL J. ECON. 466, 468 (1980) ("[B]ecause of the costs involved in enumerating and bargaining over contractual obligations under the full range of relevant contingencies, it is normally impractical to make contracts which approach completeness.").

31. *See infra* Section II.

32. *Id.*

33. Jeffrey Gordon argues that the "would have wanted" approach is also flawed because it shifts risks to the ex ante least-cost avoider but, as applied by most courts, does not in fact compensate the ex post risk bearer. Gordon, *supra* note 13, at 61 (problem with hypothetical bargain argument, "like other Kaldor-Hicks arguments, is that it doesn't guarantee that each party will in fact receive a bigger slice, or a slice of the right size." (citation omitted)).

This Article also proposes a second source of contractual incompleteness that is the focus of much of our analysis. We refer to this source of incompleteness as strategic.[34] One party might strategically withhold information that would increase the total gains from contracting (the "size of the pie") in order to increase her private share of the gains from contracting (her "share of the pie"). By attempting to contract around a certain default, one party might reveal information to the other party that affects how the contractual pie is split. Thus, for example, the more informed party may prefer to have inefficient precaution rather than pay a higher price for the good.[35] While analysts have previously explained incomplete contracting solely in terms of the costs of writing additional provisions, we argue that contractual gaps can also result from strategic behavior by relatively informed parties. By changing the default rules of the game, lawmakers can importantly reduce the opportunities for this rent-seeking, strategic behavior.[36] In particular, the possibility of strategic incompleteness leads us to suggest that efficiency-minded lawmakers should sometimes choose penalty defaults that induce knowledgeable parties to reveal information by contracting around the default penalty. The strategic behavior of the parties in forming the contract can justify strategic contractual interpretations by courts.[37]

Our analysis therefore moves beyond the received wisdom that default rules should simply be what the majority of contracting parties would have wanted. In choosing among default rules, lawmakers should be sensitive to the costs of contracting around, and the costs of failing to contract around, particular defaults. We show that different defaults may lead to different degrees of "separating" and "pooling."[38] In "separating" equilibria, the different types of contracting parties, by bearing the costs of contracting around unwanted defaults, separate themselves into distinct

34. See *infra* Section II for examples of strategic incompleteness. A third reason for contractual incompleteness is that some contingencies may simply be unforeseen by all contracting parties. In this case, the default rule will not affect the actions of the parties since by definition they do not consider the contingency in deciding what to do. There will normally be no reason to consider the rule's ex ante effect because it will have none.

There is one caveat to this statement: Behavior may be affected if parties are aware that unforeseen contingencies exist but are unable to ascertain the nature of these contingencies. For example, parties who are aware that a variety of unforeseen contingencies may affect the price at which they should transact may choose a contract that includes a reasonable price clause rather than fixing a price or a price rule as a function of foreseen contingencies. In this way the price can respond to unforeseen contingencies. See D. Kreps, Static Choice in the Presence of Unforeseen Contingencies (Aug. 1988) (unpublished manuscript on file with authors) for a utility-theoretic characterization of behavior in the presence of unforeseen contingencies. The choice of optimal defaults for such unforeseen contingencies is beyond the scope of this article. For a discussion of the appropriate default, see Posner & Rosenfield, *supra* note 29.

35. *See* K. Spier, *supra* note 29 (formalizing this strategic reluctance to reveal information).

36. *See infra* Section I-C.

37. Inefficient strategic behavior will often induce efficiency-promoting counterstrategies by other economic actors. *See* Easterbrook, *Predatory Strategies and Counterstrategies*, 48 U. CHI. L. REV. 263 (1981).

38. *See infra* text accompanying notes 113-16.

contractual relationships. In "pooling" equilibria, different types of contracting parties fail to contract around defaults, thus avoiding transaction costs but bearing the inefficiencies of the substantive default provisions.

In contrast to the majoritarian analysis, our analysis shows that it may be efficient to choose a rule that a majority of people actually disfavor. To set defaults efficiently, lawmakers must not only know what contracting parties want, but how many are likely to get it and at what cost. We recommend a greater and more explicit legal sensitivity toward the ways in which different defaults will affect the resulting contractual "equilibrium."[39]

Finally, before deciding how to fill gaps, courts must decide whether the contract even has a gap. In other words, courts must decide whether the contract already allocates a particular risk or duty. We show that this issue of whether a gap exists is identical to the issue of what is sufficient to contract around a particular default.[40] While the received wisdom is that lawmakers should minimize the costs of contracting around default rules,[41] we suggest that efficiency-minded courts and legislatures may want to intentionally increase these transaction costs to discourage parties from contracting around certain defaults.

The Article has three sections. Section I discusses the possible efficiency of penalty defaults. Section II embeds penalty defaults in a more general model of default choice, a model which suggests when penalty, tailored, or untailored defaults will be efficient. Section III then develops a theory of gap definition that determines what should be sufficient to contract around a given default.

I. Penalty Default Rules

A. *The Zero-Quantity Default*

The diversity of default standards can even be seen in contrasting the law's treatment of the two most basic contractual terms: price and quantity. Although price and quantity are probably the two most essential issues on which to reach agreement, the U.C.C. establishes radically different defaults. If the parties leave out the price, the U.C.C. fills the gap with "a reasonable price."[42] If the parties leave out the quantity, the

39. We will sometimes find it useful to distinguish between situations in which the parties negotiate in ignorance of the default rule and situations in which the parties negotiate in the shadow of the default rule. In the former case, the parties do not know how the courts will decide if the contingency in question occurs, while in the latter case the parties know the legal default (but may not know certain information about the other party). *See infra* text accompanying notes 58–60.

40. *See infra* Section III.

41. *See* Easterbrook & Fischel, *supra* note 11, at 21–30.

42. U.C.C. § 2-305(1) reads: "The parties if they so intend can conclude a contract for sale even though the price is not settled. In such a case the price is a reasonable price at the time for delivery. . . ." U.C.C. § 2-305(1) (1976).

U.C.C. refuses to enforce the contract.[43] In essence, the U.C.C. mandates that the default quantity should be zero.

How can this be? The U.C.C.'s reasonable-price standard can be partly reconciled with the received wisdom that defaults should be set at what the parties would have contracted for.[44] But why doesn't the U.C.C. treat a missing quantity term analogously by filling the gap with the reasonable quantity that the parties would have have wanted? Obviously, the parties would not have gone to the expense of contracting with the intention that nothing be exchanged.

We suggest that the zero-quantity default cannot be explained by a "what the parties would have wanted" principle. Instead, a rationale for the rule can be found by comparing the cost of ex ante contracting to the cost of ex post litigation. The zero-quantity rule can be justified because it is cheaper for the parties to establish the quantity term beforehand than for the courts to determine after the fact what the parties would have wanted.

It is not systematically easier for parties to figure out the quantity than the price ex ante, but it is systematically harder for the courts to figure out the quantity than the price ex post. To estimate a reasonable price, courts can largely rely on market information of the type "How much were rutabagas selling for on July 3?"[45] But to estimate a reasonable quantity, courts would need to undertake a more costly analysis of the individual litigants of the type "How much did the buyer and seller value the marginal rutabagas?"

43. U.C.C. § 2-201 states that a "contract . . . is not enforceable under this [provision] beyond the quantity of goods shown. . . ." U.C.C. § 2-201(1) (1976). The official comment adds that "[t]he only term which must appear is the quantity term which need not be accurately stated but recovery is limited to the amount stated." U.C.C. § 2-201(1) (official comment) (1978). In some cases, lack of a quantity term will merely be evidence that the parties did not have a meeting of the minds. But even if there are sufficient objective indicia of an intent to contract (and even if the statute of frauds is not raised as an affirmative defense), courts may refuse to enforce the contract because it is indefinite. *See* Jessen Bros. v. Ashland Recreation Ass'n., 204 Neb. 19, 281 N.W.2d 210 (1979) (contract for sod unenforceable for lack of specific quantity term); Burke v. Campbell, 258 Mass. 153, 154 N.E. 759 (1927) (contract unenforceable in part because contract did not state how much stock defendant would receive in exchange for financing corporation); King v. Krischer Mfg. Co., 220 A.D. 584, 222 N.Y.S. 66 (1927) (contract unenforceable because "a quantity of merchandise" too indefinite).

44. A simple "what parties would have wanted" approach has trouble explaining why the parties would choose reasonable price at time of delivery instead of at the time of contracting. There is no reason to think that parties would systematically prefer one risk allocation to the other. However, one can determine the efficient default rule by asking the question, "why didn't the parties explicitly contract for price?" Those parties who wish to allocate the risk of cost fluctuations to the seller will most likely contract for a price at the time of contracting. Those who wish to allocate the risk to the buyer will attempt to contract for a time-of-delivery, cost-based price. Such a clause may be costly to write into the contract explicitly because of the difficulty in measuring the seller's cost exactly. The parties may instead prefer to rely on reaching an agreement in the shadow of the court's reasonable-price default rule.

45. This analysis suggests that courts would be less likely to enforce contracts in "thin" markets in which the market price is not readily ascertainable. *See* Haddock, McChesney & Spiegel, *An Ordinary Economic Rationale for Extraordinary Legal Sanctions*, 78 CALIF. L. REV. (forthcoming 1990) (discussing how efficient legal rules will turn on "thickness" of market).

The U.C.C.'s zero-quantity default is what we term a "penalty default." Because ex ante neither party would want a zero-quantity contract, such a rule penalizes the parties should they fail to affirmatively specify their desired quantity. Because the non-enforcement default potentially penalizes both parties, it encourages both of them to include a quantity term.[46]

B. *Toward a More General Theory of Penalty Defaults*

Penalty defaults, by definition, give at least one party to the contract an incentive to contract around the default. From an efficiency perspective, penalty default rules can be justified as a way to encourage the production of information.[47] The very process of "contracting around" can reveal information to parties inside or outside the contract. Penalty defaults may be justified as 1) giving both contracting parties incentives to reveal information to third parties, especially courts,[48] or 2) giving a more informed contracting party incentives to reveal information to a less informed party.

The zero-quantity default, for instance, gives both contracting parties incentives to reveal their contractual intentions when it would be costly for a court to discover that information ex post. This justification—that ex ante contracting can be cheaper than ex post litigation—can also explain the common law's broader rule that "for a contract to be binding the terms of the contract must be reasonably certain and definite."[49] Similarly, this rationale can explain corporate statutes that give incorporators an incentive to affirmatively declare the number of authorized shares, the address of the corporation for legal process and, indeed, the state of incor-

---

46. Even if the judicial system were not subsidized, the zero-quantity default might be justified on parentalistic concerns. For example, if private parties are uninformed or systematically underestimate the costs of ex post judicial determination of a "reasonable" quantity, it might be in society's interests to dissuade parties from mistakenly failing to negotiate the contract quantity ex ante.

This rationale for this penalty default depends on the assumption that the private parties pay less than the full costs of their ex post litigation. The parties may lower their transaction costs by shifting the privately funded ex ante negotiations to publicly subsidized ex post litigation. If parties fully internalized ex post litigation costs, at first cut they should be able to choose the cheaper type of negotiation.

47. In encouraging the revelation of information, lawmakers should be sensitive to the influence that defaults can have on the incentives for private parties to acquire information in the first place. *See infra* notes 93-94 and accompanying text.

48. Penalty defaults may be established to provide information to third parties other than the courts. For example, in corporate law certain alterations to the default corporate governance can be accomplished through a by-law amendment, while other alterations can only be made by changing the articles of incorporation. *See infra* note 148 and accompanying text. Requiring certain amendments in the articles of incorporation reveals information to interested third parties, such as creditors, because these articles are publicly filed with the Secretary of State. *See, e.g.*, REVISED MODEL BUSINESS CORP. ACT ANN. § 2.01 (1987) (requiring filing of articles of incorporation).

49. Steinberg v. Chicago Medical School, 41 Ill. App. 3d 804, 807, 354 N.E.2d 586, 589 (1976); *see also* Parks v. Atlanta News Agency, 115 Ga. App. 842, 156 S.E.2d 137 (1967); 1 A. CORBIN, CORBIN ON CONTRACTS § 95 (1952 & Supp. 1989); 1 S. WILLISTON, A TREATISE ON THE LAW OF CONTRACTS § 37 (3d ed. 1957 & Supp. 1978).

poration.[50] Statutes that refuse to enforce corporate charters without these provisions create incentives similar to those created by the common law's refusal to enforce vague or indefinite contracts. In both cases, the parties can make these contractual choices more efficiently ex ante.

Lawmakers should select the rule that deters inefficient gaps at the least social cost. When the rationale is to provide information to the courts, the non-enforcement default is likely to be efficient. Non-enforcement defaults are likely to provide least-cost deterrence because they are inexpensive to enforce and give each party incentives to contract around the rule. It might seem that a penalty default set solely against one side of a contract would be sufficient to get both sides to reveal information. For example, a penalty default that makes the seller sell at one-tenth the market price would certainly encourage sellers to affirmatively fill any price gaps. But one side's penalty may be the other side's windfall. One-sided penalties can create incentives for opportunism.[51] The non-penalized buyer in the above example would have incentives to induce sellers to enter indefinite contracts in order to extract the penalty rent.[52] By taking each party back to her ex ante welfare, the non-enforcement default eliminates this potential for opportunism.

In contrast, when the rationale is to inform the relatively uninformed contracting party, the penalty default should be against the relatively informed party.[53] This is especially true when the uninformed party is also uninformed about the default rule itself. If the uninformed party does not know that there is a penalty default, she will have no opportunistic incentives.

In some situations it is reasonable to expect one party to the contract to be systematically informed about the default rule and the probability of the relevant contingency arising. If one side is repeatedly in the relevant contractual setting while the other side rarely is, it is a sensible presumption that the former is better informed than the latter. Consider, for example, the treatment of real estate brokerage commissions when a buyer breaches a purchase contract. Such contracts typically include a clause which obligates the purchaser to forfeit some given amount of "earnest" money if she breaches the agreement. How should the earnest money be

50. *See* REVISED MODEL BUSINESS CORP. ACT ANN. § 2.02 (1987).

51. Posner defines opportunism (in relation to the common-law contractual duty to act in good faith) as "taking advantage of the vulnerability of the other party to a contract . . . that is due to the sequential character of performance." R. POSNER, *supra* note 2, at 81.

52. Similar opportunistic incentives have been analyzed in other areas of contract law. *See, e.g.*, Clarkson, Miller & Muris, *Liquidated Damages Versus Penalties: Sense or Nonsense?*, 1978 WIS. L. REV. 351 (non-enforcement of penalty clauses prevents opportunistic breach inducement); Goetz & Scott, *supra* note 15, at 586 (mitigation requirement eliminates incentive for opportunism by obligee in case of breach). More generally, the inefficiency of excessive penalties has been detailed in the economics-of-crime literature. *See, e.g.*, R. POSNER, *supra* note 2, at 205-12; Becker, *Crime and Punishment: An Economic Approach*, 76 J. POL. ECON. 169 (1968).

53. *See infra* text accompanying notes 57-73.

split between the seller and the broker if their agency contract does not address this contingency? Some courts have adopted a "what the parties would have wanted" approach and have awarded all the earnest money to the seller.[54] We agree with this outcome, but for different reasons.[55] The real estate broker will more likely be informed about the default rule than the seller. Indeed, the seller may not even consider the issue of how to split the earnest money in case of default.[56] Therefore, if the efficient contract would allocate some of the earnest money to the seller, the default rule should be set against the broker to induce her to raise the issue. Otherwise, if the default rule is set to favor the broker, a seller may not raise the issue, and the broker will be happy to take advantage of the seller's ignorance. By setting the default rule in favor of the uninformed party, the courts induce the informed party to reveal information, and, consequently, the efficient contract results.

Although social welfare may be enhanced by forcing parties to reveal information to a subsidized judicial system, it is more problematic to understand why society would have an efficiency interest in inducing a relatively informed party to a transaction to reveal information to the relatively uninformed party. After all, if revealing information is efficient because it increases the value created by the contract, one might initially expect that the informed party will have a sufficient private incentive to reveal information—the incentive of splitting a bigger pie. This argument ignores the possibility, however, that revealing information might simultaneously increase the total size of the pie and decrease the share of the pie that the relatively informed party receives. If the "share-of-the-pie effect" dominates the "size-of-the-pie effect," informed parties might rationally choose to withhold relevant information.[57]

Parties may behave strategically not only because they have superior

---

54. *See, e.g.*, Dennis Reed, Ltd. v. Goody, 2 K.B. 277 (1950); *see also* J. Dukeminier & J. Krier, Property 554-55 (2d ed. 1988) (discussing evolution of common-law rule).

55. Earnest money is used to force the purchaser to internalize the cost to the seller of taking the property off the market during the time from the signing of the sale agreement to the closing or, in this case, the breach. Since these costs are largely incurred by the seller, she should receive the compensation. Furthermore, the seller may wish to give the broker incentives to find a buyer who will not default. Allowing the broker to share in the earnest money will lower or eliminate this incentive. One reason, however, that the broker and the seller would ex ante contract for the broker to receive some of the earnest money is that the breach by the initial buyer may necessitate a quick sale which may cause the seller to lower the selling price. This, in turn, would lower the broker's commission. Thus, a "what the parties would have wanted" approach might yield a default in which a risk-averse broker receives a portion of the earnest money.

56. Of course, people hire lawyers in part to ascertain the relevant negotiation issues, contingencies, and default rules. Our argument is therefore most applicable in contractual settings in which lawyers are not employed.

57. Withholding socially valuable private information to obtain private gains is common. Companies may withhold information about innovations from competitors to increase profits; car buyers may withhold information about particular options or accessories that they value if this information signals to car dealers a greater willingness to pay for the underlying automobile; and professional athletes may withhold information about injuries to increase their salaries, even though as a result their team may inefficiently hire reserves.

information about the default, but also because they have superior information about other aspects of the contract. We suggest that a party who knows that a particular default rule is inefficient may choose not to negotiate to change it. The knowledgeable party may not wish to reveal her information in negotiations if the information would give a bargaining advantage to the other side.

How can it be that by increasing the total gains from contracting (the size-of-the-pie effect) the informed party can end up with a smaller share of the gains (the share-of-the-pie effect)?[58] This Article demonstrates how relatively informed parties can sometimes benefit by strategically withholding information that, if revealed, would increase the size of the pie. A knowledgeable buyer, for example, may prefer to remain indistinguishable from what the seller wrongly perceives to be the class of similarly situated buyers. By blending in with the larger class of contractors, a buyer or a seller may receive a cross-subsidized price because the other side will bargain as if she is dealing with the average member of the class. A knowledgeable party may prefer to remain in this inefficient, but cross-subsidized, contractual pool rather than move to an efficient, but unsubsidized, pool. If contracting around the default sufficiently reduces this cross-subsidization, the share-of-the-pie effect can exceed the size-of-the-pie effect because the informed party's share of the default pie was in a sense being artificially cross-subsidized by other members of the contractual class. Under this scenario, withholding information appears as a kind of rent-seeking[59] in which the informed party foregoes the additional value attending the revealed information to get a larger piece of the contractual pie.[60]

58. If, under a given set of default rules, a seller wants to sell a sweater that she values at $50 to a buyer who values it at $150, then without contracting around any of the defaults the parties' agreement will create $100 of value. The total gain from contracting, in other words, will be $100. The parties will split this gain in value between themselves by bargaining for a price between $50 and $150. Suppose, however, that the buyer (and only the buyer) has information that would make the sweater worth $200 to him if the seller would take on a duty that is outside of the default provisions and that would cost the seller $10. The total gains from this non-default exchange would be $140 ($200 - $50 - $10). How could the buyer lose by revealing information that increased the size of the pie by $40? If the parties accept the default provisions and negotiate a $100 price (implying that each party receives a $50 share of the total gains), how can it be that revealing the value-enhancing information—by contracting for the non-default duty—would reduce the buyer's share to less than $50 (implying that the negotiated price would exceed $150 and that the seller's share would exceed $90)?

59. Most broadly, rent-seeking "arises wherever parties have an incentive to expend real resources to capture something of value." V. Goldberg, Readings in the Economics of Contract Law 49 (1989). Strategic withholding represents a species of rent-seeking because the relatively informed party commits the real resources of an inefficient contract to capture the cross-subsidization.

60. An equity-minded court might encourage information revelation to foster an equitable distribution of the gains from contracting, even if doing so reduces those gains.

C. *Penalty Defaults in Action*

1. *Uncompensated Damages in* Hadley v. Baxendale

An example of how a penalty default can restrict rent-seeking behavior can be seen in the venerable case, *Hadley v. Baxendale*.[61] In *Hadley* a miller in Gloucester contracted with a carrier to have a broken crank shaft transported to Greenwich. The shipment was delayed, and the miller sued the carrier for consequential damages of the profits lost while the mill was inoperative. The court, holding that only foreseeable consequential damages should be awarded, reversed a damage award and remanded for a new trial.[62]

The holding in *Hadley* operates as a penalty default. The miller could have informed the carrier of the potential consequential damages and contracted for full damage insurance.[63] The *Hadley* default of denying unforeseeable damages may not be consistent with what fully informed parties would have wanted. The miller's consequential damages were real and the carrier may have been the more efficient bearer of this risk. As a general matter, millers may want carriers to compensate them for consequential damages that carriers can prevent at lower cost.[64] The default can instead be understood as a purposeful inducement to the miller as the more informed party to reveal that information to the carrier. Informing the carrier creates value because if the carrier foresees the loss, he will be able to prevent it more efficiently.[65] At the same time, however, revealing

61. 9 Ex. 341, 156 Eng. Rep. 145 (1854). William Bishop has also discussed how the *Hadley* rule could promote efficient revelation of information. *See* Bishop, *The Contract-Tort Boundary and the Economics of Insurance*, 12 J. LEGAL STUD. 241, 254 (1983); L. Bebchuk & S. Shavell, Information and the Scope of Liability for Unusual Damages from Breach of Contract, (March 1983) (unpublished manuscript on file with authors).

62. *Hadley*, 9 Ex. at 356, 156 Eng. Rep. at 151-52.

63. There is some evidence that the miller in fact attempted to inform the carrier of the probable damages. Thus, it may be difficult for parties to contract around the *Hadley* default. For a discussion of how courts can alter the mutability of a default rule by varying the requirements for contracting around it, see *infra* Section III.

64. The efficient risk-sharing agreement between symmetrically-informed shippers (e.g., the miller in this case) and carriers will depend upon their relative attitudes toward risk, the ability of the carrier to prevent the damages, and the ability of the shipper to mitigate damages in case of breach.

Richard Posner and Richard Epstein argue that in many situations there are actions the shipper could take to reduce consequential damages. *See* R. POSNER, *supra* note 2, at 114-15; Epstein, *Beyond Foreseeability: Consequential Damages in the Law of Contract*, 18 J. LEGAL STUD. 105, 121-25 (1989). In such situations the parties would choose to share consequential damages through appropriate liquidated damage clauses. *See* Cooter, *Unity in Tort, Contract, and Property: The Model of Precaution*, 73 CALIF. L. REV. 1, 15 (1985). In Evra Corp. v. Swiss Bank Corp., 673 F.2d 951, 955-59 (7th Cir. 1982), Judge Posner attempts to determine what insurance arrangement the parties would have contracted for. Epstein prefers a less tailored rule that does not require the courts to analyze the relative abilities of both sides to reduce damages.

We proceed under the assumptions that the miller had no economically practical means of reducing the losses from delay (e.g., keeping a spare crankshaft in inventory would have been too expensive) and that both parties were risk-neutral. Under these assumptions the efficient contract is for the carrier who is the least-cost avoider to bear the costs of delay.

65. This is one lesson from Goetz and Scott's analysis of the anxious alumnus: A bus company driving Dean Smith to the Final Four would probably take more efficient precautions if it were

the information to the carrier will undoubtedly increase the price of shipping. Nonetheless, so long as transaction costs are not prohibitive, a miller with high consequential damages will gain from revealing this information and contracting for greater insurance from the carrier because the carrier is the least-cost avoider.

This is not to say that there could not be an equally efficient market response if *Hadley* had gone the other way. If the default required carriers to compensate for unforeseeable consequential damages, low-damage millers would have the incentive to raise the issue of consequential damages. In a competitive industry, the uninformed carrier, in effect, assumes she is facing an average-damage miller and charges a price accordingly. The market price will reflect the expected cost of insuring high-damage millers. A low-damage miller will want to contract for less-than-average insurance and, therefore, a lower price. But the gains from contracting around the default may be insignificant if the proportion of millers with high damages is small. Furthermore, it may be very difficult for a low-damage miller to determine how much of the price is an implicit insurance premium for millers with higher damages.

Thus, there may be situations in which the low-damage millers fail to contract for the low-insurance/low-price contract. In the resulting equilibrium, carriers may charge a price representing their average cost of serving both high- and low-damage millers and take an average amount of precaution (which will be relatively low if there are relatively few high-damage millers).[66] Richard Posner suggests a similar result: If the damage default changed so that manufacturers of photographic film were liable for unforeseen consequential damages, "[t]he manufacturer of the film will probably take no additional precautions . . . because he cannot identify the films whose loss would be extremely costly, and unless there are many of [the high-damage photographers] it may not pay to take additional precautions on *all* the films he develops."[67] Section II formalizes this discussion of *Hadley* to show that low-damage millers might fail to contract around a default that awarded unforeseeable damages while high-damage millers will contract around the *Hadley* rule.[68]

---

warned of how large Dean Smith's consequential damages would be were he to miss the game. Goetz & Scott, *supra* note 15, at 578.

66. The uninformed parties, the carriers, could simply exclude unforeseeable consequential damages from their standard-form contract (thereby contracting around the default at very low cost), and high-damage millers, if they want insurance, could simply contract around the contract default. In other words, if the legal default rule is inefficient, contracting parties may have ways of supplanting it with a default of their own. (This point can also be made with regard to Posner's story about film development; *see infra* text accompanying note 67.) The limits to this contractual response to the contra-*Hadley* default are discussed *infra* notes 70–71 and text accompanying notes 69–71.

67. R. Posner, *supra* note 2, at 114 (emphasis in original).

68. In the economics literature several articles examine situations in which asymmetric information induces inefficient contracting. *See, e.g.*, Akerlof, *The Market for "Lemons": Quality Uncertainty and the Market Mechanism*, 84 Q.J. Econ. 488 (1970); Myerson, *Mechanism Design by an Informed Principal*, 51 Econometrica 1767 (1983).

It is important to consider another channel for informatio ·elation. The uninformed party, the carrier, may attempt to learn the expected damages of the informed parties, the millers, by offering a menu of insurance contracts.[69] The millers might then be induced to self-select the insurance contract that is optimal for their expected damages.[70] The problem faced by uninformed parties trying to induce information revelation, however, is that in many situations the necessary menu is more complicated than in the common carrier example. Devising a menu that induces information revelation may require a great deal of sophistication by the uninformed party and may entail large transaction costs.[71]

The main lesson to draw from our discussion of *Hadley* is that there may be strategic reasons for parties' choosing not to reveal information. If the default rule awarded all consequential damages, to be sure, the low-damage millers would want to distinguish themselves from the high-damage millers. But the high-damage millers may intentionally choose to withhold information that would make their contracts more efficient. An informed party may not realize the full social value of revealing the information and, hence, her private benefits from revealing may diverge from the social benefits of having the information revealed. As elaborated below, by not distinguishing themselves, informed parties may be able to free-ride on the lower-cost qualities of others and thereby contract at a subsidized price. To counteract this strategic behavior, courts should choose defaults that are different from what the parties would have wanted.

Easterbrook and Fischel have argued that courts should choose defaults that "the parties would have selected with full information and costless contracting."[72] Their standard fittingly tracks the two reasons for contractual incompleteness that we have identified—strategic withholding and transaction costs. In a sense, their standard seeks what the parties would have selected if there were no barriers to contractual completeness.[73] We disagree, however, with their conclusion that courts should choose the default that the parties would have selected with "full information." When

69. *See supra* note 66.

70. This is in fact done by many common carriers. The Federal Express standard contract, for example, limits consequential damages to $100 but permits the shipper to buy greater insurance at stated rates. *See* Epstein, *supra* note 64, at 120.

71. *See, e.g.*, *infra* text accompanying note 81 (consumers trying to ascertain information about dealer's expected lost-profit damages may encounter significant resistance in devising menu that encourages dealers to reveal information). For an example of a menu that would require large transaction costs and sophistication on the part of the uninformed party, see Note, *Imperfect Information, The Pricing Mechanism, and Products Liability*, 88 Colum. L. Rev. 1057 (1988) (suggesting that manufacturers should be required to provide menus of warranties so that consumers can judge quality and safety of products).

72. Easterbrook & Fischel, *supra* note 11, at 20–21.

73. Full information by both parties would eliminate any opportunity for strategically withholding information, and costless contracting obviously eliminates transactions costs as an impediment to complete contracting.

relatively informed parties strategically withhold information, courts, to promote information revelation, should choose a default that the informed party does not want. Imposing ex post what completely informed parties would have contracted for may not result in the ex ante revelation necessary for efficient reliance or precaution. For example, we have shown that in *Hadley* fully informed parties may have wanted the carrier to be fully liable for consequential damages. Yet choosing full liability as the damage default may lead carriers to invest suboptimally in accident prevention. *Hadley* is inconsistent with a full-information, "what the parties would have wanted" standard. Instead, *Hadley* penalizes high-damage millers for withholding information that would allow carriers to take efficient precautions.

2. *Goldberg's Solution to the Lost-Profits Puzzle*

Victor Goldberg's analysis of the lost-volume retail seller[74] comports with our discussion of penalty defaults. Goldberg examines what a retailer's damages should be when a customer breaches a contract to buy. The U.C.C. mandates, and other commentators have suggested, that the retailer should receive the lost profits on the good.[75] Goldberg's own analysis suggests that the lost profits approximate the real loss borne by the retailer. But Goldberg instead proposes that courts deny "recovery for lost profits in the absence of explicit contract language to the contrary."[76] In other words, Goldberg proposes that the default damages be zero.

His rationale parallels our rationale for penalty defaults. The zero-damage default is intended to give retailers an incentive to come forward and contract for a nonrefundable deposit or for a liquidated damages clause. Again, the process of contracting around the default apprises the customer of her potential liability. A sales contract gives the consumer an option either to purchase the product or to pay damages. Goldberg's zero-damage default encourages retailers to inform consumers about the price of exercising the option to breach. Consumers will therefore internalize the cost to the retailer of breach and more efficiently take precautions against breach.[77] Furthermore, the consumer may not know the default rule for breach.[78] If a consumer is unaware that the default rule makes

74. Goldberg, *An Economic Analysis of the Lost-Volume Retail Seller*, 57 S. CAL. L. REV. 283 (1984).

75. *See* U.C.C. § 2-708(2) (1976); Goetz & Scott, *Measuring Sellers' Damages: The Lost-Profits Puzzle*, 31 STAN. L. REV. 323, 323 (1979); Speidel & Clay, *Seller's Recovery of Overhead Under UCC Section 2-708(2): Economic Cost Theory and Contract Remedial Policy*, 57 CORNELL L. REV. 681, 694 (1972).

76. Goldberg, *supra* note 74, at 291.

77. In this situation the uninformed party, the consumer, probably could not offer a menu of contracts to the informed retailer to induce revelation of the markup. *See supra* text accompanying notes 69-71. The information requirements, complexity, and transaction costs of such a scheme would be prohibitive.

78. This is similar to our earlier discussion of what the real estate default rule should be for

her liable for lost profits, the seller will have little incentive to bargain about damages.[79] Consumer liability for lost profits can lead to efficient breach and precaution only if consumers know the amount of their liability. The zero-damages penalty default encourages the retailer to reveal her markup.[80]

Although consumers would value this markup information, retailers still have incentives to withhold it.[81] By revealing their profits, retailers may simultaneously reduce their bargaining power. Even Goldberg's penalty default, therefore, could be too weak to induce information disclosure. Retailers may sometimes prefer to take their chances with zero damages for breach rather than disclose a high markup. If the zero-damage penalty default is insufficient to induce information revelation, a stiffer penalty may be necessary to induce the parties to contract for liquidated damages.[82]

3. *Unilateral Defaults as Penalties: The Perverse Incentives of* Lefkowitz

Some contractual rules establish defaults that individual parties may unilaterally change. Consider, for example, the legal effect of offers. The U.C.C.'s mandate that an offer intends any reasonable form of acceptance is a unilateral default that obtains "unless otherwise unambiguously indicated."[83] Consistent with the preceeding analysis, lawmakers may want to set penalty defaults that encourage offerors to reveal information to offerees. Thus, courts may want to choose the default that the offeror does not want.

In *Lefkowitz v. Great Minneapolis Surplus Store, Inc.*,[84] the Minnesota Supreme Court rejected the plaintiff's claim that the defendant, a retailer, had failed to honor two advertised offers that the plaintiff had accepted.[85] In the first offer the defendant had advertised the sale of three

splitting earnest money between the seller and the broker when a buyer breaches a purchase contract. *See supra* text accompanying notes 54-56.

79. If the seller raises the issue of damages, thereby revealing her markup, consumers can more efficiently take precautions to avoid breach. Since the consumer will learn she is liable for damages, however, she will insist on a lower price for the good.

80. Similarly, the common-law doctrine of construing ambiguities in contracts against the drafter, *see* I. MacNeil, *supra* note 11, at 372, can be viewed as a penalty default. The doctrine is not based on the judgment that the parties would have wanted the anti-drafter provision, but that such a penalty encourages drafters to draft more precise contracts.

81. For a fuller discussion of this point, see Ayres & Miller, *"I'll Sell It To You At Cost": Legal Methods to Promote Honest Retail Markup Disclosure*, 84 Nw. U.L. Rev. (forthcoming 1990) (manuscript on file with authors).

82. It is not necessarily true, however, that retailers will reveal their markups via their choice of liquidated damages. All retailers may uniformly negotiate for minimal liquidated damages that provide no more information than the zero-damage default.

83. U.C.C. § 2-206(1) (1976).

84. 251 Minn. 188, 86 N.W.2d 689 (1957).

85. The court concluded that the newspaper advertisements constituted offers and not merely invitations to make an offer. *Id.* at 192, 86 N.W.2d at 691.

fur coats " 'Worth to $100.00' " for " '$1 Each' "; in the second offer the defendant advertised the sale of one black lapin stole " 'worth $139.50' " for " '$1.00' "[86] The court, following the common-law rule that indefinite contracts are not enforceable, refused to enforce the contract arising out of the first offer but awarded the plaintiff damages for his attempted acceptance of the second.

The court reasoned that the first offer's estimate that the coat was " 'worth to $100' " was too speculative and uncertain to award damages.[87] But in applying the common-law standard that indefinite contracts are unenforceable, the court ignored the likely market response to the non-enforceability default. As argued above, non-enforceability can be viewed as a penalty default that encourages both parties to come forward and fill in the gap;[88] that is, refusing to enforce indefinite contracts drives out indefinite contracts. In *Lefkowitz*, however, the court's refusal to enforce the indefinite *offer* leads to exactly the opposite result.

Ask yourself the simple question: What kind of ad is the Great Minneapolis Surplus Store going to run the week following the court's decision? By lending its imprimatur to the indefinite ad, the court allows retailers to induce inefficient consumer reliance with impunity.[89] The *Lefkowitz* case dramatically illustrates that only by enforcing indefinite offers against the offeror can one drive out indefinite offers.

Lefkowitz was wrongly decided. The defendant's offer was intentionally vague to induce inefficient reliance on the part of the buyer (Lefkowitz incurred the "shoe-leather" costs of traveling to the store). Courts can retain the common law's general reluctance to enforce indefinite contracts so that both parties will have an incentive to make the contracts more definite.[90] But *Lefkowitz* illustrates an exception to this general rule. When the indefiniteness is clearly attributable to one party and induces inefficient reliance from the other party, punitive enforcement may be efficient to drive out inefficient indefinite offers.

D. *Summary*

Penalty defaults stand as stark counter-examples to the proposition that courts should simply choose defaults that the parties would have wanted.[91] Particularly when individual parties have private incentives to withhold

86. *Id.* at 189, 86 N.W.2d at 690.
87. *Id.* at 190, 86 N.W.2d at 690.
88. *See supra* text accompanying notes 49-52.
89. Our argument that consumers will be "suckered" into the store by non-enforceable, indefinite offers assumes that consumers are unable to distinguish between enforceable and unenforceable offers.
90. *See supra* text accompanying note 88.
91. It could be argued that rational contractual parties behind a "veil of ignorance" would want penalty defaults that increase the total gains to contracting. *Cf.* J. RAWLS, A THEORY OF JUSTICE 24-38 (1974) (discussing preferences under utilitarian assumptions of persons behind "veil of ignorance").

information, it may be desirable for the law to give them a nudge. The possibility that efficient defaults will at times be used to reflect what most people want while at other times be used to encourage the revelation of information is analogous to the disparate uses of presumptions in the laws of evidence.[92] In both instances, the law is sometimes chosen to promote the revelation of information.

Finally, having shown that lawmakers will sometimes want to set defaults that encourage one or both parties to reveal information, we now should warn lawmakers that they should sometimes protect the private incentives to become informed. In some instances forcing parties to reveal information will undermine their incentives to obtain the information in the first place.[93] Lawmakers therefore should not impose penalty defaults that have a net effect of reducing the amount of socially useful information. But in some instances, a particular party may need to acquire certain types of information before contracting, so that forcing disclosure would have minimal disincentive effects. For instance, in Goldberg's example of lost-profit damages, retailers naturally knew the profits from a sale. It is hard, therefore, to conceive how forcing retailers to disclose their profits would undermine their private incentives to calculate the profitability of a sale.[94]

---

92. The list of penalty defaults analyzed above is far from exhaustive. For example, the U.C.C. sections which establish implied or default warranties, U.C.C. §§ 2-314 and 2-315, cannot easily be justified as "what the parties would have contracted for." Instead, the defaults, consistent with the foregoing analysis, force sellers to reveal information to consumers about the extent of their coverage. Indeed, one way to identify penalty defaults is to investigate the pervasiveness with which parties contract around them, as is done with the seemingly ubiquitous use of limited warranty disclaimers.

U.C.C. § 2-207 is also inconsistent with "would have wanted" default analysis. This section supplants the common-law mirror-image rule with the default that additional terms in an acceptance that do not materially alter the terms of the offer become part of a contract between merchants. This default cannot be reconciled with a "what the parties would have contracted for" analysis, because there is no reason to think that the merchants would have wanted to include the additional terms of their contract. Instead, the rule places an informational burden on the party with the last clear chance to come forward and notify the other side if the additional terms are objectionable.

Evidentiary presumptions in litigation are sometimes used to reflect a relationship between facts and at other times to place the burden of producing evidence on the party who is more likely to be informed. *See* Allen, *Presumptions in Civil Actions Reconsidered*, 66 Iowa L. Rev. 843, 845 (1981) (suggesting that presumptions are used "to construct rules of decision to avoid factual impasse at trial; to allocate burdens of persuasion; to instruct the jury on the relationship between facts; and to allocate burdens of production").

93. *See* R. Posner, *supra* note 2, at 115; Easterbrook, *Insider Trading, Secret Agents, Evidentiary Privileges, and the Production of Information*, 1981 Sup. Ct. Rev. 309, 359; R. Allen, M. Grady, D. Polsby & M. Yashko, Confidentiality of Legal Affairs (1988) (unpublished manuscript on file with authors); *cf.* Laidlaw v. Organ, 15 U.S. (2 Wheat.) 178 (1817) (permitting relatively informed contracting party to profit by keeping information to himself). Of course, much of patent law is justified as a means of encouraging the private production of information.

94. Anthony Kronman distinguishes "deliberately acquired information" from "casually acquired information." For example, he suggests that if one side to a contract is aware that the other has entered a mistaken bid, the special knowledge of the non-mistaken party "is unlikely to be the fruit of a deliberate search." Requiring disclosure by the knowledgeable party of this casually acquired information will accordingly not undermine incentives to become informed. Kronman, *Mistake, Disclosure, Information, and the Law of Contracts*, 7 J. Legal Stud. 1, 32 (1978) (revealing lost profits from contract can undermine incentives for parties to search for undervalued assets). There may be a tradeoff between inducing efficient search by one party and efficient breach by the other. Retailers do not

II. A General Theory of Default Choice

The prior analysis of *Hadley* can be embedded in a more general model of default choice. To formalize our ideas, we begin by introducing some notation. Let the percentage of millers who had high (unforeseeable) damages be α_H and the percentage of millers who had low (foreseeable) damages be α_L.[95] Let D_H and D_L be the monetary value of damages for the high- and low-damage millers, respectively. The court chooses between two possible defaults: denying or awarding the high, unforeseeable damages. Let the costs of contracting around these defaults be c_H and c_L, where:

c_H = cost of contracting around the *Hadley* default rule that denies awards for unforeseeable consequential damages; and
c_L = cost of contracting around the default rule that awards unforeseeable consequential damages.

We assume that all parties are risk neutral, so the only goal of the insurance aspect of the contract is to induce the carrier to take efficient precaution. As argued above, in a world with full information, both high- and low-damage millers would contract for the carrier to pay for their consequential damages.[96] If the carrier knows the miller's type and bears all damages, she will choose the optimal level of precaution.[97] Let K_H and K_L equal the carrier's optimal investment in precaution for the two types of millers, respectively. Let q_H and q_L equal the probability of damages for each type of miller given the optimal level of precaution for the class.[98]

Before analyzing the likely equilibrium associated with each default, we must say a bit more about the carrier's price. Assume for the moment that the carrier is in a competitive market in which, by definition, there are zero economic profits.[99] Let the competitive price of shipping crankshafts for ***known*** high-damage millers be P_H and for ***known*** low-damage millers be P_L. With this notation, if MC is the marginal cost of shipping with no precaution, then the following equations will hold:

(1) $$P_H = MC + K_H + q_H D_H,$$
(2) $$P_L = MC + K_L + q_L D_L.$$

search for their markup information—in Kronman's terminology it is not "deliberately acquired"—so that information revelation will enhance efficiency.

95. We assume that these are the only types of millers so that $\alpha_H + \alpha_L = 1$. For a similar mathematical model of *Hadley*, see L. Bebchuk & S. Shavell, *supra* note 61.

96. *See supra* text accompanying notes 62-70.

97. We assume that the contract cannot mandate a specific level of precaution because neither the miller nor a court can observe the level of precaution. Otherwise, carriers might sort millers by offering different levels of precaution.

98. Thus, K_H is the level of K that minimizes the expression $K + q(K)D_H$, and K_L is the level of K that minimizes the expression $K + q(K)D_L$, where the function q(K) equals the probability of damages from delay for a given level of precaution, K.

99. Economic profits are the residual earnings after all implicit and opportunity costs are accounted for.

Because of competition, these prices reflect the carrier's marginal cost of shipping, precaution, and expected damages.

What will the market equilibrium look like under the alternative defaults? First consider the *Hadley* low-damage default. Since the carrier is liable only for foreseeable damages, D_L, she will choose a precaution investment of K_L. The probability of damages will therefore be q_L, and the price will be P_L. Now we can ask whether the high-damage millers will contract around the low-damage default for higher insurance. If the high-damage millers fail to contract around the low-damage default, they will pay P_L and, in addition, bear the probability of damage, q_L, multiplied by the uninsured damages $(D_H - D_L)$. Thus, the total expected cost, P_H^{in}, to the high-damage millers if they inefficiently fail to contract around the low-damage default is:

(3) $$P_H^{in} = P_L + q_L(D_H - D_L).$$

But because the carrier invests suboptimally in precaution, the millers' total expected cost in equation (3) must be greater than if the carrier had taken the efficient level of precaution and passed the cost on in the price, P_H:

(4) $$P_H^{in} > P_H.$$ [100]

This difference $(P_H^{in} - P_H)$ represents the inefficiency (f_H) associated with failing to contract for the efficient level of precaution:

(5) $$P_H^{in} - P_H = f_H.$$

"f_H," then, represents the inefficiency cost when high-damage millers fail to contract for greater precaution.[101] High-damage millers effectively pay:

(6) $$P_H^{in} = P_H + f_H$$

when they fail to contract around the *Hadley* low-damage default.

If the high-damage millers contract around this default, they should expect to bear the costs of the increased precaution as reflected in a higher shipping price (P_H rather than P_L) as well as the additional transaction costs of contracting around the default (c_H).[102] This total cost would be:

---

100. From equations (1), (2) and (3):

$$P_H^{in} = P_L + q_L(D_H - D_L) = MC + K_L + q_L D_H, \text{ and}$$
$$P_H = MC + K_H + q_H D_H.$$

So that:

$$P_H^{in} - P_H = K_L + q_L(K_L)D_H - (K_H + q_H(K_H)D_H).$$

Because K_H minimizes $K + q(K)D_H$, *see supra* note 98, $K_L + q_L(K_L)D_H$ must be larger than $K_H + q_H(K_H)D_H$. Therefore, the right side of this equation must be positive, and inequality (4) must hold.

101. From the previous note we can calculate the inefficiency cost:

$$f_H = K_L + q_L D_H - (K_H + q_H D_H) = (q_L - q_H)D_H - (K_H - K_L).$$

This latter expression illustrates that the inefficiency of low precaution derives from the fact that the costs of the higher probability of damage, $(q_L - q_H)D_H$, outweigh the lower costs of precaution, $(K_H - K_L)$.

102. The high-damage millers bear all of these additional transaction and precaution costs because competition will keep the carrier's price at marginal cost.

(7) $$P_H + c_H.$$

Thus, the high-damage millers will contract around the low-damage default if the total cost of failing to contract ($P_H + f_H$) exceeds the total costs of contracting ($P_H + c_H$):

(8) $$P_H + f_H > P_H + c_H,$$

or more simply if:

(9) $$f_H > c_H.$$

High-damage millers will contract around the *Hadley*, low-damage default when the cost of inefficient precaution (f_H) is larger than the cost of contracting around the default (c_H). If the additional costs of contracting around the *Hadley* default are sufficiently small, all high-damage millers will contract for the efficient amount of insurance. The high-damage millers will effectively pay $P_H + c_H$ for shipping, while the low-damage millers will pay P_L.

Now consider the non-*Hadley*, high-damage default.[103] If the percentage of high-risk millers, α_H, is sufficiently small, market competition may produce an equilibrium in which no one contracts around the default and the carriers take only low levels of precaution, K_L.[104] If the carriers cannot distinguish between high- and low-damage millers, competition would cause the shipping price to become:

(10) $$P^* = \alpha_L P_L + \alpha_H P_H^{in}.$$

Since in a competitive market, carriers must charge a price equal to the expected average cost of serving both high- and low-damage millers, P^* represents a weighted average of these costs. The low-damage millers cost the carriers P_L, while the high-damage millers cost the carriers P_H^{in} if the inefficient, low level of precaution is taken.[105]

This will be the equilibrium if neither the high- nor the low-damage millers have an incentive to reveal to the carrier their specific type. We might think that the low-damage millers would have an incentive to come forward and reveal their status in order to receive a lower contract price. But they will do so only if:

(11) $$c_L < P^* - P_L.$$[106]

Contracting around the high-damage default will be profitable only if the savings from the reduced shipping price ($P^* - P_L$) are greater than the

103. We assume that the costs to the court of determining the magnitude of unforeseeable consequential damages—i.e., determining whether a given miller is type H or type L—are negligible.

104. If precaution investment is a continuous choice variable (for example, the length of time spent training carriers how to drive safely), its optimal level will be between K_L and K_H. For small α_H the investment will be close to K_L. If there are discrete choices for the level of precaution (for example, use two or three horses) and α_H is small enough, the optimal investment will be K_L.

105. Substituting equations (2) and (3) into equation (10) yields:

$$P^* = MC + K_L + q_L D_L + \alpha_H q_L (D_H - D_L),$$

which, again substituting equation (2), simplifies to:

$$P^* = P_L + \alpha_H q_L (D_H - D_L).$$

106. From the prior footnote, this inequality can be expressed as:

$$c_L < \alpha_H q_L (D_H - D_L).$$

additional transaction cost, c_L. But from equation (10) we see that the equilibrium price, P*, is a positive function of α_H, the percentage of high-damage millers.[107] If this percentage (α_H) is sufficiently low, the transaction costs (c_L) will keep the low-damage millers from contracting around the high-damage default. Note that this is unlike the low-damage default in which the incentives to contract around the default rule are based on the gains to the high-damage millers and are independent of the percentage of the population that has high damages (α_H).

The high-damage millers will not reveal their true status to the carriers because they would be forced to pay more (P_H - P*) but would gain no additional coverage. The high-damage millers fail to distinguish themselves not because of transaction costs, but because they prefer to withhold this information strategically and to receive the subsidized shipping price.[108] The shipping price is subsidized because transaction costs prevent low-damage millers from contracting around the default. Even though the information is socially valuable because it leads to more efficient precaution and even though this value exceeds the transaction costs, the high-damage millers prefer to remain undistinguished from their low-risk counterparts. The high-damage millers do not mind that carriers take inefficiently low levels of precaution because, like all shippers, high-damage millers are fully insured. The low-damage millers bear the costs of this inefficiency, but are not hurt enough individually to distinguish themselves contractually.

Prior analyses of incomplete contracts have suggested that parties fail to contract around inefficient defaults because of transaction costs.[109] Our analysis is striking because it demonstrates the possibility that parties may fail to contract around defaults for strategic reasons.[110] A relatively informed party may strategically withhold information that would increase the joint gains from trade.[111] Moreover, the example illustrates two extreme forms of default equilibria. The *Hadley*, low-damage default caused all high-damage millers to contract around the rule and thus engendered

107. One could imagine situations in which the costs for low-damage millers of contracting around a high-damage default would be small. For example, the Federal Express standard-form contract limits consequential damages if the sender does not contract for more insurance. *See supra* note 70. Such a standard form would allow low-damage millers to cheaply opt for low-damage protection and consequently a lower price.

108. In other words, even if the costs of contracting for higher precaution were zero, the high-damage millers would not reveal their status.

109. *See supra* note 30.

110. In our simplified model, low-damage millers failed to contract around the pooling equilibrium because of transaction costs. *See supra* inequality (11). In a more general model, however, even without transactions costs the informed cross-subsidizing parties (such as the low-damage millers) may fail to contract around pooling equilibria if in doing so they reveal information which reduces their bargaining power. See K. Spier, *supra* note 29 for a more formal demonstration of why similar strategic concerns can keep contracts from being efficiently state-contingent.

111. This, then, is an example in which the "share-of-the-pie effect" exceeds the "size-of-the-pie" effect. *See supra* text accompanying note 57.

what economists sometimes call a "separating" equilibrium in which different types of contracting parties sort themselves through the competitive process into different groups at different prices. In contrast, the non-*Hadley*, high-damage default created a "pooling" equilibrium in which the high- and low-damage millers failed to distinguish themselves to the carriers.[112]

The tension between "pooling" and "separating" equilibria is crucial in choosing the efficient default. Separating equilibria entail the additional transaction costs of causing some parties to contract around the rule; pooling equilibria entail the costs of inefficient reliance or precaution for failing to contract around the rule.[113] In the *Hadley* example the transaction cost of the high-damage millers' contracting around the low-damage default is $\alpha_H c_H$. This is the cost of separating equilibria. The cost of the high-damage default stems from the inefficiently low precaution that carriers take with regard to the high-damage millers, $\alpha_H f_H$. This is the cost of pooling equilibria. If inequality (9) holds (i.e., if $f_H > c_H$), then the costs of pooling exceed the costs of separating, and the *Hadley* default is efficient even though it is not what the high-damage millers would have wanted.

Although the prior section described the *Hadley* rule as a penalty default, it can be alternatively conceived as an untailored default rule that provides what the majority of the parties would want (since under our assumptions, $\alpha_L > \alpha_H$). This reconception suggests that untailored defaults that apply a single rule to different types of contracting parties act as penalty defaults with regard to those parties who disfavor them. Because a majority of the millers had low damages ($\alpha_L > \alpha_H$) and would only want to contract for low damages, one might deduce that the untailored *Hadley* rule is efficient because a majority of the parties prefers it.

But the commonly accepted notion that untailored defaults should be set at what the majority of parties wants does not hold in a more general model of default choice in which the pooling and separating equilibria are not extreme. To extend the *Hadley* model, consider the choice between

112. This analysis is consonant with the economics of insurance literature. *See, e.g.*, Rothschild & Stiglitz, *Equilibrium in Competitive Insurance Markets: An Essay on the Economics of Imperfect Information*, 90 Q.J. ECON. 629, 634–37 (1976) (discussing "separating" and "pooling" equilibria). Low-risk insureds will have incentives to drop out of (or separate from) pools in which they cross-subsidize the premiums of high-risk insureds. *See generally* Priest, *The Current Insurance Crisis and Modern Tort Law*, 96 YALE L.J. 1521 (1987) (arguing that this sort of separation has occurred in third-party insurance pools and is largely responsible for recent "insurance crisis").

113. In this model all millers continue to ship crankshafts regardless of the default rule. If, however, the cross-subsidization of the non-*Hadley* default reduced the consumption of the low-damage millers (who must pay $P^* - P_L$ more) or increased the consumption of the high-damage millers (who have to pay $P_H - P^*$ less), then the pooling equilibria would additionally entail the dead-weight losses associated with inefficient amounts of contracting. *See* Note, *Contract Damages and Cross-Subsidization*, 61 S. CAL. L. REV. 1125 (1988).

two defaults: one and two. As above, there will be a certain percentage of the population of contracting parties for which each default would be preferred, α_1 and α_2, respectively.[114] Again, there will be costs of contracting around each default, c_1 and c_2: let c_1 be the cost of contracting around default two to the default one rule (and define c_2 analogously). The *Hadley* model showed that failing to contract around a default could result in inefficient levels of precaution.[115] Accordingly, let f_1 equal the inefficiency generated if a type one contracting party fails to contract for the type one rule (and analogously define f_2). Most important, in a more general model there may be intermediate amounts of pooling and separation for the different defaults. Accordingly, let:

β_1 = the percentage of type one contracting parties who in equilibrium would actually contract around default two, and
β_2 = the percentage of type two contracting parties who in equilibrium would actually contract around default one.

Thus, while α_1 percent of the contracting parties prefer default one, it is possible that if default two is the rule, a smaller percent ($\beta_1 < \alpha_1$) would contract around it for the efficient amount of precaution. And analogously, some type two contracting parties might not contract around default one if it is the rule ($\beta_2 < \alpha_2$).[116]

The completeness of the *Hadley* pooling equilibrium implies that $\beta_H = \alpha_H$, while the completeness of the non-*Hadley* separating equilibrium implies that $\beta_L = 0$. These extreme results turn on the homogeneity of, for example, f_H and c_H. More generally, if high-damage millers have heterogeneous costs of contracting or of failing to contract, then different defaults may engender intermediate forms of pooling and separating.

In this more general model, each default can engender both costs of contracting and costs of failing to contract. For example, the costs of default one will be:

$$c_2\beta_2 + f_2(\alpha_2 - \beta_2),$$

which equal the transaction costs of those type two contractors who contract around default one ($c_2\beta_2$) and the inefficient reliance or precaution costs for those type two parties who fail to contract around default one ($f_2(\alpha_2 - \beta_2)$). Default one will be optimal only if:

$$c_1\beta_1 + f_1(\alpha_1 - \beta_1) > c_2\beta_2 + f_2(\alpha_2 - \beta_2). \quad (12)$$

This expression establishes the optimal condition for choosing between two untailored defaults. In equilibrium each default may cause a portion of the population to incur the expense of contracting around the default

114. $\alpha_1 + \alpha_2 = 1$.
115. *See supra* text accompanying note 100.
116. Because we assume that parties would never bargain for a less efficient contract, α_1 and α_2 will always be greater than or equal to β_1 and β_2 respectively.

($c_i\beta_i$), and each rule may create costs ($f_i(\alpha_i - \beta_i)$) for those parties that inefficiently fail to contract around it. The efficient default minimizes the sum of these two costs, which, as stated before, are themselves the costs of separation and pooling, respectively:

$$\min_{i=1,2} [c_i\beta_i + f_i(\alpha_i - \beta_i)].$$

In contrast to the majoritarian analysis, condition (12) does not imply that efficiency-minded lawmakers should choose the default rule that most of the parties would want. In other words, condition (12) does not imply that:

$$\alpha_1 > \alpha_2.$$

Indeed, exploiting the fact that $\alpha_2 = 1 - \alpha_1$,[117] one can rearrange condition (12) in terms of α_1. Default one will be efficient if and only if:

$$(13) \qquad \alpha_1 > \frac{f_2 + \beta_2(c_2 - f_2) - \beta_1(c_1 - f_1)}{f_1 + f_2}.$$

The right-hand side of this cumbersome inequality implicitly defines a critical value of α_1^* for choosing between defaults one and two. When α_1 is less than α_1^*, default two is efficient; when α_1 is greater than α_1^*, default one is efficient.

The crude majoritarian criterion ($\alpha_1^* = ½$) only emerges from highly constrained assumptions about β_1, β_2, c_1, c_2, f_1, and f_2. For example, the majoritarian default analysis in the existing contracts literature seems to derive from two divergent sets of assumptions about these crucial variables.[118] One set of majoritarians seems to assume that transaction costs are small enough that no one fails to contract around inefficient defaults ($\alpha_1 = \beta_1$ and $\alpha_2 = \beta_2$) and that the costs of contracting around each default are the same ($c_1 = c_2$).[119] Under these assumptions, the second set of terms in condition (12) drop out of the analysis ($f_i(\alpha_i - \beta_i) = 0$), so that the costs of failing to contract are irrelevant. Inequality (13) can then be simplified to:

$$\alpha_1 > c_2/(c_1 + c_2) = ½,$$

which implies the majoritarian result that default one should be chosen only if a majority of the contracting parties prefers it.

A second set of majoritarians seems to assume that the transaction costs of contracting around a default are so great that no parties will contract around inefficient defaults ($\beta_1 = \beta_2 = 0$) and that the inefficiencies of failing to contract for the right rule are the same ($f_1 = f_2$). Under these assumptions the first terms of condition (12) drop out of the analysis ($c_i\beta_i = 0$), so that inequality (13) can be simplified to:

$$\alpha_1 > f_2/(f_1 + f_2) = ½,$$

117. *See supra* note 114.
118. *See* Craswell, *supra* note 22, at 632-39 (discussing two approaches).
119. *Id.* at 633.

which again implies that default one will be efficient only if a majority prefers it. Majoritarians are forced to make highly restrictive (and sometimes contradictory) assumptions to produce their desired rule. Most fundamentally, the majoritarian analysis errs by looking at only one of the relevant variables, α.

As an alternative, some commentators have suggested that courts fill gaps with the provisions that most parties bargain for in actual contracts.[120] Some academics have labelled this style of gap-filling as "mimicking-the-market."[121] The "mimic-the-market" approach to default rules ignores the fact that the type of parties who contract around a given rule depends upon the rule itself. Parties who dislike a given default rule will contract around it; if we change the default rule to mimic the contracts these parties write, other types of parties may contract around the new default back to the original rule. This process could cycle forever.[122] Set-

120. *See* Epstein, *In Defense of the Contract at Will*, 51 U. Chi. L. Rev. 947, 951 (1984) (a default rule "is normally chosen because it reflects the dominant practice in a given class of cases and because that practice is itself regarded as making good sense for the standard transactions it governs."). Epstein argues that the default for consequential damages should be limited because this "is what the express contracts have typically provided." Epstein, *supra* note 64, at 118. Frank Easterbrook orally suggested a similar standard for choosing corporate default rules at the Columbia conference. *See supra* note 13.

The NLRB has looked at actual collective bargaining agreements in deciding whether there should be a default limiting management's right to transfer work. *See* Milwaukee II, 268 N.L.R.B. Dec. (CCH) 601, 603 (1984) (quoting Ozark Trailers, Inc., 161 N.L.R.B. Dec. (CCH) 561, 570 (1966) (citing M. Chandler, Management Rights and Union Interests 217 (1964))). The Supreme Court has at times looked to actual contracting practices to determine whether a particular issue should be a mandatory subject of bargaining. *See, e.g.*, First Nat'l Maintenance Corp. v. NLRB, 452 U.S. 666, 684 (1981); *see also* Alchian, *Decision Sharing and Expropriable Specific Quasi-Rents: A Theory of* First National Maintenance Corporation v. NLRB, 1 Sup. Ct. Econ. Rev. 235 (1982) (suggesting how "decision sharing" default should be set); Wachter & Cohen, *The Law and Economics of Collective Bargaining: An Introduction and Application to the Problems of Subcontracting, Partial Closure, and Relocation*, 136 U. Pa. L. Rev. 1349, 1364–77 (1988) (suggesting how "default entitlements" in labor market should be set). However, in Lewis v. Benedict Coal Corp., 361 U.S. 459 (1960), discussed *supra* note 21, the Court eschewed any empirical analysis of the private reaction to a particular contract.

121. *See* Schwab, *Collective Bargaining and the Coase Theorem*, 72 Cornell L. Rev. 245, 286–87 (1987).

122. This is not to say that the mimic-the-market rule would never be desirable. If, for instance, filling a particular type of contractual gap is an issue of first impression, it may be reasonable for a court to look at existing contracts as a guide to what the parties would have wanted. If parties were unaware of the default rule when they were contracting, the cycling problem would not arise. If no well-established default exists, many contracting parties may explicitly contract for what they want in order to avoid the penalty of ex post uncertainty. In this case existing contracts provide evidence for what the parties would have done, so mimicking the market may be justified. For example, Epstein uses this approach to argue that one can ascertain the efficient form for workers' compensation legislation by observing the contractual insurance provisions that existed prior to legislation. Epstein, *supra* note 64, at 118–19.

Mimicking the market may also make sense when parties have failed to record any contract. For example, in devising their estates, many parties may not go to the trouble of writing a will, but those that do may restate even well-established intestacy defaults. Thus, looking at actual wills can give some guide to what the general populace wants. But even this argument fails if the contracting sample misrepresents the intestate class. If the reason certain parties fail to contract is related to the substantive provision that those parties want, then the inference between actual and hypothetical contracts is attenuated. For example, if only upper-class people can afford to write wills, then an upper-class preference for children over parents may not be relevant in determining the intestate preferences of

ting defaults that mimic the market therefore will not assure efficiency. A slightly more sophisticated version of mimicking the market would set the default at what most people would contract around another default for. This approach would focus solely on the β's. For example, if a larger percentage of parties were willing to contract around the first default than the second default ($\beta_2 > \beta_1$), then rule two would be chosen as the default. But maximizing the β's suffers the same flaw as maximizing the α's—neither choice rule conforms with the efficiency criterion in inequality (12).[123]

Implementing a complete theory of default choice requires attention to:

1) what the parties want (the α's),

2) whether they will get it (the β's), and

3) the costs associated with getting it (the c's) or not getting it (the f's).

It is especially important that lawmakers ascertain the degree of separating and pooling that each default engenders. For in determining the equilibrium levels of the β associated with each default, the court must estimate the importance of transactional and strategic barriers to contracting around particular default rules, as well as understand the costs associated with failing to strike the efficient contract.

We have shown that at times the efficient default will be one that a majority of contracting parties disfavors. As the number of different types of preferred contracts (and consequently the number of possible defaults) increases, any untailored default is likely to be disfavored by the majority of contractors.[124] Untailored defaults act as penalty defaults with regard to

---

the lower class.

123. Still another partial and inefficient criterion for default choice would attempt to minimize the number of people who failed to contract to their efficient rule. In the model's terminology, this would be equivalent to minimizing $\alpha_i - \beta_i$.

124. The results of this dichotomous model can be extended to a situation in which courts are choosing among more than two default alternatives. In many situations, there will be more than two possible default choices from which the lawmaker may choose. Consider a class of contracts in which tailoring is prohibitively expensive, so that the lawmaker must choose among N (N > 2) possible defaults. Assume that there are different classes of contracting parties for which different rules would be efficient. For example, heterogeneity across buyer risk preferences could lead to a range of optimal risk-sharing rules for different contracts. We assume that when parties contract around a default, they contract for the rule that is efficient for their class. *But see* Schwab, *supra* note 1, at 251 (students sometimes contracted around default to less efficient outcome). A contracting party will be called a type j contracting party if default rule j would be efficient for it. Let:

α_i = the percent of contracting parties who want default i (where $\Sigma_i \alpha_i = 1$);

β_{ij} = the percent of type j contracting parties who will contract around default i (where $\beta_{ii} = 0$);

c_{ij} = the cost for type j parties of contracting around default i; and

f_{ij} = the cost for type j parties of failing to contract around default i (where $f_{ii} = 0$).

Extending the earlier model, we can say that the cost of any default i will be:

$$\sum_{j=1,N} [c_{ij}\beta_{ij} + f_{ij}(\alpha_j - \beta_{ij})].$$

which represents for all contracting types the total costs of contracting around default i or of failing to contract around it. A lawmaker choosing the least-cost default will accordingly want to minimize:

$$\min_{i=1,N} \left\{ \sum_{j=1,N} [c_{ij}\beta_{ij} + f_{ij}(\alpha_j - \beta_{ij})] \right\}.$$

As in the dichotomous model, a penalty default may be the least costly. Even a default x that no one wants, $\alpha_x = 0$, may be optimal if most people contract around the default ($\beta_{xj} \sim \alpha_x$, for all j), and

the classes of contracting parties that disfavor them. As the diversity of contracting types grows, any untailored defaults start to resemble the types of penalty defaults we described in Section I.[125] As the number of possible defaults expands, courts must choose between a penalty default that is efficient within the class of untailored defaults or a tailored default that requires the court to ascertain what individual parties would have wanted. We have analyzed how courts should find the optimal rule within the class of untailored defaults; we now examine whether a tailored default is superior to an untailored default.

With a tailored default the court attempts to determine the default for which the particular parties would have contracted. A major cost of tailored defaults, then, is the cost of this ex post determination.[126] Instead of having the different types of parties separating themselves into different contractual groups ex ante, the court attempts the separation ex post. Instead of contracting costs, the costs of ex post tailoring are the costs of distinguishing between types of contractual parties, where each type would have contracted for a different rule.

These costs of determining what the particular parties would have contracted for can be significant. For example, in *Jordan v. Duff & Phelps, Inc.*,[127] two leading law-and-economics practitioners, Judges Easterbrook and Posner, disagreed about what the particular parties would have wanted. In *Jordan* the Seventh Circuit was called on to fill a gap in a shareholder/employment agreement. The court needed to determine whether the defendant corporation had a duty to disclose material information about a merger to an employee who was about to quit and who was, according to the agreement, thereby required to sell his shares. Predictably, both judges agreed that contractual gaps should be filled with terms that the parties would have wanted.[128]

The judges, however, strongly disagreed about what these terms would have been. Judge Easterbrook, authoring the majority opinion, found it "unwarranted to say that the implicit understanding between Jordan and Duff & Phelps should be treated as if it had such a no-duty clause; we are

---

the costs of contracting around it are low ($C_{xj} \approx 0$, for all j).

For example, consider our earlier discussion of the zero-quantity default, *supra* text accompanying notes 42-46. The default choice is non-dichotomous. Numerous quantities could be chosen as the default. Although contracting parties would not contract to exchange zero quantity ($x_0 = 0$), most people contract around this default, and the costs of contracting around it are low.

125. Any untailored quantity default would be, except for the smallest proportion of transactions, a penalty default. For example, only the smallest percentage of contracting parties would actually want a default quantity of some randomly chosen number such as, say, 39 or 2003.

126. Richard Epstein criticizes Judge Posner's analysis in EVRA Corp. v. Swiss Bank Corp., 673 F.2d 951, 954 (7th Cir. 1982), because contributory negligence requires costly ex post tailoring by courts. Epstein, *supra* note 64, at 134.

127. 815 F.2d 429 (7th Cir. 1987).

128. *Id.* at 436; *id.* at 446-47 (Posner, J., dissenting).

not confident that this is the clause firms and their employees regularly would prefer."[129]

Judge Posner, in dissent, argued that the parties would have waived any duty of disclosure because waiving such a duty would have "aligned their respective self-interests better than the legal protection that the court devises today."[130] This disagreement between sophisticated jurists suggests that tailoring costs include not only the out-of-pocket litigation expenses but also the potential costs of judicial error. Indeed, if the expected costs of ex post tailoring are sufficiently large, even a tailored rule may give the parties an incentive to contract explicitly ex ante. Ex post tailoring may be more expensive to contracting parties than ex ante contracting. Even if judicial tailoring is accomplished without error, parties may prefer to contract for the same terms that the courts would provide at a higher cost ex post.[131]

But these costs of distinguishing between different types of parties are not the only costs of tailored rules. Because courts do their tailoring after the fact, tailored rules can actually exacerbate the inefficiency of strategic incompleteness. With a tailored rule the relatively informed party—assured that the court will provide the terms that fully-informed parties would want—may have no incentive to reveal her private information to the other party. For example, in our *Hadley* model the high-damage rule was a tailored default that gave each contracting type what they would have contracted for were they fully informed—damages of D_H or D_L, depending on the miller's type. Yet, we have shown conditions under which this tailored high-damage default gives rise to the costs of inefficient reliance or precaution.[132] By not explicitly contracting for damages ex ante, the carrier cannot know if the miller is high-damage or low-damage and therefore may not choose the correct level of precaution. Even if it is costless ex post for the court to determine exactly what two specific parties would have agreed to ex ante, tailored defaults may not be optimal.

In sum, finding the efficient default can involve a complicated inquiry. Knowledgeable parties can leave holes in contracts for strategic reasons—they might prefer to remain in an undifferentiated pool than pay their full freight in an efficient but unsubsidized equilibrium. Efficiency-minded lawmakers must therefore be attuned to the sources of contractual incompleteness and to the attendant costs of pooling and separating associated with their default choice.

129. *Id.* at 436.

130. *Id.* at 448 (Posner, J., dissenting).

131. This point inverts Posner's observation that it may sometimes be "cheaper for the court to 'draft' the contractual term necessary to deal with the contingency if and when it occurs." R. POSNER, *supra* note 2, at 82.

132. *See supra* text accompanying notes 95-103.

III. A Theory of Gaps

The preceding sections have attempted to develop a theory for choosing default rules. But before implementing any default standard, courts need to establish, as a logically prior matter, rules for deciding when a contract is incomplete.[133] Indeed, the litigants in many cases will argue not only about how the gap should be filled but also about whether there is a gap at all.[134]

For example, returning again to *Jordan v. Duff & Phelps*,[135] Judges Easterbrook and Posner disagree not only on how to fill a gap in the employment-stockholding contract but also, and more fundamentally, on whether there was a gap to be filled.[136] Easterbrook's majority opinion concludes that although the fiduciary duty to disclose material information could be contracted around, the parties' agreement did not sufficiently negate this duty: "[T]he possibility that a firm could negotiate around the fiduciary duty does not assist Duff & Phelps; it did not obtain such an agreement, express or implied."[137] Easterbrook's decision then proceeds to fill this disclosure gap with the fiduciary duty default. Posner, in dissent, finds that the "stockholder agreement that defined [the employee's] rights as a shareholder 'with greater specificity' "[138] sufficiently contracted around any default fiduciary duty: "The arrangement that resulted (call it 'shareholder at will') is incompatible with an inference that Duff and Phelps undertook to keep him abreast of developments affecting the value of the firm."[139] In *Jordan*, then, two prominent legal economists disagreed not only about how the gap should be filled but also about what constitutes a gap.

---

133. At an even more basic level, courts will not be able to determine whether a contract has gaps without a prior theory of contract formation. In general, courts will need to determine:
1) whether the parties have formed a contract,
2) whether the contract has gaps, and
3) how the gaps should be filled.

We implicitly assumed in Sections I and II that there were sufficient objective indicia of the parties' meeting of the minds to infer contractual formation. *See* Barnett, *A Consent Theory of Contract*, 86 Colum. L. Rev. 269 (1986) (discussing competing theories of contractual formation). This Section's focus on legal formalities should inform courts' theories of contractual formation and contractual gaps.

134. This point is also made in M. Freed & D. Polsby, Hard Cases Make Bad Law: Employment at Will at the Edge (1988) (unpublished manuscript on file with authors). For example, Freed and Polsby criticize Richard Epstein's analysis, *see* Epstein, *supra* note 120, at 980, that the court supplied the correct "gap-filling" default in Coleman v. Graybar Elec. Co., 195 F.2d 374 (5th Cir. 1952), an employment at will/wrongful termination case: "The contract in *Graybar* was anything but silent . . . . Such an agreement could hardly 'provide otherwise' with more clarity, short of specifically reserving the employer's right to act in bad faith." M. Freed & D. Polsby, *supra*, at 2.

135. 815 F.2d 429 (7th Cir. 1987); *see supra* text accompanying notes 127-31.

136. Judge Posner argued in the alternative. Although he concluded that the contract did not have a gap, *id.* at 449 (Posner, J., dissenting) ("the parties were not silent"), he alternatively found that even if there were a gap, it should be filled differently than the way Easterbrook recommended. *See supra* text accompanying note 129.

137. 815 F.2d at 436.

138. *Id.* at 447 (Posner, J., dissenting) (quoting majority).

139. *Id.*

This question of when a contract is incomplete is identical to the question of what is sufficient to contract around a default. A court's holding that the parties' attempt to contract around a given default is insufficient is identical to a holding that there is still a gap in the contract. By answering one question, the courts necessarily answer the other. Courts need to develop a theory of gaps before they can address how best to fill them.

If the academy has been remiss in developing a theory of default choice, then to an even greater degree it has failed to address what the necessary and sufficient conditions for contracting around defaults should be. In determining these conditions, courts are determining the costs of contracting around a given default.[140] The received wisdom that transaction costs are responsible for contractual incompleteness implicitly suggests that lawmakers should minimize the costs of contracting around defaults so that if any contracting parties do not like the off-the-rack standard, they can inexpensively tailor their corporate or contractual structure to suit themselves.

But legal rules evince a greater diversity than this simple theory suggests.[141] Parties wishing to contract around both statutory and common-law defaults will encounter varying degrees of difficulty. For example, many sections of the U.C.C. establish defaults that are in force "unless otherwise agreed,"[142] but § 2-206 provides that contractual offers shall be construed as inviting any reasonable manner of acceptance "[u]nless otherwise *unambiguously* indicated,"[143] and the Official Comment punctuates this point by saying that this default obtains "unless the offeror has made *quite* clear that it will not be acceptable."[144]

Similarly, in the corporate context the common law of promoter liability requires extraordinary efforts to negate the joint and several liability default. For example, in *Stanley J. How & Assocs. v. Boss*,[145] a promoter was held liable under a contract even though he signed the pre-incorporation agreement: "By: Edwin A. Boss, Agent for a Minnesota Corporation to be formed, who will be the Obligor."[146] The court held that "[w]hile the agreement was not completely clear, the words 'who will be the obligor' are not enough to offset the rule that the person signing for the nonexistent corporation is normally to be personally liable."[147] Con-

140. These costs were represented as c_1 in the early model of default choice. *See supra* Section II.

141. *But see* Black, *supra* note 1 (arguing that corporate default rules are trivial). Black's arguments imply that corporate formalities do not impede corporations from establishing tailored forms of corporate governance. But the costs of contracting around some "strong" defaults (that is, fulfilling certain corporate formalities) are likely to give some formalities a more substantive or nontrivial nature. *See, e.g., infra* notes 148–50.

142. *See, e.g.*, U.C.C. § 2-303 (1976).

143. U.C.C. § 2-206 (1976) (emphasis added).

144. *Id.* at Official Comment 1 (emphasis added).

145. 222 F. Supp. 936 (S.D. Iowa 1963).

146. *Id.* at 939.

147. *Id.* at 942. The holding is consistent with the common-law doctrine of construing contractual

tracting around corporate statutes especially exhibits different degrees of difficulty. For example, certain default rules of corporate governance can be changed only in the articles of incorporation, while others can be overcome through less costly bylaw amendments.[148]

At times even seemingly immutable rules can be circumvented at a cost. To be sure, some methods of contracting around legal rules are better described as examples of abuse of the law.[149] But lawmakers at other times seem to allow ostensibly immutable rules to be negated if the private parties structure the transaction properly. For example, the seemingly immutable rule that limited partnerships must have at least one general partner (that is, one partner who retains unlimited personal liability) can be contractually negated in jurisdictions that allow corporate persons to serve as the sole general partner.[150]

A. Peevyhouse *and the Default-Immutable Spectrum*

As the cost of contracting around a default rule becomes extremely large, the default starts to look like an immutable rule.[151] The Oklahoma Supreme Court's classic decision in *Peevyhouse v. Garland Coal & Mining Co.*[152] exemplifies this insight. The Peevyhouses leased their land contemplating that it would be strip-mined. The contract included specific covenants that Garland would restore the land at the end of the lease

ambiguities against the drafter. *See supra* note 82.

148. Defaults that may be contracted around only in the articles of incorporation include: Board of directors may be dispensed with entirely in limited circumstances or its functions may be restricted, REVISED MODEL BUSINESS CORP. ACT ANN. § 8.01 (1984); power to compensate directors may be restricted or eliminated, REVISED MODEL BUSINESS CORP. ACT ANN. § 8.11 (1984); special voting groups of shareholders may be authorized, REVISED MODEL BUSINESS CORP. ACT ANN. § 7.25 (1987); and classes of shares may be given more or less than one vote per share, REVISED MODEL BUSINESS CORP. ACT ANN. § 7.21 (1987). Defaults that may be contracted around in either the articles of incorporation or the bylaws include: Number of directors may be fixed or changed within limits, REVISED MODEL BUSINESS CORP. ACT ANN. § 8.03 (1987); qualifications for directors may be prescribed, REVISED MODEL BUSINESS CORP. ACT ANN. § 8.02 (1987); shares may be issued without certificates, REVISED MODEL BUSINESS CORP. ACT ANN. § 6.26 (1987); power of board of directors to amend bylaws may be restricted, REVISED MODEL BUSINESS CORP. ACT ANN. §§ 10.20, 10.22 (1987). *See* REVISED MODEL BUSINESS CORP. ACT ANN. § 2.02 official comment.

149. The field of tax abounds with instances in which clever citizens abusively attempt to contract around tax liabilities in ways that Congress did not foresee or intend. *See, e.g.*, Heintz v. Comm'r, 25 T.C. 132 (1955) (stockholder of merging corporation contractually abrogates seemingly immutable rule for capital gains realization rules); Zuckman v. United States, 524 F.2d 729 (Ct. Cl. 1975) (stockholders of corporation contractually abrogate seemingly immutable rules to carry through losses).

150. In Delaney v. Fidelity Lease Ltd., 526 S.W.2d 543 (Tex. 1975), the Texas Supreme Court voided this contractual attempt to circumvent the general-partner personal-liability rule. The Texas legislature, however, amended its corporations statute to permit a corporation "[t]o be an organizer, partner, member, associate, or manager of any partnership. . . ." TEX. BUS. CORP. ACT ANN. art. 2.02A(18) (Vernon 1989).

151. Conversely, if we admit the possibility of lobbying to change current law, even immutable rules are really defaults where the costs of lobbying to change them are prohibitively expensive. This point was made by Joseph Grundfest at the Columbia conference on December 9-10, 1988, *supra* note 13.

152. 382 P.2d 109 (Okla. 1962), *cert. denied*, 375 U.S. 906 (1963).

period. As it turned out, the restoration "would involve the moving of many thousands of cubic yards of dirt, at a cost estimated by expert witnesses at about $29,000.00."[153] Garland introduced evidence that such restoration would increase the market value of the land by only $300.[154] The court was asked to choose the proper measure of damages: cost of performance ($29,000) or diminution in value ($300).

The majority opinion, which limited the Peevyhouses' damages to diminution in value, clearly claimed that the court's ruling could be contracted around.

> It should be noted that the rule as stated does not interfere with the property owner's right to "do what he will with his own," or his right, if he chooses, to contract for "improvements" which will actually have the effect of reducing his property's value. Where such result is in fact contemplated by the parties, and is a main or principal purpose of those contracting, it would seem that the measure of damages for breach would ordinarily be the cost of performance.[155]

This passage seems to emphasize that, notwithstanding the holding in this particular case, parties retain the right to contract around the diminution-in-value default standard.

The dissenting opinion, however, points to the specific provisions of the contract that had been added to the usual covenants of the defendant's coal mining leases and that seemed to place the duty of restoration on the defendant. In the face of these contractual provisions, the reader of *Peevyhouse* is left with two alternative interpretations. Either the majority opinion is 1) disingenuously creating an immutable rule; or 2) creating a "strong" default rule (that the Peevyhouses' amendments did not sufficiently override).[156] The most straightforward way to distinguish between these competing interpretations is to ask what extra words the Peevyhouses could have added to the contract to "reverse" the majority's

153. *Id.* at 111.

154. Many commentators have criticized the majority's opinion for ignoring the subjective (non-market) value of the land to the Peevyhouses. *See, e.g.*, Muris, *Cost of Completion or Diminution in Market Value: The Relevance of Subjective Value*, 12 J. LEGAL STUD. 379 (1983) (arguing that courts must recognize subjective value to fill compensatory goal of contract law). However, the courts' reliance on market value is probably more a function of the plaintiffs' trial strategy. The Peevyhouses, in trying to focus the jury's attention on cost of performance, may have strategically decided not to introduce any evidence of subjective value. And the court's opinion seems to indicate that evidence of subjective value should be included in diminution damages: "After a careful search of the record, we have found no evidence of a higher figure [than the $300 market diminution], and plaintiffs do not argue in their briefs that a greater diminution in value was sustained." *Peevyhouse*, 382 P.2d at 114. One would predict that in subsequent litigation plaintiffs would begin to introduce subjective value evidence that would be included in diminution damages.

155. *Peevyhouse*, 382 P.2d at 114 (citations omitted).

156. The majority's own use of the word "ordinarily" in the last quoted sentence seems to add some support for the immutability interpretation. After all, is the court suggesting that even if the parties explicitly attempt to contract for cost of performance, there still may be "extraordinary" situations in which the diminution in value standard will apply?

default. If the majority is really doing what it says, we should be able to write such a contract. If we cannot confidently determine what such a contract would need to say, the alternative hypothesis—that *Peevyhouse* really is creating an immutable rule—becomes more compelling.[157]

While the *Peevyhouse* opinion has been criticized for reaching the wrong result,[158] this analysis suggests that the majority also erred by not more clearly establishing what words would be sufficient to contract for the cost of performance damages. Even though the decision (rightly or wrongly) resolved uncertainty about what the default damages would be, it did little to resolve the uncertainty about how one could contract around this default. Even prospective parties who had read *Peevyhouse* and had known that it "does not interfere with the property owner's right to 'do what he will with his own' "[159] would still face considerable uncertainty about how to exercise that right.

This discussion suggests that in many instances decisions should do more than merely decide what the efficient default should be; they should establish "safeharbors" of contractual language that will be sufficient to reach other contractual outcomes.[160] As the *Peevyhouse* case illustrates, by giving prospective parties examples of explicit language, courts can dramatically reduce the uncertainty and costs of contracting around the specific default.[161]

B. *Determining the Efficient Level of Legal Formalities*

There can be good economic reasons for "strong" defaults in which the courts intentionally increase the procedural costs to parties of contracting around the default. These reasons parallel the rationales given in one of the first intuitively economic analyses of contract law, Lon Fuller's classic, *Consideration and Form*.[162] Fuller suggested that legal formalities serve

157. Tracking the majority's language, we suggest that prospective parties attempting to overcome the diminution-in-value standard include the following covenant:

> The parties specifically intend and contemplate that the lessee shall restore the land, even if the costs of performance are grossly disproportionate to the diminution in value from failing to restore the land. This is a main and principal purpose of the lease. In writing this provision, we are explicitly contracting around the holding of *Peevyhouse v. Garland Coal*.

If this provision were not sufficient, the *Peevyhouse* rule would, in fact, be immutable.

158. *See, e.g.*, Birmingham, *Damage Measures and Economic Rationality: The Geometry of Contract Law*, 1969 Duke L.J. 49.

159. *Peevyhouse*, 382 P.2d at 114.

160. Courts may face the constitutional limitation of resolving only "cases or controversies" at issue. U.S. Const. art. III, § 2, cl. 1. But other decisions have established prospective safeharbors. *See, e.g.*, Miranda v. Arizona, 384 U.S. 436 (1966) (establishing fair and effective warning requirement to persons in police custody).

161. The purpose of such contractual safeharbors should not be to preclude the parties from tailoring other standards. The safeharbor alternatives might additionally provide benefits as common-law interpretations would more fully specify their meanings. *See* J. Gordon, *supra* note 13

162. Fuller, *Consideration and Form*, 41 Colum. L. Rev. 799 (1941). In truth, the fact that the article is claimed by economists (it is, for example, reprinted in A. Kronman & R. Posner, The Economics of Contract Law 40 (1979)) is as much a tribute to the soundness of its insights as to its nexus with economics.

evidentiary, cautionary and channelling functions. The necessary and sufficient conditions for contracting around a default are examples of formalities that courts require. Our discussion accordingly tracks Fuller's categories.

In Fuller's analysis, the evidentiary function of legal formalities is to provide information to courts in order to lower the costs of subsequent decision making. This analysis is quite resonant with our earlier conclusion that penalty defaults could be justified on efficiency grounds as ways of encouraging the revelation of information.[163] In choosing the necessary conditions (the formalities) for contracting around a default, a court should consider similar informational aspects. We go beyond Fuller though and argue that the evidentiary function of legal formalities can serve to inform not only the courts but the parties within the contract as well.[164] For example, if a penalty default is chosen to encourage one party to reveal information to another, the court may want to regulate the process of contracting around the default so that meaningful information is conveyed.

Structuring formalities to facilitate internal information flows is also related to the cautionary function of legal formalities. Fuller argues that some formalities, such as certain writing requirements, serve a cautionary function by forcing the parties to undertake a minimal amount of reflection before being bound by a contract. But, as already discussed, when the parties to a contract have disparate amounts of information, lawmakers may want to establish formalities that are more directed toward protecting the relatively uninformed. For example, a holding contrary to *Peevyhouse*, in which the courts not only choose cost-of-performance damages as the default but also require extremely explicit language to opt for value diminution damages, might be justified to caution the relatively uninformed landholders of their legal rights.[165] To caution is to give information. Attention to how legal formalities will affect the flow of information should inform lawmakers' theory of gaps as well as their theory of default choice.

Finally, Fuller suggested that legal formalities could serve a chanelling function which, for example, would allow parties to channel their contractual agreements toward legal or non-legal enforcement. Fuller's theory of channelling is highly analogous to our earlier discussion of pooling and especially separating equilibria.[166] As we discussed in our *Hadley* model,

163. *See supra* text accompanying notes 47-60.

164. *See supra* text accompanying notes 53-60.

165. Similarly, if strategic withholding of information explains why employers do not reveal to employees the true probability of future termination, employees may make inefficient investments in goods such as housing and human capital. In such situations it may be efficient for courts not only to make a default rule against termination without cause but also to require employers to state specifically that they wish to be able to fire for even arbitrary reasons. *But see* Epstein, *supra* note 120 (arguing against such a rule); M. Freed & D. Polsby, *supra* note 134

166. *See supra* text accompanying notes 111-14.

different defaults can lead to different degrees of separation.[167] As with chanelling, the separating effect of legal defaults may allow parties to sort themselves into different groups.

There may be situations in which courts should increase the costs of contracting around defaults to force the majority of parties into a particular channel. For example, if a certain type of contract generates a mild externality, we may want to discourage most people from entering this type of contract. But if there is a small class of contracting parties that will be damaged more than society gains if they fail to contract, then courts may want to consider a method of "chanelling" or "separating" the socially beneficial from the deleterious classes of transactions.

One way to do this would be by direct fiat, but there may be ways of encouraging the parties to sort themselves into the correct categories through legal rules. For example, by artificially increasing the costs of contracting around a no-contract default, courts may discourage the low-benefit contractors but not the high-benefit contractors. Although such legal formalisms may engender the efficient types of contracting, they may still be inefficient because the additional transaction costs that the formalities engender are a social cost that could be avoided by simply imposing a tax of an equal magnitude. The tax would be a transfer to the government instead of a dead-weight loss. If courts are constrained from imposing taxes,[168] however, intentionally costly formalisms that increase the cost of contracting around "strong" defaults may be the most efficient rules within their choice set. The channelling function of legal formalities can also be given an informational justification because the very process of self-sorting reveals information about the parties' preferences.[169]

Such intentionally costly formalism would not be used in conjunction with a penalty default. Since the whole point of penalty defaults is to encourage parties to contract around them, formalisms that increase the cost of doing so would be counterproductive. In essence, penalty defaults encourage, and "strong" defaults discourage, contractual mutation.

C. *Legal Responses to Contracting Around Immutable Rules*

An important difference between default and immutable rules is that if parties attempt to contract around a default rule and fail, they will simply

---

167. *See supra* text accompanying notes 114–16.

168. *See, e.g.*, I. Ayres & P. Schmitt, Court-Ordered Funding of School Desegregation Remedies: Federalism Versus Minority Rights § 3 (1989) (unpublished manuscript on file with authors) (discussing constitutional limits on judicially imposed taxation).

169. The possibility that courts may intentionally want to increase the costs of contracting around a default might potentially explain their refusal to articulate alternative safeharbors. If there is uncertainty about what is sufficient to overcome a particular default, the parties will be discouraged ex ante from even trying. This argument might provide an apology for the *Peevyhouse* holding. However, in *Peevyhouse* the societal externalities of strip-mining militate toward a cost-of-performance default. This channeling explanation is therefore inapposite to the *Peevyhouse* fact pattern.

be bound by the default, whereas if parties attempt to contract around an immutable rule and fail, the law may choose to penalize the attempt by imposing a penalty different from (and, from the parties' ex ante perspectives, worse than) the immutable standard. From an ex ante perspective the possibility of receiving this ex post penalty is just another expected cost of contracting around the default rule.

The legal response to parties who try to contract around immutable rules can also be given a default interpretation. In these cases the courts remove the clauses that transgress the immutable rule and then choose a default to fill the gap. For example, in *Frostifresh Corp. v. Reynoso*,[170] the trial court established an immutable rule that retailers cannot sell at unconscionably high markups. Accordingly, the court struck out the contract's price provision (which was more than three times the retailer's cost), but it then had to decide how to fill the gap. The trial court decided that the reconstructed contract should have a price which only covered the seller's cost. The appellate court reversed and awarded the seller "a reasonable profit" instead of zero profit.[171] The difference in these holdings is very similar to the tension between a tailored default and penalty default. Reconstructing the contract to give the seller a reasonable profit is identical to the U.C.C.'s reasonable-price standard. The zero-profit standard is analogous to a penalty default, in this case imposing the penalty on the seller for trying to contract around a rule, while the penalty defaults discussed earlier penalize parties for not contracting around the rule.

This same tension arises with covenants not to compete. Courts have established an immutable rule that parties cannot make covenants of unreasonable duration. In *Fullerton Lumber Co. v. Torborg*,[172] for example, the Supreme Court of Wisconsin held that a ten-year covenant was unreasonable but then struggled in deciding whether it should reformulate the contract to impose a duty not to compete for a reasonable period or penalize the employer for transgressing the immutable limitation by allowing the former employee to compete immediately.[173]

If the goal of an immutable rule is to discourage people from even attempting to contract around a provision, then it would seem that the penalty reconstruction would be the favored result.[174] This is again analogous

---

170. 52 Misc. 2d 26, 274 N.Y.S.2d 757 (Dist. Ct. 1966), *rev'd* 54 Misc. 2d 119, 281 N.Y.S.2d 964 (App. Term 1967).

171. Frostifresh Corp. v. Reynoso, 54 Misc. 2d 119, 281 N.Y.S.2d 964 (App. Term 1967).

172. 270 Wis. 133, 70 N.W.2d 585 (1955).

173. The majority reconstructed the contract to have a covenant of "reasonable" duration. 270 Wis. at 146-47, 70 N.W.2d at 592. The dissent would have penalized the employer by allowing the employee to compete immediately. *Id.* at 148-52, 70 N.W.2d at 593-94 (Gehl, J., dissenting).

174. A penalty for even attempting to contract around a legally immutable provision may be necessary to deter attempts in a world where some disputes are not litigated. If all disputes were litigated, attempts to contract around an immutable rule would never succeed. But if some contractual parties fail to challenge unenforceable immutable rules, then imposing a penalty whenever a case does come to court might be justified to prevent underdeterrence. For example, it is widely believed that

to our earlier discussion of penalty defaults, in which we suggested that courts should choose the penalty that provided "least cost deterrence."[175] The difference is that in the earlier discussion the penalties were attempting to deter gaps and here the penalties are attempting to promote gaps (that is, deter contracting around). The preference for penalty defaults to fill the gaps left in unconscionable contracts may justify the common law "blue pencil" test which simply enforces contracts after the offending provision has been struck (with a blue pencil).[176]

Conclusion

This article has suggested how efficiency-minded lawmakers should go about filling gaps in contracts. The reasons that parties leave gaps in contracts should strongly inform this decision. Our theory of defaults should, in a sense, be guided by our theories of why there are contractual gaps. Prior theorists have argued that parties leave gaps in contracts because the cost of writing additional terms outweighs the benefit. Accordingly, they have suggested that courts should simply fill in the gap with the term the parties "would have wanted."

This article, however, has articulated a second cause of contractual incompleteness. We have shown that when one party to a contract knows more than another, the knowledgeable party may strategically decide not to contract around even an inefficient default. Because the process of contracting around a default can reveal information, the knowledgeable party may purposefully withhold information to get a larger piece of the smaller contractual pie. This possibility of strategic incompleteness leads us to embrace more diverse forms of default rules. In particular, lawmakers may be able to undercut the incentives for this strategic rent-seeking by establishing penalty defaults that encourage the better informed parties to reveal their information by contracting around the default.

Our analysis does not imply that penalty defaults should be used in all contractual settings. The decision by efficiency-minded courts or legislatures to impose a penalty, untailored majoritarian, or tailored "what the parties would have wanted" default in a particular setting is not a trivial one. The first step in the decision-making process should be to ask "why does the gap exist?" We have suggested that parties may fail to contract around inefficient defaults for strategic as well as transaction cost reasons. When parties fail to contract because they want to shift the ex ante trans-

creditors and residential landlords make a practice of including all sorts of illegal clauses in their contracts not because they think the clauses will stand up in court, but because they know that most debtors and tenants have more respect for written contracts than most courts do. The authors are indebted to conversations with Richard Craswell for this point. *See* Craswell, *supra* note 22, at 64–65.

175. *See supra* Section I.B.

176. *See Fullerton*, 270 Wis. at 43, 70 N.W.2d at 590. The "blue pencil" test is the traditional test of severability. If, after removing the unconscionable terms, the contract is still comprehensible in that the parties might have still entered into it, the court will enforce it.

action cost to a subsidized ex post court determination, a penalty default of non-enforcement may be appropriate. When strategic considerations cause a more knowledgeable party not to raise issues that could improve contractual efficiency, a default that penalizes the more informed party may encourage the revelation of information.[177]

Lawmakers should not, however, impose penalty defaults indiscriminately. Even if strategic considerations are established as a significant source of contractual incompleteness, courts or legislatures should consider the costs and benefits of penalty defaults themselves. Since the goal of a penalty default is to induce information revelation, lawmakers should consider the likelihood that the penalty will in fact result in information being revealed,[178] the benefit (in more efficient reliance or precaution) of the revealed information, and the costs of explicitly contracting around the default. If the private information is acquired with economic resources, the value of information revelation must also be weighed against the private incentives to acquire it. Penalty defaults are therefore more likely to be efficient if the private information is acquired passively. In sum, a penalty default should be used if it results in valuable information revelation with low transaction costs.[179]

Throughout the discussion we have cited examples of common-law and statutory rules that are broadly consistent with our theory's categories of penalty, tailored and untailored defaults. But we believe that both courts and legislatures should be more sensitive to the process of contracting. Lawmakers should consider explicitly the informational as well as the contractual equilibria generated by alternative default rules. Different defaults may generate different degrees of pooling and separating. When heterogeneous contracting parties separate themselves into different con-

177. In many settings, such as simple contracts for small transactions, it is easy to point to transaction costs as the source of incompleteness. In other settings, however, parties write complicated, lengthy contracts that are carefully considered by both parties and their lawyers. In these situations a contingency that is not contracted for may be sufficiently important that it is unreasonable to ascribe incompleteness to transaction costs. Some omitted clauses, for example, may be very inexpensive to include from a transaction cost perspective, such as liquidated damage clauses or non-refundable deposits. In such cases courts will find it difficult to point to transaction costs as the source of incompleteness, so penalty defaults should be considered.

178. For example, we suggested that Goldberg's zero-damage penalty default would not sufficiently encourage retailers to contract for liquidated damages, and even if a larger penalty would, the amount of liquidated damages in equilibrium might "pool" at a non-informative low level. *See supra* Section I.C.2. Courts should also consider the possibility that some parties will fail to contract around penalty defaults out of ignorance or oversight.

179. The *Hadley* rule is an example of a penalty default that 1) is cheap to contract around by including a liquidated damage clause, 2) will likely cause damage information to be revealed, and 3) will facilitate more efficient precaution.

We must add an important transitional caveat. A legal change from one default to another can be costly—especially if the move is to a penalty default. Until parties become informed about the new default, there may be transitional costs as the parties continue to bargain in the shadow of an invalid law.

Finally, we note that in many contractual settings, both parties may have private information which they choose to withhold. In such settings of "dual asymmetric information," penalty defaults may not be sufficient to ensure that all private information is revealed.

tractual agreements, they reduce the inefficiencies of strategic pooling but at the cost of increased contracting. Lawmakers need to weigh these costs of pooling and separating in choosing the right rule; but more fundamentally, they need to be able to predict how much pooling and separating different rules are likely to generate.

The analysis of the article is quite general and can be applied to a wide range of legal issues.[180] For example, courts in interpreting statutes are often called upon to fill gaps. A number of scholars have used a "legislation-as-contract" approach to resolve such questions.[181] Jon Macey has proposed a type of penalty default by suggesting that statutory gaps be filled with public-regarding legislation.[182] Macey's default is not what the legislature would have contracted for and thus forces the legislature to make their pork-barrel deals public. Justice Scalia has gone the furthest, however, in articulating a penalty default standard of statutory interpretation.[183] In *Agency Holding Corp. v. Malley-Duff & Assoc.*,[184] the Supreme Court was asked to supply a default statute of limitations for a civil RICO[185] action because the legislation was silent on the issue. While the majority established a four-year limitation as what Congress would have wanted, Justice Scalia argued that there should be no statute of limitation. Scalia was "unmoved by the fear that [this] conclusion might prove 'repugnant to the genius of our laws' "[186] and even suggested that this penalty default might encourage Congress to contract around it: "Indeed, it might even prompt Congress to enact a limitations period that it believes 'appropriate,' a judgment far more within its competence than ours."[187] Ironically, Justice Scalia is arguing for an extreme form of judicial activism. Only by choosing a default that is wholly at odds with Congressional intent can the Court ensure that Congress will reveal its intent. Scalia's ultimate message then is that extreme activism can become a form of disempowering judicial restraint. Examples such as these underscore our primary thesis that efficient defaults may at times deviate from what the parties would have wanted. More importantly, they demonstrate that our

180. *See* discussion *supra* note 10.

181. *See* Easterbrook, *The Supreme Court, 1983 Term—Foreword: The Court and the Economic System*, 98 HARV. L. REV. 4, 15-16 (1984).

182. Macey, *Promoting Public-Regarding Legislation through Statutory Interpretation: An Interest Group Model*, 86 COLUM. L. REV. 223, 236-40 (1986).

183. For a more general discussion of using penalty defaults to force Congress to enunciate the law, see L. Marshall, Let Congress Do It: The Case For an Absolute Rule of Statutory Stare Decisis (1989) (unpublished manuscript on file with authors).

184. 483 U.S. 143, 157 (1987) (Scalia, J., concurring).

185. Racketeer Influenced and Corrupt Organizations Act (RICO), 18 U.S.C. § 1964 (1982 & Supp. V 1987).

186. 483 U.S. at 170 (Scalia, J., concurring) (quoting Occidental Life Ins. Co. v. EEOC, 432 U.S. 355 (1977) quoting Adams v. Woods, 6 U.S. (2 Cranch) 336, 342 (1805)).

187. 483 U.S. at 170.

choice of default must be informed by an understanding of why contracting parties—such as legislatures—leave gaps in their texts.[188]

Finally, we suggest that teachers focus more explicitly on the difference between default and immutable rules. Often students are able to recite the various rules learned in a course without knowing whether they are obligatory or not. Teaching which rules are defaults is not a mere pedagogical conceit. To represent their clients effectively, attorneys need to know not only what the legal rules are, but how, if at all, they can be abrogated to further their clients' interests.[189] A descriptive knowledge of defaults and how to contract around them is a prerequisite of effective advocacy.

188. For example, the statute of limitation gap of RICO in *Malley-Duff* is hard to explain as hidden pork-barrel legislation.

189. In corporate law especially, the mechanism for contracting around the default may be oblique. For example, while corporate statutes do not give the board of directors the right to disapprove a merger, certain "poison pill" plans have the effect of making the board sign off on any hostile bid. *See* Dynamics Corp. of Am. v. CTS Corp., 805 F.2d 705 (7th Cir. 1986) (analyzing economic impact of "poison pill").

Part V
The Economics of Tort Law and Liability Systems

[20]

SYMPOSIUM—MODERN TORT THEORY

THE POSITIVE ECONOMIC THEORY OF TORT LAW

*William M. Landes**†
*Richard A. Posner***†

Academic literature on tort law consists largely of (1) lawyers' analysis of doctrine and (2) normative analysis, by lawyers and others, of such issues as no-fault compensation for victims of automobile accidents. Only a small proportion of the literature attempts a scientific study of the tort system, comparable to the study of organic systems by biologists or of the price system by economists. Lately, however, interest in the scientific study of the legal system has been stimulated by the "law and economics" movement, some members of which have advanced the following hypothesis: the common law is best explained as if the judges who created the law through decisions operating as precedents in subsequent cases were trying to promote efficient resource allocation. We call this hypothesis, as applied to tort law, "the" positive economic theory of tort law because no rival positive economic theory of tort law has yet appeared.

This article is designed as an introduction to the positive economic theory. Part I of the article traces the emergence of the theory from earlier scientific studies of tort law and discusses recurrent criticisms of it. Part II describes the economic model

---

* Clifton R. Musser Professor of Economics, University of Chicago Law School; Research Associate, National Bureau of Economic Research.

** Judge, United States Court of Appeals for the Seventh Circuit; Senior Lecturer, University of Chicago Law School.

† This article is based on chapters 1, 3, and 4 of an unpublished book in progress tentatively entitled "The Economic Structure of Tort Law." Research for the book has been supported by the National Science Foundation through a grant to the National Bureau of Economic Research and by the Law and Economics Program of the University of Chicago Law School.

underlying the theory and shows how it can be used to decide whether negligence or strict liability is the more efficient liability standard in particular circumstances. Part III evaluates the success of the model in explaining (1) the negligence standard itself, (2) the cases applying the standard, and (3) the areas of strict liability in tort law. Part IV discusses recent developments in tort law that may have altered its efficient character.

This article does not purport to *prove* the positive economic theory of tort law. Our aim is more modest: to show that the theory is sufficiently promising to warrant efforts by legal and economic scholars to test the theory empirically on larger bodies of data than we have thus far used.

I. Background and Criticisms of the Theory

The scholarly tradition from which the positive economic theory of tort law comes could be said to have begun with Jeremy Bentham, who first applied economics to laws regulating nonmarket behavior, or even with Adam Smith. However, we have chosen, somewhat arbitrarily to be sure, a more recent event from which to date the tradition — the publication of Holmes's *The Common Law* in 1881.[1] With the benefit of hindsight, it is possible to find in Holmes's chapters on trespass and negligence, and in slightly later articles on tort law by Ames and Terry, prefigurings of the economic approach. Holmes suggested that the only difference between negligence and strict liability as tort standards was that the latter provided a form of accident insurance.[2] This is not the whole of the difference from an economic standpoint, but it is an important part of it. Ames wrote that the law was "utilitarian,"[3] although he did not explain what he meant by the term. Terry described the negligence standard in terms of a balance of utilities.[4] The early writings do not state explicitly, however, that the tort law contains standards of conduct that promote efficient resource allocation. The writers recognized the deterrent effect of tort law,[5]

---

[1] O.W. Holmes, The Common Law (1881).

[2] *See id.* at 94-96.

[3] Ames, *Law and Morals*, 22 Harv. L. Rev. 97, 110 (1908).

[4] *See* Terry, *Negligence*, 29 Harv. L. Rev. 40 (1915).

[5] *See, e.g.*, Schofield, *Davies v. Mann: Theory of Contributory Negligence*, 3 Harv. L. Rev. 263 (1890).

In an action for negligence it is of no consequence to the law whether the particular

but they did not connect the idea that tort principles are based on utilitarian values with the idea that liability deters harmful conduct that is not justifiable on utilitarian grounds.

The next burst of scientific tort scholarship came in the heyday of legal realism, the 1920's and 1930's. The legal realists believed that it was naive to talk of "fault" in connection with accidents or to think that the law could have much effect on the accident level; legal doctrine, they believed, had little effect on how cases were actually decided (this was their "realism"). They saw the only realistically attainable function of tort law to be the provision of insurance. On this basis they recommended the assignment of liability regardless of fault to injurers having "deep pockets" and the abolition of defenses such as contributory negligence and assumption of risk that reduced the scope of liability.[6] Among the descendants of the legal realists can be found both the advocates of "no fault" compensation (in effect, compulsory accident insurance coupled with abolition or curtailment of tort liability) and many advocates of strict liability. The latter turn Holmes on his head. Holmes opposed strict liability on the ground that the state had no business providing insurance. The legal realists urge strict liability (or compulsory accident insurance) on the ground that the only proper function of tort law is to provide insurance to those who fail to insure themselves against being injured in an accident.[7] Our present interest, however, is not in the normative analysis of the legal realists but in their scientific premise that the legal system in operation diverges fundamentally from its formal functioning in accordance with legal doctrine.

The third wave of tort scholarship began in 1961 with the publi-

> defendant shall be compelled to pay damages, or whether the loss shall be allowed to lie where it fell. The really important matter is to adjust the dispute between the parties by a rule of conduct which shall do justice if possible in the particular case, but which shall also be suitable to the needs of the community, and tend to prevent like accidents from happening in the future.

Id. at 269.

[6] The writing in this genre is voluminous, and no useful purpose would be served by extensive citation. For a single good example, see Douglas, *Vicarious Liability and the Administration of Risk I*, 38 YALE L.J. 584 (1929).

[7] The most prominent advocate of the position that all accidents should be governed by either strict liability or no fault (*i.e.* no liability) is Jeffrey O'Connell. *See, e.g.*, J. O'CONNELL, ENDING INSULT TO INJURY (1975). *See also* R. KEETON & J. O'CONNELL, BASIC PROTECTION FOR THE TRAFFIC VICTIM: A BLUEPRINT FOR REFORMING AUTOMOBILE INSURANCE (1965).

cation of Ronald Coase's article on social cost and Guido Calabresi's first article on tort law.[8] This wave is the economic analysis of torts. The germ of the analysis is Jeremy Bentham's proposition that people maximize utility in all areas of life.[9] This implies that liability rules can be used to affect the level of accidents, although Bentham himself never drew this implication. A more direct antecedent of the economic approach to torts is the concept of social cost, or external cost, notably as articulated by Pigou. Using, among other examples, that of the locomotive that emits sparks which damage the crops of farmers located along the railroad right-of-way, Pigou noted the potential divergence of social from private cost.[10] The crop damage, he argued, was not a private cost to the railroad, and only private costs determine behavior. It was a social cost, however, because the farmer is a member of society as is the railroad. Therefore, unless some means were found to force the railroad to internalize the cost, there would be too much, or too careless, railroading.

Perhaps because Pigou himself thought that the proper way to force the cost to be internalized was through a tax, and thus he did not discuss liability rules, Pigou's analysis of social cost was not applied to tort law until the Coase and Calabresi articles. Coase's article is best known for its criticism of Pigou's position. Coase showed that if transaction costs were zero, the parties (railroad and farmer) would bargain to an efficient allocation of resources regardless of whether the railroad was liable (or taxed) for the crop damage. This important theoretical insight later became known as the "Coase theorem." An initially neglected aspect of Coase's article was his examination of actual English nuisance cases and his suggestion that the English courts had displayed a better (intuitive) grasp of the economics of the problem than had economists in the Pigovian tradition.[11]

Calabresi was not primarily interested in how or whether the

---

[8] Coase, *The Problem of Social Cost*, 3 J.L. & Econ. 1 (1960); Calabresi, *Some Thoughts on Risk Distribution and the Law of Torts*, 70 Yale L.J. 499 (1961). Although it bears a date of 1960, Coase's article was actually published in 1961, and Calabresi's paper was independent of Coase's.

[9] *See* J. Bentham, A Fragment on Government and an Introduction to the Principles of Morals and Legislation 125, 298 (W. Harrison ed. 1960).

[10] A. Pigou, The Economics of Welfare 134, 192 (4th ed. 1932).

[11] *See* Coase, *supra* note 8, at 27-28, 38.

courts tried to use tort principles for cost internalization. Like Bentham in this respect, Calabresi was interested in constructing an efficient system of accident law from first principles rather than in appraising the operations of the existing system of accident law, the tort system — although in later work he has criticized the tort system as failing to conform to the requirements of economic efficiency.[12]

After a ten-year hiatus following the publication of the Coase and Calabresi articles, economic scholarship on torts erupted in a sustained flow that continues to this day along two paths which can, in a rough way, be traced back to the Coase and Calabresi articles respectively. Calabresi sketched a model of efficient accident law that Peter Diamond and other theoretical economists proceeded to formalize.[13] Coase had suggested that the common law was a mechanism of social-cost internalization, and Demsetz, sketchily,[14] and Posner, more comprehensively, proceeded to develop this insight. Posner's 1972 article on negligence discussed the negligence standard itself and a number of related doctrines (contributory negligence, last clear chance, assumption of risk, and others) as methods of bringing about an efficient allocation of reources to safety and care.[15] An article published the next year, as well as the first edition of *Economic Analysis of Law*, published in 1973, extended the analysis to strict liability.[16] John Brown pro-

---

[12] *See, e.g.*, G. CALABRESI, THE COSTS OF ACCIDENTS: A LEGAL AND ECONOMIC ANALYSIS 237-87 (1970). Calabresi has also, however, made important contributions to positive analysis, in particular having to do with the distinction between property rights and liability rules and with the principles of causation in tort law. *See* Calabresi & Melamed, *Property Rules, Liability Rules, and Inalienability: One View of the Cathedral*, 85 HARV. L. REV. 1089 (1972); Calabresi, *Concerning Cause and the Law of Torts: An Essay for Harry Kalven, Jr.*, 43 U. CHI. L. REV. 69 (1975).

[13] *See, e.g.*, Diamond, *Single Activity Accidents*, 3 J. LEGAL STUD. 107 (1974); Green, *On the Optimal Structure of Liability Laws*, 7 BELL J. ECON. & MGMT. SCI. 553 (1976).

[14] *See* Demsetz, *Issues in Automobile Accidents and Reparations from the Viewpoint of Economics*, in C. GREGORY & H. KALVEN, JR., CASES AND MATERIALS ON TORTS 870 (2d ed. 1969). This is the earliest paper we know of, apart from Coase's article, in which it was suggested that the common law of torts might serve to promote economic efficiency. However, Demsetz devotes only two pages to this question. *See id.* at 873-74. Most economists in this period seem to have agreed with Calabresi that the tort system, especially in accident cases, was an inefficient system of accident regulation. *See* Vickrey, *Automobile Accidents, Tort Law, Externalities, and Insurance: An Economist's Critique*, 33 LAW & CONTEMP. PROB. 464 (1968).

[15] *See* Posner, *A Theory of Negligence*, 1 J. LEGAL STUD. 29 (1972).

[16] *See* R. POSNER, ECONOMIC ANALYSIS OF LAW 92-95 (1973); Posner, *Strict Liability: A*

duced his formal analysis of liability rules the same year.[17] Since then, Posner, Landes, Shavell, and other economic analysts of law have examined various areas of tort law with a view to evaluating their efficiency.[18]

Among the recent areas studied are intentional torts,[19] the common-law rules relating to joint and multiple tortfeasors,[20] causation,[21] the privacy and defamation torts,[22] nuisance,[23] negligent misrepresentation,[24] the "good Samaritan" question,[25] and false advertising.[26] At the same time, the theory has been criticized on various grounds. Many of the criticisms of the economic analysis of law are not, however, criticisms of the positive theory. For example, critics like Epstein and Dworkin have argued that a system of law designed simply to make society wealthier is immoral.[27] How-

---

Comment, 2 J. LEGAL STUD. 205 (1973).

[17] *See* Brown, *Toward An Economic Theory of Liability*, 2 J. LEGAL STUD. 323 (1973). Brown's work is perhaps better classified with Diamond and the other formalizers of ideal, as distinct from actual, liability rules. While Brown models concepts of negligence, contributory negligence, comparative negligence, and strict liability, he does not attempt to give these terms their legal meaning.

[18] *See* R. POSNER, ECONOMIC ANALYSIS OF LAW 119-61 (2d ed. 1977), and references cited therein for the state of the literature as of 1977. We admit to a certain unease in trying to divide economic analysts of torts neatly into two camps — formalists doing normative analysis and "informalists" doing positive analysis. For example, Steven Shavell, whose work on the economics of tort law we refer to frequently in this article, is a formal theorist; and our own economic model, expounded in part II, is formal though it is simpler than the models of those whom we have classified as formalists. As we shall explain, there is a positive correlation between formal simplicity and positive analysis but the correlation is not 100 percent.

[19] *See* Landes & Posner, *An Economic Theory of Intentional Torts*, 1 INT'L L. & ECON. REV. 127 (1981).

[20] *See* Landes & Posner, *Joint and Multiple Tortfeasors: An Economic Analysis*, 9 J. LEGAL STUD. 517 (1980).

[21] *See* Shavell, *An Analysis of Causation and the Scope of Liability in the Law of Torts*, 9 J. LEGAL STUD. 463 (1980).

[22] *See* Posner, *The Right of Privacy*, 12 GA. L. REV. 393 (1978); Posner, *Privacy, Secrecy, and Reputation*, 28 BUFF. L. REV. 1, 30-41 (1979).

[23] *See* Wittman, *First Come, First Served: An Economic Analysis of "Coming to the Nuisance,"* 9 J. LEGAL STUD. 557 (1980).

[24] *See* Bishop, *Negligent Misrepresentation through Economists' Eyes*, 96 LAW Q. REV. 360 (1980).

[25] *See* Landes & Posner, *Salvors, Finders, Good Samaritans, and Other Rescuers: An Economic Study of Law and Altruism*, 7 J. LEGAL STUD. 83, 119-27 (1978).

[26] *See* Jordan & Rubin, *An Economic Analysis of the Law of False Advertising*, 8 J. LEGAL STUD. 527 (1979).

[27] *See, e.g.*, Dworkin, *Is Wealth a Value?*, 9 J. LEGAL STUD. 191 (1980); Epstein, *A Theory of Strict Liability*, 2 J. LEGAL STUD. 151 (1972).

As will become clear when we explain our formal model in part II, we call a policy change

ever forceful a criticism this might be of a normative economic theory of tort law, it is misplaced when directed at the positive theory. We are interested in explaining rather than defending the common law of torts. Its moral inadequacy, if it is morally inadequate, is relevant only insofar as this might cast doubt on the plausibility of attributing such an approach to the judges who fashioned the common law of torts.

There are three recurrent objections to the positive economic theory of tort law that we think merit consideration here. The first, echoing the realist critique of formal law, is that the positive theory rests on unrealistic behavioral assumptions;[28] that tort doctrines, however abstractly calculated to promote efficient resource allocation, do not actually affect human behavior. Most people, it is argued, do not even know the doctrines of tort law; behavior in the face of danger is dominated by concern with personal safety rather than with the financial consequences of behavior, especially for people who carry liability insurance; and people lack sufficient information about the probability of an accident to make rational judgments concerning accident avoidance. These points, which impy that tort law probably is not an effective method of deterring inefficient behavior, draw support from a deep vein of skepticism concerning the deterrent effect of law generally.

The same points (with the exception of liability insurance) could be and have been made to show that the criminal law does not deter violent crime, yet there is now a large body of statistical evidence demonstrating that both the severity and certainty of criminal punishment have a substantial deterrent effect on such crime.[29] Moreover, although there has been little systematic study of the

---

"efficient" if the joint income or wealth of the people affected by the change is greater after the change than before. Thus, we abstract from distributive considerations. Our concept of efficiency, although it is one commonly used in economics, is ethically controversial. For a discussion of the ethical issues, see the *Hofstra Law Review*'s recent Symposium on Efficiency as a Legal Concern, 8 HOFSTRA L. REV. 485-771, 811-973 (1980).

[28] *See, e.g.*, G.E. WHITE, TORT LAW IN AMERICA: AN INTELLECTUAL HISTORY 220-23, 230 (1980); Schwartz, *Contributory and Comparative Negligence: A Reappraisal*, 87 YALE L.J. 697 (1978).

[29] *See, e.g.*, Ehrlich, *Participation in Illegitimate Activities: An Economic Analysis*, in ESSAYS IN THE ECONOMICS OF CRIME AND PUNISHMENT 68 (G. Becker & W. Landes eds. 1974); Tullock, *Does Punishment Deter Crime?*, PUBLIC INTEREST, Summer 1974, No. 36, at 103; Votey, *Detention of Heroin Addicts, Job Opportunities, and Deterrence*, 8 J. LEGAL STUD. 585 (1979).

deterrent effect of tort law, empirical evidence tends to support the proposition that tort law deters too — even in the area of automobile accidents, where liability insurance is widespread and concerns with personal safety might be thought to dominate any concern with the financial consequences of an accident.[30]

Even if it were shown that tort law does not have a significant effect on behavior, this showing would not falsify the theory that we are expounding in this article. Ours is a theory of the rules of tort law rather than of the consequences of those rules for behavior. Assume with Aristotle that the real purpose and only proper effect of tort law are to do "corrective justice," that is, to restore to a person what has been wrongfully taken from him, rather than to improve the allocation of resources.[31] It would still be necessary to inquire into the source of those norms on the basis of which conduct was judged wrongful. The source might well be economic. Efforts have been made to explain ethical concepts, including the sense of being wronged, in economic (or closely related biological) terms.[32] It would be consistent with these efforts to find that the tort concept of fault has an economic meaning also.

A second criticism of the positive economic theory of tort law is that its proponents have not explained the mechanism by which efficient tort rules might emerge in a common-law system. Twenty years ago this omission would not have seemed troublesome. In that period, one of general optimism concerning governmental intervention in the economic system, the dominant positive theory of the state was that the state supplied public goods.[33] For obvious

---

[30] *See* R. Grayson, Deterrence in Automobile Liability Insurance (1971) (unpublished Ph.D. thesis, Univ. Chi. Grad. Sch. Bus.); E. Landes, Insurance, Liability and Accidents: A Theoretical and Empirical Investigation of the Effect of No-Fault on Accidents (University of Chicago Center for the Study of the Economy and the State, 1980). Also relevant is Peltzman's study showing that drivers respond to a compulsory seatbelt law by driving less carefully. *See* Peltzman, *The Effects of Auto Safety Regulation*, 83 J. Pol. Econ. 677 (1975). *But see* Lindgren & Stuart, *The Effects of Traffic Safety Regulation in Sweden*, 88 J. Pol. Econ. 412 (1980).

[31] *See* Aristotle, The Nichomachean Ethics 114-17 (David Ross trans., rev. ed. 1980). Of course, these need not be inconsistent objectives.

[32] *See* Hirshleifer, *Natural Economy versus Political Economy*, 1 J. Soc. & Biological Structures 319, 332, 334 (1978); Posner, *Retribution and Related Concepts of Punishment*, 9 J. Legal Stud. 71 (1980); Trivers, *The Evolution of Reciprocal Altruism*, 46 Q. Rev. Biology 35, 49 (1971).

[33] *See, e.g.*, W. Baumol, Welfare Economics and the Theory of the State (1952). Public goods are goods that can be consumed without paying for them. An example is national

reasons, the provision of public goods by a free market is a problem, and it was thought until recently that the actual, as well as the ideal, function of the state was to provide such goods and thereby rectify a failure of the private market. In our positive economic theory, tort law is a public good and its provision by the state would not have seemed problematic in the period when the state was assumed to be in the business of providing public goods.

Today, however, the dominant theory of the state is redistributive.[34] Interest groups struggle for a place at the public trough, and government intervenes in the economy to redistribute wealth from politically less powerful to politically more powerful groups rather than to provide public goods. But this view seems overstated. We have armed forces, police, courts, and other (relatively) uncontroversial public goods provided by government, and it is hardly credible that these goods are produced simply as the accidental by-product of redistributive policies. Tort law may be one of those goods.

This is all the more plausible because tort law deals with activities (mainly accidents) that do not lend themselves well to redistribution in favor of politically influential interest groups.[35] The probability of being involved in an accident, either as victim or as injurer, does not vary in a regular or consistent fashion across the compact and readily identifiable interest groups that bulk so large as recipients of government largess in the redistributive theories of government. Consequently, it does not seem plausible to suppose either that an interest group would organize to seek redistribution through the accident-law system (a group consisting of the "accident prone" or of drunken drivers, for example) or that some existing group — the poor, blacks, retail druggists — would place accident law high on the agenda for legislative action. We do not wish to overstate our point. The nuclear industry obtained a limitation on liability from Congress; well-organized groups of the personal-injury bar lobby vigorously against no-fault automobile compensation plans; the railroad workers' unions fight modifications of

defense. An individual who did not contribute to the cost of national defense would nonetheless enjoy whatever deterrent or other benefits it created.

[34] *See, e.g.*, Peltzman, *The Growth of Government*, 23 J.L. & ECON. 209 (1980); Stigler, *The Theory of Economic Regulation*, 2 BELL J. ECON. & MGMT. SCI. 3 (1971).

[35] *See* Posner, *The Ethical and Political Basis of the Efficiency Norm in Common Law Adjudication*, 8 HOFSTRA L. REV. 487, 502-06 (1980).

the Federal Employers' Liability Act. However, the scope of systematic wealth redistribution in regard to accidents (and, even more clearly, in regard to intentional injuries such as assault and battery) does seem more limited than in regard to tariffs, price regulation, taxation, wages, the development of public lands, and other familiar areas of special-interest legislation. Where systematic redistribution is difficult to achieve, an interest group's best strategy may be to support policies that will increase the wealth of the society as a whole, because the members of the group can be expected to share in that increase. Hence it is consistent that the AFL-CIO should support both the minimum wage and a strong national defense. The former is a redistributive policy that benefits its members directly, the latter an efficient policy that also benefits its members, though in common with all other members of the society. We think that tort law is the latter kind of policy.

The third criticism of the positive economic theory of tort law that we shall discuss here is that the evidence used to support (or refute) the theory is spongy, meager, and equivocal, and the theory itself poorly defined.[36] Because it is a theory about rules, the principal evidence for and against it consists of interpretations of rules. There are several problems with this mode of empirical verification. First, rules are hard to quantify for purposes of sampling and hypothesis testing. What would it mean to say, for example, that eighty-two percent of the rules of tort law were efficient? Would it mean eighty-two percent of someone's catalogue of the rules of tort law? Whose catalogue? Prosser's? The American Law Institute's? Our own? Moreover, rules differ vastly in their importance. The "rule" that each dog is entitled to one bite (actually, as we shall see in part III, an oversimplified version of the principle that liability for damage inflicted by domestic animals requires knowledge or reason to know that the animal is dangerous) is not on the same level with the rule that employers are liable for the torts of their employees committed in furtherance of the employer's business (*respondeat superior*). No recognized method exists for weighting

---

[36] Our colleague George Stigler is a forceful exponent of this point of view, which he has stated in conversations with us and in an unpublished paper, G. Stigler, Is the Common Law Efficient? (Jan. 16, 1980). A number of specific criticisms of the evidentiary basis of the positive theory are made in the *Hofstra* symposium referred to in note 27 *supra* and replied to in Posner, *A Reply to Some Recent Criticisms of the Efficiency Theory of the Common Law*, 9 HOFSTRA L. REV. 775, 780-85 (1981). We do not discuss them here.

different rules of law by their importance.

There are ways around the problems, however. First, appellate decisions can be sampled randomly.[37] (A problem, however, is that rules of no liability tend, for obvious reasons, to be under-represented in such a sampling procedure.) Second, leading cases can be identified by the number of citations to them.[38] Third, casebooks, treatises, and the *Restatement of Torts* can be used as a source of authoritative cases and doctrines. Given these methods, we do not consider fundamental the sample-bias objection to our methodology for testing the positive theory.

Even if the sampling problem is overcome, there is still the problem of evaluating the outcome of each case in the sample. Rarely will there be sufficient information about the costs and benefits of alternative safety measures to enable a confident judgment that the court's outcome is the efficient one. This problem leads to another: our methodology may not enable us to distinguish between a tort system that is efficient in some meaningful sense and a system that simply is not indifferent to efficiency. We rarely will be able to say of a decision more than that it indicates a sensitivity to the economics of the situation before the court. Yet one would not want to describe the system of resource allocation in the Soviet Union as efficient merely because it allows people to marry whom they choose and pays workers on a piece-rate system. Merely because the tort law makes some crude economic distinctions, it does not follow that it is an efficient system — that efficiency is its lifeblood.

We have two answers to this criticism. First, economic analysis has identified subtle as well as gross economic distinctions that tort law makes.[39] Second, one is unpersuaded that the Soviet Union allocates resoures efficiently by isolated evidence of sensitivity to economic considerations because one knows that other principles besides efficiency guide resource allocation in the Soviet system, but there is no well-developed theory of what motivates or explains tort law besides efficiency.[40] To be sure, if asked what tort

---

[37] *See* Posner, *supra* note 15, at 34-36.

[38] On the use of citations to identify and weight precedents, see Landes & Posner, *Legal Precedent: A Theoretical and Empirical Analysis*, 19 J.L. & Econ. 249 (1976).

[39] Such as the activity-care and joint-alternative care distinctions discussed in parts II and III of this article.

[40] However, there are hints of a positive theory in the work of Epstein, Fletcher, and

law is based upon, most tort lawyers would answer that it is based upon notions of justice, equity, fairness, or morality — not efficiency. But all of these terms may be, in the tort setting, synonyms. It is not as if efficiency cosiderations entered as constraints (as apparently they do in the Soviet system) on allocative choices made on different grounds; so far as torts scholars have been able to discover, the only force operating in a systematic fashion to shape tort law is a concern with efficiency.

Another objection to our empirical procedure is that it consists of rationalization rather than prediction. We know the rules of tort law, it is argued, and knowing them we always can come up with a plausible rationalization based on economic theory. If a rule seems allocatively inefficient, considerations of administrative cost are available to save the theory from a contradiction. Or, if allocative and administrative costs appear to dictate a different rule from the actual rule, we may be able to appeal to risk aversion to bail us out. This procedure is quite different, it is said, from formulating a theory and then testing it on unknown bodies of data.

The difference, however, is more theoretical than practical. Much of economic theory is directed toward explaining known data, and this article is an example of applying a theory originally developed and tested on one body of data to a different body. The danger to which the criticism points, however, is a real one. One can complicate a theory to the point where any empirical observation is consistent with it. When that point is reached, the theory cannot be refuted, and a theory that cannot be refuted cannot be confirmed either. Concern with this problem has led us to propose an extremely simple economic model of tort law — a model in which, for example, risk aversion plays no role. In explaining this model in part II of this article, we shall comment further on the importance of a simple model to a theory designed to guide empirical research.

Another objection to our empirical procedure, this one more likely to be made by lawyers than economists, is that we use as

---

Dworkin and of Abraham Harari and Mario Rizzo, both of whose approaches resemble Epstein's. *See* Dworkin, *Seven Critics*, 11 GA. L. REV. 1201, 1203-23 (1977); Epstein, *supra* note 27; Fletcher, *Fairness and Utility in Tort Theory*, 85 HARV. L. REV. 537 (1972); A. HARARI, THE PLACE OF NEGLIGENCE IN THE LAW OF TORTS (1962); Rizzo & Arnold, *Causal Apportionment in the Law of Torts: An Economic Theory*, 80 COLUM. L. REV. 1399 (1980).

evidence only some features of the appellate opinions in tort cases — the outcome of the case and the rule that can be extracted from the opinion — and ignore the language, concepts, and reasoning in the opinion. Thus, it is argued, in explaining judicial opinions in economic terms we ignore the terms in which the authors themselves thought and wrote. A partial reply is that none of the actors whose behavior the economist seeks to explain uses an explicit economic vocabulary to describe his actions: not the consumer, not the worker, not the criminal, not even the businessman. The rejoinder is that the consumer, worker, criminal, and businessman are not engaged in a self-conscious, expressive activity comparable to drafting a judicial opinion. They are not required by their occupation to articulate reasons for their actions, but the judge is. The judge's reasoning ought to be considered by the theorist and not brushed aside as an irrelevance.

We agree that judicial reasoning is relevant to the economic analysis of law. It is always material and sometimes essential to determining the scope and meaning of the rule that can be extracted from the judicial opinion. Our quarrel is with the narrower proposition that the refusal of judges to speak in the language of economics shows that the rules they formulate are not based on efficiency. People can apply the principles of economics intuitively — and thus "do" economics without knowing they are doing it. Indeed, economic principles may be encoded in the ethical vocabulary that is a staple of judicial language. The language of justice and equity that dominates judicial opinions could represent simply the translation of economic principles into ethical language.

Another methodological criticism is that by drawing precedents indiscriminately from the fourteenth through twentieth centuries, we conceal significant trends in the common law — including a recent and pronounced trend away from efficiency. Far from denying that the common law has changed over the years, however, we regard changes in the law as important tests of the positive economic theory. If a relevant social circumstance (such as the relative costs of buyer and seller in determining whether a product is defective) changes, we predict that the law will change. But perhaps recent changes in products liability law, medical malpractice, and other areas of tort law are not justified by any changes in the relative costs of safety; this is a serious and important argument which we examine in part IV of this article.

A related criticism is that the efficiency theory of tort law is poorly defined. Does the theory hold that *all* tort rules and outcomes are efficient? If not, how can it be refuted? Or, is the theory temporally limited, perhaps to exclude the last twenty years? Is it a theory equally applicable to all common-law jurisdictions or does it exclude, for example, California, which has led the recent movement away from efficiency as a ruling principle of tort law? These are legitimate questions. Our tentative answer is that, throughout the history of the common law, efficiency has been the dominant value embodied in tort law but not the only value. The distributive and other nonefficiency concerns that have shaped legislative interventions in safety questions from workmen's compensation through no-fault automobile accident compensation have indeed influenced the courts, especially in recent years.

If our theory is that efficiency has been the dominant rather than the only value served by tort law, the question arises how it can be refuted. To repeat an earlier point, a positive theory that cannot be refuted even in principle cannot be confirmed either. Under the formulation offered here, if a rule of tort law cannot be explained on efficiency grounds, this is not a contradiction of the theory or even a puzzle; it is consistent with the proposition that most rather than all tort doctrines are efficient. However, this point does not show that our theory cannot be refuted. A theory that most rules are efficient is refuted by evidence that most are inefficient, or that a nonefficiency theory explains more tort rules than an efficiency theory.

We could discuss the criticisms of the positive economic theory of tort law at greater length, but the discussion would be inconclusive — most debates over methodology are. The reader who is unconvinced by our rebuttals should suspend judgment at least until the end of the article (or, if he is very patient, until he has read the book upon which it is based). The reader will be better able then to judge what we consider the most troubling criticism of our approach: the difficulty of forming confident judgments about the efficiency of specific case outcomes without knowing more than the opinions reveal about the facts.

II. The Model of Efficient Tort Law

This part of this article presents the formal model that underlies the positive economic theory of tort law. There is nothing new about the model.[41] If there is any novelty in this part of the article, it is in our effort to exposit the model in a way that will enable lawyers with little or no mathematical or economic background to understand it.

A. A Model of Accidents

1. Choice under Uncertainty. There is a problem in attaching values to, and hence choosing among, uncertain prospects. How is one to value the prospect of a 10% chance of \$20 and a 90% chance of \$1 compared to a certain income of \$2? Or a 10% chance of suffering a \$10 injury compared to a 1% chance of a \$100 injury? Fortunately, there is a well-developed model of choice under uncertainty. The basic assumption of the model is that an individual ranks uncertain prospects by their expected utility and chooses that prospect with the highest expected utility.

In presenting the expected-utility model, it is convenient to assume that the individual's utility depends upon a single composite good called "income" (or "wealth"), as in

$$U = U(I), \tag{1}$$

where I is income. Thus, for example, if a person is injured in an accident, his injury can be expressed in terms of a loss in units of the composite good, I. We assume that the individual prefers more to less income or, in other words, that the marginal utility of income is positive — *i.e.*, the increment in utility from a \$1 increase in income is positive. Hence, $U(\$1000) > U(\$500) > U(\$499)$, and given the choice among these incomes, \$1000 would be chosen. We can extend the analysis to uncertainty by defining the expected utility of a prospect as

$$U = \sum_{i=1}^{n} p_i U(I_i) \tag{2}$$

where there are n mutually exclusive states of the world or outcomes, $U(I_i)$ is the utility associated with the income in state i ($i=1, \ldots, n$), p_i is the subjective probability of each state i, $0 \leq p_i \leq 1$, and $\sum p_i = 1$. (Notice that if $p_i = 1$, we are back at

[41] It is essentially the same model introduced in Brown, *supra* note 17. We have used the model in our previous work. *See* Landes & Posner, *supra* note 20; W. Landes & R. Posner, *supra* note 19.

an analysis of choice under certainty.) The assumption of expected utility maximization implies that the individual will select that prospect with the greatest expected utility.[42]

There are three important classes of utility functions in the expected-utility model: risk-averse, risk-neutral, and risk-preferring.[43] These are shown in Figure 1. Although marginal utility of income is positive for all three functions, it is diminishing for the risk-averse function, constant for the risk-neutral function, and increasing for the risk-preferring function (*i.e.*, $U' > 0$ for all three functions but $U'' \gtreqless 0$ depending on whether the individual is risk-preferring, risk-neutral, or risk-averse).[44]

Figure 1

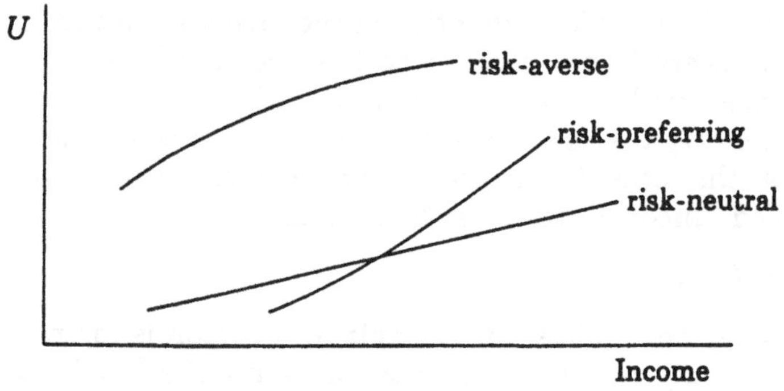

[42] One can obtain a more intuitive understanding of expected utility analysis by assuming that there are only two possible states of the world, for example, an accident and no-accident state where

p = probability of an accident

$(1 - p)$ = probability of no accident.

Expected utility equals

$$\overline{U} = pU(I^a) + (1 - p)\,U(I^n) \tag{3}$$

where I^a and I^n are the incomes in the accident and no-accident states respectively, and $I^a < I^n$. We can compare the expected utility from this prospect with that of other prospects involving different income levels or accident probabilities, or to the prospect of receiving a certain income between I^a and I^n. The expected-utility model enables us, for example, to determine how much an individual would pay, if anything, for insurance against the accident, or the level of care that maximizes expected utility, assuming p depends upon care.

[43] A single utility function also could have segments that are risk-averse, risk-neutral, and risk-preferring. To simplify, we assume the utility function exhibits only one of these characteristics.

[44] U' denotes marginal utility of income (the derivative of utility with respect to income) and U'' denotes the rate of change of U' (the second derivative of utility with respect to income). A derivative is simply a rate of change. Where, as with the risk-averse function, the function is increasing but at a decreasing rate, the first derivative is positive but the second negative.

Generally, people are assumed to be risk-averse. It seems intuitive that the marginal utility of money income does diminish eventually, so that a person will not gamble his entire net worth for a fifty percent chance of doubling it, particularly if losing it means starvation. There is a good deal of evidence for the prevalence of risk aversion in the behavior of securities investors, in the purchase of insurance,[45] and in other areas. Nevertheless, our analysis of the economics of tort law assumes that the utility functions of both injurers and victims are risk-neutral rather than risk-averse.

Our principal reason for adopting so seemingly unrealistic an assumption is that a risk-neutral model of liability rules yields more definite predictions than a model that assumes risk aversion. To assume risk aversion would give us too many degrees of freedom in explaining common-law rules and would make the efficiency theory of those rules difficult to refute (and hence to confirm). This would be an inadequate reason for assuming risk neutrality if we were analyzing an institution patently designed to reduce risk, such as insurance. But there is no compelling reason to assume that common-law judges in formulating efficient rules of accident control would think it important to try to reduce risk as well as accident and accident-avoidance costs. Both accident and liability insurance have long been available to prospective victims of accidents and prospective injurers alike,[46] and before there was market insurance there was informal insurance provided through the family.[47] If people who want insurance and are willing to pay for it can obtain insurance in the insurance market or in some informal substitute for it, there is no reason to use the tort system to provide insur-

---

[45] The purchase of insurance is intelligible only on the assumption of risk aversion: because of administrative costs, the insurance premium is always greater than the expected value of the insurance.

[46] *See, e.g.*, O.W. HOLMES, *supra* note 1, at 961 ("Universal insurance, if desired, can be better and more cheaply accomplished by private enterprise.").

[47] The role of the family as an insurance mechanism is emphasized in Posner, *A Theory of Primitive Society, with Special Reference to Law*, 23 J.L. & ECON. 1, 10-18 (1980).

Contract law, in contrast to tort law, has been analyzed in several studies that assume risk aversion. *See, e.g.*, S. CHEUNG, THE THEORY OF SHARE TENANCY (1969); Posner & Rosenfield, *Impossibility and Related Doctrines in Contract Law: An Economic Analysis*, 6 J. LEGAL STUD. 83 (1977). The difference between tort and contract law in this respect is that moral-hazard problems greatly complicate the provision of market insurance for breach of contract and for injury caused by such breach. For example, it is difficult to purchase market insurance against a rise in the price of an essential input. Thus, risk-shifting may be an important function of contracts and contract law but not of tort law.

ance also.[48] The tort system then can treat injurers and victims as if they were risk-neutral. The adequacy of insurance outside the tort system is, to be sure, a matter of fair debate, and we lack enough data to form a judgment on the costs of insurance through tort liability relative to those of market insurance or insurance through the family (and lately through the state). However, given the availability of insurance to people involved in accidents, whether as injurers or as victims, it is not grossly unrealistic to posit risk-neutral utility functions for purposes of the positive economic analysis of tort law.

2. *Optimal or Due Care.* What actions should prospective parties to an accident take to minimize the social costs of accidents? Each party is assumed to be risk-neutral and therefore to have a utility function that in terms of Figure 1 is linear. That is, $U = a + bI$ where $a \geq 0$ and $b > 0$. Observe that U is positive for all levels of income and increases at a constant rate equal to b, the marginal utility of income, as income increases. Because a person's expenditure on care or insurance will be the same for all values of a and b, provided $b > 0$, it is convenient to assume that $a = 0$ and $b = 1$, and therefore that $U = I$. If, in addition, we let social welfare equal the sum of all utilities, then assuming $U = I$ has the computational advantage of allowing us to measure social welfare as the sum of all incomes, thus equating efficiency with income or wealth maximization. This does not mean that social welfare actually is, or should be, simply the sum of all incomes, or even that there is such a thing as a social welfare function. The purpose of assuming a particular social welfare function is to enable us to define the term "social costs of accidents" and then to test the hypothesis that the rules governing tort liability are best explained as efforts to minimize these costs.

Assume that an accident, if it occurs, involves two people, A and B, where A is the victim (plaintiff) and B the injurer (defendant). Defining x as A's inputs of care and y as B's inputs of care, we can

[48] It can be shown that if insurance is actuarially fair, a risk-averse person will (1) insure until his income is equalized in all states of the world, and (2) act as if he is risk-neutral with respect to expenditures on care. *See* Ehrlich & Becker, *Market Insurance, Self-Insurance, and Self-Protection*, 80 J. Pol. Econ. 623 (1972).

express p, the probability of accident between A and B, as a function of x and y; that is

$$p = p(x,y). \tag{4}$$

We assume that p_x and p_y, the marginal products of care, are both negative and diminishing, meaning that a small increase in A's or B's inputs of care, x and y, will reduce p but at a decreasing rate. (Diminishing marginal product is denoted by $p_{xx} > 0$ and $p_{yy} > 0$.)[49] Let D denote the dollar equivalent of the injury to A if the accident occurs, and $A(x)$ and $B(y)$ the costs of care to A and B respectively. We then can write the expected utilities (equal to expected incomes under the assumption of risk neutrality) of A and B respectively as

$$\begin{aligned}\bar{U}^a &= p(I^a - D - A(x)) + (1 - p)(I^a - A(x)) \\ &= I^a - pD - A(x)\end{aligned} \tag{4a}$$

$$\begin{aligned}\bar{U}^b &= p(I^b - B(y)) + (1 - p)(I^b - B(y)) \\ &= I^b - B(y)\end{aligned} \tag{4b}$$

and the sum of their expected utilities (or expected income) as

$$\bar{U}^a + \bar{U}^b = I^a + I^b - pD - A(x) - B(y). \tag{4c}$$

If it is assumed that everyone else's utility is independent of A's and B's utility, social welfare is maximized when $\bar{U}^a + \bar{U}^b$ is maximized. Because I^a and I^b are fixed, this is equivalent to minimizing the social costs of accidents defined as the sum of the expected accident losses and the costs of care (or avoidance). That is, we want to pick the levels of x and y that minimize

$$L(x,y) = p(x, y)D + A(x) + B(y) \tag{5}$$

where $L(x,y)$ is the social cost of accidents. Let x^* and y^* be the values that minimize $L(x,y)$, *i.e.*, the "due care" levels, and assume the marginal costs of care, A_x and B_y, are positive and nondecreasing. Then x^* and y^* can be found by taking the first partial derivatives of L with respect to x and y and setting the resulting expression equal to zero.[50] This requires that x^* and y^*

[49] P_x and P_y are the first partial derivatives of p with respect to x and y, and p_{xx} and p_{yy} are the second partial derivatives. Throughout the article we denote derivatives by subscripts unless indicated otherwise.

[50] Our assumptions of diminishing marginal products ($p_{xx} > 0$ and $p_{yy} > 0$) and increasing or constant marginal costs of care ($A_{xx} \geq 0$ and $B_{yy} \geq 0$) assure that x^* and y^* yield the

satisfy the following conditions:

$$A_x = -p_x D \qquad (6a)$$
$$B_y = -p_y D. \qquad (6b)$$

The results are intuitive. A should keep adding inputs of care until the reduction in expected damages $(-p_x D)$ is equal to the marginal costs of the last unit of care. Before that point is reached, an additional input of care would confer a greater social benefit in reducing A's expected damages than it would cost in additional expenditures on care; beyond that point an additional input of care would cost more than it was worth in accident prevention. The analysis of B's optimal care is parallel.

The optimal or due care levels are shown graphically in Figures 2 and 3. In both diagrams, the demand curves show the expected reduction in the victim's damages from additional units of care and the supply curves show the marginal costs of taking care. Demand curves are shown downward sloping, indicating decreasing marginal products of care, and supply curves are shown upward sloping, indicating increasing marginal costs of care. The due care levels, x^* and y^*, occur at the intersections of the demand and supply curves.[61]

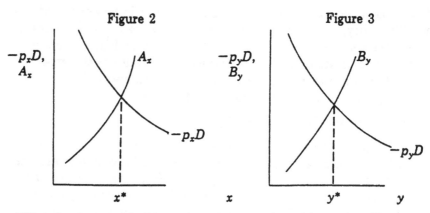

Figure 2

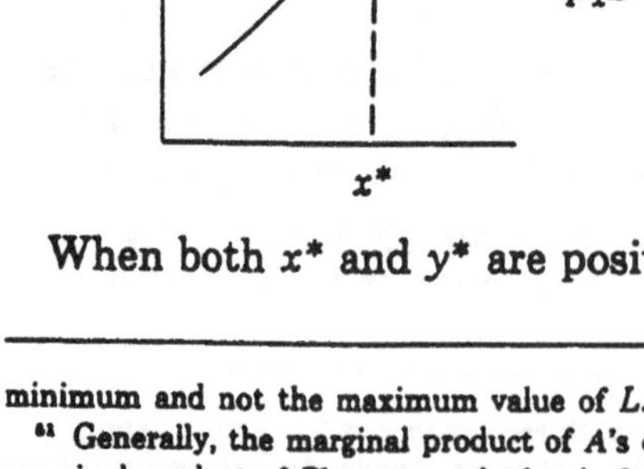

Figure 3

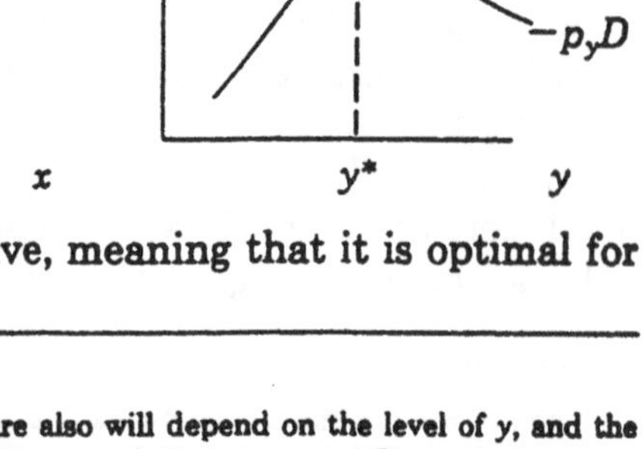

When both x^* and y^* are positive, meaning that it is optimal for

minimum and not the maximum value of L.

[61] Generally, the marginal product of A's care also will depend on the level of y, and the marginal product of B's care on the level of x (*i.e.*, $p_{xy} \neq 0$). In terms of Figure 2, therefore, a different demand curve exists for each level of y and in Figure 3 a different demand curve for each level of x. To simplify the diagrams, the demand curve in Figure 2 is drawn assuming $y = y^*$ and in Figure 3 assuming $x = x^*$.

both *A* and *B* to take some care, we speak of the situation as one of "joint care." Where it is optimal for either *A* or *B* to take care, and for the other party not to take care, we refer to the situation as one of "alternative care."[52] The distinction will become clear in due course. A further point to bear in mind is that inputs of care, x and y, can take two forms. One is doing an activity more carefully; the other is doing less of the activity. For example, while one way of reducing crop damage from locomotive sparks is to reduce the level of the activity, either railroading or farming, another is to conduct the activity more carefully. For example, the railroad could run the same number of trains but install spark-arresting equipment on each locomotive, or the farmer could plant the same amount of crops and as close to the railroad tracks as before but spray them with some fire-retardant chemical. Though unimportant in our formal analysis, the distinction between carefulness and activity will become important when we compare the legal standards of negligence and strict liability as methods of creating incentives for accident avoidance. These standards have different effects on the incentive to avoid an accident by reducing the level of one's activity as distinct from conducting the activity more carefully.[53]

Some other assumptions of our formal analysis should be noted briefly. We assume that the parties' inputs of care affect only the probability of an accident and not the cost of the accident (D) if it occurs. The model could easily, indeed trivially, be expanded to allow x and y to affect D as well as p — to deal, for example, with the case where wearing seatbelts will reduce the cost of an accident if it occurs while not affecting the probability it will occur. We also assume that people can be sorted into potential injurers and potential victims, rather than that they are symmetrical. Other economic analysts of accidents, notably Peter Diamond, have assumed that injurers and victims are drawn from an identical pool, and that when they encounter each other in an accident it is a matter of pure chance who is victim and who is injurer.[54] Our model is

[52] This distinction was introduced into the literature in Landes & Posner, *supra* note 20. Alternative care, for example where $x^* = 0$, would be depicted in Figure 2 by a demand curve that was everywhere below the supply curve.

[53] The distinction between care and activity as methods of accident avoidance is discussed in Posner, *supra* note 16, at 208-09, and formalized and elaborated upon in Shavell, *Strict Liability versus Negligence*, 9 J. LEGAL STUD. 1 (1980).

[54] *See* Diamond, *supra* note 13; Diamond, *Accident Law and Resource Allocation*, 5 BELL

simpler than Diamond's and there appear to be no important differences in substantive implications.[65]

Finally, we assume that A and B are complete strangers and that the costs of a voluntary negotiation between them are prohibitive. Without this assumption liability rules would not affect the level of care; the Coase theorem implies that the parties would agree to use x^* and y^* inputs of care, because these are the levels of care that maximize their joint incomes.[66] With the assumption that a transaction is infeasible, we confront, as noted in part I, a serious externality problem. Why should B expend any resources on care when the benefits of that expenditure will inure to A? And if B takes no care, will not A be led to take excessive care from an overall social standpoint? The question to which we turn next is how liability rules can internalize the cost of accidents and thereby induce A and B to buy x^* and y^* inputs of care, respectively.

B. *A Model of Liability Rules*

1. No-Liability. A no-liability rule is a genuine liability rule because it affects the incentives of the parties. It is sometimes the optimal rule. Although B has no incentive to take care because he is not liable for A's accident costs, A has an incentive to invest in care up to the point where $A_x = -p_xD$ given $y = 0$. This point will be optimal if $y^* = 0$, *i.e.*, in the alternative-care case where A, the potential victim, is the more efficient accident avoider. If the case is one of joint care, so that x^* and y^* both are positive, a no-liability rule is inefficient. Moreover, if the care inputs of injurers and victims are partly substitutable, the victim's care level under a rule of no-liability will be greater than x^*.[67] For example, if some

J. ECON. & MGMT. SCI. 366 (1974); Diamond & Mirrlees, *On the Assignment of Liability: The Uniform Case*, 6 BELL J. ECON. & MGMT. SCI. 487 (1975).

[65] *See* Appendix to this article, where we extend our model to the symmetrical case.

[66] Although our formal analysis focuses on accidents between complete strangers (in the sense that transaction costs are prohibitive), it easily can be extended to torts that arise out of a contractual setting (*e.g.*, where A buys a product or service from B). Assuming risk neutrality, the parties to a contract would maximize its joint value by agreeing to use x^* and y^* inputs of care. Thus, in an accident between parties to a contract, one would define negligence and contributory negligence in the same way as one defines it in an accident between strangers — *i.e.*, as a level of care less than due care.

[67] By "substitutable" we mean that a reduction in y raises the marginal product (p_x) of x — *i.e.*, $p_{xy} > 0$. Since p_x is negative, a higher marginal product as y declines means a larger negative number (*e.g.*, -6 instead of -4) for p_x and therefore a positive value for p_{xy}.

care by drivers is optimal, a pedestrian probably will take more care than x^* if drivers are not liable for running down pedestrians, but he might take less. Measures of victim accident avoidance that were feasible when drivers took some care against pedestrian accidents might become infeasible (unproductive) when drivers took no care against such accidents, and no other pedestrian-care measures might be feasible either.

2. *Strict Liability*. Strict liability is symmetrical to no liability. Under strict liability (with no defense of contributory negligence), the victim, *A*, has no incentive to take care, because he is fully compensated for his injury, *D*. But *B* has an incentive to invest in care up to the point where $B_y = -p_y D$ given $x = 0$, because under strict liability *D* is a cost to *B* if an accident occurs. Just as no liability is efficient where the case is one of alternative care and $y^* = 0$, so strict liability is efficient where the case is one of alternative care and $x^* = 0$, *i.e.*, where there is no reasonable (cost-justified) measure that the victim can take to avert the accident or reduce the probability that it will occur. There is, however, an important asymmetry between no liability and strict liability that appears once we relax the implicit assumption that there are no costs of operating the legal system: no liability is cheaper to administer. Strict liability is costly to administer because (ignoring possible defenses to strict liability) every accident that occurs gives rise to a legal claim for compensation and thus a possible lawsuit. No liability is administratively costless. Administrative costs are discussed in more detail later.

3. *Negligence*. Under a negligence rule (and ignoring for the moment contributory negligence), an injurer is liable for his victim's damages if and only if the accident resulted from the injurer's failure to take due care, which for now we will assume (an assumption to be relaxed later) means a failure to use y^* inputs of care (*i.e.*, $y < y^*$). So defined, a negligence rule gives *B* an incentive to use the optimal amount of care, y^*.

If we put to one side the problem of contributory negligence by assuming that $x^* = 0$, *L* is minimized when

$$L(0,y^*) = p(0,y^*) + B(y^*). \tag{7}$$

We then can state the negligence rule as follows: if an accident occurs, *B* must pay *A*'s damages (*D*) if *B*'s actual inputs of care are lower than y^*, the due care level; conversely, *B* is not liable if $y \geq$

y^*. Let y_0 be any level of y (including 0) less than y^*. B will choose to be negligent or nonnegligent depending upon whether

$$p(0, y_0)D + B(y_0) \lesseqgtr B(y^*). \qquad (8)$$

We know, however, that

$$L(0,y_0) = p(0,y_0)D + B(y) > L(0,y^*) \qquad (9)$$

because, by definition, y^* minimizes $L(0,y)$. Because $B(y^*) < L(0,y^*)$, it is also less than $L(0,y_0)$; hence a negligence rule creates an incentive for a potential injurer to use due care.

4. *Strict Liability and Negligence Compared.* Conventional legal scholars long have assumed that strict liability would induce potential injurers to be more careful than they would be under a negligence standard; economic analysis suggests that their analysis is superficial. Assuming that $x^* = 0$, B will choose y^*, the due care level, whether he is strictly liable or liable only if negligent. The intuitive explanation is straightforward. Even if strictly liable, meaning that he must pay D whether he was at the due care level or not, B will not exceed that level. By definition, at any level of care greater than y^*, the cost of the marginal unit of care to B is greater than the expected reduction in his liability for A's damages. Therefore, B's expected net income $(I^b - pD - B(y))$ is greater at y^* than $y > y^*$, and he will never use care greater than y^*. But neither will he under a negligence rule ever use care greater than y^*, because he will not be liable for any accident that occurs when he is at the due care level, y^*. Notice also that the victim's care level will be zero under both strict liability and negligence (assuming a case of alternative care where $x^* = 0$). Under strict liability, A has no incentive to take care because he is compensated for his injury should an accident occur. Under negligence, A does not expect to be compensated for his injury but he still has no incentive to take care, because the costs of care are greater than the resulting reduction in expected damages.

Strict liability and negligence are not, however, economically identical standards. They differ in two major respects. The first involves the costs of administering the liability rule. These costs are of two types, which we shall call with some looseness "information costs" and "claim costs." The former we define as the costs of ascertaining whether B's actual level of care, y, was equal to y^*. These costs are zero under strict liability because due care is not an issue in a case decided under a strict liability standard, but they may be substantial in a negligence case. The second kind of cost, claim costs, comprises the costs (other than information costs as defined above) of processing and collecting a legal claim; that is, of determining damage, causation, and other issues not involving the level of care of the defendant, and of transferring money from injurer to victim if the injurer is held liable. These costs are higher under strict liability than under negligence because the number of claims is larger. Under strict liability, a claim arises every time there is an accident caused by someone worth suing; under negligence, there is a claim only if the victim thinks he can show that the defendant failed to use due care. Defenses to liability may reduce the scope of liability under both negligence and strict liability, but presumably not more so under the latter; thus the relative administrative costs are unaffected.

Because information costs are higher under a negligence rule and claim costs higher under strict liability, we would expect that, other things unchanged, a fall in information costs would result in a shift away from strict liability and toward negligence. Looking broadly at the history of liability rules and at the differences between liability rules in primitive and modern societies, we find that the secular decline in the costs of information associated with growing literacy and knowledge of how the physical world operates has been accompanied by a movement away from strict liability and toward negligence as the dominant rule of liability. The evidence for these trends, presented elsewhere,[58] supports our theory that tort law has been shaped by economic considerations.

The other major respect in which negligence and strict liability differ economically is in incentives to avoid accidents by reducing the level of activity rather than by increasing the care with which the activity is conducted. We mentioned earlier that y^* might involve running fewer trains as well as installing spark-arresting equipment on each locomotive. Under strict liability, a potential injurer will interpret y^* broadly. He is interested in any measure that would reduce his expected liability by more than the cost of the measure; it is a matter of indifference to him whether the cost results from having to purchase some safety input or from forgoing the profits from a higher level of productive activity. However,

[58] *See* Posner, *supra* note 49, at 42-52; Posner, *supra* note 32, at 90-91.

when a court determines y^*, as it must when the rule is negligence rather than strict liability, it may take a narrower view of the potential injurer's options. The court will consider how the defendant might conduct his activity more carefully but it may not consider the benefits and costs of the defendant's avoiding accidents by reducing his activity. For example, a court in an automobile-accident case would consider whether the defendant had driven carefully when the accident occurred but it would not consider whether the trip was really necessary in the sense that the benefits of the trip exceeded all of its costs including expected accident costs.

This is essentially a point about information costs. One way of economizing on the costs of determining y^* is for the court to look at only a subset of care inputs — those that relate to the safety with which the activity is carried out, as distinct from the amount of the activity. If courts in negligence suits constrict their vision in this way, strict liability may result in fewer accidents than negligence — not by inducing the defendant to be more careful but by inducing him in some cases to reduce the level of his activity and with it the expected number of accidents.

Before concluding that strict liability is allocatively more efficient than negligence,[59] however, we must consider a heretofore neglected factor, the victim's activity level. Put aside any issue of the victim's being careless in a negligence sense by assuming that there is a defense of contributory negligence under both a strict liability and a negligence standard. Assume also that contributory negligence resembles negligence in that the activity of the victim is not considered in determining whether he used due care. On these assumptions, strict liability and negligence have opposite, and potentially offsetting, effects on injurer and victim activity. Under strict liability, the injurer has an incentive to change or reduce his activity where such an adjustment is an optimal method of accident avoidance, because he bears the costs of any accident that could be avoided by such an adjustment; but the victim has no incentive to adjust his activity because he is compensated for any injury not resulting from his own failure to be careful. Under negligence, the injurer has no incentive to adjust his activity level but the victim does, because he is not compensated for any injury that occurs un-

[59] By the "allocative" dimension of a rule, we mean its effect in internalizing external costs; by its "administrative" dimension, we mean the costs of administering the rule.

less it could have been avoided by the injurer's being more careful rather than by the injurer's reducing his activity level. Hence the different effects of strict liability and negligence on activity do not provide an economic reason for preferring strict liability to negligence, unless an adjustment in the defendant's activity, but not in the plaintiff's, would be an efficient method of accident avoidance. Strict liability may not result in fewer accidents than negligence; it will reduce the defendant's activity level but it will increase the plaintiff's, and the number of accidents may be greater, fewer, or the same as under a negligence standard.

This analysis yields predictions concerning the pattern of strict liability and negligence that one will observe in the law if the positive economic theory of tort law is correct. If a change in the plaintiff's activity is unlikely to be an efficient method of accident avoidance, but a change in the defendant's activity is likely to be an efficient method, strict liability is an attractive rule. It will deter many accidents, and what we have called the claim cost of strict liability will be reduced. However, where greater care rather than less activity is the optimal method of accident avoidance by potential injurers, the case for negligence is strengthened, for now the claim costs of strict liability are likely to be high relative to its allocative effect, compared to negligence. Whether the pattern of strict liability and negligence follows the predictions of our analysis is considered in part III.

The activity point is not relevant only to the choice between strict liability and negligence. In the *Restatement*'s formulation of the nuisance standard, the utility of both the plaintiff's and the defendant's activities must be considered and compared in deciding whether there is an actionable nuisance.[60] Often a change in activity levels is a feasible means of avoiding damage in a nuisance case where greater care in the activity would not be. The reduction in property values caused by a funeral parlor cannot be eliminated by conducting funerals more discreetly or carefully, but it can be eliminated by relocating the funeral parlor — a change in activity rather than care.[61] The nuisance standard illustrates the common

---

[60] *See* RESTATEMENT (SECOND) OF TORTS § 826 (1977), and comments thereto.

[61] W. PROSSER, HANDBOOK OF THE LAW OF TORTS 599-601 (4th ed. 1971), stresses the importance of relocating either defendant's or plaintiff's operations as a mode of avoiding damage in nuisance cases.

law's recognition that when the place, kind, or amount of activity is an important factor in bringing about an optimal level of damage, it should be part of the legal standard.

Activity occasionally is considered in negligence cases as well. The utility of the plaintiff's activity was one of the factors singled out by Henry Terry in his formulation of the negligence standard,[62] a formulation that foreshadows the Hand formula discussed in part III. Terry was discussing rescue cases, one of the principal areas where the activity point is considered under the negligence standard. Suppose that *A* rushes into a burning building to save his hat. His behavior would be deemed negligent even if he did everything possible to minimize the hazard to himself — short of not entering the building in the first place. Because the cost of curtailing the activity is less than the expected accident cost, his behavior is, as we shall see, held to be negligent. The costs to the factfinder of determining the optimal activity level are low in this case, so the concept of due care is enlarged to include the level of the activity as well as the care with which it is undertaken. Where it is difficult to ascertain the optimal activity level, however, the courts applying a negligence standard generally do not attempt to do so. They do not consider, for example, whether the best way to avoid certain accidents at railroad crossings is for railroads to run fewer trains, or for travelers using the crossing to travel less. The determination of the opportunity costs of a lower activity level would in this case be very difficult. In the rescue case it is simple.

There is thus a trade-off between the information costs of considering the injurer's activity level as an aspect of due care and the allocative costs of ignoring the activity level. If the common law has made this trade-off correctly, there is no merit to the argument that the movement from strict liability to negligence in nineteenth-century tort law amounted to a covert subsidizing of productive but dangerous activities.[63] To be sure, strict liability increases the private costs of injurers compared to negligence liability, but if the imposition of those costs on them is not the best method of acci-

---

[62] *See* Terry, *supra* note 4.

[63] *See, e.g.*, M. Horwitz, The Transformation of American Law, 1780-1860, at 99-100 (1977). For criticism of Horwitz's argument, see Williams, *Transforming American Law: Doubtful Economics Makes Doubtful History*, 25 U.C.L.A. L. Rev. 1187 (1977).

dent control, the removal of those costs cannot be regarded as a subsidy. The repeal of an unjustified tax is not a subsidy to the former taxpayer.

One question remains to be considered in our comparison of strict liability and negligence: why are there *any* negligence cases? It is easy to see why there will be some cases under a rule of strict liability even if all potential injurers take due care (y^*). Although the probability of an accident will be lower than if injurers took less care (assuming that the plaintiff's optimal care level is zero or negligible), the number of accidents will still be positive and injurers will be liable for the damages resulting from them, so claims will be generated. Under negligence, however, it would seem that the number of cases should be zero. If the injurer maintains a care level of y^*, he is not liable for any accidents that occur; and he will not set a lower level of care because, as we showed earlier, he minimizes his private costs by adhering to that level.

There are several reasons for observing a positive number of negligence cases even if the courts set a care level of y^* for nonnegligent behavior and injurers are all rational economic maximizers:

(1) Either the court or the injurer may make a mistake in applying the standard to the facts. (Victims may make the same mistake, but their mistakes would result in cases in which negligence was alleged rather than in cases where it was found.) Mistakes give rise to the possibility that the parties will have divergent expectations of the likely outcome of litigation and divergent expectations can lead to litigation.[64]

(2) As emphasized by Peter Diamond, care has a stochastic (random) element.[65] For example, suppose that a potential injurer tries to achieve a level of care y^*, but his realized care is $y = y^* + e$, where e is a random error term with a mean of zero. Although $E(y)$, the injurer's expected care, is y^*, there will be instances when e will be negative and y will fall below y^*. If an injury occurs when $y < y^*$, a court that ignored the stochastic element of care would deem the injurer negligent. Because an omniscient court would take account of the stochastic character of care and decline to find negligence whenever $E(y) = y^*$ even though the realized level of care was below y^*, Diamond's is really a point about the

[64] *See, e.g.*, Landes, *An Economic Analysis of the Courts*, 14 J.L. & ECON. 61 (1971).
[65] *See* note 13 *supra*.

information costs of determining negligence in difficult cases.

(3) A related reason for expecting there to be some negligence cases, also introduced into the economic literature by Diamond, is the "average man" or "reasonable man" concept of negligence law. Due care is judged by the capabilities of the average individual rather than by those of the particular defendant (again, presumably because of information costs). If the defendant's capabilities are below average, the costs of his taking care will be above average and he may choose a care level below the average y^*. If an accident occurs, he will be held liable.[66] (Stated differently, reasons (2) and (3) both imply a strict liability element in negligence.)

(4) If judicial factfinding and law-applying were so accurate that nobody behaved negligently, was accused of negligence, or was adjudged negligent, there would be for a time no cases, supposing reasons (2) and (3) above were not operative either. But this happy situation could not last. As time passed, the precedents defining the standard of care would become stale, the difficulty of predicting the outcome of negligence cases (if they should arise) would therefore grow, and people would begin to behave negligently or be sued for negligence because of misapprehension of what the legal standard was or how it would be applied to them.[67] Presumably, then, the common-law equilibrium is one where there are some negligence cases in the courts at all times.

5. *Negligence Plus Contributory Negligence*. Our analysis of strict liability and negligence was simplified by assuming that $x^* = 0$, *i.e.*, that optimal avoidance requires no inputs of care by the potential accident victim. If we assume instead that the social costs of accidents, $L(x,y)$, are minimized only when both x^* and y^* are positive, we have an important reason why the legal system would favor negligence with a defense of contributory negligence over strict liability with no such defense.

Assume that contributory negligence, defined as x less than x^* (just as negligence was $y < y^*$), is a complete bar to the victim's recovering damages from the injurer. Under a standard of negligence plus contributory negligence so defined, and denoting by s^a

[66] Although his optimal care level is less than y^*, a below-average person (provided he is not too far below average) may bring his care level up to y^* under a negligence rule to avoid liability if an accident occurs.

[67] *See* Landes & Posner, *supra* note 38, at 271-72.

the share of damages (D) that falls on the victim A and by s^b the share of damages that is shifted by the liability system to the injurer B, we have the following relationship between care and liability:

Care	Liability
x^*, y^*	$s^a = 1; s^b = 0$
$x < x^*, y^*$	$s^a = 1; s^b = 0$
$x < x^*, y < v^*$	$s^a = 1; s^b = 0$
$x^*, y < y^*$	$s^a = 0; s^b = 1$

For example, when both parties take due care (x^*, y^*) or both take less than due care ($x < x^*, y < y^*$), none of A's damages are shifted to B (*i.e.*, $s^a = 1$ and $s^b = 0$). If only the injurer is negligent, A's full damages are shifted to B (*i.e.*, $s^a = 0$, $s^b = 1$).

Assume that each party acts to minimize his expected loss (or equivalently to maximize his expected income), taking account of the particular liability rule and the likely behavior of the other party. First consider the potential victim's behavior. Table 1 shows the victim's expected loss for different levels of his and the injurer's care. If A expects B to be negligent and use y_0 inputs of care,[68] A will minimize his expected loss by choosing x^*.

Table 1

A's Expected Losses

B's care	A's care	
	$x_0 < x^*$	x^*
$y_0 < y^*$	$p(x_0,y_0)D + A(x_0)$	$A(x^*)$
y^*	$p(x_0,y^*)D + A(x_0)$	$p(x^*,y^*)D + A(x^*)$

Because $p(x_0,y_0)D + A(x_0)$ in Table 1 may be written as $L(x_0,y_0) - B(y_0)$, and $L(x^*,y^*)$ is by definition the minimum expected social cost of an accident, the best choice for A given $y = y_0$ is x^* because $L(x_0,y_0) - B(y_0) > L(x^*,y^*) - B(y_0) > A(x^*)$. Alternatively, if A expects B to choose the due care level y^*, A will also choose x^* because by definition $L(x^*,y^*) - B(y^*) < L(x_0,y^*) -$

[68] Y_0 inputs may be zero or any amount less than y^*. Similarly, x_0 may be zero or any amount less than x^*.

$B(y^*)$.

Now consider B's behavior. Table 2 gives B's expected loss for different assumed values of A's and B's care.

Table 2

B's Expected Losses

A's care	*B*'s care	
	$y_0 < y^*$	y^*
$x_0 < x^*$	$B(y_0)$	$B(y^*)$
x^*	$p(x^*,y_0)D + B(y_0)$	$B(y^*)$

Obviously, the best possible outcome for B is (x_0,y_0) because he can use zero care and still not be liable for A's injury should it occur. We have shown, however, that A has an incentive always to use x^*. Thus, B will expect that potential victims are using due care. Hence B's choice is limited to the second row of Table 2. From the definition of due care we know that $B(y^*) < L(x^*,y^*)D - A(x^*) < L(x^*,y_0) - A(x^*) = p(x^*,y_0)D + B(y_0)$; therefore B will choose y^*.

The intuition behind this result is straightforward. Each party knows that if he is careless, the other party will have an incentive to be careful as a way of throwing the entire liability onto him; knowing this, each has an incentive to be careful. Thus, suppose a \$100 injury to B can be averted if A spends \$50 and B \$40, and each will be deemed negligent (in A's case, contributorily negligent) for failing to make that expenditure. B knows that if he fails to spend \$40, A will spend \$50, for by doing so A shifts a \$100 loss to B at a cost of only \$50; knowing this, B will invest his \$40 so as to avert a loss of \$100 (resulting in a net gain of \$60). Conversely, A knows that if he fails to spend \$50, he will be barred from recovering damages from a negligent B by the doctrine of contributory negligence. Moreover, even if A expects B to be nonnegligent, A can avoid a \$100 loss by spending \$50 on care. Knowing this, A will spend \$50.

The rule of contributory negligence is only one possible allocation of loss between injurer and victim. Other allocations — as under a strict liability rule with a defense of contributory negligence (where $s^a = 0$ and $s^b = 1$ when $x = x^*$ and $y = y^*$) or a comparative negligence rule (where the parties divide the losses if an accident occurs and both have used less than due care) — would have the same effect on the parties' levels of care. No proof of this proposition will be presented here,[69] but an arithmetical example for comparative negligence will indicate the underlying intuition. Suppose the rule were that the negligent victim could collect 90 percent of his damages from a negligent injurer — *i.e.*, when $x < x^*$ and $y < y^*$, $s^a = .10$ and $s^b = .90$. Then, in the above example, *A* might appear to have no incentive to take care because 10 percent of \$100 is less than \$50. *B* would have an incentive to take care, however, because by doing so he could avoid an expected liability of \$90 at a cost of only \$40. Therefore, *A* will expect *B* to spend \$40 on care. *A* knows that he thus will incur the full \$100 loss unless he spends \$50, so he will do so. Although comparative negligence has the same allocative effect as contributory negligence, at least in a joint-care case, it is more costly to administer, and hence less efficient in terms of our analysis. Its traditional rejection by common-law courts is thus consistent with the positive theory.

III. The Model Applied: Negligence and the Choice Between Negligence and Strict Liability

Having presented a formal model of the basic principles of tort liability in accident cases, we turn now to a comparison of that model with the actual doctrines of tort law. The liability rules modeled in part II were *economic* concepts of liability; it remains to inquire whether the actual rules of tort liability correspond to the predictions of the economic model. The scope of such an empirical inquiry is as broad as tort law itself, and no effort to explore the full range of tort principles will be made in this article. We shall merely begin the empirical inquiry by examining (1) the basic negligence standard, encapsulated in the Hand formula; (2) contributory negligence, and some defenses thereto; (3) the application of the negligence standard in representative cases; and (4) the common law's choice between strict liability and negligence as the liability standard in particular classes of case.

---

[69] For a proof, see Landes & Posner, *supra* note 20, at 539 n.51.

A. The Hand Formula

In *United States v. Carroll Towing Co.*,[70] the question was whether the owner of a barge owed a duty to keep an attendant on board while the barge was moored in the harbor, because on occasion unattended barges would break loose from their moorings and cause damage to other ships. Judge Learned Hand defined the owner's duty as a function of three variables:

P = probability that the barge will break away;
L = gravity of resulting injury, if it does break away;
B = burden of precaution adequate to prevent it from breaking away.

According to Hand, the owner would be negligent if the burden of precautions (B) was less than the probability times the gravity (PL); *i.e.*, if $B < PL$. This is the "Hand formula" of negligence.

Because *Carroll Towing* is a recent decision by common-law standards and because few if any other decisions have used this or any other algebraic formulation, it has been questioned whether the Hand formula states the legal meaning of negligence accurately. Since Hand was purporting only to make explicit what had long been the implicit meaning of negligence, however, the comparative recency of the case does not establish the novelty of the definition. Something like the Hand formula has long been used to decide negligence cases. For example, in a case decided in 1864, the court stated that

> in all cases the amount of care which a prudent man will take must vary infinitely according to circumstances. No prudent man in carrying a lighted candle through a powder magazine would fail to take more care than if he was going through a damp cellar. The amount of care will be proportionate to the degree of risk run and to the magnitude of the mischief that may be occasioned.[71]

The Hand formula obviously resembles the economic model of due care (see equations (6a) and (6b) in part II), but how close is the resemblance? The Hand formula makes no reference to care by

---

[70] 159 F.2d 169 (2d Cir. 1947).

[71] Mackintosh v. Macintosh, 2 M. 1357, 1362-63, 36 Scot. Jur. 678, 681 (Scot. Ct. Sess. 1864).

the accident victim; we take up this problem in the next section. In addition, the formula is inexplicit on whether accident costs and benefits are to be considered in the correct marginal, rather than total, terms. If for B, the burden or cost of precautions, we substitute B_y, the marginal cost of care, and for PL, the expected damage from the accident, we substitute $-p_yD$, the marginal reduction in accident damage, the Hand formula for negligence can be written as $B_y < -p_yD$. This means that it is negligent to use a level of care at which the marginal cost of accident avoidance is less than the marginal benefit from avoidance; that is, to use a care level less than y^*.

This is the correct economic standard of negligence, but have we altered the meaning of the Hand formula by expressing it thus in marginal terms? To answer this question requires a consideration of actual cases, which we provide below. To anticipate, we find that the courts do consider marginal rather than total values in applying the standard. This is an unexpected benefit of the constricted focus which critics of the fault system consider a weakness of case-by-case determination of fault issues. The court asks, "What additional care inputs should the defendant have used to avoid this accident, given his existing level of care?" The focus on the particular accident and the particular inputs that could have prevented it invites a marginal analysis.

B. *Contributory Negligence and Some Defenses Thereto*

The common law used the doctrine of contributory negligence to evaluate the victim's care. Because the legal standards of negligence and contributory negligence are the same, we can infer that Judge Hand would have applied his formula to victims as well as injurers in any case where contributory negligence was alleged. Thus, if A_x is less than $-p_xD$, the victim is barred from recovering damages.

The negligence-contributory negligence approach, defined in marginal Hand formula terms, yields optimal results in cases of joint care (*i.e.*, cases where x^* and y^* are both positive), provided that the law applies the Hand formula to each party *on the assumption that the other party is exercising due care.*[72] Here our

[72] Recall from part II that if x and y, the inputs of care, are complementary or substitutable, the marginal products of one will depend upon the other; hence, x^* can be determined

interest is in the application of this principle to the victim. Suppose that if a railroad makes no effort to limit the emission of sparks from its locomotives, the expected damage to the farmer's crops will be $150, but this damage can be averted by the farmer's not planting crops near the tracks, at a cost to the farmer of $100. The damage also will be averted if the railroad spends $50 on a spark arrester and the farmer $5 on keeping a small space between his crops and the tracks. Obviously, the second method of avoidance, involving joint care by the railroad and the farmer, is more efficient, but if the Hand formula is applied to the farmer without the qualification suggested above, because $100 is less than $150 the farmer will be deemed contributorily negligent and will be led to relocate his crops. The accident will be averted, but at a cost that is $45 higher than necessary. If, instead, the farmer is required to protect himself only against accidents that will not be averted by due care on the part of the railroad, then he will maintain only the small space between crops and tracks, at a cost of $5.

Under this interpretation of contributory negligence, the defense comes into play only where neither party exercises due care, defined as the care that is optimal if the other party to the interaction is using optimal care.

This analysis explains the remark in Justice Holmes's concurring opinion in *LeRoy Fibre* (the most famous American railroad spark case) that "as a general proposition people are entitled to assume that their neighbors will conform to the law . . . and therefore will not be negligent."[73] In that case the railroad's locomotive, as a result of negligent operation by the railroad's employees, spewed large quantities of sparks and live cinders which ignited a pile of flax stacked eighty-five feet from the tracks. The accident no doubt could have been prevented by removing the flax to a greater distance from the track, but if this fact in itself were deemed to make the owner of the flax contributorily negligent, the railroad would have had an incentive to spew sparks and cinders with total abandon, in order to induce the owner of the flax to remove it to as great a distance as possible, thus minimizing the railroad's own damage-prevention costs. The real question in the case was

---

by assuming $y = y^*$, and y^* by assuming $x = x^*$. If x and y are independent ($p_{xy} = 0$), then due care for one party can be determined without reference to the other party's care.

[73] LeRoy Fibre Co. v. Chicago, Milwaukee & St. P. Ry. Co., 232 U.S. 340, 352 (1914).

whether the flax should have been more than eighty-five feet from the tracks to prevent damage from a nonnegligently operated train — in which event plaintiff should not have been allowed to recover.[74]

Although the legal position on contributory negligence yields correct results in the joint-care case, it may yield incorrect results in the particular alternative-care case where x^* is zero given y^* but positive given $y = 0$. Suppose that an expected accident cost of \$100 can be avoided by an expenditure of either \$20 by *A* (the victim) or \$10 by *B* (the injurer), and that the best avoidance strategy from a social standpoint is for *B* to spend \$10 on care and *A* nothing; that is, $x^* = 0$ given y^*. If *B* spends nothing on care and an accident occurs, *A* will be deemed contributorily negligent for having failed to take care (because \$20 < \$100). *A* therefore will take care and the accident will be avoided, but at a higher social cost than necessary (\$20 instead of \$10). The problem does not arise when the victim is the cheaper accident-cost avoider. In that situation, the rule of contributory negligence brings about the correct allocation of resources even in the alternative-care case. But where the case is one of alternative care and the injurer is a cheaper accident-cost avoider than is the victim, comparing each party's costs of care with expected reductions in accident cost brings about a misallocation of resources.

This misallocation would be avoided if, instead of examining negligence and contributory negligence separately, the courts explicitly compared the parties' costs of avoidance. However, to do so in every case — obviously at some price in higher costs of information — would be a dubious strategy, because the comparison would, as we have seen, yield an allocative improvement in only a subset of cases. It would yield no gain in any joint-care case, in any alternative-care case where the victim was the cheaper cost avoider, or in any alternative-care case where the costs of accident avoidance were the same to victim and injurer. In the limited group of alternative-care cases where a comparison of the victim's and injurer's avoidance costs would yield an improvement, there is an alternative to case-by-case comparison: creating defenses to

---

[74] Justice Holmes thought this question should have been left to the jury; the majority disagreed, perhaps because of the way in which the certified questions that the Court had been asked to answer were phrased.

contributory negligence that deal on a category rather than an individual-case basis with the recurring cases where the costs of accident avoidance are lower to injurer than to victim.

In nineteenth-century tort cases there is considerable talk of the "degrees" of negligence — slight, ordinary, and gross. These were (and to some extent still are) used in other tort contexts, but for now our interest is in their use in comparing plaintiff's and defendant's negligence. Several state courts held during this period that contributory negligence was a bar to plaintiff's recovering only if the plaintiff's negligence was of the same or a higher degree than the defendant's.[75] Thus, if defendant was grossly negligent and plaintiff only slightly or ordinarily negligent, plaintiff could still recover damages. This approach, however, yields no allocative improvement in joint-care cases. Consider a case where the expected accident cost is $150, optimal care requires that the potential injurer spend $5 and the potential victim $50, neither party takes care, and an accident occurs. One way to think of the degrees of negligence is in terms of the ratio of the costs of care to the expected reduction in accident damages: the lower the ratio, the greater the negligence. In the case just put, the ratio is 1/30 for the injurer and 1/3 for the victim. A fair translation of these ratios into words would be that the injurer was grossly negligent and the victim ordinarily negligent. But if, on this ground, the victim is awarded damages, there is no allocative benefit. In future cases, the potential injurer will spend $50 on care, and knowing this the victim will have an incentive to spend $5 to avoid an accident for which he would not be compensated because the injurer would not be deemed negligent. As we saw earlier in discussing *LeRoy Fibre*, the same result is reached under a simple negligence standard. The degrees of negligence add nothing in a joint-care case — except administrative costs when deterrence fails and a court must decide liability.

The degrees-of-negligence approach to the problem of different victim and injurer costs of avoiding accidents soon fell into disfavor, but other defenses to contributory negligence proved more durable and seem more sensible because they are not applicable in joint-care cases, where, as we have seen, they are not needed. We shall discuss briefly two of these defenses, beginning with the doc-

[75] *See* W. PROSSER, *supra* note 61, at 434.

trine of "last clear chance" as illustrated by *Kumkumian v. City of New York.*[76] Kumkumian jumped or fell onto a subway track in front of an approaching train. The train struck him — without fault on the part of the defendant or its employees — and immediately stopped. Kumkumian's body had triggered an automatic mechanism that halted the train whenever it hit an object on the tracks. The subway motorman reset the mechanism without bothering to see what was on the track. The train started up, struck Kumkumian again, and again stopped. Once again the motorman reset the automatic tripping mechanism without looking to see what was on the track. Kumkumian's fatal injuries, it seems, occurred not when he was first struck by the train but when he was struck the second and third times, after the motorman restarted the train. The court assumed that Kumkumian had no business on the track in the first place, that he was a trespasser who could have avoided the accident simply by not trespassing. Because the motorman had the "last clear chance" to avoid the accident, however, Kumkumian's status as a trespasser (contributorily negligent) did not bar the suit. The cost to the motorman of seeing what it was that was tripping the automatic mechanism was lower than the cost to Kumkumian, once he already had been struck by the train, of avoiding a further injury.

Whether *Kumkumian* and the last clear chance doctrine in general really is explainable on economic grounds is more problematic than just suggested. The correct perspective for judging the efficiency of a legal rule is an *ex ante* one[77] — *i.e.*, does the rule create incentives for parties to behave efficiently in the future? Suppose, for example, that Kumkumian could have avoided trespassing (and hence any injury) at a cost of $1, but once he had trespassed the cost rose to $1 million. Suppose further that the subway could have avoided injuring Kumkumian at a cost of $5. Because the cost of accident avoidance is either $1, $5, or $1 million, this would be an example of alternative care where the injurer's optimal care level was zero. A rule of no liability therefore would seem to be efficient. Applying the last clear chance doctrine in these circumstances would be inefficient because the victim, knowing the in-

---

[76] 305 N.Y. 167, 111 N.E.2d 865 (1953).

[77] As emphasized in Wittman, *Optimal Pricing of Sequential Inputs: Last Clear Chance, Mitigation of Damages, and Related Doctrines in the Law*, 10 J. LEGAL STUD. 65 (1981).

jurer would be liable if an accident occurred unless the injurer had spent $5, would not take care. Knowing this, the injurer would have an incentive to spend $5 to avoid liability. The accident would be prevented but at a social cost $4 greater than it would have been if the victim had used due care.

On closer analysis, however, two reasons appear why the last clear chance doctrine may create incentives for efficient behavior. One is that even from an *ex ante* perspective, the cost to the injurer may be lower than the cost to the victim of not trespassing. In the typical last clear chance case, the injurer's costs are indeed negligible — the cost of blowing a whistle or slamming on the brakes. In *Kumkumian* we do not know what the victim's cost would have been, because we do not know why he was on the track. However, the statement of facts in the court's opinion suggests he may very well have been mentally ill, in which event his cost of accident avoidance may have been high. The subway's costs appear to have been trivial. The subway train was equipped with a tripping mechanism for the safety of its passengers and crew and the cost of the mechanism would have been no lower had Kumkumian never trespassed. Given the mechanism, it was virtually costless for the motorman to look under the track to see why the train had stopped. Indeed, he probably should have done so for the safety of himself and his passengers, in which case the cost was negative.

The other economic reason behind the last clear chance doctrine is related to our earlier point that care has a probabilistic rather than a certain effect on safety. Suppose that if Kumkumian spends $1 on care (including avoiding trespasses) there will still be a .01 probability that he will trespass on the subway tracks and receive an injury (assuming that the subway takes no care) of $1000. Suppose that the subway could spend $5 on care to reduce the probability of injuring Kumkumian, if he trespasses, from 1.0[78] to .5 and that if it fails to do so and an accident occurs it will be liable for Kumkumian's injury under the last clear chance doctrine. The subway will, of course, spend $5 to avoid a certain liability of $1000 if it observes a trespasser on its tracks, and this is efficient given that the victim is already on the tracks. The critical question

[78] This is the conditional probability of hitting Kumkumian given that he trespasses; the probability that he will trespass, we said, was only .01.

is whether Kumkumian will still spend $1 on care (as we want him to do), knowing that, if he trespasses, the threat of liability under the last clear chance doctrine will induce the subway to take care.

To answer this question, we must consider Kumkumian's options. If he spends $1 on care, the sum of his expected injury costs and costs of care will be $6 (= (.01)(.5) $1000 + $1) compared to $500 (= (.5) $1000) if he doesn't take care. Thus, he will take care. The last clear chance doctrine will give him an incentive not to take care only when the subway's taking care will reduce the probability of an injury to near zero. (In the nonprobabilistic case discussed earlier, it was assumed that the subway's expenditure of $5 did in fact reduce this probability to zero.) For example, if the subway's $5 expenditure would reduce the probability of injury to less than .001 (instead of to .5), Kumkumian will not take care.[79] Surprisingly, this is the efficient outcome. Because the subway's $5 expenditure will reduce Kumkumian's expected damages to $1, it would be inefficient for him to spend $1 to reduce his expected damages from trespassing by 99 cents, *i.e.*, from $1 to (.01) (.001) ($1000) = $0.01. While counter-examples could be constructed where the last clear chance doctrine would yield inefficient results (too much care by the subway and not enough by Kumkumian), our analysis suggests that in a broad range of plausible cases the doctrine yields efficient results.

Another interesting defense to contributory negligence is the "attractive nuisance" doctrine. Children are attracted to various dangerous conditions on land, including railroad turntables and swimming pools or holes. As trespassers, they ordinarily would be barred from recovering damages if injured by one of these conditions even if the cost of fencing to the landowner was also less than the expected accident cost, so that the landowner was negligent. The economic explanation is that the cost of not trespassing is usually negligible relative to the landowner's cost of fencing. Under the attractive nuisance doctrine, however, the landowner's negligence is not excused by the child's status as a trespasser.[80] The economic basis of this result is that the costs to the children —

[79] If Kumkumian takes care, the sum of his expected injury costs and his cost of care is $1.01 (= (.01) (.001) ($1,000) + $1), compared to $1.00 (= (.001) ($1000)) if he does not take care.

[80] *See* W. Prosser, *supra* note 61, at 364-76.

more realistically, to their parents — of avoiding the lure of the attractive nuisance probably are greater than the costs to the landowner of fencing out the children. It is an alternative-care setting because either fencing in or fencing out will avoid the accident; doing both would be redundant. We shall discuss later an interesting analogy to the attractive nuisance doctrine in the law relating to damages caused by straying cattle.

The notorious *Britt* case, long regarded as an illustration of Justice Holmes's hard side, further illustrates the economic logic of the attractive nuisance doctrine.[81] Two children were killed when they dove into a pool that they thought contained just water but that actually contained sulphuric acid as well. The Supreme Court held that the attractive nuisance doctrine was inapplicable because the pool was not visible from the public highway from which the boys had entered the defendant's land.[82] This fact made the pool less dangerous to children, because the only children who would be attracted by it would be those who *already* had entered defendant's land despite the absence of any visible attraction. Hence the cost-justified level of defendant care was less than in the usual attractive nuisance case. It may not have paid to fence the pool given the low probability that any children would be attracted to it. Furthermore, the costs of accident avoidance by the victims and their parents were lower because they did not have to fight the lure to trespass created by the sight of an apparent swimming hole.

C. *Judicial Applications of the Hand Formula (Economic) Approach*

We could give other examples of defenses to contributory negligence, but rather than do that we will examine further how the courts apply the fundamental negligence doctrine, encapsulated in the Hand formula, to both injurer and victim negligence.

Hendricks v. Peabody Coal Co.[83] illustrates how courts approach the question of determining B_y, the effect on the injurer's cost of care of adding another input of care. Plaintiff, a youth of sixteen, was seriously injured while swimming in defendant's abandoned strip mine which had become filled with spring water. Defendant

---

[81] United Zinc & Chem. Co. v. Britt, 258 U.S. 268 (1922).

[82] Or, if visible, was not shown to have been the lure that drew the boys to the site.

[83] 115 Ill. App. 2d 35, 253 N.E.2d 56 (1969).

knew that the water hole was used frequently for swimming, knew also of the hazard (a concealed shelf beneath the water's surface at the point where plaintiff dived) that caused plaintiff's injury, and "undertook to police the area but did not do so effectively."[84] Considering measures that the defendant might have taken to avert the accident, the court noted: "The entire body of water could have been closed off with a steel fence for between $12,000 and $14,000. The cost was slight compared to the risk to the children involved . . . ."[85] Alternatively, the defendant could have barricaded the road to the site to prevent entry, or at the very least could have posted warning signs. Because the plaintiff's damages had been assessed at $200,000 and the swimming hole was heavily used, a fact which suggests that accidents of comparable severity were likely to happen in the future, the court seems to have been on safe ground in concluding that the defendant had failed to use due care.

An older case, *Adams v. Bullock*,[86] illustrates the situation where the cost of care is disproportionate to the expected accident cost, and where accordingly the failure to take care is not negligent. Plaintiff, a twelve-year-old, while crossing a bridge under which defendant's trolley line ran, swung a wire eight feet long over the side of the bridge. The wire touched the defendant's trolley wire, which ran underneath the bridge. The trolley wire was not insulated and when plaintiff's wire touched it there was a shock which burned him. Because "[t]he trolley wire was so placed that no one standing on the bridge or even bending over the parapet could reach it," the court regarded the accident as an

> extraordinary casualty, not fairly within the area of ordinary prevision. . . . No special danger at this bridge warned the defendant that there was need of special measures of precaution. No like accident had occurred before. No custom had been disregarded. We think that ordinary caution did not involve forethought of this extraordinary peril.[87]

Although the court spoke in terms of foreseeability, it seems to

---

[84] *Id.* at 46, 253 N.E.2d at 61.
[85] *Id.* at 45, 253 N.E.2d at 61.
[86] 227 N.Y. 208, 125 N.E. 93 (1919).
[87] *Id.* at 210, 125 N.E. at 93.

have meant simply that there was only a slight probability that the trolley wire beneath the bridge would injure anyone.

Regarding the burden of precautions, the court stated:

> There is, we may add, a distinction not to be ignored between electric light and trolley wires. The distinction is that the former may be insulated. Chance of harm, though remote, may betoken negligence, if needless. Facility of protection may impose a duty to protect. With trolley wires, the case is different. Insulation is impossible. Guards here and there are of little value. To avert the possibility of this accident and others like it at one point or another on the route, the defendant must have abandoned the overhead system, and put the wires underground.[88]

This is as clear a statement as one might ask of the proposition that the optimal level of care is a function of its cost, other things being equal. On the one hand, even if the probability of harm were slight, if the cost of avoiding the harm were also slight, failure to avoid it might be negligence. On the other hand, even if the probability and magnitude of harm were the same for trolley and electric wires, electric companies might be liable and trolley companies not, simply because the cost of care was lower for the electric companies.

Just as the optimal level of care varies with the cost of care (B_y), so it varies with the probability of an accident. In *Nussbaum v. Lacopo*,[89] plaintiff was struck by a golf ball which the defendant had hit out of the golf course. The court alluded to the cost of care by noting that "even the best professional golfers cannot avoid an occasional 'hook' or 'slice,' "[90] but its emphasis was on the low probability of this particular accident. Not only was plaintiff's property situated at a substantial angle to the direction in which the ball was shot, but the ball had to traverse a rough area twenty to thirty feet wide between the golf course and plaintiff's property, and the rough area contained trees forty-five to sixty feet in height, with their full summer foliage. The court stated: "The mere fact that a person may have been careless in the performance of an

[88] *Id.* at 211, 125 N.E. at 94.

[89] 27 N.Y.2d 311, 265 N.E.2d 762 (1970).

[90] *Id.* at 319, 265 N.E.2d at 767.

act does not necessarily result in actionable negligence. It is only required that the care be commensurate with the risk and danger."[91] Maybe defendant could have hit the ball more carefully, but the cost of care would have been disproportionate to the cost of the accident discounted by the extremely low probability that a careless shot would injure plaintiff or anyone else. And as the court pointed out, it is not easy, even for an experienced golfer, to avoid an occasional hook or slice shot that might carry out of the course.

Nussbaum resembles the famous English negligence case of *Bolton v. Stone*,[92] where a cricket ball hit with unusual force by a member of a cricket team playing in defendant's cricket grounds carried out of the grounds and hit a pedestrian in the street near her home. Defendant was held not liable. The probability that a cricket ball would carry outside the cricket grounds and injure a pedestrian was remote. Moreover, the cost of avoiding the accident would have been substantial. The cricket grounds would have had to be enlarged, or an extremely high fence erected,[93] or the players instructed to hit the ball less hard — an instruction that would reduce the satisfactions of the game to both participants and spectators.

Another well-known English case where defendant was held not to be negligent because of the low probability of harm is *Blyth v. Birmingham Waterworks Co.*[94] Plaintiff suffered water damage when the defendant's water main opposite his house burst because of an extraordinary frost. As one judge explained:

> A reasonable man would act with reference to the average circumstances of the temperature in ordinary years. The defendants had provided against such frosts as experience would have led men, acting prudently, to provide against; and they are not guilty of negligence, because their precautions proved insufficient against the effects of the extreme severity of the frost of 1855, which penetrated to a greater depth than any

---

[91] *Id.*

[92] [1951] A.C. 850 (H.L.).

[93] The ball that hit the plaintiff had carried over the 12-foot fence surrounding the cricket ground, and because of a rise in the ground the fence started from a point 17 feet above the road on which the plaintiff was walking when she was struck. Thus, the fence was, in effect, 29 feet high.

[94] 11 Exch. 781, 156 Eng. Rep. 1047 (1856).

> which ordinarily occurs south of the polar regions. Such a state of circumstances constitutes a contingency against which no reasonable man can provide. The result was an accident, for which the defendants cannot be held liable.[95]

This passage indicates an implicit concern with marginal or incremental, rather than total, costs of care. The court was not interested in whether the total costs of burying the main to a depth at which it would not have burst even in the unusually severe frost of 1855 were less than the expected accident costs. It was interested in whether, given that the mains had been buried to a depth that would prevent their freezing in any ordinary frost, the incremental expense of protecting against an unusually severe frost would have been justified by the incremental reduction in accident costs brought about by such an expense.

A case that illustrates judicial awareness of the importance of the magnitude of the loss if an accident occurs (*D* in our notation), as well as of the probability of the accident and the cost of care, is *Paris v. Stepney Borough Council*.[96] Plaintiff was a workman who had only one good eye. While working as a garage man for the defendant, he struck a bolt with a hammer, and a chip flew off and injured him seriously in his good eye. He claimed that defendant's failure to supply him with goggles was negligent. The parties agreed that, given the unlikelihood of such an accident in this line of work, it would not have been negligent to fail to supply goggles to an employee who had two good eyes. The court nevertheless held that failure to supply this employee with goggles was negligence because of the greater harm that would accrue to him if an accident occurred. As one judge stated, "the more serious the damge which will happen if an accident occurs, the more thorough are the precautions which an employer must take."[97]

All of the elements of the Hand formula come together, in the context of contributory negligence, in *Eckert v. Long Island Railroad*.[98] Defendant was running its train at excessive speed and without adequate signals in a densely populated area. Eckert saw a small child sitting in the track in front of the advancing train. He

---

[95] *Id.* at 784-85, 156 Eng. Rep. at 1049.
[96] [1951] A.C. 367 (H.L.).
[97] *Id.* at 385.
[98] 43 N.Y. 502 (1870).

ran to rescue the child and managed to throw it clear but was himself killed. The court held that he had not been negligent. Had Eckert

> for his own purposes attempted to cross the track, or with a view to save property placed himself voluntarily in a position where he might have received an injury from a collision with the train, his conduct would have been grossly negligent, and no recovery could have been had for such injury.[99]

However, "it was not wrongful in him to make every effort in his power to rescue the child, compatible with a reasonable regard for his own safety. It was his duty to exercise his judgment as to whether he could probably save the child without serious injury to himself."[100]

Let us translate the court's discussion into economic terms. Assume hypothetically that the railroad could negotiate costlessly with Eckert to rescue the child. Because the railroad was negligent, it would be liable for the injury to the child who, we assume — plausibly enough on the facts — was certain to be killed if not rescued by Eckert. In deciding whether to "buy" Eckert's services, the railroad would compare the reduction in the probability of killing the child (equivalent to the reduction in the probability of the railroad's liability), multiplied by the value of the child's life, with the costs of Eckert's services, in this case an uncertain cost equal to the probability of Eckert's being killed times the value of his life. In terms of our notation, $-p_xD$ is the benefit of Eckert's rescue services and A_x is the cost of his services. So long as $-p_xD$ was not less than A_x, the railroad and Eckert would have contracted to have Eckert rescue the child. Although the transaction costs between the railroad and Eckert were in fact prohibitive, we still can use the zero-transaction-cost model to infer that Eckert was not negligent if $-p_xD \geq A_x$, because the railroad would have "bought" Eckert's services had a transaction been possible.[101] If the child's

---

[99] *Id.* at 505.

[100] *Id.*

[101] An alternative but equivalent way to model Eckert's behavior is to define the expected cost of the rescue to Eckert, A_x, as the injury to him discounted by the probability that he would be hit by the train. To determine the benefits of care, $-p_xD$, we must ask what care Eckert would have had to give up if he had forgone the rescue and thereby averted the expected accident cost to himself. The answer is the value of the child's life discounted by

life and Eckert's are assumed to have roughly the same value, the question whether Eckert was negligent is reduced to whether the probability of his rescuing the child was less than the probabiliy of being killed himself. If it was less, then $-p_xD$ (the probability of rescuing the child times the value of the child's life) would be greater than A_x (the probability of losing his own life times the value of that life). In asking whether Eckert "could probably save the child without serious injury to himself," the court was comparing these probabilities, for if Eckert probably could have saved the child without serious injury to himself, this implies that the probability of a successful rescue was greater than the probability of his being hit by the train himself.

If the object of the rescue had not been a child but instead property of slight value, $-p_xD$ would have been lower because one of its components, the value of the object rescued, would have been smaller. This much the court made clear, but presumably it did not mean to imply that it is *never* prudent to risk life for property. In a subsequent case, *Liming v. Illinois Central Railroad*,[102] plaintiff, in an effort to rescue some horses, ran into a building that was on fire because of the defendant's negligence and was burned. The court stated that

> a person would not be justified in exposing himself to as great danger in saving property as he would in saving human life, and whether the person injured acted with reasonable prudence would, in most cases, be a question of fact depending upon the circumstances under which the act was done.[103]

The court refused to hold plaintiff contributorily negligent *per se*.

This discussion of cases has been designed to establish several points. First, the Hand formula is an accurate formulation of the negligence standard (including contributory negligence) in diverse periods and jurisdictions. Second, it is applied in marginal rather than total terms, and thus coincides with the economic model of negligence. This is clearest in *Blyth*, but in the other cases also the courts seem to have been evaluating the costs and benefits of safety measures at the margin. Third, in none of the cases is it

---

the probability of a successful rescue. Eckert would not be negligent if $-p_xD \geq A_x$.

[102] 81 Iowa 246, 47 N.W. 66 (1890).

[103] *Id.* at 254, 47 N.W. at 68.

likely that optimal accident avoidance required a change in the level of activity of either plaintiff or defendant.[104] For example, in *Adams v. Bullock*, eliminating trolley lines would not have been an efficient way of preventing the accident. This suggests that cases where activity is an important factor in achieving an efficient level of accidents are not decided under the negligence standard; further evidence of this point is presented later. Finally, in none of the cases was the sequential application of the Hand formula (*i.e.*, first to negligence and then to contributory negligence) a source of problems. In *Hendricks*, an alternative-care case where the defendant probably was the cheaper accident-cost avoider, the defense of contributory negligence was precluded by the attractive nuisance doctrine. In *Eckert*, another alternative-care case, it seems plain that the cost of accident avoidance was lower to the railroad than to the victim, who was allowed to recover damages.

To all this it may be replied that we have discussed only a tiny, and perhaps deliberately selected, sample of cases applying the negligence standard. However, one of us once examined a random sample of 1,500 tort cases decided between 1875 and 1905 and found considerable congruence between the economic model and the legal practice.[105] The cases discussed here should be regarded as an addition to that large sample. Furthermore, most of the cases we have discussed in this section are leading cases on negligence. Certainly *Eckert, Blyth, Stepney, Bolton*, and *Carroll Towing* are in this category. These are not legal "sports" that happen to coincide with economic analysis.

However, in an effort to construct a sample that is immune to a charge of bias, we also have examined all the cases reprinted in the current edition of Kalven, Gregory, and Epstein's torts casebook that deal with the meaning of negligence.[106] Those authors cannot be accused of undue partiality to the economic theory of tort law. Professor Kalven once wrote that the concern of tort law is with

---

[104] Except possibly *Lacopo*, where the golfer-defendant was a trespasser on the golf course. However, his trespass was probably not a cause of the accident when "cause" is interpreted in legal terms; but we defer explanation of this point to the causation chapter of our forthcoming book.

[105] *See* Posner, *supra* note 15.

[106] *See* C. Gregory, H. Kalven, & R. Epstein, Cases and Materials on Torts 102-30 (3d ed. 1977). This section is entitled "Calculus of Risk" and is described as an exploration of "the judicial efforts to fashion and apply a standard of reasonable care." *Id.* at 102.

equity rather than efficiency,[107] and Professor Epstein is, of course, a pertinacious critic of both the positive and normative economic theories of tort law. Nevertheless, every one of the cases included by those authors to illustrate the legal meaning of negligence appears to be consistent with the Hand formula interpreted in economic terms.

Three of the cases reprinted in the relevant section of the casebook have been discussed already: *Blyth*, *Eckert*, and *Carroll Towing*. We did not, however, analyze the facts in *Carroll Towing*. Defendant's bargee had left his barge for twenty-one hours, and during this period the barge broke away from its mooring and caused damage. No good reason for the bargee's protracted absence was offered. The harbor was a busy one (it was the height of World War II), the days short, and the danger of collision manifest. Hence $-p_yD$ was substantial, while the lack of a satisfactory explanation for the bargee's absence implied that B_y was very low. The court properly found negligence.

The casebook reprints the portion of the opinion in *Osborne v. Montgomery*[108] that discusses the negligence standard. The discussion is consistent with the economic approach. For example, the court states:

> Circumstances may require the driver of a fire truck to take his truck through a thickly populated district at a high rate of speed, but if he exercises that degree of care which such drivers ordinarily exercise under the same or similar circumstances, society, weighing the benefits against the probabilities of damage, in spite of the fact that as a reasonably prudent and intelligent man he should foresee that harm may result, justifies the risk and holds him not liable.[109]

In *Cooley v. Public Service Co.*,[110] another case reprinted in the casebook to illustrate the meaning of negligence, a power line owned by the defendant electric company broke during a storm and hit a telephone cable which was strung below it, causing a loud

[107] *See* W. Blum & H. Kalven, Public Law Perspectives on a Private Law Problem 65 (1965).

[108] 203 Wis. 223, 234 N.W. 372 (1931).

[109] *Id.* at 232-33, 234 N.W. at 376. The court did not discuss the application of the standard to the actual facts of the case.

[110] 90 N.H. 460, 10 A.2d 673 (1940).

noise on the telephone line that plaintiff was using. She fainted. The evidence showed that the only devices that the power company might have used to prevent the accident would have increased the risk of electrocution to people on the street below from the power line. Balancing the risk of electrocution (which is part of the cost of taking care) against the expected reduction in the injury from noise, the court held that the power company had not been negligent in failing to adopt either device suggested by plaintiff. B_y was much higher than $-p_yD$.

Union Oil Co. v. Oppen[111] upheld the right of commercial fishermen whose livelihood had been impaired by an oil spill in the Santa Barbara Channel to recover damages from the oil companies that had caused the spill. The defendants' negligence was stipulated, which makes the inclusion of the case in this part of the casebook somewhat puzzling, and the only issue was whether the plaintiffs could recover for a purely "economic" loss (the fish that were destroyed were not their property). The court held that they could. The opinion contains a confused discussion of the economic approach to tort questions,[112] but the outcome seems correct. Giving the plaintiffs a tort right was a method of internalizing some of the external costs of the oil spill.[113]

Next in the casebook come a pair of railroad accident cases, *Hauser v. Chicago, R.I. & P. Railway*[114] and *McDowall v. Great Western Railway*.[115] In *Hauser*, the plaintiff, a passenger on defendant's railroad, fainted in the toilet compartment and was burned severely when her face came into contact with a hot steam pipe that ran along the wall of the compartment beneath the sink. The court held that the railroad had not been negligent in the design or construction of the toilet compartment. The court thought the probability that a passenger would fall and wedge his face or other exposed part of the body against the hot steam pipe too remote to require the railroad to have relocated or shielded the pipe, assum-

---

[111] 501 F.2d 558 (9th Cir. 1974).

[112] *See* Posner, *Some Uses and Abuses of Economics in Law*, 46 U. CHI. L. REV. 281, 297-301 (1979).

[113] *See* Posner, *Epstein's Tort Theory: A Critique*, 8 J. LEGAL STUD. 457, 467-68 (1979).

[114] 205 Iowa 940, 219 N.W. 60 (1928).

[115] [1903] 2 K.B. 331 (C.A.), *rev'g* [1902] 1 K.B. 618. Both the lower-court and the court of appeal decisions are reprinted in the casebook; because the court of appeal is more authoritative, we discuss its opinion.

ing that this would have been practicable. In economic terms $-p_yD$ was lower than B_y, and it was not negligent not to have taken greater care. In *McDowall*, some boys broke into a railroad car parked on an incline and decoupled and unbraked it. The car rolled down the incline and caused damage. Plaintiff argued that the railroad should have placed the car on the other side of a "catch-point" which would have prevented it from rolling down. In rejecting this argument and exonerating the railroad from the charge of negligence, the court of appeal made two points. First, although the boys previously had broken into railroad cars to steal apples and the like, they never before had tried to decouple and unbrake a car and the probability that they could do so was slight. Second, opening the catch-point would have been a simpler operation for the boys than decoupling and unbraking the car, so presumably it would not have been a significant obstacle to their plan. Thus, $-p_yD$ was low and (from the second point) probably negative, suggesting that it would have been inefficient to make even a negligible expenditure to move the car.

The last two cases reprinted in the relevant section of the casebook, *Quintal v. Laurel Grove Hospital*[116] and *Lucy Webb Hayes National Training School v. Perotti*,[117] are medical malpractice cases. In *Quintal*, the plaintiff, while being operated on by an ophthalmologist for an eye condition, suffered cardiac arrest which resulted in permanent brain damage. One negligence issue was whether the ophthalmologist should have known how to perform a thoracotomy (open heart massage) and, if not, whether a surgeon competent to perform such an operation should have been present. There was evidence that the standard of care prevailing in the locality where the operation was performed required that a surgeon capable of performing an open heart massage be present at every operation involving general anesthesia. Cardiac arrest is a risk in every such operation and can have terrible consequences — death or severe brain damage — if not terminated within three minutes, which is too short a time in which to procure a surgeon from another part of the hospital. Another negligence issue was whether the ophthalmologist and the anesthesiologist may have been negligent in failing to heed certain warning signs (fever and

[116] 62 Cal. 2d 154, 397 P.2d 161, 41 Cal. Rptr. 577 (1964).
[117] 419 F.2d 704 (D.C. Cir. 1969).

apprehensions) in the plaintiff which increased the risk of cardiac arrest. A judgment for the defendants was reversed.

In *Perotti*, plaintiff's decedent, who was confined in defendant's hospital because of mental illness (including suicidal tendencies), slipped out of his closed ward and while being escorted back to it broke away from his escort and plunged to his death through a closed window. There were two negligence issues: whether the window should have been either barred or made of a stronger kind of glass, and whether the decedent should have been allowed to escape from the closed ward. The court held for the hospital on the first issue and for the plaintiff on the second. The negative effects of barred windows on the therapeutic activities of the hospital provided a strong reason against barred windows and there was no expert evidence that thicker glass than that used by the hospital — bulletproof glass, for example — would have been feasible. The hospital, however, had established a standard requiring confinement of mental patients such as the plaintiff's decedent and had violated its own standard without justification.

> This was not a case where a determined patient managed to commit suicide in a mysterious or unexpected fashion. Nor is this a case where a calculated risk was taken for therapeutic reasons with a patient of known suicidal tendencies, nor where a hospital had concluded after examination that a patient was not suicidal and hence did not require precautions.[118]

In other words, $-p_yD$ was high relative to B_y given that the hospital had established a closed ward for such patients and had only to secure it against a patient not shown to be "determined . . . to commit suicide in a mysterious or unexpected fashion."

In both cases, the court's resolution of the negligence issues seems consistent with the economics of the situations presented. The reference to and deference accorded customary standards of care in both cases are also appropriate from an economic standpoint. The existence of a preexisting voluntary relationship between doctors and patients suggests that transaction costs are not prohibitive and hence, via the Coase theorem, that customary standards are efficient.

[118] *Id.* at 710.

D. The Areas of Strict Liability in Accident Law

We now consider whether the choice that the common law has made between strict liability and negligence to govern particular kinds of accidents is consistent with the predictions of the economic model. We said that strict liability is more likely to be the superior regulatory device in cases where optimal accident avoidance requires altering the defendant's activity rather than his care or the plaintiff's activity or care. Is this the pattern of the law?

We begin with rules relating to damage caused by animals. The common law distinguished between domestic animals, such as dogs, pigs, and sheep, and wild animals, such as bears and tigers. The owner's liability for damage caused by wild animals was absolute. If *B*'s pet lion clawed *A*, *B* was liable for *A*'s damages even if he had used all reasonable care to prevent the lion from attacking people. With regard to domestic animals, the owner's liability again was strict — provided that he had notice of the animal's vicious disposition. This principle is the origin of the famous "one bite" rule for dogs. Before a dog has bitten anyone, its owner usually will have no reason to think it vicious; once it has bitten someone, however, he is on notice of its vicious disposition. The common law was not in fact so mechanical:

> A single incident does not necessarily place the owner on notice the animal is dangerous or vicious. The test is whether the incident was of such a nature as to lead a reasonable person to believe the dog was sufficiently dangerous as to be likely to cause injury to a person at a later date.[119]

Within the class of domestic animals, there was an important exception: owners of trespassing cattle or other livestock were strictly liable for property damage (though not for personal injury) caused by their animals.[120]

We have put our statement of the common law relating to liability for damage caused by animals in the past tense because of important developments that have led to changes in the traditional common law. First, with the growth of zoos and animal parks, there has been a tendency to relax the rule of strict liability for

[119] Rolen v. Maryland Cas. Co., 240 So. 2d 42, 46 (La. App. 1970).

[120] On the common-law principles governing liability for damage caused by animals, see W. Prosser, *supra* note 61, at 496-503; G. Williams, Liability for Animals (1939).

wild animals when they are kept for purposes of exhibition as in a zoo.[121] Second, many of the western American states rejected the English common-law rule of strict liability for property damage caused by wandering livestock.[122]

This pattern is consistent with what economic analysis of the choice between strict liability and negligence liability predicts. In the case of a dog not known to be dangerous, the expected accident cost is too small to warrant the dog's owner either in expending substantial resources to restrain the dog from biting people or in substituting another domestic animal. Moreover, many bites by gentle dogs are due to provocation by the victim rather than to carelessness by the owner. However, once a dog is known to be dangerous, the probability of its biting people, and hence the expected accident costs associated with the dog, rise sharply. Yet as any dog owner knows, it is difficult to restrain a dog at all times. Because care alone may not be sufficient to avoid an accident, we want the owner of the animal to consider whether the animal is worth keeping — an activity-level point. Were vicious dogs so valuable that the prospect of having to pay repeated damages to dog-bite victims would never deter an individual from keeping such a dog, no allocative purpose would be served by imposing liability for a bite that could not have been averted by greater care. But because a gentle dog is ordinarily a good substitute for a vicious one, imposing strict liability on the owner of a dangerous dog, and thereby forcing him to consider whether the extra benefits of having such a dog exceed the social costs, may have allocative benefits.

The argument for making the owner of a wild animal strictly liable for damage caused by the animal is even stronger. On the one hand, care undertaken by owners and potential victims may not be effective in preventing the animal from endangering people. On the other, keeping such an animal is not so valuable an activity that the threat of substantial tort liability will have no effect in inducing people to substitute toward a less dangerous animal — again an activity-level point. The situation is different when the wild animal is kept not as a pet, curiosity, or watch animal, but in a zoo

---

121 *See, e.g.*, City of Denver v. Kennedy, 29 Colo. App. 15, 476 P.2d 762 (1970).

122 *See, e.g.*, Beinhorn v. Griswold, 27 Mont. 79, 69 P. 557 (1902); Delaney v. Errickson, 10 Neb. 492, 6 N.W. 600 (1880); 3 T. Shearman & A. Redfield, A Treatise on the Law of Negligence 1719-22 (6th ed. 1913); 1 E. Thomas, Negligence 998-1002 (2d ed. 1904).

or animal park. In a carefully operated zoo, the probability of an animal's harming people is very low, and activity changes are unlikely to be optimal (what would a zoo be without dangerous animals?). These considerations may explain the trend away from strict liability for such harm.

The special rule applicable to straying farm animals, and the rejection of the rule in the western states, is a good illustration of the economic rationale of strict liability. It is difficult through fencing to prevent cattle, sheep, and other domestic farm animals from straying. It is impractical to keep fences always in good repair, and cattle and sheep are forever finding ways through and around fences. These straying animals do considerable damage, particularly in areas of dense cultivation. The alternative of fencing them out is also costly in such areas because of the amount of cultivated land that would have to be fenced. Abandoning cultivation would not be a feasible means of reducing this damage either. These circumstances make a rule of strict liability economically attractive, because the rule forces the rancher to consider either a reduction in his herds or flocks or a relocation of his activity to a less densely cultivated area. But the western United States was not densely cultivated, and livestock raising was not a marginal activity. Fencing out may well have been a more feasible method of controlling damage to crops from cattle and sheep than fencing in because the area under cultivation was smaller than the area being used for ranching.[123] The analogy to the attractive nuisance doctrine, where fencing out is chosen in preference to fencing in because the area to be fenced out is so much smaller than the area that would have to be fenced in, should be evident. If limiting herd size or substituting other land use for ranching was not a feasible means of limiting crop damage in the western states, strict liability for such damage would not be the optimal approach — and that approach was not followed.

The greater density of population and cultivation in England than in the United States also may explain the stricter liability for fire damage under English, as compared to American, common law.[124] For example, in England, in the absence of statutory privi-

---

[123] This issue was debated extensively at the time. *See* W. Webb, The Great Plains 282-83 (1931).

[124] *See* W. Prosser, *supra* note 61, at 503-05; Note, 16 Va. L. Rev. 174 (1929).

lege, a railroad that caused spark damage to crops along the right-of-way was strictly liable for the damage caused even if its locomotives were equipped with the latest and best spark-arresting equipment. In the United States, the railroad was liable only if negligent, negligence being defined for these purposes as not having the state-of-the-art spark-arresting equipment.[125] Not only were locomotive sparks a greater hazard in England because of the greater density of population and cultivation, but railroads were probably a more valuable activity in the United States because of the greater distances. On both of these counts, limiting the number of trains was less likely to be a feasible method of damage control here than in England, so strict liability was less likely to be adopted as the liability rule here.

Many of the areas of strict liability in the common law are grouped under the rubric of ultrahazardous or abnormally hazardous activities.[126] The keeping of wild animals, and in England the setting of fires, are examples of such activities. The roots of this principle in the economics of optimal accident avoidance are suggested by the *Restatement*'s list of the factors to be considered in determining whether an activity is abnormally dangerous:

> (a) existence of a high degree of risk of some harm to the person, land or chattels of others;
> (b) likelihood that the harm that results from it will be great;
> (c) inability to eliminate the risk by the exercise of reasonable care;
> (d) extent to which the activity is not a matter of common usage;
> (e) inappropriateness of the activity to the place where it is carried on; and
> (f) extent to which its value to the community is outweighed by its dangerous attributes.[127]

The elements in this definition are, first, a high expected accident cost (factors (a) and (b)); second, the impracticability of avoiding accidents through exercising greater care (factor (c)); and third,

---

[125] *Compare* Jones v. Festiniog R. Co., L.R. 3 Q.B. 733 (1868), *with* Burlington & M.R. Co. v. Westover, 4 Neb. 268 (1876).

[126] *See* W. PROSSER, *supra* note 61, at 505-16.

[127] RESTATEMENT (SECOND) OF TORTS § 520 (1977).

the feasibility of reducing accidents by curtailing (factors (d) or (f)) or relocating (factor (e)) the activity. The first element shows that there are substantial social benefits from reducing the accident rate, the second that this cannot be done economically simply by conducting the activity with greater care, and the third that maybe it can be done economically by curtailing or relocating the activity, because the activity, either in general or in the particular place where it is being conducted, is marginal and can be changed or eliminated without great social loss. The *Restatement's* definition of ultrahazardous activities thus coincides with the economic principles that make strict liability the preferred liability rule for some activities.

The leading case in England on strict liability, *Rylands v. Fletcher*,[128] from which the modern concept of ultrahazardous activities is descended, held that a landowner was strictly liable for any "nonnatural" use of his land, in that case the storage of water in a reservoir. The general principle of *Rylands*, that of strict liability for nonnatural land uses, was absorbed into the American law as an element in the definition of an ultrahazardous activity — the "not a matter of common usage" provision of the *Restatement*. But the application of that principle in *Rylands* to the storage of water in a reservoir was generally rejected, especially in the western states. Because water is abundant in England, the construction of a reservoir was, at least when the case was decided, an unnatural land use. The western United States, however, is dry and the building of reservoirs was not "unnatural" in the sense of a marginal use of the land which might be abandoned if the landowner bore the costs of accidents caused by his use.[129] The more valuable

---

[128] L.R. 3 H.L. 330 (1868).

[129] As stated in Turner v. Big Lake Oil Co., 128 Tex. 155, 96 S.W.2d 221 (1936):

> In Texas we have conditions very different from those which obtain in England. A large portion of Texas is an arid or semi-arid region. . . . The country is almost without streams; and without the storage of water from rainfall in basins constructed for the purpose, or to hold waters pumped from the earth, the great livestock industry of West Texas must perish . . . .
>
> Again, in England there are no oil wells, no necessity for using surface storage facilities for impounding and evaporating salt waters therefrom. In Texas the situation is different. . . . Producing oil is one of our major industries. One of the by-products of oil production is salt water, which must be disposed of without injury to property or the pollution of streams. The construction of basins or ponds to hold this salt water is a necessary part of the oil business.

Id. at 165-66, 96 S.W.2d at 226.

a land use relative to its alternatives, the less likely it is to be altered by the imposition of liability for accidents that can be avoided only by altering the activity and not by using greater care, and the weaker therefore is the case for strict liability.

Judging by the number of cases, the most common example of an ultrahazardous activity is blasting with explosives. This is, of course, a dangerous activity and considerable danger remains even after all reasonable care has been used to confine the effects of the blast. Moreover, people who are injured or suffer property damage as a result of debris or vibrations from blasting can do little either by taking greater care or by altering their activity to avoid or reduce damage. In addition, because blasting usually is done in connection with construction, which is ubiquitous, potential victims cannot, by relocating their activities, feasibly avoid blasting damage. Finally, there are substitutes for blasting, so that strict liability may very well alter the level of the activity. Strict liability makes economic sense here.

Another traditional, but now waning, example of ultrahazardous activity is flying. Airplane owners traditionally were held strictly liable for damage caused to people or property on the ground, although collisions between airplanes, and injury to passengers and crew, were governed by the negligence standard. An old case, *Guille v. Swan*,[130] illustrates the economic basis of strict liability for ground damage. A balloonist descended into plaintiff's garden, damaging plaintiff's vegetables, and additional damage was caused when a crowd of onlookers broke into the garden to help the balloonist land safely. The balloonist was held strictly liable for all the damage. As the court noted, the balloonist had no control over the balloon's horizontal motion and hence little ability to control its descent. Thus it was not a case where the accident could have been avoided by the exercise of due care, and there was no suggestion that the balloonist was careless. But the accident could have been prevented by his not ascending in the balloon in the first place. The reason for the balloon ride is not disclosed in the opinion but the court seems to have regarded balloon riding, at least over New York City, as a rather frivolous activity. If the activity was not a valuable one, abandoning it may well have been the optimal method of accident avoidance, in which event strict liability

[130] 19 Johns. (N.Y.) 381 (1822).

would have induced abandonment. Plainly, it would not have been more efficient for plaintiff to have switched from gardening to some land use less sensitive to damage from balloons and crowds of onlookers; thus, a no-liability rule was not an attractive alternative to strict liability.

The situation in the early days of the airplane was much the same as in the balloon case. Flying was a marginal activity, avoidance of damage to the subjacent property could not be assured simply by taking care, and the subjacent property owners could not protect themselves by altering their activity. As flying became both an established and a relatively safe activity, the likelihood that strict liability for ground damage would reduce the amount of flying, and with it the amount of ground damage, fell. Hence the economic analyst is not surprised that strict liability for ground damage is giving way to negligence.[131]

The situation with regard to airplane collisions has always been different. The parties to a collision are in a symmetrical position insofar as reducing accidents through reducing activity is concerned; moreover, virtually all collisions result from failure to exercise due care. In these circumstances, the economic argument for strict liability is weak. Moreover, because each party is both an injurer and a victim, there is no obvious way to apply a strict liability standard. Our analysis in the appendix shows how a negligence standard in these circumstances leads both parties to take due care.

The situation of passengers and crew is also different from that of people on the ground who suffer damage from an airplane crash. The passengers and crew have a contractual relationship with the airline. In such a relationship, the Coase theorem implies, there are powerful incentives to attain the optimal safety level regardless of the rule of liability. Here strict liability is unlikely to produce a lower accident rate than negligence liability.

The above analysis suggests a more general hypothesis. During the early stages of development of a new product or activity, we lack sufficient experience to determine whether the benefits of the product exceed its full costs including costs to third parties (*e.g.*, property owners who suffer ground damage from airplane crashes).

---

[131] *See, e.g.*, Southern Cal. Edison Co. v. Coleman, 150 Cal. App. 2d 829, 310 P.2d 504 (1957).

One way to gather such information is to hold the producer or user strictly liable for accidents to third parties resulting from the activity. Strict liability forces the innovator to internalize all the costs of his activity. If the activity still flourishes in spite of a strict liability standard, we can be confident that its benefits exceed its full costs or, equivalently, that eliminating or greatly reducing the new activity would not be optimal. At this point the argument in favor of strict liability weakens. Experience already has demonstrated that the activity's benefits exceed its full costs, and society is now being burdened with the greater administrative costs associated with an increasing number of claims brought about by the growth of the activity. We would predict, therefore, a shift toward negligence and away from strict liability as a new industry or activity matures. Notice that this hypothesis is the reverse of the "infant industry" or "subsidy" arguments sometimes made for the use of the negligence standard in the nineteenth century.

There are, however, two factors that may work against the hypothesis. First, strict liability may not provide information on the full costs of a new activity because an accident may result in a large number of small claims, each of insufficient amount to provide an incentive to bring a suit. If there is no feasible means of aggregating small claims, we are in effect in a world of no liability and can offer no hypothesis on the relative advantages of different liability rules. The other factor is that strict liability, even at the early stages of a new activity, reduces the incentives for the potential victim to take care or alter his activity level to minimize risk. These disadvantages of strict liability will tend to be minor, however, when the activity begins on a small scale, when the probability of being a victim is small, and when the victim would have to take care or change his activity level to avoid the accident before he had knowledge of whether he was likely to be a victim. If the victim's care is an important component of due care in the early stages of an activity, as it was for airplane collisions and injuries to pedestrians from automobiles (because the cost of pedestrian care is often trivial), strict liability would be inefficient even initially and we would predict that it would not be adopted.

A number of activities have been classified as ultrahazardous, and hence subjected to strict liability, on an *ad hoc* basis. The considerations used by the courts seem to be those listed by the *Restatement* in its definition of ultrahazardous activities, a definition that, as we have seen, tracks closely the economic model. In *Cities Service Co. v. State*,[132] for example, defendant, in connection with its phosphate rock mining, impounded billions of gallons of phosphatic slimes behind an earthen dam. The dam broke, causing substantial damage to the surrounding area. The court held defendant strictly liable for the damage. Potential victims were apparently helpless to avoid or reduce the damage, while defendant, although not careless, might have been induced by strict liability to reconsider its decisions to build an earthen dam.

Another recent case, *Siegler v. Kulhman*,[133] illustrates a different element of the economic model of the choice between negligence and strict liability: information costs. Defendant's trailer tank broke free and spilled thousands of gallons of gasoline. The gasoline exploded, destroying the car driven by plaintiff's decedent and killing decedent. In holding that this was an appropriate case for strict liability, the court pointed out that when large quantities of gasoline transported by truck explode, the explosion is likely to destroy the evidence necessary to establish whether the accident was caused by negligence. The information costs of applying the negligence test prevented use of that test in *Siegler*. Therefore, as between strict liability and no liability, the former was the preferable standard because it was more likely that defendant could have prevented such an accident at reasonable cost than that plaintiff's decedent could have done so.

One result the courts have reached may seem puzzling in light of the blasting cases. We refer to cases holding that the storage of gunpowder is not an ultrahazardous activity that subjects the owner of the storage facility to strict liability for damage caused by an explosion. If blasting subjects the blaster to strict liability, why should not storage of the material used for blasting also give rise to strict liability?

Tuckashinsky v. Lehigh & Co.[134] illustrates the economic distinction between these cases. The defendant was engaged in coal mining and kept several kegs of black powder near the mine shaft for use in blasting. A bolt of lightning hit the powder and the concussion from the explosion injured the plaintiff, who was standing

[132] 312 So. 2d 799 (Fla. Dist. Ct. App. 1975).

[133] 81 Wash. 2d 448, 502 P.2d 1181 (1972).

[134] 199 Pa. 515, 49 A. 308 (1901).

in the doorway of her father's house nearby. The court stated:

> The evidence in this case shows that the powder magazine had been in use by the defendant company for more than 30 years, and that plaintiff has resided within about 700 feet of it for some 16 years. Yet there is no testimony to show that any apprehension of danger, or any fear of explosion, was felt or expressed by any one during that time. No objection to the location or maintenance of the magazine has been shown. The explosives were stored in small quantities to meet current needs. Such materials are always dangerous, but, as their use is essential to the work of mining, it is impossible to protect, absolutely, persons or property in the immediate vicinity. The risk is similar to that arising from the operation of steam boilers and other machinery and apparatus necessary to the prosperity of great communities.[135]

The difference between *Tuckashinsky* and the blasting cases is that in *Tuckashinsky* plaintiff's optimal activity level was an important choice variable. People cannot relocate to avoid the danger from blasting because blasting may accompany any new construction and new construction is ubiquitous, but they do not have to live 700 feet from a mine or, as in the *Kleebauer* case, near a plant that manufactures high explosives.[136] *Tuckashinsky* was really a nuisance case rather than an accident case. The issue was the optimal pattern of land development, and there was no presumption that defendant's use of his land to store gunpowder was less appropriate than use by plaintiff's father of his land for a residence.

An interesting feature of the strict liability standard is that contributory negligence, as such, is not a defense. In a wild-animal case, for example, plaintiff is barred from recovery only by (in the language of the *Restatement*) "knowingly and unreasonably subjecting himself to the risk that a wild animal . . . will do harm to his person . . . ."[137] Under this rule, one who enters a lion's cage and is mauled by the lion is barred from recovering damages, but the question whether the cost of accident avoidance to the victim

[135] *Id.* at 518, 49 A. at 309.

[136] *See* Kleebauer v. Western Fuse & Explosives Co., 138 Cal. 497, 71 P. 617 (1903).

[137] RESTATEMENT (SECOND) OF TORTS § 515(2) (1977). *See, e.g.*, Keyser v. Phillips Petroleum Co., 287 So. 2d 364 (Fla. Dist. Ct. App. 1973). The standard is similar in cases of strict liability for ultrahazardous activities. *See* RESTATEMENT, *supra*, § 524(2).

was less than the expected accident cost is not examined beyond this; the Hand formula is not applied. At first glance, this result seems inconsistent with the economic model in part II, but the inconsistency is superficial. Recall the possible consequences of applying the Hand formula sequentially to injurer and victim conduct in an alternative-care case where the victim's cost of accident avoidance, while lower than the expected accident cost, is higher than the injurer's avoidance cost. Ultrahazardous activities are by definition activities in which the expected accident cost is high. Often it will be higher than the cost of care to the victim. If your neighbor keeps a pet lion in his backyard, the expected accident cost may justify extraordinary measures of self-protection. The cost of these measures probably will be greater than the cost to the lion's owner of avoiding an accident simply by substituting a less dangerous watch animal. The optimal solution is obtained by *not* applying the Hand formula to the victim's care, and this is what is done. Where, however, the cost of care to the victim is low (and possibly negative) relative to the cost of curtailing the activity, as where the victim enters the lion's cage, the defense of "knowingly and unreasonably subjecting himself to the risk" brings about the efficient solution.

Probably the most important principle of strict liability in tort law (other than in the products liability area, which is not discussed in this section), at least as measured by the number of cases in which it is applied, is that of *respondeat superior*: an employer is strictly liable for the torts of his employees committed in furtherance of the employment. This principle has been thought to be an example of the law's sympathy for accident victims. Employees often lack sufficient assets to pay a tort judgment, and *respondeat superior* allows the victim to reach into the employer's "deep pocket." This is an unsatisfactory explanation. The principle of *respondeat superior* is not recent but dates back to a period in which the common law was not otherwise noted for sympathy for accident victims. Moreover, the employer is strictly liable only for damages resulting from the negligence of his employees. A victim injured by an employee who is exercising due care has no claim against the employer.

The economic explanation of *respondeat superior* focuses on the fact that employees often are unable to pay a tort judgment against them, and therefore lack adequate incentive to take due care. The employer could use the threat of termination or refusal to promote as a substitute inducement to careful conduct, but he will do so only if the employee's carelessness is a cost to him. There are also activity-level measures that employers might take to reduce the number of accidents caused by negligent employees, such as making greater use of independent contractors or giving their employees simpler tasks requiring less care.

In view of these arguments for employer liability for the torts of employees,[138] is there any justification for the common law's refusal to hold parents liable for the torts of their children? One difference is that it is unlikely that imposing liability on parents would significantly affect people's choice of whom to marry or how many children to have; in other words, activity-level adjustments do not seem a promising method of reducing torts by children.[139] Second, children are generally less dangerous than employees; this is, of course, just another reason for not expecting that liability would call forth many activity changes. The principal exception to parental nonliability is consistent with these distinctions: the "family car" rule that many common-law jurisdictions have adopted.[140] Under this rule, the owner of a car is liable for the torts of family members committed while they are driving it. Not only does the car make even (or perhaps especially) a child dangerous, but there is a simple activity change to reduce expected accident costs — preventing the child from driving the car.

A notable exception to *respondeat superior* is the "fellow servant" rule, which existed in the days when accidents to workers were subject to tort rather than workmen's compensation law. Under this rule, the employer was not liable for the tortious injury to one of his workers by another unless the employer had reason to know that the tortfeasor was careless. The rule encouraged workers to monitor each other's level of care and report careless workers to the employer. Because workers have better information in this respect than the employer himself, this rule should produce a lower accident rate than if each worker is insured by his employer

---

[138] The arguments are developed more fully in Landes & Posner, *supra* note 20, at 526-28, 534.

[139] Of course, parents who are negligent in supervising their children are liable for such negligence and principles of vicarious liability do not come into play.

[140] *See* W. PROSSER, *supra* note 61, at 483-86.

against the carelessness of his co-workers.

Even if the reader is convinced by our discussion that the areas of strict liability in tort law make economic sense, he still may object that we have not shown that the areas of tort law governed by negligence rather than strict liability are not equally or more appropriate for treatment under strict liability. We shall not attempt such a showing here beyond noting that the principal areas of tort law not governed by strict liability involve collisions and professional (chiefly medical) malpractice. Neither is an area suitable for strict liability. In collision cases, due care typically requires both parties to exercise care, and there is no presumption that altering the injurer's activity level is a more efficient method of accident avoidance than altering the victim's activity level. Hence there is no allocative advantage to strict liability. (Whether there is a savings in administrative costs depends upon whether the higher information costs of the negligence standard exceed the higher claims costs of the strict liability standard; as a first approximation, it seems best to treat these costs as offsetting.) As for medical malpractice, to treat every case in which medical treatment injures the patient as one of strict liability would entail much loss-shifting for small allocative gains. Most medical procedures involve a risk of injuring the patient. Under a standard of strict liability, every one of these procedures, however carefully administered, would give rise to a claim for damages if injury occurred.[141]

IV. Is Tort Law Growing Less Efficient?

Part III of this article revealed considerable congruence between the legal doctrines of negligence, contributory negligence, and strict liability and the economic model of efficient tort law explicated in part II. But while giving some examples of how the law had changed to adapt to changing economic circumstances, we did not ask whether the law as a whole was becoming less responsive to

---

[141] It also may be more difficult, and therefore more costly, to determine in a medical malpractice suit, as compared to an ordinary accident case, whether the victim's injury was caused by the injurer's behavior. This would make the claims cost of a medical malpractice suit greater than the cost of an ordinary accident case. Although causation would be a requirement under both strict liability and negligence (and there are important economic reasons why this is so), the fact that the claims cost of a medical malpractice case is great would tend to make the savings in administrative cost an important factor in preferring negligence to strict liability.

efficiency. That question now must be faced in light of frequent assertions that whatever the situation may once have been, tort law as interpreted and applied in recent years, especially since 1970, is not efficient.[142]

The best way to evaluate this contention would be to draw a random sample of recently decided tort cases and compare them with the cases and doctrines discussed in part III of this article. To do so, however, would extend the article to an unmanageable length. Instead, we shall offer some summary impressions of recent trends in tort law, leaving to another day the more rigorous inquiry that the question deserves.

(1) The formulation of the negligence standard has not changed in recent years; it is still the Hand formula, or some verbal counterpart to it. What does seem to have changed is the amount of control that judges exercise over juries. Judges in the nineteenth century were quick to withdraw cases from juries where they disagreed with the jury's assessment of the defendant's negligence. Judges today are more deferential to juries. This trend apparently has coincided with a decline in the quality of juries. The rising value of time has made productive people increasingly reluctant to serve on juries. If, as is likely, juries bias the application of the Hand formula in favor of the accident victim, then the two trends we have mentioned are increasing both random and biased error in applying the formula.

(2) The demarcation between negligence and strict liability has not changed, at least in the areas discussed in this article, except as dictated by changes in the economic environment (*e.g.*, the growing safety of flight and the establishment of zoos). If anything, the scope of strict liability has been contracting, because some activities have been reclassified from ultrahazardous to normally hazardous, as discussed in part II. This trend rebuts any simple claim of a uniform expansion in tort liability.

(3) Not every expansion in liability is inefficient. For example, the trend in recent years toward broader recovery for negligently inflicted emotional distress[143] probably is making tort law more,

---

[142] *See, e.g.*, Epstein, *The Static Conception of the Common Law*, 9 J. LEGAL STUD. 253 (1980).

[143] *See, e.g.*, Barnhill v. Davis, 300 N.W.2d 104 (Iowa 1981); Sinn v. Burd, 486 Pa. 146, 404 A.2d 672 (1979).

rather than less, efficient. Such distress — the horror, for example, that the mother feels when seeing her child run over by a car — is a real social cost. Courts formerly were inhibited about granting recovery in such cases by the difficulty of determining accurately the causal relationship between a physical accident to one person and emotional distress to another and of quantifying those damages. The growth of our knowledge of emotional illness, slow as that growth has been, has, by lowering the costs of establishing these facts, increased the net social benefit of allowing damages to be awarded in such cases.

(4) Economics is beginning to be used explicitly in the trial and decision of tort cases, especially with reference to damages. Sophisticated treatments of such questions as the value of a child to his parents[144] and the proper treatment of inflation in calculating lost earnings[145] now may be found in the cases.

(5) The recent and dramatic expansion in products liability may seem to undermine our claim that the boundaries between negligence and strict liability have been shifting only in response to changes in the economic environment. However, the real problem with modern products liability is not the encroachment of the strict liability principle on the negligence principle. That encroachment has been only modest, because the requirement of proving a defect preserves a strong foothold of the negligence concept in strict liability products cases. The real problem with modern products liability law is, rather, the growing reluctance of courts (1) to allow the market to set the standard of safety even where the market can be expected to work with reasonable efficiency, and (2) to allow the plaintiff's contributory fault to bar him from recovering damages.[146] The first of these trends is illustrated by design-defect cases,[147] where courts inappropriately use the Hand formula to decide whether a product should have been designed more safely. Because transaction costs between manufacturer and user are low, the market can be expected to generate the product design that minimizes all costs, including expected accident costs. There is no

[144] *See, e.g.*, D'Ambra v. United States, 481 F.2d 14 (1st Cir. 1973); Wycko v. Gnodtke, 361 Mich. 331, 105 N.W.2d 118 (1960).

[145] *See, e.g.*, Doca v. Marina Mercante Nicaraguense, S.A., 634 F.2d 30 (2d Cir. 1980).

[146] These trends are documented in R. EPSTEIN, MODERN PRODUCTS LIABILITY LAW (1980).

[147] *See, e.g.*, Dawson v. Chrysler Corp., 630 F.2d 950 (3d Cir. 1980).

occasion for the court to substitute its own conception of what an optimal design would be. A parallel trend in the area of medical malpractice has led some courts to disregard the customary standard of care and to substitute their own conception of due care.[148]

The second trend in the products liability area, the withering away of defenses based on plaintiff's status or conduct, deserves attention because it appears to be a general characteristic of tort law in recent years. Some of the developments in this area, to be sure, may be consistent with, or even required by, efficiency. For example, more and more courts are abandoning the traditional principle that the status of being a trespasser or licensee bars one from recovering damages for an accident caused by the landowner's (or occupier's) negligence.[149] The victim's status *vis-à-vis* the landowner is relevant to the negligence calculus because the cost of avoiding trespassing may be lower than the cost to the landowner of avoiding harm to the trespasser. It is not always lower, however, as the common law recognized in such defenses to the no-duty-to-trespassers principle as last clear chance and attractive nuisance, discussed in part III. To eliminate the common law categories and substitute a standard whereby the plaintiff's status is relevant to, but not determinative of, his right to recover damages — the course taken by the California court in *Rowland v. Christian* and followed by many other courts — may actually be superior to the common-law approach. It does, however, interact disturbingly with another trend we have noted — the expanding discretion of the jury. The common-law categories kept from the jury certain cases where plaintiff's cost of accident avoidance was low; the approach of *Rowland v. Christian* makes the plaintiff's cost of accident avoidance just another issue for the jury to weigh, with minimal judicial control.

Other tendencies relating to plaintiff status or conduct as a bar to recovery of damages are less easy to reconcile with efficiency. These include the substitution of comparative for contributory negligence in thirty-seven states,[150] the widespread abolition of

---

[148] *See, e.g.*, Helling v. Carey, 83 Wash. 2d 514, 519 P.2d 981 (1974).

[149] The leading case is Rowland v. Christian, 69 Cal. 2d 108, 443 P.2d 561, 70 Cal. Rptr. 97 (1968).

[150] *See* Alvis v. Ribar, 85 Ill. 2d 1, 421 N.E.2d 886, 891-92 (1981). A cognate trend that we cannot explain on efficiency grounds is that toward substituting contribution among joint tortfeasors for the common-law rule of no contribution. *See* Landes & Posner, *supra* note

assumption of risk as a defense,[161] and the increasing reluctance of courts to enforce clauses limiting liability for negligence.[162]

Have such trends reached the point of changing the basic character of the common law? It is difficult to say. The common law remains an area of incremental rather than radical change; not all the changes in recent years have been opposed to efficiency; and the pattern of change has been uneven across jurisdictions — much more rapid in California than elsewhere. We think it would be an exaggeration to say that recent tort decisions have changed the character of the common law fundamentally; but if the adverse trends traced above continue, the day is not far distant when that character will be profoundly different from that described in this article.

Will these trends continue? The expansion of tort liability that is the dominant trend of the recent period seems related to the general expansion of social-insurance principles during that period. At this writing, the legislative expansion has stopped; indeed, contraction may be beginning. Perhaps the judicial expansion of tort liability will be reversed also.

V. Conclusion

In this article we have attempted to introduce to a nonspecialist audience the positive economic theory of tort law — the theory that the common law of torts is best explained on the "as if" assumption that the judges are trying to maximize efficiency. The purpose of the article has been introductory, not definitive. We have described the history, and replied to the recurrent criticisms, of the theory; explicated the economic model that underlies it; discussed the congruence between the model and some basic tort doctrines relating to negligence, contributory negligence, and strict liability; and, very briefly, reflected on recent trends in the law that threaten, but have not yet fundamentally changed, the efficient character of tort law. We have not proved that the theory is

---

20.

[161] The leading case here is Meistrich v. Casino Arena Attractions, Inc., 31 N.J. 44, 155 A.2d 90 (1959).

[162] *See, e.g.*, Tunkl v. Regents of Univ. of Cal., 60 Cal. 2d 92, 383 P.2d 441, 32 Cal. Rptr. 33 (1963).

correct. We hope that this article will stimulate the additional empirical research that is necessary to confirm or refute it.

APPENDIX: THE MODEL EXTENDED TO THE SYMMETRICAL CASE

In part II, we assumed, to simplify the exposition, that parties to an accident could be divided into injurers and victims — *i.e.*, that only one party to the accident was injured. The assumption is unrealistic for many accident cases, especially those involving a collision between vehicles. Here we extend the model to the symmetrical case (*i.e.*, where both parties are simultaneously potential victims), and show that the implications of the model are not substantively affected by the modification.

One possibility in a collision is to let the damages lie where they fall. *A* and *B* would select care levels to minimize respectively

$$\lambda^a p(x,y)D + A(x) \quad (10)$$

$$\lambda^b p(x,y)D + B(y) \quad (11)$$

where λ^a is the fraction of the total damages (D) incurred by *A* and λ^b is the fraction incurred by *B* (before in our analysis $\lambda^a = 1$ and $\lambda^b = 0$). Each party will take the other's care as given and some pair (x,y) would be selected. How does that pair compare with the due care level (x^*,y^*)? It will tend to be lower, because each party is in equilibrium when his share of expected reduction in damages is equal to the cost of an additional unit of care. For example, suppose that $\lambda^a = .5$, $-p_xD = \$2$, and $A_x = \$1$ at 5 units of x. *A* would be in equilibrium because $-\lambda^a p_x D = A_x$. From society's viewpoint, however, an additional \$1 in care reduces expected damages by \$2. Therefore, it would be optimal for *A* to go beyond $5x$. The problem with a rule that lets losses lie where they fall is that neither party has an incentive to take account of the benefits to the other party.

A possible alternative would be to make one of the parties, say *B*, liable for the entire damages caused by the accident. This would be tantamount to a rule of strict liability with no contributory negligence, and would yield inefficient results (assuming x^* is positive) because *A* would have no incentive to take care. Now consider negligence. Here losses lie where they fall only if both parties are negligent or both use due care. The distribution of losses for both *A* and *B* are illustrated in Table 4.

Table 4
A's and *B*'s Expected Losses

A			*B*		
B's Care	*A*'s Care x_0	x^*	*A*'s Care	*B*'s Care y_0	y^*
y_0	$\lambda^a pD + A(x_0)$	$A(x^*)$	x_0	$\lambda^b pD + B(y_0)$	$B(y^*)$
y^*	$pD + A(x_0)$	$\lambda^a pD + A(x^*)$	x^*	$pD + B(y_0)$	$\lambda^b pD + B(y^*)$

Note: To simplify the table we have written $p(x,y)$ as p.

First, consider *A*'s behavior. If *B* selects due care, *A* will compare $p(x_0,y^*)\ D + A(x_0)$ with $\lambda^a p(x^*,y^*)D + A(x^*)$. We know from the definition of due care that $L(x_0,y^*) - B(y^*) > L(x^*,y^*) - B(y^*) = p(x^*,y^*)D + A(x^*) > \lambda^a pD(x^*,y^*)D + A(x^*)$. Therefore, *A* will select x^* if *B* chooses y^*. Similarly, *B* will select y^* if *A* chooses x^*. Suppose, however, that *B* chooses y_0. What will *A* do? *A* will choose x_0 or x^* depending upon whether

$$\lambda^a p(x_0,y_0)D + A(x_0) \lesseqgtr A(x^*). \tag{12}$$

It seems possible that if λ^a is relatively small and $A(x^*) - A(x_0)$ is relatively large, *A* will prefer to be negligent. A similar argument holds for *B*. That is, *B* will choose y_0 or y^* (if *A* chooses x_0) depending upon whether

$$\lambda^b p(x_0,y_0)D + B(y_0) \lesseqgtr B(y^*). \tag{13}$$

It would appear, therefore, that we do not have a unique solution:

1. If one party chooses due care, the other will also choose due care; or
2. If one party chooses less than due care, the other may also behave negligently.

Although it *seems* that either (x_0,y_0) or (x^*,y^*) are possible equilibrium solutions, this is not so. For both *A* and *B* to behave negligently would require that

$$\lambda^a p(x_0,y_0)D + A(x_0) < A(x^*) \tag{14}$$
$$\lambda^b p(x_0,y_0)D + B(y_0) < B(y^*) \tag{15}$$

which implies (by the addition of (14) and (15)) that

$$p(x_0,y_0)D + A(x_0) + B(y_0) < A(x^*) + B(y^*) \tag{16}$$

which contradicts the definition of (x^*,y^*) as care levels that minimize $L(x,y)$. Hence only (x^*,y^*) is an equilibrium.

The intuitive explanation for this result is similar to that in the parallel case of negligence-contributory negligence. If *A* does not use due care, *B* certainly will have an incentive to do so, because he thereby can throw the full costs of the accident onto *A*; knowing this, *A* will exercise due care also. An identical argument can be made for *B*. To illustrate, suppose that the total damages from the accident are \$100, they fall equally on both parties ($\lambda^a = \lambda^b = .5$), and $x^* = \$25$ and $y^* = \$25$. If *A* fails to use due care, *B* will see an opportunity to avert damages of \$50 by using due care at a cost of only \$25. Knowing this, *A* will use due care also to avert having to pay both his damages and *B*'s. The particular numbers are immaterial so long as the costs of $x^* + y^*$ are less than \$100 (if their sum exceeded \$100, it would not be efficient to avoid the accident). For example, suppose that the injury to *A* if the accident occurs will be only \$10, but the injury to *B* will be \$90. Initially, it may seem that *A* would have no incentive to invest \$25 in care to avoid an accident that would cost him only \$10. However, *B* will have an incentive to avert a \$90 injury by expending \$25 on due care; once *B* does so, *A* will face expected accident costs of \$100 (\$10 in injury costs to *A* that he cannot recover from *B*, and \$90 in injury costs to *B* that *B* can recover from *A*), which he can avert by expending \$25 on care.

[21]

STRICT LIABILITY VERSUS NEGLIGENCE

*STEVEN SHAVELL**

I. Introduction and Discussion

The aim of this article is to compare strict liability and negligence rules on the basis of the incentives they provide to "appropriately" reduce accident losses. It will therefore be both convenient and clarifying to abstract from other issues in respect to which the rules could be evaluated. In particular, there will be no concern with the bearing of risk—for parties will be presumed risk neutral—nor with the size of "administrative costs"—for the legal system will be assumed to operate free of such costs—nor with distributional equity—for the welfare criterion will be taken to be the following aggregate: the benefits derived by parties from engaging in activities less total accident losses less total accident prevention costs.

Because the analysis of the rules will employ a mathematical model, it seems desirable to consider first in an informal way the points to be made and the logic behind them. Since this discussion will not serve as a complete summary, readers will probably also want to at least look at the statements of the propositions in the later parts of the paper and will almost certainly wish to read the concluding comments (which are not focused on the details of the model).

Accidents will be conceived of as involving two types of parties, "injurers" and "victims," only the latter of which are assumed to suffer direct losses. The category of accidents that will be examined initially are *unilateral* in nature, by which is meant that the actions of injurers but not of victims are assumed to affect the probability or severity of losses. The unilateral case is studied for two reasons. First, it is descriptive of situations in which whatever changes in the behavior of victims that could reasonably be expected to result from changes in liability rules would have only a small influence on accident losses.[1] The second reason is pedagogical; it is easier to understand the general *bilateral* case after having studied the unilateral case.

* Associate Professor of Economics, Harvard University, and Visiting Professor, Harvard Law School. I wish to thank the National Science Foundation (NSF grant SOC-76-20862) for financial support and Peter Diamond, Douglas Ginsburg, Henry Hansmann, Duncan Kennedy, and, especially, A. Mitchell Polinsky and Richard Posner for comments.

[1] Examples of accidents occurring in such situations and which therefore might be considered

Unilateral Case

This case (as well as the bilateral case) will be considered in each of several situations distinguished by the nature of the relationship between injurers and victims.

Accidents between strangers (see Proposition 1): In this subcase it is supposed that injurers and victims are strangers, that neither are sellers of a product, and that injurers may choose to engage in an activity which puts victims at risk.

By definition, under the negligence rule all that an injurer needs to do to avoid the possibility of liability is to make sure to exercise due care if he engages in his activity.[2] Consequently *he will not be motivated to consider the effect on accident losses of his choice of whether to engage in his activity or, more generally, of the level at which to engage in his activity;* he will choose his level of activity in accordance only with the personal benefits so derived. But surely any increase in his level of activity will typically raise expected accident losses (holding constant the level of care). Thus he will be led to choose too high a level of activity;[3] the negligence rule is not "efficient."

Consider by way of illustration the problem of pedestrian-automobile accidents (and, as we are now discussing the unilateral case, let us imagine the behavior of pedestrians to be fixed). Suppose that drivers of automobiles find it in their interest to adhere to the standard of due care but that the possibility of accidents is not thereby eliminated. Then, in deciding how much to drive, they will contemplate only the enjoyment they get from doing so. Because (as they exercise due care) they will not be liable for harm suffered by pedestrians, drivers will not take into account that going more miles will mean a higher expected number of accidents. Hence, there will be too much driving; an individual will, for example, decide to go for a drive on a mere whim despite the imposition of a positive expected cost to pedestrians.

However, under a rule of strict liability, the situation is different. Because

---

unilateral are not hard to imagine: a water main breaks and floods the basement of a home; a plane crashes into a house; a surgeon performs the wrong procedure on an anaesthetized patient. Concededly, even in these examples the victim could have taken *some* protective action (the surgeon's patient could have hired another surgeon to watch over the operation), but, we may plausibly assume, not at a cost nearly low enough to make it worthwhile.

[2] It is assumed for ease of exposition that courts have no difficulty in determining if a party did in fact exercise due care; the reader will have no trouble in appropriately modifying the arguments to be made so as to take into account relaxation of such simplifications as this.

[3] Specifically, while he will choose to engage in the activity just up to the level at which the personal benefit from a marginal increase would equal zero, it would be best from society's viewpoint for him to engage in the activity only up to the level at which his benefit from a marginal increase would equal the (positive) social marginal cost in terms of accident losses.

an injurer must pay for losses whenever he is involved in an accident,[4] he will be induced to consider the effect on accident losses of both his level of care *and* his level of activity. His decisions will therefore be efficient. Because drivers will be liable for losses sustained by pedestrians, they will decide not only to exercise due care in driving but also to drive only when the utility gained from it outweighs expected liability payments to pedestrians.

Accidents between sellers and strangers (see Proposition 2): In this subcase it is assumed that injurers are sellers of a product or service and that they conduct their business in a competitive market. (The assumption of competition allows us to ignore monopoly power, which is for the purposes of this article a logically tangential issue.) Moreover, it is assumed that victims are strangers; they have no market relationship with sellers either as their customers or as their employees.

Under the negligence rule the outcome is inefficient, but the reasoning is slightly different from that of the last subcase. While it is still true that all a seller must do to avoid liability is to take due care, why this results in too high a level of activity has to do with market forces. Because the seller will choose to avoid liability, the price of his product will not reflect the accident losses associated with production. This means that buyers of the product will face too low a price and will purchase too much, which is to say that the seller's level of activity will be too high. Imagine that the drivers are engaged in some business activity—let us say that they are taxi drivers. Then, given that they take due care, the taxi drivers will not have liability expenses, will set rates equal to "production" cost (competition among taxi drivers is assumed), will experience a greater demand than if rates were appropriately higher, and will therefore carry too many fares and cause too many accidents.

Under strict liability, the outcome is efficient, and again the reasoning is a little different from that in the last subcase. Since sellers have to pay for accident losses, they will be led to take the right level of care. And since the product price will reflect accident losses, customers will face the "socially correct" price for the product; purchases will therefore be appropriately lower than what they would be if the product price did not reflect accident losses. Taxi drivers will now increase rates by an amount equal to expected accident losses suffered by pedestrians, and the demand for rides in taxis will fall.

Accidents between sellers and customers—or employees (see Proposition 3 and Part III. B (iii)): It is presumed here that victims have a market relationship with sellers as either their customers or their employees; and since both situations are essentially the same, it will suffice to discuss only that when victims are customers. In order to understand the role (which is important)

[4] Causal or other reasons for limiting the scope of liability are ignored.

of customers' knowledge of risk, three alternative assumptions will be considered: customers know the risk presented by each seller; they do not know the risk presented by each seller but they do know the average seller's risk;[5] they misperceive even this average risk.

Under the negligence rule, the outcome is efficient only if customers correctly perceive risks. As before, when the victims were strangers, sellers will take due care in order to avoid liability, so that the product price will not reflect accident losses. However, now the accident losses are borne by the customers. Thus, the "full" price in the eyes of customers is the market price plus imputed perceived accident losses. Therefore, if risks are correctly perceived, the full price equals the socially correct price, and the quantity purchased will be appropriate. But if risks are not correctly perceived, the quantity purchased will be inappropriate; if customers underestimate risks, what they regard as the full price is less than the true full price and they will buy too much of the product, and conversely if they overestimate risks.[6]

Think, for example, of the risk of food poisoning from eating at restaurants. Under the negligence rule, restaurants will decide to avoid liability by taking appropriate precautions to prepare meals under sanitary conditions. Therefore, the price of meals will not reflect the expected losses due to the (remaining) risk of food poisoning. If customers know this risk, they will correctly consider it in their decisions over the purchase of meals. But if they underestimate the risk, they will purchase too many meals; and if they overestimate it, too few.

Under strict liability, the outcome is efficient regardless of whether customers misperceive risks. As in the last subcase, because sellers have to pay for accident losses, they will decide to take appropriate care and will sell the product at a price reflecting accident losses. Thus customers will face the socially correct price and will purchase the correct amount. Their perception of the risk is irrelevant since it will not influence their purchases; as they will be compensated under strict liability for any losses, the likelihood of losses will not matter to them. Restaurant-goers will face a price that reflects expected losses due to food poisoning when meals are prepared under sanitary conditions; they will buy the same—and appropriate—number of meals whether they think the probability of food poisoning is low or high, for they will be compensated for any losses suffered.[7]

[5] If sellers are assumed to be identical (as they are in the formal model) and therefore to act identically, the average risk will in fact be the risk presented by each seller. But it will be seen from the discussion of the situation when sellers are not liable that the first and second assumptions are nevertheless different.

[6] It may be instructive to mention the parallel situation in regard to employee victims. If employees correctly perceive risks at the workplace, then they will (appropriately) choose to work for a firm only if the "net" wage—the market wage less the expected accident losses they bear—is at least equal to their opportunity elsewhere. But if, say, they underestimate risks, they might choose to work for a firm when the net wage is in fact below their opportunity elsewhere.

[7] However, it is worthwhile noticing that if they could not possibly be compensated for a kind

When sellers are simply not liable for accident losses, then the outcome is efficient only if customers know the risk presented by each seller. For, given this assumption, because customers will seek to buy products with the lowest full price (market price plus expected accident losses), sellers will be induced to take appropriate care (since this will lower the accident-loss component of the full price). While it is true that if a restaurant took inadequate precautions to prevent food poisoning, it could offer lower-priced meals, it is also true that customers would respond not just to the market price of meals but also to the likelihood of food poisoning—which they are presumed to know. Therefore customers would decide against giving the restaurant their business. Consequently, restaurants will be led to take adequate precautions and to charge accordingly. Moreover, because customers will base purchases on the correctly perceived full price, they will buy the correct amount.

If, however, customers do not know the risk presented by individual sellers, there are two sources of inefficiency when sellers are not liable. The first is that, given the risk of loss, the quantity purchased by customers may not be correct; of course, this will be true if customers misperceive the risk. The second source of inefficiency is that sellers will not be motivated by market forces to appropriately reduce risks. To understand why, consider the situation when customers do correctly perceive the average risk (when they do not correctly perceive this risk, an explanation similar to the one given here could be supplied). That is, assume that customers know the risk presented by sellers as a group but do not have the ability to "observe" the risk presented by sellers on an individual basis. Then sellers would have no inducement to exercise adequate care. Suppose that restaurant-goers know the risk of food poisoning at restaurants in general and it is, say, inappropriately high. Then if a *particular* restaurant were to take sufficient precautions to lower the risk, customers would not recognize this (except insofar as it eventually affected the average risk—but under the assumption that there are many competing restaurants, this effect would be negligible). Thus the restaurant could not charge a higher price for its meals—customers would have no reason not to go to the cheaper restaurants. In consequence, a situation in which sellers take inadequate care to reduce risks would persist; and similar reasoning shows that a situation in which they take adequate care would not persist. (Notice, however, that since customers are assumed to correctly perceive the average risk, at least they will purchase the correct number of meals—correct, given the high risk.)

---

of loss from food poisoning, then misperception of risk certainly would matter. For instance, if there were a risk of death from food poisoning and if restaurant-goers underestimated it, then they would expose themselves to a higher risk of death by eating restaurant meals than they would truly want to bear. Thus, the conclusion of this paragraph that misperception of risk does not matter under strict liability holds only in respect to risks compensable by payment of money damages.

Finally, it should be observed that the discussion of liability in the present subcase bears on the role of tort law in a contractual setting. When customers make purchases, they are willingly entering into a kind of contract—in which they agree to a price and pay it, receive goods, and expose themselves to a risk (in the absence of liability).[8] Therefore, our conclusions may be generally expressed by the statement that, when customers' knowledge of risks is perfect, the rule of liability does not matter; the "contractual" arrangement arrived at in the market is appropriate. But when the knowledge is not perfect, there is generally scope for the use of liability, and the relative performance of liability rules depends on the precise nature of the imperfection in knowledge. The force of this point, and the fact that it is not always an obvious one, is perhaps well illustrated by the situation described in the previous paragraph. In that situation, customers did correctly perceive average risk, so that there was "assumption of risk," but this did not lead to a desirable result. The situation was one therefore in which, under our assumptions, courts ought not to allow the defense of assumption of risk to be successfully asserted.

Bilateral Case

In this case, account is taken of the possibility that potential victims as well as injurers may influence the probability or magnitude of accident losses by their choices of both level of care and of level of activity.

Accidents between strangers (see Propositions 4 and 5):[9] Under the negligence rule,[10] the outcome is not efficient. As was true in the unilateral case, since all that an injurer needs to do to avoid liability is to exercise due care,

[8] It should be remarked that the possibility of contractual arrangements that go beyond mere agreement on price is not considered here; for example, the possibility that sellers might give customers some form of guarantee is not allowed for in the discussion or in the analysis. However, our conclusions do have some relevance to what contractual arrangements might be made. This is because what is "efficient" is, by definition, what maximizes benefits minus costs, which is in turn what is in the mutual interest of the sellers and customers to do. (To illustrate, if customers *realise* that they do not know the risk of loss, then they might wish for, and insist on, a blanket guarantee, in effect making the seller strictly liable, and thereby giving him an incentive to reduce the risk of loss.) Of course, the reason this is not considered here is that a satisfactory treatment would require us to study at the least the value of explicit arrangements over the arrangements that inhere in the applicable tort and contract law, the costs of making explicit arrangements as opposed to the expected costs of reliance on the applicable law, and the willingness of courts to enforce what is at variance with the applicable law.

[9] The explanation given in this and in the next subcase for why neither strict liability with a defense of contributory negligence nor the negligence rule results in an efficient outcome is in its essence that given by Richard Posner, Economic Analysis of Law 139-40 (2d ed. 1977). See also Duncan Kennedy, A History of Law and Economics or the Fetishism of Commodities (1979) (unpublished mimeographed paper at Harvard University) which makes related points at 54-63.

[10] In the present discussion, it will make no difference whether or not the reader thinks of this rule as incorporating the defense of contributory negligence.

he will choose too high a level of activity. In regard to victims, however, the situation is different. Since a victim bears his accident losses, he will choose an appropriate level of care *and* an appropriate level of his activity, given the (inefficient) behavior of injurers. The drivers will exercise due care but will go too many miles. And the pedestrians, knowing that they must bear accident losses, will exercise due care (in crossing streets and so forth) and they will also reduce the number of miles they walk in accordance with expected accident losses per mile.

Under strict liability with a defense of contributory negligence, the outcome is symmetrical to the last—and again inefficient.[11] Because all that a victim needs to do to avoid bearing accident losses is to take due care, he will have no motive to appropriately reduce *his* level of activity; this is the inefficiency. However, because injurers now bear accident losses, they will take the appropriate amount of care and choose the right level of activity, given the inefficient behavior of victims. Drivers will exercise due care and go the correct number of miles. Pedestrians will also exercise due care but will walk too many miles.

From this discussion it is apparent that the choice between strict liability with a defense of contributory negligence and the negligence rule is a choice between the lesser of two evils. Strict liability with the defense will be superior to the negligence rule when it is more important that injurers be given an incentive through a liability rule to reduce their activity level than that victims be given a similar incentive; that is to say, when it is more important that drivers go fewer miles than that pedestrians walk fewer miles.

Because neither of the familiar liability rules induces efficient behavior, the question arises, *"Is there any conceivable liability rule depending on parties' levels of care and harm done that induces efficient behavior?"* It is proved below (Proposition 5) that the answer is *"No."* The problem in essence is that for injurers to be induced to choose the correct level of activity, they must bear all accident losses; and for victims to choose the correct level of their activity, they also must bear all accident losses. Yet it is in the nature of a liability rule that both conditions cannot hold simultaneously; clearly, injurers and victims cannot each bear all accident losses.[12]

Accidents between sellers and strangers (see Proposition 6): Because the reader will be able to appeal to arguments analogous to those already made and in order to avoid tedious repetition, explanation of the results stated in this and the next subcase will be abbreviated or will be omitted.

[11] It is of course clear that under strict liability without the defense the outcome is inefficient, for victims would have no motive to take care.

[12] However, when other means of social control are also employed, it is possible to achieve an efficient outcome. For example, if use of the negligence rule were supplemented by imposition of a tax on the level of injurer activity, an efficient outcome could be achieved.

Under both the negligence rule and strict liability with a defense of contributory negligence, the outcome is inefficient, as was true in the last subcase. Under the negligence rule, sellers will take appropriate care, but since the product price will not reflect accident losses, too much will be purchased by customers. Also, since victims bear accident losses, they will take appropriate care and choose the right level of activity. Under strict liability with the defense, sellers will take appropriate care and the product price will reflect accident losses, so the right amount will be purchased. Victims will exercise due care but will choose too high a level of activity. In addition, as in the last subcase, there does not exist any liability rule that induces efficient behavior.

Accidents between sellers and customers—or employees (see Propositions 7a and 7b and Part IV.B (iii)): As before it will be enough to discuss here only the situation when victims are customers. If customers have perfect knowledge of the risk presented by each seller, then the outcome is efficient under strict liability with a defense of contributory negligence or the negligence rule or if sellers are not subject to liability at all. For instance, in the latter situation, since customers wish to buy at the lowest full price, sellers will be led to take appropriate care; and since customers will make their purchases with the full price in mind, the quantity they buy will be correct; and since they bear their losses, they will take appropriate care.

There is, however, a qualification that needs to be made concerning the way in which it is imagined that customers influence accident losses. If one assumes that customers influence losses only by their choice of level of care and of the amount purchased, then what was stated in the previous paragraph is correct; and in regard to services and nondurables (such as meals at restaurants) this assumption seems entirely natural. But in regard to durable goods, it might well be thought that customers influence accident losses not only by their choice of level of care and of purchases, but also by their decision as to frequency of use per unit purchased. The expected number of accidents that a man will have when using a power lawn mower would seem to be influenced not only by whether he in fact purchases one (rather than, say, a hand mower) and by how carefully he mows his lawn with it, but also by how frequently he chooses to mow his lawn. In order for customers to be led to efficiently decide the frequency of use, they must bear their own accident losses. Thus, in regard to durables, the outcome is efficient under the negligence rule or if sellers are not liable, but the outcome is inefficient under strict liability with a defense of contributory negligence; for then if the man buys a power lawn mower, he will have no motive to appropriately reduce the number of times he mows his lawn.

Now suppose that customers correctly perceive only average risks. Then, subject again to a qualification concerning durables, the results are as follows. The outcome is efficient under strict liability with a defense of contributory negligence or under the negligence rule, but the outcome is not efficient if sellers are not liable, for then they will not take sufficient care. The qualification is that if the sellers produce durables, strict liability with the defense is inefficient, leaving the negligence rule as the only efficient rule.

Last, suppose that customers misperceive risks. Then the outcome is efficient only under strict liability with a defense of contributory negligence; and the qualification to this is that, if sellers produce durables, even strict liability with the defense is inefficient, so that there does not exist a liability rule which is efficient.

II. The Model

The assumptions here are much as described in the introduction. There is a single physical good, called "income." The utility (or disutility) of any action which a party takes is assumed to have a well-defined equivalent in terms of income; and, henceforth, when reference is made to income, what will be meant is the amount of literal income plus income equivalents. The (von Neumann-Morgenstern) utility of income is assumed to be equal to income. Thus, parties are risk-neutral; expected utility is expected income. Since the social-welfare function is taken to be the sum of expected utilities, social welfare is the sum of expected incomes.

Accidents are assumed to involve two types of parties, injurers and victims. The number of injurers is assumed equal to the number of victims (and equal to the number of customers in the market case described below); this assumption is inessential and could obviously be modified. In the absence of liability rules, all accident losses fall on victims. The class of injurers and the class of victims are themselves each comprised of identical parties.

Injurers either engage in a nonmarket activity—the "nonmarket" case—or are sellers of a product or service—the "market" case. In the market case, sellers are expected to be profit-maximizing price takers and to face constant production costs per unit. Thus, they earn zero profits in competitive equilibrium. Victims are either strangers, customers, or employees. If victims are customers or employees, three alternative assumptions (which were discussed in the introduction) are made about their knowledge of accident risks.

Parties take liability rules as given; they do not circumvent the rules by contractual arrangement.[13] They also take the behavior of others as given.

[13] The justification is the familiar one, that some "transaction cost" stands in the way. In the nonmarket case and the market case involving strangers, it is that it would be very difficult for each potential injurer to get together with and make a contractual arrangement with each of his potential victims. In the market case, the assumption is that the costs of

Under these assumptions, the (Nash) equilibrium associated with the use of a liability rule can be determined.

An analysis of equilibrium outcomes under liability rules for the nonmarket and market cases is made both in the part of the paper concerned with unilateral accidents and in the one dealing with bilateral accidents. In the nonmarket case, victims are assumed to engage in their activity at a fixed level and to exercise a fixed level of care. Their only role in the market case is, if they are customers, to decide how much to buy or, if they are employees, to decide where to work. The liability rules examined are no liability, strict liability, and the negligence rule. In the bilateral case, two additional liability rules are considered, strict liability with a defense of contributory negligence and the negligence rule with that defense.

If a liability rule results in the outcome that maximizes social welfare, it will be called efficient. The efficient values of variables will be denoted with an "*".

Because the notation used changes somewhat in the different cases analyzed, it will be easiest to present it and to modify it as needed.

III. Unilateral Accidents

Define the following variables,

$x \geqq 0$ care level of an injurer.
$y \geqq 0$ activity level of an injurer,
$l(x)$ expected accident losses per unit of injurer activity level.[14]

Expected accident losses are assumed to fall with care, so $l' < 0$, but at a decreasing rate, so $l'' > 0$. Notice that the model allows for the possibility that injurers may choose not to engage in their activity at all; this corresponds to $y = 0$.

Under strict liability, an injurer is assumed to pay for all accident losses suffered by victims of accidents in which he is involved. Under the negligence rule an injurer has to pay for accident losses only if his care level is less than a due care level. Define

$$\tilde{x} = \text{injurer's due care level.}$$

bargaining and perhaps of recording an agreement make it easier for the involved parties to rely on a liability rule.

[14] We are implicitly assuming that increasing the activity level corresponds to a physical repetition of an activity and causes a proportional rise in expected accident losses. For example, doubling the activity level would double expected accident losses (the level of care held constant). This assumption often seems to be the natural one to make, but it will be clear that the qualitative nature of our results would not be altered if expected accident losses were a more general function of x and y.

Thus, as emphasized in the introduction, y does not enter into a determination about negligence.

A. *The Nonmarket Case: Accidents between Strangers*

Recall that in this case, injurers are not sellers of a product or service but they may decide to engage in an activity which puts victims at risk. Define

$a(x,y)$ = income equivalent of the utility to an injurer of engaging in his activity at level y and exercising care x.[15]

Assume that taking more care reduces this, so $a_x < 0$.[16] Assume also that, given the care level, increases in the activity level up to some point result in increases in utility; beyond that point, however, utility falls with increases in the activity level. Specifically, for any x, $a_y(x,y) > 0$ for $y < y(x)$ and $a_y(x,y) < 0$ for $y > y(x)$. Here $y(x)$ is (uniquely) defined by either $a_y(x,y) = 0$ or, if this never holds, by $y(x) = 0$.

Social welfare W is given by[17]

$$W(x,y) = a(x,y) - yl(x). \quad (1)$$

Note that what enters into W is not only expected accident losses (through yl) and prevention costs (through a_x), but also the benefits of participating in the activity (through a_y). The efficient values x^* and y^* maximize W.

Since under strict liability an injurer must pay for accident losses to possible victims, an injurer's position is

$$a(x,y) - yl(x). \quad (2)$$

The injurer's problem, maximizing (2) over x and y, is the social problem. Strict liability is therefore efficient.

Under the negligence rule, assume that the due care level $\bar{x}$ is sufficiently low so that injurers decide to act in a nonnegligent way, that is, to choose $x = \bar{x}$.[18] Thus, the injurer's problem becomes one of choosing y to maximize

[15] The reader might find it convenient to think about the case $a(x,y) = z(y) - v(x)y$, where $z(y)$ is the benefit of engaging in the activity at level y and $v(x)$ is the cost of taking care x per unit of activity.

[16] Subscripts denote partial derivatives. The arguments of derivatives will frequently be suppressed in the notation.

[17] We need only consider social welfare for a "representative" injurer and victim pair—recall that we have assumed for simplicity that their numbers are equal. An injurer's expected income is $a(x,y)$ − expected liability payments, and a victim's is expected liability payments $- yl(x)$. Adding these gives W.

[18] If $\bar{x}$ were so high that injurers decided to be negligent, they would be, in effect, strictly liable. It does not seem natural to analyze this possibility as one having to do with the negligence rule.

$$a(\bar{x},y). \tag{3}$$

The injurer therefore increases y to the point at which it yields no marginal benefit; in other words, he selects $y(\bar{x})$. Let $y^*(\bar{x})$ be the efficient y given $\bar{x}$ (that is, $y^*(\bar{x})$ maximizes W over y given $\bar{x}$). Then the injurer's activity level is excessive in the sense that $y(\bar{x}) > y^*(\bar{x})$, and for this reason one can immediately conclude that the negligence rule is not efficient.[19] The socially optimal due care level, say $\bar{x}^*$, is determined by maximizing

$$W(\bar{x},y(\bar{x})) = a(\bar{x},y(\bar{x})) - y(\bar{x})l(\bar{x}) \tag{4}$$

over $\bar{x}$ (where $\bar{x}$ must be in the range low enough so that injurers decide to set $x = \bar{x}$). Under fairly weak assumptions, it is true that $\bar{x}^* > x^*$.[20] The optimal due care standard exceeds the efficient care level because it is socially desirable to compensate for inability to control the activity level by forcing injurers to exercise special care (and because this in itself reduces the value of the activity, inducing injurers to lower the activity level).

If there is no liability, the outcome is generally worse than that under the negligence rule (with $\bar{x}^*$ as the due care standard), since injurers exercise no care. That is, $x = 0$ and $y = y(0)$ is the outcome.[21]

The conclusions about the welfare comparison of liability rules may be summarized as follows.

PROPOSITION 1. *Suppose that injurers and victims are strangers. Then strict liability is efficient and is superior to the negligence rule, which is superior to not having liability at all.*

B. *The Market Case: Accidents between Sellers and Victims*

Injurers are now assumed to be sellers of a product or service. The precise interpretation of care x will be explained in the various subcases, which are distinguished by whether the victims are strangers, customers, or employees. The activity level y will be interpreted as the seller's output.

[19] Assume that W is concave in y, that $\bar{x} > 0$, and that $y(\bar{x}) > 0$. Then $y(\bar{x})$ is identified by the first-order condition $a_y = 0$. But $y^*(\bar{x})$ is determined by $a_y = l$. Since $l > 0$ and W is concave, $y^*(\bar{x}) < y(\bar{x})$. Note, however, that the concavity assumption is not needed to show that the negligence rule is not efficient; without it we can still conclude that $y^*(\bar{x}) \neq \bar{y}(\bar{x})$.

[20] Let $[0, \hat{x}]$ be the range of $\bar{x}$ such that injurers would choose $x = \bar{x}$. It is easy to show that $\hat{x} > x^*$. Thus, assuming concavity of (4) in $\bar{x}$, we need only argue that $dW/d\bar{x} > 0$ when evaluated at x^*. But $dW/D\bar{x} = W_x - y'l$ and it is plausible that both terms should be positive at x^*. Assuming that W is concave in x and that the optimal x given $\bar{y}(x^*)$ exceeds x^*, we have $W_x > 0$. Also, assuming that $y' < 0$, $-y'l > 0$.

[21] To show that the negligence rule would be better, we need only demonstrate that $\bar{x}^* > 0$ (for $\bar{x} = 0$ corresponds to no liability). This is plausible for the reasons given in the previous footnote: A sufficient condition for $dW/d\bar{x} > 0$ at $\bar{x} = 0$ is that $W_x(0,y(0)) > 0$ and $y'(0) < 0$.

Before considering the subcases, additional notation is needed, as is a description of competitive market equilibrium. Define

$$c(x) = \text{production cost per unit given } x,$$
$$p = \text{product price,}$$

and assume that $c' > 0$ and $c'' > 0$. The seller's full cost per unit produced and sold is

$$c(x) + \text{expected liability payments per unit.} \tag{5}$$

Since sellers maximize expected profits and are price takers,

$$x \text{ is chosen by sellers to minimize } c(x) + \text{expected liability payments per unit.} \tag{6}$$

Also, in equilibrium, price must equal full cost,

$$p = c(x) + \text{expected liability payments per unit.} \tag{7}$$

(However, (6) and (7) will be slightly modified when the victims are customers and can observe x.) Now define

$$b(y) = \text{income equivalent of gross benefits enjoyed by a customer who purchases } y.$$

These benefits are gross of any expected accident losses he has to bear. We assume $b' > 0$ and $b'' < 0$. The customer's position u is

$$u(y) = b(y) - py - \text{any expected accident losses he has to bear.} \tag{8}$$

The customer's demand is therefore determined by

$$u(y) \text{ is maximized over } y. \tag{9}$$

Equilibrium p, x, and y are determined by (6), (7), and (9).

Social welfare W is given by

$$W = b(y) - yc(x) - yl(x), \tag{10}$$

the gross value of output to customers minus production costs—note that the increase in c with x corresponds to prevention costs—minus expected accident losses. As in the nonmarket case, maximizing W requires taking into account the benefits of y as well as accident costs and prevention costs. From (10), it is clear that the efficient value x^* is determined by

$$\text{minimize } c(x) + l(x) \text{ over } x \tag{11}$$

and that y^* is then determined by

$$\text{maximize } b(y) - y(c(x^*) + l(x^*)) \text{ over } y. \tag{12}$$

(i) *Victims are strangers.* Here x is interpreted as the care the seller exercises in the conduct of his operations.

Under strict liability sellers are induced to choose the care level that minimizes production costs plus accident losses. Moreover because customers pay a price that reflects production costs plus accident losses, they are induced to purchase the socially correct output. To prove this, note that full cost per unit is $c(x) + l(x)$, which (see (6)) sellers minimize. Hence (see (11)), x^* is the care level. Therefore (see (7)), price p equals $c(x^*) + l(x^*)$. Hence (see (8) and (9)), consumers maximize $b(y) - py = b(y) - (c(x^*) + l(x^*))y$. This implies (see (12)) that y^* is chosen. Consequently, strict liability is efficient.

Under the negligence rule, an efficient outcome is not achieved. This is because sellers escape liability by acting nonnegligently. Hence the price charged customers reflects production costs but not accident losses. Since customers face too low a price, output is too high. To demonstrate this, assume (for the reason given in the nonmarket case) that $\bar{x}$ is low enough so that sellers decide to be nonnegligent. Then production cost and price must be $c(\bar{x})$. Consequently, customers choose y to maximize $b(y) - py = b(y) - c(\bar{x})y$. Let $y(\bar{x})$ be the customers' choice and $y^*(\bar{x})$ the efficient y given $\bar{x}$. Then $y(\bar{x}) > y^*(\bar{x})$, output is excessive, which also implies that the negligence rule cannot be efficient. The optimal due care level $\bar{x}^*$ is determined by maximizing

$$W(\bar{x},y(\bar{x})) = b(y(\bar{x})) - c(\bar{x}) - y(\bar{x})l(\bar{x}) \qquad (13)$$

over $\bar{x}$ (in the range such that sellers choose to be nonnegligent). As in the nonmarket case, it can be shown that $\bar{x}^* > x^*$, and for analogous reasons.[22]

If there is no liability, sellers have no motive to prevent accidents nor do customers have a motive to buy a socially appropriate quantity, since price does not reflect accident losses. Therefore, the outcome is worse than under the negligence rule. Specifically, production cost and price are $c(0)$ and customers choose $y(0)$.[23]

In summary, the conclusions are just as in the nonmarket case.

PROPOSITION 2. *Suppose that injurers are sellers and that victims are strangers. Then strict liability is efficient and is superior to the negligence rule, which is superior to not having liability at all.*

(ii) *Victims are customers.* In this subcase x might still be interpreted as the care the seller exercises in the conduct of his operations. This would be

[22] This and other claims made in this paragraph can be proved using arguments analogous to those in notes 19 & 20 *supra.*

[23] That no liability is inferior to the negligence rule can be shown by establishing, as in note 21 *supra,* that $\bar{x}^* > 0$.

appropriate if one is thinking about accidents which occur at the time and place of sale of a product or service. On the other hand, if one is considering accidents which occur after the time of purchase and involve a product that the customer takes away with him (a car, a piece of industrial machinery), then x should be interpreted as an index of the safety and reliability of the product.

Under strict liability, an argument virtually identical to that given in (i) shows that the efficient outcome results. Sellers again choose x in accord with (11). Thus price is $c(x^*) + l(x^*)$, and as customers do not bear accident losses, they select y in accord with (12). Note that this argument in no way depends on customers' knowledge of the risk of accident losses.

However, under the negligence rule, the analysis changes. Assume first that customers know what expected accident losses are either for particular sellers or only on average. Then the efficient outcome results if the due care level $\bar{x}$ is set equal to the efficient level x^*. To prove this, suppose that sellers choose x^*. Then, as they are nonnegligent, price equals $c(x^*)$. Since customers bear losses $l(x^*)$ per unit and know their magnitude, they maximize over y their utility position, $b(y) - py - l(x^*)y = b(y) - (c(x^*) + l(x^*))y$. Thus, they choose y^*. Therefore, to complete the proof, we need only show that sellers would choose x^* or, more precisely, that no seller would have a motive to choose an x other than x^* if there were an equilibrium in which x^* was the commonly chosen care level. To show this, suppose, on the contrary, that some seller chooses $x > x^*$. If customers can't observe *his* x, then he gets no benefit in the price from raising x but does incur greater production costs. On the other hand, if customers can observe his x, it is easy to show they wouldn't purchase from him if he charged his cost of production. If he did that, a customer's utility position would be the maximum over y of $b(y) - (c(x) + l(x))y$ which (since $x \neq x^*$) must be less than $b(y^*) - (c(x^*) + l(x^*))y^*$, the utility position of the customer if he buys from a seller who chooses x^*. Now assume that some seller chooses $x < x^*$. Then, as he will be liable for accident losses, his problem is to minimize full unit costs, namely $c(x) + l(x)$. But this implies that he chooses x^*, a contradiction.

Consider now the outcome under the negligence rule given the assumption that customers misperceive risks. Specifically, suppose that if expected accident losses are really $l(x)$, customers think they are $(1 + \lambda)l(x)$. Thus $\lambda > 0$ means that customers overestimate risk and $\lambda < 0$ that they underestimate risk. Assume that $\bar{x}$ is such that sellers choose $x = \bar{x}$. The price is therefore $c(\bar{x})$ and customer purchases are determined by maximizing over y the perceived utility position $b(y) - py - (1 + \lambda)l(\bar{x}) = b(y) - (c(\bar{x}) + (1 + \lambda)l(\bar{x}))y$. Therefore customers buy too little (less than $y^*(\bar{x})$) if they overestimate risk and too much if they underestimate risk. In particular, an efficient outcome cannot result.

Finally, consider the situation if there is no liability. Assume initially that customers can identify expected accident losses for particular sellers. Then competitive forces would induce sellers to choose an efficient care level and customers' purchases would be efficient. To show this we demonstrate that a situation in which sellers choose x^* is an equilibrium which results in an efficient outcome. Assuming that x^* is chosen by sellers, price must equal $c(x^*)$. Thus, customers (recognizing that they bear $l(x^*)$) choose y to maximize $b(y) - py - l(x^*)y = b(y) - (c(x^*) + l(x^*))y$. Consequently, they choose y^*. If a seller chose $x \neq x^*$, no customer would choose to buy from him. For if the customer were charged the production cost, his utility would be the maximum over y of $b(y) - (c(x) + l(x))y$. Since $x \neq x^*$, this must be less than $b(y^*) - (c(x^*) + l(x^*))y^*$, which is the customer's alternative.

If there is no liability and customers know expected accident losses only on average, then an efficient outcome would not result, for sellers would have no motive to take care. That is, $x = 0$ would hold. Also price would equal $c(0)$. Since they would realize that they bear $l(0)$, customer purchases would be determined by maximizing $b(y) - py - l(0)y = b(y) - (c(0) + l(0))y$. Thus, at least purchases would be efficient given the inefficiently low care level.

When there is no liability and customers misperceive average risks, then, as in the last paragraph, sellers choose $x = 0$, but in this instance customers purchase the wrong amount given that $x = 0$. Thus the outcome is worse than in the previous paragraph.

These results are summarized below.

Proposition 3. ***Suppose that injurers are sellers and that victims are customers. Then the relative performance of liability rules depends on the knowledge customers have about risk.*** (See Table 1.)

As for the ranking of the inefficient outcomes in Table 1, it was shown that (a) is superior to (c) and it can also be shown that (b) is superior to (c) (using the argument of note 21 *supra*); however there is no necessary relationship between (a) and (b).

(iii) *Victims are employees*. In this subcase the results and their proofs are exactly parallel to those in the last subcase (in Proposition 3 merely substitute the word "employee" for "customer"). Therefore, it will not be necessary to verify all the results. However, it will be described how the model changes and, to provide a pattern for the reader, a proof that strict liability is efficient will be given.

The variable x is interpreted as the care the seller exercises in his production process.

It is assumed that an employee's wage minus the expected accident losses that he has to bear must equal his "opportunity wage," which is set by economy-wide forces of supply and demand and is therefore taken as exogenous. Define

TABLE 1

Knowledge of risk of accident loss	Form of Liability: Strict Liability	Negligence	No Liability
Accurate knowledge about each seller's risk	efficient	efficient	efficient
Accurate knowledge only of the average risk	efficient	efficient	inefficient (a)
Misperception of average risk	efficient	inefficient (b)	inefficient (c)

w = wage paid to employee,
$\bar{w}$ = opportunity wage,

so that[24]

$$\bar{w} = w - \text{expected accident losses borne.} \tag{14}$$

The seller's unit cost of production is

$$c(x) = w + k(x), \tag{15}$$

where $k(x)$ are nonlabor production costs given x.

Under strict liability the efficient outcome results because, on the one hand, firms are induced to choose a care level that minimizes nonlabor production costs plus expected accident losses and, on the other, because customers face a price that reflects total production costs plus expected accident losses. To see this, note that since employees do not bear accident losses, $\bar{w} = w$. Hence, firms minimize $c(x) + l(x) = \bar{w} + k(x) + l(x)$, which means that they choose x^*. Price therefore equals $c(x^*) + l(x^*)$ and customers choose y to maximize (12).

IV. Bilateral Accidents

Define the following additional notation,

$s \geq 0$ care level of a victim,
$t \geq 0$ activity level of a victim.

Expected accident losses are assumed to fall with victims' care and to rise with victims' activity levels. Also, if victims do not engage in their activity (t

[24] The wage is normalized so that it is the amount paid per unit of labor time necessary to produce one unit of output.

= 0)), then losses are zero. More will be said later about how expected accident losses are related to s and t.

As previously noted, along with the liability rules examined in the last section, both strict liability and the negligence rule will be considered when there is a defense of contributory negligence. Therefore, define

$$\bar{s} = \text{due care level for victims.}$$

However, there will never be need to distinguish between the negligence rule with and without the defense. This is because in this model the two negligence rules are equivalent (as is true in most models which assume that injurers are identical).[25]

The results and proofs of this section closely parallel those of the last. Therefore, although formal statements of the results will be given, proofs will usually either be omitted or only sketched.

A. *The Nonmarket Case: Accidents between Strangers*

Define

$h(s,t)$ = income equivalent of the utility to a victim of engaging in his activity at level t and exercising care s

and assume that h has properties analogous to those of the function $a(x,y)$ (namely, assume that $h_s < 0$, $h_t(s,t) > 0$ for $t < t(s)$, etc.). Also define

$l(x,s)$ = expected accident losses per victim per unit of injurer activity and of victim activity,

where $l_x < 0$ and $l_s < 0$. Thus, expected accident losses as a function of x, y, s, and t are $ytl(x,s)$.[26]

Social welfare is

$$W(x,y,s,t) = a(x,y) + h(s,t) - ytl(x,s), \tag{16}$$

the sum of the benefits of engaging in their activities for victim and injurer less the expected cost of accidents.

[25] While it is true that if an injurer is negligent, whether there is a defense of contributory negligence matters, it turns out that, in the situations which we consider, all injurers decide to act in a nonnegligent way. Therefore, whether there is a defense of contributory negligence is irrelevant.

[26] Expected accident losses have this form if we make the same assumption about the victim's activity level as we have made about the injurer's: an increase in the activity level is a physical repetition of an activity which causes a proportional rise in expected accident costs. This makes analysis easier (principally, the proof to Proposition 5), and it will be clear that the qualitative nature of the results would not change were expected accident costs to depend in a more general way on $x,y,s,$ and t.

Under strict liability with a defense of contributory negligence, an efficient outcome cannot be achieved, for assume otherwise. Then, in particular, it must be that $s = \bar{s} = s^*$. This means victims will never have to bear losses. Consequently they will have no motive to reduce accident losses by lowering their activity level, and t will exceed t^*.

An argument similar to this one (and to the basic argument made in the last part) shows that an efficient outcome cannot be achieved under the negligence rule. Under the negligence rule injurers are not given an incentive to reduce accident losses by lowering their activity level.

Thus, as stated before, the choice between strict liability with a defense of contributory negligence and the negligence rule is a choice in favor of the lesser of two evils.

However, a rule of strict liability without a defense of contributory negligence would never be desirable, as it would always be dominated by strict liability with the defense. (The argument showing this is essentially that of note 21 *supra*). Similarly, it would never be desirable not to have liability, for this would result in an outcome inferior to that under the negligence rule. No welfare comparison can be made between strict liability and not having liability without knowing whether it is more important to control victim or injurer behavior.

In summary,

PROPOSITION 4. *Suppose that injurers and victims are strangers. Then none of the usual liability rules is efficient. Strict liability with a defense of contributory negligence is superior to the negligence rule if it is sufficiently important to lower injurer activity levels. Strict liability without the defense and no liability are each inferior to whichever rule is better: either strict liability with the defense or the negligence rule.*

The next result states that there is no conceivable liability rule that induces parties to act efficiently.

PROPOSITION 5. *Suppose that injurers and victims are strangers and consider any liability rule which may depend on any or all of the following variables: the victim's losses, the care he exercises, the care the injurer exercises. Then the liability rule is not efficient.*

To prove this, note that under a liability rule of the type under consideration, expected payments by the injurer must be of the form $ytq(x,s)$. Now suppose that the rule is efficient. If the injurer is to select the efficient activity level, then y^* must be the solution to

$$\underset{y}{\text{maximize}}\ a(x^*,y) - yt^*q(x^*,s^*). \qquad (17)$$

On the other hand, since y^* maximizes $W(x^*,y,s^*,t^*)$, y^* must be the solution to

$$\underset{y}{\text{maximize}}\ a(x^*,y) - yt^*l(x^*,s^*). \tag{18}$$

Consequently, it must be that $q(x^*,s^*) = l(x^*,s^*)$. Similarly, if the victim is to choose his efficient activity level, then t^* must solve

$$\underset{t}{\text{maximize}}\ h(s^*,t) + y^*t(q(x^*,s^*) - l(x^*,s^*)). \tag{19}$$

But since t^* must also solve

$$\underset{t}{\text{maximize}}\ h(s^*,t) - y^*tl(x^*,s^*), \tag{20}$$

it must be that $q(x^*,s^*) = 0$, which is a contradiction.

B. *The Market Case: Accidents between Sellers and Victims*

The same assumptions are made about the market as in Part III.B. However, victims now play a role in accidents.

(i) *Victims are strangers*. In this subcase, the results are just like those described in the nonmarket case, and for reasons which combine the arguments given there and in Part III.B(i). (See also the discussion in the introduction.)

PROPOSITION 6. *Suppose that injurers are sellers and that victims are strangers. Then the results are as given in Propositions 4 and 5.*

(ii) *Victims are customers*. In this subcase, the customer care level will have the usual interpretation. However, the customer activity level could be interpreted in several ways. First, think of it as the quantity of the good the customer purchases. This is the interpretation that will be made in regard to purchases of services or of products which are not durables. In this situation, then, the victim's activity level and the injurer's activity level are one and the same, namely, the level of output (so $t = y$); expected accident losses are given by $yl(x,s)$; and the following result holds.

PROPOSITION 7a. *Suppose that injurers are sellers of a nondurable good or service and that victims are customers. Then the relative performance of liability rules depends on the knowledge customers have about risks.* (See Table 2.)

Now consider the situation when customers buy durable goods—say lawn mowers or, if the customer is a firm, industrial machinery. In this situation,

TABLE 2

Knowledge of risk of accident loss	Form of Liability: Strict Liability with Defense of Contributory Negligence	Negligence	Strict Liability	No Liability
Accurate knowledge about each seller's risk	efficient	efficient	inefficient	efficient
Accurate knowledge only of the average risk	efficient	efficient	inefficient	inefficient
Misperception of average risk	efficient	inefficient	inefficient	inefficient

it is assumed that the customer contributes to expected accident losses not only through the choice of care level and quantity purchased but also by the rate of use, denoted by r, of each unit purchased (number of times a mower is used per week, the frequency of operation of a machine). Therefore, the income equivalent of the utility of use to the customer will be written $h(s,t,r)$ (with $h_r > 0$) and the expected accident losses, $yrl(x,s)$. The results must now be modified as follows.

PROPOSITION 7b. *Suppose that injurers are sellers of a durable good and that victims are customers. Then the relative performance of liability rules depends on the knowledge customers have about risks.* (See Table 3.)

The point to be noticed here is (as explained before) that strict liability with a defense of contributory negligence never leads to an efficient outcome. It is true that in order to avoid being contributorily negligent, customers exercise due care and, because price reflects accident losses, they purchase the socially correct amount. However, they have no motive to lower expected accident losses by reducing their frequency of use of the product they buy. In contrast, under the negligence rule, provided that customers have knowledge of accident risks, an efficient outcome is achieved. Sellers exercise due care to avoid being found negligent. Customers choose the socially desirable care level, quantity to purchase, *and* rate of use since they bear accident losses.

(iii) *Victims are employees*. In this subcase, there is some difficulty in interpreting what the activity level would mean. In many situations, there is no obvious aspect of the discretionary behavior of the employee that would not come under the rubric of care. If so, the results turn out to be identical to

TABLE 3

	Form of Liability			
Knowledge of risk of accident loss	Strict Liability with Defense of Contributory Negligence	Negligence	Strict Liability	No Liability
Accurate knowledge about each seller's risk	inefficient	efficient	inefficient	efficient
Accurate knowledge only of the average risk	inefficient	efficient	inefficient	inefficient
Misperception of average risk	inefficient	inefficient	inefficient	inefficient

those reported in Proposition 7a. However, in situations where there is a type of employee decision that fits the description of activity level given here, then the results are those of Proposition 7b.

V. Concluding Comments

1. A question which is in a sense logically prior to the analysis of this article must be mentioned, namely, *"Why isn't the level of activity usually considered in the formulation of a due care standard?"* After all, the inefficiencies discussed here were viewed in the main as deriving from the fact that in order to avoid being found negligent (or contributorily negligent), parties are not motivated to alter their level of activity.[27] The answer to the question appears to be that the courts would run into difficulty in trying to employ a standard of due care expanded in scope to include the level of activity. In formulating such a broadened due care standard, courts would, by definition, have to decide on the appropriate level of activity, and their competence to do this is problematic. How would courts decide the number of

[27] Were the level of activity included in the "due care" standard, a party would, by definition of due care, have to choose both the level of activity and the level of care appropriately in order to avoid liability; thus the inefficiencies analyzed in this article would be eliminated. However, A. Mitchell Polinsky, Strict Liability versus Negligence in a Market Setting (1979) (unpublished mimeographed paper, Stanford University) makes a point of qualification to this. He observes that in the market case it is not enough for the level of activity to be incorporated in the due care standard for each firm within the industry, for then too many firms would enter it; rather, the level of activity would somehow have to be made part of the due care standard for the industry as a whole. He also notes a similar point in respect to the nonmarket case.

miles an individual ought to drive or how far or how often a pedestrian ought to walk?[28] How would courts decide the level of output an industry—much less a firm within an industry—ought to produce? To decide such matters, courts would likely have to know much more than would normally have to be known to decide whether care, conventionally interpreted, was adequate.[29]

2. From the logic of the arguments presented here, it can be seen that what is important about the variable "level of activity" is only that it is not included in the due care standard. Any other variable omitted from the standard would also be inappropriately chosen in many of the circumstances in which we said the same of the level of activity. For example, in regard to accidents involving firms and strangers it has been noted that, if the scale of a firm's research in safety technology is not comprehended by the standard of due care, then under the negligence rule the firm would not be expected to invest sufficiently in such research.[30]

3. Commentators on tort law have in recent years frequently pointed to the reciprocal nature of harm, especially in the sense that the victim must be present in order to suffer harm. This has unfortunately engendered a misleading piece of folklore: that the very concept of harm is rendered ambiguous. While it is undeniable that for harm to occur there must be a victim, I can see no sense in which this truism leads to conceptual problems in instrumentalist analysis. Here, under the heading of bilateral accidents, the situation when victims as well as injurers could vary their level of activity (and of care) was studied; and one such possibility for victims was a level of activity of zero, which is to say, the "victims" are not around to be harmed. Thus, for example, the result (Proposition 4) concerning strict liability (with the defense of contributory negligence) versus negligence in regard to accidents between strangers might be expressed by saying that strict liability is preferable if it is more desirable to control whether injurers are present than it is to control whether victims are present; and the next result (Proposition 5) might be expressed by saying that there is no liability rule which generally induces both victims and injurers to make the efficient decision as to whether they should be present.[31]

[28] There might also be evidentiary problems. The courts might find it difficult to learn how many miles an individual drives or a pedestrian walks.

[29] On this argument, we would expect that when courts could easily discern what the level of activity ought to be, then it would be incorporated into the standard of due care. One legal doctrine which appears to confirm this is that of "coming to the nuisance," for the doctrine is applied in precisely those situations when the *activity* of coming to the nuisance—which is quite distinct from the level of *care* exercised once one is near the nuisance—may be seen as clearly socially undesirable.

[30] See Posner, *supra* note 9, at 139 & 140.

[31] It should be noted that Proposition 5 holds if one thinks of the level of activity as a binary variable (and/or if there is no variable "care"), for the proof does not depend on the level of activity being a continuous variable (nor on the existence of the variable care).

4. The analysis presented here does appear to help to explain certain features of tort law. A notable example is provided by the so-called pockets of strict liability: for ultrahazardous activities, ownership of wild animals, and so forth. These areas of strict liability seem to have two characteristics. First, they are such that injurer activity has a distinctive aspect (which makes the activity easy for the law to single out) and imposes nonnegligible risks on victims (which make the activity worthwhile controlling). And, second, they are such that victim activity is usually not at all special—on the contrary, it is typically entirely routine in nature, part of what it is to carry on a normal life—and is therefore activity that cannot and ought not be controlled. Consequently, it is appealing to explain the pockets of strict liability by the idea (expressed in Propositions 4 and 6) that strict liability is preferable if it is more desirable to control injurers' activity than victims'.[32]

However, there are many features of tort law which the analysis by itself does not seem to satisfactorily explain. And this is not unexpected, for it is in the nature of the formal approach to isolate selected factors of interest by ignoring others; the formal approach aims for a particular kind of insight, not for true balance or comprehensiveness.[33] Two examples will illustrate various limitations in our ability to employ in a direct way the results of this article. The first concerns the trend in decisions in product-liability cases toward expansion of manufacturer's liability. If this trend can be likened to one toward holding manufacturers strictly liable, we may be tempted to explain it as broadly rational given some of our results (Propositions 2, 3, 6,

[32] Posner, *supra* note 9, at 140-41, makes essentially this point. Also George P. Fletcher, Fairness and Utility in Tort Theory, 85 Harv. L. Rev. 537 (1972), explains the pockets of strict liability (at 547-49) by appeal to the notion that strict liability is imposed when parties create "nonreciprocal" risks. Our discussion might be viewed as helping to explain why it is that when parties create nonreciprocal risks, they should be strictly liable (but Fletcher would probably not welcome this interpretation).

[33] Of course, the informal instrumentalist approach is more flexible, aims for, and achieves greater balance and generality. But, whether formal or informal, the instrumentalist approach has been subject to the limitation that it does not refer to "moralist" argument or explanation—that which sounds in terms of what is "right" or "fair" or "just" to do in the particular situation at hand. (Fletcher, *supra* note 32, is a recent and valuable discussion of the contrast between the instrumentalist and moralist approaches. See also Richard Epstein, A Theory of Strict Liability, 2 J. Legal Stud. 151 (1973).) Perhaps a few tentative remarks about this will not be out of order. Given that (i) we believe that to an important extent legal institutions are/should be shaped by moralist notions and that legal decisions are/should be made in consideration of them; and that (ii) the instrumentalist approach has some merit (I am not saying how much) in descriptive and normative analysis of law, it seems plausible (by implicit reasoning) that (iii) moralist notions must encapsulate instrumentalist goals (and, of course, there are explicit arguments for this, such as those of the utilitarian ethical theorists). Yet it also seems that (iv) to an important extent the moralist notions (or many of them) must be viewed as having a life of their own—cannot be fruitfully, or at least naturally, viewed as embodying what would normally be conceived of as instrumentalist goals. One would hope that discussion of such issues in the future might help to clarify the extent to which the division between instrumentalists and moralists merely reflects use of a different mode of discourse, and is therefore not "real," and the extent to which the division is in fact substantive.

7a). However, realism requires us to look at other, complementary explanations of the trend, such as that strict liability may provide a better means of risk sharing than the negligence rule, or that strict liability may be easier to apply than the negligence rule. Moreover, realism requires us to ask whether there even is an explanation of the trend based on its social rationality—whether in fact the trend might be socially undesirable, say on the ground that the expansion in the scope of liability has led to an excessively costly volume of disputes. Similar questions may be asked in respect to the second example, which concerns the fact that the negligence rule is the dominant form of tort liability in Anglo-American and in Western European legal systems today. Our analysis certainly does not suggest why this should be so, since, at least as often as otherwise, strict liability (with a defense of contributory negligence) is superior to the negligence rule. We are therefore led to ask again about such matters as risk sharing, administrative simplicity, and (especially) the social costs of expansion of the scope of liability.

5. Many of the points made in this article have been discussed before, and doubtless numerous times.[34] For example, the literature on enterprise liability virtually always considers the effect of such liability on product price, and the influence of this on purchases. The contribution made here would therefore seem to lie principally in the attention given to context—to the specifics of the relationship obtaining between injurers and victims—and in the unified way in which the variety of problems is viewed.

[34] But it is hard to find the points stated in explicit and general form. However, the reader should certainly refer to "Strict Liability vs. Negligence" in Posner *supra* note 9, at 137-42, which is the clearest discussion of our subject of which I am aware, and on which this article may properly be regarded as building. The reader should also refer to Guido Calabresi, Optimal Deterrence and Accidents, 84 Yale L. J. 656 (1975). And the reader might also want to look at the following papers by economists: John Prather Brown, Toward an Economic Theory of Liability, 2 J. Legal Stud. 323 (1973); Peter A. Diamond, Single Activity Accidents, 3 J. Legal Stud. 107 (1974); Jerry Green, On the Optimal Structure of Liability Laws, 7 Bell J. Econ. 553 (1976); and Steven Shavell, Accidents, Liability, and Insurance (forthcoming in Am. Econ. Rev.). In these papers liability rules are studied when parties can affect accident losses only by altering their levels of care; levels of activity are implicitly regarded as fixed (but see Section 11 of Diamond's paper). The reader may also find relevant Michael Spence, Consumer Misperceptions, Product Failure, and Producer Liability, 44 Rev. Econ. Stud. 561 (1977). He studies the use of strict liability and fines in the case of unilateral accidents; and he allows for sellers to offer guarantees and for consumers to be risk averse and to misperceive risks.

[22]

LIABILITY FOR HARM VERSUS REGULATION OF SAFETY

*STEVEN SHAVELL**

I. INTRODUCTION

LIABILITY in tort and the regulation of safety represent two very different approaches for controlling activities that create risks of harm to others. Tort liability is private in nature and works not by social command but rather indirectly, through the deterrent effect of damage actions that may be brought once harm occurs. Standards, prohibitions, and other forms of safety regulation, in contrast, are public in character and modify behavior in an immediate way through requirements that are imposed before, or at least independently of, the actual occurrence of harm.

As a matter of simple description, it is apparent that liability and safety regulation are employed with an emphasis that varies considerably with the nature of the activity that is governed. Whether I run to catch a bus and thereby collide with another pedestrian will be influenced more by the possibility of my tort liability than by any prior regulation of my behavior (informal social sanctions and risk to self aside). Similarly, whether I cut down a tree that might fall on my neighbor's roof will be affected more by the prospect of a tort suit than by direct regulation. But other decisions—whether I drive my truck through a tunnel when it is loaded with explosives or mark the fire exits in my store, or whether an electric utility incorporates certain safety features in its nuclear power plant—are apt to be determined substantially, although not entirely, by safety regulation. There are also intermediate cases, of course; consider, for instance, the

* Professor of Law and Economics, Harvard Law School. I wish to thank Bruce Ackerman, Susan Rose Ackerman, Lucian Bebchuk, Paul Burrows, Louis Kaplow, Mark Kelman, and Richard Stewart for comments and the National Science Foundation (grant no. SES-8014208) for financial support. A formal version of the main argument of this article is made in my Harm as a Prerequisite for Liability (1979) (unpublished manuscript, Harvard Univ. Dep't of Econ.); and in A Model of the Optimal Use of Liability and Safety Regulation (forthcoming, Rand J. Econ.). The present article will provide the basis for a chapter in the part on torts of *A Theoretical Analysis of Law*, a book on which I am at work.

[*Journal of Legal Studies*, vol. XIII (June 1984)]

behavior of ordinary drivers on the road and the effects of tort sanctions and regulation of automobile use.

What has led society to adopt this varying pattern of liability and safety regulation? What is the socially desirable way to employ the two means of alleviating risks? These are the questions to be addressed here, and in answering them I use an instrumentalist, economic method of analysis, whereby the effects of liability rules and direct regulation are compared and then evaluated on a utilitarian basis, given the assumption that individual actors can normally be expected to act in their own interest.[1] In making this evaluation, I have not counted compensation of injured parties as an independent factor on the grounds that first-party insurance (augmented if necessary by a public insurance program) can discharge the compensatory function no matter what the mix of liability and regulation. Likewise, for simplicity I ignore the complications that would be introduced by considering interest group theories of regulation.[2] Also, I do not make an explicit attempt to determine the extent to which the conclusions reached may be separately attributable to either of the two dimensions in which liability and safety regulation differ: employed only after harm is done versus beforehand; employed only at the initiative of private parties versus a public authority.[3]

Subject to these caveats and assumptions, this article first discusses four general determinants of the relative desirability of liability and regulation. It then argues in light of the determinants that the actual, observed use of the two methods of reducing risks may be viewed as socially desirable, or roughly so. The article concludes with several qualifying remarks and with comments on how the analysis could be extended to incorporate additional means of social control including the fine and the injunction.

II. Theoretical Determinants of the Relative Desirability of Liability and Safety Regulation

To identify and assess the factors determining the social desirability of liability and regulation, it is necessary to set out a measure of social welfare; and here that measure is assumed to equal the benefits parties

[1] This is the general approach adopted by two influential legal scholars in their analyses of tort law; see Guido Calabresi, The Costs of Accidents, 1970; and Richard Posner, Economic Analysis of Law (2d ed. 1977), ch. 6.

[2] See, for example, George Stigler, The Theory of Economic Regulation, 2 Bell J. Econ. 3 (1971); and Sam Peltzman, Toward a More General Theory of Regulation, 19 J. Law & Econ. 211 (1976).

[3] But the concluding discussion may help the reader to make a judgment about this issue.

derive from engaging in their activities, less the sum of the costs of precautions, the harms done, and the administrative expenses associated with the means of social control. The formal problem is to employ the means of control to maximize the measure of welfare.

We can now examine four determinants that influence the solution to this problem. The first determinant is the possibility of a *difference in knowledge about risky activities* as between private parties and a regulatory authority. This difference could relate to the benefits of activities, the costs of reducing risks, or the probability or severity of the risks.

Where private parties have superior knowledge of these elements, it would be better for them to decide about the control of risks, indicating an advantage of liability rules, other things being equal. Consider, for instance, the situation where private parties possess perfect information about risky activities of which a regulator has poor knowledge. Then to vest in the regulator the power of control would create a great chance of error. If the regulator overestimates the potential for harm, its standard will be too stringent, and the same will be the case if it underestimates the value of the activity or the cost of reducing risk. If the regulator makes the reverse mistakes, moreover, it will announce standards that are lax.

Under liability, however, the outcome would likely be better. This is clear enough under a system of strict liability—whereby parties have to pay damages regardless of their negligence—for then they are motivated to balance the true costs of reducing risks against the expected savings in losses caused. Now assume that the form of liability is the negligence rule—according to which parties are held responsible for harm done only if their care falls short of a prescribed level of "due" care—and suppose further that once harm occurs, the courts could acquire enough information about the underlying event to formulate the appropriate level of due care. Then parties, anticipating this, would be led in principle to exercise due care.[4] The situation is altered for the worse if the courts are unable to acquire sufficient information to determine the best level of due care; but the outcome would still be superior to that achievable under regulation if the information obtained ex post at trial would be better than that which a regulator could acquire and act upon ex ante.

These conclusions are reversed, of course, if the information possessed by a regulator is superior to private parties' and the courts'; converse reasoning then shows that the use of direct regulation would be more attractive than liability.

[4] See John Prather Brown, Toward an Economic Theory of Liability, 2 J. Legal Stud. 323 (1973).

The question that remains, therefore, is when we can expect significant differences in information between private parties and regulators to exist. And the answer is that private parties should generally enjoy an inherent advantage in knowledge. They, after all, are the ones who are engaging in and deriving benefits from their activities; in consequence, they are in a naturally superior position to estimate these benefits and normally are in at least as good a position to estimate the nature of the risks created and the costs of their reduction. For a regulator to obtain comparable information would often require virtually continuous observation of parties' behavior, and thus would be a practical impossibility. Similarly, the courts—when called upon under a negligence system—should have an advantage, though a less decisive one, over a regulator. One would indeed expect courts to adjust the due care level to take into account the facts presented by litigating parties more easily than a regulator could individualize its prior standards or modify them to reflect changed conditions.

Yet this is not to say that private parties or the courts will necessarily possess information superior to that held by a regulatory authority. In certain contexts information about risk will not be an obvious by-product of engaging in risky activities but rather will require effort to develop or special expertise to evaluate. In these contexts a regulator might obtain information by committing social resources to the task, while private parties would have an insufficient incentive to do this for familiar reasons: A party who generates information will be unable to capture its full value if others can learn of the information without paying for it. For parties to undertake individually to acquire information might result in wasteful, duplicative expenditures, and a cooperative venture by parties might be stymied by the usual problems of inducing all to lend their support.[5] Continuing, once a regulator obtains information, it may find the information difficult to communicate to private parties because of its technical nature or because the parties are hard to identify or are too numerous. Thus we can point to contexts where regulators might possess better information than private parties to whom it cannot easily be transmitted, even if the usual expectation would be for these parties to possess the superior information.

The second of the determinants of the relative desirability of liability and regulation is that *private parties might be incapable of paying for the full magnitude of harm done*. Where this is the case, liability would not furnish adequate incentives to control risk, because private parties would treat losses caused that exceed their assets as imposing liabilities only

[5] See generally Kenneth J. Arrow, Essays in the Theory of Risk Bearing (1971), ch. 6.

equal to their assets.[6] But under regulation inability to pay for harm done would be irrelevant, assuming that parties would be made to take steps to reduce risk as a precondition for engaging in their activities.[7]

In assessing the importance of this argument favoring regulation over liability, one factor that obviously needs to be taken into account is the size of parties' assets in relation to the probability distribution of the magnitude of harm; the greater the likelihood of harm much larger than assets, the greater the appeal of regulation.

Another factor of relevance concerns liability insurance. Here the first point to make is that a party's motive to purchase liability insurance against damage judgments exceeding his assets will be a diminished one, as the protection will in part be for losses that the party would not otherwise have to bear.[8] A party with assets of $20,000 might not be eager to purchase coverage against a potential liability of $100,000, as four-fifths of the premium would be in payment for the $80,000 amount that he would not bear if he did not buy coverage. Hence, it might be rational for the party not to insure against the $100,000 risk. If this is the case, then the assertion that liability does not create an adequate motive to reduce risk is clearly unrebutted.

Suppose, however, that the party does choose to purchase liability insurance covering losses substantially exceeding his assets or is required by statute to do so. What then is his incentive to take care? The answer depends on whether insurers can easily determine risk-reducing behavior—so that they can link the premium charged or the other terms or conditions of coverage to the party's precautions. Where this linkage can be established, the party's incentive to take care should be tolerably good. But if insurers find it too costly to verify insureds' efforts at risk reduction, then their incentives to take care may be insufficient; plausibly, they could be lower than if no insurance coverage had been obtained. Consider a requirement that the party facing a $100,000 risk purchase full coverage against it and assume that the insurer cannot observe anything about the party's exercise of care. Then as the party would not have to pay a higher premium or be otherwise penalized for failure to take

[6] See more generally Steven Shavell, The Judgment Proof Problem (1984) (unpublished manuscript, Harvard Law School).

[7] The parties could be made to do this through the exercise of the state's police powers; force could be used to prevent a business from operating that disobeyed safety regulations. Where, however, monetary penalties are relied upon to induce parties to satisfy regulations, the fact that their assets are limited might lead to problems.

[8] See William Keeton & Evan Kwerel, Externalities in Automobile Insurance and the Underinsured Driver Problem, 27 J. Law & Econ. 149 (1984); and Shavell, *supra* note 6.

proper care, he would have no reason to do this. Yet if he had not owned the liability coverage, at least his $20,000 assets would have been at risk, supplying him with some motive to take care. Thus, it appears that the problem of inadequacy of incentives to take care which arises when parties' assets are less than potential harms can either be mitigated or exacerbated by the (mandatory or voluntary) purchase of liability insurance, depending on insurers' ability to monitor insureds.

An additional factor of relevance in considering the effects of inability to pay for harm done concerns firms and their employee decisionmakers. What is of special interest in this regard is that the activities of firms are prone to result in liabilities much larger than the assets of their employees—quite apart from whether firms themselves have assets sufficient to cover their liabilities.[9] This means that employees' personal liability or ex post sanctions imposed on them of a firm's devise may not result in proper incentives to reduce risks; an employee with assets of $50,000 might not take suitable precautions to reduce the risk of a $1 million corporate liability if only his assets or his job is at stake.[10] Hence, some sort of regulation of employees may be necessary to reduce risks appropriately.

But as firms themselves would wish to avoid large liabilities, they would have good reason to establish, ex ante, internal controls over the behavior of their employees. Thus we cannot conclude that there ought to be social regulation without supplying an argument for why it would be superior to a firm's own form of regulation. Now such an argument can be given in respect to the highest level of management—those individuals whose activities are overseen only by the board of directors and the shareholders—assuming that the board and the shareholders lack the time and the necessary expertise to control management's behavior as effectively as a regulator. This argument cannot be made, however, in respect to members of lower-level management, for they have superiors within the firm who presumably have better knowledge than a regulator and are thus able to set up a better scheme of ex ante controls. On the other hand, the desire of these superiors to regulate lower-level management might be inadequate precisely because the assets of the superiors could be less than the firm's potential liability. Thus, the situation is complex, but especially

[9] For a general discussion of closely related issues, see Christopher D. Stone, The Place of Enterprise Liability in the Control of Corporate Conduct, 90 Yale L. J. 1 (1980); and see also Lewis A. Kornhauser, An Economic Analysis of the Choice between Enterprise and Personal Liability for Accidents, 70 Calif. L. Rev. 1345 (1982).

[10] Risk aversion is a qualifying factor here. If the individual is sufficiently risk averse (and does not own liability coverage), he might still take adequate care; but beyond some magnitude of corporate liability—perhaps $2 million if not $1 million—the appropriate level of care would exceed that which the individual would be led to take.

in relation to the decisions of higher-level management we can see that there exist arguments in favor of social regulation independently of whether firms' assets are large enough to cover their liabilities.

Let us turn next to the third of the four general determinants, the chance that *parties would not face the threat of suit for harm done*. Like incapacity to pay for harm, such a possibility results in a dilution of the incentives to reduce risk created by liability, but it is of no import under regulation.

The weight to be attached to this factor depends in part upon the reasons why suit might not be brought. One reason that a defendant can escape tort liability is that the harms he generates are widely dispersed, making it unattractive for any victim individually to initiate legal action. This danger can be offset to a degree if victims are allowed to maintain class actions, whose application has problematic features, however. A second cause of failure to sue is the passage of a long period of time before harm manifests itself. This raises the possibility that by the time suit is contemplated, the evidence necessary for a successful action will be stale or the responsible parties out of business. A third reason for failure to sue is difficulty in attributing harm to the parties who are in fact responsible for producing it. This problem could arise from simple ignorance that a given harm or disease was caused by a human agency (as opposed to being "natural" in origin) or from inability to identify which one or several out of many parties was the cause of harm.[11]

The problems here are aggravated when the potential liability rests on large firms, where complications analogous to those mentioned before exist. Namely, even if the harms can be attributed to an individual firm, the prospect of a successful suit may exert only slight influence on the behavior of corporate decisionmakers. With the passage of time, for example, there might be no clear way of determining which were the responsible employees, or those who were responsible may no longer be with the firm. The actual decisionmakers therefore may be beyond both the threat of suit and the prospect of sanctions internal to the firm.

The last of the determinants is the magnitude of the *administrative costs incurred by private parties and by the public* in using the tort system or direct regulation. Of course, the costs of the tort system must be

[11] Discussion of modifications of the tort system that would alleviate this problem of attribution—notably, imposing liability in proportion to the probability of causation—is beyond the scope of the present article. On this matter, see Comment, DES and a Proposed Theory of Enterprise Liability, 46 Fordham L. Rev. 963 (1978); David Rosenberg, The Causal Connection in Mass Exposure Cases: "Public Law" Vision of the Tort System, 97 Harv. L. Rev. 851 (1984); Steven Shavell, Uncertainty over Causation and the Determination of Civil Liability (1983) (unpublished manuscript, Harvard Law School).

broadly defined to include the time, effort, and legal expenses borne by private parties in the course of litigation or in coming to settlements, as well as the public expenses of conducting trials, employing judges, empaneling juries, and the like. Similarly, the administrative costs of regulation include the public expense of maintaining the regulatory establishment and the private costs of compliance.

With respect to these costs, there seems to be an underlying advantage in favor of liability, for most of its administrative costs are incurred only if harm occurs. As this will usually be infrequent, administrative costs will be low. Indeed, in the extreme case where the prospect of liability induces parties to take proper care and this happens to remove all possibility of harm, there would be no suits whatever and thus no administrative costs (other than certain fixed costs). Moreover, there are two reasons to believe that even when harm occurs administrative costs should not always be large. First, under a well-functioning negligence rule, defendants should in principle generally have been induced to take due care; injured parties should generally recognize this and thus should not bring suit. Second, suits should usually be capable of being settled cheaply by comparison to the cost of a trial. A final cost advantage of the liability system is that under it resources are naturally focused on controlling the behavior of the subgroup of parties most likely to cause harm; for because they are most likely to cause harm (and presumably most likely to be negligent), they are most likely to be sued.

Under regulation, unlike under liability, administrative costs are incurred whether or not harm occurs; even if the risk of a harm is eliminated by regulation, administrative costs will have been borne in the process. Also, in the absence of special knowledge about parties' categories of risk, there is no tendency for administrative costs to be focused on those most likely to cause harm, again because these costs are incurred before harm occurs. On the other hand, a savings in administrative costs can typically be achieved through the use of probabilistic means of enforcement.[12] But there is a limit to these savings because there is some minimum frequency of verification necessary to insure adherence to regulatory requirements.[13]

[12] See Donald Wittman, Prior Regulation versus Post Liability: The Choice between Input and Output Monitoring, 6 J. Legal Stud. 193 (1977), for a discussion of probabilistic enforcement in a setting similar to that of this article.

[13] This minimum frequency of verification is determined by the maximum fine—the size of parties' assets—that can be paid for noncompliance. To induce a party with assets of $10,000 to make a precautionary expenditure of $500, for example, his compliance must be verified with a probability of at least 5 percent; for otherwise, even were the fine to equal his entire assets, the probability-discounted fine would be less than $500. But if the likelihood of harm were negligible or lower than 5 percent, then under liability administrative costs could easily be smaller than under regulation, despite its probabilistic enforcement.

Joint Use of Liability and Regulation

Examination of the four determinants has thus shown that two generally favor liability—administrative costs and differential knowledge—and the other two favor regulation—incapacity to pay for harm done and escaping suit. This suggests not only that neither tort liability nor regulation could uniformly dominate the other as a solution to the problem of controlling risks, but also that they should not be viewed as mutually exclusive solutions to it. A complete solution to the problem of the control of risk evidently should involve the joint use of liability and regulation, with the balance between them reflecting the importance of the determinants.

If, then, some combination of liability and regulation is likely to be advantageous, two questions immediately arise: Should a party's adherence to regulation relieve him of liability in the event that harm comes to pass? On the other hand, should a party's failure to satisfy regulatory requirements result necessarily in his liability? Our theory suggests a negative answer to both questions.

As to the first, if compliance with regulation were to protect parties from liability, then none would do more than to meet the regulatory requirements. Yet since these requirements will be based on less than perfect knowledge of parties' situations, there will clearly be some parties who ought to do more than meet the requirements—because they present an above-average risk of doing harm, can take extra precautions more easily than most, or can take precautions not covered by regulation. As liability will induce many of these parties to take beneficial precautions beyond the required ones, its use as a supplement to regulation will be advantageous.[14] At the same time, just because this is true, regulatory requirements need not be as rigorous as if regulation were the sole means of controlling risks.

A similar analysis is appropriate for the second question. If failure to satisfy regulatory requirements necessarily resulted in a finding of negligence, then some parties would be undesirably led to comply with them when they would not otherwise have done so. In particular, there will be some parties (*a*) who ought not to meet regulatory requirements because they face higher than usual costs of care or because they pose lower risks

[14] To illustrate, suppose that a $500 expenditure is desirable for typical firms to make to prevent $1,000 in losses, but for atypical firms, an additional $500 expenditure will prevent another $1,000 in losses. If the regulator is unable to tell the atypical firms apart and tailor regulations to them, then only through the deterrent of liability will these firms be led to make the extra $500 expenditure. Note, however, that use of liability alone would not be desirable, as then firms with low assets or ones likely to escape suit might not make even the first $500 expenditure.

than normal and (*b*) who will not have been forced to satisfy regulatory requirements due to flaws in or probabilistic methods of enforcement. By allowing these parties to escape liability in view of their circumstances, the possibility that they would still be led to take the wasteful precautions can be avoided.[15]

III. Activities Controlled Mainly by Liability: The Typical Tort

In this section and the next I will attempt to show that the theoretically desirable uses of tort liability and regulation correlate roughly with their uses in fact. In speaking first about activities controlled primarily by liability rules, I will for concreteness make reference to two activities mentioned earlier—to my chopping down a tree that might fall on my neighbor's home and to my running to catch a bus and possibly colliding with another person. A consideration of the relevance of the four determinants to activities such as these will suggest strong advantages of the liability system and acute drawbacks of regulation.

As regards the first determinant, there is ample reason to believe that private parties would possess much better information about risks and whether and how to reduce them than would a regulator. Because I would know the precise position of my tree and of my neighbor's home, I would likely have superior insight into the chance of an accident and the opportunity to lower it by use of guy wires, or by cutting down the tree in stages. Likewise, I would presumably be better able to determine whether I should do the work myself or hire an independent contractor to do it. Similarly, my knowledge of the probability of knocking someone down when running for a bus at that particular corner under these particular conditions of visibility and weather would be better than a regulator's, and I would surely know more about the importance of catching the bus.

In these situations private parties possess the better information because they apparently do obtain it as an ordinary by-product of their

[15] Suppose that, unlike in note 14 *supra*, the atypical parties ought not to make the first $500 expenditure because for them it would not reduce losses at all. Then, assuming that the regulator is unable to identify atypical parties, a single regulatory standard must be used, and suppose that it corresponds to the $500 expenditure (as the typical parties for whom this is appropriate are so numerous). Now consider the question whether an atypical party who for some reason was not made to satisfy the standard should be found negligent for that, if he happens to cause an accident. Clearly, if such an atypical party were not found negligent, then he would not make the $500 expenditure, the desirable result; but if he were found negligent, he might be led to make the expenditure. Hence it is best for atypical parties to escape liability for negligence if they did not adhere to the regulatory standard. (And note again that the use of liability alone would not be desirable, for without regulation typical parties with low assets or who would escape suit would fail to make the $500 expenditure.)

activities and can take into account the changes in circumstance that influence the risks and the value of their activities. Consequently, parties should make reasonably satisfactory decisions under liability, while costly mistakes would be unavoidable under regulation. Were the regulatory authority to set forth rules on the felling of trees or the pursuit of buses, it is a certainty that the rules would sometimes be too restrictive, imposing needless precautions that would not be taken due to a concern only over liability; conversely, the rules would fail to identify desirable precautions that parties would obviously be motivated to take to avoid liability.

Turning next to the ability to pay for harm done, there is admittedly a potential problem, but sometimes not one of great magnitude. The damage to my neighbor's roof, for example, will probably be limited in scope, and I am likely to have assets plus liability insurance sufficient to cover it whether I own or rent my house. While inability to pay for harm counts as a weakness of liability in respect to the typical tort, it does not stand out as a problem of unusual dimension, at least by comparison to many of the situations to be discussed in the next part of the article.

The likelihood that suit would be brought against a liable defendant, moreover, appears to be relatively high for the typical tort, as none of the reasons for failure to bring suit seems to apply. Harms generally will not be dispersed among victims; my tree will fall on one, not many, roofs; I will collide with one or at most several pedestrians. Harms will not take a long period of time to manifest themselves; rather, any injury that I cause to a pedestrian or any damage to my neighbor's roof will be an immediate and direct consequence of my behavior. Further, harms will normally be readily attributed to responsible parties; there will be no mystery over whose tree damaged my neighbor's roof or over how the damage came about. There is thus no argument favoring regulation for fear that proper defendants would systematically escape suit.

Finally, liability should enjoy a significant administrative cost advantage over regulation in controlling the risks of typical torts. One does have the impression that it should be much less costly for society to incur administrative costs only when falling trees happen to descend on neighbors' homes and only when individuals chasing buses happen to collide with pedestrians, fairly unlikely events, than for society to formulate and enforce regulations on when and how trees may be cut down and on when individuals may be allowed to hurry after a bus.[16] Indeed, virtually all our

[16] Suppose, for instance, that the likelihood of my tree's striking my neighbor's roof is 0.1 percent; that should this happen, the chance there would be a dispute over my negligence is 50 percent; that given this, the probability of a settlement before trial would be 75 percent;

routine activities—walking, mowing a lawn, playing catch—are perfectly innocuous in the overwhelming majority of instances, so that the savings achieved by limiting the bearing of administrative costs to those few occasions when harm occurs must be great.

The notion of effective regulation of the activities of everyday life even seems fanciful to contemplate, particularly because it would necessitate the use of extremely frequent and intrusive verification procedures. This is because what would usually need to be determined by a regulatory authority are aspects of modifiable behavior rather than "fixed" physical objects. While it may be enough to inspect elevator cables annually, because their condition will change little over that period, effective regulation of ordinary behavior such as whether I chase after buses clearly requires much more frequent monitoring.

Also of importance is the tendency for administrative costs to be incurred primarily in controlling the parties most likely to cause harm. Because those who fail to prevent their trees from falling on their neighbors' roofs must be a disproportionately awkward group, it is a good thing that the liability system's costs be concerned only with them; it would be a waste for society to incur costs to monitor the majority of careful individuals whose trees fall safely to the ground; yet that is just what the regulatory approach requires.

Let us now summarize our discussion. Of the four determinants, differential knowledge and the size of administrative costs pointed strongly in favor of use of liability to reduce the risk of the typical tort, while inability to pay for harm done worked with only moderate force against it, and the possibility of escaping suit did not constitute an argument against it. Thus, the use in practice of liability to control the familiar category of risks known as torts seems to be the theoretically preferred solution to the problem.

IV. Activities Subject to Significant Regulation

This section will argue that it is desirable that society resort to safety regulation where it generally does—in controlling the risks of fire, the production and sale of many foods and drugs, the generation of pollu-

that the administrative costs of a settlement would be $100 and those of a trial $1,000. Then the likelihood of a dispute ending in settlement would be 0.0375 percent, of one ending in litigation 0.0125 percent, so that the expected administrative costs associated with my chopping down my tree would be .000375 × $100 + .000125 × $1,000, or about 16 cents. It is hard to think of any regulatory scheme that could, ex ante, verify satisfaction of safety requirements at comparable cost.

tants, and the transport and use of explosives and other dangerous materials. A consideration of the four determinants in these areas will lead to the conclusion that substantial regulation is not a coincidence but rather is needed, both because liability alone would not adequately reduce risks and because the usual disadvantages of regulation are not as serious as in the tort context.

First, what typifies much of regulation in the areas of concern is that its requirements can be justified by common knowledge or something close to it. Presumably most of us would agree that it is well worthwhile for explosives to be transported over designated routes that avoid the drastic risks of explosions in tunnels or in densely populated locations; that expenditures on very strong elevator cables are warranted by the resulting reduction in the probability of fatal accidents; that milk should be pasteurized to decrease the chances of bacterial contamination. In these and similar cases, the regulatory authority can be reasonably confident that its requirements are justified in the great majority of situations. To be sure, they will not always be justified; there will be some occasions when milk will be consumed soon enough that failure to pasteurize it would lead to no significant risk. But these occasions will be few in number, and the error due to inappropriate regulation will be small.

Furthermore, even where the proper design of regulation must be based on much more than common knowledge, the regulatory authority may not suffer an informational disadvantage, but instead may enjoy a positive advantage relative to private parties. Notably, in dealing with many health-related and environmental risks, a regulatory agency may have better access to, or a superior ability to evaluate, relevant medical, epidemiological, and ecological knowledge. A small fumigating company, for example, might know little about, and have limited ability to understand, the nature of the risks that the chemicals it uses create. The same might be true of a large producer of pesticides; it may be uneconomical for the producer to develop and maintain expert knowledge about the dangerous properties of pesticides, especially where there are economies of scale in acquiring this knowledge and where it would benefit others.

Consideration of the determinant concerning inability to pay for harm done also suggests why we regulate the activities that we do. A fire at a nightclub or hotel could harm a large number of individuals and create losses greater than the worth of the owner. The harm caused by mass consumption of spoiled food or by inoculation with vaccines with adverse side effects could easily exhaust the holdings of even a large corporation, and so too with the losses resulting from explosions, oil spills, or the release of toxic agents or radioactive substances. Clearly, in many areas of regulation, potential liability could exceed the assets of the firms involved (certainly of their employees), and the deterrent effect of tort law is therefore diluted.

Deterrence is similarly diluted by the likelihood that responsible parties would not be sued for a wide class of environmental and health-related harms. Many of these harms are sufficiently dispersed that individual victims do not find it worth their while to bring suit. In addition, these harms often become apparent only after the passage of years, either because ecological damage or the disease process itself is slow (as with asbestosis) or because the substance generating the risk retains its potency for a long period (as with anthrax bacillus or radioactive wastes). In consequence, it may be difficult for victims to assemble the evidence necessary to succeed in a suit, the responsible individuals may have retired or died, or the firms themselves may have gone out of business. Last, it is frequently hard to trace environmental and health-related harms to particular causes and then to particular firms. Many different substances may combine to produce a given type of harm, and the mechanism that links cause to effect may be complex and incompletely understood. There are, then, a variety of reasons to believe that parties responsible for environmental and health-related harms would not be sued, and hence to find the use of regulation attractive.

Finally, regarding administrative costs, several factors may offset the underlying advantage of liability in the major regulated areas. First, what regulation often requires is the presence of particular safety devices—fire extinguishers, guard rails, lifeboats—making enforcement less costly than if regulation demanded particular modes of behavior. And where regulation does demand a type of behavior, there may be features of the situation making lack of compliance hard to conceal. How easy would it be for a dairy to keep secret its failure to pasteurize milk when samples can be tested at low cost and when numbers of employees would be aware of the violation? Second, probabilistic methods of enforcement of regulation are often employed; firms are subject to spot visits by regulatory authorities; products and services are randomly selected and examined. Thus, the administrative costs of verifying adherence to regulatory requirements appear sometimes to be low per party, while other times some savings are realized by verifying compliance on a probabilistic basis.

We conclude that the importance of the four determinants is different for the major regulated areas from what it is for the typical tort. In the regulated areas, there is a larger likelihood that responsible parties will be unable to pay for or will escape detection and suit for harms that they bring about; and the disadvantages of regulation involving administrative costs and differential knowledge are less troublesome. Of course, the relative weights of these determinants will change from one case to the next—the possibility of escaping suit, for example, is of significant concern for harms due to pesticides although of little concern for damage caused by fire. But the overall balance of the determinants in the various cases should indicate the desirability of substantial regulation.

This general claim of theoretical consistency is further supported by considering the "second-order" choices society has made over which *aspects* of an activity to regulate given the initial choice that the activity is one that should be subject to important controls. While fire regulations will often contain requirements concerning the installation of smoke alarms and sprinkler systems, they inevitably will not cover many routine practices, such as whether to store flammable furniture polish in a closet through which a heating pipe passes. Regulating these practices would usually be very expensive (closets would have to be checked frequently) or require a highly contextual sort of knowledge (type of polish and of heating pipe). It therefore appears that the two disadvantages of regulation—the magnitude of administrative costs and the regulator's inferior information about risk—help explain what aspects of a regulated activity are left unregulated.

The claim of theoretical consistency is also confirmed by the observed interrelationship between regulation and imposition of liability, especially in the basic rule that compliance with regulation does not necessarily relieve a party of liability.[17] Moreover, the cases often say that it is "unusual circumstances" or "increased danger" that makes additional precautions desirable, which is exactly what our theory suggested ought to give rise to liability despite satisfaction of regulation.[18] Similarly, the failure to conform to regulation does not in fact automatically result in liability.[19] And the explanation that is furnished here—that a party's "violation of the [statutory] law" does not imply his negligence if the special circumstances justify the apparent disobedience—again comports with the theory.[20]

[17] See William L. Prosser, Handbook of the Law of Torts (4th ed. 1971), at 203.

[18] See *id.* at 204. Also, at 203, Prosser writes, "The statutory standard is no more than a minimum, and it does not necessarily preclude a finding that the actor was negligent in failing to take additional precautions. Thus the requirement of a hand signal on a left turn does not mean that . . . a driver . . . is absolved from all obligation to slow down, keep a proper lookout, and proceed with reasonable care." This statement is in perfect agreement with our explanation from Section II, *supra*, where we said that the statutory standard ought to be regarded as a minimum since there would be parties who ought to take greater care and would not do so were they to escape liability on account of simply complying with the statutory standard.

[19] *Id.* at 197.

[20] *Id.* at 198. At 198 and 199, Prosser writes that "it has been held not to be negligence to violate . . . a statute because of physical circumstances beyond the driver's control, as

V. Concluding Comments

a) The basic purpose of the last two sections of this article has been to demonstrate how the observed use of liability and regulation can be explained by looking to the four determinants discussed at the outset. As would be true of any simple theory, however, the fit between the theory presented here and reality is only approximate.

Indeed, we often encounter the view that major mistakes have been made in the use of liability and regulation. On the one hand, it may be asserted that regulation has proved inadequate, as for instance in controlling the disposal of toxic wastes. This particular claim may well have merit, for until recently toxic wastes were little regulated, while the threat of tort liability probably provided an insufficient deterrent against improper disposal—due to manifold problems faced by victims in establishing causation and to the possibility that responsible parties would be unable to pay for harm done.[21] Conversely, there are frequent charges that certain regulations are too restrictive, as in complaints that various OSHA requirements and antipollution standards are unduly constraining or impose excessive costs on industry.[22]

That there are such examples of apparent social irrationality is to be expected, for the choices actually made about regulation and liability are obviously influenced by factors lying outside the framework of this analysis, and in any event often will not reflect a conscious, careful use of a cost-benefit calculus. Moreover, the complexity of the relationship between liability and regulation and the many unanswered empirical questions also afford ready explanations for differences between observed and ideal results.

b) The theoretical determinants examined here would be of relevance to

---

where his lights suddenly go out on the highway at night. . . . Another valid excuse is that of emergency, as where one drives on the left because the right is blocked, or a child dashes to the street . . ." Such results obviously agree with what we said in Section II. That is, we do not want the driver to stay on the right-hand side of the road when the child dashes out; holding him liable for being on the left would give him a socially undesirable incentive to drive on the right.

[21] See, for example, Note, Allocating the Costs of Hazardous Waste Disposal, 94 Harv. L. Rev. 584 (1981) and references cited therein; Richard A. Epstein, The Principles of Environmental Protection: The Case of Superfund, 2 Cato J. 9 (1982); and "Public Threat Feared in Loopholes in Laws on Toxic Waste Dumping," New York Times, June 6, 1983, at 1.

[22] See, for example, Stephen Breyer, Regulation and Its Reform (1982), ch. 14; Albert L. Nichols & Richard Zeckhauser, Government Comes to the Workplace: An Assessment of OSHA, 49 Public Interest 39 (1977); and, for a general introduction to the issues, ch. 5 of Environmental Law and Policy (Richard B. Stewart & James E. Krier eds. 2d ed. 1978).

a more comprehensive analysis of the social control of risk, and specifically to one allowing for the use of public fines measured by harm done,[23] and of the private right to enjoin others from engaging in harmful activities. The general conclusions that would emerge from such an analysis seem clear.

First, the fine is identical to liability in that it creates incentives to reduce risk by making parties pay for the harm they cause. Thus the fine enjoys essentially the same advantages as liability rules—the private parties balance the costs of reducing risks against the benefits, while society bears administrative costs only when harm occurs. Also, the fine suffers from similar disadvantages—inability to pay for harm done dilutes its effectiveness, as does the possibility that violators would escape detection.

But the fine differs from liability in its public nature; private parties do not institute suits to collect fines nor benefit financially when they are paid. The principal implication of this difference is that the likelihood of imposition of a fine may be less than the likelihood of a private suit. Private parties should ordinarily be more likely to know when harm occurs than a public agency and, as just observed, will not profit from reporting harm but may from bringing suit. Nevertheless, in some circumstances the advantage may lie with the fine. A fine could be imposed where suits would not be brought due to difficulty in establishing causation or where harms are widely dispersed, as in many environmental and health cases.

The injunction, unlike the fine, resembles safety regulation, for it works in a direct way to control risk; the injunction prevents harm simply by proscribing certain behavior. Hence the injunction shares the main advantages of safety regulation. Its use is in no way impeded by the possibility that a party would not be able to pay for the harm he does,[24] or by the chance that the harm would be highly dispersed or hard to attribute to him under tort principles. Just as, for instance, the regulation of nuclear power plants might be justified by both these factors, so too might enjoining their operations in certain circumstances.

The injunction, however, differs from safety regulation in that it is brought at the behest of private parties. The injunction accordingly has an advantage where private parties would have superior information about

[23] Thus, from the point of view of parties who pay fines, it is as if they were strictly liable for harm done.

[24] This point is made in Robert C. Ellickson, Alternatives to Zoning: Covenants, Nuisance Rules, and Fines on Land Use Controls, 40 U. Chi. L. Rev. 681 (1973).

the harm they might suffer, as is perhaps true of ordinary nuisances. But safety regulation would be more attractive where parties are not easily able to assess dangers or where many parties are involved and "free rider" and associated problems make it difficult to coordinate a collective action.

As this discussion indicates, the injunction and safety regulation may be viewed as substitutes, but not perfect ones, and similarly with the fine and liability. Thus, although an analysis of all four methods of controlling risk would be complicated, the conclusions would parallel our own. Where the theoretical determinants had indicated a relative advantage of regulation over liability, they would now indicate an advantage of regulation or the injunction over liability or the fine.

[23]

ECONOMIC ANALYSIS OF PUNITIVE DAMAGES*

ROBERT D. COOTER**

Litigating a tort dispute involving punitive damages, much like navigating the Straits of Magellan, runs the risk of incurring grave losses from colliding with unseen objects. There is no clear standard for deciding when punitive damages are appropriate or for computing their magnitude when awarded. This paper develops such standards with the help of economic theory.

Imagine any potentially harmful activity in which liability is governed by a fault rule. The legal standard of care represents a threshold, on one side of which the injurer is liable and on the other side he is not liable. Crossing this threshold causes an abrupt jump in the costs which the injurer expects to bear, with profound effects upon rational behavior. The economic model developed in this paper is based upon an analysis of these threshold effects, which have not been explained previously in a systematic fashion.

I begin with a brief, nontechnical explanation of the policy conclusions of this analysis. For most potential injurers, it is far cheaper to comply with the law than risk liability, so noncompliance will usually be unintentional. If fault is unintentional, then imposing punitive damages in addition to compensatory damages is both unnecessary for deterrence and undeserved as punishment. However, there may be a small group of unusual persons who derive illicit pleasure from noncompliance or incur exceptional costs from compliance. Such people may cross the threshold of fault intentionally and, once crossed, it usually pays them to cross it a long way. The situation is analogous to the historical conflict between France and Germany in which armies did not cross the Rhine merely to occupy the far bank. This fact provides a behavioral test for intentionality: Intentional fault is usually aggra-

* Helpful comments were provided by Steve Shavell, Steve Sugarman, and the participants in the Liberty Fund Seminar in Punitive Damages, held under the auspices of the Law and Economics Center at Emory University.

** Professor of Law, University of California, Berkeley. B.A. 1967, Swarthmore College; M.A. 1969, Oxford University; Ph.D. 1975, Harvard University.

vated and constitutes gross negligence, willful and wanton disregard for others, and the like. Three policy conclusions follow from this analysis: (1) punitive damages should be restricted to intentional faults; (2) a criterion for identifying intentional fault is that it is gross or repeated; and (3) punitive damages should be computed to offset the injurer's illicit pleasure from noncompliance or exceptional cost of compliance.

In Part I of this paper, the distinction between intentional and unintentional fault is explained by the distinction between equilibrium and disequilibrium behavior, and the concept of a threshold is explained by discontinuities in cost functions. In Part II, the theory is used to determine whether the purpose of punitive damages is to punish the defendant, to deter potential injurers, to reward victims for suing, or to correct a shortfall between actual harm and allowable damages. In Part III, the difference between negligence and strict liability is explained by the presence or absence of threshold effects. Finally, Part IV discusses some applications of the model, including the conclusion that consumers injured by defective products should not be awarded punitive damages unless they prove that the manufacturer knew that his behavior was negligent and likely to cause a defect. The paper concludes with a mathematical appendix.

I. FAULT RULES AND INCENTIVES

Economists often explain a person's behavior by observing that the costs and benefits of a change are perfectly balanced at the margin, so there is no gain from acting differently. However, a threshold in costs can create an unbalanced situation in which the costs of a change substantially exceed the benefits. For example, the cost of complying with a negligence rule will be far less than the cost of noncompliance for most people. In technical language, the difference is between an "internal equilibrium" where the marginal costs and marginal benefits of change are equal, and a "corner solution" where the costs of change exceed the benefits. This distinction is important for liability law because a fault rule creates a corner solution in which the potential injurer will not change his precaution in spite of moderate changes in the costs or benefits or precaution.

A simple numercial illustration is provided by Tables 1 and 2, which depict the costs associated with exploding pop bottles. In this example, precaution against exploding bottles takes the form of testing bottles for weaknesses in the glass. There are two possible levels of testing: sampling one bottle in fifty or sampling one bottle in one hundred. An increase in the sampling ratio from 1/100 to 1/50 causes the cost of precaution to rise from 40 to 65, as indicated in column 1. However, this increase in precaution causes the cost of the harm suffered by victims to fall from 80 to 40, as indicated in column 2. The social cost is the sum of the cost of precaution and the cost of the harm, as indicated in column 3. Efficiency requires the bottler to sample at the ratio which minimizes social costs, namely 1/50.

TABLE 1: COSTS OF EXPLODING POP BOTTLES

	(1) Cost of Precaution	(2) Cost of Accidents	(3) Social Costs[a]	(4) Cost of Precaution Plus 50% Accident Costs
Sample 1 in 50	65	40	105	85
Sample 1 in 100	40	80	120	80

[a]Social cost is the sum of the cost of precaution and the cost of accidents.

TABLE 2: COSTS BORN BY BOTTLER

	Negligence Rule		Strict Liability Rule	
	100% Liability	50% Liability	100% Liability	50% Liability
Sample 1 in 50	65 (not negligent)	65 (not negligent)	105	85
Sample 1 in 100	120[a] (negligent)	80[a] (negligent)	120	80

[a]The cost to a negligent bottler is the sum of his cost of precaution and the costs of the accidents for which he is sued (100% or 50% of the total number, as the case may be).

Table 2 depicts the incentives for precaution created by a rule of strict liability and a negligence rule. Assuming that the standard of negligence requires a sampling ratio of 1/50, a negligence rule presents the bottler with a choice between sampling at the ratio 1/50 and escaping liability, in which case his costs are 65, or sampling at the ratio 1/100 and assuming liability. If the bottler assumes liability, then his costs are 120 or 80, depending upon whether he is liable for 100 percent or 50 percent of the harm. The important point is that the bottler's costs are lower under a negligence rule when he complies, even if fault exposes him to liability for only half of the actual harm. Thus, in this example, a negligence rule provides efficient incentives even though a negligent injurer does not bear the full cost of accidents.

By contrast, consider the bottler's costs under a rule of strict liability. If he is liable for 100 percent of the harm, then it is cheaper to sample at the ratio 1/50 and bear costs of 105, than to sample at the ratio 1/100 and bear costs of 120. However, if he is liable for 50 percent of the harm, then it is cheaper to sample at the ratio 1/100 and bear costs of 80, than to sample at the ratio 1/50 and bears costs of 85. This illustrates the fact that strict liability does not provide efficient incentives to the injurer unless he bears 100 percent of the cost of harm.

The reader may wonder why a negligence rule may provide efficient incentives without fully internalizing costs, whereas a strict liability rule cannot provide efficient incentives unless the injurer bears 100 percent of accident costs. The reason is that the level of precaution defined in the legal standard of negligence is a threshold at which costs jump abruptly, rather than increase marginally. In order to understand this fundamental difference between negligence and strict liability, it is necessary to use some simple graphs and mathematical notation.

Let x denote the injurer's expenditure on precaution, let A denote the dollar value of the harm caused by an accident, and let p denote the

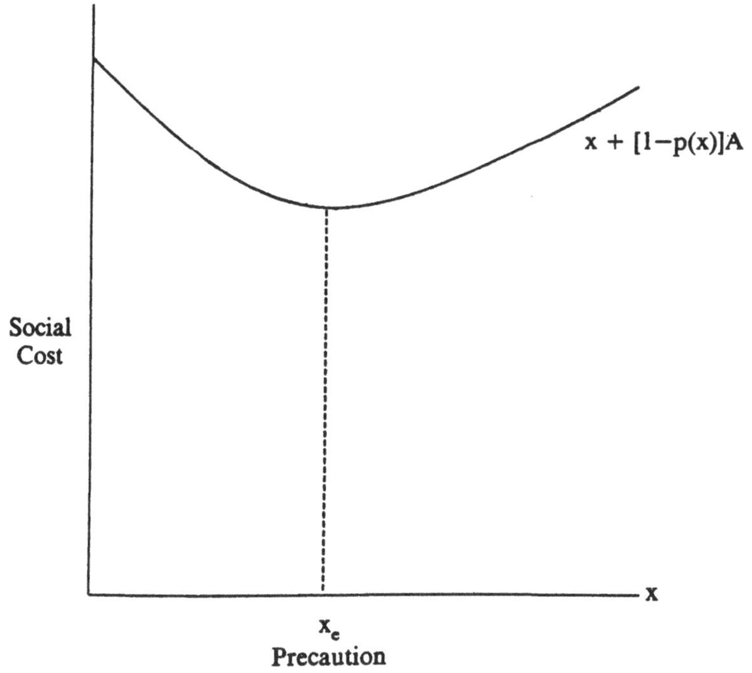

FIGURE 1: SOCIAL COSTS OF ACCIDENTS

probability of avoiding an accident. The social cost, SC, is the expenditure on precaution plus the expected harm, or $SC=x+(1\text{-}p)A$. Figure 1 graphs the relationship between social cost and precaution. The probability p of avoiding an accident is an increasing function of the expenditure on precaution, x, or $p=p(x)$, where $p'>0$. At low levels of precaution, a little more precaution saves more than it costs, but the opposite is true at high levels of precaution. The efficient level of precaution, x_e, is an intermediate value at which social costs are minimized.

It is easy to to represent graphically the injurer's costs under a fault rule. For simplicity, assume that negligent injurers must fully compensate their victims, and assume that the legal standard of fault, x^*, corresponds to the efficient level of precaution, x_e, that is, $x^* = x_e$.[1]

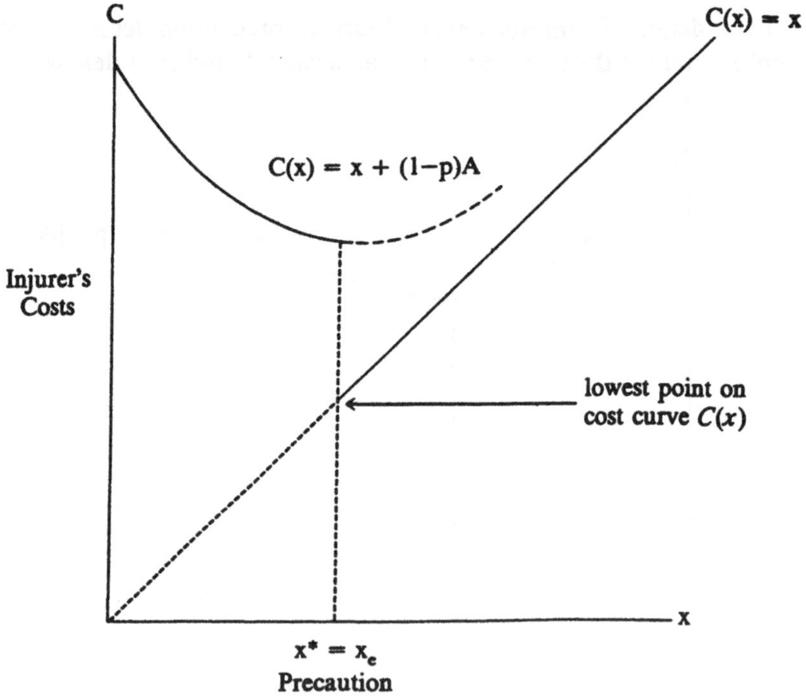

FIGURE 2: INJURER'S COSTS

1. Social costs, $x + [1-p(x)]A$, are minimized when x is chosen to satisfy the inequality:

As depicted in Figure 2, if the injurer's precaution is less than the legal standard, $x<x^*$, then he bears the social cost of accidents. Thus, the injurer's cost curve *C(x)* in Figure 2 is identical to the cost curve in Figure 1 for values of x below x^*. If his precaution is above the legal standard, $x \geq x^*$, then he only bears the cost of his precaution, in which case his costs *C(x)* equal his expenditure on precaution, x. Thus, his cost curve is in two pieces, with a jump or discontinuity at $x = x^*$. The

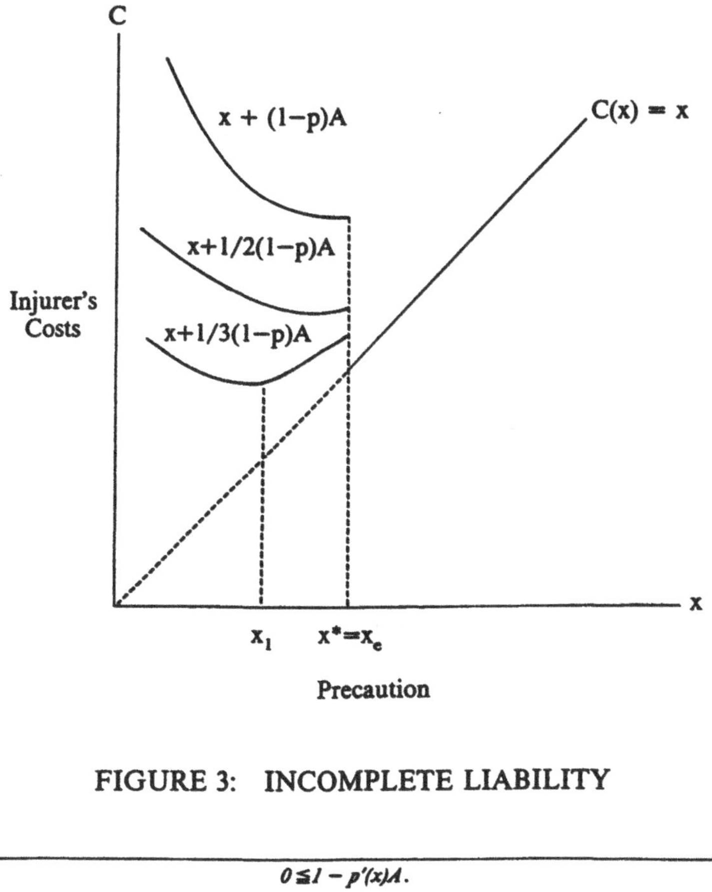

FIGURE 3: INCOMPLETE LIABILITY

$$0 \leq 1 - p'(x)A.$$

Solving this inequality for x gives the efficient level of precaution x_e. This formula also gives the legal standard of fault, x^*, prescribed by the marginal Hand Rule. This rule was formulated in Brown, *Toward an Economic Theory of Liability*, 2 J. LEGAL STUD. 323, 332 (1973). There is a fundamental misconception, however, in Brown's account of the Hand Rule in that he concludes that courts cannot find the correct legal standard when they have limited information about the costs of precaution. This misconception is addressed in Cooter, Kornhauser & Lane, *Liability Rules, Limited Information, and the Role of Precedent*, 10 BELL J. ECON. 366, 369-73 (1979) (where variations in injurer behavior determine the information available to the court, rather than the legal standard itself, a sequence of precedents tends toward efficiency).

injurer's costs jump from x to $x + [1-p(x)]A$ at the point where he crosses the threshold of liability.

The cost curve in Figure 2 reaches its lowest point at $x=x^*$, so a cost-minimizing injurer will exactly satisfy the legal standard of care. But Figure 2 is drawn under the assumption that negligent injurers must fully compensate their victims. Instead, assume that imperfections in the law prevent complete internalization of social costs. For example, suppose that damages cover only a fraction of the harm A, or that only a fraction of victims actually bring suit. Figure 3 depicts such a situation. If the injurer's liability equals half the actual harm, then his costs are still minimized by satisfying the legal standard, $x=x^*$. If the injurer's liability equals one-third of the actual harm, then his costs are minimized by taking precaution at the level denoted x_l, which is well below the legal standard, x^*. Figure 3 illustrates the fact that, under a negligence rule, liability must fall far short of the actual harm before the cost-minimizing injurer will reduce his precaution below the legal standard of care.

A. Unintentional Fault

In the preceding examples, the injurer complies with fault rules even though damages do not fully compensate victims and some victims do not sue. Would such an injurer ever be at fault? The answer is yes, because such an injurer might be at fault unintentionally. For instance, he might be mistaken about the legal standard, x^*, and believe that he is complying, when in fact he is not. Such mistakes can easily occur since the standard of "reasonable care" is so vague in tort law.

In economic jargon, unintentional fault corresponds to "disequilibrium behavior." An economic equilibrium is a condition in which expectations are fulfilled, or, equivalently, in which actions have their intended effects.[2] An economic disequilibrium is a situation in which expectations are disappointed, intentions are unfulfilled, decisionmakers are surprised, and so on. If the injurer thinks he is complying with the law, but at trial he learns that he is liable because he is in fact not complying, then the injurer will be disappointed and will want to revise his behavior. An equilibrium will be reached when he per-

2. For a general discussion of this topic, consult any microeconomic textbook. For an advanced treatment, see K. Arrow & F. Hahn, General Competitive Analysis (1971).

ceives the legal standard accurately and satisfies it, ending the possibility of further surprises.

As explained, unintentional fault can be corrected by awarding compensatory damages. Of course, it is also true that unintentional fault will be eliminated if the injurer bears more than the full cost of the harm that he causes. Adding punitive damages provides a second reason for compliance where the first suffices. When punitive damages are imposed for unintentional fault, the cost of making errors increases, causing injurers to invest more in avoiding mistakes. Thus, punitive damages for unintentional fault will not change the injurer's equilibrium behavior,[3] but the movement from disequilibrium to equilibrium will be more rapid.

An argument can be made against imposing punitive damages for unintentional faults because punishment is unjust where no harm was intended.[4] This claim is important, but this paper will not consider such moral arguments. Instead, it considers next the small number of cases where fault is intentional.

B. Intentional Fault

Suppose the courts face an unusual individual who intended to breach his legal duty, despite liability for the actual damage.[5] Requiring him to pay compensation will not cause surprise or disappointment. In a situation such as this, the court confronts equilibrium fault. Although intentions are difficult to prove in court, there is a behavioral guide that often distinguishes intentional from unintentional fault. Unintentional fault usually involves a moderate degree of noncompliance, whereas intentional fault usually involves gross noncompliance. Intentional fault is gross because a person who deliberately exposes himself to liability crosses a threshold, after which aggravation of the fault is less costly.

Table 3 illustrates why intentional fault is usually gross. It shows the options of a father who will miss his daughter's wedding if he complies with traffic laws. Assume the father is willing to pay up to $1,000

3. For elaboration of this point, see discussion of Figure 5 in the text.

4. The scope and purpose of imposing punitive damages is discussed in K. Redden, Punitive Damages §§ 2.2 (origin and development of punitive damages), 4.1-4.36 (cases in which punitive damages may be awarded) (1980 & Supp. 1981).

5. This paper is concerned with intentional fault, rather than intentional harm. Thus, a driver may intend to speed but hope that his speeding will not result in harm. Several meanings of an intentional tort are distinguished in Landes & Posner, *An Economic Theory of Intentional Torts*, 1 Int'l Rev. L. & Econ. 127, 127-39 (1981).

not to miss the wedding. If he does not speed, he will miss the whole wedding and suffer a loss valued at $1,000. If he speeds a little, then he will miss much of the wedding, with a loss valued at $400. If he speeds a lot, then he will miss some of the wedding, with a loss valued at $300. Even a little speeding makes him liable for all the damage resulting from a collision with another motorist who is not at fault. Thus, his expected civil liability jumps from $0 to $500 when he speeds a little. If he decides to speed a lot, the expected civil liability increases from $500 to $550 to reflect the increase in the probability of an accident. There is a threshold in liability costs when he decides to speed a little, but there is no abrupt jump when he decides to speed a lot. If it pays to cross the threshold at all, then it pays to cross it a long way. Thus, the father will minimize his costs by speeding a lot, as is apparent from column 3 of Table 3.

To explain this point more fully, suppose there is a special class of injurers who derive an illicit benefit from wrongful behavior or who experience exceptional costs from compliance. For notational simplicity, let b represent such illicit benefits, where the benefit b is a decreasing function of precaution x, or $b=b(x)$. If the injurer satisfies the legal standard, his costs are precaution costs less illicit benefits, or $x-b(x)$. If the injurer is at fault, then he bears these costs minus the illicit benefits, or $x-b(x)+[1-p(x)]A$. This situation is depicted in Figure 4, where there is a discontinuity or jump in costs at the legal standard, x^*. The difference between Figure 4 and Figure 2 is that the existence of illicit benefits causes the injurer to minimize his costs at the level of precaution, $\bar{x}$, a point at which he is at fault, rather than at the legal standard, x^*.

It is clear from Figure 4 that the level of precaution, $\bar{x}$, that minimizes the injurer's costs cannot be just a little below the legal standard,

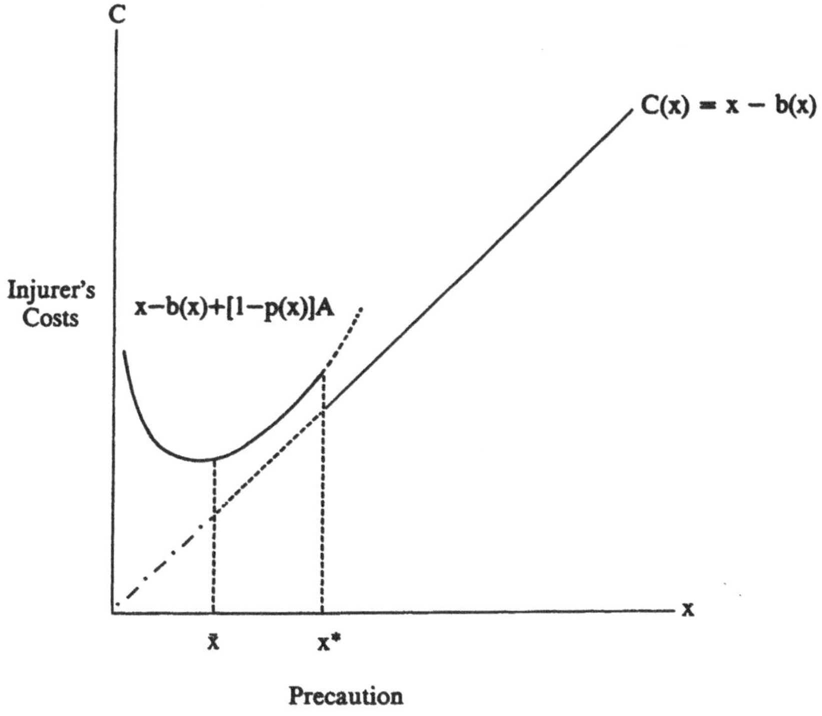

FIGURE 4: INTENTIONAL FAULT

x^*. The jump or discontinuity guarantees that the injurer's cost-minimizing level of precaution, $\bar{x}$, must be *far* below the legal standard, x^*.[6] In technical terms, intentional fault must be gross because the discontinuity in costs at the legal standard creates a nonconvexity in the injurer's cost function. Consequently, there are two local minima, one at the legal standard and one far below it.[7]

6. If gross fault triggers punitive damages, then an injurer may attempt to avoid punitive damages liability through noncompliance at a level of fault that is not gross enough to trigger punitive damages. For example, newspapers that specialize in gossip may publish libelous material that stops just short of causing public figures to sue. Repetition of mild fault is an indication that the fault is intentional, even though each individual act is not gross. A more detailed treatment of strategic behavior is beyond the scope of this paper.

7. For a discussion of nonconvexities and the law, see Cooter, *How the Law Circumvents Starrett's Nonconvexity*, 22 J. ECON. THEORY 499, 500-01 (1980) (courts can distinguish between local and global optima by assigning liability rights according to a calculation of benefits and costs).

If punitive damages are added to compensatory damages, it is possible to restore a situation in which compliance minimizes the injurer's costs. This is accomplished by imposing punitive damages equal to the illicit benefits of non-compliance, b.[8] If punitive damages exactly offset the injurer's illicit benefits, then his cost function will look just like that of an ordinary injurer in the zone of liability, as depicted in Figure 2. Thus, a good measure by which to set punitive damages is the illicit benefit or extraordinary cost that prompts the intentional fault. If this measure is adopted, then the amount of money awarded in punitive damages will usually be large, because the illicit benefit or extraordinary cost of gross fault is large.

It is important to consider the conditions under which intentional fault should be deterred. From the utilitarian or economic perspective, intentional fault should be deterred if its social cost exceeds its social benefit, but not otherwise. If the illicit pleasure from noncompliance is given no social weight, then the social cost of intentional fault will exceed the social benefit and deterrence will be appropriate. For example, the pleasure of defaming your enemy or breaking his nose is given no social weight by the courts, and punitive damages are therefore assessed to deter such behavior. However, a person who breaks into a cabin in the woods and eats food to keep from starving will not face punitive damages, even though his fault is intentional. Similarly, most courts would not excuse speeding on the grounds that the driver was late for his daughter's wedding, but speeding to bring a pregnant woman to the hospital might be excused under the emergency doctrine.

II. PURPOSES OF PUNITIVE DAMAGES

The model presented above highlights three broad characteristics of an economic view of punitive damages: (1) punitive damages should be restricted to intentional faults; (2) these faults will usually violate the legal standard of care by a wide margin; and (3) the awards for punitive damages should be large. These characteristics are essential to the

---

8. It may be best for reasons not stated in this model that punitive damages should internalize social costs exactly. To internalize social costs fully, the punitive damages should be set equal to the illicit benefit, b, plus the expected shortfall of compensatory damages from actual damages. If D denotes compensatory damages, q denotes the probability that the injurer will be held liable, and P denotes punitive damages, then

Social Costs $= x + (1-p)A$

Injurer's Costs $= x - b + (1-p)q(D+P)$.

Punitive damages internalize social costs if the preceding values are equal, which implies:

$$P = \frac{A-qD}{q} + \frac{b}{(1-p)q}$$

institution of punitive damages and can clarify the purposes of that institution. Purposes that have been suggested for imposing punitive damages include punishing offenders, deterring injurers, rewarding plaintiffs who otherwise would not sue, and fully compensating victims. In this section, I consider which of these purposes are consistent with the three characteristics of punitive damages identified by economic analysis.

The first characteristic to consider is intentionality. As explained, compensatory damages are sufficient to deter unintentional faults and insufficient to deter intentional faults. Furthermore, punishment is often regarded as unjust if the fault is unintentional. Thus, restricting punitive damages to intentional faults is consistent with the purposes of deterrence and punishment. By contrast, there is no necessary relationship between the injurer's intentions and the completeness of compensatory damages or the victim's reluctance to bear the cost of a suit. If the purpose of punitive damages were to achieve complete compensation or to reward plaintiffs for suing, then the intentionality restriction would make no sense.

The second characteristic, restriction to gross faults, also seems consistent with punishment and deterrence. The fact that fault must be gross to trigger punitive damages can be viewed as a safeguard against mistakes in civil proceedings, which afford less protection to defendants than criminal proceedings. Such a safeguard seems desirable when punishment is at issue. Furthermore, restriction of punitive damages to gross fault is consistent with my analysis of deterrence based upon threshold effects, as explained in the preceding section.

The fact that punitive damages are often large is also consistent with deterrence and punishment. As noted, a substantial increment in damages is needed to offset the illicit pleasure from noncompliance or the exceptional costs of compliance which prompt intentional fault. Furthermore, intentional fault is more serious morally than unintentional fault, so an increase in the sanction is warranted. By contrast, small awards of punitive damages would be appropriate if the purpose were to reward plaintiffs for suing or to fully compensate victims.

Therefore, the three characteristics of punitive damages are consistent with the purposes of punishment and deterrence of exceptional injurers, but inconsistent with the purposes of rewarding plaintiffs for suing or fully compensating victims.[9] I will now consider the difference

9. There is a troublesome question which remains: Why give the money to the victim,

between strict liability and negligence.

III. STRICT LIABILITY VERSUS NEGLIGENCE

The economic model developed in this paper is based upon the observation that a negligence rule creates a threshold or jump in the potential injurer's costs. No such threshold or jump exists in the cost function of an injurer under a rule of strict liability. This observation can be developed into a theory about the difference between strict liability and negligence rules.

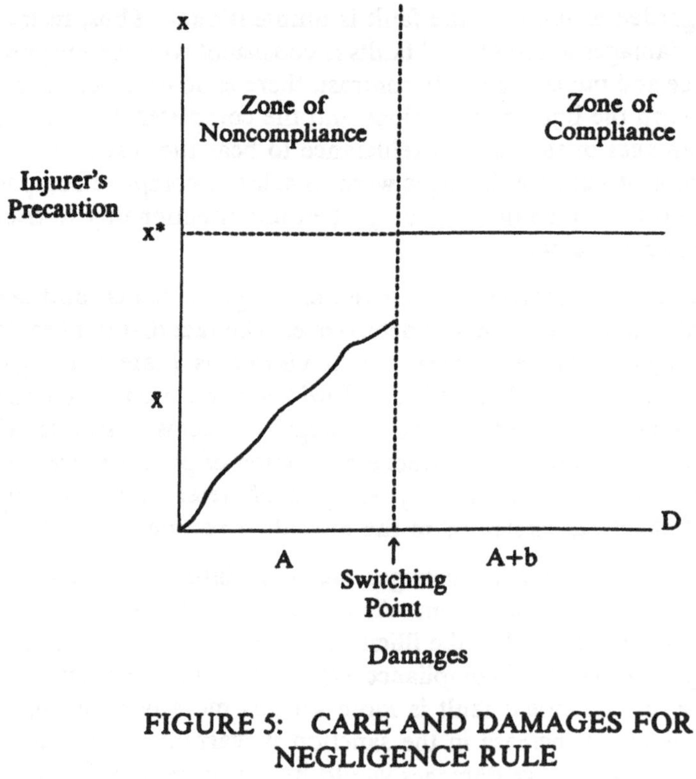

FIGURE 5: CARE AND DAMAGES FOR NEGLIGENCE RULE

To develop this theory, Figure 5 depicts the precaution of a potential injurer under a negligence rule as a function of the extent of his liability. If negligent injurers are liable for only a small fraction of

instead of to the state as with a fine? The answer is that the plaintiff requires a reward for undertaking the additional burden of proving that the injurer's fault was intentional. It is desirable for the plaintiff to undertake this burden, since it saves the state the cost of a criminal trial.

accident costs, A, then a cost minimizing injurer will take a level of precaution, x, which is below the legal standard of care, x^*. As the fraction of liability increases, the cost minimizing level of precaution increases, which is represented in Figure 5 by the upward sloping line to the left of the switching point. Eventually, a switching point is reached at which damages are high enough so that the cost minimizing level of precaution is the legal standard, x^*. The switching point is by definition the lowest level of damages at which compliance with the legal standard of care is cost minimizing. Once total damages are high enough to induce compliance, further increases in damages do not influence the injurer's precaution. This fact is represented in Figure 5 by the horizontal line $x=x^*$ to the right of the switching point.

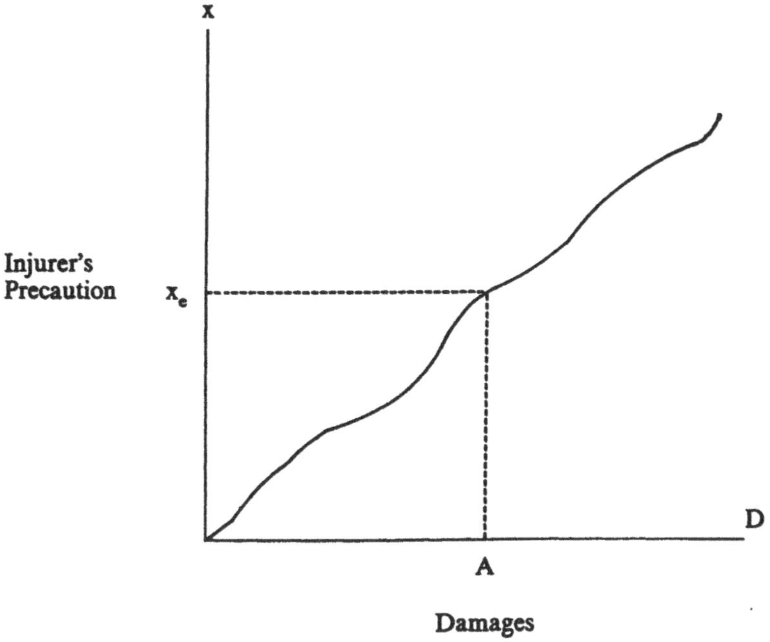

FIGURE 6: CARE AND DAMAGES WITH STRICT LIABILITY

Figure 6 illustrates the relationship between damages and the amount of precaution taken by an injurer under a rule of strict liability. The injurer is liable at all levels of care, so precaution increases continuously, without jumps, as damages increase. If social costs are perfectly internalized, so that damages equal the harm A suffered by accident victims, then the injurer's precaution will be at the socially optimal level x_e. If some costs are externalized, however, then the injurer will not take enough precaution. In either case, an increase in damages causes the injurer's precaution to increase.

There is a disadvantage of fault rules which is illustrated by a comparison of Figures 5 and 6. Whenever damages exceed the switching point in Figure 5, the injurer will satisfy exactly the legal standard of care. If the standard is too high, then his precaution will be too high, and if the standard is too low, then his precaution will be too low. In brief, fault rules make the injurer's precaution sensitive to variations in the legal standard and insensitive to variations in damages. By contrast, strict liability makes the injurer's precaution sensitive to variations in the legal standard and insensitive to variations in damages. Thus, the danger with fault rules lies in imperfect standards of fault, not imperfect computation of damages, while the opposite is true for strict liablity rules.

From an efficiency viewpoint, the choice between fault rules or strict liability rules should be guided by considering the kinds of errors the courts are likely to make. A fault rule is preferable if the courts are likely to make errors in setting damages and unlikely to make errors in setting the legal standard of care. Conversely, a strict liability rule is preferable if the courts are likely to make errors in setting the legal standard of care and unlikely to make errors in setting damages. Computing damages involves measuring the harm suffered by the victim, whereas setting an efficient legal standard of care involves balancing the marginal cost and benefit of precaution. Thus, the choice between negligence and strict liability should be guided by whether the court is more likely to make errors in computing the harm suffered by the victim or in computing the marginal value of precaution.

Courts are likely to set damages below the actual harm if part of the harm is speculative or intangible. Harm which is speculative or intangible is difficult to prove in court and may be excluded from damages as a matter of law. By contrast, the courts are likely to set the legal standard of care incorrectly if the costs and benefits of marginal changes in the injurer's precaution are difficult to observe.[10] Returning

10. As explained in the first footnote, the marginal Hand Rule sets the legal standard, x^*, at the value of x which solves the inequality:

$$0 \leq 1 - p'(x)A.$$

If damages, D, underestimate accident costs, A, however, so that $D < A$, then courts may solve the inequality this way:

$$0 \leq 1 - p'(x)D,$$

to the example of exploding pop bottles, the courts may have difficulty determining how many accidents would be eliminated if the bottler sampled at a higher rate. Such a determination is particularly hard for the courts if it involves understanding technology and evaluating statistics.

IV. SOME APPLICATIONS OF THE MODEL

In the preceding analysis, the economic model of punitive damages concerned gross negligence, but the original cases involved intentional torts such as assault or slander, and many contemporary cases involve consumer injuries for which the rule to be applied is strict liability. Thus, one issue is whether the formal model applies to cases involving a rule other than negligence.

The applicability of the model to assault is obvious after reinter-

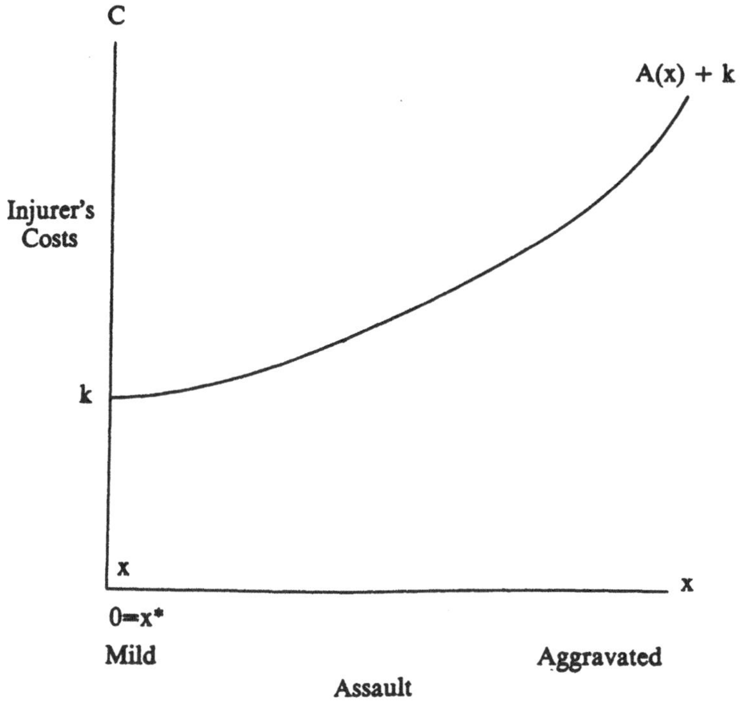

FIGURE 7: INJURER'S COST OF ASSAULT

in which case x^* will be below the efficient value.

preting its variables. Assault can be scaled from mild to aggravated, so the variable x can be reinterpreted to denote the level of assault. Any level of assault is prohibited, so legal standard x^* is taken to be nil, $x^*=0$. Crossing the threshold creates the possibility of a costly dispute and criminal sanctions, so let k denote the threshold costs. Besides the threshold costs, the injurer's costs increase with the seriousness of the assault, that is, $A=A(x)$. The increase in costs is due to an increase in civil and criminal liability that goes with a more serious assault. The injurer's costs can be graphed as in Figure 7, with a threshold in costs at x^*, just as in Figure 2.

From a mathematical viewpoint, there is little difference between Figures 2 and 7. This is why the formal model presented here applies to assault as well as to negligence. The argument that most potential injurers will minimize costs by compliance with the law is still true, as well as the fact that a few injurers will intentionally violate the standard because they either enjoy illicit pleasure from noncompliance or incur exceptional costs from compliance. The only substantial difference between the model of assault and the model of negligence is the manner in which the jump in costs is interpreted. With assault, the jump is caused by the injurer's risk of criminal sanctions and his need for defense. By contrast, the jump in costs in negligence cases is caused by the injurer's abrupt assumption of liability when he crosses the threshold of fault.

Another aspect of the model that warrants attention is its application to consumer injuries.[11] The conventional rule of law holds the manufacturer strictly liable for accidents caused by defective products. To recover compensatory damages, the injured consumer must prove that a defective product caused his injury. However, to recover punitive damages, the economic model suggests that the consumer should also be required to prove that the manufacturer knowingly caused the defect. If there is no fault in the manufacturer's quality control, but a defective product slips through and injures someone, then punitive damages are unwarranted. As noted in the preceding section, awarding supercompensatory damages distorts the incentives of potential injurers when the rule is strict liability. If punitive damages are awarded to consumers without requiring proof of intentional fault, then manufacturers will take excessive precaution.

11. *See* R. Cooter & R. Weissler, Economic Analysis of Strict Product Liability (unpublished manuscript in preparation).

Before concluding this paper, there are several applications which should be mentioned in passing, even though space does not permit a detailed treatment. In modern cases, the injurer is often the agent of a corporation, which raises the question of vicarious liability for the intentional faults of employees. From an economic standpoint, the appropriateness of vicarious liability turns upon whether it is cheaper for courts to control the employees by punishing them directly or to do so indirectly by punishing the employers. Generally, increasing an employer's liability will cause the employer to increase his vigilance over the actions of his employees. It is impossible to discuss in detail the question of efficient vigilance, but economic theory favors vicarious liability for punitive damages if the cost of the resulting increase in employer vigilance is less than the harm that it averts.[12]

Another issue that warrants attention concerns the propriety of allowing liability insurance to cover punitive damages. The primary objection to allowing these types of insurance contracts to be written is the fear that this practice will lead to an increase in the very behavior that the courts are trying to deter. In most situations, however, it would seem that such insurance would be desirable to both injurers and victims. Injurers can decide for themselves whether they are better off with or without the insurance, so prohibiting its sale would not be in their best interest. And, when punitive damages are awarded in addition to compensatory damages, victims are usually overcompensated. Thus, even if critics are correct and such insurance leads to an increase in injuries, victims who receive compensatory plus punitive damages may be better off than if they never suffered the accident at all. If both parties are better off as a result of insurance, it should not be prohibited. Of course, insurance companies may be unwilling to write such contracts,[13] but there is no need for the state to prohibit them.

The insurance issue raises another important problem: the eager victim. The eager victim is one who wants to suffer an injury in order to recover damages. If punitive damages overcompensate, they can create disincentives for precaution by victims. This problem has been

12. Application of the Coase Theorem to this issue leads to the conclusion that it does not matter which rule of law is used in vicarious liability cases, as long as that rule presents no impediment to private contracts. The Coase Theorem suggests that the law regulating vicarious liability should be structured to save transaction costs in private contracts.

13. If punitive damages are awarded only for cases of intentional fault, then any injurer who wishes to insure against a punitive damages assessment must, at the least, conceive of a situation in which he intends to be at fault. This prospect is enough to cause any insurance company to approach such a contract with trepidation.

extensively investigated in the economic analysis of law.[14] Generally, a defense such as contributory negligence will prevent inadequate precaution by victims.

The arguments against awarding punitive damages when the rule of law is strict liability explain why punitive damages are rarely awarded for breach of contract.[15] Absent specific defenses or excuses, a party who breaches a contract is strictly liable for the resulting harm. There is no threshold of fault that must be crossed to assume liability. Consequently, the potential injurer's precaution against events that would cause him to breach increase continuously with his liability. If punitive damages are imposed in addition to damages that compensate the victim, then the precaution against breach will be excessive.

As a final remark, there is a disparity between the economic model of negligence developed in this paper and the actual rules used by courts. The standard of fault discussed in my model, namely that level which minimizes social costs, is clear and precise, which is why it could be represented by the variable x^*. On the other hand, the standard used by courts, the behavior of a "reasonable" person, is vague. The potential injurer cannot always predict whether or not courts will hold him negligent for exercising a particular level of care. Fortunately, vagueness in the standard of fault does not alter the conclusions of the model, although demonstrating this fact involves some technical arguments.[16]

CONCLUSION

It is characteristic of moral and legal systems that fault is a discrete judgment:[17] either the behavior crosses the threshold of fault or it does not. If liability is contingent on fault, then the potential injurer's costs will jump at the threshold of fault. Consequently, an injurer concerned

14. The economic analysis has usually allowed precaution to be bilateral, by which I mean both the injurer and the victim can reduce the probability or extent of an accident. *See, e.g.*, Brown, *supra* note 1; Cooter, Kornhauser & Lane, *supra* note 1.

15. Sullivan, *Punitive Damages in the Law of Contract: The Reality and the Illusion of Legal Change*, 61 MINN. L. REV. 207, 207-08 (1976-1977); Comment, *Punitive Damages on Ordinary Contracts*, 42 MONT. L. REV. 93, 93 (1981). *Cf.* Harman, *An Insurer's Liability for the Tort of Bad Faith*, 42 MONT. L. REV. 67, 78-79, 87-88 (1981) (punitive damages sometimes available for breach of insurance contract when insurer's conduct was tortious).

The similarity of structure between the model of torts and contracts is discussed in R. Cooter, Utility in Torts, Contracts, and Property (Fall 1981) (unpublished manuscript).

16. For a detailed exposition of this point, see *infra* Mathematical Appendix.

17. The relationship between economic reasoning and the discontinuous logic of the law is explored in R. COOTER, JUSTICE AND MATHEMATICS: TWO SIMPLE IDEAS (1979).

with minimizing costs is likely to be slightly at fault only through bad judgment or an honest mistake. An injurer whose fault is intentional is likely to be grossly at fault, and a large punishment is needed to deter him. Thus, the economic model shows the relationship among the three broad characteristics of punitive damages noted above: the fault must be intentional, the fault usually must be gross or repeated, and the punitive damage award must be large.

The economic model suggests that punitive damages serve the purposes of deterring future injuries and rewarding plaintiffs for undertaking the additional burden of proving that fault was intentional. The economic model, however, does not support the view that punitive damages should correct the shortfall between actual harm and allowed compensation, or reward plaintiffs who otherwise would not sue. The social efficiency of fault rules is not disturbed by externalization of costs, provided its size is moderate. Rather, the efficiency of fault rules is disturbed by failure to compute correctly the legal standard of fault. By contrast, rules of strict liability are socially inefficient even if only some costs are externalized.

The economic model does suggest how courts might improve the consistency of their punitive damages rules. First, punitive damages should be regarded as an unusual measure, appropriate only for gross, intentional fault. Punitive damages should not be used to correct small imperfections in computing damages or in bringing suits. Second, punitive damages should be computed at a level that offsets the illicit pleasure of noncompliance or the exceptional costs of compliance that motivated the injurer. Fortunately, this computation does not have to be exact to achieve deterrence. Finally, punitive damages should be awarded in strict liability cases only if the plaintiff can prove intentional fault.

MATHEMATICAL APPENDIX

This appendix provides a brief formal statement of the model used in this paper. The notation used is as follows:

x = injurer's precaution, where $x \geq 0$ (dollars);
x^* = precaution required by law (dollars);
p = probability of no harm, where $p=p(x)$ and $0 \leq p \leq 1$;
q = probability that the victim will press his claim against the injurer;
A = dollar value of harm (dollars);
D = damages (dollars);
b = extraordinary compliance costs (or illicit benefit from non-compliance), where $b=b(x)$ (dollars);
C = injurer's costs, where $C=C(x)$ (dollars).

Behavior of the Injurer

Assume there is a legal standard, x^*, and a rule that the injurer is liable if and only if $x < x^*$. The injurer's costs, $C(x)$, under this fault rule would be:

$$C(x) = \begin{cases} x + b(x) + [1-p(x)]qD, & \text{if } x < x^* \\ x + b(x), & \text{if } x \geq x^*. \end{cases}$$

The cost function $C(x)$ has a discontinuity at x^* whose size is given by

$$-[x^* + b(x^*)] + [x^* + b(x^*) + (1 - p(x^*))qD] = (1 - p(x^*))qD.$$

If the injurer's cost minimizing precaution x is x^* for some values of q and D, then the cost minimizing precaution will not vary with moderate changes in q and D.

By contrast, the injurer's costs under a rule of strict liability are:

$$C(x) = x + b(x) + [1-p(x)]qD.$$

The value of x that minimizes the expression is sensitive to variations in q and D.

Social Costs

The social costs are:

$$SC = \begin{cases} x + [1-p(x)]A & \text{or} \\ x + b(x) + [1-p(x)]A, \end{cases}$$

depending upon whether weight is given to $b(x)$. Let x_e minimize SC. Let $\bar{x}$ denote the value of x which solves $\inf_x C(x)$. Incentives are efficient when x_e is equal to $\bar{x}$. Efficient incentives are achieved under a fault rule for a range of values of q and D if the legal standard is efficient, or $x^* = x_e$.

Suppose that fault is an equilibrium behavior:

$$\left[\inf_{x < x^*} [x + b(x) + (1-p(x))qD] \right] < \left[\min_{x \geq x^*} [x + b(x)]. \right]$$

The purpose of punitive damages is to reverse the inequality. This can be achieved by a sufficiently large increase in D.

Unclear Standards

This explanation of punitive damages has relied upon a discontinuity in the injurer's costs at the level of care equal to the legal standard, or at $x = x^*$. Legal standards are vague, however, so injurers may not face a sharp discontinuity. I want to show that the same conclusions can be reached if standards are unclear. When standards are unclear, the injurer's cost function will contain a nonconvexity that has the same effect as a discontinuity.

Reformulating the model with a vague standard of negligence is straightforward. Let $\pi(x^*)$ be the probability that the standard of negligence applied by the courts is x^*. Thus, the probability that precaution level x will be judged to be nonnegligent can be written as:

$$\pi(x) = \int_0^x \pi(x^*)dx^*.$$

The expected cost function for the injurer is the same as before, except that it contains a new probability term:

$$C(x) = x + [1-\pi(x)][1-p(x)]qD,$$

or

$$C(x) = x + [1-\pi(x)][1-p(x)]qD - b(x).$$

Assume the standard of negligence is vague, but not wholly unknown. Thus, the probability density $\pi(x^*)$ clusters around a certain value of x^*. The discontinuity has disappeared from $C(x)$ and has been replaced by the cluster of probability. In this case the cost function $C(x)$ will be nonconvex as depicted in Figure 8. There will be two local minima, one near the cluster point for the legal standard and the other at the far lower level of precaution. The nonconvexity in Figure 8 plays the role of the discontinuity in Figure 2. As before, potential offenders will be divided into those who try to satisfy the legal standard but sometimes fail because a very high standard is sometimes applied by courts, and those whose fault is intentional. The policy conclusions and analysis of the purposes of punitive damages are the same when legal standards are vague as when the standards are clear.

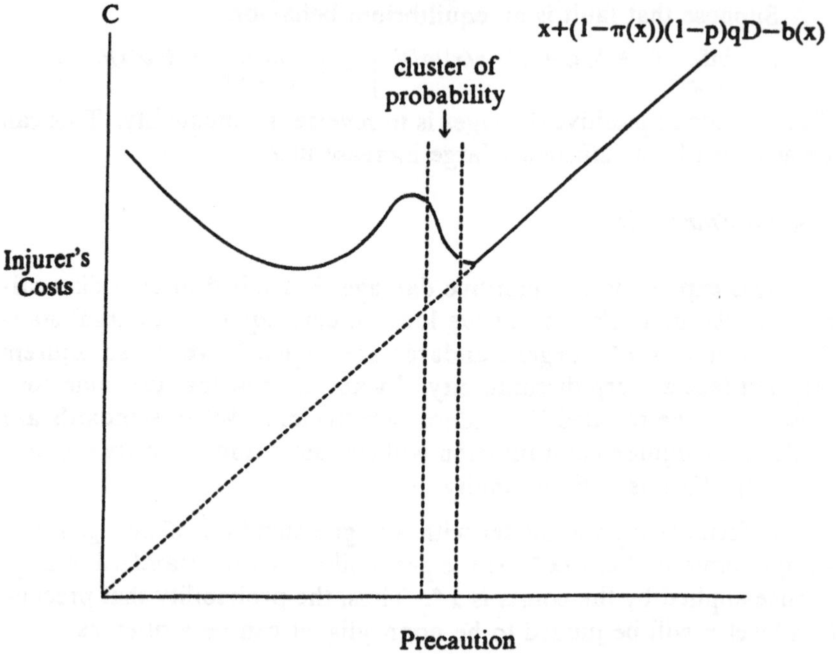

FIGURE 8: INJURER'S COSTS WITH UNCLEAR STANDARDS

Name Index

Printed and bound by CPI Group (UK) Ltd, Croydon, CR0 4YY

16/04/2025

14658435-0002